American publishing and engraving co

Illustrated Boston

The Metropolis of New England

American publishing and engraving co

Illustrated Boston
The Metropolis of New England

ISBN/EAN: 9783743317468

Manufactured in Europe, USA, Canada, Australia, Japa

Cover: Foto ©ninafisch / pixelio.de

Manufactured and distributed by brebook publishing software (www.brebook.com)

American publishing and engraving co

Illustrated Boston

ILLUSTRATED BOSTON

THE METROPOLIS OF NEW ENGLAND

1889

PUBLISHED BY
AMERICAN PUBLISHING AND ENGRAVING CO.
102 CHAMBERS STREET
NEW YORK

Copyright, 1889, by
THE AMERICAN PUBLISHING AND ENGRAVING CO.

INTRODUCTORY.

 A NATION'S growth is centred in the freedom of its institutions, the multiplication and expansion of its workshops and factories, and the increase of its commercial establishments and facilities. Herein lie the attractions to the sons and daughters of other nations where freedom is restrained, despotism paramount, and commerce crippled, to come and abide with us and help us to build up this grand Republic into the greatest and most powerful nation the world has known.

Upon the historian rests the responsibility of chronicling the progress and achievements of communities from age to age, and of conveying to present and oncoming generations a faithful representation of the times in which he lives. The publishers of this volume have been actuated by a desire to place before the readers of these pages, not merely an account of Boston as it was in the past, but as it exists to-day — with its vast emporiums of commerce; its thousands of industrial establishments; its hundreds of wharves, to and from which the merchantmen belonging to all the countries of the world come and go; its half a million of people, representing every nation and tongue; its halls of learning; its institutions for the cultivation of the arts and dissemination of the sciences; its charitable associations and religious edifices; its beautiful parks and drives; its memorials of by-gone heroes by flood and field; its improvements over the past, in buildings and thoroughfares; its civic government; and its attainment to the distinction of the manufacturing and commercial metropolis of New England.

To every American citizen, some knowledge of the history of his country, and of its leading cities, is indispensable; and in the compiling of this work, telling of the origin of the second city founded on American soil, of its subsequent growth and present *status*, the publishers believe that they have not uselessly employed, and that the reader will rise from the perusal of its pages with an increased knowledge of Boston and its progressive people. This book is intended for the average American; for the manufacturer and merchant, who have neither time nor disposition to plod through ten or twenty volumes of elaborate historical dissertations; for the practical man of the shop, the counter, and the plough. The story of the coming of the first settlers to the pear-shaped peninsula on which they began the building up of the present giant city of Boston is briefly but interestingly told; the great work of converting that which was but a narrow neck connecting the city to the mainland, into what is now the broadest part of the municipality, is adequately described; the valiant deeds of the forefathers, who sounded the tocsin and fired the first guns of the Revolution, have been concisely but truthfully related, and old landmarks pointed out. But the ambition of the authors has been to give a pen-picture, with beautiful new illustrations, of the city as it is in this year of grace 1889; to tell of the character of its multifarious manufactures, and of its miscellaneous commerce; and to make the reader acquainted with its representative business men, who have won fame for themselves and made the name of Boston known and honored in all the corners of the earth.

The *data* given touching the various business enterprises have been drawn from the most authentic sources, have been carefully collated and intelligently revised; and the utmost care has been exercised in order that the information herein given may be relied upon, since it is highly desirable that the most accurate knowledge

INTRODUCTORY.

with regard to a community so useful and progressive in trade and manufactures as Boston is should be as widely diffused as possible. While it is not claimed that the work is free from imperfections and shortcomings, it is confidently asserted that no previous publication of a like character has contained so much new and valuable points for reference. The preparation of the work has needed much labor, patience, and perseverance; but, great as the task has been, the drudgery of compilation has been shorn of unpleasantness by the universal courtesy extended to us, and the cheerful manner in which information has been afforded wherever it was applied for. Without such help, this work could not have been issued in the form in which it now is. To so many are our thanks due, that it would be impossible to tender them individually; and though we do so collectively, our sincerity of appreciation of favors received is none the less.

Designed for distribution among persons residing in other localities, as well as among the citizens of Boston, and especially among those who are unacquainted with the real magnitude of the city and its extraordinary manufacturing and mercantile facilities, we are assured that this work will perform a mission of the highest utility. It is dedicated to the manufacturer, the merchant, the household, and to the libraries of the rich and of the poor. It is inscribed to the business man, to the father, the mother, the son, and the daughter of the American family. If the man of business, the father, mother, son, and daughter shall be more proud of their ancient city, the "Athens of the New World," and love it and their country better, if they shall understand more clearly and appreciate more fully the founding, progress, and growth of liberty in the New World, and be brought to a more perfect knowledge of the giant strides that are being made in manufactures and commerce in the capital of the Old Bay State, the publishers will be abundantly repaid.

THE PUBLISHERS.

GENERAL INDEX.

	PAGE
Abbott, H. E., insurance	189
Adams, Blodget & Co., bankers	264
Adams, Taylor & Co., wine importing merchants	122
Adams, F. P., & Co., flavoring extracts	156
Allee, H. L., & Co., manfrs. folding-beds	301
Allee, Brown & Co., stoves, ranges, etc.	287
Albion Milling Co., merchant millers, etc.	164
Alden Furniture Spring Co., The	102
Aldrich, H., & Co., eggs, butter, and cheese	102
Allan Line of Royal Mail Steamships	135
Allen, E., & Co., woolens	248
Allen & Whitney, marine insurance brokers	213
Allen, A. G., hardware, etc.	242
Allen & Ginter, manfrs. cigarettes, etc.	266
Allen Bros., manfrs. rubber and steel stamps	280
Alliance Insurance Ass'n, The, of New York	207
Almy, R. T., & Co., clothiers	226
American Loan and Trust Co. of Omaha, The	135
American Grip Machine Co.	227
American Loan and Trust Co.	198
American Fire Alarm Co.	136
American Investment Co., The	147
American Manfg. Co., manfrs. fertilizers	183
Amsden, J. F., & Son, bankers	175
Anderson, Wm. G., window screens, etc.	188
Andrews, Jno. A., & Co., wholesale grocers	124
Andrews & Co., truckmen	209
Appleton, G. C., real estate	271
Appleton, C. F., boots and shoes	217
Appleton, S., insurance	144
Appleton, Geo. B., & Co., cutlery, etc.	178
Archer & Pancoast Manfg. Co., gas fixtures	177
Ateshian, O. H., & Co., Turkish and Persian goods	150
Atkins, H. & Co., wine merchants	122
Atwood, F. L., teas, coffees, etc.	256
Atwood & Co., commission merchants	272
Atwood, H. & R., oysters	203
Babson, C., Jr., American and foreign patents	137
Bacon, W. M., architect	259
Bacon, F. H., shirts, etc.	256
Bailey, J. W., & Sons, mouldings, brackets, etc.	190
Baker, J. Y., & Co., oysters	231
Balderston & Daggett, rubber goods	145
Ballance & Sorrell, manfrs. boots and shoes	166
Bangs & Horton, coal	150
Banks, D S., tea broker	284
Barber Bros., cigars, etc.	267
Barbour Bros. Co., The, manfrs. thread	137

	PAGE
Barker & Starbird, photographic apparatus, etc.	250
Barnard's Bakery	270
Barnes, F. G., & Son, auctioneers, etc.	177
Barnes & Cunningham, bankers and brokers	174
Barnes, E. B., & Co., manfrs. gold and bronze frames	160
Baron & Co., manfrs. cigars	295
Barzelle & Co., auctioneers, etc.	182
Barry, J. A., millinery	262
Bartlett, S. L., teas, cocoas, etc.	305
Bartlett, H. F., periodicals, cigars, etc.	262
Bastey & Sutherland, manfrs. harness, etc.	248
Batcheller, E. & A, H., & Co., manfrs. boots and shoes	133
Bates, A. M., carriages, etc.	122
Bates, H. M., & Richards, stock brokers	115
Battey, W. A., commission merchant	163
Baxter, Stoner & Schenkelberger, manfs. cut soles and taps	104
Bay State House, Geo. O. Pattee, propr.	135
Bay State Boiler Compound Co., manfrs. boiler compound, etc.	136
Bay State Manfg. Co., egg-beaters, etc.	150
Beal, J. W., architect	144
Beale, C. C., publisher, and teacher of phonography	169
Beals & Co., wholesale leather remnants, etc.	184
Beals, J. W., Jr., timber land investments	180
Beals, Col. Wm., public decorator	264
Beaman Bros., commission merchants	228
Beebe, L., & Co., cotton	179
Beiermeister & Spicer, manfrs. collars and cuffs	240
Bent, C. T. A., boots and shoes	246
Berry, C., bottler of lager beer	266
Berry, A. C., engraver and stationer	255
Berry, H. W., pianos	185
Besses, R. & J., caterers	277
Bicknell & Robinson, fire insurance	198
Billman, C., rigger loft	284
Bird, H., & Co., beef, pork, lard, etc.	231
Blackstone National Bank of Boston, The	103
Blake, C., Furniture Co., desks, hall-stands, etc.	167
Blake, C. D., & Co., publishers of music	172
Blakemore, W. B., real estate	141
Bliss, J., & Co., grocers, etc.	198
Block, E., & Sons, distillers	217
Boardman, E. A., wine merchant	189
Bolles & Co., bankers and brokers	307
Bond, W., & Son, chronometer and watch makers	127
Boston Consolidated Produce Co.	152
Boston Dyewood and Chemical Co.	195

GENERAL INDEX.

	PAGE
Boston Daily Globe, The	129
Boston Dash Stitching Works, J. L. Taylor, Propr.	244
Boston & Gloucester Steamboat Co.	207
Boston Ice Co.	168
Boston & Lockport Block Co., manfrs. self-lubricating metaline tackle blocks, etc.	157
Boston Mercantile Business Co	279
Boston Paste Co., manfrs. paste	289
Boston Photogravure Co., fine art publishers	137
Boston Plating Co.	285
Boston Rubber Shoe Co.	125
Boston Type Writer Co., The	165
Boston Tavern, Robinson & Fitzsimmons, Propts.	119
Boston Watch Co., W. W. Farr, propr.	199
Bourne & Co., commission merchants	141
Bowen & Co., real estate, etc.	296
Bowler, W. F., driving and working horses	244
Boyce, E. J., manfg. jeweler	293
Boyce Bros., furniture	171
Boyle Bros., furniture, etc.	186
Boynton & Co., commission merchants	291
Brackett, C. A., manfr. paper boxes, etc.	237
Bradbury, B. F., pharmacist	275
Bradley's Troy Laundry, G. E. Bradley, Propr.	292
Braman, D. & Co., bankers and brokers	150
Bray, E. L., manfr. curtain fixtures	283
Brett, Wm. H., The Engraving Co.	148
Brewster, Cobb & Estabrook, bankers	110
Brigham & Co., engravers on metal	244
Brigham & Pillsbury, commission merchants	219
Brine & Norcross' Reliable Stores, hosiery, gloves, etc.	119
Broadway Hat Store, Wm. McCarthy, propr.	255
Brockway, J. L. & Co., wholesale grocers	179
Brooks, S. P., manfr. pianos	280
Brooks, J N., cotton buyer	303
Brown, G. D & Co., mutton, lamb, etc.	125
Brown, E. J. & Co., cotton	252
Brown, H F. & Co., manfrs. blackings and dressings for leather	126
Brown, Riley & Co., bankers and brokers	175
Brown, DeLoriea & Co., commission merchants	176
Brown, A. H. & Bros., millers agts	293
Browne, E. J., insurance, etc.	206
Brunswick-Balke-Collender Co., billiard tables, etc.	183
Bumstead, J. F. & Co., paper hangings, etc.	171
Bunker Laundry & Towel Supply	186
Burbank, E. R., real estate, etc.	202
Burke, J. B., undertaker, etc.	251
Burnham, D S., real estate, etc.	192
Burrell & Dutton, saws.	246
Butler, W. S. & Co., millinery goods, etc.	232
Butler, E. E., & Co., produce commission merchants	298
Caley, J., & Co., engravers, etc.	261
California Insurance Co. of San Francisco	145
Call & Carlton, butter, cheese, etc.	283
Campbell Bros., loan brokers	284
Campbell, C. A., & Co., coal	120
Canning & Patch, pharmacists	194
Canny, P., West India goods, groceries, etc.	191
Cantwell, M., plumber	258

	PAGE
Cape Ann Granite Company	172
Carleton, R H., & Co., manfrs. boots and shoes	281
Carleton, A. D., silver and gold plater	265
Carr, C., mechanical engineer	229
Carr, D. A., stoves, ranges, etc.	273
Carrie, W. A., bank stationer, etc.	304
Carrington, R., bookbinder	266
Carter, C. N, cloaks, suits, and furs	164
Carter's Band, T. M. Carter, leader	250
Casey, H. D., manfr. and gilder of frames	298
Caswell, Livermore & Co., salt and pickled fish	176
Chamberlin, S. W., manfrs. steam cookers	277
Chandler & Farquhar, hardware, etc.	275
Chapin, Troll & Co, distillers of rum	146
Chapin Bros., wholesale produce commission	159
Chapman, A. F., publisher	199
Chard, D. T., & Co., cigars	301
Chase, R. G., & Co., proprs. Chase Nurseries	252
Chase, W. P., book lettering and stamping, etc.	186
Chessman, G. H., & Co., general commission merchants	219
Chester Manufacturing Co., suspenders, braces, etc.	221
Chicago Lumber Co., A. H. Bolton & Co., agts	202
Chicago, Milwaukee & St. Paul Railway	160
Child, A. J., boarding and baiting stable	263
Cigarmakers' Co-operative Association, The	153
Citizens' Mutual Insurance Co.	197
Clark, C. C., printer and publisher	279
Clark, G. A., broker in chemicals	225
Clark, H. H., & Co., book printers	233
Clark, C., insurance	250
Clark, R. F., stock broker	168
Clark & Haley, commission merchants	172
Clarke, G. R., & Co., interior decorations	216
Clarke, G. A., designer	294
Clapp, A, & Co., wholesale lumber	232
Clatur, A. A., leather remnants	102
Clayton, F. I., tailor	212
Cleaves, J. H., weigher and gauger	246
Clement, H. E., & Co., watches, jewelry, etc.	302
Codman & Hall, drugs, etc.	239
Cohn, L., & Co, manfrs. picture frames, etc.	241
Cohn, I., clothing, etc.	303
Coffin, Geo. W., insurance	126
Collins & Co., real estate, etc.	180
Comer's Commercial College	159
Commonwealth Loan & Trust Co.	155
Condell, W. S., agt. Union Pacific Railway	299
Condon, T. J., provisions, etc.	268
Conner, W N., propr. London Hair Store	290
Coolidge House, Wm P. Comee, propr.	199
Coon, H. J., & Co., grain shippers	252
Coon, H., & Co., masons, contractors, etc.	300
Cosmopolitan Dining Room, The	255
Costigan, E. A., shipwright and caulker	303
Cotton & Haley, commission merchants	187
Cousens & Pratt, sail makers	295
Cowan, H., watch materials, etc.	232
Coy, S. I., restaurant	156
Crafts & Co., druggists	299
Crawford House	102

GENERAL INDEX.

	PAGE
Cressy, M. D., & Co., teamsters and forwarders	245
Crine, H., manfr. for garments, etc.	133
Crocker & Eldridge, wholesale grocers	103
Crosby, Geo. E., & Co., printers	295
Crowell, S. R., ship broker	293
Cullen, J. P., provisions	259
Cummings, J. A., Printing Co.	114
Curtis, J. G., & Co., coffees and spices	214
Curtis & Motley, stock and bond brokers	152
Curtis & Weld, costumers	154
Cushing, Wm., & Co., real estate, etc.	237
Dale, J. P., & Co., publishers and bookbinders	196
Damm & Penkert, manfrs. clarinets, flutes, etc.	191
Damrell & Upham, bookseller	238
Dana, T., & Co., wholesale grocers	210
Dasey, C. V., steamship agt.	143
Davenport, Peters & Co., lumber	260
Davenport, Chas. L., salt	151
Davis, Stebbins, & Co., hardware, etc.	274
Davis, J., & Son, ship stores, etc.	265
Dawson, J. F., gold gilder	125
Dean, S. B., cut soles and leather	235
Deering, Wm., & Co., grain and grass cutting machinery.	122
De Loe, G. V., & Co., carpenters and builders	246
Demain, W. C., & Son, manfrs. blank-books, etc.	229
Denham, M. T., treasr. and agt. for Eastern Forge Co.	208
Dennett, J. A., paper hangings, etc.	292
Derry, C. T., & Co., granite, etc.	208
Desk Exchange, office and library furniture	202
Dewey, S. W. & Co., cotton buyers	200
Diamond Cutting	134
Diaz, R. M., & Co., wholesale hardware	184
Dickerman, G. H., & Co., manfrs. paper boxes	152
Dickey, L., manfr. whips, etc.	270
Dinner, I. H., ladies' traveling caps, etc.	305
Dixon, J. B., & Co., lumber	201
Doane & Co., ship brokers	282
Doane, A. S., & Co., engravers and printers	242
Doane, F., & Co., manfrs. blank-books, etc.	114
Dole, C. G., mutton, lamb, etc.	105
Doll & Richards, fine arts	212
Dooling, J., caterer and confectioner	125
Dorr, C. A., note broker	265
Dow, E. C., outer and inner soles, etc.	293
Dowling, P. F., fish and oysters	255
Downer & Co., bankers and brokers	207
Drew Bros., groceries, etc.	298
Driscoll, J., manfr. cigars	288
Dutton & Carroll, manfrs. cigars	266
Dunbar, D. A., poultry and game	231
Dunbar, W. H., & Co., tailors	223
Dunning, G. H., beef, pork, lard, etc.	247
Dunshee & Co., photographers	302
Dyer, L. M., mutton, lamb, etc.	219
Dyer, Rice & Co., straw goods, robes, furs, etc	127
Dyer, J. T., & Co., gents' furnishers	167
Dyke, Shute & Co., weighers	184
Eames, C. E. druggist	182
Earle, J. H., publisher, etc.	272
Earle, J. & Co., tailors	224

	PAGE
Eastern Lobster Co., S. S. Poole, mgr.	192
Eddy, P. E., insurance	215
Eddy, R. H., solicitor of patents	175
Edmonds, W. H., optician	164
Egin, Wm., manfr. pipes	304
Elliot, C. E., & Co., tailors	275
Elliott, C. D., civil engineer, etc.	162
Ellis, J. D., paper and linen collars	275
Emerson, W. R., architect	153
Emerson, T. W., & Co., seeds	173
Emerson, W. H., molasses and sugar	302
Emerson, H. P., & Co., manfrs. agts.	304
Emery, J., Jr., & Co., wholesale fish	192
Emery, W. H. & S. L., coal, etc.	202
Epples & Adams Sewing-machine Co.	238
Essex Boot & Shoe Co., L. F. Keene, propr.	236
Eustis & Aldrich, genl. commission merchants	228
Eutebrouk, C. H., importer and gun maker	289
Everett, E. F., insurance adjuster	195
Eyelett Tool Co., G. W. Robbins, agt	177
Faccini, L., & Co., wines, brandies, etc.	214
Fairbank, N. K., & Co, lard refiners	160
Family Grocery and Wine Store	278
Faneuil Hall National Bank	114
Farmers' Loan & Trust Co.	167
Farrell, J. R., tailor	287
Favor, E. W., groceries, etc.	270
Faxon, C. A., genl. agt. Cheshire, Central Vermont & Del. & Hudson Canal Co.'s Railroads	255
Farley, Harvey, & Co., dry goods	111
Fisher & Fairbanks, rock cordials, etc.	186
Fisher, A. P., & Co., brokers in grain, etc.	134
Fisher's Restaurant	125
Fisk, M., cigars	233
Fisk's Lunch and Dining Rooms.	277
Fitzpatrick, D. W., tailor	260
Fitzmeyer, W. J., japanner	282
Fletcher, J. V., beef, pork, lard, etc.	209
Flitner, J. H., & Co., general commission merchants	190
Florence Shirt Co., The	244
Fobes, Hayward & Co., (incorp.), manfrs. confectionery	106
Fogg, A. T., embroideries, etc.	220
Fogg Bros. & Co., bankers, etc.	166
Foss & Gault, hosiery, etc.	276
Foster, D. W., manfr. horse blankets, etc.	270
Foster, H. H., & Co., coal and wood	254
Foster, C., & Son, groceries, etc.	115
Fowle, Hibbard & Co., produce commission merchants	140
Fowle, E. M., & Co., shipping and commission merchants	151
Fox, A., & Co., manfrs. cloth hats and caps	120
Frank, D., & Co., cigars	188
Franklin Rubber Co., Fuller, Leonard & Small, propr.	213
Frazier, L. B., stockbroker	227
French Bros., provisions, groceries, etc.	111
French, C. E., distiller of N. E. rum	187
French, W. C., bedsteads, etc.	196
French, J., & Sons, real estate, etc.	203
French, F., employment Agency	177
Frink & Hayes, builders of gas and water works	135

GENERAL INDEX.

	PAGE
Furness Line of Steamships	139
Gattcomb, L. B., & Co., manfrs. banjos, guitars, etc.	153
Gay & Jeffrey, provisions, etc.	267
Gay, A. R., & Co., manfrs. account books	140
Gendron, Miss A. M., photographer	247
George, I. M., & Co., commission merchants	228
Gilman, J. T., apothecary	279
Gill, J. W., fish, oysters, etc.	278
Gillespie & Hutchinson, dry and fancy goods, etc.	255
Gillette & Hennigan, wholesale apples, oranges, etc.	175
Gillis, F. E., photographer	268
Gleason & Kimball, commission merchts. in fruits, etc.	204
Gleeson, T. W., & Co., electricians	281
Glen Shirt and Collar Co.; A. B. Rice, manager	232
Goldberg, H. H., manfr. cigars	267
Goldsmith, Silver & Co., manfrs. cigars	106
Goodman, J., & Co., fire insurance	118
Goodridge, M. E., stable	260
Gore, T. W., average adjuster	214
Gossler & Co., bankers and importers	162
Gould & Co., wholesale paint	297
Gould's Hat, Trunk, and Glove Depot	262
Graham, T. J., & Co., manfrs. trunks, etc.	251
Grant Jett, water filters	111
Gray, E. F., commission merchant	276
Great Atlantic & Pacific Tea Co., The	175
Green, C., & Co., clothing	154
Green, B. F., & Co., tailors	168
Grose, J. R., manfr. paper boxes	195
Gustin, H. E., & Co., country produce	292
Harley, A. G., stair builder	249
Haines, F. H., jeweler and optician	283
Haley's Fashionable Millinery	272
Hall, G. O., dentist	290
Hall, J., & Son, carriages, etc.	172
Hall, C. E., & Co., marble	115
Hall, D. F., meats, provisions, etc.	254
Hall & Cole, commission merchants	221
Hall, J. M., & Co., house painters	261
Hallett, F. E., commission merchant	284
Halma, H. P., sailmaker, etc.	275
Hamlin & Martin, furniture, etc.	291
Hammett, J. L., school furniture, etc.	179
Hammond Type Writer Co.	141
Hancock Inspirator Co., The, manfrs. inspirators	103
Hano, Sam'l Co., manfrs. manifold books	220
Hanson, M. F., boarding, hack and livery stable	302
Harrington & Freeman, watches, diamonds, etc.	249
Harrison, Heard & Co., manfrs. furniture, etc.	302
Harrison, E. S., & Co., proprs. Dr. Harrison's Peristaltic Lozenges, etc.	245
Harmon, J. W., manfr. spirit levels, etc.	216
Hartnett, E. J., millinery	292
Haskell, H. A., manfr. Eureka Pipe Bender	128
Haskins Bros., isinglass, Irish moss, etc.	159
Haskins, W., & Son, lumber	195
Hastings, H. C., bookseller, etc.	239
Hatch, L. P., hats, caps, etc.	143
Hatch, S., & Co., auctioneers	251
Hatch, D. H., manfr. paper and wood boxes	256

	PAGE
Hatch, H., & Co., steel and stencil letter-cutting	250
Hatchman, J., manfr. moldings and picture-frames	263
Hathaway, Soule & Harrington, manfr. men's shoes	131
Hatheway & Co., ship and freight brokers	185
Hawes, G. W., manfr. suspenders, etc.	190
Hawes, J. P., broker in fertilizers	248
Hawkes & Crawford, plumbers, etc.	256
Hawkes, B. L., stationery, etc.	244
Hayden, Geo. E., costumer	284
Hayden, A. L., boots and shoes	266
Hayes, S. C. & Co., commission merchants	280
Haynes, A., manfr. white wine and cider vinegar, etc.	246
Hazeltine, H. & Co., butter, cheese, and eggs	162
Heald, A. V., meats, etc.	267
Hearn, T. H., apothecary	274
Heath & Co., apothecaries	216
Heath, L., & Co., manfg. opticians	184
Hewes & Mayo, sign and office painters	275
Hewins & Hollis, outfitters	234
Higgins, R. R., & Co., wholesale oysters	152
Highton, W., & Sons, manfrs. of hot-air registers, etc.	210
Hills, R., watchmaker	282
Hilton, H. C., commission merchant	272
Hilton & Woodward, mutton, lamb, etc.	238
Hinckley Bros., & Co., cordage, chains, etc.	184
Hitchcock & Browne, druggists	255
Hixon, W. S., & Co., manfrs. soapstone	181
Hobbs, H. B., sign painter, etc.	251
Hoblay, Thos. W., mechanical draughtsman	241
Hodges, L. L., japanner	185
Hodgdon, W. S., manfr. tongues, stays, etc.	254
Hodgman Rubber Co., manfrs. India-rubber goods	131
Holden, C. W., insurance	190
Holden, F., & Co., beef, pork, lard, etc.	297
Holland, Dr. A. J., dentist	266
Hollis, C. N., commission merchant	196
Hollis, T., drugs, etc.	227
Holman, J., & Co., bedding and bed lounges, etc.	249
Holmes, E. D., lumber, etc.	301
Holmes, W. A., &. Co., grocers	221
Holmes, T. J., specialist in atomizing tubes, etc.	261
Holway Bros., & Woodbury, sailmakers	277
Homer, J. W., real estate	181
Hood, R. S., scrap iron, etc.	303
Houghton & Colby, grain and feed	156
Howard, M. E., & Co., printers	290
Howard National Bank of Boston, The	106
Howe, I. A., manfr. shirts, etc.	227
Howe, O. F., wooden and willow ware	203
Howe, J. M., real estate, etc.	247
Howes, A. C., hotel and restaurant supplies	269
Howland, F. H., men's furnishings	282
Hoyt, G. T., & Co., sailmakers, etc.	273
Hoxt & Tripp, mechanical draughtsmen	291
Hubbard, J., & Co., manfrs. Hubbard's Deodorizer and Germicide	183
Hubbard, J., & Co., manfrs. and proprs. Hubbard's Deodorizer	193
Humphrey, B. F., blank-book manfr.	274
Hunnewell, J. W., & Co., wholesale petroleum	132

GENERAL INDEX.

	PAGE
Hunt, Rodney, Machine Co.	155
Huston, W. A., druggist	291
Hutchinson, J. F., & Co., wholesale and commission butter, cheese, etc.	170
Hyde, E. J., insurance, etc.	296
Ingalls, Brown & Co., leather	119
Ingersoll Rock Drill Co., Mellen S. Harlow, mgr.	213
International Trust Co.	123
Irving, K., flour mill products	113
Isburgh & Co., carriage dealers	252
Jacobs, S., & Bros., manfrs. cigars	272
Jeaneret, A. E., watchmaker and manfr. of Diamond Luster	145
Jellison, J. M., & Co., Boston and Maine Drug Co.	227
Jeselsohn, L., tobacconist	281
Jewell & Co., bankers and brokers	145
Jewett, F. P., coffee broker	248
Johnson, J. P., produce and provisions	267
Johnson, B., mutton, lamb, etc.	231
Johnson, F. H., & Co., fish	230
Jones, M. D., & Co., manfrs. ornamental iron work	212
Jones, J. F., & Co., oils, etc.	245
Jordan, Lovett & Co., insurance	151
Judge, R., tailor	176
Kansas Investment Co.	106
Keenan, M. H., printer	272
Keenan, J., wool and wool stock	272
Keenan, M. T. J., glass cutter	255
Keene, C. S., agt. Buchanan and Lyall's tobaccos	130
Kelley, S. D., architect	243
Kellogg, H. Jr., note broker	262
Kelly, T., & Co., birds, etc.	271
Kendall, G. A., feathers, etc.	181
Kenney, A. E., furniture, etc.	255
Kent, John; agt., A. French Spring Co., Limited, and Carnegie Phipps & Co., Limited	106
Kent, J. L., & Co., commission brokers	157
Kerr, W., & Son, watches, etc.	257
Keys, D. W., & Co., produce commission merchants	293
Kilborn, Whitman, & Co., manfrs. furniture	301
Kimball, Chas., photographer	264
Kimball Bros., beef, pork, lard, etc.	225
Kimball, L. L., & Co., wholesale fruit and produce	109
Kimball's Fine Confectionery, R. H. Kimball, propr.	223
Knapp, J. M., machine and tool forging	287
Knowles & Co., grain shippers	215
Koeller, F., cutler	211
Koschwitz & Co., lithographic engravers and printers	286
Ladd, N. M., boots, shoes, etc.	263
Laforme and Frothingham, commission merchants	127
Lalley, C. H., wholesale bottles	273
Lamb, B. F., & Co., lumber	161
Lamkin, G., & Co., manfrs. boots and shoes	305
Lane, F. A., painter, etc.	268
Lane & Small, machinists	300
Lapworth, J., carving, etc.	279
Laycock, R., tailor	291
Law, G. H., musical instruments	265
Lawrence & Robinson, real estate	240
Lawrence, H. L., & Co., poultry, etc.	211

	PAGE
Lawson, W. S., & Co., bankers and brokers	195
Learnard & Bird Oil Co., The	230
Learnard, S. S., beef, pork, lard, etc.	204
Leavitt, A., manfr. church organ keys	198
Leavitt, M. L. H., Ph.G., pharmacist	251
Leighton, R. B., insurance, etc.	200
Leland, A. M., music goods	294
Leman, F. N., sign painter	231
Lennon & Co., brass founders and finishers, etc.	156
Lent & Braham, tailors' trimmings	296
Levy, D., manfr. clothing	170
Levy, B., & Co., French perfumers	193
Levy, B., & Co., French perfumers	193
Lewando's French Dyeing and Cleansing Establishment and Laundry, W. L. Crosby, mgr.	194
Lewis, D. W., sewer and drain pipes, etc.	148
Lewis, B., stationery, etc.	240
Lewis' Wharf Tow-boats, N. P. Doane, agt.	274
Libbie, C. F., Jr., printer	250
Lincoln, W., & Son, insurance	196
Lincoln, F. H., real estate, etc.	175
Lindall's Band, Lindall, C. E., mgr.	263
Litchfield, H. C., & Co., manfrs. of fishing tackle, etc.	153
Littlefield, W. H., & Co., apothecaries	262
Littlefield, G. E., old books, etc.	190
Livermore, A. H., dentist	278
Lloyd, G. H., manfg. optician	118
Locke, H., beef	236
Lockett, W., & Co., merchandise brokers	295
Lockhart, W. L., manfrs. coffins, etc.	138
Logan, S. B., auctioneer, etc.	303
Lombard, H. S., clothing, etc.	278
Lombard, N. C., mechanical engineer, etc.	203
Loring & Clark, insurance	237
Lougee, G. F., & Co., cotton brokers and buyers	127
Lovell, A. J., grocer	286
Low, O., real estate, etc.	206
Lowe, W. W., real estate, etc.	146
Lowell, R. M., plumber	294
Lundahl, E. W., photographic printer	284
Lydon, P. W., music plate printer	258
Lyman & White, stationers and printers	144
Macdonnell, Mrs. S. A., gloves	223
Macullar, Parker & Co., clothing	104
Manning, W. E., & Co., real estate, etc.	110
Manning & Bro., oils, etc.	156
Mariner & Williams, shipping agts.	294
Market National Bank	110
Marshall, H., & Co., printers	253
Marshall, J. E., manfr. Saratoga potato chips	194
Marston, J. W., & Co., wholesale lobsters	271
Martin, W. H., window tickets, show cards, etc.	290
Martin, A. P., & Co., manfrs. boots and shoes	139
Mason & Co., coin dealers	189
Massachusetts Mutual Fire Insurance Co.	114
Massachusetts Loan and Trust Co., The	146
Massachusetts Real Estate Co., Geo. Leonard, genl. agt.	147
Matison, J., & Co., real estate and insurance	243
Mazeppa Sign Co., F. F. Applequist, mgr.	185
McAdams, W. M. L., stationer, etc.	248

GENERAL INDEX.

	PAGE
McArthur, A., & Co., furniture and carpets	142
McCarthy, J. H., mutton, lamb, etc.	202
McCarthy, C. F., manfg. jeweler	191
McCarthy, N. F., & Co., flowers, etc.	234
McClean, A., & Co., lumber, etc.	294
McCleery, A. L., sawing, planing, and moulding	214
McCoster, T., photographer	304
McDonald, A., manfr. trunks, bags, etc.	250
McElwin, D., manfr. show cases, etc.	297
McFarland, F. J., grocer	283
McFarlin, G. R., china, glass, etc.	234
McGrath, J., real estate, etc.	204
McGreenery Bros., cigars, etc.	240
McIntyre, P., & Co., wholesale grocers	188
McKay, H. S., architect	171
McKenney, C. H., & Co., manfrs. gas fixtures	149
McKey, J. W., crockery, china, etc.	257
McLean, Ella C., artist	279
McMahon, T., cigars, etc.	263
McPherson Bros., commission merchants	203
Measures, J., brass foundery	286
Mekelburg & Cube, manfrs. cigar	199
Melledge, R. J., mortgages	243
Mercantile Fire & Marine Insurance Co.	140
Merchandise National Bank	136
Merchants' National Bank of Boston, The	171
Merchants' & Miners' Transportation Co.	174
Messer, G. E., & Co., black walnut and amber work	201
Metropolis Land Company of Boston	124
Metropolitan Steamship Co.	132
Miller & Son, manfg. confectioners	305
Miller, The, Boot and Shoe Trees, O. A. Miller, propr.	204
Miller, E. W., manfr. Miller's Reform Boot	235
Miller, R., & Co., manfrs. sails, etc.	250
Mills & Gibb, lace curtains, etc.	225
Mills, Miss V. L., corsets and panniers	263
Missouri Pacific Railway Co., The	154
Mitchell, A. R., & Co., cigars and tobacco	235
Mitchell, A. S., auctioneer, etc.	151
More, C. H., & Co., granites	170
Morrill, F. W., & Co., butter, cheese, etc.	254
Morrill, J. Jr., & Co., manfrs. soap and candles	158
Morrison, E. L., & Co., commission merchants	222
Morse, H. A., & Co., coal	300
Morse, E., manfr. billiard tables	202
Morse, R., wines, liquors, etc.	242
Moulton, B. S., & Co., art gallery, etc.	176
Mugridge, C. R., carpenter	286
Munch, C. R., Jr., hat tip printer	275
Munch, H. W., manfr. ribbon badges for societies, etc.	257
Murphy, M. J., undertaker	271
Murphy, W. T., watchmaker, etc.	191
Murray, R. F., provisions	266
Myers Bros. & Co., tobacco manfrs.	194
Nardi, J., & Co., manfrs. Moorish and Nubian figures	240
Nash, M. E., furnaces, stoves, etc.	265
National Supply Co., J. Brooke, mgr.	193
National Supply Co., clothing, dry goods, etc.	193
National Mortgage & Debenture Co.	116
National Bank of the Commonwealth	155

	PAGE
National Plating Co.	292
Naylor, R. F., real estate, etc.	202
Ness County Bank, Ness City, Kansas, A. E. Alvord, Eastern mgr.	132
Newell, J. S., & Co., mechanical engineers, etc.	289
Newhall, F. C., wood easels, fire screens, etc.	238
Newhall & English, costumers	262
Newhall, J. Q., pattern maker	211
New England Weston Electric Light Co., The	123
New England House, J. T. Wilson, prop.	113
New England Furniture Exchange	285
New England Supply Co., clothing, dry goods, etc.	278
New England Steam Cooperage Co., manfrs. tanks, casks, etc.	139
New England Grip Co.	224
New England Lobster Co., G. L. Young, mgr.	190
New England & Savannah Steamship Co.	170
Newman, J., & Sons, floral artists	220
Niagara Fire Insurance Co., Henry B. Turner, genl agt.	205
Nichols & Fish, manfrs. cigar boxes, etc.	282
Nichols, L. E., watches and clocks	275
Nichols, O., & Co., manfrs. Residene Heeling	246
Nickerson, W. E., patentee of Nickerson's Hydraulic Elevator Safety	229
Nickerson & Glidden, commission merchants	206
Nims, O. F., apothecary	268
Norris & Cortheil, insurance, etc.	187
Norris Piano & Diamond Co.	112
North, C. H., & Co., packers and curers of pork, etc.	185
Northern Assurance Co., of London	155
Nowell, C., real estate, etc.	204
Noyes, E. W., printer	269
Noyes, B., mortgages	236
Ober, C. S., & Co., manfrs. table sauce	108
Oberle, F. X., manfr. cigars	260
O'Brion, T. L., insurance	200
O'Callaghan, T., & Co., carpetings, etc.	128
Ocean Steamship Berth Co.	110
O'Hara, F. J., & Co., wholesale fish, etc.	177
Old Boston National Bank	154
Old Colony Grocery, Wm. C. Cooledge, propr.	304
Oliver, D. M., & Co., pork, lard, hams, etc.	216
Oriental Coffee House Co.	287
Orne, C. W., butchers' scales, saws, etc.	247
Osgood, J. H., & Co., printers' rollers	218
Otis, G. D., & Co., bonded truckman, etc.	151
Page, M. S., & Co., merchandise and money brokers	205
Paine, A. W., tailor	246
Palmer, Parker & Co., mahogany and veneers	222
Park House, W. D. Park & Son, props.	129
Parker, F. M., provisions, etc.	267
Parker, G. S., real estate, etc.	210
Parkinson & Burr, bankers and brokers	239
Patten & Stratton, photographers	300
Patterson, R. A., & Co., tobacco manfrs.	156
Patterson & Lavender, manfrs. show cases, etc.	179
Paul, W. F., paper stock	247
Pazolt, T. C., & Son, furs	224
Pease, C. F., bindings for carpets, etc.	296
Peck Bros., printers, etc.	126

GENERAL INDEX.

Pelonsky, M., dry and fancy goods, etc............ 287
Peninsular Novelty Co., The, manfrs. button attaching
    machines and fastners........................... 297
Percival, J. P. T., pharmacist..................... 133
Peretti, L., cigars................................ 242
Perkins, A. D., mutton, lamb, etc.................. 221
Perkins, C. L., manfr. candies, etc................ 162
Perry, J. P., & Co., plumbers, etc................. 259
Perry, W. A., real estate, etc..................... 297
Pettee Machine Works, manfrs. cotton mill machinery 228
Phelps, F. S., insurance........................... 118
Phenix Hotel, I. M. Southwick, propr............... 268
Phillips, W. P., manfr. lubricators, etc........... 177
Pickens, L. W., planing mill....................... 249
Pinkham, H. W., provisions, etc.................... 286
Pino-palmine Co., George C. Stewart, mgr........... 104
Plumer & Co., commission merchants in flour, etc... 151
Pollock, C., photographs........................... 230
Pond, G. L., & Co., real estate brokers............ 239
Porter, J. W., insurance........................... 120
Porter, W., & Co., fire insurance.................. 165
Porter, A., optician............................... 175
Post, J., jr., & Co., mechanical engineers 115
Potter, C. D., commission merchant, etc............ 142
Power, J. E., designer and engraver................ 269
Power, T. C., employment agency.................... 244
Power, J., manfr. corks............................ 293
Powers, C., musical goods, etc..................... 264
Pratt, I. L., & Co., metals........................ 303
Pray, B. S., commission merchant................... 210
Pray & Tillson, diamond cutters.................... 299
Preston, G., commission merchant................... 303
Prior, W. H., mutton, lamb, veal, etc.............. 218
Pullen, O. C., market.............................. 267
Quimby, M. T., & Co., manfg. jewelers, etc......... 164
Quincy, The, G. G. Mann, propr..................... 117
Quincy Club Stable, H. W. Miller, manager 218
Rand, C. F., auctioneer, etc................197 & 306
Raymond, G. P., costume parlors.................... 242
Read, Hawkins & Co., flour and produce............. 195
Read Furniture Co., The Geo. E..................... 140
Read W., & Sons, guns, sporting goods, etc 296
Reardan, J., & Co., engraved and painted signs..... 272
Reardon, M., manfr. horse collars.................. 303
Redding Electrical Co., manfrs. electrical supplies 130
Reed & Bro., fire insurance........................ 226
Reed, W. G., fire insurance........................ 146
Revere House, J. F. Merrow & Co., propes........... 105
Reversible Collar Co., manfrs. collars and cuffs... 188
Reynolds, A. N., & Co., manfrs. oils............... 116
Rice, J. S., & Co., manfrs. tin cans, etc.......... 264
Rice & Holway, commission merchants................ 148
Richards & Co., tin plates. etc.................... 211
Rink, J. J., blacksmith, etc....................... 250
Ritchie & Brown, auctioneers....................... 158
Ritz, E. F., photographic artist................... 182
Roach, G. F., & Co., furniture, etc................ 210
Roberts, J. N., collateral banking rooms........... 152
Robbins, N., poultry and wild game................. 241
Robinson, W. F., & Co., wholesale beef, pork, etc.. 157

Robinson, C. F., produce commission merchant....... 265
Roby, W. G., & Co., metal dealers.................. 112
Rockwell, G. C., & Son, produce commission merchants 264
Rockwood, E. E., apothecary........................ 259
Rodocanachi, J. M., Smyrna and Mediterranean products 304
Rogers, L. A., & Co., commission merchants......... 209
Rollins, L. B., & Co., commission merchants........ 274
Rowe, R., insurance, etc........................... 142
Rowe, A. A., & Son, forwarding agts. and truckmen.. 285
Ruggles & Buss, commission merchants............... 250
Russell, B. B., publisher.......................... 283
Russell Counter Co., manfr. waterproof moulded stif-
    fenings....................................... 133
Russell, J. M., publisher of sheet music........... 245
Russell, C., & Co., wholesale ice.................. 192
Russell, D., steam and gas pipe, etc............... 298
Rydingsvard, K. A., wood carver.................... 139
Sages Trunk Depot, O. F. Sage, propr............... 295
Samuels, E. A., publisher.......................... 111
Sanborn, C. B., & Co., produce commission merchants 255
Sanderson & Son, genl. agts. Wilson Line of Steamers 225
Sargent, F., & Co., manfrs. carriages, etc......... 191
Sargent, E. P., jr., & Co., manfg. stationers, etc. 200
Savory, T. C., banner painter...................... 222
Sawyer, G. A., mutton, lamb, veal, etc............. 131
Sawyer, N., & Son, printers........................ 101
Sawyer, E., civil and mechanical engineer.......... 146
Scanlon & Dillon, fruit, vegetables, etc........... 170
Schaefer, W. R. & Son, sporting goods, etc......... 236
Schloss, N., wholesale cigars and tobacco.......... 225
Schmidt, S., manfr. jewelery, etc.................. 246
Schwarz, R., toys.................................. 258
Scribner, H. M. & Co., photographers, etc.......... 279
Schofield, W. J., printer.......................... 247
Scott, Jesse, confectionery........................ 276
Scull & Bradley, fire and marine insurance......... 103
Sears People's Drug Store, G. T. Sears, propr...... 166
Sears, J. H. & Co., shipping commission merchants.. 161
Seavern, H., hair felt, etc........................ 226
Security Investment Co............................. 235
Sewell & Day Cordage Co............................ 210
Sewing Machine Supplies Co., The................... 245
Sexauer, W. L., manfr. cigars...................... 263
Sharp, S. T., foreign exchange and insurance....... 247
Shattuck & Jones, fish, etc........................ 228
Shaw, E. A., cotton buyer.......................... 237
Shedd & Crane, leather............................. 222
Sheehan, D. C., fruits and produce................. 256
Shepard & Morse Lumber Co.......................... 144
Sherman, C. J. F., & Son, watches, clocks, etc..... 271
Sherman, J. W., stationery, toys, etc.............. 258
Shurtleff Bros., commission merchants.............. 281
Siebert, H., leather and findings.................. 267
Silsby, B. F., confectioner........................ 261
Simonds, C. H., & Co., printers.................... 264
Simmons, Amsden & Co., fruit and vegetables........ 218
Simpson Bros., asphalt floors, etc................. 150
Singleton, T., & Son, manfrs. glassware............ 269
Siskind, L., & Co., 5 and 10 cent goods............ 278
Skillings, Whitneys & Barnes Lumber Co............. 150

GENERAL INDEX.

	PAGE
Slade, L., butter, cheese, etc.	289
Slayton & Boynton, commission merchants	264
Smith, J., & Son, fish, etc.	208
Smith, E. F., photographer	256
Smith, T. E., cigars, etc.	256
Smith, T. J., tea broker	135
Smith & Blanchard, wholesale lumber	131
Smith, W. E., fruits, etc.	206
Smith, Wm. A., diamonds	250
Smith, H. W., watchmaker	115
Smith, L. H., & Co., manfrs. machine screws, etc.	159
Smith, F. A., & Co., commission and wholesale paper	164
Smith, J., & Co., manfrs. harness, etc.	173
Smith, Geo. W., insurance	289
Snow, P., ladies' and gents' furnishings	271
Snow, J. P., railroad lands	153
Snow & Higgins, groceries	171
Snow, T. G., manfr. Commonwealth Solid Cream, etc.	288
Soule, Dillingham & Co., pavers and street railway contractors	230
Sowden, C., signs and show cards	284
Spalding, Elms & Co., tailors' trimmings	231
Spencer, S. M., stencil and stamp works	187
Sprague Mrs. H., dry and fancy goods	251
Spring Lane Furnishing Co., gents' furnishing goods	101
Stahl, H., manfr. cigars	286
Standard Cordage Co., manfrs. cordage and binders' twine	103
Stanwood, F., cotton buyer	273
Starratt, D, W., & Co., tailors	273
Stearns, W., & Co., wholesale grocers	283
Stedman & Kellogg, bankers and brokers	166
Stetson, A. M., & Co., coal, wood, etc.	143
Stevens, C. D., millinery	252
Stevens, E. F., photographer	137
Stewart, Miss M. B., typewriter, etc.	254
Stewart, H., manfr. carriages, etc.	258
Stillings, E. B., & Co., stationers and printers	109
Stockwell, F. F., engraver	284
Stone, C. D., & Co., grocers	186
Story & Stevens, wholesale fish	176
Story, O. L., scenic artist	198
Stratton, G. F., mouldings	245
Strecker, L., & Co., manfrs. pants, etc.	209
Stubbs, J. A., wholesale oysters, etc.	164
Sturtevant Mill Co., manfrs. mills for crushing ores, etc.	121
Suffolk National Bank of Boston, The	130
Sullivan Consolidated Gold Mining Co.	124
Sumner, F. H., & Co., bankers and brokers	188
Swain, Earle & Co., teas and coffees	163
Swift, T. S., horse-shoer	268
Sylvester, W. A., mechanical draughtsman	270
Tamarack Mining Co.	174
Tarbox & Clarke, flour, etc.	249
Taylor, H. W., real estate, etc.	222
Taylor, Dr. E. S., dentist	212
The Quincy, G. G. Mann, propr.	117
Thomas, F., manfr. candies	282
Thompson, A. T., & Co., manfrs. stereopticons, etc.	137
Thompson, E. W., N. E. Pass. Agt. C., R. I. & P. Ry.	291

	PAGE
Thorndike Bros., beef, mutton, etc.	291
Tighe & Burke, grocers	223
Tilton, S., & Co., tobacco	162
Tinkham, J., undertaker	260
Todd, Thomas, printer	123
Todd, F. W., & Co., real estate, etc.	210
Tower, H. C., commission merchant	247
Townsend, T. W., real estate, etc.	264
Toy, D., tailor	304
Tracey, photographer	186
Tregurtha, J., machinist	271
Trickey, F. P., boarding, baiting, and sale stable	165
Triggs, F. J., representing Arthur & Bonnell, lithographers	298
Troeder, A., Elint Loan Co.	251
Tryon, S. C., beef, pork, lard, etc.	219
Tucker, J. A., & Co., phosphate	112
Turnbull, W., & Co., dry-goods commission merchants	217
Turnbull, G. L., clothing, etc.	230
Turner & Kaupp, silver platers, etc.	218
Turner, R. W., real estate, etc.	207
Turton, T., & Sons (Limited), manfrs. spring steel, etc.	209
Tuttle, A. & J. E., mechanical draughtsmen	273
Tuttle, C. F., real estate	263
Tuttle, J. W., & Sons, wholesale commission merchants	178
Twitchell, C. A., & Co., engravers	270
Tyler, G., & Co., agricultural machinery	140
Union Debenture Co.	109
Union Investment Co., W. M. Mick, mgr.	133
Union Steam Sponging Works, M. Crohn, propr.	300
Valentine, L., ladies' tailor	258
Van Dalinda, W. H., manfr. barbers' supplies	292
Van Derveer & Holmes Biscuit Co.	209
Varney, N. R., watchmaker	284
Ver Planck, E. D., sugar, hemp, etc.	144
Vinton & Jenkins, manfrs. boots and shoes	261
Virginia, Tennessee & Georgia Air Line	260
Vorenberg, S., & Co., clothing	199
Wainwright, H. C., & Co., stock brokers	207
Wait & Cutter, architects	205
Wakefield, E. H., real estate, etc.	171
Walker, G. A., Machine Co.	183
Walker, H. E., & Co., manfrs. stoves, ranges, etc.	233
Walker & Pratt Manfg. Co.	215
Walker, S., & Co., oils, naphtha fluid, etc.	246
Wall, J. E., manfr. bamboo furniture, etc.	230
Ward, C. M., & Co., manfg. jewelers	294
Ware, Geo. H., printer	274
Ware, G. A., barbers' supplies	302
Warner & Jarvis, salt	196
Warner, R., & Co., manfrs. wooden ware, etc.	171
Warren, M. C., & Co., hardware	104
Warren's Military Band & Orchestra	264
Washburn, I., insurance, etc.	199
Wasserboehr, J. E., & Son, manfrs. cigars	290
Waterhouse, W. A., lumber	208
Waters & Litchfield, beef, pork, lard, etc.	224
Watts & Willis, commission merchants	243
Waverly Manfg. Co., confectioners' specialties	163
Webb, J. H., engraver	261

GENERAL INDEX.

	PAGE
Weber, F. E., confectioner and caterer	194
Webster, H. P., tea and coffee	191
Weiss, Max, clothing	291
Wells Manufacturing Co., manfrs. brass and wire goods	240
Wemyss Concert Co. of Boston, Alex. J. Wemyss, mgr.	134
West, W., & Co., manfg. confectioners	298
Weston Lumber Co.	211
Wetmore & Story, tailors	279
Wheatland, P. D., stock broker	187
Wheeler, G. H., real estate, etc.	258
Wheelock, C. W., & Co., oil stoves, etc.	142
Wheildon, L. B., & Co., real estate brokers	285
Whidden, Curtin & Co., furniture, etc.	235
White & Johnson, provision, etc.	292
White, W. H., Jr., & Co., boots and shoes	287
White, C. H., & Co., manfrs. hot air furnaces, etc.	143
White, C. E., cigars, etc.	278
White's, T., Sons, truckmen and forwarders	226
Whitaker, N. C., & Co., tortoise shell and horn goods	276
Whitaker Bros., ecclesiastical decorative painters	161
Whitmore, C. E., & Co., brokers	132
Whitney, J. E., East India goods	149
Whiton Bro. & Co., agts. for the Woodbury Cotton Duck Mills	176
Whiton & Knight, printers	295
Whitten, Burdett & Young, clothing	107
Whittington, H., & Co., horse clothing	113
Wilson, B. O. & G. C., wholesale druggists	283
Wilson, Cassells & Co., New England representatives of Hall's Safe & Lock Co.	241
Wilson, E. M., D.D.S., dentist	302
Wilcox, Geo. B., printer	219
Willard, J. H., picture framer	270
Winegar, M. B. & Co., stationery, etc.	305
Winn, Ricker & Co., commission merchants, etc.	206
Winship, W. W., manfr. trunks, bags, etc.	257
Winslow Furniture Co., S. Winslow, mgr.	298
Winslow, Geo. S., & Co., provisions, poultry, etc.	259
Wise, Harris & Co., manfrs. cigars	160
Wolff, A., watchmaker, etc.	267
Wood, Kilbourne & Co., pianos	254
Wood L., Jr., manfr. cabinet work, etc.	293
Wood Bros., paints, oils, etc.	301
Woodbridge, S. F., & Co., wholesale beef, pork, etc.	206
Woodbury, Shaw & Co., wholesale oysters, etc.	152
Woodcock, S. S., architect and landscape gardener	160
Woodman, J. H., manfr. boots and shoes	282
Woodward, S. T., lumber	274
Woodward, W. E., architect	201
Woodward, H. E., & Co., wholesale salt and pickled fish	173
Woolson, H. H., tailor	285
Wright Bros. & Co., manfrs. umbrellas, etc.	281
Wright, C., & Co., lard refiners	207
Yale, R. M., & Co., sail makers	285
Yarrington, P., & Co., agents Automatic Water Gas Co	138
Ybarra, General A., coffee and cocoa importer	147
Yenetchi, G. V., wholesale wines and liquors	117
Yeretsky A., tailor	254
Young A., & Co., building materials, etc.	140
Young, J. A., wholesale lobsters	288
Young's Hotel, J. Reed Whipple, propr.	120
Ziegler, J. J., & Co., real estate, etc.	262
Zohrlaut H., Leather Co., Leavitt & Libbey, mgrs.	214

ILLUSTRATED BOSTON

THE METROPOLIS OF NEW ENGLAND.

BOSTON, from whatever point of the compass approached,—whether by any of the eight railway lines which radiate from it as a centre; or by the numerous broad, well-kept highways that cleave the fragrant gardens and verdant pastures of its vicinage on the land sides; or by the ocean, whose shimmering waves dash and spend their force against the numerous wooden wharves which skirt the shore,—presents one object—a golden one, flashing in the rays of the hot summer sun, or dully glimmering under the fleecy winter sky—that arrests the attention of the traveller. It is a gilded dome, towering above all the thousands of buildings that cluster around it. It is the pivot of industrial, cultured, and fashionable Boston: in the characteristic language of Dr. Oliver Wendell Holmes, it is "the hub of the solar system,"—whence Boston's sobriquet, "The Hub." While from every side of the city this gold-leaf-covered cupola is seen to stand out prominently like a tall monarch overlooking ambitious minions compactly crowded on gentle slopes, its interior, which is open to visitors at certain seasons of the year, commands a view of unsurpassed grandeur. It is a vantage-ground from which the

eye can encompass the outlay and form of the city; the deep blue sea, dotted with innumerable islands and sailing craft of every kind, and stretching out to the level eastern horizon, whence the sea meets the sky; the picturesque Blue Hills of Milton and the rocky heights of Essex; the scores of white villages, towns, and hamlets, strewn, as it were, at random, and interlineated with tortuous rivers, like so many silvery belts; and the dark, wide-spreading forests which form the background of a beautiful landscape stretching to the westward sky line.

This "hub of the solar system" is the dome of Massachusetts' capitol, which stands on Boston's highest ground, the breezy crest of Beacon Hill, whereon for more than fourscore years "the wise men and foolish, noble men and petty," constituted by the suffrages of the people "The Great and General Court," have managed and mismanaged the public affairs of the State, and influenced more or less the greater and more important national councils.

BEACON HILL

and its immediate surroundings are rich in historic associations. Historians tell of a time when there was only one solitary log hut nestling on the breast of this far famed hill, and of this being the only habitation on the whole of Boston's domain. It was the abode of an eccentric gospel minister, the Rev. William Blackstone, who, after fleeing from the haunts of men in old England, sought seclusion here. He it was who first purchased from the Indians the entire peninsula on which Boston now stands. At this time there were three hills on the peninsula, and these had given to them the name of Treamount, while the whole peninsula was designated Trimountaine, instead of Mushauwomuk, as called by the Indians, and since abbreviated to Shawmut. Mushauwomuk is variously assumed to have signified in the Indian tongue "living fountains," "free land," and "land unclaimed." These hills came to be separately known as Beacon, Copp's, and Fort Hills. Beacon Hill, however, had three peaks, and some writers claim that the name Treamount was derived from this fact. In 1634, Wood, the voyager, wrote of Beacon Hill as "three little hills on top of a high mountain." Blackstone's hut was situated near Pinckney and West Cedar Streets. East of the hut was the clergyman's garden; and a spring, from which he drew his water supply, and which proved to be the earliest inducement to the founders of New England's metropolis to come and settle here, was not far from the centre of the grass plat in the present enclosure of Louisburg Square.

A number of people from Dorchester, England, had in 1628 purchased the territory now known as the Massachusetts Bay State Colony. They were one of two parties of dissenters — Puritans and Separatists — from the Episcopal Church of England, and the laws of Britain made it a crime to worship God in any other form than that prescribed by this church, by law established. The religious dissenters, who came to the old Bay State for conscience' sake, were Puritans, who lamented the evils in the church, and hoped to reform it from within. The pilgrims who settled in the neighboring colony of Plymouth, about thirty miles from Boston, in 1620, were Separatists, who, believing Episcopalianism utterly corrupt, came off from it. The Puritans were a strait-laced sect, and came to the new colony accompanied by John Winthrop as their Governor, and by Thomas Dudley as lieutenant-governor. The colonists settled at Charlestown, which for a long time was a distinct municipality, but is now a part of the city of Boston. Experiencing at Charlestown a lack of wholesome water, a number of the colonists crossed the stream in a boat to Blackstone's peninsula to search for some. Here they found it in abundance, and this discovery led to overtures between Blackstone and the colonists. The negotiations resulted in Blackstone and many of the Puritans becoming close neighbors. Winthrop had at this time built himself a house at Charlestown, and there the headquarters of the colonists was located. Though a few houses rapidly grouped around that of Blackstone's, no thought had yet been entertained of establishing here a city which should one day be the most noted one in the Republic, and which should play an important part in the creation of the great United States. It is true the governor and his lieutenant had decided upon looking up a tract of country more suited for the seat of government than Charlestown was believed to be; but Boston had not been considered—if indeed any place had been thought of—as eligible for the distinction. Accordingly, one day in 1630 the governor and his lieutenant mounted their horses and started out to explore the plains and swamps and forests lying to the westward, and find a suitable site for a capital. The spot they finally picked out, with the help of some assistant magnates, lay about three miles west of Charlestown, on the banks of the tortuous little river since sung of by poets, and already named the Charles by Captain John Smith, who never saw it. The location seemed to Winthrop "a fit place for a beautiful town;" and accordingly, on the 29th of December, a goodly number of persons bound themselves with Governor Winthrop to build houses there in the following spring. The village they named Newtown, and this has since developed into the present Cambridge. The town was laid out regularly in squares, and early in 1631 houses began to arise. Governor Winthrop set up the frame of his dwelling on the very spot where he had first pitched his tent. But the people who had gone over from Charlestown to Boston had been promised by Winthrop that he would never move away anywhere unless they accompanied him, and of this

Scollay Square.

promise they now reminded him in pretty strenuous terms. Bound by two solemn agreements, and under the necessity of breaking one of them, Winthrop found himself in a "fix;" but his conscience yielded to the promise he had first made. So, in the fall of 1631, he disappointed his Newtown friends by taking down the frame of his unfinished dwelling and by setting it up in Boston, near Beacon Hill. Dudley had completed his house and installed his family into it; and he and the rest of the Newtown colonists refused to accompany Winthrop. This led to an open quarrel between Winthrop and Dudley, and a coolness existed between them for years. Winthrop's excuse for quitting Newtown was somewhat strengthened in his own mind by the fact that Chickatabut, the chief of the neighboring Indians, had promised to be friendly, so that the necessity of having a fortified settlement in the colony, three miles west, was somewhat less urgent. The commercial prospects of Boston, too, had begun to look brighter than those of Newtown. Making the best of their opportunities, the remaining settlers at Newtown proved thrifty and prosperous, and in 1632 received accessions to their number from Braintree, England. The quarrel between Winthrop and Dudley continuing, the ministers justified the lieutenant-governor by ordering Winthrop to get a clergyman for Newtown, failing in which he should pay Dudley £20. This sum Winthrop had to render, but the pacified Dudley was magnanimous in his triumph, and returned it with a polite note, in which he courteously intimated that he would rather lose £100 than Winthrop's friendship. Their difficulties settled, the two magnates lived on friendly terms thereafter, and

BOSTON BECAME THE COLONIAL CAPITAL.

Of the new State no one could become a citizen unless he was a member of the Puritan Church. Under a stern, theocratic discipline, the town and colony grew steadily and surely, and sanguinary edicts were issued against the Baptists, Episcopalians, and Quakers who came to reside here. Rigid sumptuary laws were enforced. A high official was reprimanded by the governor for indulging in the luxury of a wainscot in his house; a clergyman was reproved for the vanity of painting his house on the outside. Fast riding, ball-playing in the streets, absence from church, speaking disrespectfully of the clergy, using tobacco publicly, charging high prices, denying the Scriptures, a man kissing his wife on the street or on a Sunday, and sheltering Quakers or Baptists, were all crimes in the sight of the lawmakers. Watchmen patrolled the streets by night, and walked "two by two together, a youth joined with an elder and more sober person." Their instructions set forth: "If after ten o'clock they see lights, to inquire if there be warrantable cause; and if they hear any noise or disorder, wisely to demand the reason. If they find young men and maidens, not of known fidelity, walking after ten o'clock, wisely to demand the cause; and if they appear ill minded, to watch them narrowly, command them to go to their lodgings, and if they refuse, then to secure them till morning." The people were warned by the ringing of public bells when to go to bed, when to rise in the morning, and when to eat and drink. The ringing of the Boston town bells, at nine o'clock in the evening, was instituted in 1649, and was doubtless originated from the curfew, a custom introduced in England before the Norman conquest to command the people to put out their fires. The ringing of the nine o'clock bell remained a custom in the city within living memory, and the practice is still kept up in some New England villages. Josselyn, describing the town as it was between 1660 and 1670, says: "On the south there is a small but pleasant common, where the Gallants a little before sunset walk with their marmalet madams, as we do in Moorfields, etc., until the nine o'clock bell rings them home to their respective habitations, when presently the Constables walk their rounds to see good order is kept, and to take up loose people." The "morning bell," in those days of early rising was rung "half an hour after four." In 1664 an "eleven o'clock bell" was ordered "for the more convenient and expeditious dispatch of merchants' affairs." In course of time this bell became the recognized signal for the worthy tradesmen to adjourn from their places of business to the nearest tavern, there to take a "nip" of rum, Holland or Cognac (whiskey was not a beverage in those times). This ringing of the town bells at 11 o'clock continued until 1835, when the hour was changed to 1 P.M., or, as it was said, "from the hour of drinking to the hour of dining." Various bills in the city clerk's files, however, show that different hours were chosen in the different neighborhoods. In 1718, £3 were voted "to pay a Bell Ringer at the New South Meeting House for a year," he to officiate at five in the morning and nine at night, "as other Bell Ringers did."

The religious bigotry and civic intolerence on the part of his neighbors proved too much for minister Blackstone, the proprietor of the peninsula, for, said he, "I came from England because I did not like the

Post Office.

Lord Bishops, but I cannot join with you, because I would not be under the Lord's Brethren." Accordingly, about four years after the removal of the colonists to the peninsula, and being ill at ease among them, he agreed to sell to them the whole of the peninsula, except six acres where his house stood on Beacon Hill, for £30 ($150), and the money was raised by a rate, each householder paying six shillings (about $1.50). Compared with the price paid for Manhattan Island, the site of the commercial metropolis of the country, that peak for the peninsula on which New England's leading city stands was six times greater; but the former was bought from the Indians and the latter from an Englishman, and a parson at that. With the money received from the sale, Blackstone bought cows and other things, and travelled farther into the wilderness, establishing a new home, which he called "Study Hill," not far from Providence, R. I., on the banks of the picturesque river, which is now known as the Blackstone.

Since Blackstone shook the dust of Boston off his shoes forever, and looked for the last time upon the first house his own hands had reared on the site of the new prosperous city, Beacon Hill, with its three peaks, has undergone great transformations. The peaks have long since disappeared. One was located behind where the State House now stands, near Mount Vernon, Temple and Hancock Streets (where the beacon stood), and was for a time designated Centry Hill; another, situated farther west, was named Copley's Hill, and subsequently Mount Vernon, from which the present Mount Vernon Street derived its name; and the third, located to the east of Centry Hill, was first known as Cotton's Hill, and then as Pemberton's Hill, from which the present Pemberton Square took its name. The original Treamount stretched from the head of the present Hanover Street on the east to near the present Charles Street on the west, and near West Cedar Street was a high bluff known as West Hill. From Cambridge Street on the north, the hill extended to the Common on the south, and its highest point was 138 feet above sea level.

The beacon—a fiery alarm to the surrounding country of invasion or other danger—was fixed on the summit of the hill, just below the present Mount Vernon and Temple Streets, in 1634, by order of the General Court, and thenceforward the eminence became known as Beacon Hill. The beacon consisted of an iron

Lief Ericsson, Commonwealth Avenue.

skillet, filled with combustibles always ready for use, and was suspended from a crane of iron at the top of a tall mast, into which were driven tree-nails that served the purposes of a ladder. The times in which this beacon was erected were troublous, and the beacon had often to render important service to the struggling and harassed colonists, of whom twenty thousand came to the colony in the first ten years after the settlement of Boston. When the beacon was raised on the hill, a rude castle arose on an island before the town, and war vessels were commissioned, because at various times the port was menaced with attacks from Dutch, Spanish, and French fleets. In 1639 a thousand well-armed men mustered on the Common, and powerful contingents went out from Boston to aid the British expeditions against Louisburg, Quebec, Acadia and Havana; and the colonists, marching side by side with the best troops in the world, became veteran and skilful soldiers. One of the earliest colonists wrote to his folks in the old country that the new land was "a hideous wilderness, possessed by barbarous Indians, very cold, sickly, rocky, barren, unfit for culture, and like to keep the people miserable."

The first beacon that was erected fell, through some unknown cause, and a new one was erected in 1768. In the dark days of the Revolution the British troops tore down the beacon and erected a small square fort in its stead; but as soon as the English left the town in 1776 the inhabitants again placed the beacon in position. During a gale in 1789 it was blown down. On its site, in 1790–94 was erected a monument of brick to commemorate the heroic deeds of those patriots who fell in the sanguinary struggle on Bunker Hill. The monument, which was sixty feet high and four wide, had a tablet on each of its four sides, and it was surmounted by a gilded eagle with outstretched wings. The inscription on the east-side tablet read: "Americans! While from this eminence, scenes of luxuriant fertility, of flourishing commerce, and the abodes of social happiness meet your view, forget not those who have by their exertions secured to you these blessings." That on the south side: "To commemorate that train of events which led to the American Revolution and finally secured liberty and independence to the United States, this column is erected by the voluntary contributions of the citizens of Boston. MDCCXC." The west and north-side tablets contained lists of the principal events connected with the War of the Revolution.

This hill formed a part of the public lands, and in 1811 the town sold off many of these, including the hill, to raise money to reduce its debts, which were pressing heavily upon it. Following the sale, a spirit of improvement set in, and the various eminences of Treamount were removed, much of the soil being used to raise the low land in the neighborhood of Charles Street, and to reclaim from the waters of the ocean the whole of the land now lying west of that thoroughfare. The tablets of the monument were placed in Doric Hall in the State House, and the gilded eagle occupies a place over the speaker's chair in the House of Representatives. The work of improvement lasted for about a dozen years, and the whole aspect of Beacon Hill was changed.

That side of the hill, overlooking the Common and the Public Garden, has for a hundred and fifty years been occupied by the most aristocratic houses in the city. Indeed, Beacon Street has been famed as the patrician street of New England, and as corresponding with Fifth Avenue in New York, though much less splendid than that grand thoroughfare, being lined with tall, sombre, brown stone structures, with no rich architectural grandeur in church edifices to relieve the monotony as in the avenue. Beacon Street runs in a straight line from Tremont Street over the crest of the hill, and has been extended by recent improvements to the aristocratic suburb of Longwood, running for a considerable distance close to and parallel with the river Charles. Along it and beyond it are the finest driveways in the country. On the hilly section of the street are the most fashionable and select clubs of the city, and here are or were several houses of interest to literary men. One of these—now rebuilt—was for twoscore years the abode of the late George Ticknor, the bosom friend of Hawthorne, the fast friend of Southey and Scott, and the historian of Spanish literature. Another was the residence of the famous blind scholar, W. H. Prescott, the historian of the Spanish Conquests of Mexico and Peru, etc. Among other residences may be pointed out that of C. C. Perkins, whose works on Tuscan sculptors and Italian art have had a world-wide circulation; that of one of the best poets of a past generation, Richard H. Dana; and that of Charles Sumner, the famous leader of the anti-slavery movement, also many others too numerous to particularize in this work.

Louisburg Square, situated on the western slope of the hill, and between Mount Vernon and Pinckney Streets, is an historic spot. Here was Blackstone's garden and spring. It is now private property, and in 1834 was enclosed and given its present name to commemorate the victory at Louisburg, upon which the French had spent twenty years and 30,000,000 livres in fortifying, as a menace to New England. In 1745 an army of 4000 undisciplined Yankee farmers and artisans left Boston and, joining a powerful British squadron, overthrew the fortress. The enclosure has many fine, noble trees, and two fine Italian statues of Aristides and Columbus.

In late years, even on the patrician Beacon Street, trade has planted its vigorous foot, and the aristocracy, as it has multiplied its members, has moved in a westerly direction, but under the shadow of the time-honored Beacon Hill. The sturdier rank and file of humanity and the representatives of commerce have taken possession of the other slopes of the hill, and, among the changes of recent years, a massive, gloomy structure of granite on Doane Street, built in 1849 for a distributing reservoir, has been removed, and the heavy stone work has gone to form the Charles River embankment, and to aid in constructing a wilderness into a beautiful park in the Back Bay district, thereby adding much to the beauty of that section.

THE METROPOLIS OF NEW ENGLAND.

THE STATE HOUSE.

Whose gilded dome is, as we have already said, the first object that strikes the eye of the stranger approaching Boston in any direction by land or sea, stands majestically on the highest point of Beacon Hill, a fitting position for the capitol of the State. Its foundations are more than one hundred feet above water level. Its dome, which rises to an altitude of one hundred and ten feet, has, ever since it was reared, been a well-known land-mark in every direction; and since it was covered with gold leaf, in 1874, it has been an object prominent above all its surroundings, and an ornament to the city. Near to the State House stood the old Hancock House, the residence of Governor Hancock of Revolutionary fame, and it was one of the noblest private mansions of the colonial period. It was razed in 1863, and private residences now

Washington Street, Looking North.

occupy its site. The site of the State House was Governor Hancock's pasture, and over ninety years has slipped by since the town of Boston purchased it and presented it to the State. On July 4, 1795, there was a pompous display of Puritan burghers, the Freemasons marching to the strains of bands of music to lay the corner stone of the State House, under Grand Master Paul Revere, and Governor Samuel Adams, not long before exiled for liberty's sake, giving the speech of dedication. The stone itself was drawn up the steep slope of Beacon Hill by fifteen white horses, representing the number of States forming the Union. The edifice was erected under the direction of Charles Bulfinch, and in January, 1798, the members of the Legislature marched in solemn procession from the Old State House, at the head of State Street, and took possession of the new capitol, which is a plain enough brick building, constructed massively, but at small cost, and seeking ornament only in a dark colonnade of Corinthian pillars and its shining Byzantine dome. Lofty flights of stone steps lead from the street to the main entrance, and the high terraces are kept enlivened by masses of brilliant flowers, in the midst of which stand bronze statues of the great orator, Daniel Webster, and of the famous educator, Horace Mann. The steps lead into a large hall, known as Doric Hall, where, in the recesses, protected by plates of glass, are shown the tattered remnants of several scores of flags carried by the Massachusetts regiments through the fierce struggles of the war for the Union. Here are also statues of Washington and Governor Andrew; busts of Samuel Adams, Charles Sumner, Henry Wilson, and Abraham Lincoln; fac similes of the tombstones of the ancestors of Washington, from England; the tablets from the Beacon monument, and many rare remembrances of ancient days in the Old Bay State. The Hall of Representatives has accommodation for five hundred legislators. Over the speaker's chair is the gilded spread eagle which once did duty on the summit of Beacon monument; and opposite hangs suspended from the ceiling the ancient wooden codfish brought from the Old State House, and typical of one of the foremost industries of the State. The Senate Chamber, where the Upper House meets, is adorned with notable trophies, and portraits of ancient worthies of Massachusetts; and near it is the State library, where more than forty thousand volumes are kept. Younger States—States that have sprung into being since this old edifice was built—have reared, where a few years ago were wildernesses, capitols with marble walls, fretted with sculpture and carving; but no State can be prouder of its capitol than that of Massachusetts, whose State House is typical of that simplicity and solidity which characterized the founders of the government. Plans have been prepared for enlarging the capitol and providing increased accommodation therein. On the slope and at the base of the hill, overlooked by the capitol, is

THE COMMON,

probably the most famous bit of land on the American Continent. It is an undulating natural park of forty-eight acres, surrounded by an iron fence over a mile long, crossed by five walks, shaded by a thousand ancient and graceful elms. It is located in the heart of the city, is surrounded on all sides by line upon line of busy and populous streets, and is the admiration not only of our own citizens, but of every visitor to the city, American and foreigner. When the early settlers purchased, more than two and a half centuries ago, the whole peninsula from Blackstone, they laid out this place for a "training field," and "for the feeding of cattle." Until 1830 cattle continued to be grazed on the Common, which is still sometimes used as a training field. Originally the Common extended in one direction as far as Tremont House, and in another to Mason Street, bordering westerly on the Back Bay, then a marshy tract, the waters of the ocean then flowing up to Charles Street and to the foot of the Roxbury Hills. Where Park Street now is an almshouse, a bridewell, and a granary stood, and was called Sentry Field. Forty-three and three fourths of the Common was enclosed in 1835 at a cost of $80,000, and later the remainder was enclosed. The Common is now surrounded on its four sides by Tremont, Boylston, Beacon and Park Streets, and it is one of the most beautiful and attractive parks in the country, rich in its greensward, its thousands of trees with umbrageous boughs, its ponds, monuments, and lovely walks.

The Common is not valued by Bostonians alone for its beauties and for the opportunities for outdoor recreation it affords, but for its historic associations. In the old granary referred to were made the sails of the frigate "Constitution," or "Old Ironsides," concerning the threatened destruction of which Boston's favorite citizen, Dr. Oliver Wendell Holmes, wrote in pencil, in his attic room in Cambridge, in 1829, and when he was but twenty years old:

> "And one who listened to the tale of shame,
> Whose heart still answered to that sacred name,
> Whose eye still followed o'er his country's tides
> Thy glorious flag, our brave Old Ironsides!
> From yon lone attic, on a summer's morn,
> Thus mocked the spoilers with his school-boy scorn."

The troops who captured Louisburg, the troops enlisted by Amherst, and who conquered Quebec, and the soldiers whose fights brought about the American Revolution, mustered here. Boston, as more copious histories will tell the reader, handled the torch that set aflame the Revolution. It had resisted the imposition of taxes by England time after time, and given the mother country to understand it was prepared to conduct business on its own account, if let alone. Its sons had boarded vessels in the harbor and thrown taxed tea into the sea rather than have it. They had resented the Stamp Act and other imposts, and made themselves so obnoxious to the English government that the latter declared the former rebels, and ordered the army of soldiers quartered on the town to send them to England for trial. Between the soldiery and the citizens there was, of course, no kindly feeling, and the dislike was intensified by an event known as

THE "BOSTON MASSACRE,"

which, it is not too much to say, was one of the most important events which united the interests and feelings of the colonists, and brought on the revolutionary war. After the elapse of more than a century the event has been commemorated by the recent raising on the Common of a monument, known as the Attucks Memorial, which stands on the greensward near the Tremont Street Mall. The massacre occurred toward evening, on Monday, March 5, 1770, in the very centre of the business part of the town, in the rear of the State

Boylston Street, from Copley Square.

House, on King Street—known since, for nearly a hundred years, by the more appropriate name of State Street. Of the five victims of the massacre, four of them, namely, Samuel Gray, Samuel Maverick, James Caldwell and Crispus Attucks, where buried on the Thursday following, March 8, in what is still known as the old Granary burying ground, on the present Tremont Street. On the occasion of the funeral the bells of the town were rung, places of business were closed, and vast numbers of all persons of citizens were in attendance. Various accounts have been written and published of the Boston massacre, not differing, however, much in their essential particulars, and all appear to agree in condemning the outrage as a natural result from the quartering of troops in the town. The soldiers belonged to the 14th and 29th Regiments, and it has been well said that it was a more highly criminal to quarter troops in such a town as Boston then was. The people hated the soldiers, and this feeling was reciprocated by the latter with interest. The inhabitants could not go about their ordinary avocations without being challenged at every corner by sentinels, and often insulted and assaulted. Some outrage, it is said, was complained of every day; and if soldiers in all cases of misconduct and violence were not the offending parties, their presence induced them, and they generally had the credit of them. "From the time the troops arrived in September, 1768," says one account, "until they left the town, there were complaints against them and trouble with them." On the afternoon before the massacre the soldiers posted the following in writing as a warning to the people:—"Boston, March ye 5, 1770. This is to Inform ye Rebellious People in Boston that the soldiers in ye 14th and 29th Regiments are determined to Joine together and defend themselves against all who Oppose them. Signed, Ye Soldjers of ye 14th and 29th Regiments."

"The evening of the 5th came on. . . . Parties of soldiers were driving about the streets, making a parade of valor, challenging resistance, and striking the inhabitants indiscriminately with sticks or sheathed cutlasses. A band poured out from Murray's barracks, in Brattle Street, armed with clubs, cutlasses and bayonets, provoked resistance, and a fray ensued. One soldier after another levelled a firelock and threatened to make a lane through a crowd. At about nine o'clock, a party of soldiers issued violently from the main guard, in King Street, their arms glittering in the moonlight, hallooing. 'Where are they? Where are they? Let them come on!' Presently twelve or fifteen more, uttering the same cries, rushed from the south-side into King Street, and so by way of Cornhill (Washington Street) toward Murray's barracks. They knocked a small boy down, and abused and insulted several persons at their doors and in the street, while their outcries of fire caused the bells to be rung. A body of soldiers came up Royal Exchange lane, crying, 'Where are the

Statue of Gen. John Glover.

cowards?' and, brandishing their arms, passed through King Street, a crowd of boys following them. A parley occurred with the sentinel, who had previously knocked one of the boys down, and loaded his gun and threatened to shoot them. 'Stand off!' said the sentry. 'They are killing the sentinel,' reported a servant, running to the main guard. 'Turn out! why don't you turn out?' cried Preston, captain of the guard. A party of six, two of whom, Kilroi and Montgomery, had been previously worsted in a fight at the ropewalk, formed with a corporal in front and Preston following. With bayonets fixed they rushed through the people upon the trot, cursing them and pushing them as they went along. They found about ten persons round the sentry, while about fifty or sixty came down with them. 'For God's sake,' said Henry Knox, who was passing by, holding Preston by the coat, 'take your men back again; if they fire your life must answer for the consequences.' 'I know what I am about,' said he, hastily and much agitated. None pressed on them or provoked them till they began loading, when a party of about twelve in number, with sticks in their hands, moved from the middle of the street, where they had been standing, gave three cheers, and passed along in front of the soldiers, whose muskets some of them struck as they went by. 'You are cowardly rascals, they said, 'for bringing arms against naked men. Lay aside your guns and we are ready for you!' . . . Just then Montgomery received a blow from a stick which had hit his musket, and the word 'fire!' being given by Preston, he stepped a little on one side and shot Attucks, who at the time was quietly leaning on a long stick. The people immediately began to move off. 'Don't fire,' said Longford, the watchman, to Kilroi, looking him full in the face; but yet he did so, and Samuel Gray, who was standing next to Longford, with his hands in his bosom, fell lifeless. The rest fired slowly and in succession on the people who were dispersing . . . Three persons were killed, eight were wounded, two of them mortally. Of all the eleven, not more than one had any share in the disturbance. So infuriated were the soldiers that when the men returned to take up the dead they prepared to fire again, but were checked by Preston, while the 29th regiment appeared under arms in King Street. 'This is our time,' cried the soldiers of the 14th, and dogs were never seen more greedy for their prey.

"The bells in all the churches were rung, and the cry of the people was 'To arms! To arms!' 'Our hearts,' said Warren, 'beat to arms, almost resolved by one stroke to avenge the death of our slaughtered brethren.' The people would not be satisfied or retire till the regiment was confined to the guard room and the barracks, and Governor Hutchinson gave the assurance that instant inquiries should be made by the county magistrates.

Such, as we have described, was the Boston massacre and some of the attending circumstances. It was a rude and brutal and unnecessary murdering of the people, in support of unjust and wrongful claims and pretensions of the British ministry, Parliament and the King. It was the first blood spilled by British soldiers upon American soil, and, in fact, the initiation of the war which followed between the colonies and the mother country. From this time forward there was no longer agreement or concord of action between the government (king, ministry and Parliament) and the people of the American colonies.

On the morning following the massacre, the Sons of Liberty gathered in great numbers in Faneuil Hall, and resolved that the people and soldiers could no longer live together in safety. In the afternoon over three thousand persons assembled at the Old South Church and appointed a committee to wait upon the governor and Colonel Dalrymple, the commander of the forces, and to demand that the soldiers should be removed from the town if the peace of the province was to be preserved. The governor and his council and

Clarendon Street.

Colonel Dalrymple were in a dilemma, but seeing that the people meant business unless their demand was complied with, took the responsibility upon themselves of ordering the soldiers to remove to Castle Island, in the Harbor.

Captain Preston and eight of his men were put on trial for murder. The court, on a pretence of its inability to determine whether it was Preston or some one else who gave the order to fire, acquitted him. Two of the soldiers, who declared that they had simply done their duty in obeying orders to fire, were found guilty of manslaughter and sentenced to be branded in the hand in open court. For a long time the anniversary of the massacre was annually celebrated by Bostonians, but it was not until Wednesday, November 14, 1888, that a permanent memorial of the event was completed and unveiled on the Common with much ceremony, to immortalize Crispus Attucks and his fellow victims. Attucks was a negro, and the monument is named after him. By publicly immortalizing the name of a negro who, it is presumed, was a patriot, race distinction in this country has received a blow that should be fatal. By inference a man is now declared a man, be he white, black, rich or poor. This is undoubtedly the highest thought suggested by the dedication ceremonies, though they were confined chiefly to eulogy of the victims of the massacre by Professor Fiske and other orators on the occasion. The monument, while an ornament to the Common, stands as a silent encouragement to the valor of future generations. It is the work of Mr. Robert Kraus. It bears in bas-relief, a representation of the event as it occurred in King (State) Street. The soldiers are in the act of firing upon the people, at the command of their captain, while the victims are seen falling among the crowd of people which surrounds them. The work is very vivid, life-like, and a very excellent representation of the scene. The sentiments which have been inscribed upon the monument, with the names of the authors, indicate the public estimation of the event at the present time almost as emphatically as compelling the troops to leave the town did more than a hundred years ago. These sentiments are the following: "From that moment we may date the severance of the British empire."—DANIEL WEBSTER. "On that night the foundation of American independence was laid."—JOHN ADAMS.

After the massacre England continued to tighten the screws of exaction and oppression, while the Bostonians grew more obstinate. In March, 1774, the English Parliament ordered the closing of Boston port, and in the following September instructed the newly appointed governor of Massachusetts, General Gage, to reduce the colonists by force. A fleet and an army of ten thousand soldiers were sent to aid in the work of subjugation. Boston Neck was seized and fortified by the governor's orders; the military stores in the arsenals at Cambridge and Charlestown were conveyed to Boston; and the General Assembly was ordered to disband.

The Common became the fortified camp. Earthworks were thrown up on several of its eminences, of which all traces have long since disappeared. The British artillery was stationed upon Flagstaff, or Powderhouse Hill, where there were intrenchments and a powder house. A battery was located on Fox Hill, which stood near the present Charles Street. On the Boylston Street side, opposite the present Carver Street, was a strong fortification. The marines were located near the Tremont Street side of the Common, and the infantry were scattered over the old "training field." Deep trenches were cut near the present Charles Street Mall, within a short distance of which was then the water front. Here during the winter of 1775-76 over 1700 British warriors waited in expectation of being attacked by Washington, for the whole town was in a state of siege.

When it became apparent what General Gage's instructions were, the Bostonians, concealing their guns and ammunition in cartloads of rubbish, conveyed them to Concord, sixteen miles away. Gage discovered the movement, and on the 18th of April, 1775, dispatched a regiment of 800 men to destroy the stores. Another purpose was to capture John Hancock and Samuel Adams, who were supposed to be hidden at Lexington or Concord. The fact was that they were not hidden anywhere, but were abroad encouraging the people. The plan of the British general was made with great secrecy; but the patriots were on the alert, and discovered the movement, and when the regiment, under the command of Colonel Smith and Major Pitcairn left the foot of the Common at Boston about midnight for Concord, under Gage's orders, the people of Boston, Charlestown and Cambridge were roused by the ringing of bells and the firing of cannons by the patriots. Two hours before, William Dawes and Paul Revere had started off on horseback to spread the alarm through the country, and at two o'clock in the morning a company of one hundred and thirty armed patriots had assembled on the Common at Lexington, with guns loaded. At five o'clock the English regiment hove in sight, and Pitcairn rode up and shouted: "Disperse, ye villains! Throw down your arms, ye rebels, and disperse!" The minute men stood still; Pitcairn discharged his pistol at them and cried "Fire!" The first volley of the Revolution whistled through the air, and sixteen of the patriots fell dead or wounded. The rest fired a few random shots and then dispersed. But the end was not yet. The British pushed on to Concord, but the inhabitants had removed the greater part of the stores to a place of safety, and there was but little destruction. Two cannons were spiked, some artillery carriages were destroyed, and a small quantity of ammunition thrown into a mill pond. While the English were pillaging the town the minute men gathered from all quarters, and came in contact with a company of soldiers guarding the North Bridge, over Concord River. For the first time the Americans fired under the orders of their officers and two English soldiers were killed. The bridge was taken by the patriots and the enemy began a retreat, first into the town and then through the town on the road to Lexington. Then the minute men attacked the enemy from every side, and kept up a terrible fire from behind rocks, trees, fences and barns. Nothing but good discipline and reinforcements which, under the command of Lord Percy, met the fugitives just below Lexington, saved the English from total rout and destruction. The fight continued to the precincts of Charlestown, the patriots becoming more and more audacious in their onslaughts. At one time it seemed that the whole

British force would be obliged to surrender. Such a result was prevented only by the fear that the English fleet would burn Boston. The American loss in this, the first battle of the war, was forty-nine killed, thirty-four wounded and five missing; that of the enemy was two hundred and seventy-three—a greater loss than the English army sustained on the Plains of Abraham.

The battle of Lexington inspired the patriots everywhere, and within a few days an army of twenty thousand men had gathered in the vicinity of Boston. A line of intrenchments encompassing the city was drawn from Roxbury to Chelsea, and the talk of the camp was to drive Gage and his army into the sea. On the 25th of May, Generals Howe, Clinton and Burgoyne arrived with more men, and the British army at Boston was increased to 10,000 strong. Gage issued a proclamation styling all in arms as rebels, and offering pardon to all who would submit to the King's authority except two, Samuel Adams and John Hancock, who were to be put to death, if caught, as traitors. A well-founded rumor was set on foot that the English intended to sally out of Boston and burn the neighboring towns and devastate the country. The Americans with a view to preventing this, seized and fortified Bunker Hill, but afterwards removed to a neighboring height, subsequently called Breed's

Park Street Church.

Hill, which was within easy cannon range of Boston. On the 17th of June the British advanced against the stronghold, and a fierce struggle ensued, the patriots being only driven from the trenches at the point of the bayonet. It was, however, a costly victory for the English, who lost 1054 men in killed and wounded while the American loss was 115 killed, 305 wounded and 32 prisoners.

The Bunker Hill fight showed that the British army was not invincible, and it was followed by increased enthusiasm among the Americans everywhere; and in all parts George the Third's authority was set at nought. Fifteen days after the Bunker Hill engagement General Washington arrived at Cambridge and took command of the patriotic army, while General Howe succeeded General Gage in command of the British troops in Boston. Washington besieged the city all winter, and by the middle of February the American army had increased to 14,000 men. Washington was frequently urged to force a fight with the enemy, but until the spring he contented himself with narrowing his lines, strengthening his works, and waiting his opportunity. On the north, Boston was commanded by the peninsula of Charlestown, and on the south by Dorchester Heights. Since the battle at Bunker Hill the former position had been held by the British; the latter was, as

Boston Museum of Fine Arts, Art Square and Dartmouth Street.

yet, unoccupied. Washington resolved to take advantage, by a strategic movement, of the enemy's oversight, to seize the Heights and drive Howe out of Boston. To distract the attention of the British, heavy cannonading was kept up from the American batteries for two days, and during the night of the 4th of March a detachment of Americans ascended the Heights and established a line of formidable intrenchments and cannon frowning upon the city. Howe was astonished next morning when he saw how he had been out-generalled, and that he must either drive the Americans from the Heights or abandon the city. He directed Lord Percy to place himself at the head of 2400 men and storm the redoubts before nightfall. It was the anniversary of the "Boston Massacre," and the patriots were eager for vengeance. Percy got as far as Castle Island, when a violent storm arose and rendered the harbor impassable all day, so that the attack could not be made. The Americans continued to strengthen their position until Howe found himself in the extremity of giving up the capital of New England to the rebels. By an informal agreement between Washington and Howe, the latter was allowed to retire from the city unmolested, on condition that he did not burn the place. On the 17th of March, Howe and his army and some 1500 loyalist citizens left, and from that date the contending hosts transferred their struggles to other parts of the country. On the 20th, Washington rode triumphantly into the city, and the ten months' siege had ended. The whole country was exultant, and Congress ordered a gold medal to be struck in honor of Washington, who went in pursuit of the enemy to Long Island, but not before he had strengthened the defences of Boston.

The Common not only played an important part in the Revolutionary era, but in the days of the Rebellion it was the mustering and encamping ground of the Massachusetts regiments which were sent to do battle with the armed hosts of the Southern Confederacy. The Common is yet the place on which military bodies muster on anniversary days and public events, and it has been the scene of celebrations of many military and naval victories. In ante-Revolutionary times, on this historic ground frequent executions occurred under the ancient trees, especially in 1676, when the Narragansett Indians had been subjugated in a fierce battle among the swamps of Rhode Island, and when many a valiant red-skinned warrior was brought hither in chains and suspended from the boughs of the wide-spreading elms. Thirty Indians were thus put to death in a single day. Here, too, Whitfield preached and Quakers were hanged for conscience' sake. The famous old Common has been swept by shot and shell by night and by day, and nobles, generals, and statesmen have plotted and planned, under the leafy shades, the fate of dynasties and empires; and, within its cool retreats, lovers have for ages held their trystings, built airy castles, and whispered "sweet nothings." Orators have fretted and fumed on the greensward over real and fancied public wrongs; youngsters have, year after year, made the air ring with their merry shouts and laughter as they have swiftly glided on the winter ice on the hill-slopes; musicians have filled, and do fill in the summer months, the balmy air with pleasant sounds; and on festival days the old Common is a scene of jollity, presenting many of the sights of a country fair.

The glories of statesmen, warriors, and scholars are commemorated on the Common by monuments and statues. On the highest point of the Common, long known as Flagstaff Hill, or Monument Hill, as it is now called, is the Army and Navy Monument, which is worthy of a city that gave to the cause of the Union in the War of the Rebellion 24,434 soldiers and 685 officers. This magnificent specimen of the sculptor's art was the work of the late Mr. Martin Milmore, and cost $75,000. The cornerstone was laid September 18, 1871, and at its dedication, September 17, 1877, militia, veterans, and civic societies, numbering 25,000 men, marched in procession. This monument bears this record: "To the men of Boston, who died for their country on land and sea in the war which kept the Union whole, destroyed slavery, and maintained the constitution, the grateful city has built this monument, that their example may speak to coming generations." The base is cruciform, three steps rising to a pedestal which is faced with large bronze reliefs, representing the departure of the State troops, battle scenes in which the army and navy were engaged, the work of the hospitals in the field, and the return of the volunteers to the city. Between and above these stand four heroic bronze statues: The Soldier, fully equipped, with his musket and bayonet fixed; the Sailor, facing seaward, with drawn cutlass; History, a female figure, laurel-wreathed, clad in Greek costume, and about to write on a tablet; and Peace, another classic female figure, seated and holding an olive-branch toward the South. Above these rises a tall Roman Doric Shaft of white Maine granite, with allegorical figures representing the North, South, East, and West at its base and four marble eagles at the top. The summit of the monument, seventy feet high, is a colossal bronze statue of the Genius of America, crowned with thirteen stars, holding a bare sword and two laurel wreaths in one hand, and a banner staff in the other, and with her face bowed towards the south. Of this great and imposing memorial we give a fine illustration in these pages.

At the foot of the hill, within an iron inclosure, stood an old tree, known as the "Old Elm," until the winter of 1876, when it was destroyed in a gale. It was believed to have been there even before Blackstone set foot on the peninsula, and was regarded as the oldest of its kind in Boston. It was decrepit even in 1775, and was tenderly cared for for more than a hundred years. It had been the scene of many stirring events. Witches, Quakers, murderers, pirates, and others had been hanged from its branches; the "Sons of Liberty" had illuminated it with lanterns in Revolutionary days; duels had been fought under its shadow; and it had been a tryst for generation after generation of Bostonians. A foot above the ground, its circumference was 22½ feet, and it rose to a height of over 72 feet. A shoot off the "Old Elm" is now thriving on the spot where the old monarch of the forest stood.

THE PUBLIC GARDEN

lies just to the westward of the Common, with which it forms one of the handsomest parks in the country. The Garden, which is only separated from the Common by Charles Street, is in form varying little from a parallelogram, and contains over twenty-four acres. The site of the Garden was formerly a dreary expanse of marshy flats, overflowed by high tides, and was known as Round Marsh, or "the marsh at the bottom of the Common." After a great fire among some rope-walks in the present Congress Street in 1794, the city, in a fit of generosity, gave the marsh to the burned-out ropemakers. In 1819 their rope-walks on the marsh were burned out, but, as the land round about had increased much in value, they determined that it would pay them better to sell the marsh for building purposes than to reconstruct their rope-walks. The citizens were indignant, but the ropemakers were determined, and finally, in 1824, the city fathers concluded to buy back their gift of thirty years before, for $54,000 to make a public garden out of the marsh. In this they have succeeded admirably. In the centre is an artificial lake, with fountains, swan-houses, pleasure-boats, etc. The Garden is intersected with fine, graveled, sinuous walks, the velvety lawns are kept in splendid order, and the floral displays are the finest in America. The Garden contains many fine statues, among them being a colossal equestrian one of General Washington, bronze statues of Charles Sumner and Edward Everett, and a granite and red marble monument to commemorate the discovery in Boston of ether as an anæsthetic. By night the Garden is illuminated by electric lights, and the place is a popular resort for persons of all conditions.

ORIGINAL AND PRESENT AREAS OF BOSTON

In the preceding pages frequent reference has been made to the first settlement of Bostonians being on a peninsula. When Blackstone was here "lord of all he surveyed," his landed possessions formed a pear-shaped peninsula, and up to the beginning of the last half century the territorial area of the city was limited to the land owned by him. Its extreme length was less than two miles, and its greatest breadth a little more than one. The peninsula "hung to the mainland, at Roxbury," says one writer, "by a slender stem, or neck of a mile in length, so low and narrow between tide-washed flats that it was often submerged. Now the original 783 acres of solid land have become 1829. The broad, oozy salt-marshes, the estuaries, coverts, and bays once stretching wide on its northern and southern bounds have been reclaimed; and where then the area was the narrowest, it is now the widest. The hills have been cut down—some, Fort Hill, entirely removed; the whole surface of the original ground has been levelled and graded, and every square inch turned over and over; new territory has been added by annexing adjoining suburban cities and towns, until now the area of the city, with all its districts, is 23,661 acres ($36\frac{7}{8}$ square miles)—more than thirty times as great as the original area. The areas of the districts are as follows: South Boston, 1002 acres; East Boston, 836; Roxbury, 2700; Dorchester, 5614; West Roxbury, 7848; Brighton, 2277; Charlestown, 586; Breed's Island, 785; Deer Island, 184.

The following islands in the harbor of Boston belong to the city, viz.: Deer Island, containing 184 acres upland, and 50 acres flats, conveyed to the inhabitants of Boston, March 4, 1634-35; Thompson's Island, annexed to Boston by act of March 15, 1834; Great Brewster Island, containing 16 acres, purchased in 1848 for $4000; Gallop's Island, containing 16 acres, purchased in 1860 for $6600; Apple Island, containing 9½ acres, purchased 1867 for $3750; Rainsford Island, containing 11 acres, purchased, together with all hospital buildings and dwellings thereon, in 1871, for $40,000. Male paupers whose settlement is established in this city are now located in the large hospital building upon this island. Moon Island, containing about 30 acres, was taken by right of eminent domain from the heirs of James Huckins and others in 1879, and constitutes the point of discharge of the great sewer of the city of Boston. The city has within it 125,268,652 feet of marsh-land flats; and the measurement of the city from north to south is eleven miles, and from east to west nine miles. The principal business section of the city, lying between the harbor and Charles River, is a mile and a quarter across.

The various annexations that have been made to the city have necessitated the building of many bridges over the water-ways that separate the city proper from the districts annexed. These bridges are: Broadway Bridge, over Fort Point Channel to South Boston; Cambridge Bridge, Western Avenue and North Harvard Street bridges, from Brighton to Cambridge; Canal, or Craigie's Bridge, Leverett Street to East Cambridge; Charles River Bridge, Charlestown Street to Charlestown; Chelsea bridges (North and South), Charlestown to Chelsea; Chelsea Street Bridge, East Boston to Chelsea; Commercial Point Bridge; Congress Street Bridge, over Fort Point Channel; Dover Street Bridge, to South Boston; Essex Street Bridge, Brighton to Cambridge; Federal Street Bridge, to South Boston; Granite Bridge, Dorchester to Milton; Malden Bridge, Charlestown to Everett; Meridian Street Bridge, East Boston to Chelsea; Mount Washington Avenue Bridge, to South Boston; Neponset Bridge, Dorchester to Quincy; North Beacon Street Bridge, Brighton to Watertown; Prison Point Bridge, Charlestown to East Cambridge; Warren Bridge, Beverly Street to Charlestown; West Boston Bridge, Cambridge Street to Cambridgeport; Western Avenue Bridge, to Watertown; Winthrop Bridge, Breed's Island to Winthrop. A new bridge is now in course of construction from the Back Bay lands across the Charles River to Cambridgeport, and will be of vast service to the people located in these thriving sections.

CREATED LAND.

Proudly as she sits by the sea, majestic as she appears in her thrift and grandeur as the metropolis of New England, Boston has not acquired her present domain, her pre-eminence among the cities of the New

Post Office Square.

World, and her prosperity as a great manufacturing and commercial centre on the Atlantic seaboard, without a patient and prolonged struggle with natural obstacles and manifold adversities in varied forms. From statistics, given in a previous page, it will be seen that what are now the most valuable sections of the city have been stolen, as it were, by engineering skill from the boundless and restless ocean. Much of the original peninsula was rocky, and what is now the Common was liberally strewn with boulders deposited there ages ago. The first settlers found the peninsula abounding in abrupt and gradual elevations; large inlets of sea-water, that nearly divided it; broad fringes of ooze, and mud, and extensive marshes; an inner bay and with but a slender neck connecting it with the mainland. The greatest breadth of the Neck was at Beach Street, and its narrowest at Dover Street. From the latter point, says Drake, "it increased gradually in width to the neighborhood of Dedham Street, thence expanding in greater proportion to the line at the present car-stables, nearly opposite Metropolitan Place." In Revolutionary times the Neck was known as that part lying south of Dover Street, and at high tides the road was in some places covered with water which reached to the knees of horses passing through it. A sea-wall was built on the west side and a dyke on the east. A little south of the present Dover Street a fortification was built, and here were gates which were closed at night and which prevented any one from coming into or leaving the town on that side after a certain hour at night.

Since that time the city has been enlarging its area on every hand by making inroads upon the domain of Old Neptune, and this at fabulous cost, for the materials with which to do this have had to be carried from a distance. Trees were not found numerous on the peninsula by the first customers, though bushes were abundant; and to what extent the trees growing on the site served for house-building, the records are silent. But, when it was found necessary to construct piers or wharves, or to form solid borders to the territory over marshlands, or to push out to deep water, piles and timber had to be brought chiefly from the islands in the harbor. For a long time cargoes for sea going vessels had to be carried in small boats between the shore and the ships. It would be a curious calculation, were it possible, to estimate the number of forest trees which, from the earliest days to the present, have been driven into the marginal or alluvial soil of Boston, as solid land has been made over the water-flowage. These trees, covered with granite from the blowing up of local quarries and from Cape Ann, and with sand and gravel from hills a score of miles inland, illustrate the conditions by which a foothold has been secured on the peninsula. It is interesting, however briefly done, to inquire what has been achieved in this direction in the various

SECTIONAL DIVISIONS OF THE CITY.

In the early days the "Old Canal," or Mill Creek, which ran on the line of the present Boston & Maine Railroad, from Causeway Street to Haymarket Square, thence through Blackstone Street and North to the old town dock, where North Market Street now is, divided the city into the North and South Ends. At the beginning of the present century the whole of what is now Haymarket Square—the termination of Union, Washington, Sudbury, Cross, Merrimack, Canal, Haverhill, Charlestown, and Blackstone Streets—was a pool, known as Mill Cove and Mill Pond, and this was spanned by a bridge. This waterway was known as the Middlesex Canal, by which canal-boats came down from the up-country, along the Merrimack, to the East-Side wharves of Boston. The Canal was filled up and Blackstone Street opened as a thoroughfare in 1834. At this time, and for some years afterwards, Commercial Street, from the Old Battery, or Battery Wharf, to Long Wharf, was a water-front; and, until Broad Street was laid out, in 1808, Battery-march, to its junction with Kilby Street, marked the water-line. Where Dock Square now is, was formerly the Town Dock, which ran along the foot of the Market Place, about where Faneuil Hall now stands; and near the junction of North and Union Streets was the "Watchhouse." Near the latter was a reservoir of water, raised in the centre and sloping at the sides, and was called the "Conduit." It was about twelve feet square, and the top was utilized as a meat-market on Saturdays. At the foot of Merchant's Row was a swing-bridge over the dock. What is now Atlantic Avenue was at one time the site of an ancient harbor defence known as the Barricado, but sometimes called the "Sea Wall" or "Out-Wharves." It connected the South Battery, which was on the spot where Rowe's Wharf now is, with the North Battery, which was at the North End, opposite Charlestown. It formed a line of about 2200 feet in length, about 15 feet in height, and 20 feet in breadth at the top. It was erected in 1673, and was provided with openings to allow shipping to pass within its line, where it was calculated to mount heavy guns *en barbette*. It was of little use, fell into

Odd-Fellows Monument.

decay, and finally gave way to improvements. It will be seen that all the present water-front extending to a line with Commercial Street, and, in places beyond it, is made land, and the most valuable in the city. Atlantic Avenue, extending from the junction of Commercial Street and Eastern Avenue to Federal Street, was constructed by the city at a cost of $2,404,078, and is 100 feet in width. Here are immense wharves, huge warehouses, and immense traffic, which is facilitated by the railroad cars running along the line of docks. It was at one of these wharves—the Liverpool (formerly Griffin's) Wharf—where the famous "Boston Tea Party" took place, and to which we shall revert hereafter.

The term "North End" is usually applied to that section of the city lying towards Charlestown, between the Boston & Maine Station and Faneuil Hall. This was the first settled part of the town, and it is historic ground, and once the residential quarter for Boston's aristocracy, and now the abode of thousands of the

State House.

humbler classes. North Square, the small triangular inclosure between North and Moon Streets, was, in the early days, the heart of the "court end" of the town. In the immediate neighborhood the first families dwelt. For years the "Old North," the "Church of the Mathers," occupied one side of the Square, near where the Mariner's House now is. This church was torn down by the British during the siege of the city, and was used by them for firewood. In 1734 one of the three town markets was located in the Square, in which was located the residence of the Revolutionary hero, Paul Revere. Near the Square, on corner of North and Richmond Streets, was the famous hostelry, the Red Lion Inn, kept by a Quaker, one Nicholas Upsall, who, in the days of religious persecution, was put to death because of his Quakerism. In time this section became a "dangerous" quarter, the habitation of the immoral and vicious, but street improvements and electric lights have done much to take away from the locality a large measure of its unsavoriness. Till within a comparatively few years the North End retained the quaint, old-fashioned look of the town as it was a hundred and more years ago. Many of the ancient houses still remained, with "gambrel roofs and overhanging stories, standing close upon the narrow, crooked and winding streets that characterize the older portion of most old cities." But the hand of improvement has been busy here, as elsewhere; for streets have been straightened and widened, and the old houses sliced off, set back, torn down, or decorated with new fronts. The most marked improvement is in Hanover Street, stretching from Court Street, on the slope of the Pemberton Hill,— one of the peaks of the ancient Treamount,—to the water-front on Atlantic Avenue. This thoroughfare was opened out about a quarter of a century ago, since which time many old store edifices have given place to fine business blocks of spacious character, and Hanover Street is to-day one of the best-known business avenues of the city. Salem Street (which runs off obliquely from Hanover Street, and then runs nearly parallel with it), and the streets which cross it, offer to the lover of the antique and curious much to interest him. Modern innovations in the building art are here and there apparent, but on Salem and the intersecting streets there are still many good examples of the colonial style of building yet extant, with the second story projecting over the first. Salem, Cross and adjacent streets are to-day chiefly occupied by Jews, and their stores are the centres for trade in second-hand clothing, jewelry, and "odds and ends" of every description. From the left of Salem Street, through Baldwin Place, is the Home for Little Wanderers, where poor children, many of them orphans, are received and cared for, and ultimately given permanent homes in the country and in Western States on farms. Farther down Salem Street, opposite Sheafe Street, is the Industrial Home, where poor children and adults are instructed to become useful workpeople. The most interesting part of Salem Street is below Prince Street. The picturesque features are the old Christ Church, which fronts on Hull Street, and the ancient Copp's Hill Burying-ground near by. Christ Church is associated with the outbreak of the Revolutionary War. It was

> "Here the patriot hung his light
> Which shone through all that anxious night
> To eager eyes of Paul Revere."

An inscribed stone in the front of the steeple declares, in spite of some writers who have found time to argue to the contrary: "The signal lanterns of Paul Revere displayed in the steeple of this church April 18, 1775, warned the country of the march of the British troops to Lexington and Concord." Here, too, is the oldest chime of bells in America. The inscriptions on them tell their history. On the first is, "This peal of eight bells is the gift of a number of generous persons to Christ Church in Boston, New England, anno 1744, A. R.;" on the second, "This church was founded in the year 1723, Timothy Cutler, doctor in divinity, the first rector, A. R. 1744;" the third, "We are the first ring of bells cast for the British empire in North America, A. R. 1744;" the fourth, "God preserve the church of England, 1744;" the fifth, "William Shirley, Esq., Governor of the Massachusetts Bay in N. E., anno 1744;" the sixth, "The subscription for these bells was begun by John Hammock, Robert Temple, Robert Jenkins, and Ino Gould, church wardens, 1744;" the seventh, "Since generosity has opened our mouths, our tongues shall ring aloud its praise, 1744;" the eighth, "Abel Rudhall, of Gloucester, cast us all, anno 1744." The aggregate weight of the eight bells is 7272 pounds; they cost £560; the freight by ship from England was given by John Rowe, and the charges for wheels and hanging were £93.

These bells relate their own story so concisely that one wishes they could chronicle with equal clearness the events which have occurred around them since first they rang their opening peal. What an interesting tale it would be! But they have had their share in making history, and their voices have often been lifted in behalf of liberty and humanity, as well as for the sacred cause of religion. The belfry in which the bells now are is not, however, the same that first received them. That was blown down by a tempest early in the present century, and the present erection, though old as things go in America, is modern compared with the main edifice. In the times that tried men's souls to the uttermost, the bells here tolled when danger for the colonists was at hand; they called meetings of patriots, and rang merrily when the independence of the United States was declared.

Near by the church is the ancient burial-ground of Copp's Hill, once the site of the homestead of William Copp, an industrial cobbler. The hill was originally much higher than it is now, but, notwithstanding changes affected in its surroundings, the old graveyard, where the bones of many noted old Bostonians have been laid at rest, has been carefully preserved, and is a place of great attraction to all who find interest in old-time associations. At one time a small mill stood on the summit of the hill, which in 1660 was laid out for a graveyard, and this for a long time was known as the Old North Burying-ground. In the siege of Boston the British established a redoubt on this hill, and from the battery here they fired upon the American earthworks on Breed's Hill in the battle of Bunker Hill. From here, too, the English poured hot shot into Charlestown, and destroyed the village. It is said that the British, while here, made targets of the gravestones of the burying-ground. When the English evacuated Boston, on March 17, 1776, three of the heaviest guns of the battery here were found to be spiked and clogged so as to prevent their immediate use.

In late years the whole of the North End has undergone great transformations. New churches have arisen, streets have been straightened and widened, and large warehouses, and factories, and workshops have taken the place of what were once habitations of the humblest and least favored of the population. Haymarket Square, once a pond with a bridge over it, is now one of the busiest centres in the

The New Old South Church.

city, with streets branching off from it to all points of the compass. The Boston & Maine Railroad Station site fronting on the Square, and all the ground in the rear of it is made land, and now of enormous value. When the projected new Union Railroad Depot shall have been erected on Causeway Street and on the water's edge, the whole of the space now occupied by the railroad between Causeway Street and Haymarket Square will be thrown open for improvement and new buildings, and as important a change will be effected as was achieved in 1873-4 by the opening up of Washington Street from Dock Square to Haymarket Square at a cost of $1,500,000. But let us for a moment turn from the North End (which is the designation of that part of the city lying towards Charlestown, between the Boston & Maine Station and Faneuil Hall), to

THE SOUTH END.

This appellation now applies to that part of the city lying to the south of Dover Street and extending to the Roxbury district. All this area is largely made land, and the newer portion, towards the West, joins the New West End, or Back Bay district; but in the early days the canal which ran through Causeway Street, Haymarket Square, and Blackstone Street to the old town dock, where North Market Street now is, divided the city into the North and South Ends. The Old South Church, on the corner of Washington and Milk Streets, was, when erected, out at the South End; hence its name. For many years the South End contained the principal shops, the finest mansion houses, and the Common. What is now known as the South End was then the Neck Field. At a later date the present Winter Street formed the down-town boundary. Then the boundary was extended to Boylston Street, and next to Dover Street, which is now recognized as the line between the Central portion of the city and the South End.

For over thirty years subsequent to the settlement of Boston all that part of the South End embraced in the territory included between Kneeland and Eliot Streets north, and Castle Street south, was one unbroken field, the property of Deacon William Colbron. The "highway to Roxberrie," as it was termed, leading from North End, made a detour at Kneeland Street eastwardly, following thence the margin of the Old South Bay to Castle Street, whence a return was made to the road leading over the Neck, which, a short distance beyond the present Dover Street, had a gate across it to keep out marauding animals, and as a sort of protection against the incursions of Indians. In 1663, however, a straighter line was made for the highway by an opening through the Colbron field. When Washington Street—now a continuous thoroughfare from Haymarket Square, through the heart of the city, to the Highlands—existed under several titles, that portion of it south-ward from the intersection of Essex Street bore the name of Orange Street, and at this point the Neck of former days actually commenced. The tide came up to within a stone's throw of old Orange Street on the easterly side and to Pleasant Street on the westerly margin. From Essex Street the width gradually diminished, until there was a mere thread of land, which was often overflowed by the high tides. This part of the territory of Boston, a century back, was practically in the "country." There were not more than seventy-five families on the whole of it, extending from Essex Street to the Roxbury line and including all adjoining territory, and these families were distributed widely apart in the manner common with outlying precincts of villages. Each householder had and cultivated more or less of a garden for the growth of fruits and vegetables. Some of these residences were the abodes of persons of affluence who had retired from the active channels of trade. The district, too, was noted for several prominent distilleries a century ago. Following this period the town had a healthy growth, on the recovery from the depression consequent upon the Revolution, and there was excited and exploring spirit for new habitations. This led many seekers to the Neck district, and to the filling up of the vacant places with residences. Streets were opened intersectingly; and those openings which had previously been simple places or courts leading to single houses were rearranged for the purposes of thoroughfares.

In 1809 the Boylston Market was erected on the corner of Washington and Boylston Street, and its site was then on the outer margin of the town. This building (removed during the last three years) was named in honor of Ward Nicholas Boylston, a great benefactor of Harvard College. He it was who presented the clock that for so long a period did faithful duty in the tower of the quaint-looking old market, which contained three floors and basement. The land upon which the building was erected cost 75 cents per foot and the building itself $20,000. In 1859 the building was extended 40 feet, and in 1870 was bodily removed back from the street 11 feet. The lower floor served as the market, and the Boylston Hall, above it, was used for church services, musical, theatrical, and miscellaneous entertainments, drill-room, armory, etc. A new, elegant structure of larger dimensions, covering about 15,000 square feet and costing about $250,000 to build, has just been erected on its site. The lower floor is a clothing store, and the upper floors are divided into offices. In its day the old Boylston Market was a great factor in promoting good living, and it drew its patronage from the élite of the city. Its erection led to the building in its vicinity of other public edifices of considerable note, among these being Mellish Motte's Unitarian Church, Dr. Phelp's Congregational Church, the Franklin Schoolhouse, etc.

The work of creating the area comprised within the modern South End was begun, about the year 1853, by widening the Neck. This was done by reclaiming the flats on either side of it. Before this time, however,—in 1844,—Harrison Avenue had been laid out, and in 1852 Tremont Street, on the west side of the Neck, had been extended to the Roxbury line. When in 1856 the street-railroad system was introduced,— the first line of the Metropolitan Company running from the old Granary Burying-ground, on Tremont Street, to Roxbury—the South End at once became the favorite residence portion, and building was extensively begun. Until the building up of the Back Bay district, the South End was the best residence section, and large portions of it still contain fine estates occupied by the most substantial citizens of the city. Legrange Street, once known as Legrange Place, was formerly one of the most charming spots in town, having nice houses, in a secluded position, handy to business. For some unexplained reason, however, the tenants were restless, and made frequent changes, but for many years tenants were drawn from the better class of citizens engaged in mercantile life. In time "boarding-places" were opened, and later Langrange Place had become

Liberty Square, showing Mason Building and Kilby Street.

a centre for residences of musical people. Since the place was opened out as a thoroughfare from Washington Street to Tremont Street, it has been a headquarters for the sporting fraternity, besides being the *locale* of one of the most lively police stations in the city. In former days the atmosphere of the South End was permeated with an aromatic and pungent odor derived from various distilleries. There were two distilleries in the vicinity of Harvard Street, one of which was quite extensive, and was owned by W. C. Fay. Another, kept by Gardner Brewer, was situated on the corner of Washington Street and the present Indiana Street (then known as Distill house Street). Luther and Artemas Felton each prosecuted the distillery business a little farther up-street, and, on Castle and Suffolk Streets, Alexander Meldrum carried on an extensive brewery, where old-fashioned ale was made, and which was a popular resort for all thirsty South-Enders.

While three score years ago the air was redolent with the flavor of hops and the color of new rum, there were three churches in this region exerting a "powerful influence in exhibiting the religious tendencies of the inhabitants. They were all flourishing to their utmost. Dr. John Pierpont's society, in Hollis Street, represented the most rigid Unitarians, and embraced in its congregation several who, like Francis Jackson, held advanced views upon moral questions, in common with their pastor. He was talented, and his independence often took an offensive form. On the corner of the present Motte Street stands a relic of what was one of the most fashionable Unitarian churches in town. Here Rev. Mellish Motte preached, and here Charlotte Cushman (before her theatrical days) sang in the choir, along with several members of the Handel and Haydn Society, including John G. Roberts, before alluded to. The immediate neighborhood of this church had then recently been improved and occupied by the residences of a number of its members. Orange Street then was a charming place, and its houses were eagerly sought for when erected. The houses are there now, but the street has a forbidding appearance. In placing the railroad bridge near by, it was made necessary to raise the grade, and the corners of Orange Street were demolished. On the lower corner the building contained an elegant hall, where fashionable parties and dances were held. Across the street, at its entrance, was sprung a tasty iron arch, holding a handsome lantern in the centre, which threw its rays down the street, giving a cheerful aspect after nightfall. The other church in allusion was known as the Pine Street Church. The old shell of this edifice still remains. The society held a first-class position under the ministration of Rev. Amos A. Phelps, and is perpetuated to-day by the church corner of Berkeley and Appleton Streets, as Mr. Motte's society is by that known as Edward E. Hale's." The site of the Hollis Street Church, which was built in 1819, is now occupied by the Hollis Street Theatre, and the congregation of the old church have now comfortable quarters in a fine new edifice on the corner of Exeter and Newbury Streets.

The avenues and streets of the South End section of the city are wide and handsome. It needs but little discernment for one familiar with the territory and its properties lying between Washington and Tremont Streets, and extending from School to Dover Streets, to divine the purpose of enterprising citizens in 1868 of laying out a new thoroughfare to the South End, midway between the then and now main arteries of the city. Shawmut Avenue did not then exist except as Suffolk Street, and that had not then been extended and widened to intersect with Tremont Street. Washington Street was narrow and crowded with traffic and stores, and Tremont Street was just beginning to develop into a business property. The improvements made, of what had been rear property, valuable front building lots, and new residences and stores soon lined the avenue. Shawmut Avenue and Tremont Street are of generous width, as also is Washington Street and likewise Columbus Avenue on the west, while on the east side the chief thoroughfares are Albany Street and Harrison Avenue. These are the main thoroughfares running from north to south, and all, with the exception of a small strip on Washington Street, are on made land. The streets crossing these are very numerous, several of them containing many beautiful residences, and the most of them lined with comfortable dwellings. The principal cross streets include Canton, Brookline, Union Park, Newton, Rutland, Concord, Worcester, Springfield, and Chesterpark Streets. The "through" streets are spoken of as East or West, taking Washington Street as the dividing line. Scattered all through the South End are many large public and private buildings, a

Young Men's Christian Association New Building

number of noted church edifices, numerous large manufactories, and some of the finest apartment houses in the city and country.

The leading streets and avenues stretching from north to south extend for miles, and are lined with richly equipped marts of trade and attractive residences, sanctuaries, hospitals, halls, and educational institutions. Building operations have been actively prosecuted in late years, the entire region of the South End has been changed in its aspect, and real estate has increased immensely in value. The whole district is intersected with horse railroads, and an old-time Bostonian can find much here to interest him in comparing the present with the past. Let him take a horse-car on Tremont Street, and as the vehicle sweeps round the corner of the Common into Boylston Street he espies on the opposite corner the Hotel Pelham, the first building of the "French flats," or "family hotel" class in Boston. The edifice was erected a little over a quarter of a century ago by Dr. John Dix, and has always been regarded as the finest and most popular of its kind. The building is valued at $420,000; the whole is assessed at $434,300, and the tax paid by the proprietor, Mr. J. L. Little, is $11,500. Some years ago, when Tremont Street was not as wide at this point as it is to-day, this hotel was raised up bodily and moved about twenty feet down Boylston Street, without disturbing the occupants, or in the least disarranging the interior. This was the greatest engineering feat of the age, being the first instance of the moving of such a large mass of masonry; and it not only excited the wonder of people at home but of those in Europe, where the newspapers published full descriptions of the work of removal. On the opposite corner is the Hotel Boylston, originally erected as an apartment house, with the kitchens in the upper story. It belongs to the estate of Charles Francis Adams. The total valuation of this house is $119,000, the building being assessed at $180,300, and the tax paid by the trustees amounting to $30,000. Adjoining the Pelham Hotel is one of the most useful and most appreciated institutions in the city—the Public Library. As the car sweeps along Boylston Street, the traveller notices many changes that have been made and that are being made in the buildings fronting on the deer park and the old burying-ground at the foot of the Common. A few years ago these buildings were occupied as residences by noted wealthy Bostonians; now they are being utilized for business purposes. Turning into Park Square, one notices here many improvements which did not exist a few years ago. A prominent feature in the Square is the "Emancipation Group" monument, representing Lincoln with the figure of a slave kneeling at his feet in gratitude for the Emancipation Proclamation, the broken fetters falling from his limbs. This group is of bronze, designed by Thomas Ball. It was presented to the city by Hon. Moses Kimball, proprietor of the Boston Museum. On one side of the Square is the station of the Providence Division of the Old Colony Railroad, built at immense cost, and forming one of the handsomest and best-equipped railroad stations in the world. The property in this Square and in the streets branching off from it has increased phenomenally within the past few years, and vast improvements are distinguishable on every hand. This increase between the Square and Church Street may be said to be greater than in any other section of the city. Ten years ago this property was held at a very low valuation, and some of it could hardly be given away, so to speak—that is, could not find a purchaser. Now some of it is immensely valuable, and all of it is very desirable, and with a great future before it. The corner building on the Square was erected by William J. Rotch of New Bedford, at a cost of $75,000. This estate is so valuable that it is assessed at about $40 a foot for tax purposes. The Hollander Building, adjoining, another fine business structure, cost $100,000 to build. The Hotel Thorndike, on Church Street, extending from Boylston to Providence Street, cost about $75,000. It is owned by the heirs of the late Dr. Thorndike. Many of the buildings between the hotel and the Square have been altered over for business purposes, and command high rents.

Let the voyager continue his ride, or his walk along Columbus Avenue; in fact, explore the whole of the South End, and he will be amazed to witness the transformations that have been effected within a lifetime. Where the sea water once rolled unhindered in majestic waves there are beautiful, wide, well-shaded streets, lined with buildings varying from the plainest to the most splendid in architecture. On two corners of Columbus Avenue and Berkeley Street stand the handsome People's Church (Methodist Episcopal) and the equally attractive First Presbyterian Church, while to the right and to the left are costly apartment houses and mansions betokening affluence on the part of the occupants. Passing over the railroad bridge one sees on the corner of Clarendon Street the fine Columbus Avenue Universalist Church, the pastor of which is the Rev. Dr. A. A. Miner. Farther on, and located on the corner of the avenue and West Rutland Square, is a picturesque structure with ivy-covered walls. This is the Union Church (Congregational Trinitarian). The visitor may

ILLUSTRATED BOSTON.

vary his journeyings as he pleases and find something to interest him at every turn in noting the improvements effected and the air of refinement which characterizes this residential section. If at Columbus Square he turns down Warren Avenue to reach the far-stretching Tremont Street, his attention will be arrested by the Church of the Disciples standing out prominently on the corner of Warren Avenue and West Brookline Street, where the late Rev. Dr. James Freeman Clarke was for a long period the pastor. Beyond, on the corner of

Paine Memorial Building, Appleton Street.

West Canton Street, is the Warren Avenue Baptist Church, and on the corner of Warren Avenue and Dartmouth Street stands one of the most noteworthy structures of its kind in the country — the building of the Latin and English High Schools, containing seventy-eight rooms and halls, drill hall, gymnasium, etc., standing on an area of 423x220 feet. Beyond the avenue a little, and to the left on Dartmouth Street, is the old Rice School building, now occupied by the Normal School for girls, and herein is a training-school. On the

Army and Navy Monument, Boston Common.

lot adjoining the site of the Latin and English High School, and forming the corner of Montgomery and Clarendon Streets, stands the Clarendon Street Baptist Church, of which the Rev. Dr. A. J. Gordon is the pastor.

Continuing the walk along Warren Avenue until Berkeley Street is reached, there, standing on the corner, at the left, is the handsome Berkeley Street Congregational Trinitarian Church, and on the opposite corner, to the right, the handsome Odd Fellows' Hall building, with its marble front. Near the latter, on Berkeley Street, is the famous Parker Memorial Building, with the Parker Memorial and Summer Halls; while alongside of this edifice is the Paine Memorial Building, with its Paine and Investigator Halls. In the same vicinity are two notable circular buildings, with fortress-like entrances,—the Cyclorama of Gettysburg and the Cyclorama of the Battle of Bunker Hill, both of which are worth visiting.

Turning into Tremont Street, and proceeding up it, the Clarendon Hotel and the St. Cloud Hotel are reached, and opposite the latter is Union Park Street, with a trim, neat parkway in the centre. Through this a view is gained of what was once Edward Everett Hale's South Congregational (Unitarian) Church, but now a Hebrew synagogue. Farther along Tremont Street, and at the corner of West Brookline Street, the Shawmut Congregational Church (Congregational Trinitarian) stands; and when the corner of Pembroke Street is reached we get a glimpse, on looking down the latter street, of the imposing school building occupied by the Girl's Latin and the Girl's High School. Journeying farther up Tremont Street the corner of West Concord Street is reached, and here stands one of the most handsome churches of the Methodist denomination in the city. On Springfield Street, to the left of Tremont Street, is the Home for Aged Men, a most popular and well-managed institution.

Reaching Chester Square, a pleasant little park is seen, intersected with walks; and taking the centre path we reach Washington Street, where, on the left, between Springfield and Worcester Streets, looms up the large marble front building, the Commonwealth Hotel, recently remodelled at a cost of $100,000. Near it, standing in the midst of ample grounds on the corner of West Concord Street, is the building long occupied as the State Normal School for the training of teachers of drawing in the public schools of the State. The school is now located on Newbury Street.

While here it is worth while to turn into East Concord Street, then into Harrison Avenue, and inspect the City Hospital buildings, covering the entire block on this avenue, between East Concord and Springfield Streets. Near these buildings, on East Concord Street, are seen the Homœopathic Hospital and the Massachusetts Medical School. In the immediate neighborhood is the Church of the Immaculate Conception, possessing one of the richest and most impressive interiors of the Roman Catholic Churches in the city. Attached to it is the Boston College of the Roman Catholic body.

Passing into East Newton Street the New England Conservatory of Music—once the St. James Hotel, and now one of the largest and most useful educational institutions in the country—presents itself for inspection. This, started as a music school, is now a general college, with and without boarding conveniences. It is proposed to enlarge the building by making a large music hall, into which is to be placed the "Great Organ," long a noteworthy feature of the Boston Music Hall on Winter Street. In the rear of the Conservatory, and occupying the lot fronting on Washington Street, is the Old South Burying-ground, laid out in 1810. Here are two small, but much appreciated parks, lying on either side of Washington Street, and extending from Newton to Brookline Streets. That on the east side of Washington Street is Franklin Park, and that on the west side Blackstone Park.

Walking along Washington Street in the direction of Boylston Street, one recognizes vast changes in store and other buildings lining this magnificent thoroughfare that have been effected in recent years. Old buildings, of diminutive size, have given place to high, towering structures that are now busy, prosperous marts of trade. One of the most noteworthy edifices on this thoroughfare is the great Cathedral of the Holy Cross, located on the corner of Union Park Street. It is the largest and finest Roman Catholic edifice in the city. It covers more than an acre of ground and its style is of the early English Gothic, cruciform, with nave, transept, aisle and clerestory, the latter supported by two rows of clustered metal pillars. The total length of the building is 364 feet; width at the transept, 170 feet; width of nave and aisles, 90 feet; height to the ridgepole, 120 feet. The entire interior is clear space, broken only by two rows of columns, extending along the nave, and supporting the central roof. The arch separating the spacious front vestibule from the nave is of bricks, taken from the ruins of the Ursuline Convent on Mt. Benedict in Somerville, which was burned by a mob on the night of August 11, 1834. The interior is very rich in decoration, and has pew accommodations

THE METROPOLIS OF NEW ENGLAND.

for 3,000 persons. There are two main towers in front, and a turret, all of unequal height, and all to be eventually surmounted by spires, that on the southwest corner to the height of 300 feet, and that on the opposite corner to 200 feet. At the rear of the Cathedral, on the corner of Union Park Street and Harrison Avenue, is the residence of the Archbishop.

Another notable edifice, erected in 1887, is the Grand Opera House, a building of great size on Washington Street, just above Dover Street. At the corner of Washington and Dover Streets is the Grand Museum, opened in 1888. This was formerly the Windsor Theatre, and was the first "uptown" theatre in the city proper. It was at about this spot that the old fortifications at the "Neck," we have already spoken of, were located. On reaching Hollis Street it is well worth while paying a visit to the handsome theatre which has been erected on the site of the old Unitarian Church, and by the time Boylston Street—the starting point for the tour through the South End—has been reached, a most comprehensive idea of the wonders which have been wrought, and of the vast wealth now centred in the South End will have been gained.

THE BUSINESS DISTRICT.

The region between the North End and South End, the Common and the Harbor, is occupied by the "Business District," where the chief wholesale and retail shops are grouped, the theatres, the city and national buildings, and the older hotels. It is a region bristling with old time associations, is full of historic spots hallowed by the tread and blood of bygone heroes, and was the battleground where the forefathers dared to risk limbs and lives in resisting foreign oppression, to throw before them warlike shields, and, as Macbeth, call to their political taskmaster to "Lay on, Macduff; and damn'd be him that first cries, 'Hold, enough!'" It is a region where the "Cradle of Liberty" has vigilantly rocked, where justice has been gagged and unbound, where fortunes have been won and lost, where statesmen have harangued and poets sung, where fire swept off buildings of generations and men's indomitable pluck and busy hands reared edifices more majestic and beautiful than those which went before, and where modern Bostonians love to point with pardonable pride to past achievements. Here are "items of interest" that would fill volumes, but the limits of these pages necessarily enforce conciseness.

Let us, however, take a hasty run through some of the principal avenues of this renowned, busy centre, and notice in brief some of the relics that have been preserved and link the past with the present, and jot down such chief improvements and alterations in latter days that catch the eye during the journey. Let our starting point be Scollay Square, through which Court Street passes, and from which Tremont Street at the south, and Cornhill at the north, begin. Here is a puzzle for a stranger to start with, for the Court Street which runs through the Square, and off which Brattle, and Hanover and Sudbury Streets shoot, is only a one-sided street, the other side of the thoroughfare—a busy shopping quarter—being designated Tremont Row, the why and wherefore of which it is difficult to discover. Scollay Square, now a great street railroad centre, takes its name from Scollay's Building, which for a long period stood in the middle of the Square, and had a streetway on each side of it. Scollay's Building was the last of a row of buildings, of wedge shape, that extended from the line between Tremont

Crawford House.

Street and Cornhill to Hanover Street. It was owned by William Scollay, an apothecary, hence its name. It was removed in 1871, and the site was then officially given the name Scollay Square, where, since September 17, 1880, a final bronze statue of Governor Winthrop has stood.

The two main streets of the city are Tremont and Washington. As we turn into the former from the

Square, we notice on the left corner that one of Boston's old landmarks has vanished. This was an old-time mansion, where Washington lodged on the occasion of his visit to Boston in 1789, but for a long period prior to its demolition in 1883 was devoted to business. It was originally a three-story building, and another story was added when it ceased to be used as a residence. On the Court Street front of the building, between the second and third stories, was a stone tablet, bearing the inscription, "Occupied by Washington, October, 1789." For half a century the lower story was occupied by S. S. Pierce & Co., grocers, and in the upper rooms Daniel Webster, Harrison Gray Otis, Judge R. I. Burbank and other notabilities had their offices. On its site now stands a high, towering brick structure of many stories, named the Hemenway Building, erected at a cost of $220,000. The old grocery firm are the occupants of the lower part of the building, the upper floors of which are used for offices. On the opposite side of the street, on the corner of Tremont Street and Pemberton Square, a number of old buildings, crowded with lawyers' offices, have within the past two or three years given place to a most imposing brick edifice of many floors, built at a cost of $75,000 by the heirs of Ebenezer Chadwick, and named the Chadwick Building. Here, as of old, the lawyers still "do most congregate." Adjoining the Hemenway Building is the Boston Museum, erected in 1846 at a cost of a quarter of a million of dollars. It is the oldest of the existing theatres in the city, and on its stage have appeared the most celebrated actors and artistes of the time. The granite building next beyond, at Nos. 30 and 32, extends backward into Court Square. It is jointly occupied by the Suffolk County Probate Office and the Massachusetts Historical Society, which possesses a valuable library, a lot of rare relics, paintings, busts and unique curiosities.

Adjoining this building is the King's Chapel Burial Ground and the Old King's Chapel itself, occupying the corner of Tremont and School Streets. These are among the most cherished landmarks in the city, and the chapel still preserves in its name the memory of the ancient time when Boston was loyal to England's King. Now a Unitarian church, it was the first Episcopal church erected in New England. In the year 1646 a few Episcopalian citizens timidly craved the Puritan authorities to allow them to worship with the Book of Common Prayer "till inconveniences hereby be found prejudicial to the churches and colony;" but the stern old Roundheads would have none of it. The chaplain of Charles Second's Commission, however, introduced the Episcopal ritual by royal order twenty years later, and in twenty years more a church was erected. On the same site the present King's Chapel was built, in 1749-54, a small and massive structure of blackish stone, whose lower windows, deep set and square, gave point to Matthew Byles's pun, that he had heard of the canons of the church, but had never seen the port-holes before. The interior, with its high, old-fashioned pews, its tall pulpit and sounding-board, its massive pillars, stained glass window, mural tablets and monuments, is remarkably attractive, and the organ, selected by Handel, the great composer, and sent hither from England in 1756, still serves the church. When the English army evacuated Boston in 1775, the rector left also, and carried with him the vestments and registers and the communion service, a gift of the King, and amounting to 2800 ounces of silver. In 1787 this parish, under the lead of its rector, exchanged Episcopalianism for Unitarianism, and King's Chapel became the first Unitarian Church on the American continent. The old burial ground is rich in coats-of-arms and quaint epitaphs on its monuments, and headstones, and here lie the remains of Winthrop, Shirley and others of the colonial governors, several of the early Puritan clergy, Isaac Johnson and other founders of Boston. Johnson's wife was Lady Arabella, daughter of the Earl of Lincoln, and the climate of New England proved too severe for both of them, for three months after her arrival she died at Salem, and a month later her husband was buried in the King's Chapel Burial Ground. In 1878 the city discussed a proposal to utilize the sites of the chapel and burial ground for a new court-house, but old landmarks were permitted to remain untouched.

In the rear of the chapel, and fronting on School Street, is the handsome City Hall, a costly white granite structure, in the Renaissance style of architecture, built in 1862-65. The city government, on its organization in 1822, was located in Faneuil Hall. Later the Old State House, at the head of State Street, was used as the City Hall, and in 1840, the old Court-House, which occupied the site of the present City Hall, because the seat of the civic government. When the present edifice was erected it was thought to be on a large scale, and sufficient for the needs of the city for many years; but it became overcrowded and for a long time past quite a number of departments have been located in other buildings in the immediate neighborhood. The building, which cost over half a million of dollars to erect, contains five floors and an attic, above which is a high louvre dome, surmounted by a balcony, from which rises a flag-staff 200 feet high. The attic and the dome are utilized as the centre of the fire-alarm telegraph system which spreads all over the city, and the rest of the building is utilized for the offices of the municipality. The structure is handsome and substantial, and is elegant in its appointments throughout. In front of the building is a neatly kept lawn, and this is adorned on one side with a statue of Benjamin Franklin, and on the other with one of Josiah Quincy, the second mayor of the city (in 1823). Probably when the new Court-House, now being erected in Pemberton Square, has been completed, the present Court-House, on Court Square, in the rear of the City Hall, will be utilized for the enlargement of the latter.

School Street (so called because of the old Latin school having been located here) is famous for its ancient corner bookstore. It has stores of a varied character, and lawyers' offices in considerable number, and is noted as the *locale* of the famous Parker House, which, before its costly enlargement, Dickens called the best hotel in America. Originally, it was a spacious six-story marble structure, and during the past four or five years it has been extended on to the corner of Tremont Street, the front of the addition being also of marble and towering higher than the older part of the building. The addition cost to construct over $100,000, and it forms one of the most imposing attractions on Tremont Street.

Revere House.

Opposite King's Chapel, and on the corner of Tremont and Beacon Street, Messrs. Houghton & Dutton have, within the past three years, erected, as an addition to their extensive store, a nine-story, fire proof structure at a cost of $190,000. On the opposite corner is the famous old Tremont House with heavy, dark granite walls, where Henry Clay, Andrew Jackson, the Prince of Wales, Charles Dickens and other notables have sojourned. Dickens wrote of it: "It has more galleries, colonnades, piazzas, and passages than I can remember, or the reader would believe." It has been recently considerably modernized. The heavy portico and flight of granite steps in front have been removed, and the office, reading-room, etc., brought down to the street level. It is said that Mr. Fred. L. Ames has acquired this property and purposes building upon its site a monster hotel in the near future. Adjoining the present building is the famous Old Granary Burying Ground, once a part of the Common. The title of the Old Granary Burying Ground was given to it because of its proximity to the old town granary, which stood where the Park Street Church now stands. More distinguished persons have been buried here than in any other place in the city. Here are entombed the remains of nine governors of Massachusetts, two signers of the Declaration of Independence, six famous divines, the victims of the Boston Massacre, John Hancock, Samuel Adams, Peter Faneuil, Paul Revere, Samuel Sewall, the parents of Benjamin Franklin, and many other notable Americans. Until about sixteen years ago, the crowded sidewalk in front of the burying ground was partly occupied by a line of noble elms, which were imported from England in 1672. To meet the demand of the street railways they were cut down at night, for the civic authorities feared the opposition of the people, who were indignant. Admission to the burying ground is by permit, obtained at the City Hall. On the side of this "God's Acre," is the Park Street Church, built in 1809. It was the first Congregational Trinitarian Church established after Unitarianism had won over from orthodox ranks its principal members. With such persistent earnestness was Calvinism contended for from its pulpit that the "ungodly" of the other sects nick-named the locality "Brimstone Corner." It has now a large and wealthy congregation.

Hotel Brunswick, Boylston Street cor. Clarendon.

Opposite the Tremont House is a notable building, the Tremont Temple, sandwiched between parts of trade. Its site was formerly occupied by the Tremont Theatre, in which Charlotte Cushman, the famous actress made her début on April 8, 1835. In 1843 the Baptists bought the building and erected in its stead a Temple, which was destroyed by fire, as was also its successor, the present structure having been erected in 1870. It is the place of worship of the Union Temple Free Church, the headquarters of the New England Baptists, and a popular place for public meetings. The main hall is one of the finest in the country, and contains an organ of great power and singular beauty. The hall is 66 feet high and 122 x 72 feet in dimensions and has two galleries. There is seating accommodation for 2,600 persons. Beneath this hall is a smaller one, called Meionaon Hall, with a seating capacity of nearly one thousand. Farther along the street, and facing the Old Granary Burying Ground is the Horticultural Hall, a handsome granite edifice, standing between Montgomery Place and Bromfield Street. This is the headquarters of the Massachusetts Horticultural Society. It contains offices and large, handsome halls for meetings, exhibitions, etc. During a fire which occurred on December 29, 1888, many valuable paintings of past presidents of the society were ruined.

Bromfield Street is one of the many cross streets which connect Tremont and Washington Streets. It contains several publishing houses, offices, varied business stores, and a largely attended Methodist Episcopal Church, of which the Rev. G. A. Crawford is pastor. Some of the buildings adjoining the church have recently undergone extensive alterations and effected a marked improvement in the business aspect of the street. At the corner of Bromfield and Tremont Street is a handsome edifice, the Studio Building, devoted to offices, etc. It has quite recently been reconstructed to a considerable extent internally. Side by side with this building are art and other stores fronting on Tremont Street, and extending to the corner of Hamilton Place, whence Tremont Street is built up only on one side as far as where it is crossed by Boylston Street, the other side of the thoroughfare being occupied by the Common. This length, during shopping hours, presents at all times an animated aspect, the broad sidewalk being at all times crowded with persons good-naturedly elbowing their way through the moving throng.

At the corner of Hamilton Place and in the "place" itself two magnificent buildings have been lately erected at a cost of about $225,000 by the heirs of Jonathan Phillips, and on the opposite side of the "place" most of the old buildings have been rebuilt. In the "place" is one of the entrances to the great Music Hall, another entrance being on Winter Street. It was built in 1852, and is almost entirely concealed by surrounding buildings and is devoid of architectural pretensions. It contains two halls, one seating 2600 and the other 800 persons. The main hall used to contain the largest and finest organ in the world, and it is said it will soon be introduced into the New England Conservatory of Music on East Newton Street. The Music Hall seems to have outlived its usefulness as the home of musicians, and of late years it has been occupied for all sorts of purposes, including fairs, public meetings, balls, cat and dog shows, foot races, walking and wrestling matches, beer garden, etc. More than once the idea has been entertained of demolishing the building to make way for business improvements and to extend Hamilton Place straight through to Washington Street.

Near the corner of Winter Street and fronting on Tremont Street and the Common, is St. Paul's, a church of the Episcopal Communion, erected in 1819-20, and built of dark granite, with a fine Ionic portico and colonnade of sandstone. The ceiling is panelled and cylindrical, and the chancel contains modern frescos and a brilliant stained window. Winter Street, like Temple Place and West Street, is a fashionable retail shopping centre, filled with elegant stores, many of which have been improved and enlarged in recent years. On the corner of Temple Place used to stand the Masonic Temple, always an attractive feature from the time of its erection in 1832 owing to its peculiar formation. It was five stories high and was built of rough Quincy granite. The entrance was a low, broad Norman doorway, and the various floors were lighted by long arched windows. The building was surmounted by battlements and pinnacles and had two towers, each sixteen feet square and ninety-five feet high. The Masonic body held their lodges here until they erected their new Temple on the corner of Boylston Street, and then it was for years occupied as the United States Circuit Court. Three or four years ago the property was purchased by R. H. Stearns & Co., and the building was raised bodily and two stories built under it, while its outward aspect as well as its interior arrangements was entirely changed. It is now devoted to the dry-goods business.

From West Street to Boylston Street high, imposing buildings have been erected on the sites of old houses, and this quarter is now chiefly occupied by the Boston Conservatory of Music, and by so many piano manufacturing concerns as to have earned the name of "Piano Row." The new Masonic Temple, on the corner of Tremont and Boylston Street, built in 1867, is seven stories high, with octagonal towers rising 120

Dock Square.

feet. It contains three magnificent halls for meetings, one being furnished with splendor in the Corinthian style, another in the Egyptian, and the third in the Gothic.

We now turn into Washington Street, and retrace our steps northward along this busy thoroughfare, filled at all hours of the day with a seething mass of human beings. As we turn from Boylston Street (anciently called Frog Lane) into Washington Street, a tablet, with a representation of a spreading tree, will be observed on the front of the building on the east side of Washington Street, corner of Essex. Here stood the "Liberty Tree" under which the "Sons of Liberty" were organized in 1765, and under which meetings were held to give expression of opposition to the revenue oppressions of the English government. When a meeting was intended to be held the signal was given by placing a flag in the branches of the tree, and the flag is still preserved in the Old South Church. In the siege of Boston the tree was purposely destroyed by the British, to the grief of the people.

The present Washington Street has always been the chief artery of the town, though it has not always been known by the name it now bears nor was it formerly so far-stretching in its length. The name Washington was given in honor of General Washington on the occasion of his visit to the town in 1789. At first the present Washington Street was a series of streets from down-town to the Roxbury line, known as Cornhill, Marlborough, Newbury, Orange and Washington; and it was not until 1824 that the old names were dropped, and the entire thoroughfare named as now. Until 1873-4, the down-town end of Washington Street was at the present Cornhill and Old Dock Square, in that year, as noted elsewhere, the street was extended through to Haymarket Square, from which point it now stretches through the city and the Roxbury district to the Dedham boundary. A few doors north of Boylston Street corner we enter the theatre district, where are the Park, Globe, Boston and Bijou theatres, the neighborhood of which presents a very brilliant appearance at evening or just after matinees. In the bend of the street, near the Boston Theatre, is the Adams House, a splendid hotel built in 1883 on the site of the old Adams House, which itself long stood on the site of the Lamb Tavern, whence the first stage to Providence started before the days of railroads. Recently the proprietors of this house have acquired, on a lease for fifteen years at a rental of $30,000 a year, two estates on which they have erected an extension of the hotel. In this immediate neighborhood are the great retail dry-goods houses of the city, notably those of R. H. White & Co. and Jordan, Marsh & Co., with their acres of floorage space. Congregated about these are stores where every variety of merchandise is to be obtained; and the sidewalks are filled from morning till night with an ever-moving throng, while the carriage-way is frequently choked with vehicular traffic. Much of the property here was destroyed in the great fire of 1872, of which more anon. Most of the buildings lining this thoroughfare have, during the past sixteen or eighteen years been greatly altered or entirely rebuilt upon an expensive and ornamental scale; but the street is too narrow for these improvements to be seen to advantage and also for the accommodation of great traffic constantly found here.

Farther on we come to the corner of Milk Street, where stands the famous old South Church, that relic of revolutionary times, that tells on a tablet in its tower that the church was erected, first, in 1669, rebuilt in 1729, and that it was "desecrated by the British in 1775," by using it as a riding school and liquor saloon. In those troublous times, however, neither the British nor the colonists hesitated to use the churches for the exigencies of war, for of the latter it is said that they took away the lead pipes from the then church at Cambridge and converted them into bullets with which to kill the armed hosts of England. The site of the old church was originally occupied by the house of Governor Winthrop, who lived and died here. The property was bequeathed by Mrs. Mary Norton (wife of Rev. John Norton) for the erection of a meeting-house. In the days immediately prior to the Revolution, meetings of citizens were held here to discuss their grievances, and such meetings British officers sought to repress. One such meeting was held here when the famous Boston Tea Party, which culminated in the Revolution, occurred on December 16, 1773. Paul Revere, Samuel Adams and about twenty other kindred patriots, had been concocting a plan for some time to rid the port of some hateful tea chests that were at the wharves, or soon to arrive there—hateful because of the obnoxious tax of the British government, imposed upon it after the repeal of the "odious Stamp Act." It is said that Sam Adams had contrived this meeting to draw off the attention of the English officers from the scheme to destroy the tea brought over by the ships Dartmouth and Eleanor and the brig Beaver, then at Griffin's (now Liverpool Wharf). When the meeting opened, British officers, with wonted effrontery, crowded the pulpit, so that Dr. Warren, the pastor and the orator on the occasion, had to climb through a rear window to get into the pulpit, which he did. During the proceedings, John Rowe asked, "Who knows how tea will mingle with salt water?" a question which was greeted with shouts of laughter. About sunset an Indian yell was heard outside the church, and a band of men, disguised as Mohawk Indians filled the street. The meeting at once broke up; and the Indians in disguise marched down to the ships, whence they threw into the harbor 342 chests of tea. After the war, the church was used for divine service until the society erected the New Old South Church in the Back Bay district. The old edifice just missed falling a prey to the great fire in 1872, and was then for a time used as a post-office. It is now used for the exhibition of historic relics, lectures, etc., and the basement is occupied as an old bookstore. In the vicinity of the church on the opposite side of the street, formerly stood the Old Province House, of whose quaintness Hawthorne wrote so charmingly. It was built in 1679, and became the vice-regal residence of Shute, Burnet, Shirley, Pownall, Sir William Howe, and a long line of British governors, when the court ceremonies of the province were conducted within its halls, and the royal proclamations were read from its high balcony. The present Province Court was the way to the stables. From its high estate the vice-regal residence descended to the level of a shabby gin-mill and concert hall, and finally to that of a cheap lodging-house, while it became hidden almost from view to pedestrians on Washington Street by the tall buildings erected about it. Now, a handsome six-story hotel, to be named the Boston Tavern, is being erected on its site. In the same vicinity, too, is the great publishing centre, and the oldest bookstore in the city. Book houses are plentiful, and the leading newspaper offices are crowded into this locality. Opposite the church, in Milk Street, is the *Post* building, occupying the site of the house in which Benjamin Franklin was born. Near too, on Washington Street, is the *Transcript* building, and farther north, crowded near each other, are the offices of the *Herald*, *Journal*, *Globe*, *Advertiser*, and *Record*, all occupying tall, costly, well-appointed buildings, the *Globe* building being the latest accession and which is a fitting monument to its enterprise. The *Globe* Newspaper Company is comprised of some of Boston's most highly esteemed and public-spirited citizens, with Mr. Ed. Prescott as president and cashier, and Colonel Charles H. Taylor as manager. This representative and progressive Newspaper Company are proprietors of the daily, Sunday, and weekly *Globe*, which are the recognized leading newspapers of New England. The *Globe* Newspaper Company was duly incorporated in 1872 under the laws of Massachusetts. It was reorganized in 1878, with a paid-up capital of $125,000, and now its daily and Sunday issues of the *Globe* have a larger circulation than any other Boston newspaper. The first editor of the *Globe* was Maturin M. Ballou, and the first paper, issued March 4, 1872, contained eight pages of seven columns, the price being four cents. He was succeeded, in August, 1873, by Colonel Chas. H. Taylor, who has been the editor and manager of the *Globe* from that time until the present. The success achieved has been due to his enterprise and industry. The building is one of the finest and largest in Boston, and was built expressly for the *Globe*. The building is admirably equipped with all modern appliances, including elevators, electric lights, etc., and no

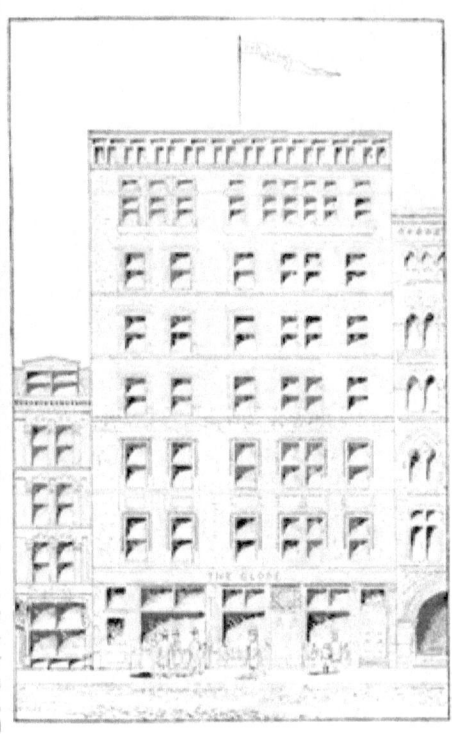

Globe Building.

pains or expense have been spared to make this establishment complete in every detail. In the printing-rooms are three splendid single and two double Hoe presses, which are able to print 1400 papers in a minute. The machinery is driven by two superior 125 horse-power steam-engines, and the total number of persons employed in the various departments is about 500. There are likewise two elevator and electric-light engines on the premises, of the latest type. Eight editions of the *Globe* are turned out daily, which consume fifteen tons of paper. The daily, Sunday, and weekly *Globe* are got up in the highest style of the typographical art. An able and superior staff of editorial writers, reporters, and correspondents is employed. It has regular letters from its own correspondents abroad, and carefully covers all political, local, and foreign news; while at the same time it gives ample descriptions of races, base-ball, and all kinds of manly sports and pastimes. Its editorials are able, crisp, direct to the point, and treat all matters of interest in an impartial and fearless manner. The circulation of the Sunday *Globe* in November was 127,923, and the daily *Globe* 148,710. Its advantages as a splendid advertising medium have been recognized very generally by all classes of the community; and in this line it conducts the largest and most lucrative business in Boston. In consequence of its large size and vast amount of original and able reading-matter, it is not only the cheapest, but unquestionably the best, paper in the city. Colonel Chas. H. Taylor, the manager, was born in Charlestown, Mass., and during the civil war was a private in the 38th Mass. Vol. Infantry. He served one year, and was seriously wounded at the battle of Port Hudson, Miss., and eventually retired from the service, for disability. He was private secretary to Governor Claflin, and was also clerk of the House of Representatives. Colonel Taylor is a popular member of the Press, Temple, Central, and Algonquin Clubs, etc., and is one of Boston's highly esteemed and public-spirited citizens. The circulation of the *Globe* is steadily increasing, not only in Boston, but in all sections of New England, and its present prosperous status augurs well for the future. In "Printing House Square"—and Dock Square, are many old-time buildings, relieved by but few new edifices, prominent among which are Rogers' and Sears' Buildings, magnificent structures at the head of State Street. The whole of the

Bunker Hill Monument.

buildings, except a few on the east side that line the remaining length of Washington Street from Dock Square to Haymarket Square, have been built or rebuilt since this section of the street was opened, and no city in the country can show a finer range of business blocks than those to be seen here. Dock Square, on the site of the old Town Dock, which was spanned by a swing bridge at the foot of Merchants' Row, is now a busy centre, and standing in the middle of it is a statue of Samuel Adams erected in 1880. From here is seen the front of Faneuil Hall, and off Washington Street, at this point, Cornhill and Brattle Street swing round to Scollay Square. The famous hostelry, Quincy House, stands on the corner of Brattle Street and Brattle Square; and in this square stood formerly a church which the British turned into a barrack during the siege of Boston. Cornhill, renowned for its old book-stores and up which we must now pass once more to Scollay Square, was so named in 1828, having previously been called Market Street, because it lead to the market, the original Cornhill being at the foot of Washington Street before its extension. Having returned to Scollay Square, we must now prepare for a journey, through the principal sections of the great

FINANCIAL AND WHOLESALE BUSINESS CENTRES

of the city. These centres are confined between the harbor on the one hand, and the streets of Essex, Washington, and Hanover on the other, and lie chiefly south of Blackstone Street. A large portion of this area is frequently spoken of as the "Burnt District," laid waste by the "Great Fire" in 1872. At 7.45 P.M. on November 9th in that year a fire broke out in a building on the corner of Summer and Kingston Streets, and spread with terrible speed, in spite of all the efforts that could be brought from far and near to suppress it, and, before the conflagration was quenched, it had spread over sixty-five acres, and destroyed about eighty million dollars' worth of property and many lives, leaving the entire district bounded by Summer, Washington, Milk, and Broad Streets a smoking chaos of ruins. This was a terrible blow to Boston, but the city soon recovered from it, and the "Burnt District" is to-day a section of imposing and substantial warehouses, its appearance greatly improved, and the wealth and convenience of this part of the city thereby increased. The financial centre is circumscribed by Washington, State, Brook, and Milk Streets. The great dry-goods and clothing quarter covers a large area. The wholesale trade is chiefly centred in Devonshire, between Milk and Franklin Streets, Franklin and its lateral streets, Winthrop Square and Otis Street, Summer and its lateral streets. The great woodhouses are located principally on Federal, Pearl, and High Streets; the boot, shoe, and leather, and hardware trades on Pearl, High, Purchase, lower part of Summer, South, Bedford, and parts of Lincoln and contiguous streets; the paper trade, on Federal Street and vicinity; crockery, on Federal and Franklin Streets; drugs, on Milk Street and vicinity; grocery trade in neighborhood of Broad, Commercial India streets; fish, on Commercial Street and Atlantic Avenue; flour and grain, on Commercial Street, near the principal wharves; fruit and produce, Merchants' Row, Chatham and South Market, Commercial, Commerce, and Clinton Streets; and provisions, on streets about Faneuil Hall Market and the new meat market on Mercantile Wharf.

As we start from Scollay Square, in the direction of State Street, the County Court-house, on Court Street (called Queen Street in pre-Revolution days), claims attention. It is a ponderous, gloomy granite building, with a heavy Doric portico in front, and formerly had a similar portico at the rear end of the building, facing the City Hall. Here numerous courts are held, and, as a consequence of its inadequacy to meet the demands upon it, the new court-house on Pemberton Square is being erected. On the old court-house, which was erected in 1836, an intense excitement centred many years ago, when the fugitive slave cases were under trial; and the citizens of Boston, indignant that men should be carried from their free soil into a terrible and degrading servitude, came near rebelling against the United States and rescuing the doomed negroes by force of arms. In the vicinity of this seat of justice are the Tudor Buildings, on the site of the home of Colonel William Tudor, a statesman and jurist of many years ago. In this neighborhood, also, Smibert, the canny Scot, painted "Landskips," more than a century and a half ago; and Franklin printed his pioneer newspaper; and Captain Kidd, the famous pirate, was jailed; and Sir John Leverett, the friend and veteran of Cromwell, resided. Standing near the Court-house is the famous Young's Hotel, adjoining which is the splendid Sears' Building, occupying the corner of Court and Washington Streets.

Directly opposite this, occupying the head of State (once King) Street, is the old State-house, occupying the site of what was originally the old village market-place. A town-house was first erected here in 1658, and in 1748 a new building arose on the same ground, which was used for the Provincial Council, and also at different times for an exchange, a post-office, an enginehouse, barracks for British troops, and a capitol in which the State Legislature met for fifteen years. Here, according to John Adams, "Independence was born;" here the death of George II, and the accession to the throne, of George III, were proclaimed; here Generals Howe, Clinton and Gage held a council of war before the battle of Bunker Hill; and a year later the Declaration of Independence was read from the balcony to the rejoicing soldiers and people below; and the constitution of Massachusetts was planned; and Governor Hancock gave a grand reception to the Count d'Estaing; and Washington reviewed the militia and was welcomed by the people. The quaint old steeple lost part of its height and the lion and unicorn disappeared from the angles of the roof after the Revolution and were burned; but otherwise the building maintained its original aspect. Some six or seven years ago the building was completely restored, to preserve its historic features, even to the fixing of the lion and unicorn on the west front, a fact which raised the ire of Irish citizens, who could recognize nothing even that was good out of the land of the hated Anglo-Saxon. Attempts were made to destroy these emblems in secret, but too strict a watch was kept on the toothless lion and blind unicorn, and they were permitted to remain; still the grumblers declined to be quiet until something of a counteracting character was put on the Washington Street end of the building, to balance it, to hold it down, or something of that kind. A gorgeous gilt eagle was accordingly spread on the outer wall, accompanied with the State's motto in gold characters on a broad ribbon—"Ense Petit Placidam Sub Libertate Quietem." And it did "quiet 'em;" so the old lion and unicorn are now at peace. It was near here—on the corner of State and Exchange Streets, where the Custom-house then stood—that the Boston Massacre, described elsewhere, occurred. On the building now on the corner the Bostonian Society, in 1886 placed a tablet bearing this inscription: "Opposite this spot was shed the first blood of the American Revolution, March 5, 1770." On the opposite side of the street, near the Old State-house, the first church was built in Boston. Brazer's Building now occupies the site, and near this is the office of the *Traveller* newspaper.

On State Street are numerous banks and insurance offices, and the headquarters of many mining and man-

Massachusetts Horticultural Society Building.

ufacturing companies and railways, shipping-offices, etc. The Merchants' Exchange, the Board of Trade, and the Stock Exchange are in the building No. 53, opposite 'Change Avenue. Great changes are projected here. The entire lot of buildings extending from the Tremont Bank Building to Kilby Street will soon be torn down to make room for a new Stock Exchange, to be erected at a cost of millions of dollars. Messrs. Peabody & Stearns have for some time been engaged in making designs, and the plans, sections, and elevations are completed. Builders will soon be at work, and the building they will raise will be the largest of its kind in the city. It will be ten stories high above the basement, and in parts eleven stories high. From the sidewalk on the State Street front to the cornice there will be a height of about 160 feet. It will have a frontage of 171 feet on State Street from the Tremont Bank Building (which is five stories high) to Kilby Street, about the same on Kilby Street, and 52 feet on Exchange Place and Post-office Avenue, the last named leading from Congress Street, just in the rear of the Tremont Bank building. Stone will be the material for the two lower stories, the rest being of brick, with stone trimmings. The interior finish will be plain but very serviceable, in marble, natural woods, and plastered walls suitably tinted. Steam heat, open fire-places, electric lights, and all the modern conveniences, together with six fast-running elevators, will make the building desirable in every way for the purposes to which it is to be put. The main entrance will be on State Street. A broad corridor, finished in marble, will lead direct to the entrance of the Stock Exchange Hall, and another corridor, at right angles to it, will lead from the Kilby Street entrance to an entrance at Post-office Avenue, a short alley leading from Congress Street. Near the junction of these corridors will be the large main staircase. In the basement, at the right of the main entrance on State Street, will be rooms and vaults for a safe-deposite company. In front is the large banking-room, 50 by 60 feet, and in the rear the vaults for about 10,000 boxes of varying sizes, as well as "coupon-rooms" for the patrons of the company. A novelty here is a number of coupon-rooms, eight feet square. At the left of the main entrance, and along the Kilby Street front, are half a dozen offices of varying size, the largest being the one on the corner, and this has a separate entrance at the intersection of the streets. In the wing of the building extending to Exchange Place are a couple of desirable offices fronting on that street, and several smaller ones. The Boston Stock Exchange, as already stated, will occupy a hall in the first story under a twenty years' lease. This hall will have an area of about 5000 feet, and will be in the Exchange Place wing. Here also are three large rooms for "puts" and "calls," and the bond and telephone rooms. The Stock Exchange will have a private entrance on Exchange Place. The main portion of this floor, with frontage on State and Kilby Streets, will be devoted to banking and insurance offices, which will be subdivided to suit tenants. The arrangement of the second story is very similar to the first, the Exchange Place wing being taken up by the Stock Exchange Hall, which is two stories in height, and the State and Kilby Street fronts being divided up into banking and insurance offices. Upon this story begins the light-well, 116x30 feet, situated west of the central stairway and over the safe-deposit vaults, which, as well as the rear of the offices on the first story, are lighted by it. This well extends from the Tremont Bank Building, parallel with State Street, and is nearly as broad as Kilby Street. By means of it, an additional row of well-lighted offices is obtained in the upper stories. Above the second story the arrangement of the floors will be substantially alike, as represented in the third-floor plan. The floors will be devoted to offices, ranging in size from 12x20 to 20x20 feet, which are reached by broad corridors following the several frontages of the building. The central stairway stops at the second story, and from thence upward there are flights of stairs in front and rear, directly opposite the elevator-wells. The third and the stories above have toilet-rooms over those in the basement, thus concentrating the plumbing as far as possible. There are 350 offices in the building. Changes in the floor plans will be freely made to suit tenants. In the interior finish, no elaborate effects will be sought, and the exterior convenience has nowhere been sacrificed for architectural effect. Nevertheless,

Commonwealth Avenue, showing Hotel Vendome.

the building will be an exceedingly handsome addition to the business blocks of Boston. It will be a year and a half before the building will be completed; and the cost of building and land will probably be upwards of $3,000,000.

On the north side of State Street the Hospital-Life Building has just been completed at a cost of $800,000, and opposite Merchants' Row there is now nearing completion a nine-story building erected by Mr. J. N. Fiske at a cost of half a million of dollars. State Street is, in fact, becoming a region of tall, costly buildings, and has changed much of its aspect of a dozen years or so ago.

Proceeding through Merchants' Row, the historic Faneuil Hall, the "Cradle of Liberty," and the New Faneuil Hall, or Quincy Market, are reached. The latter, built in 1825-26, is a granite structure two stories high, and covers 27,000 feet of land. The centre part rises to a height of 77 feet, and is ornamented by a graceful dome. The height of the wings on either side of the central part is thirty feet. The market is on the lower floor, the stalls are well arranged, and the place is always a busy one and worthy of a visit. The upper floor is used for offices, and a large hall under the dome is occupied by the Boston Chamber of Commerce, for whom it is proposed to erect, at an early date, a separate building. Faneuil Hall was built in 1742, and presented to the town by Peter Faneuil, a prosperous Huguenot merchant, as a market and public hall; and the present city charter contains a provision forbidding its sale or lease. The lower floor is occupied as the market, and the upper floor as a hall, which contains no seats, and which gives standing room to thousands of people. In the galleries, however, there are settees. The platform is spacious, the walls are adorned with copies of large and valuable historic oil-paintings, the originals being deposited in the Art Museum for safe keeping; and the quaint and antiquated architecture is very interesting. When any great popular question takes definite form, the people say, "Let's go down and rock the cradle," and assemble in the hall, to be addressed by their favorite orators and leaders. It was so before the Revolution; it has been so since. It has, in fact, during its history, been used for all sorts of purposes. The coronation of George III. was celebrated in it, pirates and robbers have been tried in it, and the Earl of Elgin was feasted there. "Every political party in the country has had its use at one time or another. Anarchists, Socialists, Fenians, and Land-leaguers have spoken there. The Chinese have been told to go, and the poor Indian pitied by large audiences. The Constitution of U. S. has been styled 'a covenant with death and a league with hell' in this hall." In June, 1887, the British Charitable Society obtained the consent of the Mayor and Board of Aldermen for its use on the occasion of a banquet on the 21st of that month to celebrate the jubilee of Queen Victoria. It provoked a howl among the Irish residents against such a "desecration" of the hall, the use of which they themselves secured to protest against the "desecration" and to say hard things against Britisher, generally. The Aldermen reconsidered their resolution granting the use of the hall, but without change, and the Britishers held their banquet, and that a lively one, for a mob of about 15,000 persons gathered about the hall ready to turn the "cradle" over. The whole police force, of over 800 men, were called out, armed with revolvers, and 400 were stationed around the hall. Several of the military companies were under arms, and Gatling guns were placed in position to rake the mob if necessity required. Several persons were seriously injured, and during the night an attempt was made to pull, with ropes, the lion and unicorn from off the Old State-house. The occasion served as a lesson to the English, who had generally been indifferent to naturalization; they formed the British-American Association, with branches all over the country, the object of which was to encourage Englishmen to become American citizens and to vote against class rule.

North Market and South Market Streets, Chatham, Clinton, and Commerce Streets, running parallel with Faneuil Hall and Quincy Markets, and Blackstone, Fulton, and Commercial, and other neighboring streets are great centres for the wholesale trade in all kinds of food products. The conversion of the so-called Mercantile Wharf property, at the foot of Clinton Street and on Atlantic Avenue, into a country market, as well as a wholesale meat market, has attracted provision-dealers and grocerymen to that section of the city, and naturally the wholesale grocers in that vicinity, and especially on Commercial Street, have pushed their trade. Below this market, on Atlantic Avenue, is the Fish Market, another attraction to dealers. Property between Richmond Street and Faneuil Hall Market has improved recently in value, in keeping with the improved surrounding conditions. On Fulton Street the wholesale fruit trade is advancing, and tall warehouses have been and are being erected. To meet the exigencies of the shipping trade, costly warehouses have been erected along Atlantic Avenue, from near the corner of which, and extending almost close up to the Custom-house, on State Street, a magnificent, extensive granite block of spacious warehouses of pleasing exterior has been put up.

The Custom-house was built between 1837 and 1849, at a cost of over one million dollars, and rests on ground reclaimed from the sea, the foundation being composed of a deep bed of granite masonry, laid in hydraulic cement on the heads of three thousand piles. It is a massive granite structure, built to stand for generations. It is Doric in style, cruciform in shape, and fire-proof in construction, with thirty-two fluted monolithic columns, weighing forty-two tons each, fronting its stately porticoes and extending around the sides, surmounted by classic cornices and pediments, and sustaining a roof and dome of granite slabs. Under the dome is a handsome rotunda, surrounded by twelve tall Corinthian columns of white marble. This building is one of the principal attractions on State Street, which maintains its old-time supremacy as the financial centre, though in some of its off streets, notably Devonshire, Congress, and Kilby Streets, banks and brokers' and insurance offices are to be found in great numbers. These are located in buildings of large size and of great architectural beauty. Congress, Devonshire, Milk, and Water Streets, at their crossings, form Post-office Square, wherein stands the Government Building, an immense but very ornamental pile of Cape Ann granite. The erection of the building was begun in 1871 and some fourteen or fifteen years elapsed before it was entirely completed, the cost being upwards of six millions of dollars.

Fronting on Post-office Square are several fine specimens of the modern business structure, designed both for architectural effect and utility. On the south side of the square is a magnificent white marble building, with a majestic clock-tower. This is by some considered the handsomest block in New England and it cost $900,000 to build. It is owned and occupied by the Mutual Life Insurance Company of New York. The tower is surmounted by gilded crests and an iron flag-staff, and the height from the street to the top of the flagstaff is 234 feet. At a height of 198 feet from the sidewalk is a balcony on the tower; and from this balcony a charming view of the city and harbor is to be obtained. Adjoining, and occupying the corner of Congress Street, is the handsome building of the New England Mutual Life Company, erected at a cost of $1,000,000. In the basement of the building are the extensive fire and burglar-proof vaults and the superb reading-room of the Security Safe Vaults Co. From the roof of this building a fine view is to be obtained. A few yards away, occupying the corner of Devonshire and Milk Street, is the splendid building of the Equitable

Boylston Street and Copley Square.

Life Assurance Society of New York, built in 1873 at a cost of between one and two millions of dollars. In 1885-86 the building was extended, and its Milk-street façade altered, at an immense outlay of capital. It stands on the site of the house of Robert Treat Paine, one of the signers of the Declaration of Independence. Within about a stone-throw from here, and bounded by Milk Street and Kilby Street, is Liberty Square, whereon stands an immense, imposing, solidly built business structure, presenting a rounding front on Kilby Street, and possessing a peculiar, dome-like roof. This is the Mason Building, occupied by banks and offices. Contiguous thereto are the great wholesale trade thoroughfares of Broad Street (opened in 1806 and originally called Flounder Lane) and India Street (opened in the following year for the East India trade).

Nearly opposite the Milk-street end of Mason Building, we enter Oliver Street and the "Burnt District," and by way of this street attain Fort Hill Square, where used to stand Fort Hill, one of the three noted hills of "Treamount." Half a century ago this was an aristocratic residential quarter. The hill has been carried away; and the work of doing this was started in 1869, and continued for years. A park occupied the summit of the hill, on which at one time were fortifications. Within the fort here Sir Edmund Andros, in 1689, sought shelter from, and was subsequently surrendered to, the enraged colonists, whose rights he had usurped. A neat circular grass-plat occupies the centre of Fort Hill Square, now the highest point of the hill. From here the entire area, stretching to Essex and Washington Streets on the one hand, and from Atlantic Avenue to Milk Street on the other, is occupied by Oliver, Pearl, Franklin, Purchase, Congress, Devonshire, Summer, Bedford, Kingston, Arch, Chauncey, and Hawley Streets and Winthrop Square; and here are centred the great wool, boot, shoe and leather, hides, fur, oil, dry-goods, paper, hardware, and crockery jobbing-houses. This was the area swept and laid waste by the great fire of 1872. Here are now to be found some of the finest specimens of modern architecture; and no business section of any of our American cities presents more solid and attractive features than this one does. The buildings are palatial in character, and new structures are continually arising and others being altered and extended. From the corner of Congress Street down to the property of the New York & New England Railroad, adjoining its passenger station, there is a row of six magnificent blocks of business buildings of recent erection the equal of which it would be difficult to match in the country. Five of them are occupied by extensive wool firms, and the sixth for other kinds of business. They are all six stories in height, of enough difference in façade to break up the monotony of equality in other respects. They are of solid and substantial construction, and have passageways on the sides and rears for receiving and shipping, which preclude the necessity of blocking sidewalks and stopping travel, as is too frequently the case in all cities. These buildings cost $444,000 to erect. On one corner of Purchase and Pearl Streets formerly stood a Protestant Church, which subsequently became a Catholic Church, and now it has been replaced, at a cost of $60,000, by a handsome six-story business building. On the opposite corner stand the remains of an old building that escaped the fire. This lot and one on the corner of Oliver and Purchase Street, are the only two which remain unimproved in the "Burnt District." The prospectus of the year 1889 indicates a large increase in building operations within the city proper, as well as the outlying districts. Plans now matured and presented, but for which permits have not yet been issued, are for some of the most palatial business structures, which will rival, if not surpass, any now erected in the Union.

THE BRIGHTON DISTRICT

constitutes the 25th ward of the city, and was annexed to Boston in 1873, and increased the city's dimensions by 2277 acres. The situation is one of the finest in the vicinity of Boston. The neighborhood generally is one of high lands, possessing fine facilities for drainage, and abounding in the finest locations for dwelling purposes to be found anywhere. A great feature of the Brighton District is Chestnut Hill Reservoir and the parkways about it. The construction of the reservoir was begun in 1865, and the city of Boston became possessed of 2123 acres of land, the work costing about $120,000 before it was finished. It is, in fact, a double reservoir, divided by a water-tight dam into two basins of irregular shape. Their capacity is 730,000,000 gallons, and the water-surface is 123¼ acres. A magnificent driveway, varying from 60 to 80 feet in width, surrounds the entire work. In some parts, the road runs quite close to the embankment, separated from it by only a smooth, gravelled walk.

The splendid driveway around the reservoir is reached from Boston by the Brighton Road, which is a continuation of Beacon Street, and a noted trotting and driving course that at almost all seasons in the year is, especially on afternoons, crowded with gay equippages, worth coming from afar to see. Brighton can also be reached by the Boston & Albany Railroad, and by horse and electric cars.

Originally, Brighton formed a part of Cambridge, and was known as Little Cambridge. It became a separate town in 1807, and remained so until it was absorbed by Boston, in 1873. The elevated lands of Brighton afford charming views, and the streets are pleasant and shady. Brighton has long been noted for its extensive abbatoirs; and persons who know little about the place have pictured its streets as being crowded with cattle and hogs, and as being ill-smelling. The abbatoirs, however, are situated near the line of the Boston & Albany Railroad; and while thousands of cattle, sheep, and pigs are slaughtered here weekly, so retired are the slaughter-houses that the most refined inhabitant of Brighton may abide here in happy ignorance of their presence.

Brighton contains many beautiful mansions. Within the last few years, building operations have been active, land has increased in value, the population has multiplied; and it is predicted that the range of hills in this District, running southwest from Covey Hill, and including the latter, will in time be the "court end" of Boston. The opening up of Commonwealth Avenue, from Arlington Street to Chestnut Hill Reservoir — four and three quarters miles in length, — and also of Beacon Street, thus offering the finest facilities for travel, brought much low-priced farm lands into the market for building purposes. The route from the city proper to this section is a magnificent series of parks; and in the District itself are several fine parks, in the improvement of which considerable expense has been incurred. On Brighton Square is a splendid branch of the Boston Public Library. This branch was originally founded in 1864 as the Holton Library, by the town of Brighton; and on the annexation of the town the library became a branch of the now main library of Boston. The building is a very convenient one and well-stocked with books. Brighton was one of the first places in the State to erect a monument to the soldiers and sailors who fell in the War of the Rebellion. The monument, a very handsome one, stands in Evergreen Cemetery, and was dedicated July 26, 1866. It is 30 feet high and of Quincy granite. Brighton is assured a progressive and prosperous future.

SOUTH BOSTON

was set off from Dorchester and joined to Boston in 1804. The district extends about two miles along the south side of the harbor, an arm of which, known as Fort Point Channel, separates it from the city proper. This channel has been much narrowed by filling up, and the "made" land is chiefly occupied by the railroads. The channel is crossed by bridges. When South Boston was added to Boston, the city acquired 1002 additional acres of land; but at that time there were only ten families on the territory. The annexation, it is said, was the outcome of a real-estate speculation; and the most active promoters of it were actuated by a belief that in the near future this district would become a very populous and fashionable one. But their expectations were not as rapidly realized as they predicted. Soon after the annexation, a bridge was built across the channel at the "Neck," at Dover Street, and was opened in March, 1804, with a military display and great civic "pomp and circumstance."

State Street.

It was 1550 feet long, and cost $50,000 to construct it. In recent years there has been substituted a fine, substantial iron bridge. In 1828, a second South Boston Bridge was built, from the foot of Federal Street; and now in the matter of bridges the city proper and South Boston are adequately connected, the latest important addition in this respect being the magnificent iron bridge extending from Broadway to Harrison Avenue. The building of the earliest bridges led to an increase of the population of South Boston; and though the district failed to become, as had been predicted, the "court end" of the city, many fine residences were reared upon the sightly bluffs towards the South Boston Neck. South Boston experienced its most rapid growth after the street-railway system had been established, in 1854. Then it was that building operations multiplied. Dwellings arose on every hand, and several important and notable public institutions were erected here, while factories, foundries, work-shops, etc., kept on increasing, parks were laid out and the place in many ways made attractive. The street system of South Boston is very regular, which is more than can be said for the city proper, especially in its most ancient parts. Broadway is the principal thoroughfare, and runs through the centre from Albany Street, in the city proper, to City Point, at the extreme end of South Boston. The parallel streets on either side are generally numbered, and the cross-streets lettered. Broadway, on which are located many fine business blocks, splendid church edifices, and neat-looking mansions, is divided into West and East, that portion from Albany Street to Dorchester Street being designated as West Broadway, and that from Dorchester Street to City Point, East Broadway. A walk or ride up Broadway is interesting, particularly so beyond Dorchester Street. City Point is the common terminus for the horse-car lines, and is one of the two chief places of interest for the mere spectator, the other being Dorchester Heights. The Point is a favorite resort in the summer season, when the place presents a lively appearance, visitors finding all necessary facilities for fun and frolic and everything that can contribute to their enjoyment. The Point commands magnificent harbor views, and yachting sights innumerable. Indeed, this is the greatest rendezvous on the Eastern Massachusetts coast for yachts, as respects numbers; for there are other places where yachts of larger tonnage than those which anchor here are more numerous. Southerly, a fine view is obtained of Dorchester, the Blue Hills, and parts of Quincy. The Point abounds in seaside hotels and cafés. Here, too, is the new Marine Park, with its long promenade pier extending nearly to Fort Independence (the old Castle Island) in the harbor.

In the immediate neighborhood is the School for Idiotic and Feeble-minded Children, at No. 723 East Eighth Street; also the City Asylum for the Insane, and the Suffolk House of Correction on First Street. Standing on a high elevation on the corner of Broadway and Emerson Street, and commanding charming views over land and water, is the building of the world-renowned charity, the Perkins Institution for the Blind, over which the late learned Dr. S. G. Howe presided successfully for many years. Near by are the historic Dorchester Heights, famous in Revolutionary lore. These heights were included in the territory annexed to Boston in 1804, and are sometimes spoken of as Telegraph Hill (though it is many years since it was used for marine telegraphing purposes) and also as Mount Washington. As mentioned elsewhere in this work, Washington, during the siege of Boston, by a strategic movement, seized upon these heights and fortified them, to the astonishment of the British, who were in possession of the city. All other points of vantage were in the hands of the English; and Washington, seeing they had neglected to hold the heights, determined, in March, 1776, to seize them and throw up formidable works with despatch. The ground was frozen and the weather bad, and his army was scattered over East Cambridge and Roxbury. When night set in, he caused a heavy cannonading to begin from both East Cambridge and Roxbury that should claim the attention of the English soldiery and prevent the work going on on the heights from being heard. To still further deaden the noise of the carts passing over the frozen ground, their wheels were bound with whisps of straw, and straw was strewn over the roads through which they passed. When daylight dawned on the morning of the 4th of March, the British were not only surprised, but alarmed, by the fortifications they saw on the heights. Howe, the English commander, determined to storm the fortifications on the following night, and to this end sent three thousand men to Castle Island (now Fort Independence), to make an attack from that side. A storm, however, arose, that prevented the carrying out of the design; and meanwhile the Americans kept on vigilantly strengthening their works until the British recognized they were too formidable to overthrow, and decided to evacuate the town. This they did on the 17th; and Washington, to the great delight of the citizens and the whole country, then marched with his soldiers into Boston, where he was hailed as a deliverer. This is regarded as one of the greatest military achievements of the "Father of the Country."

On the slope of hill on Old Harbor Street is Carney Hospital, a public institution of great excellence, conducted by the Sisters of Charity, and its usefulness is extended to both Catholics and Protestants alike.

A vast area of land has been reclaimed and is being reclaimed from the Bay at South Boston, and the place is renowned for its numerous and varied foundries, sugar-refineries, breweries, and other noteworthy industries. These are for the most part located along the water-sides of the district and afford employment to vast numbers of workpeople. Among the most noted works here are those of the South Boston Iron Company, on Foundry Street. The concern covers nearly seven acres, and is the largest of its kind in the country. It was founded by Cyrus Alger, the famous metallurgist and inventor, who constructed the first perfect bronze cannon for the national and State governments. Here have been produced the largest cannon ever made in America.

Handsome as South Boston is as a residential section, noted as it is for its cottages, and populous as it is, it has never been very attractive to the aristocratic citizens as a place of residence; and a peculiarity attached to it is the falling in value of property in what were once the most select sections and the growth in value of building lots in others. The old-timers who owned the fine hill residences have been attracted to more fashionable sections of the city, or made homes in the suburbs; and, on putting their property into the market, have found that they could sell only at from thirty to fifty per cent below the cost of building. The consequence is that there has been considerable falling off in the valuation of property in this section of South Boston; but it has been more than made up by the advances realized elsewhere through the erection of tenement-houses and moderate-priced dwellings. Since 1883, about 600 houses (chiefly of the tenement class) have been erected in the district, most of them in the territory east of Dorchester Street and well toward the Point. These are occupied mostly by mechanics. Many single houses, too, have been erected, costing from $3000 to $4000. In Ward 13, there is a large co-operative tenement building on Second Street, corner of Athens, near Dorchester Avenue. It is a four-story building, and contains about thirty tenements, ranging from three rooms and upward each. There have been many improvements made at and near the Boston wharf property. Among others is the establishment at this place of the Chace Confectionery Works. To show how, on the other hand, land has varied in value, it may be stated that the local gas company, some ten or fifteen years ago, paid $2 a foot for a piece of land on the corner of B and Third Streets, for which a dollar a foot can now be hardly realized. There has been an offer of 75 cents a foot for it. Another peculiarity of land values is that, while vacant land on the south of Broadway is taxed at from 40 to 50 cents a foot, on the north side of that thoroughfare, it is taxed at only from 20 to 25 cents per foot. The valuation of the three wards, 13, 14 and 15, comprised in South Boston has increased in the last five years $2,939,100, and the population, according to the number of polls, about 7000.

EAST BOSTON.

This now populous and busy centre little more than half a century ago was a wilderness, and was occupied by only one family, while to-day it has upon it more than forty thousand people; is crossed and recrossed with streets lined with stores, factories, foundries, workshops, dwellings, churches, schools, etc., by the thousands; its thoroughfares are kept lively with the eternal jingle of the bells of railroad car horses and the din of the wheels of traffic; from its piers ferry-boats flit hither and thither by day and by night; and to and from its extensive wharves ocean steamers come and go at will burdened with merchandize and human freight; while its shipyards turn into the deep vessels that plow the billows from coast to coast. And all this is the achievement of half a century!

East Boston is an island situated at the confluence of the Mystic and Charles Rivers, and is connected with the city proper by ferry, and with the mainland at Chelsea and Winthrop by bridges. Its original name was Noddle Island, and it received this appellation on account of having been occupied by one William Noddle, who, by old writers, was designated "an honest man from Salem." Its "settlement"—if such a term can be legitimately used—dates back to the earliest accounts of Massachusetts Bay, and its history includes many interesting incidents, both of a local and general character. From the time of its discovery it became, owing to its close proximity to Boston, a favorite pasture-ground. In this way both it and the other islands in the harbor yielded considerable revenue, and at the time of the Revolution all the islands were well-stocked with domestic animals. Noddle Island was also a favorite fishing-ground.

On November 3, 1620, King James I. granted the territory hereabouts to the council of Plymouth, who, on December, 13, 1622, gave to Robert Gorges, youngest son of Ferdinando Gorges (who had expended £20,000 in fruitless attempts to make settlements in various parts of Massachusetts) various lands. This gift included Noddle Island. Robert died, and his brother John, who succeeded him as proprietor in January, 1628, conveyed the island and other lands to Sir William Brereton, of Handforth, Co. Chester, England, who sent over servants to improve the lands and make leases; but neither the Plymouth council nor his own own government seem to have recognized his authority, and he does not appear to have ever come to the country himself. But be that as it may, it seems that according to the colony records, the General Court, on April 1, 1633, granted the island to Samuel Maverick, and this under the title of Noddle Island. This fact demonstrates that William Noddle, who is believed to have been one of Sir W. Brereton's colonists, and who was made a freeman in 1631, occupied the island previously. Prior to Maverick coming into possession the General Court seems to have exercised a care over the island, for in 1631 it passed an order restraining persons from "putting on cattell, felling wood or raising slate" on this island. Like all the islands in the harbor, there appeared to be forests growing upon Noddle's Island in former times, and apparently a similar fate befel them all to be bereft of this growth. In 1632 the following order was passed: "Noe p'son wt'soever shall shoot att fowle upon Pullen Poynte or Noddle's Ileand, but the sd places shalbe reserved for John Perkins, to take fowle with netts." The following is a copy of the orders passed in favor of Mr. Maverick, who acquired all John Perkin's privileges:

"Noddle's Ileland is granted to Mr. Sam'l Mavack to enjoy to to him and his heires for ever. Yielding and & payeing yearly att ye Generall Court, to ye Gov'n'r for the time being, either a fatt weather, a fatt hogg, or Xs in money, & shalle give leave to Boston and Charles Towne to fetch woode contynually, as theire neede requires, from ye southerne p'ts of sd ileand." It appears that the "neede" of Boston and Charlestown re-

Museum of Fine Arts, St. James Avenue.

quired all the wood growing, and these two enterprising towns appear to have used it pretty freely, for by 1833 they had removed all the timber on the island except two trees!

Noddle's Island was "layd to Boston," as it was termed, in 1636. It originally contained about 663 acres, together with the contiguous flats to low-water mark. Before any alterations in topography had been made the island was fancifully stated to resemble a great bear, described as follows: "The bear's head, an elevated tract of land, was known as the 'middle farm,' with Hog Island marsh at its northeast. The small, round pond in this part called Eye pond in consequence of the loss there of the eye of a noted gunner helps out the fancied figure. The bear's back, fronting the mouth of Mystic River, was the most elevated part of the island, and was known as Eagle Hill, and its abrupt termination at the confluence of Mystic River and Chelsea Creek as West Head, and more recently as Eagle Point. The two fore feet of the assumed bear were called Eastern and Western Wood Islands, being isolated from the Great Marsh, which also isolated Camp Hill and its marsh, the two hinder paws from the same. The heel of the hinder leg was called Smith's Hill, the site of the old buildings which anciently stood on the island, and was separated from Camp Hill by Great Creek, since the canal of the water-power company, lying between the present Bainbridge and Decatur Streets. The old houses on Smith's Hill were destroyed in 1775, during the seige of Boston, and were rebuilt soon after the British evacuated the town from materials taken from the old barracks used by Washington's army in Cambridge. In 1776 a fort was erected on Camp Hill. This or Snow's Hill may have been the site of Mr. Maverick's fort of four guns erected in 1630." In 1814 another more substantial fort was placed on Camp Hill, called Fort Strong, in compliment to the governor then. This was long ago removed, and Belmont Square now occupies its site.

Samuel Maverick, who was the son of the Rev. John Maverick of Dorchester mentioned in the foregoing pages, was born in 1602. He was evidently in his day a man of considerable importance, and exercised great hospitality at his island home, where he was frequently visited by Governor Winthrop and other notabilities. When Mt. Wollaston in Quincy belonged to Boston, Maverick was there granted the use of five hundred acres for the pasturing of his cattle. In 1645 he made a loan to the town toward fortifying Castle Island, which the town guaranteed should be refunded "in case said garrison be defeated or demolished, except by adversary power, within three years." From the earliest settlement of Boston religious persecutions characterized the colonists, though they had fled from their native land on account of similar intolerance. Maverick was a devout Episcopalian and because of the persecutions to which he was subjected he gave up his residence, and, conjointly with his wife and son, Nathaniel, sold his property to Captain George Briggs of Barbadoes, who, in the same year (1650) conveyed it to Nathaniel, and the latter on October 28, 1650, conveyed it to Colonel John Burch of Barbadoes. In 1656

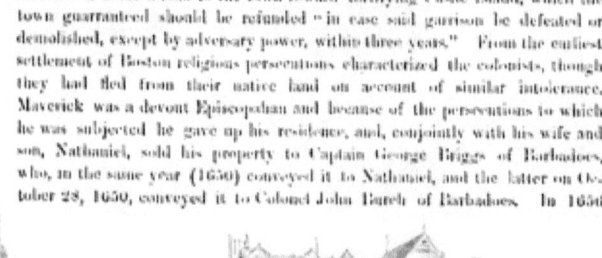

Boylston Street.

Thomas Boughton purchased the island through Richard Louder, his attorney, who took the deed in his own name and that of Richard Newbold. On account of financial embarrassment Boughton, on April 19, 1659, conveyed the island and other property to Henry Shrimpton and Richard Cooke of Boston, and Walter Price of Salem, in trust for his creditors. Shrimpton declined this trust, as full possession of Noddle Island had been previously given to Walter Price. In 1664 Sir Thomas Temple purchased Cooke's interest, and in 1657 Newbold's interest (as creditors of Boughton) in the island and became sole owner. In 1670 Temple sold out to Samuel Shrimpton, who, in 1682, by the payment of £30 to the State, cleared the island of all the conditions in the grant to Maverick, and thus became the first person who held it in his own right in fee-simple. The property descended to his widow, Elizabeth, who became the wife of Richard Stoddard, and by her will, dated April 11, 1713, she devised the island to her granddaughter, the daughter of her son, Samuel Shrimpton, Jr. This granddaughter married into the Stoddard and Yeamans families, and her three daughters married into the Chauncy, Greenleaf and Hyslop families, one of the Hyslops and a descendant of Shrimpton, also becoming the wife of Governor Increase Sumner. The representatives of these families came to have interests in the island, and finally death carried off some of the owners and the island came to be owned by David Stoddard, who held, in fee, three-sixths of the island; David Hyslop, who held one sixth; and Elizabeth (Hyslop) Sumner, who held two sixths. General W. H. Sumner, son and successor of the latter, purchased the others' interests, and in 1833 formed the East Boston Company, to accomplish the great object of his life—to make Noddle Island a valuable addition to the metropolis of New England.

One of the early arrangements made for travel to and from Noddle Island appears in the following order, passed October 30, 1637, authorizing Edward Bendall to "keepe a sufficient ferrie-boat to carry to Noddle's Island and to the Shipps riding before the Towne, taking for a single p'son ijd. and for two 3d." Prior to 1833, the island shores were resorted to by pleasure-parties, to cook their fish and to have a jollification, to which end they were aided by the hospitality of the one resident, Mr. Thomas Williams, as long as he lived. This gentleman and his father, Mr. Henry Howell Williams, held the lease of Noddle Island for seventy years; and as a consequence the place came to be frequently spoken of as Williams' Island. In the war of the Revolution, the island was occupied by the British, who carried off Williams' flocks and herds and made a bonfire of his farm dwelling. After the British evacuated Boston, General Washington gave, as a recompense, the building which had been used as barracks at Cambridge, to Williams, who removed the structure to the island.

After the East Boston Company was incorporated, on March 25, 1833, the island property, according to the survey of 1801, consisted of 663 acres of upland and marsh, surrounded by several hundred acres of flats, which were declared, by an act of the legislature, "to belong to the ordinary cove water marke." The island was separated from Boston by a distance of 142 rods, which distance was afterwards diminished by the extension of the wharves. The island and the city of Boston, to which it was annexed in 1836, were originally reputed to be of about equal size, each being supposed to contain about a thousand acres, some three hundred acres of the island having been washed or worn away by the action of the sea.

Shares in the company were rapidly taken up, lands reclaimed and mapped out into streets, and building-lots set off and sold. In street nomenclature, the plan was of a judicious nature. The selection of names of American towns, commemorative of their services in connection with struggles for liberty, was not only thoughtful, but comprehensive. The names of Bennington, Lexington, Saratoga, Princeton, Eutaw, Monmouth, and Trenton were out of commonplace, and of a sterling character. Maverick, the early owner of the island, was not forgotten; nor were those patriots, Sumner, Webster, and Everett. These all made good names for streets. There can be little objection, also, to the names of Paris, London, Liverpool, and Havre, which constitute the other principal street names.

A census was made in 1833, but the numbering of the people was an easy task, for there were only eight persons—three males and five females—on the island, and these comprised three families. From 1833, to 1835, however, great progress was made, and the tax valuation rose from $60,000 to $806,000. In 1836, the Eastern Railroad Company was organized to construct a line of railway from East Boston to Salem, and at East Boston the company's depot was located until 1854, when it was removed to Boston. In 1839, the Cunard line of ocean steamships made East Boston their entrepot, and the construction of railway and wharves and the establishment here of a sugar-refinery gave an impetus to the settlement in that locality, of mechanics and others engaged about the wharves, depot, and in building operations. Portions of the land were laid out in sections, comprising those known as sections 1, 2, and 3; lots were then apportioned and sold off at auction. In a short time, as if by magic, a handsome edifice appeared upon the highest summit of the southerly portion, near the remains of an old fort which occupied that eminence in former days. This mansion was for the use of one of Boston's affluent citizens, Benjamin Lamson; and a more delightful situation could not be found in the vicinity, as it commanded a fine panoramic view of the city and harbor. This was the pioneer settler in that section of the island. Soon, however, others came in his train. Elegant mansions and more terraced gardens followed, until the whole southern slope, with Webster Street for a foreground, became a blooming paradise. Mr. Lamson also built a block of nine five-storied, swelled-front brick houses near his residence; and these had gardens in the rear. Beyond this block, and directly overlooking the fort, James Cunningham erected a princely mansion. The view from this house was the most extensive of any on the island, it being more lofty than others. Advancing to the extreme southerly point, passing several pretty cottages, there was seen at the terminus, like a bird's-nest overhanging the water, the unique and romantic residence of Dr. Jeffries. This point is still known as "Jeffries' Point," in perpetuation of the doctor.

The only wharves at East Boston forty years back were those known as Cunard's (where the British steamers stopped); Locke's, on Marginal Street; Miller's, foot of Maverick Street; and Tuttle's, foot of London Street. It remained for after-developments to form a fringe of piers all along the harbor front. In the early

40's, there was considerable of a flow of population to East Boston, and by 1857 the residents numbered 16,618. There were 1879 dwellings, 11 churches, 10 schoolhouses, 24 manufactories and mills, 76 warehouses and stores, 109 mechanics' shops, several hotels, 5 fire-engine houses, 12 counting-rooms, and 77 stables; while 17 miles of streets had been laid out. The story of the building of bridges, the construction and operation of ferries, the creation of manufacturing enterprises, the growth of the ship-building interest, and other ventures would fill a volume. There are two ferries now — known as North and South — connecting East Boston with the city proper; and these are owned by the city. A ferry, owned by the Boston, Revere Beach & Lynn Railroad (whose depot is at East Boston) is run between the island and Atlantic Avenue.

East Boston and the other harbor islands comprise the first and second wards of the city, the "harbor islands" being included in the second ward. It is to-day one of the most populous sections of Boston; where the well-to-do people of industrial callings principally have homes. It is indeed a district of homes, and has not within its limits a modern apartment-house, though there are many blocks where two or more tenements

Public Garden, showing Commonwealth Avenue and Arlington Street.

for family housekeeping exist. It has abundant school and church accommodations. Its population is now computed at forty thousand. Its valuation has grown to $17,964,700, the increase since 1883 having been $4,865,900.

The building improvements in East Boston during the year 1888 have been far in advance of those made within the past twenty years. Many of the unsightly vacant lots on Chelsea, Paris, Havre, Bennington, and other adjoining streets have been brought up to the street grade, and fine tenement-house structures erected thereon. In the first section the most notable improvements have been made at the foot of Everett Street, where a long line of houses have been put up. On Maverick Street, east of Chelsea Street, it is intended shortly to make many improvements in the neighborhood of the dump, in anticipation of laying out new streets and giving citizens a straight road over the marsh to the fourth section. The Atlantic Works, which were burned last summer, have been fully rebuilt at a cost of over $50,000, and 300 men are at work. The new structure is the handsomest machine-shop in East Boston. The New England Cooperage Company recently vacated its extensive building on Summer Street, to take up new quarters on Chelsea Street, and is employing a larger number of hands than ever. In the third section the most noticeable building is that of the new Trinity Baptist Church. It is an imposing structure and an ornament to the hill upon which it stands. The most extensive of recent improvements is that of the construction of the machine-works of the Boston Tow-boat Company, on Border Street. They cover several acres. In the fourth section over twenty houses and tenement blocks have been built. At Orient Heights and Winthrop Junction a number of new dwellings have been erected.

Among the improvements now making in the district are those of the East Boston Company. This company own about 110,000 square feet of land, bounded by Meridian, West Eagle, and Falcon Streets, which is from 25 to 30 feet above grade. The company also own about 36 acres of high marsh land, bounded by the city parkway, the Boston, Revere Beach & Lynn Railroad, Prescott Street, and the track of the Boston & Albany Road. The material from the high lands is being carted on to the marsh property, on which the street and cellar grades will be brought up to the city standard, viz.: 14 feet for cellars and 18 feet for streets. This is one of the choicest locations in East Boston, being on the harbor front and near the new city park. Some of the best houses recently built in East Boston was located in this neighborhood.

CHARLESTOWN.

The Charlestown District, an old-fashioned, quaint place, once a distinct city of itself, has formed an important section of Boston since its annexation in 1873. It now comprises the third, fourth, and fifth wards of Boston. It has an interesting history, dating from the very earliest settlement of the colony, for it was here that Governor Winthrop and his associates landed from their ship and established their abodes. Before they came the Indians were here, and the place was called Mishawum. Then it took unto itself the name of Charlestown, and as a town it embraced the areas of what are now the town of Burlington and the cities of Woburn, Malden, and Somerville, as well as parts of Reading, Medford, Cambridge and West Cambridge (now Arlington). Charlestown was a difficult place to get to from Boston until after the Revolution, for such ferries as existed between the two places were of a very primitive character, and wagons from the North End had to travel roundabout by way of Roxbury, over the "Neck," to reach Charlestown or Cambridge.

Charlestown, for all that, was a flourishing place in colonial times. It was founded in 1629, and in the following year many hundreds of English were trying to live in huts and tents on or around the Town Hill, at the foot of which was the great house, sheltering the Governor and his chief officers. A part of the inhabitants went across the water to keep minister Blackstone company and to found the city of Boston. Charlestown, however, continued to grow, if slowly, and when the revolutionary era arrived, there were some three hundred dwellings and from 150 to 200 other buildings in the place. There is nothing to be found now to tell us what the little settlement was like then, but whatever there was of it was wiped out by fire started by the British forces then located in Boston. General Gage had repeatedly warned the people that he would burn their town if they allowed it to be used as a basis of hostilities against his army, and he kept his word, for he wrote home to his government on June 26th, 1775, that the town "was set on fire during the engagement, and most part of it consumed." The engagement referred to the Bunker Hill fight, for this is the home of the far-famed Bunker Hill.

After the outbreak of the war at Lexington, armed colonists to the number of twenty thousand, formed an encampment around Boston from Roxbury to the Mystic River, and General Gage received powerful reinforcements, accompanied by Generals Howe, Clinton, and Burgoyne from England. Gage had the idea that the Americans wanted to drive him into the sea, and the colonists suspected that Gage and his troops intended to sally out into the country and burn up and destroy everything they could. The Americans determined to anticipate this movement by seizing and fortifying Bunker Hill, a height which commanded the whole peninsular of Charlestown. Orders were accordingly issued on the 16th of June, 1775, to Colonel Prescott, father of the historian of the same name, to proceed with a thousand men to occupy and entrench the Hill; but by some mistake, or designedly, as some assert, Breed's Hill was marked out instead of Bunker Hill, seven hundred yards distant. Bunker Hill was higher, but Breed's Hill was near Boston, and within common range of the city. Under cover of darkness, Prescott and his men reached the hill without being observed, and on the summit the men labored from midnight to dawn in building a redoubt, which the British viewed with considerable astonishment as soon as daylight appeared, for Prescott's cannon commanded the city. "We must carry these works immediately," said General Gage to his officers, and soon the ships in the harbor began to cannonade the new fortifications. The British battery on Copp's Hill also opened a heavy fire. But little damage was done in this way, and the Americans returned but few shots, as their supply of ammunition was very limited. Soon after noon, three thousand English, commanded by Generals Howe and Pigot, landed at Morton's Point to carry the hill by assault. The Americans numbered only one half of the British, and were wearied with their night's work and hungry as well; but they had a big stock of courage. When the cannonading was at its hottest, Prescott climbed out of the defences and walked leisurely around the parapet in full view of the British officers. Generals Putnam and Warren volunteered as privates and entered the trenches. At three o'clock in the afternoon Howe ordered his column to advance, and at the same time every gun in the fleet and batteries was turned upon the American redoubt. Then it was that Charlestown was set on fire and destroyed. The people mounted the house-tops in Boston to behold the engagement. On came the British with steady march, and not until they were within a hundred and fifty feet of them did the Americans show any signs of their presence. "Fire!" cried Prescott, and instantly from breastwork and redoubt every gun was fired, and the front rank of the British melted away. There was a recoil, and fifteen minutes afterwards a precipitate retreat. When beyond musket range, Howe rallied his men and led them to the second charge. Again the American fire was withheld until the enemy was but a few rods distant. Then, with steady aim, volley after volley was poured upon the charging column until it was broken and a second time driven to flight. The British officers grew desperate, and the vessels of the fleet changed position until the guns were brought to bear upon the interior of the American works. Then for the third time the assaulting column was put in motion, and the men came on with fixed bayonets up the hillside where were strewn the dead and dying. The Americans had but three or four rounds of ammunition left, and these were fired into the advancing enemy. Then there was a halt. The British climbed over the ramparts, and after a fierce struggle drove the patriots out. Prescott lived through the fight, but Warren was numbered among the slain. In this terrible engagement the English paid dearly for their victory, for they lost 1054 men in killed and wounded. The American loss was 115 killed, 305 wounded, and 32 prisoners. Prescott and Putnam conducted the retreat to Prospect Hill, where a new line of entrenchments was formed, and which still commanded the entrance to Boston. The fight showed that the British soldiers were not invincible, and the Americans were proud of their achievement, though defeated. The event is yearly celebrated at Charlestown on June 17th, by a holiday, processions, etc.

The event, too, has been commemorated by the building on the site of the redoubt a great granite obelisk, rising to a height of $221\frac{1}{2}$ feet. It has a base 30 feet square and the column tapers gradually to $15\frac{1}{2}$ feet at the apex. Inside the shaft is a hollow cone, surrounding which is a spiral flight of 295 stone steps, ascending to a chamber 11 feet square and 17 feet high, whence a beautiful view is obtained from the four windows. The capstone of the apex, above this observatory, is in one piece, and weighs $2\frac{1}{2}$ tons. The room contains two small cannons, the inscriptions upon which tell their story. The corner-stone was laid June 17th, 1825, by General Lafayette, and it was dedicated June 17th, 1843. The orator on both occasions was Daniel Webster. The monument cost over $150,000, and at the foot of it is a building containing a marble statue of General Warren and various memorials of the battle. The surroundings of the monument are handsomely laid out, and in the main path of the grounds, on the spot where he is supposed to have stood encouraging his men, is a bronze statue of General Prescott, erected in 1881. The celebration of the centennial of the battle on June 17th, 1775, was an event which drew together military representatives and others from all sections of the country. The real Bunker Hill is crowned by a Catholic Church.

In 1777 the people began to rebuild their town, and by the end of 1785 there were 279 buildings and 999 inhabitants. In 1786 the Charles River bridge to Charlestown was built at a cost of $50,000. It was then considered one of the grandest enterprises ever undertaken in the country. It was 1503 feet long, and 42 feet wide, with a 30 foot draw. It was opened amid great rejoicings on the anniversary of the battle of Bunker Hill. In the following year (1787), a bridge was opened between Charlestown and Malden, another to Chelsea in 1803, and one to East Cambridge in 1820. These established communications of immeasurable benefit, and in 1793, when the work of constructing the Middlesex Canal was begun, it was of immense advantage to the town. It was one of the earliest undertakings of the kind in the country, and was to connect tidewater with the upper Merrimack. The canal was completed in 1804, but was never very profitable. The railroads came and took away the traffic. The charter was forfeited in 1860 and the canal destroyed.

Charlestown is adequately supplied with railroad and other transportation facilities. Formerly the Fitchburg passenger and freight stations were located here, but in 1848 were removed to Boston. The district has many objects of interest to visitors. The "Neck," over which the Bunker Hill warriors went to give battle, and over which they retreated when worsted, connects Charlestown with the mainland of Somerville beyond. It was washed by the tides in the early days, but has been entirely changed by the filling up of the marshes and flats on its borders. The Neck property begins near the foot of Bunker Hill and ends at the boundary line over the Maine & Eastern Railroad Bridge, between the Charlestown district and Somerville. The Navy Yard stands on what was once Moulton's Point, at the confluence of the Charles and Mystic Rivers, and was founded in 1800. The Yard and buildings cover an extensive area, and as they are daily open to visitors, an inspection is to be commended. Another object of interest is the handsome Soldiers and Sailors' Monument

Public Garden, showing the Lake.

in Winthrop Square, once the military training-field. On Main Street is Edes House, the birthplace of S. F. B. Morse (the inventor of the electric telegraph), and the oldest house in the district. On the same thoroughfare is the oldest burying-ground, where a granite monument surmounts the grave of John Harvard, the founder of Harvard College; and near by is the tomb of Thomas Beecher, ancestor of the Beecher family of America. The district also contains the old state prison, a free dispensary and hospital, several other charitable institutions, public free library, and schools, churches of all denominations, and many fine mansions and neat cottages. The streets are wide and well kept, and illumination is supplied by gas and electric lights, while the water supply is abundant in quantity and excellent in quality.

While Charlestown has not been what is called a manufacturing place, it has numerous industrial establishments of a varied and extensive character, and these are constantly being multiplied. The principal thoroughfare, Main Street, is lined with stores, in which every conceivable class of merchandise is to be secured.

Charlestown never had a theatre or concert-room, yet it has occasionally been favored by visits of a circus. Plays and concerts, however, have been given in the old Town Hall (where the public library now is), and in the Waverley and Monument Halls and Navy Yard, but in no regular places. The growth of population is in-

THE METROPOLIS OF NEW ENGLAND.

stanced by the following statistics: In 1785 the population was 900; in 1800, 2734; in 1805, 2600; in 1810, 4736; in 1834, 10,000; in 1840, 10,872; in 1850 15,933; in 1855, 21,742; in 1865, 26,398; in 1870, 28,324; in 1885, 37,073; and now it is computed to be over 40,000. Values of property, however, have been but little increased during the past few years by the erection of new buildings. As in the case of South Boston, noted elsewhere,—though in a greater degree,—much of the former high-cost property in residences has largely depreciated in value, owing to the desire on the part of owners to move into more fashionable quarters, and other causes that would induce vacation and sacrifice of property. Houses worth $10,000 and upward have shrunk in value, while lower-priced buildings hold their own. There have been some dwellings and a few apartment-houses erected in Charlestown in the past five years, but the decrease in residential property on the hill—where the wealthy people of the district mostly resided—has so largely offset the increase of real-estate values thus acquired, that in that period the gain in real-estate valuation has been only $1,717,300. The gain in population has not been large, as would naturally be expected from the fact that the district is pretty thickly built over, the only vacant land, and that limited in extent, being on the Neck.

THE NEW WEST END, OR BACK BAY DISTRICT.

The reader has seen, in the perusal of the foregoing pages, how the original boundaries of Boston have been extended, not merely by the annexation of out-lying districts, but by the reclamation of thousands of acres of new valuable lands, from the ocean. He has, however, yet to be told of the greatest achievement of creating building land, and that the most attractive and valuable in the city. It comprises the whole region of the now showy and fashionable "New West End" or "Back Bay District," the "Court End" of the city.

When the present century was ushered in, the appearance of Back Bay was like unto that of Dorchester Bay to-day. At that time the waters of the bay flowed up to the present Washington Street at the "Neck," and swept over the present Public Garden to the coast now forming Charles Street. At flood tide the bay was a beautiful sheet of water spreading out far and wide, with the Brookline Hills in the distance, much as the Blue Hills are observed from South Boston, with no bridge, dam, or causeway intercepting the view of rustic Cambridge lying amid forest surroundings at the foot of Mount Auburn, between the West Boston and Brighton Bridges. In 1814, the Boston & Roxbury Corporation was organized to utilize the water-power of the great basin by dams thrown across it, and to use these dams as causeways for communication between Boston and Roxbury and the western suburbs. The "Mill-dam," now lower Beacon Street; the "Cross-dam," now Parker Street; and the causeway, now known as Brookline Avenue, were made to divide the waters. The Mill Dam was completed in 1821, and three years later the business of the corporation was divided, the Boston Water-power Company being then chartered to use the water-power of the mill company, which retained the roads and the lands north of the dam, while the new company became possessed of the mills and water-power. In 1831, the Boston & Worcester and the Boston & Providence Railroad Companies were given authority to construct lines across the Back Bay, and the riparian owners power to fill up their flats—concessions which so interfered with the water-power as to lead to the Boston Water-power Company converting itself into a land company. Much of the sewage of the city was thrown into the basin, until it became a nuisance and the filling up of the bay an absolutely necessary sanitary act. Below the line of riparian ownership the State had the right to the flats, and in 1849 the State appointed a commission to deal with the subject of creating new land here. A comprehensive plan was reported in 1852, and it was arranged that the mill corporation should fill up the area north of the Mill Dam; that the State should attend to that north of an east-and-west line drawn from near the present Boston & Providence Railroad Station; and that the water-power company should see to all south of that line. The contractor for filling in and making marketable the whole of this section (in which work millions of piles were used) was Norman C. Munson, who received as payment for his first work 260,000 square feet out of upwards of a million square feet of land reclaimed. By continuous contracts, the work extended over twenty years, and finally Munson received about seven million dollars as reward for his enterprise. The work was planned by the famous architect Arthur Gilman.

The State filled in its section at a cost of $1,750,000, and it has since sold land for $4,625,000 and has yet 250,000 feet unsold. The water-power company found the work alike profitable. The city, too, has for years been engaged in filling up swamps, levelling lands, constructing avenues, driveways, and parks, and ornamenting the whole of this region, which for beauty and residential magnificence has no counterpart in either the New or Old Worlds. Let the reader spread before him a map of the city as it exists to-day and strike a line through Charles,

Boylston, and Essex Streets, running crookedly from Charles River on the west to the Fort Channel dividing the city proper from South Boston. All the area represented below this line up to the foot of the Highlands is "created" land, save where Washington Street runs, and this thoroughfare is over the Neck, which was itself frequently lapped by the waters of the ocean. All the land lying to the south of the Boston & Providence Railroad, including Columbus Avenue, is now territorially identified with the "South End," already referred to in these pages. The "Back Bay District" includes all the "made" land on the other side of the railroad.

In this district, running from Arlington Street (the western border of the Public Garden), and parallel with Beacon Street, are Commonwealth Avenue, Newbury, Marlborough, and Boylston Streets, with Huntington Avenue branching off the latter street at the junction of Clarendon Street. Parallel with Arlington Street are Berkeley, Clarendon, Dartmouth, Exeter, Fairfield, Gloucester, and Hereford Streets, West Chester Park, etc. As we have said, vast improvements are now in progress in this district, the most prominent of which is the opening up of Boylston Street to public travel in its entire length. This street, which skirts the Common on its southern end, as Beacon Street does on the northern side, is in every way a more available and convenient avenue from the business section of Boston to the Back Bay; but, owing to the fact that it crossed the tracks of the Boston & Albany Railroad near its junction with West Chester Park, and the difficulty and expense of bridging the railway, its completion was delayed, to the great inconvenience of the public, as well as to the stagnation of values of property on the unfinished line of the street. This condition is now in active process of being remedied. Boylston Street had been completed to Exeter. From this point down to where the line crossed the railway, the grade had to be raised, the filling in some places, viz., from Gloucester to Hereford Street, being from 15 to 18 feet. The work of filling in this section of street, as well as the portions west of the bridge and beyond to the Back Bay Park, was begun in the fall of 1887, and completed in February, 1888. The north abutment of the bridge, just beyond Hereford Street, was first built to enable the filling in of this section of the street to be accomplished, and to render available the use of the new police station and engine house which had been erected at the corner of Hereford and Boylston Streets. The work of grading and macadamizing is, at this writing, in active operation on the section of street in question, in conjunction with the construction of double street-railway tracks by the West End Railway Company. The railway tracks, it may be said, are now completed up to Hereford Street, and the street department is now macadamizing the driveways on each side in the most substantial manner. Every part and detail of this work is done thoroughly, and, when the street is opened, it will present one of the best driveways on the Back Bay. From the corner of Hereford Street to the bridge, the roadway will be paved, for the purpose of providing against the wear and tear of running in and out of the engine-house where the fire apparatus; and the city will join with the railway company in this work. Beyond West Chester Park to the new Back Bay Park, the roadway of Boylston Street is completed, and now forms one of the entrance driveways to that attractive place. When this latter improvement was undertaken, it was found that, in order to conform to the grade established by the park commissioners and that already existing on West Chester Park, it would be necessary to raise the grade of Boylston Street about five feet near and at the point where Parker Street leads out from it. A block of new brick buildings on the south side of Boylston Street at the junction of Parker had to be raised in consequence of this elevation of the roadway, at an expense of over $30,000 to the owner, the city allowing but $5,000 toward the work. The cost to the city of the construction of the roadway of Boylston Street from Exeter Street to the park, not including filling in, of course, will be about $25,000.

The bridge over the tracks of the Boston & Albany Railroad is, owing to the acute angle at which the street crosses it, a structure of peculiar form and details. The width of the railway road-bed under the street is only 60 feet, yet on the line of the street there is a distance of about 210 feet between abutments. The north abutment has a length of 185 feet, with flanking walls or abutments of 100 feet in length on the north side of the street and 122 feet on the south side. The south abutment is 174 feet in length, with a southern flank of 36 feet and a northern one of 105 feet. The piles for the foundation are driven in concrete to the depth of 3½ and 4 feet is filled in, on which rubble masonry is laid. Then succeed granite blocks on the railway fronts. The height of the roadway above the track of the railroad is 20 feet, the distance from track to under side of bridge being but 14 feet. The length of the truss-spans of this bridge is each 216 feet, being the longest of any bridge-truss span in the city. The total weight of the bridge—that is, of the structure of iron and steel composing it—is about 400 tons. The total width of the bridge is 80 feet, which is the full width of the street. The width of the roadway inside the trusses is 44 feet. The construction was by the

Boston Bridge Works, of Cambridgeport. The bridge cost about $50,000, and is one of the best, as well as the most unique, of its kind in the city. The cost of the abutments of this bridge was about $80,000, which, added to that of the bridge superstructure, would make the total cost of the bridge $230,000. This is a costly improvement, to be sure, but one of great utility and public importance. With the completion of the bridge, the tracks of the West End Railway will be quickly pushed forward and united to those on West Chester Park; and a direct line of communication, not only to the Back Bay residences south of Commonwealth Avenue established, but to the Back Bay Park, which can thus be readily and quickly reached, and the round-about way through Marlboro Street avoided. Altogether this work of completing Boylston Street is one that

Statue of Washington—Public Garden.

adds another to the many great improvements that the city government is making on the Back Bay district of Boston.

In addition to these public improvements the whole of the Charles River embankment, beginning at Leverett Street near Craigie's Bridge, and extending to Cottage Farms Bridge, is being enlarged, fronted with a sea wall and laid out as a park, 200 feet in width, and will connect with a park at Brighton. Near West Chester Park a bridge—to be known as Harvard Bridge—is in course of construction across the Charles River to Cambridge, and will, when completed, be a great boon to residents on both sides of the river. West Chester Park is not a park but a street ninety feet wide. It crosses Commonwealth Avenue, about five blocks west of the Hotel Vendome, and beginning at Charles River, and varying its direction at Falmouth Street, runs across the city. Between Tremont and Shawmut Avenue it broadens into Chester Square, a modest park of 1½ acres. East of Washington Street, it is called East Chester Park.

Back Bay has, or will have, its park, however. It is now being laid out and will contain ponds fed by the waters of the Stony Brook, promenades, driveways, etc., connecting with Beacon, Parker, and Boylston Streets, and also with Commonwealth, Westland, Longwood, Huntington, and Brookline Avenues. The work is a costly one, but when the park is completed it will, in addition to its own attractions, have a surrounding of beautiful scenery, and will be a connecting link in a long splendid parkway stretching from the Common and Public Garden, through Commonwealth Avenue, along the Muddy River Improvement, Jamaica Pond, the Arnold Arboretum and ending in the spacious and picturesque Franklin Park. The Charles River embankment will be separated from the Back Bay Parkway, only by Beacon Street, which is itself a popular driveway, extending along the Mill Dam, the surrounding of Chestnut Hill Reservoir and the shady, rustic lanes of Brighton.

Back Bay is the richest section in the city, and it takes the lead in expensive dwellings and in the constant advance in the value of real estate. That portion of the district which is bounded by Charles River, Arlington Street, the Boston & Providence railway tracks and West Chester Park, in 1883 had a total valuation as follows: Land, $26,182,600; buildings, $22,315,200. In 1888, land in this section had increased to $34,056,500, and buildings to $39,501,500, a total increase of rising of $16,000,000. But Back Bay has, in fact, two districts. One is the ultra-fashionable and aristocratic section, and extends west from Arlington Street to West chester Park, and is bounded on the south by the line of the Boston & Albany Railroad, and thence northward to Charles River. South of the railroad line, out to the Back Bay Park at least, the section is less aristocratic, and land is not much, if any, over one half the price that it is on the other side. No very costly residences are erected. On Huntington Avenue and on the back streets large apartment houses are being put up. West Chester Park, south of the Boston & Albany Railway track, besides family hotels, buildings with stores on the street level are being occupied; and, with the completion of the bridge at this point over the Charles River, this street promises to become an important thoroughfare.

But what shall be said of the Back Bay District as a whole? Volumes might be written descriptive of its magnificent thoroughfares, its architectural splendor, its palatial mansions and hostelries, its public institutions, and its creation from out of the sea into one of the most attractive and beautiful habited spots the world can show; but we are compelled to dismiss the whole in a page or two.

Commonwealth Avenue is undoubtedly the chief attraction in this charming section. It is, in reality, two streets in one, with a fine park in the centre, containing rows of ornamental trees, neatly kept paths, benches, and several statues. The width of the thoroughfare, from house to house, is 250 feet, and from curb to curb 175 feet. It extends through the new Back Bay Park to Brookline Avenue, and is lined with costly and beautiful residences, in the erection of which architects have had no limit to the exercise of their talents, nor had their plans marred by lack of capital. Commonwealth Avenue, from Arlington Street to West Chester Park, may be said to be practically built up.

The cost of Mr. Fred L. Ames' residence, on the corner of Dartmouth Street and the avenue, was very great. The residence of Governor Ames, corner of West Chester Park, is said to have cost $180,000, exclusive of the land. Mr. Nathaniel Thayer's house, on the corner of Fairfield Street cost about $135,000 to build; and on the corner of Gloucester Street and the avenue, Mr. Eugene V. R. Thayer recently completed a residence which cost $135,000. This is about as sightly a dwelling as there is on the avenue. On the corner opposite, Mr. Charles Francis Adams has erected a very fine dwelling which cost about $80,000. The residence of Congressman John F. Andrew, on the corner of Hereford Street, cost about $100,000 to build. One of the handsomest residences on the avenue is that of Mrs. William Powell Mason, located between Dartmouth and Exeter Streets, and built at a cost of $61,000. It is of the coming-into-fashion colonial style, and maintains the dignity of its ancestry even amid the more modern and artistic structures which are in its vicinity. Between Exeter and Fairfield Streets Mr. Alexander Cochran has an elegant residence, which cost in the neighborhood of $100,000 to build. The above are all on the north side of Commonwealth Avenue. On the south side of the avenue there are also many fine and costly residences of recent erection, ranging all the way from $30,000 to $50,000.

Beacon Street (from the corner of Arlington Street) has in recent years shown more activity in the erection of mansions than any other thoroughfare in this section. This is the most noticeable in the vicinity of and beyond West Chester Park. It contains some of the finest residences to be found in this section of palatial homes. General Whittier has put up a magnificent building at a cost of $145,000, and a number of other dwellings have been erected at a cost varying from $20,000 to $125,000. Beacon Street during the past two

THE METROPOLIS OF NEW ENGLAND.

years, has shown a marked advance in building improvements, and real estate quotations have consequently been increased.

Boylston Street, in that section overlooking the Common and the Public Garden—once a fashionable residential quarter—is rapidly being given up to business, but beyond the Public Garden, there are many handsome residences and the opening out of the street in the region of West Chester Park, will lead to more buildings being put up. The Boston & Albany Railroad owns the land on the south side of this thoroughfare, west of Exeter Street, and may build a passenger station there. Owing to these conditions and other contingencies, the north side of the street has not been built upon, with two solitary exceptions, west of Exeter Street. That section of Boylston Street, between the Old South parsonage and Exeter Street, north side, has been built up mostly within the last five years, with a good class of dwellings, costing on an average about $20,000 each. The Hotel Kensington, one of those fashionable family hotels, is located on the corner of Boylston and Exeter Streets. It was erected by Mr. Henry B. Williams, at a cost of about $200,000. Land prices have all along this street increased amazingly within the last few years, and in many places building lots commanded from $12 to $15 per square foot.

West Chester Park will soon be a busy scene of operations among builders, for the opening up of Boylston Street and the erection of the Harvard Bridge has brought this district into the market, and as both the thoroughfares just named are the only Back Bay Streets on which there are no restrictions as to business structures, it is likely that both will, ere long, become great centres of trade.

Almost everywhere in this section of the city new buildings are arising. In this region are some of the finest hotels in the country, chief among which are the marble Vendome, the imposing Brunswick, and the Victoria (the new "Delmonico"). Then there are numerous first-class apartment houses, the Hotel Berkeley being the first erected in the district. On Boylston Street is the handsome building of the Young Men's Christian Association, also the Natural History Society Building, the famous Institute of Technology, Trinity Church (Rev. Dr. Phillips Brooks, pastor), one of the finest and most impressive church edifices in the country; and the Second Church (Congregational Unitarian) with chapel adjoining (Rev. E. A. Horton, pastor). The society worshipping here once occupied the Old North Church, on North Square, torn down and used for firewood by British soldiers during the siege of Boston. At one time Ralph Waldo Emerson was the pastor of the present church. Near this church is the far-famed Chauncy School. Opposite to it, with entrance on St. James's Avenue, is the Museum of Fine Arts, and beyond, on the corner of Boylston and Exeter Streets, is the Harvard Medical School. Near by, on the corner of Exeter and Newbury Streets, is the Prince School building, the only public school in the district. The other corners of Exeter and Newbury Streets are occupied by the South Congregational Church (Unitarian); the First Spiritual Temple, a costly, curious edifice; and the Massachusetts Normal School. Farther on, on the corner of Boylston and Hereford Streets, is a handsome, new Romanesque building, occupied by the Back Bay police and fire departments. On Dartmouth Street, nearly opposite Trinity Church, the immense new Public Library building is being erected and will take years to complete. On Exeter Street and St. James Avenue, on December 29th, 1888, was opened the new Athletic Association building (erected at a cost of nearly $300,000), the finest edifice of its kind in the world. The New Old South Church—one of the costliest church buildings in the city—stands on the Dartmouth Street side of Copley Square, on the corner of Boylston Street. The society worshipping here formerly occupied the historic Old South, on the corner of Washington and Milk Street. Near the New Old South, on Dartmouth Street is the handsome new building of the Art Club. Located on the corner of Commonwealth Avenue and

The Chauncy Hall School, Boylston Street.

Clarendon Street is the massive stone edifice of the First Baptist Church (formerly the Brattle Square Congregational Unitarian). The First Church (Congregational Unitarian) is located on Marlborough Street and Berkeley Street. It is the direct descendant of the first church established in Boston. The church was first formed in Charlestown, and the members of it, on coming to Boston, built the first meeting house on State Street, near where the Brazer Building stands. The church was afterwards removed on to Washington Street near top of State Street, then to Chauncy Place, and, finally to its present location. The Protestant Episcopalians have a fine church, with a very rich interior, on Newbury Street, known as the Emmanuel Church.

Boston Common—Beacon Street Mall.

A short distance from it, on the corner of Newbury and Berkeley Streets is the handsome Central Church (Congregational Trinitarian), which possesses the tallest spire in the city, the height being 236 feet. On Berkeley Street is the Notre Dame Academy, and at the corner of Boylston and Arlington Streets is the widely known Arlington (Unitarian) Church, of which Rev. Hereford Brooke is pastor. Huntington Avenue has upon it the famous exhibition building of the charitable Mechanic Association, covering an area of 96,000 square feet, and erected in 1881. A short distance from it is the Children's Hospital, a useful and well-conducted institution. There are many other notable residences and buildings, but space will not allow us to treat of them separately.

ROXBURY.

The thoroughfares leading to it are four, namely, Harrison Avenue, Washington Street, Shawmut Avenue and Tremont Street. This is the order of their succession, viewed laterally, Tremont Street being the most westerly. Columbus Avenue, which lies more to the westward, will in the future be extended through to the Roxbury district. At present Washington Street, Shawmut Avenue, Tremont Street and Huntington Avenue are available throughout by horse-cars, but the Washington Street route is to be preferred by the stranger and sight-seer. The Roxbury district includes the old city of Roxbury, which was annexed to Boston in 1867. It comprises wards 19, 20, 21, and 22, the latter being bounded on the east by West Chester Park, and including, therefore, a portion of the Back Bay territory. When first settled it was called Rocksbury, or Rocksborough, and was recognized as a town on October 8, 1630. The town originally included the present West Roxbury district (set off in 1851) and annexed to Boston in 1873, Jamaica Plain, and the present town of Brookline, known in the early days as "Punch-bowl Village." William Wood, the first historian of New England, writing in 1633, says, after describing Dorchester:—"A mile from this Town (Dorchester) lyeth Roxbery, which is faire and handsome Country-towne; the inhabitants of it being all rich. The Towne lieth upon the Maine, so that it is well-wooded and watered; having a cleare and fresh Brooke running through the Towne; up which although there come no Alewives, yet there is great store of Smelts, and therefore it is called Smelt-brooke. A quarter of a mile to the North-side of the Towne is another River called Stoney-river, upon which is built a water-milne. Here is good ground for Corne and Meadow for Cattle. Up westward from the Towne it is something rocky, whence it has the name of Roxberry," etc. Another writer (1654) describes the town as "being filled with a very laborious people, whose labours the Lord hath so blest, that in the roome of dismall Swamps and tearing Bushes, they have very goodlie Fruit-trees, fruitfull Fields and Gardens, their Heard of Cowes, Oxen and other young Cattell of that kind about 350, and dwelling houses neere upon 120. Their streetes are large and some Fayre Houses."

If inquiries were made of a hundred persons resident in Boston as to where the dividing line existed between the domains of the two former municipalities, no doubt 99 would not pretend to guess at what the hundredth would be likely to miss, yet that line is distinctly marked to-day. One at all curious in this regard needs only to bestow his glances when enjoying a horse-car ride in the direction of the suburbs over Washington Street, upon a granite curbstone post of the horse-hitching kind, which stands on the sidewalk abutting the old car station at the extremity of the Neck, near Lenox Street, where it has stood so long that it may be considered a landmark. On one side of this stone, in deep-engraved work, is, "B., A.D. 1823." On the reverse is a similar inscription, save that R. takes the place of B. This indicates Roxbury and Boston. At present the top of this puny shaft is black and greasy, looking as though it had received the caresses of many dirty hands, which has doubtless been the case during the last 66 years of its standing as a monitor.

What, in the parlance of the inhabitants of Roxbury of former days, was denoted as "the street," or "Roxbury Street" (now Washington Street), commenced at this line and terminated at Vernon Street. Here were concentrated the shops; and a considerable degree of business was performed in them, especially before omnibus days. There were several local inns on this street, stopping-places for stages plying to and from Providence, as well as for transient travel, and local imbibing and feasting, to which, if rumor is to be believed, the ancient "gudemen" were somewhat devoted. On this "street" in later days were stores that prosecuted a large business; and hereabouts reside many old-timers. The "street" of to-day has been considerably elongated, and includes a great number and variety of stores, presenting quite a metropolitan aspect, both for this reason and for the magnitude of business performed there. At no place in the city, save in the main shopping district, two miles distant, is there more life and activity noticed, especially on Saturday evenings, when the citizens of the neighborhood turn out en masse, seemingly to do their shopping, thereby crowding the large clothing, dry-goods, boot and shoe, and furniture stores, likewise the many food-providers, the variety shops, the several gayly illuminated tea-stores, etc., to repletion, and forming kaleidoscopic throngs surging along under the electric lights. There is "a sight" of difference in this respect, compared with the "fayre" street views of the forefathers.

The territory now lying between the Lenox Street horse-car stables and the Roxbury stables at the Providence Railroad crossing, and including the contiguous streets and places, was formerly called Grab Village; and the name is still sometimes applied to it. This is a picturesque and unique locality, especially that part lying towards Tremont Street; and the business signs contain, for the most part, Teutonic names. It is, in fact, the mercantile portion of Germantown which is concentrated in this vicinity in consequence of the number of breweries in Roxbury, Boylston Station and Jamaica Plains, with which hundreds of the inhabitants are connected. Where or when the sobriquet of "Grab Village" came to be applied is a profound mystery to the present generation. The oldest inhabitant of the region knows naught regarding the inception of such a queer name.

Sixty years ago this territory was flooded by the tides of the Back Bay, and its only inhabitants were fishes and birds. In 1832, the Tremont Road (now Tremont Street) had been filled in, laid out, and became open for travel from Pleasant Street, South End, to Roxbury. Both sides of this roadway were marshes covered with water when the tide was in. Other land was acquired in the vicinity by the process in which most of the present South End and all of Back Bay were secured. Lots were quickly taken, and houses sprung up like magic. The outflow from South End—then a contracted and crowded region—took this direction naturally. Practically, it amounted to an exodus from the city to suburban homes, for there existed no means of public conveyance; and this necessitated the keeping of horses or long walks with business men who located there. In many respects it proved to be a charming place for residence, and, in fact, that portion of the city has always borne a good reputation for healthfulness. Gardens were planted, fruit-trees were set out, and shortly the locality gained credit for its lovely show of flowers and the quality of its fruit. While it has lost much of its former aspect, Grab Village has assumed other peculiarities which make it a very lively part of the city. The Tremont Street portion, from end to end of its three-fourths-mile length, is a busy mart of traffic. Stores of many kinds line both sides of the street. In no other part of Boston, away from the shopping district, excepting perhaps on Broadway, South Boston, is such a condition to be found. Some of these stores, in extent and appearance, with their large plate-glass windows filled with nice dress goods, etc., rival downtown concerns, and no doubt their patronage is commensurate with their spirit of enterprise. Veritably, Grab Village is a city in itself, covering over portions of several wards, and numbering a population high up in double numbers of thousands. Despite its seemingly derisive title, it constitutes a portion of the city that bears a good reputation; and that is highly cherished by the residents.

But let us return to the old boundary line between Boston and Roxbury—at the Neck, near the horse-railway stables, beside Lenox Street, for this is a historic spot. It was here that the American troops who were engaged in the siege of Boston erected strong fortifications and planted heavy batteries, to resist any attempt of the British troops to get into the country from the city. A few rods beyond this point is one of Roxbury's old landmarks—the venerable buryingground, corner of Eustis and Washington Streets, where the remains of the Apostle Eliot lie. This ground has been sadly neglected in the past, and bears marks of desecration at present. In its vaults were deposited many of the bodies of the notabilities in Roxbury of colonial times. A writer of the olden time describes Eliot as " a young man at his coming thither, of a cheerful spirit, walking unblameable, of a godly conversation; apt to teach, as by his indefatigable paines both with his own flock and the poore Indians doth appeare; whose language he learned purposely to helpe them to the knowledge of God in Christ," etc. His body, together with those of five other pastors of the First Parish, rests in the "parish tomb," and near by it are the graves of Governor Thomas Dudley, Governor Joseph Dudley, and Chief Justice Paul Dudley.

Proceeding a little beyond this resting-place of the forefathers, and still continuing on Washington Street, we reach Eustis Street, where the travel is divided into three principal lines. To the right, Roxbury Street stretches to Eliot Square, better known as Norfolk House neighborhood, on account of the large hotel there. To the left, Warren Street sweeps away through what were recently rural pastures toward Central Dorchester by the way of Grove Hall. At these points of divergence the principal stores, banks, public institutions, post-office, public halls, etc., of Roxbury are located. Washington Street extends towards Jamaica Plains, sweeps past Forest Hill Station and the noted cemetery of that name; and along its course is beautiful scenery and several old-fashioned mansions, each with an interesting story of its own of the past. The old First Parish Church, on Eliot Square, is an object of great interest as a splendid specimen of Puritan church architecture. It stands on elevated land, which was fortified by General Washington to command the roads from Boston. About a quarter of a mile to the southwest were still stronger works, known as the Roxbury Fort, whereon is now located the standpipe of the Boston Water-works, which, as an architectural column, is an object of great beauty.

Roxbury, small as she was, had a conspicuous part in the events of the Revolution. It was the native place of the immortal Warren, Heath, and Greaton, and the residence and burial-place of Dearborn—all generals in the Continental Army. The old Roxburyites have shown in various ways that they have not forgotten the heroes of those trying times.

Here is the great public pleasure-ground of forests and fields, formerly known as Roxbury, and now as Franklin Park, to which thousands daily find their way in the summer from all parts of the city. Not alone is the park an object of beauty, but the whole region of Roxbury, which in late years has become a favorite residential quarter, and consequently has experienced a large growth in population.

As we have already observed, Roxbury comprises four wards of the city. These wards contain more than one sixth of the polls of the city of Boston, which is a good index of the extent of their population. The same thing will show their growth in population in the past five years. In 1883, the number of polls in them was, in round numbers, 19,000; in 1888, it was 23,000—an increase of 4000 in the five years. The valuation of these four wards will also show their advance in material wealth. In 1883, their total valuation was $59,324,000; in 1888, it was $74,394,000—an increase of $15,069,000 in five years, a most encouraging showing. This great advance in population is due, in the first place, to Roxbury, with its high lands, abounding in the finest sites for residence, and being so situated that Boston seems to naturally merge into it, and to

Boston Common—Tremont Street Mall.

form a part of the city itself in reality, while still retaining many rural features. Another important fact is that there are several parallel lines of horse-railway penetrating every section of the district, and these led to the more convenient localities being seized upon for dwellings, and to the building of apartment-houses in great numbers. But even these failed to provide for all who wanted homes, and the territory beyond was encroached upon. On one of the main avenues, Warren Street, as far as Grove Hall, the drift of population found a way, as well as on Washington Street on the west and Blue Hill Avenue on the east, which crosses Warren Street in its course at Grove Hall. These streets and their affluents furnished land for dwelling purposes, which was utilized from time to time, until to-day there is but little land, comparatively, left in the limits of old Roxbury to build on, the last of the considerable farm properties (the Horatio Harris estate) being now in process of arrangement to be put upon the market. Land has consequently appreciated in value; for lots which five years ago or less were bought for 15 to 20 cents a foot are now held at from 40 to 60 cents per square foot. Walnut Avenue, running in a southwesterly direction from Warren Street, and nearly parallel to Washington Street, up to Franklin Park, opened up a district for settlement, in which many fine and costly mansions have been constructed in the past fifteen years or more. In the territory northwest and southeast of this avenue, and especially in the latter sections, there have been built in the past five years a large number of very fine dwellings. This section is known as Elm Hill; and on Elm Hill Avenue, and between it and Walnut Avenue, some of the best houses are located. Many of these are veritable palaces, representing all styles of architecture and varying in cost from $12,000 to $60,000. Many of them are surrounded with trees, shrubbery, flower gardens, or grassy lawns, adding to the beauty and attraction of the streets and avenues as excellent driveways. Walnut Avenue, Humboldt Avenue, and Elm Hill Avenue all lead up to Franklin Park, and the two latter end at Seaver Street, which skirts its northern side. The park is of vast extent, and, as no residential buildings can be put upon it, the rush of settlement in that direction to some extent has been stopped, and the operations here in the future will be the filling up of the gaps now existing, with the result in a few years of a compactly built district, though, compared with that north of it, owing to the nature of its settlement, it will be a great many years before houses in it are crowded so closely together. In other sections of the district, dwellings are rising rapidly. On nearly every street, from Dudley Street to Grove Hall, new houses have been erected in the past five years, either by those who had them built for their own use or to let or for sale; but there have been but few erections for business purposes in the district in the same period.

On the northwest side of the Roxbury district is Parker Hill, a splendid location, overlooking the city, and on which is located the Parker Hill Reservoir. Its high and favorable location places it in the line of future occupation.

THE DORCHESTER DISTRICT

which forms the twenty-fourth ward of the city, is delightfully situated on Dorchester Bay, an arm of Boston Harbor, and in a healthy, attractive and picturesque region. It is to-day one of the most interesting of the outlying districts of the city, and is a favorite place of suburban residence. It is, too, an historic place, and was established as a town on the same date as Boston itself. On the 20th of March, 1629-30, "that great ship of 400 tons," the Mary and John, set sail from Plymouth, England, for the New World, and during the ten weeks of the voyage the party on board, including two clergyman, Revs. Meverick and Warham, spent every day "in preaching or expounding the word of God." The ship, which was commanded by Captain Squeb, landed on May 30, 1630, at Nantasket (now Hull), where the captain turned his passengers adrift into the "forlorn wilderness," though his contract bound him to carry them to the Charles River. They found their way to Dorchester, then called Mattapan by the Indians, by whom they were well received. They at once changed the name to Dorchester, after the town of the same name in England. Dorchester has its quaint old town-hall; its ancient meeting-house and magnificent soldiers' monument on Meeting-House Hill; at Upham's Corner the graves of several eminent public men of the Colonial and Provincial periods; and Jones's Hill affords from its summit one of the finest and most extensive views in the neighborhood of Boston. Northward is seen the old city and the famous Dorchester Heights. Westward is presented an amphitheatre of hills and villages. Southward is a wide and deep intervale, the famous Blue Hills of Milton showing up on the horizon. Near at hand in this direction is observed Meeting-House Hill, capped by the First Parish Church and by the Soldiers' Monument of red Gloucester granite, rising to a height of 31 feet, and erected in 1867. Looking eastward the eye embraces within the range of vision nearly all the islands of the harbor, the harbor itself and its shipping, and the ocean in the extreme distance, while near at hand is Savin Hill, rich in rustic beauty and commanding charming views. An object of special interest and one meriting inspection is the Lyman Fountain, which is located on Eaton Square, a sightly and beautiful spot, well chosen for its situation. The fountain occupies the sight of a famous old tavern—the Eaton Tavern, kept by a once equally famous Captain Eaton.

Of this handsome fountain we give a fine illustration in these pages. It was erected in memory of one of Boston's noblest and revered sons, the late Theodore Lyman, Jr., who was mayor of the city in 1834-35. Mr. Lyman was a descendant from one of the pilgrim fathers who came from England to the Old Bay State in 1631 in the same ship that brought John Eliot. Mr. Lyman was born in Boston on February 20, 1792, and his father was one of the city's merchant princes. He received his early education at Phillips Academy, Exeter, N. H., and graduated at Harvard College in 1810. He afterwards became a student in the famous University of Edinburgh, Scotland, and then travelled extensively throughout Europe. In 1820 he published a work of much merit entitled "The Political State of Italy," and in the same year delivered the Fourth of

THE METROPOLIS OF NEW ENGLAND.

July oration before the town authorities of Boston. In 1826 he published an important work, "The Diplomacy of the United States." From 1820 to 1823 he was aide-de-camp to Governor Brooks, and from 1823 to 1827 was commander of the Boston Brigade. From 1820 to 1825 he was a member of the Massachusetts Legislature, occupying a seat in the Senate in 1824. In 1834 and 1835 he was mayor of Boston, and gave the city a dignified, fearless, and able administration, during a period that called for unusual qualities in her chief magistrate. He was a large hearted, generous man, and many noble public institutions had their usefulness developed by his munificence. One of his most intimate friends spoke of him as "a pure, loving, devoted man, of unusual grace of bearing and manly beauty," who "used the gifts of God as His steward, and not for his own indulgences." He died on July 18, 1849, but he continued to live in the memories of his friends, who, thirty-six years after his demise, determined to erect some tangible memorial of him. The leader in this movement was the Honorable Nahum Capen, and the erection of a water fountain was decided upon. A sum of two thousand dollars was quickly subscribed, and an application was made for an allowance from the Phillips Fund, the munificent gift of Jonathan Phillips, who gave by his will to the city of Boston, in 1860, the sum of $20,000, as a trust fund, the income of which shall be annually expended to adorn and embellish

Erected in Memory of Theo. Lyman, Jr., in Eaton Square, Dorchester.

the streets and public places in the city. The authorities voted from this fund towards the cost of the fountain $4050, and a further sum of $175 for incidentals.

The site for the fountain in Eaton Square was selected by Mr. William Doogue, the city forester, and the commission to design and construct the fountain was entrusted to Mr. M. D. Jones, of the firm of M. D. Jones & Co., No. 76 Washington Street. The design is original. The structure is of fine proportions, rich in ornamentation, and is believed to be the highest and handsomest fountain in the New England States. It rises to an altitude of 26 feet. The basin is of Monson granite, and 33 feet in diameter. The first pan is 12 feet and 6 inches in diameter; the second pan 6 feet and 8 inches. The surmounting groups of figures represent Venus, Cupid and swan, while the figures about the pedestals stand for the four seasons. The supply of water is from three pipes attached to a 3-inch main, a sixty-pound pressure providing ample force. One of these pipes discharges through the swan's mouth and through four dragons on the first pedestal and four griffins, between the first and second pans. Another furnishes a supply for one hundred and forty-four jets in the rim of the first pan, and eighty in the second, while the third pipe feeds the four cascades at the base of the pedestal. The water from the jets does not overflow the pan, but discharges through four gargoyle heads. The fountain proper is of bronzed iron and zinc. The whole reflects the highest credit upon Mr. Jones. His experience as a designer and builder of fountains in various parts of New England has been extensive, but this is one of his most ambitious undertakings as well as one of his most successful achievements. The basin was constructed by Mr. John Kelly, a Boston contractor. The fountain, in its playing power, has realized all expectations. Cut in the granite basin is this legend:—"In memory of Theodore Lyman, Jr., mayor of Boston in 1834–35;" and upon a bronze plate attached to the basin is this inscription.—"This fountain as a memorial was originated by Nahum Capen, designed and constructed by M. D. Jones, Boston, located by William Doogue, city forester, accepted and dedicated by Hugh O'Brien, Mayor, October 24, 1885."

The occasion of the dedication service was a red letter day in the annals of Dorchester. Around the fountain a large and interested company of prominent persons gathered, the Germania Band was in attendance, the fountain was accepted by Mayor O'Brien as a gift to the city, and speeches were delivered appropriate to the occasion by Honorable Marshall P. Wilder, Honorable C. Winthrop, Rev. Peter Ronan, Honorable Leverett Saltonstall, and Honorable Nahum Capen.

Dorchester, which was annexed to Boston, June 22, 1869, has, since it was accorded good railway and horse-car accommodation, enjoyed a large and steady growth in population and in popularity as a residential section. Hotels, apartment-houses and costly dwellings are more numerous than they were a few years ago. Farm lands are being constantly cut up into streets and offered to those who desire to build, and as a result there is a steady increase in the value of property. Since 1883, it is safe to say that there have been built in the Dorchester district from 700 to 1000 houses of various styles and grades of cost, the great majority of them being single dwellings. In that year the real estate valuation of Dorchester was $17,797,600. In 1888, it was $22,913,300, being gain of $5,115,700 or at the rate of over $1,000,000 of gain in this item of valuation per year. The number of polls in 1883 was 4981, and in 1888 it was 6803, or nearly 2000 gain. The gain in population has been a substantial one, and is due quite largely to the good railway accommodation afforded, as well as to the horse-railway lines and low fares.

STREETS AND AVENUES

Boston is the most like an English city of any place on the American continent both in the peculiarity of its ancient buildings and in the tortuous windings of its oldest streets. The crookedness of the streets, formed on the lines of old cow-paths, makes an unceasing puzzle to strangers to find their way about, and yet these twists and turns afford good opportunity for the display of architectural qualities of buildings, and add much to the picturesque appearance of the city. Millions of dollars have been expended in straightening old thoroughfares and in effecting improvements, but there are curves and bendings that will ever remain unless another conflagration like that of 1872 should involve the old parts of the city in ruins and provide an opportunity for remapping the section in "square cuts." The modern wards of the city, however, are laid out in Babylonian rectangularity, with streets that are broad and straight, and vistas ending on hills in the suburbs. Streets and avenues are being increased in number or length year by year, for there are thirty-two more miles of streets now, in 1889, than there were four years ago, the total number now being 412. The streets are most efficiently sewered, for Boston has the most perfect sewerage system of any city in the country; and this has been attained at immense cost. The thoroughfares are sufficiently illuminated. At this writing there are within the city limits the following street lamps in use: Gas, 10,104 ; oil, 2994; electrics, 704; large gas-lamps, 74; naptha lamps, 49; total, 13,925.

The streets are divided up into twenty-five wards, and there are 262 miles of street-railway tracks. Formerly there were some six street-railroad companies in Boston, and some opposition in consequence but a year or two ago these corporations amalgamated, or formed a "trust," so that one huge corporation now controls the whole street-railroad system, not only in the city, but the suburbs also. The company have in use 1912 cars, and are now introducing electric cars through the Back Bay district, Brighton, Brookline, etc. and ere long it is likely these cars will come into general use. One need not be a prophet, however, to foresee the time when the elevated railroad will be one of the institutions of Boston. The Meigs plan of elevated railroad, now being introduced into Chicago, has been proposed, and a short experimental line built in Cambridge. By this plan the use of a ponderous, smoke-producing locomotive is entirely done away with, and in its stead is used the most improved form of the electric motor, the power of which is transmitted through a third rail and applied to every third car by a simple device hidden in the bottom of the vehicle, and which is under the immediate and perfect control of an attendant. The weight and size of the supporting posts are reduced to the minimum compatible with safety; and, as all the structure is of iron and steel, the obstruction to light and traffic is almost inconsiderable. Every precaution has been taken in regard to safety, and the speed that can be acquired is one of the especial feature of the system. The expense at which the road can be constructed is marvellously small, and its operating expenses will also be much less than those of any other road—facts which will result immediately to the public benefit by allowing the fares to be placed at a very low point.

Of the architectural changes to be noticed in a walk through Boston's streets, the following, written recently by Mr. A. W. Barrett, is apropos:

"In place of the old buildings destroyed by the devouring element, have sprung up huge edifices imposing in their size and extent, and in some cases of architectural beauty. It is a fact easily proven that the architectural styles of Boston have closely followed the prevailing ones of the same period in Europe. Early in the century there was a Greek revival, the principal monuments of which are the Court and Custom houses, the Tremont House, Quincy Market and St. Paul's Church. In 1838 began the Gothic period, an example of which is found in Old Trinity Church. Then followed the 'French-roof' style. The Deacon House on Washington, Concord, and Worcester Streets, was probably the first building of this style in the country. With the increase of popular travel, the influence of foreign models became more strongly felt in a great variety of styles. Northern and Southern Gothic, Romanesque and Renaissance, French Renaissance, became extremely popular and are the styles of many business and public buildings, including the City Hall and Post-office. Gothic has remained the favorite for churches. A peculiarity of Boston architecture is the richness and variety of the building-material. The prevailing material is red brick, but there is an abundance of light, dark, and red granite, brown, yellow, and buff sandstones; a variety of marble, Roxbury pudding-stone, and other material. When a 'big building' is mentioned, one naturally thinks of a huge edifice conspicuous for its size, and standing alone like a giant pine above the scrubby undergrowth. Examples of this kind of buildings are not uncommon in Boston; and yet it must be borne in mind that there are hundreds of 'big buildings,' side by side for blocks and blocks that are worthy of the title, though they do not strike a spectator so forcibly as a building like the Mason Building, which stands by itself."

TRANSPORTATION FACILITIES AND COMMERCE.

At the close of the war of the Revolution, Boston was the most influential community in America, but now there are two cities of greater importance and four larger in population. Then she took the lead in commerce, now, although her trade is immense, she occupies a second-rate position. Her shipping interests are, however, multiplying, and she is growing in popularity as the western port of several lines of British steamships, doing an immense and increasing freight business, and favored by the depth and security of the harbor and by the marginal railways, which allow freight vans to be run directly out upon the docks. The distance from Boston to Liverpool is shorter than from Philadelphia to Liverpool by 370 miles, New York to Southampton, by 260 miles, and New York to Liverpool by 160 miles. The harbor of Boston is the most picturesque on the coast, is of ample dimensions, and of sufficient depth to accommodate the largest vessels afloat. Her wharves are extensive, and upon them are built large warehouses. The city, too, is the starting-point for eight extensive railway lines, and the headquarters for numerous railroad corporations. Her transportation facilities are therefore of the most extensive and complete character. The Inman Steamship Company, it is reported, intends to establish a line of steamers between Boston and Europe to compete with the Cunard and other lines already located here. The tendency of recent railroad construction in the Northwest, and the developments in trade that are promised in that quarter, all have the outlook of largely increasing the merits of Boston as a point of shipment for the export and import trade of this country. The old combinations made by the trunk lines have given in the past certain advantages in rates to New York and Philadelphia; but it is questionable whether these can be maintained in the future. Then, beside having a large advantage, so far as ocean distance is concerned, over Philadelphia, and a considerable gain over New York, Boston has hitherto enjoyed the merit, when compared with the latter place, of lower port charges for the vessels which come here. Boston may perhaps never hope to compete with New York as the great centre of the export and import trade of this country; but, as this trade is constantly increasing, there is no reason why it should not maintain its relative position; and there are some reasons for thinking that it may in the next few years have a larger proportionate share of this business than it has enjoyed in the past. As an indication of the extent of the foreign shipping trade now done, it may be here stated that the receipts for duties at the Custom-house amounted in 1888 to $21,166,212.31.

Boston is the great centre, too, for internal traffic, especially in food products, shoes, leather, machinery, rubber, dry goods, etc.; and in all these great commodities there is an increase year by year, the record for last year being largely in excess of that of previous years. The city has its Shoe and Leather Exchange, Boston

Faneuil Hall Square, showing Faneuil Hall and Quincy Markets.

Commercial Exchange, Produce Exchange, Chamber of Commerce, New England Furniture Exchange, Fish Bureau, Board of Trade, Firemen's Exchange, Boston Board of Marine Underwriters, Boston Board of Trade, Boston Fire Underwriter's Union, Boston Grocers' Association, Boston Merchants' Association, Master Builders' Association, National Association Wool Manufacturers, New England Cotton Manufacturers' Association, New England Retail Grocers' Association, New England Saddlery Hardware Association, Mechanics' Exchange, Merchants' Exchange and Reading-room, etc.

Financial facilities are afforded by sixty national and several private banks, seven trust companies, and thirteen savings banks; and numerous home and foreign insurance companies afford protection against losses by fire to buildings, merchandise, and other property.

SCHOOLS AND CHURCHES

Boston has always occupied a prominent position among the American cities in respect to literary and scientific culture. She has been liberal in her provision of public libraries and schools, which are renowned all over the country for their number, affluence, and efficiency. The public schools are under the direction of a school committee, elected by the popular vote, a superintendent, and several supervisors. There are 530 regular schools with 1253 teachers and over 58,000 pupils, and 21 special schools with 151 teachers and 4086 pupils,

In addition to these, there are evening schools, attended by about 1900 pupils. On June 12, 1888, the school board discontinued Swinton's "Outlines of History" from the textbooks of the English High-school, at Rev. Theodore A. Metcalf's instigation, for a harmless paragraph about the sale of indulgences while Leo X. was pope. This would not have created any great amount of popular feeling, perhaps, but, on the 19th of June, the school board accepted a report transferring Mr. C. B. Travis from his post as teacher of history in the English High-school, to another duty. This action of the board created much public indignation, which was expressed in various ways. A tremendous meeting was held at Faneuil Hall on the evening of July 11th, and an overflow meeting at Tremont Temple, to protest against the displacement of Swinton's "Outlines" from the textbooks of the English High-school and transferring Mr. Travis from the historical department of that school. This was one of the most memorable meetings held in Faneuil Hall during recent years. It took the initial steps towards forming a committee of one hundred that wielded a marked influence upon the city election. Women were enlisted in the movement to reconstruct the school board so that it might be freed from mischievous ecclesiastical control, and several associations were formed to promote the assessment and registration of women to vote for school committee. The Loyal Women of American Liberty, Independent Women Voters of Boston, School Suffrage Association, Bunker Hill Educational Association, and Women's Christian Temperance Union took an active part in this work. The assessment of women elicited a spirited trial of strength be-

New England Conservatory of Music

tween Protestants and Catholics. The Republican city convention to nominate mayor and school committee assembled on the evening of Nov. 16th, and on the first ballot nominated Thomas N. Hart for mayor. A committee was selected to nominate eleven members of the school board. Subsequently the Republicans nominated a ticket for school committee, which was indorsed by the committee of one hundred and the women's associations affiliating with them. A vigorous canvass was made in its behalf by the committee of one hundred and the women's organizations acting with them. This ticket had no Catholics upon it, but a women's ticket was sent to every woman registered, having upon it the names of Messrs. Williamson, Dunn, and Canning, then members of the school board, who voted to reject Swinton's "Outlines" and transfer Mr. Travis. Besides this, there was a regular Democratic woman's ticket. Mr. Hart accepted the Republican nomination on a non-partisan platform entirely. A citizens' movement, into which the British element threw all its influence and zeal, was started in his favor, and subsequently put a school committee ticket in the field, embracing, among others, the names of Caroline E. Hastings, Messrs. Williamson, Dunn, Canning, and Collison of the present school board. The Republican canvass for the city government was made on the issue of reform and the necessity of an entire change in methods at City Hall. The appeal was made to all parties, but a potent factor was the determination of the women to rebuke the school board for submitting to priestly control. Mr. Hart was elected mayor on the 11th of December by a plurality of 2621. The Republicans elected two thirds of the aldermen, and gained in the Common Council. It was a rout of the City Hall ring. The people emphatically condemned the school board by electing the entire Republican ticket for school committee, which has been indorsed by the Committee of One Hundred. The city voted for license by a majority of 17,651, against 8483 last year. An enormous vote was polled, considering the heavy, penetrating rain which prevailed. The total for mayor fell short of the presidential vote only 1550. Of the twenty-one thousand women registered, seventeen thousand voted under the most disagreeable circumstances as regards the weather. But this did not appear to daunt them in the least. They labored zealously and effectively from the opening to the closing of the polls, were everywhere treated with consideration, and had the satisfaction of having contributed very materially to the election of the Republican school committee ticket, made up wholly of Protestants. The school committee, as elected, consists of: Caroline Hastings (one year), W. A. Mowry (two years), Lalilah B. Pingree, W. S. Allen, R. C. Humphreys, T. J. Emery, S. B. Capen, Dr. W. C. Green, Solomon Schindler, J. P. G. Winship, Dr. Liberty Packard.

There are over 220 churches in the city, representing all sects of religionists, and some of these and their pastors have won fame both at home and abroad.

THE CITY GOVERNMENT.

Boston received its city charter in 1822; and the government comprises a mayor, a board of 12 aldermen and a common council consisting of 73 representatives of the 25 wards. The executive power was formerly vested in the mayor and aldermen, but the law of 1885 (Stat. 1885, ch. 266), amending the charter of Boston, vests all executive power in the mayor, but retains, with very few exceptions, all the boards, commissions, trustees, and separate departments or offices existing at that time or since established. The number of these separate bodies exceeds 50, some of whom are not even required to publish regular reports. The election takes place annually on the Tuesday after the second Monday in December. From what has already been stated in connection with the election of the school committee (conducted at the same time) that of the mayor, aldermen and councilmen was, in December, 1888, an excitable one, and resulted in arresting the executive power so long held by the Democrats, by the Republicans, with the aid of the women and the British citizens.

The police force, numbering 800 men, some three years ago was taken from under the control of the civic authorities and placed under that of the State. Not including druggists, 1564 places were in 1888 licensed in the city for the sale of intoxicating drink, or one to every 263 persons, the population of the city on January 1, 1889, being computed at 410,688. The law of 1888 (chapter 340) demands the reduction of these licenses to 781, or exactly one half. The fire department is one of the most efficient in the country, and the water-supply is of a most adequate and excellent character.

THE CLIMATE AND HEALTH.

The climate of Boston is severe, especially in winter and spring; but the intense heats of summer are tempered by refreshing east winds, which fill the streets with the salty smell of the adjacent ocean. The death-rate in 1888 was 24.57 for each 1000 inhabitants, against 25.18 per 1000 in 1887.

THE SUBURBS.

No city has more attractive and picturesque suburbs than Boston, and it would take volumes to consider the traits and beauties of those outlying districts.

Many popular summer resorts are by the sea, and the most charming and most visited of these are Nantasket Beach, Revere Beach, and Point of Pines. A sail down the beautiful harbor is one of the special delights of Bostonians, and a pleasure which no visitor should forego.

ILLUSTRATED BOSTON.

The pages that follow contain many of the representative houses of this metropolis, and in connection with the illustrated portion of the work will be found profitable and interesting.

SPRING LANE FURNISHING COMPANY, Gents' Furnishing Goods, No. 279 Washington Street.—A point of interest and comfort, close to the Old South Church, at No. 279 Washington Street, and two doors from School Street, is a spot, which though it at first presents no striking appearance on the outside, is nevertheless in a quiet way one of the best known and most largely frequented of any of the places in this busy locality; for it is always productive of comfort and satisfaction to Bostonians and visitors. The reason why this is the headquarters for the business men of this vicinity, as well as the stopping for those who are on their way to or from the various railway stations are these: First, At this store can be obtained all the best and latest varieties of gents' furnishing goods. Second, Immediate attention is given; no time is lost by customer in waiting, at the times when the patronage is very large the number of clerks is doubled. The Spring Lane Furnishing Company buys direct from the most reliable manufacturers and is one of the first in the city to import latest novelties in neckwear (every known style), shirts, collars, cuffs, underwear, hosiery, suspenders, gloves, and umbrellas with hundreds of notions for gents' outfits. The beautiful display of goods, artistic arrangement of store, and scrupulous neatness and politeness of clerks are very pleasing. Laundry work. In order to meet the large demand in this direction a slide has been made into which parcels can be dropped from the outside any time, day or night, without stopping to come into store. Three of the best laundries make daily calls. This company is especially to be congratulated in having for the person in charge at the store Mr. W. B. Draper, who has been so long connected with this business and whose management and attention have been so universally acceptable.

MACULLAR, PARKER & CO., A Representative New England Clothing House, Nos. 398 and 400 Washington Street. The recent addition of a department for boys' and youths' clothing to the other branches of business at Macullar, Parker & Co.'s advances that house still another step in the cloth and clothing trade. They carry on a great business, as will be seen by the following summary of operations: To begin with, they are direct importers of fine woolens, with a sampling office at No. 30 Golden Square, London; they are jobbers of piece goods, having correspondence with merchant tailors in almost every state and territory in the United States, with agencies in New York and Chicago. In connection with the jobbing department, they employ a force of specialists, who shrink and finish, after the London manner, all goods requiring that treatment. Entrance to this department is from Hawley Street. They run a series of shops or halls for manufacturing ready-made clothing, and others for custom work. They sell at retail to men, youths and boys everything needed for dress and general equipment, except hats and shoes—their furnishing goods and shirt department being a familiar feature of trade to all Bostonians. They employ upwards of six hundred men and women, by whom, all the year round, the words "hard times and dull season" are never heard, and to whom every favorable consideration in the way of satisfactory wages, vacations, early closing, and weekly half holidays all through July and August, cheerful, well lighted, well-ventilated, and commodious working quarters, is accorded as a matter of simple right and propriety. All these things can only go with a prosperous and well-ordered house. One great feature here also is the exceptional variety and quantity of fine piece goods distributed to the merchant tailoring trade, as well as the amount cut up in the shops on the premises. The constant services of one hundred and fifty people are required in the custom department, nine of whom are cutters, with but very few idle hours in the year. This also implies an immense stock of piece goods, and the ready-made shops are of more than twice that capacity. In respect of operations in strictly fine goods, therefore, this firm is not surpassed by any other in America. The great Scotch mills on the Tweed and Yarrow, and the Dee and Don, and the equally celebrated looms in the west of England and in France and Germany, contribute their standard coatings and suitings; while the best home mills are called upon for their leading specialties notably the Middlesex yacht cloths and the excellent rough-faced goods from the George's River Mills in Maine. Many people wear ready-made goods than formerly in proportion of ten to one, and they dress better, too, in proportion simply as they take pains in finding the best shops. It is only a matter of a little discernment and discrimination. A house like Macullar, Parker & Co. keeps the standard advanced so high that all trade novelties and betterments gravitate naturally to its quarters in search of recognition and illustration. Its reputation gives immediate character and circulation to meritorious devices in loom-work. Chemistry and the elements are cited to attend here in the interests of pure woolens. The sun and the rain being so light and view all surface crudities and all half-way coloring. The dyer's hand must be cunning, indeed, that can evade these irresistible natural forces. Is there a suspicion of cotton where the contract calls for all-wool? Then in goes a sample section of the cloth to contend with boiling chemicals in a crucible heated to the hottest degree of Fahrenheit. Sometimes the result justifies the suspicion. The mass gradually revolves itself to its original elements. The wool, being of the animal, takes on the appearance of a formless solution, while a tell-tale insoluble residuum of intact cotton fibre (being of the vegetable kingdom and proof against the acid) attests at once the scope of chemistry and the finesse practiced by certain weavers. The house of Macullar, Parker & Co. dates back to 1849. It has gone on from year to year without a single interruption save one sharp trial by fire, gaining strength and popularity as a conservator of correct business principles, and with a wide-spread reputation for producing the best clothing at prices proportioned to intrinsic values, and therefore upon a scale fairly adjusted as between buyer and seller. Its outlook for a great business, bounded by no local lines, was never fairer than it is to-day.

CRAWFORD HOUSE, European Plan, Goodwin & Rimbach, Proprietors, Nos. 83 Court to 19 Brattle Streets.—One of the most popular, most largely patronized and most ably conducted hotels in Boston is unquestionably the Crawford House. It is just such comfortable and perfectly run houses as this that are full and make money while the badly kept old style hotels make poor showings. The Crawford was established fully twenty-five years ago by Messrs. Stumcke & Goodwin, and whose liberal policy, able methods and central location of house, secured to them a large and growing patronage. In 1886, Mr. Stumcke died after a lengthy career of efficient and progressive management, and was succeeded by Mr. Henry Goodwin, under the name and style of Henry Goodwin & Co. On Jan. 1st, 1889, he took into copartnership Mr. George H. Rimbach, nephew of the late Mr. Stumcke, a native of Boston, and though still a young man, thorough system of organization. The restaurant and bar are on the Brattle Street side, and are strictly first-class in every respect. The large measure of patronage enjoyed, including the best classes of the commercial and traveling public, permanent residents, etc., indicates the superior inducements offered, and no hotel in Boston is more worthy of an extended and influential class of patronage.

ALFRED A. CLATUR, Dealer in All Kinds of Leather Remnants, No. 177 Summer Street.—One of the most important adjuncts to the shoe and leather trades of Boston, is the scrap leather business. From an insignificant branch of Massachusetts' great industry, it has grown within a few years to immense magnitude, and has now an invested capital of about a million dollars. Large quantities of remnants of leather, that used

brings to bear fifteen years of experience in the business. As thus constituted the firm stands second to none in regard to every qualification. On Jan. 1st, there was added an annex containing sixty rooms, particularly adapted for families; large square commodious rooms, with steam heat and all modern convenience, elegantly furnished, and connected by iron bridge with main house. The Crawford House is the most centrally located of any hotel in Boston as regards all the depots, theatres, lines of street cars, and points of interest. It is a handsome and substantial structure, facing on Scollay Square, Hanover and Brattle Streets, five stories in height, and embracing all the modern improvements. There are steam heat, electric light, gas, safety passenger elevator, etc. On the first floor are the office, newsstand, reading-room and dining-room, the floors are tiled; the office and other apartments are very handsomely furnished and decorated. On the second floor are the ladies' and gentlemen's parlors elegantly furnished. There are 200 rooms, single and double, all comfortably and newly furnished throughout, and carefully looked after by a staff of servants. The house is conducted upon the European plan, and accommodations can be had at remarkably low rates for a first-class hotel, viz: single rooms, from $1 per day upwards, and double ones from $2, to $4 per day. A staff of 100 hands are employed, and Messrs. Goodwin and Rimbach are noted for the exercise of the highest order of ability, and for enforcing a to be regarded as nearly worthless, are now gathered up, assorted, and made of considerable commercial value. Nothing in the leather line now goes to waste. Among the numerous merchants in Boston who make the scrap leather business a specialty, is Mr. Alfred A. Clatur. He was one of the first to give it close attention. He started with a small capital in 1864, on Pearl Street, which was then the centre of the shoe and leather trade. From there he removed to No. 100 High Street in order to secure more commodious quarters. He was burnt out in the great fire of 1872, but immediately obtained temporary quarters, and kept his trade going without a break, meeting all his obligations promptly, and rapidly increasing his sales. He followed the extension of the leather trade southward, and removed to his present location, No. 317 Summer Street, corner of South Street, July 1, 1879, where he occupies two spacious floors, besides filling one floor in building No. 90 South Street. He carries a large and varied line of stock, including remnants of sole and upper leather, moulded stiffenings, inner soles, heels and boot counters. Having a thorough knowledge of the business in all its detail, she knows what stock is required to supply the demands of the trade, and being in a position to take advantage of the market, and to at all times discount his bill, he is thus enabled to give his customers the benefit of the lowest current rates. Mr. Clatur has always taken a deep interest in political affairs.

THE METROPOLIS OF NEW ENGLAND.

SCULL & BRADLEY, Fire and Marine Insurance, No. 85 Water Street.—Throughout the United States, Boston is recognized as one of the principal centres of all business interests, and so important is this fact, that all the more prominent corporations and companies are represented in this city by responsible and energetic agents. In insurance affairs this is equally noticeable, and the leading companies both of the United States and Great Britain find it essential to maintain branches or agencies in this city. Prominent among our most reliable and widely known insurance agents, is the firm of Messrs. Scull & Bradley, whose well equipped offices are centrally located at No. 85 Water Street. This business was established in 1868 by G. E. Foster, who was succeeded by Foster & Coe, Foster & Scull and Scull & Bradley. The members of this copartnership, Messrs. Gideon Scull, Fred. Bradley and Geo. P. Field, are expert and prudent underwriters, fully conversant with every detail of fire and marine insurance and the requirements of property owners and merchants. They represent the following first-class companies, viz: The Insurance Company of North America, Philadelphia; Pennsylvania Fire Insurance Co., Philadelphia; American Fire Insurance Co., Philadelphia; Royal Insurance Company, Liverpool, England. Messrs. Scull & Bradley are prepared to take risks to any amount, and write policies in any of the above named companies at the lowest rates of premium, and losses on risks placed by them have always been promptly adjusted and paid, and numbers of our prominent citizens testify to the just and straightforward manner in which Messrs. Scull & Bradley conduct all transactions. Outside manufacturers, property and ship owners will study their best interests by insuring with this agency, securing to them in every case the lowest rating rates and entire security. The partners are popular members of the Underwriters' Association, and are highly esteemed in business circles for their promptness and integrity. Mr. Bradley takes charge of the marine department, while Messrs. Scull and Field devote themselves to the fire branch.

THE BLACKSTONE NATIONAL BANK OF BOSTON, Joshua Loring, President; James Adams, Cashier; No. 132 Hanover Street.—One of the representative financial institutions of Boston, which is contributing largely to the prosperity of the city and maintaining its reputation at the highest standard throughout every section of the United States, is The Blackstone National Bank of Boston, whose banking rooms are located at No. 132 Hanover Street, corner of Union. This successful bank was originally incorporated in 1851, and eventually in 1864 became a national bank. It has a paid up capital of $1,500,000, which has been further augmented by a surplus of $196,000. The interests of the Blackstone National Bank have always been intimately allied with the material progress and prosperity of Boston, and its policy has ever been to promote, as far as is consistent with its own safety, the well-being of the manufacturing industries and commerce of the city. The following gentlemen are the officers and directors:—Joshua Loring, president ; James Adams, cashier. Directors—Geo. W. Chipman, Eleazar Boynton, Joshua Loring, Wm. A. Rust, Eustace C. Fitz, Ebenezer N. Blake, John S. Paine, J. Otis Wetherbee, John Edmunds and Geo. F. Blake. The bank transacts a general banking, exchange and collection business, and receives upon favorable terms the accounts of banks, bankers, merchants, corporations and individuals. Its management is thoroughly conservative, its business is rapidly growing, and it is one of the strongest financial organizations in New England. The directors are men intimately identified with the best interests of the City of Boston, and whose names are synonymous of integrity, prudence and stability. Mr. Joshua Loring has been with the bank since its incorporation, as cashier till 1874, when he was elected president. He is a judicious, able financier, and a vigorous exponent of the soundest principles governing banking and finance. Mr. Adams, the cashier, has held office since 1878. He is an experienced and capable bank officer, with every qualification for his important position. The deposits of the Blackstone National Bank now amount to $1,300,000 and its future prospects are of the most favorable and encouraging character.

THE HANCOCK INSPIRATOR COMPANY, Manufacturers of Inspirators, Ejectors, and general Jet Apparatus, Office, No. 81 India Wharf, foot of Atlantic Avenue.—This representative company was duly incorporated under the laws of Massachusetts in 1878 with a paid up capital of $50,000, and since its organization at that date has built up an extensive and permanent patronage not only in all sections of the United States and Canada, but also in Europe. The works of the company which are fully equipped with all the latest improved tools and machinery, and furnish constant employment to 120 skilled workmen, are situated on Watson Street. The Hancock Inspirator Company make a specialty of the manufacture of the famous Hancock inspirator, the Hancock ejector or lifter and all kinds of general jet apparatus. The Hancock inspirator is the best appliance known for feeding all kinds of boilers, on account of its simplicity of operation, the great range of its duties, and the fact that all the steam used in operating it is returned to the boiler, there being no loss, excepting by radiation, from the pipes used in connecting. It has one set of tubes for lifting, and another set of tubes for forcing, water—a combination entirely new, reliable and efficient. Water can be delivered at a high or low temperature, as may be desired. Each inspirator is carefully tested before leaving the factory, and is guaranteed to perform all that is claimed for it. The Hancock ejector or lifter is highly recommended for use in raising water either for filling or emptying tanks, for pumping out wheel pits, or for raising and transferring liquids, hot or cold, in tanneries, dye houses, etc.; also for filling railroad tanks, and locomotive tenders. To be permanently attached by the side of the road, in the vicinity of water supply, whether well, brook or pond; or to be attached to tender or engine as may be most convenient, taking steam from the locomotive boiler to operate the elevator in either case. The company has already sold 10,000 inspirators and great numbers of ejectors. Numerous testimonials from the leading railroad companies, not only of the United States but also of Europe, bear undoubted testimony to their efficacy, reliability and superiority over all competitors. These splendid inspirators and ejectors were invented by Mr. John T. Hancock, who died in 1881. The company's principal agents in America are Fairbanks & Co., of New York, Boston, Chicago, Cincinnati, St. Louis, San Francisco, etc. Messrs. John G. Rollins & Co., of London, England, are the agents for supplying Great Britain and other European countries.

STANDARD CORDAGE COMPANY, Manufacturers of Cordage and Binders' Twine; Silas Potter, President; Chas. H. Pearson, Treasurer and General Manager; Office: No. 127 State Street.—The extent and importance which the manufacture of cordage of all kinds, and binders' twine has attained in the United States, within comparatively recent years, can scarcely be over-estimated. The large amount of capital invested, the wide sphere covered by its operations and the great number of operatives to whom it affords employment, all impart to this great branch of industry a special interest and importance. Prominent among the leading houses actively engaged in this growing trade in Boston, is that known as the Standard Cordage Company, whose office is situated at No. 127 State Street. This company was incorporated under the laws of Massachusetts in 1884 and has a paid up capital of $150,000, and since its organization has built up a liberal and permanent patronage, which now extends throughout the entire United States, Canada and South America. The chief executive officers of the company are Mr. Silas Potter, president, and Mr. Chas. H. Pearson, treasurer and general manager. The Standard Cordage Company manufactures extensively cordage and binders' twine, manilla and sisal goods, which are unrivalled for quality, finish, strength and general excellence. The company's factory which is fully equipped with modern appliances and machinery and furnishes constant employment to 150 operatives, is situated in Camden Street. The output of the factory is about twenty tons daily of cordage and twine. Messrs. Potter and Pearson, the officers, are highly regarded in trade circles for their sound business principles, enterprise and integrity. Mr. Silas Potter was previously president of the Boston Cordage Company. He is a director of the Shawmut National Bank and of the Merchandise National Bank, and is one of Boston's progressive and public spirited citizens. Mr. C. H. Pearson has had twenty-six years' experience in the manufacture of cordage and twine, and is as widely known for his ability and sterling integrity as for the just and prompt manner in which he attends to the interests of patrons in all sections of the country.

BAXTER, STONER & SCHENKELPERGER, Manufacturers of Cut Soles & Taps, Nos. 70-74 Lincoln Street.—The leather trade with its numerous tributary branches constitutes a feature of colossal proportions and commanding importance in the commercial activity of this city, and one of the principal branches of this industry is that so ably represented by Messrs. Baxter, Stoner & Schenkelberger, manufacturers of cut soles and taps, at Nos. 70-74 Lincoln street. Owing to the increase of improved machinery and the general tendency toward specialties, many shoe manufacturers have been compelled to confine themselves to the production of certain lines of goods; in this way only requiring the soles suitable for each grade, and, in place of buying their leather in sides, as formerly, they go direct to the sole-cutter who supplies them with just the grade of sole they require in their special line of goods. The custom shoemakers and repairers are now, almost without exception, buying soles and taps instead of side leather. The advantages of buying the bottom stock cut, instead of buying the leather in the side are manifest. The business has been brought to such a degree of perfection that the manufacturer can buy any desired quality and thickness; he knows just exactly what his soles cost, which knowledge he is unable to obtain accurately by cutting his own stock. He is relieved of the necessity of being constantly on the lookout for desirable and suitable leather to cut, for reliable men to cut it, for men to oversee that it is cut properly, without waste and loss. He avoids accumulating grades that he cannot use to good advantage, and which must be worked in where best they can be, at a loss, of course. When the manufacturer cuts his own leather he cannot get the uniformity in his soles that the sole cutter can give him. The sole cutter has a market for all his soles, and by being able to place all his grades where they will bring what they are worth, he is enabled to sell his soles as low and often lower than the manufacturer can cut them. Baxter, Stoner & Schenkelberger are thoroughly practical and experienced in the cut sole business. Their policy has been to make the best, and they are winning in this line. They occupy a fine seven-story building, fully equipped with new and improved machinery and give steady employment to upwards of fifty skilled and experienced workmen. The general arrangement is systematic and convenient, and every facility is afforded for the advantageous prosecution of the business. They have just made arrangements with the tanner of the celebrated Camden Hemlock sole leather, whereby they are henceforth the only sole cutters in the United States who cut this leather. Made from a straight Texas packer hide, thoroughly tanned and solid, it is to-day the best leather for taps in the country. Cutting as they do, only one tannage of hemlock leather, the firm is able to give a uniformity of stock, quality and assortment that no other cutter can give. They follow this pshirople in Union and Oak leather also, cutting in the former the firm and solid West Branch backs, and in the latter the celebrated Cover—pure Virginia Oak. Their specialties are in heavy and steadily increasing demand throughout the United States. Always at the head, and offering superior inducements in quality, it is no wonder that the productions of this house have a standard value in every market into which they have been introduced, and they bid fair to retain the position they have achieved at the head of the cut sole trade of this country.

M. C. WARREN & CO., Jobbers and Retailers of Hardware and Building Materials, No. 9 Dock Square.—An oblesstablished and well-known hardware house is that of M. C. Warren & Co., located at No. 9 Dock Square. For more than a century Dock Square has been a recognized centre of the hardware trade in Boston, and though few of the present day will recall the names of those engaged in the business in the earlier part of this century, there are probably many who will remember those of John Bradford, Charles Brooks & Co., West & Paakman, Thomas P. Barnes, Otis Vinal and A. J. Wilkinson, who were located there some fifty years ago, and several of whom continued for many years after, but there are none now remaining except the one who is the subject of this sketch. This firm was was established April 14, 1841, by the present senior member, in the same building as that now occupied, and was conducted by him with but few changes until 1874, when his son, William H. Warren, and Messrs. John E. Norton and Eugene B. Stoddard were admitted to partnership under the firm name of M. C. Warren & Co. Messrs. Norton and Stoddard retired in 1885, and the business has since been conducted by the father and son under the same title. It is now, and has always been considered one of the most responsible firms devoted to this line of business in the city, and receives a large patronage, not only from residents of Boston and the surrounding cities and towns, but from various parts of the New England States, many goods being shipped to Maine, New Hampshire and Vermont, and there are at times shipments made to some of the more remote states in the Union, both in the south and west; and even to some of the far away countries of the earth, as orders from Burmah and China will testify. The business premises occupy four 25x60 feet floors, and a complete stock of goods are constantly on hand, and a force of salesmen employed sufficient to meet the requirements of the trade, it being a cardinal principle of this house that its patrons should be well-served, and with as little delay as possible. The stock on hand comprises a full assortment of the latest styles and best grades of builders' hardware and carpenters' tools, to which the business, which is both wholesale and retail, is almost exclusively devoted. There are, however, many other articles in general use, such as table and pocket cutlery, scissors, razors, butchers' tools, shovels, spades, rakes, etc., together with an almost innumerable variety of other goods, selected with care to meet the wants of the mechanic, the farmer or the family. The Messrs. Warren & Co. have always been strictly honorable and just in all their dealings.

PINO PALMINE COMPANY, Geo. C. Stewart, Manager; No. 130 Commercial Street.—One of the greatest improvements and valuable aids to health, adding to our comfort and promoting nature's sweet restorer—balmy sleep, that has been brought to the notice of the public during the past few years is the pine needle bedding or pino-palmine, which is without exception, the driest, purest and most healthful bedding material in the world and is endorsed and recommended by the medical faculty in all parts of the country. Pino-palmine Bedding is made from the leaves of the Florida pine tree, called the Fox-tail Pine, from its bushy appearance while on the stock. These leaves are about fourteen inches in length, of a peculiar odor, strong, but not rank, and agreeable to every one. They occupy a high place in materia medica. From them come the balsams, turpentines, tars, frankincense and, in general, the oleo resins in medicines. They act as a tonic and diuretic, checking disease of the mucous membrane, etc. Its beneficial influence depends on its stimulant and diaphoretic operation, especially in old or debilitated persons. The great merit of this filling for mattresses, pillows and comforts is its toughness, dryness and elasticity of its fibers together with its delightful fragrant, pleasant aromatic odor. The medical properties of the pine and its balsams are clearly defined in the United States Dispensatory, the highest standard authority, on Materia Medica as valuable remedies in asthma, bronchitis, catarrh, hay fever, nervousness, insomnia, neuralgia, rheumatism and other diseases. Pino-Palmine was first introduced by Mr. George C. Stewart who was an invalid with rheumatism for a long time, and derived such benefits from sleeping on this material, that he caused several beds to be made for his friends, and in 1879 he manufactured about thirty mattresses, and such were the remarkable results and benefit derived by those who were using them, that in 1886 he determined to place the Pino-Palmine before the public. The premises of the company consist of two floors, each 35x125 feet in extent, which are convenient and capacious. Two assistants are employed, and a business extending to all parts of the United States is carried on. The following experiment made by Dr. H. L. Bowker, May 12th, 1881, speaks for itself. Gentlemen:—At your request I made a series of experiments with various articles of bedding, with a view to test their merits as to dryness, and the amount of moisture they will retain. 100 grains of best quality of curled hair, feathers, excelsior and Pino-Palmine were selected and thoroughly dried, and immersed in water for fifteen minutes, after which they were pressed so as to remove all the water except what had been absorbed or adhered to the surface, with the following result:—100 grains of excelsior retained 246 per cent. of moisture. 100 grains of feathers retained 121 per cent. of moisture. 100 grains of hair retained 107 per cent. of moisture. 100 grains of Pino-Palmine retained 65 per cent. of moisture.

THE METROPOLIS OF NEW ENGLAND.

REVERE HOUSE, Bowdoin Square; J. F. Merrow & Co., Proprietors.—There is nothing which adds so much to the prestige of a city, as first-class hotel accommodations, and in this respect Boston stands pre-eminent. One of the leading and most successful hotels on the European plan in the city is the favorite Revere House, eligibly located on Bowdoin Square, and of which Messrs. J. F. Merrow & Co. are the popular and energetic proprietors. This noted hotel was first opened to the public in 1847 by Paran Stevens, who was the originator of our present American first-class hotel system. In 1881 the Revere House was thoroughly renovated, refurnished and remodelled, when Mr. J. F. Merrow assumed the management. He has introduced all modern improvements including, safety passenger elevator, electric lights, electric bells, steam heat, hot and cold water on every floor. Then the Revere while conducted strictly on the European plan, now so

The night clerk is Mr. E. W. Hall, and the cashier, Mr. W. D. Merrow. All these gentlemen are experienced and are noted for their obliging and courteous manners. Mr. J. F. Merrow, the proprietor was born in New Hampshire. He is thoroughly conversant with the management of first-class hotels, and has made hosts of friends owing to his promptness, business ability and integrity. The Revere House has been rejuvenated under his careful management, and is now always full, at all seasons of the year.

C. G. DOLE, Mutton, Lamb, Veal, Etc., Stall No. 19 New Faneuil Hall Market.—Among those dealers who have attained prominence and popularity in the meat and provision trade of Boston is Mr. C. G. Dole, who occupies Stall No. 19, in the New Faneuil Hall Market. This gentleman has been established in the business here since

generally preferred by the travelling public, has the finest restaurant considering price and quality to be found in Boston. Its cuisine is renowned and no pains or expense are ever spared to make it a leading feature of comforts and excellence. The hotel is finely built and is attractive in appearance both inwardly and outwardly. It contains 200 rooms available for guests, graduated in price according to location and size from $1.00 per day and upwards. There are also a number of suites, varying from $5.00 per day, etc. All the rooms are commodious, handsomely furnished and elegant in all their appointments, fixtures and upholstery, while the halls and corridors are spacious and beautifully tiled. The ladies' and gentlemen's parlors and reception rooms are richly furnished, and the offices are fitted up in a convenient and attractive style. The sanitary arrangements are perfect in every detail and the means of escape in case of fire, ample. In the office is one of the new improved Howard electric clocks, which compels the night-watchman to make rounds at stated intervals, and pass every point in the house. In the yard enclosed by the house is a handsome fountain constantly playing. The bar is supplied with the finest wines, liquors and cigars, which are obtained direct from the most reliable houses. We would observe that the parlors of the Revere are far more spacious than those of any other American hotel, while the accommodation for dinner parties is absolutely unsurpassed. The day clerks are Messrs. O. H. Thornton and C. M. Green for many years connected with the Tremont House and two of the best hotel clerks in the United States.

October, 1865, and has built up a large and influential trade as a wholesale and retail dealer in mutton, lamb, veal, etc. He commands all the advantages naturally accumulated by long years of identification with a special line of trade, and possesses the best possible facilities for conducting all operations under the most favorable auspices. He exercises the greatest care in the selection of his stock and in preparing it for the market which justifies him in claiming to offer the trade and consumers a line of meat products that cannot be excelled for quality, reliability and excellence. He is prepared to supply hotels, restaurants, families and large buyers with meats in quantities to suit with the utmost promptness and at prices which are safe from unsuccessful competition. Having always been earnest and unremitting in his endeavors to meet every demand of his customers in a prompt and satisfactory manner, he has developed a patronage of great and gratifying proportions, which is in itself the best possible proof of the superiority of the goods he offers, and of the honorable and straightforward methods that have ever characterized his dealings. His trade extends to all parts of the city and to the surrounding towns, and is annually increasing in volume and value under enterprising, reliable and painstaking management. Mr. Dole is a native of Acton, Mass, and well and favorably known in the social and business circles of this city for his strict probity and integrity, his liberal and obliging methods of dealing, and his business tact and ability, all of which his customers derive the benefit of in their dealings with him.

FOBES, HAYWARD & CO., (Incorporated) Manufacturing Confectioners, A. F. Hayward, President; Nos. 42 to 52 Chardon Street.—Americans, especially the rising generation, are probably the largest consumers of candy and confectionery in the world, and the productions of our manufacturers of these delicious luxuries can now compete favorably with those of France, which country for a very long period has been considered the most successful in this particular line. One of the most prominent and representative houses, extensively engaged in the manufacture of confectionery of all kinds in New England, is that of Fobes, Hayward & Co. (incorporated), whose office, factory and salesrooms are located in Boston at Nos. 42 to 52 Chardon Street. This business was established in 1848. In 1860 Messrs. Fobes, Hayward & Co., succeeded to the management. Eventually in 1886 it was duly incorporated under the laws of Massachusetts, with a paid up capital of $150,000. The following gentlemen being the officers viz.: A. F. Hayward, president; E. F. Fobes, vice-president; F. H. Woodward, secretary. The premises occupied comprise a spacious six-story and basement building 150x120 feet in dimensions. The manufacturing departments are fitted up with the latest improved machinery, apparatus and appliances necessary for the systematic conduct of this extensive industry. Here 200 operatives are employed, and the machinery is driven by a superior 80 horse power steam engine. Purity in the main essential with these goods, and to-day the difficulty to obtain candies and confectionery devoid of adulteration and deleterious substances is so great, that the advantage of dealing with a house like that of Fobes, Hayward & Co., whose reputation is so high for making none but the purest and best goods, is at once manifest. All their productions are warranted to be exactly as represented, and the creditable position that their goods have in the market, is due to the determination of the officers to always maintain their standard. The company manufactures in large quantities plain and decorated creams, marshmallows, plain and fine chocolate creams, mixed candy of all kinds, vanilla chocolate, cream almonds, macaroons, etc., which are unexcelled in this country or Europe for quality, purity and uniform excellence. All orders are promptly and carefully filled at the lowest possible prices, and the trade of the house which is steadily increasing, now extends throughout all sections of the United States and Canada. The officers are thoroughly able and honorable business men. Retailers and jobbers will find it greatly to their interests to make a factor of this responsible house, and will obtain such advantages here, as will fully sustain all that has been stated in this editorial article.

GOLDSMITH, SILVER & CO., formerly the Mass. Co-Operative Association, Manufacturers of Cigars, No. 108 State Street.—Among the various industries represented in the City of Boston, few deserve more attention than that of the manufacture and handling of cigars. This business involves the investment of a large amount of capital and gives employment to hundreds of operatives. A thoroughly enterprising and progressive house engaged in this industry is that of Messrs. Goldsmith, Silver & Co., whose office and factory are located at No. 108 State Street. The gentlemen comprising the firm are Mr. I. N. Goldsmith, Mr. S. C. Silver, Mr. Henry Mack and Mr. H. Van Uhm, all of whom were formerly connected either as officers or members of the cigar manufacturing house known under the title of the Massachusetts Co-operative Association; who entered into this present copartnership on January 1st, 1889, under the existing firm name, and, although of such recent organization they have acquired already a very large and increasing patronage, such as is not often accorded to much older houses in this line of business. The business premises comprise three floors, each 25x60 feet in dimensions, which are fully equipped with all conveniences and employment is given to from thirty-five to forty skilled operatives. Competition in the cigar trade is very keen, but this firm owing to the evident superiority and standard quality of their productions have had no difficulty thus far in convincing their trade, which extends throughout New England, that their goods are honestly made from the purest materials. It is the aim of this concern to make a thoroughly good cigar, well worthy the attention of connoisseurs and experts and to maintain their brands at a high and uniform standard of excellence. That they are successful in this laudable endeavor is evidenced by the extensive demand created for their cigars wherever they are introduced, which is the best possible assurance of the continued success and permanent prosperity of this house. They make a leading specialty of their famous brands M. C. A., a ten-cent, and 10s a five-cent cigar, which have quickly become among the most popular cigars in this market, and are handled by the best dealers and retailers throughout New England and eagerly sought for by experts and good judges of fine tobacco. Dealers and large buyers requiring a high grade of cigars at moderate prices should give their orders to this reliable house, which is prepared to offer inducements and advantages not easily obtained elsewhere. The members of the firm have had a wide range of experience in this line of trade, and devote their entire attention to their business. They are well and favorably known in the commercial and trade circles of this city and vicinity and are thoroughly identified with every interest effecting the city's welfare and prosperity.

JOHN KENT, New England Agent of The A. French Spring Co., Limited, and Carnegie, Phipps & Co., Limited, Nos. 52 Mason Building, No. 70 Kilby Street.—Prominent among the important manufacturing enterprises of the country represented in this city are those under the management of Mr. John Kent, whose office is located at Room 52, Mason Building, No. 70 Kilby Street. This gentleman is the New England agent of Carnegie, Phipps & Co., manufacturers of steel plates, merchant iron and forgings, of Pittsburgh, Pa.; the A. French Spring Co., Limited, manufacturers of springs of all kinds, of Pittsburgh, Pa.; and has been established in the business here since 1882 and enjoys a large wholesale trade throughout New England. His connection with the above powerful corporations and prominent manufacturers enables him to conduct all branches of the business upon the largest scale. He ships direct from the manufactories to his customers in all cases, and is in a position to guarantee the prompt and perfect fulfilment of all orders, of whatever magnitude; and also to offer inducements to the trade as regards both superiority of goods and liberality of terms and prices, which challenge comparison and defy successful competition. Controlling the entire trade of these mammoth manufactories in New England, Mr. Kent is prepared to battle on even terms with his most formidable contemporaries from any part of the country, and is transacting an immense and constantly increasing business. The great resources at his command endow him not only with advantages for the successful prosecution of the trade, but also insure to the benefit of all his patrons, rendering business relations once entered into with this agency not only pleasant for the time being, but of a character to become lasting and permanent. Mr. Kent has been identified with the iron business for many years, has a foundation understanding of all the details and requirements of the trade, and is eminently popular and successful in meeting all its demands.

THE HOWARD NATIONAL BANK OF BOSTON, R. E. Demmon, President; S. F. Wilkins, Cashier; No. 19 Congress Street.—The Howard National Bank of Boston is the successor of the Howard Banking Co., which was incorporated in 1852 with a capital of $400,000. In 1858 the name was changed to the Howard Bank, and under that style the institution continued until January, 1865, when having re-organized under the national banking law it assumed the present title. In March, 1865, the capital was increased to $750,000, and in October, 1869, it was further increased to $1,000,000. The bank has been located since January 1, 1879, at No. 19 Congress Street, occupying the first floor of the Howard Bank Building. Its total dividends as a National bank have been $1,800,000 and its present surplus fund is $377,000 besides other profits of $47,000. The Howard has among its depositors many of the best firms and corporations in the city and has also a large number of bank and mercantile correspondents. The president is R. E. Demmon and the cashier is Samuel F. Wilkins. The directors are A. B. Butterfield, John W. Candler, Samuel D. Capen, R. E. Demmon, Francis Flint, J. M. W. Hall, A. P. Matin, N. W. Rice, and Samuel F. Wilkins. Among the principal American correspondents of the bank can be named the Importers' and Traders' National Bank, of New York; Mercantile National Bank, of New York; National Bank of Commerce, New York, and the Corn Exchange Bank, of Chicago.

THE METROPOLIS OF NEW ENGLAND.

WHITTEN, BURDETT & YOUNG, Manufacturers and Jobbers of Men's and Boys' Clothing, Nos. 3 Winthrop Square and 36 Otis Street.—Boston's supremacy in the wholesale clothing trade is assured by the possession of such an eminent and enterprising house as that of Messrs. Whitten, Burdett & Young, whose sound judgment, marked executive capacity and perfected facilities have secured for the fine clothing of their manufacture the national reputation of being fully the equal of custom made in every respect. The immense industry centred in the magnificent modern structure, corner Winthrop Square and Otis Street, was established upwards of fifty years ago by Messrs. John Gove & Co.; in 1858 Mr. Chas V. Whitten entered the house, organizing the firm of Whitten, Hopkins & Co., and who thus continued up to 1862 when he and Mr. Horatio S. Burdett formed a copartnership under the name and style of Whitten, Burdett & Co. In 1862, Mr. Amos S. Young came into the firm under the now long familiar title of Messrs. Whitten, Burdett & Young. As the business enlarged and departments increased in magnitude two other partners were admitted, viz: Mr. Jules M. Burns in 1884, and Mr. James Rankin in 1885. As thus constituted this house has no equal for every qualification insuring efficiency and success and their concern is the recognized, largest and the model establishment of the kind in Boston, and one from which the leaders of the New York clothing trade can secure valued suggestions. From the start Messrs. Whitten, Burdett and their colleagues were animated with the laudable ambition to excel—to lift the wholesale manufacture of fine clothing from the rut into which it had fallen, and their efforts were from the start crowned with a legitimate and lasting success, their enlightened policy practically revolutionizing the trade and securing for their goods the eager demand of the most celebrated retail clothiers and jobbers of Boston and the country at large. The firm make the finest clothing put on the market—in every respect the equal of custom work. The firm occupy five immense floors, splendidly lighted, and most handsomely and conveniently fitted up, all the modern improvements being at command. The premises are 80x140 feet in dimensions, which figures give a faint idea of the immense area of floor space here utilized. A thorough system of organization is enforced and housebosmen, cutters, clerks, examiners, porters, etc. are here busily engaged in the work of preparing the cloths and woolens for the cutters, (who include the best talents and the reception of the made up clothing and suitable disposition, packing, shipping, etc. Messrs. Whitten, Burdett & Young exercise sound judgment and the greatest enterprise in the selection of their woolens and suitings, bringing ample resources to bear and being the first to secure all the newest shades, patterns and textures in American and foreign fabrics; their styles are ever the leaders, correct, fashionable and elegant. Their cutters, as before remarked, are all trained experts from fine custom shops; all goods are critically examined and the slightest imperfection or blemish condemns the piece of material. All goods are duly sponged and made up in the most thorough manner by experienced workmen, of whom the firm employ no less than 2,200, thus bringing their industrial army up to the round number of 2,500—the equal of three big regiments—all busy in producing the clothing that is first sought for by shrewd and careful buyers in Boston and all over New England and the west. The business has attained proportions of enormous magnitude growing up on the sound lines of the best clothing of every grade, at the lowest prices commensurate with honest workmanship. The firm's policy is synonymous with integrity, and the popular demand for its clothing became so urgent that to meet it the concern opened large retail stores in such great cities as Worcester, Mass.; Providence, R. I.; Hartford, New Haven and Bridgeport, Conn., and in Minneapolis, Minn. Each one has been a pronounced success and as a further instance of their enterprise, we may state what is already so familiar to the Boston public, the opening in December, 1888, of their magnificent and mammoth clothing store in the prominent new building, corner of Washington and Kneeland Streets. It is

FACTORY AND
WHOLESALE STORE,
NO. 3 WINTHROP SQUARE.

RETAIL STORE,
COMMONWEALTH CLOTHING HOUSE,
COR. WASHINGTON AND KNEELAND STREETS.

admittedly the finest clothing store in Massachusetts, and is 80x 165 feet in size and is fitted up as only the accurate taste, ripe experience and ample resources of this eminent house could dictate. There are displayed in profusion, every possible form and style of garment worn by man or boy in season, all of the firm's perfection of manufacture, and quoted at prices, which quality considered, cannot possibly be duplicated elsewhere. The sales have far more than met the most sanguine anticipations of the firm and their store has at once taken rank as the leading representative in Boston. Mr. Charles V. Whitten was born in Maine. Early in life he came to Boston and has ever been prominently identified with the wholesale clothing trade. The remarkable progress manifest is very largely due to his skill and enterprise. He saw the need of progress and so did Messrs. Burdett and Young, and these three gentlemen are veritable public benefactors in their line. Mr. Burdett was born in Massachusetts, and Mr. Young in New Hampshire, thus they represent the three principal New England States. Mr. Whitten is a public spirited citizen and has been and is active in public life, has as chairman of the Boston Board of Aldermen, most ably and creditably presided over the deliberations of that body and doing much to secure to the city an efficient and economical administration. He is a director of the Mechanics' National Bank, while Mr. Burdett is a director of the Lincoln and Exchange National Banks, both gentlemen being vigorous exponents of the soundest principles governing banking and finance. Mr. Burns is a native of New Hampshire, and Mr. Rankin of Maine; both are valued factors in guiding the immense business of this famous old house, whose wise guidance is so noteworthy, whose facilities are unequalled, connections the most influential and which has brought such a lasting source of credit and value to Boston and an enduring monument to the industry and enterprise of the copartners.

KANSAS INVESTMENT COMPANY, Topeka, Kansas, Eastern Office: No. 101 Devonshire Street, George C. Morrell, Vice President and Manager.—The rapid growth of the fertile west in population, wealth and material improvements of every kind, would have been greatly retarded without the free bartering of eastern capital by the sturdy farmers and stock raisers, who have turned the bleak prairies into waving wheat fields and productive cattle ranges. In this connection special reference is made in this commercial review of Boston, to the reliable and successful Kansas Investment Company of Topeka. The company's home office is at No. 535 Kansas Avenue, Topeka, Kansas. This company was duly incorporated under the laws of Kansas, in 1883, with a paid up capital of $500,000, and since its organization at that date has built up an extensive and liberal patronage. The company's business is confined exclusively to the negotiation of first mortgages and debenture bonds to savings banks, insurance and trust companies, trust estates and individual capitalists. The company employs ten expert examiners six of whom are stockholders and two directors in the company. These examiners are paid a salary, and have no interest except to protect the company. Every property on which a loan is made is carefully inspected by one of these examiners before the loan is granted. The western managers and examiners have had a successful experience of from ten to fifteen years in this line of work, and not a dollar has been lost of the millions that have passed through their hands. The fact that the company has a Boston office should not mislead any one. The company is a Kansas institution; its western managers and officers are Kansas men, on the ground, to give personal attention to the important work of making loans—the work that is the key to the safety of the whole business. The directors of the company, east and west, are among the heaviest stockholders, and have a deep interest in the success and prosperity of the company. The company urges all interested parties to examine minutely into its methods, its personnel and its general status. It begs careful inquiry of competent judges, and has no doubt of fear as to what the answer will be. The following gentlemen, who are highly regarded in financial and business circles for their executive ability, prudence and just methods are the officers, H. E. Ball, president; Geo. C. Morrell, vice president; B. R. Wheeler, secretary; P. T. Bartlett, assistant secretary; S. L. Leavitt, manager city dept.; G. J. Wilmot, general examiner; Jones & Mason, counsel; Byron Roberts, Rankin Mason, auditors; O. S. Bowman, cashier; J. P. Goggin, assistant cashier; Boston Safe Deposit and Trust Company, trustee. Directors: Wm. Lloyd Garrison, Boston, Mass.; Hon. Joshua G. Hall, Dover, N. H., ex-member of Congress, director Dover National Bank; Lewis W. Anthony, Providence, R. I.; Greene, Anthony & Co., wholesale dealers in boots and shoes, director Traders' National Bank; Isaac J. Carr, Gardiner, Me., president Gardiner National Bank; Edwin A. Smith, Providence, R. I., cashier City National Bank; W. H. Winants, Kansas City, Mo., cashier Armour Bros., Banking Company; Hon. N. C. McFarland, Topeka, Kansas, ex-commissioner General Land Office; William Sims, Topeka, Kansas, president State Board of Agriculture, vice president First National Bank; Dr. Reid Alexander, general surgeon, Chicago, Kansas and Nebraska Railway; Herbert E. Ball, president, Topeka, Kansas; George C. Morrell, vice president, Boston, Mass.; Bennett R. Wheeler, secretary, Topeka, Kansas; Sylvanus L. Leavitt, manager city department, Topeka, Kansas; director Kansas National Bank; G. J. Wilmot, general examiner, Kansas City, Mo., manager Kansas City Office; Byron Roberts, auditor, Topeka, Kansas, treasurer Shawnee County, Kansas; Rankin Mason, auditor, Topeka, Kansas, Jones & Mason, attorneys at law; B. M. Davies, Topeka, Kansas, vice president Bank of Topeka; Hon. Albert H. Horton, Topeka, Kansas, Chief Justice Supreme Court; Hon. Samuel T. Howe, Topeka, Kansas, president Kansas National Bank, ex-treasurer State of Kansas. The following statement as at the close of business October 31st, 1888, shows the company's affairs to be in a most substantial and nourishing condition: Resources: Loans secured by mortgage on real estate, $1,591,005.91; remittances for interest within sixty days, $2,181.09; other past-due interest remitted for but not paid us, $1,706.95; cash on hand and in bank, $27,813.69; special trust fund mortgage loans, $7,361.30; total, $1,825,398.54. Liabilities: Capital stock paid in, $500,000.00; surplus fund, $100,000.00; undivided earnings, $27,723.52; debenture bonds outstanding, $1,000,000.00; trust savings deposits, $6,046.16; trust fund interest account, $1,172.28; certificates of deposit bearing interest, $151,151.20; other deposits and funds awaiting investment, $136,872.58; total, $1,825,398.54. The company employs no commission men, make no loans on personal property, or second mortgages—business confined to the exclusive loaning of money on first mortgages of real estate. Deposits may be made to the credit of the Kansas Investment Company, with any of the following banks: National Bank of Redemption, Boston, Mass.; Bank of Topeka, Topeka, Kansas; Ninth National Bank, New York City; Amoskeag National Bank, Manchester, N. H.; Kansas National Bank, Topeka, Kansas; The British Linen Company Bank, Edinburgh, Scotland, and London, England; Boston Safe Deposit & Trust Company, Boston, Mass.; Central National Bank, Topeka, Kansas; Armour Bros., Banking Company, Kansas City, Mo.; Gardiner National Bank, Gardiner, Me. We would observe that the company's debenture bonds are rapidly becoming a popular form of investment with cautious and careful investors and capitalists. First: Because these bonds are negotiable by delivery, just as a government or railroad bonds, and can be sold by the holder without assignments or transfers in writing, which have to be made when mortgages are sold and transferred. Second: For purposes of collateral, the bonds are preferable to the mortgages. Third: They can be held by parties without publicity, and if any holder desires, he can cut the coupons off and send them directly to the company and receive a New York draft therefor. Fourth: The amount of security behind each series of $100,000 is $5,000 more than the par value and interest of the bonds, besides the further security found in the entire assets of the Kansas Investment Company, which in law may be exhausted to meet these bonds in case of any default by the company. These bonds are sold at par and accrued interest, and the company recommends them as the most desirable and remunerative investment that can be made in any form of western securities, and as absolutely safe as Government bonds. In conclusion it may be justly stated, that this responsible company aims solely for the absolute safety of the lender, and makes no loans to applicants who are not known to be sober, industrious and honest men with capacity to accomplish what they undertake and meet their obligations promptly.

C. S. OBER & CO., Manufacturers of Wiesbaden and Devonshire Table Sauces; New England Depot for "Scourene," Etc., Nos. 134 and 136 Commercial Street.—The increased attention given of late years in this country to the preparation of a superior quality of table delicacies, condiments, flavoring extracts and kindred specialties has resulted, as it is scarcely necessary to remark, in very notable improvement having been made in these palatable articles. Indeed, some of those engaged in this line here in Boston have achieved a signal success, and on absolute merit, too. Among those referred to, special mention should be made of C. S. Ober & Co., manufacturers of Wiesbaden and Devonshire table sauces, Ober's flavoring extracts and grocers' sundries, whose connections establishment is located at Nos. 134-136 Commercial Street, and whose productions have secured an enduring hold on popular favor throughout the country owing to the uniformly high standard of excellence at which the same are maintained. These goods are articles of exceptional merit, being noted for their choice flavor, purity and quality, and as a consequence they are in steady, extensive and growing demand in the trade. This now flourishing enterprise was started in 1878 in a rather modest way, and no better criterion of the superiority of its productions need be offered than the unequivocal success that has attended the efforts of the firm since the inception of the venture. The business premises, including salesroom and factory, occupy three 25x75 feet floors, and are well ordered and equipped in every respect, the establishment being under the capable and efficient management of W. F. Fraser. A heavy and A1 stock is constantly kept on hand, the concern being New England depot for "Scourene" and goods manufactured by George A. Moss, of New York, while a large staff of hands is employed on the premises, besides half a dozen travelling salesmen on the road, and the trade of the firm, which is principally located in the Eastern States, is of a highly gratifying character. Their trade is of that conservative class that they continually retain.

THE METROPOLIS OF NEW ENGLAND.

UNION DEBENTURE COMPANY, John C. Taylor, President; Julius L. Clarke, Secretary.—The Union Debenture Company: The almost magical growth of the state of Minnesota during the last twenty-five years has made great demands on eastern capital. There are at the present day very few sections of the country which offer more profitable, and, at the same time, more absolutely safe methods for the investment of funds than in carefully selected first-class farm mortgages in this thriving state, as also in some of its neighboring jurisdictions. In connection with these remarks, special attention is directed in this commercial review of the City of Boston, to the representative and reliable Union Debenture Company, whose office is located at Nos. 5½ Congress and 49 Water Streets. The company has likewise offices in Chicago and Minneapolis. The Union Debenture Company was incorporated under the laws of Minnesota, in 1887, with authority to commence business on a paid up capital of $100,000, which has since been more than doubled, so that its present surplus as regards patrons is upwards of $250,000. The gentlemen associated with its management are highly regarded in financial and commercial circles for their executive ability, prudence and just methods. Among its present officials are:—John C. Taylor, president; I. R. Berry, vice-president and general manager; Julius L. Clarke, secretary; A. S. Burt, assistant secretary, Hon. George C. Wing, John C. Taylor, William Oswald, A. S. Burt, Hon. Julius L. Clarke, and I. R. Berry, directors. The debenture bonds issued by this company are in denominations of $100, $500, and $1,000 at 6 per cent. interest, each series being specially and fully secured by real estate mortgages deposited with the American Loan and Trust Company of Boston. The company also issues $500 ten year investment bonds, which are sold on the installment plan and delivered on the first payment, the purchaser paying $50 a year, or $5.00 in ten years, and receiving in return $500, or a compound interest accumulation of over 9 per cent. on the investment. These bonds are non-forfeitable after two annual payments, their values with compound interest accumulations after each payment being definitely stated thereon. Being transferable, they have at all times a present market value, increasing with every year approaching maturity. For the protection of these bonds a sinking fund is specially provided, which, with the large interest accumulations realized on its mortgage investments, fully enables the company to guarantee the generous return assured to its patrons. The company confines its operations to farm mortgages chiefly in Minnesota, Nebraska and Dakota. Its stock and bond holders represent persons in every calling and condition of life; while its loaning agents are mostly bankers and stockholders in the company, and therefore personally interested in each and every loan. The following financial statement issued November 1, 1888, shows the affairs of the company to be in a satisfactory condition: Resources—Bonds and real estate securities, $458,359.45; bills and accounts receivable, $77,238.82; accrued interest, $9,527.50; office furniture, expense and supplies, $3,500.00; cash and cash items on hand and in bank, and with St. Paul Trust Company for investment, $6,467.16; total $37,558.83. Liabilities—Capital stock paid up, $216,800.00; investment bond sinking fund, debenture bonds and all other liabilities, $83,499.43; total, $286,099.49. Surplus—$16,487.51. Surplus as regards patrons, $222,687.51, being over $257 for each $100 of liability. This exhibit, which has been officially attested by proper authority, and the company's compliance with the laws of states requiring statutory supervision, coupled with the benefits so easily available to its patrons, may well claim the attention of all classes of investors.

E. B. STILLINGS & CO., Stationers and Printers, No. 55 Sudbury Street.—No Boston house has achieved a more enviable reputation than that of Messrs. E. B. Stillings & Co., the widely celebrated stationers and printers, whose office is conceded to be the best in the country for a high artistic class of printing, engraving and blank book work. Mr. Stillings established this business in 1867 and early became noted for the elegance, accuracy and durability of all jobs executed by him. The growth of trade taxed his facilities to the utmost and repeated enlargements and introduction of new and improved presses and machinery attest to not only his popularity but the determination to maintain the lead for the execution of the finest work. At No. 55 Sudbury Street Mr. Stillings has the model office of its kind. He has here twelve job presses and four Hoe presses run by steam, including the recent addition of one of Hoe's latest stop cylinder presses, costing over $6,000, adapted to the fast printing of the finest work and insuring beautiful typographical execution. With his equipment and having a staff of fifty of the most skillful and experienced workmen he offers substantial inducements to customers in every department of the stationery and printing trade. A specialty is made of the engraving and printing of bonds and stock certificates, engraved either on wood, stone or steel. They do only strictly first-class work, and among their patrons may be mentioned such concerns as "The Thomson

Houston Electric Company;" Noyes Brothers; Thayer, McNeil & Hodgkins, New York and New England Railroad, leading Masonic Lodges, Grand Army Posts, Societies, Woman's Relief Corps, etc., etc. An important department is that devoted to the manufacture of account books, ledgers, journals, day books, etc., produced to order of the very best materials, promptly and always at the most reasonable prices. Mr. Stillings is a man of inventive ability, who has effected several important improvements in his line, and has devised a system of books for keeping records and accounts, so comprehensive, handy and concise as to receive general public endorsation and which has been adopted by the Grand Army of the Republic, and Woman's Relief Corps. Mr. Stillings executes all kinds of book, commercial and job printing, and in fancy chromatic and high class circular and other letter, press as of ornamental printing, has become one of the leading representatives in New England and second to none in the United States. His energy, enterprise and skill are proverbial; his printing house is thoroughly typical of the best methods and most skillful work, and Mr. Stillings is worthy of the enviable reputation achieved and of the heavy growing trade developed in his branch of industry.

LYMAN L. KIMBALL & CO., Wholesale Fruit and Produce, Nos. 29 and 31 Richmond Street.—Among the representative houses engaged in the handling of produce and fruits at wholesale in this city is that of Messrs. Lyman L. Kimball & Co., the well known shipping and commission merchants. The proprietor of this concern, Mr. L. L. Kimball was born at Barry, Mass., forty-eight years ago, and has resided in Boston since he was seven years of age. He has been identified with the fruit and produce trade for the past thirty years, and for five years was connected with his father's establishment, Charles Kimball & Co. In 1868, Mr. Kimball started business on his own account, and removed to his present premises in 1878. The premises are very commodious and in every way admirably adapted for the purposes to which they are devoted. They are equipped with every appliance and convenience that can be suggested for facilitating the transaction of business—the receiving and storage of supplies and the shipping of orders to all points. Every description of domestic and foreign fruit and produce is handled, a leading specialty being made of potatoes. Indeed this house is the most extensively engaged in the handling of potatoes of any in the city. Consignments are received, quick sales are effected, and prompt and satisfactory returns are made.

MARKET NATIONAL BANK, Charles J. Whitmore, Esq. President; Richard H. Weld, Esq., Vice President; Josiah Q Bennett, Esq., Cashier, No. 86 State Street.—The importance of Boston as a great financial centre is forcibly demonstrated by the record and solid prosperity of her leading banks. Commercial stability is largely dependent on the extended facilities accorded by these fiscal institutions and they are intimately linked with the growth of every interest in Boston and New England. One of the oldest, and thoroughly representative in every respect is the Market National Bank, which was duly organized in 1852 as a state bank, and in 1864 was reorganized under the National Banking Act. The Market Bank has ever been a favorite with the business world, its unusually extended lines of deposits are largely those of active merchants, while it discounts much of the most desirable commercial paper on the market. The bank has a capital of $800,000 held by leading citizens, as one of the choicest and remunerative of investments. Its board of directors is as follows: Messrs. Benjamin P. Cheney, Charles W. Hubbard, George Hyde, Herbert Nash, Francis H. Raymond, Richard H. Weld, and Charles J. Whitmore. The above gentlemen are prominent and influential in commercial circles; their names are synonymous with stability and integrity, and there is no fiscal institution in the city which enjoys greater confidence, or whose management is more signally prudent or sagacious. Its president, Mr. Charles J. Whitmore, is recognized as as one of Boston's ablest financiers; an energetic and far-sighted head of the Executive, and whose services of the bank are justly appreciated. He was born in Boston and has ever accorded a hearty support to all measures best calculated to advance the city's prosperity. He is also treasurer of the Ames Plow Company, and is connected with other important enterprises. Mr. Richard H. Weld, the Vice president, is a native of Boston, and is prominently identified with her great shipping and import trade, being member of the firm of Aaron D. Wells Sons, the leading importers of hemp and sugar. Mr. Weld is an authority in financial circles, and has devoted himself indefatigably to the discharge of the onerous duties devolving upon him. The cashier, Mr. Josiah Q Bennett is a native of Somerville, Mass., and is a bank officer of the greatest practical experience, and thoroughly qualified for the duties of his responsible post. His acquaintance is most widespread throughout American financial circles, he is a vigilant officer, of sound judgment, and is a thorough exponent of the great principles governing banking and finance. Mr. Bennett is a resident of Cambridge, and is president of the Cambridge Electric Light Company, as also of the Fresh Pond Ice Company. The Market National Bank transacts a general business. It has great and remunerative lines of loans and discounts and makes extended series of collections, among its correspondents being the Hanover and Fourth National Banks of New York; the National Bank of Illinois, of Chicago, etc. The bank has safely weathered every financial crisis; its present management is eminently conservative and Boston is to be congratulated upon the possession of such a valued financial factor.

W. E. MANNING & CO., Real Estate and Mortgages, No. 266 Washington Street, (Room No. 3).—Among the best known and most responsible firms engaged in the real estate line in Boston, may be mentioned that of W. E. Manning & Co., whose office is located at No. 266 Washington Street, Room 3. Established in 1873, this popular and reliable firm has from its inception steadily won its way to public favor and confidence and numbers among its clientele some of the staunchest citizens in the community. The firm transacts a general real estate business, buying, selling, exchanging and letting city and suburban property of every description, and attends also to the collection of rents and the management of estates. Loans are procured also and mortgages negotiated, while investments are desirably placed and insurance effected in first-class fire companies, and, altogether a very fine business done. Mr. Manning, who is the sole member, the company being nominal, is a gentleman of middle age, and a native of this city. He is a man of entire probity in his dealings, as well as energy and excellent business ability, and prior to embarking in this line had been for many years engaged in manufacturers' supplies and importing and exporting chemicals and naval stores.

BREWSTER, COBB & ESTABROOK, Bankers, No 35 Congress Street.—This is an old established and thoroughly representative Boston banking house, its origin dating back to 1881, when it was founded by Brewster, Sweet & Co. They were succeeded by the firm of Brewster, Bassett & Co., and eventually in 1887 the present firm assumed the management. The individual members of this copartnership are Messrs. Henry F. Cobb, Arthur F. Estabrook, Charles E. Eddy, C. H. Watson and Arthur L. Sweetser. These gentlemen are intimately identified with the best interests of Boston, and their house has ever been a recognized exponent of just methods and legitimate enterprise in the financial world. Messrs. Brewster, Cobb & Estabrook conduct a general banking and brokerage business, and are advantageously connected with a large circle of banks, bankers and copartners in various parts of the country. They buy and sell government, state and city bonds, make collections on all available points, and also act as agents and advisers to a number of wealthy residents and capitalists. The firm have private wires to New York, Providence and New Bedford, and execute all commissions in a prompt and satisfactory manner. Messrs. Brewster, Cobb & Estabrook make a specialty of placing loans for state, city and railroad companies. The partners are popular members of the Boston and New York and Chicago Stock Exchanges. In conclusion we would observe, that they ably cover all branches of financial activity as bankers and brokers with zeal, integrity and well organized methods, which reflects great credit on the facilities, ability and resources of this responsible firm.

OCEAN STEAMSHIP BERTH COMPANY, Sole owners of the Letters Patent and Property of the Brunswick Ships' Berth Company, No. 7 Exchange Place.—The time is rapidly approaching when no person going to Europe or to foreign countries, will patronize a steamer which is not fitted with self-leveling berths. When once the traveling public has experienced the delightful repose afforded by these berths, it will demand them for ocean use, equally as much as the Pullman cars are required for land transit, for, in point of fact, the self-leveling berth is the "Ocean Pullman." In connection with these remarks we desire to make suitable reference in this commercial review of Boston, to the representative and successful Ocean Steamship Berth Company, sole owners by purchase of the letters patent and property formerly owned by the Brunswick Ships' Berth Company. The Ocean Steamship Berth Company was duly incorporated under the laws of Maine in 1887 with an authorized capital of $250,000, and since its organization at that date has already obtained a liberal and influential patronage. The executive officers of the company, are Dr. H. E. Townsend, president, and Mr. Chas. H. Tucker, Jr., treasurer. When the Pullman car was first brought to the attention of the traveler but little interest was manifested in it, and its obvious merits carelessly passed over. Many people regarded it as an extortion, and were disinclined to pay for its use, while some regarded it as an aristocratic exclusion inconsistent with the American democratic idea. For years the Pullman cars were but sparingly patronized and the railroad corporations disliked to haul them. To-day, owing to the untiring energy of the Pullman company, the public has been convinced, railroad companies have been compelled to haul them on account of the demand, and no thoroughly equipped passenger train is complete without them. Analagous to the Pullman experience is that arising from the introduction of the self-leveling berth of the Ocean Steamship Berth Company. It was with difficulty that passengers could at first be induced to try them and steamship companies be led to adopt them, and even to-day but comparatively few of the traveling public are cognizant of the merits of the berth. Numerous attempts have been made to invent a berth which should be self-leveling, that is, one that would always maintain a horizontal position no matter how great the roll of the steamer, and one that would rotate and not swing. This has only been achieved in the berth now owned by this company, and is secured to it by letters patent of the United States and foreign countries. The berths are now in use upon the steamers of the Inman and North German lines, and it is the purpose of the Ocean Steamship Berth Company to introduce them extensively and as rapidly as possible to the ocean-traveling public, affording them the greatest degree of comfort.

THE METROPOLIS OF NEW ENGLAND.

FARLEY, HARVEY & CO., Importers and Jobbers of Dry Goods, Nos. 61 and 67 Chauncy, and Nos. 39, 41 and 43 Bedford Streets.—The wholesale dry goods trade of Boston has attained proportions of the greatest magnitude, and the supremacy maintained by this city in that field of commerce is almost wholly due to the exercise of an able and energetic business policy, on the part of our leading representative houses, coupled with the ample resources at their command. One of the oldest, largest and best known houses thus referred to, is that of Messrs. Farley, Harvey & Co., located at Nos. 61 and 67 Chauncy, and Nos. 39, 41 and 43 Bedford Streets. This firm enjoys an enviable reputation as extensive importers and jobbers of dry goods. The business was founded in 1848, by Mr. N. W. Farley. In 1867 Mr. G. D. Harvey be-

came a partner and in 1880, Mr. A. C. Farley, a son of the founder, was also admitted to partnership, comprising the firm as at present constituted. The premises occupied by the firm were destroyed by fire in 1872, on Summer Street, and the present site has been occupied since 1877. Here a spacious salesroom, basement and lofts are utilized, having a frontage of eighty, and a depth of one hundred feet, where is displayed a most excellent stock in fancy and staple lines, chief among which may be named imported and domestic dress fabrics, linens, domestics and white goods, woolens, and many valuable specialities in complete assortment. Messrs. Farley, Harvey & Co., are recognized as among the most active and extensive importers in this city, being always in the forefront of the trade in securing the freshest novelties and latest patterns in all fabrics of the loom. The partners are thoroughly experienced in catering to the demands of buyers from every section of the country, and their widespread and influential trade has been developed by reason of a thoroughly enterprising, liberal and honorable business policy. A force of from fifty to sixty experienced clerks and salesmen are required for the exigencies of the business. Mr. Farley, senior came from the Granite State to Boston in 1848 and has continuously been engaged in his present line of business from that date. Mr. Harvey is also a New Hampshire man by birth, and identified with the Boston dry goods trade for many years. Mr. A. C. Farley is a gentleman in the early prime of life, and trained to the business from his boyhood. All are prominent members of the Boston Merchants' Association.

FRENCH BROTHERS, Wholesale and Retail Dealers in Provisions, Groceries, and Ship Stores, Fruit and Vegetables, Nos. 300, 202 and 204 Hanover Street.—A careful review of the business interests of Boston reveals the existence of a class of houses, prepared to compete in the several lines they represent with the rival establishments of any city in the United States. Their complete stocks, ample resources and remarkable enterprise are matters of which our citizens have every reason to be proud. In connection with these remarks, special reference is made in this commercial review to the representative and progressive firm of Messrs. French Brothers, wholesale and retail dealers in provisions, groceries, ship stores, fruit and vegetables, whose store and salesrooms are located at Nos. 300 to 204 Hanover Street. This business was established eight years ago by Messrs. Byron L. and Elmer L. French. Both partners have ever been identified with the best class of trade, and in all departments of their establishment have successfully aimed to give entire satisfaction to their numerous patrons, while at the same time they possess great practical experience in all details, and personally attend to all orders. The premises occupied comprise a superior store, having a frontage of sixty feet, by a depth of seventy feet, with a spacious basement and second floor. The store is utilized for meats, canned goods and vegetables, the second floor for groceries and ship chandlery. The different departments are arranged and fitted with special reference to the trade, which involves the handling of a vast quantity of meat, provisions, etc., and it may be safely asserted that in freshness, quality and general excellence, the stock of Messrs. French Brothers' has no superior in the city. The store is a model of neatness and cleanliness, and the provision department is supplied with a large refrigerator for the preservation of meat, etc. Messrs. French Brothers deal only in the finest groceries, teas, coffees, etc., and pay particular attention to the furnishing of vessels. In such staples as canned goods, sugars, syrups and soaps, the firm is always prepared to offer substantial inducements to patrons. They promptly and carefully fill orders at the lowest possible prices, and their trade extends not only throughout all sections of Boston and its vicinity, but also largely among the leading steamship lines. The firm employ twelve clerks, assistants, etc. Both Messrs. Byron L. and Elmer L. French were born in Vermont, but have resided in Boston for the last eighteen years, where they are highly esteemed in business circles for their enterprise, energy and integrity. To those who desire a high grade of provisions and groceries, this popular house commends itself as one that may always be implicitly relied on, to furnish only such supplies as shall rank superior in every respect.

EDWARD A. SAMUELS, Publisher of Choice Band Music, Band Books, Etc., No. 86 State Street.—The most extensive and representative band music publishing house of the city of Boston, is that of Mr. Edward A. Samuels. This business was established twenty years ago by Mr. Samuels, who has since, built up a liberal, influential and permanent patronage in all sections of the United States and Canada. Mr. Samuels publishes extensively choice band music, band books, albums for military bands, cornet and piano music, which are offered to customers at extremely low prices. He has already supplied music for 10,000 bands in the United States and Canada and his patronage is steadily increasing, owing to the superiority and excellence of his publications, which are general favorites with a critical public wherever introduced. Though the American people have not yet produced such famous musicians as Handel, Mozart and Beethoven, yet the present generation has made marked advances in musical culture. Music is an unfailing source of pleasure and a powerful means for development and advancement, and its importance to society is now universally acknowledged and recognized. This taste for music has been cultivated in no small degree by Mr. Samuels, whose publications are now everywhere recognized and appreciated by eminent musicians. The premises occupied are commodious, and the stock is systematically arranged in all departments and full and complete in every particular. Mr. Samuels is a native of Boston, well known throughout a large portion of Massachusetts and is highly esteemed by the community for his sound business principles and integrity, and has ever evinced the greatest anxiety to assist in any measure of movement, which have been brought forward to advance musical literature and studies.

ILLUSTRATED BOSTON.

NORRIS PIANO AND DIAMOND COMPANY, Dealers in Pianos and Organs, Diamonds, Watches and Jewelry, No. 37 Court Street (Opposite Court House).—These articles of universal demand in the refined, intelligent and wealthy communities of civilization—musical instruments and jewelry and precious stones, are of varying degrees of value and merit, so largely so, indeed, as to necessitate the average purchaser dealing with an honorable and responsible firm if they wish to avoid all chance of imposition and deception and rest assured that every article is absolutely as represented. In Boston, and as regards New England, the most justly celebrated and reliable concern in the above lines is the Norris Piano and Diamond Company of No. 37 Court Street. This extensive business was founded in 1852 at No. 3 Tremont Row by the late Mr. G. W. Norris, father of the

present proprietors and was continued at No. 1 Pemberton Square by the name of the Palace of Music, and, so remained until 1882 when the style was changed to the American Piano and Diamond Company, with headquarters at No. 604 Washington Street. Eventually in 1887 it was removed to the more commodious quarters, No. 37 Court Street, under the above style and title. Mr. Norris became nationally famous for the superior goods he handled and his liberal, honorable policy. Upon his lamented decease in August, 1887, he was succeeded by his sons, Messrs. L. W., A. M. and E. E. Norris, all natives of Somerville, and now residents respectively of Everett, Winthrop, and this city. They occupy very spacious, and magnificently-equipped and furnished premises, 150 feet in dimensions, where they carry a large stock of the popular Norris pianos, with a department larger than the average jewelry store devoted to their splendid and comprehensive stock of diamonds, watches and jewelry. This is the bargain store of New England for everything in the above lines. For instance pianos ranging all the way from $40 up to $600, any one of which can be purchased by paying from $5 to $25 down, and from $3 to $5 monthly thereafter. These pianos are of the company's own make, constructed of the best materials and upon the most approved principles, embodying all the modern improvements, and justly renowned for perfect action, purity and brilliancy of tone, great compass and power, and elegance and durability. The firm also sell the best organs on easy terms, do all kinds of tuning and repairing, and are leaders in this important branch of trade. This is also headquarters for the popular music boxes, of which the company imports a large assortment of all sizes from Geneva, Switzerland, and which are kept in their miscellaneous musical depot and are made a leading specialty, selling at prices ranging from $1 to $125, for cash or on instalments. Here are the best make of cornets, drums, piccolos, zithers, flutes, accordeons, guitars, banjos, violins, harmonicas, metallophones, children's pianos, etc., all at prices which, quality considered, cannot be duplicated elsewhere. This is the place to buy diamond jewelry, where the largest stock and choicest diamonds can be had at a small margin above cost. For instance, diamond rings, $5 to $400; diamond ear jewels, $10 to $600; diamond studs and collar buttons, $6 to $300, etc., etc.; also full lines of solid gold jewelry in all the latest styles. A feature of the company's business worthy of attention and affording opportunities that will be gladly availed of by many is, that diamonds, watches and jewelry at reduced prices are taken in exchange for pianos, organs, etc. Many are thus enabled to secure a piano at but slight cash outlay. Their stock of watches is equally desirable, comprising ladies' and gents' gold and silver watches from $5 to $150; also plain and fancy clocks, optical goods, etc. The warerooms are divided into three departments, viz: The piano department, under the supervision of Mr. L. W. Norris; the diamond department, under the supervision of Mr. A. M. Norris, and the small musical instruments' department, under Mr. E. E. Norris' supervision. The copartners bring to bear vast practical experience; they are leading authorities as to all goods they handle, selecting with the utmost care and selling in such enormous quantities as to be able to place prices away below those of dealers doing a limited trade. The company publishes about four months in the year, during the holiday season a very handsome eight-page paper, and which is full of interesting stories, sketches, valuable receipts and other information, besides advertisements of the company's specialties. Every one of our readers should send for a copy, and when they want a piano, or musical instrument, any jewelry, watch or clock, they can by selecting here save money and feel certain of securing the best bargain obtainable in New England. The Messrs. Norris are popular and respected business men and have ever retained the confidence of leading commercial and financial circles. In conclusion we would state, that the late Mr. G. W. Norris was the originator of the now celebrated instalment plan, having been the first to inaugurate the sale of pianos on monthly payments.

J. A. TUCKER & CO., Original Bay State Bone Super-Phosphate, No. 13 Doane Street.—The growing demand for fertilizers for agricultural operations indicates that farmers and growers of special crops have come to realize the absolute necessity of making liberal use of the best manures if they desire to derive increased returns from their lands. As in every other branch of industry in Boston, so in that of the fertilizer trade there are numerous competitors for public favor, and prominent among the number is the representative and reliable firm of Messrs. J. A. Tucker & Co., manufacturers of the Original Bay State Bone Super-Phosphate, whose office is located at No. 13 Doane Street. The firm's factory, which is fully supplied with the latest improved machinery and appliances, is situated at Chelsea. This business was established twenty-eight years ago by Mr. J. A. Tucker, who eventually, in 1880, admitted his brother, Mr. H. F. Tucker, into partnership, the firm being known by the style and title of J. A. Tucker & Co. They make a specialty of manufacturing the Original Bay State Bone Super-Phosphate, which is especially suitable for the nourishment and forcing of crops of all kinds. This super-phosphate is carefully prepared to meet a long-felt want, and is found by practical results to be absolutely unrivalled. The firm fill all orders at the lowest possible prices, and guarantee entire satisfaction to patrons. They ship direct from their factory, and their trade, which is steadily increasing, extends throughout all sections of New England and New York. Mr. J. A. Tucker was born in Dunstable, Mass., but has resided in Boston for the last thirty-nine years. He established the first post-office at East Pepperell, Mass., and was the postmaster until he retired and came to Boston. Mr. J. A. Tucker was in office under the administration of President Fillmore and remained so till he requested President Pierce, whom he knew personally, to place another man in his position. President Pierce appointed the person Mr. Tucker recommended. The position is now worth $4,400 per annum. Mr. Tucker was a member of the Boston School Board for nine years, an alderman three years, and is now President of the City Hospital Board. His brother, Mr. H. F. Tucker, is a native of Pepperell.

W. G. ROBY & CO., Metal Dealers, No. 11 Broad Street.—Copper, in its native state is generously distributed throughout the United States. Our copper mines in importance rank with iron, coal, gold and silver. A prominent and well established house, dealing extensively in metals, in the city of Boston, is that of W. G. Roby & Co., No. 11 Broad Street, who are among the oldest metal houses in the city. Their stores are fully stocked with every variety of crude and manufactured metals, which are offered to buyers at the lowest ruling market rates. Mr. Roby is also selling agent for the well known TAUNTON YELLOW METAL and COLORADO INGOT COPPER, Copper Nails, Sheet and Bolt Copper, Yellow Metal Bolts and Nails, which are unrivalled for quality and general excellence. The increasing trade of this reliable house extends throughout all sections of the United States and Canada.

THE METROPOLIS OF NEW ENGLAND.

NEW ENGLAND HOUSE, Corner Blackstone and Clinton Streets.—Boston is favored with the benefits and advantages derived from having located in her midst some of the best hotels in existence, which are recognized by travelers and experts as a true type of the modern art of hotel-keeping. One of the most popular and best-patronized is the New England House, situated at the corner of Blackstone and Clinton streets. This famous hostelry was opened about the year of 1836, and was successfully managed by numerous parties, among them being such well-known hotel men as Paran Stevens, who left it to take possession of the Revere house; Lambert Maynard who was its proprietor for twenty-eight years; Joel Gray, Bell & Bailey —the latter firm being succeeded in 1873 by the present popular proprietor, Mr. Josiah T. Wilson. These are among those whose names have been linked with the New England House in the past, and from whose fund of experience, laudable ambition and sound judgment,

many a landlord has since taken a leaf for his guidance and support. Its location is excellent. The site is the centre of all the markets, fruit and provision dealers, and in close proximity to the Faneuil Hall and Quincy markets. It is a four-story structure, conducted on both the American and European plans, and contains ninety-nine rooms for the use of guests. Its spacious and inviting dining-room has a seating capacity for one hundred and fifty persons, while a fine lunch-room is also provided, where is provided all kinds of hot meats, vegetables, tea and coffee, salads, pastry and hot lunches to order, and which is largely patronized by the general public, who are attracted by the fair prices and excellent menu. The best table for the price in Boston is set right here at the New England house. Mr. Wilson is a liberal and painstaking caterer. He believes in the best and plenty of it, and to travelers who desire the comforts of life we would recommend this old-established and deservedly popular house. Rates are but $2 and $2.50 per day on the American plan, and its service, cuisine and accommodations are unsurpassed. A word as to its host. Mr. Wilson is a native of New Ipswich, N. H., where he was born Dec. 18, 1836. At the age of fifteen he entered the hotel of his brother, Geo. A. Wilson, at Watertown, Mass., where he stayed two years. Then, desiring to learn a trade, he chose that of a machinist, and became an apprentice of Capt. Seth Wilmarth, of the South Boston Locomotive Works, where he thoroughly learned the trade in all its various departments. In 1855 he occupied the position of machinist and engineer for Messrs. Fulton & Perkins' large establishment of machinists and millwrights in Chicago, remaining there and in Fulton, Ill., until 1858, when he returned to Brighton, Mass., and entered into partnership with his brother in the then famous Brighton Hotel, continuing in the hotel business ever since. His record as a hotel man exceeds in continuous service that of any other Boniface now in Boston, while his reputation as a genial, prompt, enterprising and agreeable host is second to none in the whole country.

HIRAM WHITTINGTON & CO., Manufacturers of Horse Blankets, Carriage Robes, Etc., No. 22 Federal Street and No. 121 Congress street.—The elements of commercial success are seldom found in happier combination than in the case of Mr. Hiram Whittington of this city, who has secured for the goods manufactured and dealt in by his house such celebrity coupled with a trade of great and growing magnitude. Mr. Whittington was born in Massachusetts, and after acquiring an education, he decided to embark in commercial pursuits, and perceiving an opening in the line of better and cheaper grades of horse blankets, carriage robes, etc., he in 1878 began their manufacture under the name and style of Hiram Whittington & Co. He began with but limited experience and little or no capital, financially speaking, more than counterbalanced however by his sound judgment, great energy of character and sterling integrity. He speedily secured the recognition and patronage of the best class of the trade throughout the United States, and once introduced into any section, his horseblankets, carriage robes, saddlery and carriage hardware, rapidly enlarged their sales strictly on their merits. The substantial inducements offered by him both as to price and quality, have had their natural result, and Mr. Whittington though the youngest, is now the leading representative of any house in the above lines in Boston or New England. He manufactures horse blankets and carriage robes very extensively and of all weight and grades, adapted to every class of trade throughout the United States. Quality has ever been his first consideration and his personal attention is given to the selection of the wools, yarns, etc., for the purposes of manufacture. He has introduced the most popular original shades and patterns in robes, and the attractive array of these goods to be seen in his large establishment is sufficient evidence of his cultured, refined taste. Mr. Whittington also imports and deals heavily in all kinds of saddlery and carriage hardware, riding saddles and everything connected with these lines, all bearing the most famous brands of European and American manufacturers, and the best in their line His store is centrally located at No. 22 Federal street, running through to No. 121 Congress street, securing a double frontage, and abundance of light. A thorough system of organization is observable, and buyers can at once see any goods called for, a number of obliging and courteous clerks being always in attendance for this purpose. Mr. Whittington is a recognized authority in everything appertaining to his branch of trade, and successfully solved several problems insuring greater efficiency and security. He is the inventor of a patent hame bolt handy, simple, strong and durable, and which is now largely used by both Boston and New England street car and teaming companies. It is destined to supersede all other hame bolts for heavy harness and is such a marked improvement that will lead the trade to expect further inventions from the same source. Mr. Whittington has been a permanent resident of this city for eighteen years past, and during this period has won the confidence and esteem of the leading social and business circles of Boston. He is a type of New England's intelligent and educated young business men and to whom is so largely due the renewed spirit of capacity and ability, which permanently retains to this section its due share of national trade supremacy.

FANEUIL HALL NATIONAL BANK, J. V. Fletcher, President; T. G. Hiler, Cashier; Corner South Market Street and Merchants' Row.—The city of Boston as a great national centre of financial activity has in no branch attained such a remarkable degree of development, as the prosperity and usefulness of her banks and fiscal corporations. Their management is in the hands of men whose ability, prudence, and just methods have won the admiration and confidence of the financial world. In this connection, special reference is made in this commercial review to the old established and successful Faneuil Hall National Bank, which was originally organized in 1857 as a State Bank. In 1865 it was reorganized under the national banking laws with a paid-up capital of $1,000,000, which has been further augmented by a surplus of $330,000 and undivided profits of $60,000. The Faneuil Hall National Bank receives upon favorable terms the accounts of manufacturing firms, corporations, merchants and others. It likewise issues sight drafts available in the principal cities of the United States and Canada, makes collections on all available points, negotiates and collects bills of exchange, discounts commercial paper and attends carefully and promptly to all kinds of legitimate banking business. Its career has been a very prosperous one and closely allied with the growth and development of the city's business interests. The following gentlemen, who are widely and favorably known in financial circles for their integrity and prudence, are the officers: J. V. Fletcher, president; T. G. Hiler, cashier. Directors: J. V. Fletcher, J. H. Curtis, Ralph Warner, Chas. E. Morrison, S. S. Leannard, A. J. Adams, G. W. Fiske, and L. M. Haskins. The bank occupies spacious and handsome banking rooms in the four-story brick building fronting on Faneuil Hall Square, Merchants' Row and South Market Street. Mr. Fletcher, the president, is also president of the Belmont Savings Bank, trustee of the Belmont Public Library and is the Republican Senator to the Massachusetts Senate from the Second Middlesex District. Mr. Fletcher is an able financier, and a vigorous exponent of the soundest principles governing banking and finance. During four years membership of the Legislature of Massachusetts, he was one of the committee on banks and banking, and for the last two years has been Senate Chairman of that committee. Mr. Hiler, the cashier, has been connected with the bank for many years, and is eminently qualified for his important position. The business of this substantial bank is steadily increasing, and its deposits at the present time are about $1,600,000, while its future prospects are of the most encouraging character.

MASSACHUSETTS MUTUAL FIRE INSURANCE COMPANY, Chas. B. Cumings, President; John M. Corbett, Secretary; No. 28 State Street.—Insurance, that element in society which guarantees against loss that may arise to property or merchandise from the ravages of fire, is one of the most potent influences in the development of business activity and human progress. Of the varied phases of the principle of fire insurance none presents such popular and beneficial features, as the mutual system, of which the old established and substantial Massachusetts Mutual Fire Insurance Company is one of the most successful exponents in the United States. The main office of the company is at No. 28 State Street, Boston. This company was originally organized in 1798 and after many years of success, was reorganized and duly incorporated in 1852, under the laws of Massachusetts. The following gentlemen, who are widely and favorably known in mercantile circles for their prudence, energy, and integrity, are the officers and directors, viz: Chas. B. Cumings, president; John M. Corbett, secretary. Directors: H. H. Hunnewell, Thomas Wigglesworth, Nathaniel J. Bradlee, C. Wm. Loring, Chas. B. Cumings, George A. Gardner, William P. Kuhn, William Minot, Jr., Moses Williams, William Endicott, Jr., Peter C. Brooks, Franklin Haven, Jr., Nathaniel B. Emmons, and John L. Thorndike. The business of the company is confined to the insurance of dwellings, house property, etc. The company's statement to policy holders January 1st, 1885, was as follows: cash assets, $828,706.32; contingent assets, $147,087.60; total, $475,854.01. Liabilities (including capital and reinsurance fund), $372,126.95; cash surplus, $56,569.27; amount at risk, $19,461,560.00. Although the cost in the Massachusetts Mutual Fire Insurance Company has been less than other companies, it has always paid its losses promptly, while it need scarcely be added to prudent and able business men. that the true principle of insurance is to become your own insurer. In this carefully managed company there are no inducements to take specially hazardous risks, as the object is to save more than to make money. All policies cover against loss and damage by lightning, as well as by fire. There is a large amount of insurance in New England and the adjacents states, in which the risk is very slight, yet it is not prudent to be without protection. To this class especially this responsible company is well adapted. In conclusion we would observe that this noted corporation is in every way worthy the attention of all persons desirous of placing their property in a company's hands, which is abundantly able and makes a specialty of immediately adjusting and paying all losses as soon as they are properly determined.

J. A. CUMMINGS PRINTING COMPANY, Printers, Publishers and Stationers, No. 262 Washington Street.—In some lines of business the mere mention of the name of a house carries with it the idea of strength, reliability and success. The printing, publishing, and stationery establishment of the J. A. Cummings Printing Company, at No. 262 Washington Street, is one of this sort. The foundation of the business of this house was laid in 1868 by Mr. J. A. Cummings, who died in 1886, and in 1887 the present company was incorporated with a capital of $12,000, and with the following board of officers, viz: President, John Haskell Butler; secretary, S. Z. Bowman; treasurer, G. W. Cummings. Mr. Guy P. Cummings, son of the founder, and Mr. Wm. A. Wood are the business managers. Under such favorable auspices, the business has grown in extent and reputation until it stands well in the front rank of all the houses in New England. The business premises comprise two floors, 25x125 feet, which are thoroughly equipped with new and improved machinery and appliances, including nine presses, operated by steam power, and employment is given to from twenty-five to thirty skilled hands. In later years, while devoting prompt and skillful attention to the general mercantile line, this house has made a long step forward in the direction of the very highest class of book, illustrated catalogue and magazine work. They are also the publishers of the Knights of Honor Reporter, the best society paper in the country, with a circulation of 40,000 monthly, which is the largest of any society paper known. Its methods of business, while recognizing the competition of the hour, do not go to the length of placing its prices at the lowest rate offered for inferior work, but parties who deal with this house will find its motto to be "a fair price for fair work," and that proves the most satisfactory in the long run. The patronage is large, first-class and influential in this city and throughout New England, and it is clearly evident that both the facilities of the company and the policy of its management have met with the approval of the trade. Orders and commissions by telephone or otherwise, are given prompt and careful attention, and all transactions are placed upon a thoroughly substantial and successful basis. The officers of the company are among the best known citizens and prominent business men of Boston. The president, Mr. Butler, is a leading member of the legal profession, and is also Mr. Bowman, the secretary, who has served his fellow-men as a member of Congress. Mr. Cummings, the treasurer, is a brother of the founder of the business, and cashier of the Francestown National Bank. The curriculum embraces everything in the job printing line.

FRANCIS DOANE & CO., Manufacturers of Blank Books, Stationers, Etc., No. 116 State Street.—This business was established in 1825. In 1867 Messrs. Doane & Greenough succeeded to the management and continued it till 1884, when on the retirement of Mr. Greenough, Mr. Francis Doane became sole proprietor. The line of business includes everything required in the routine of office work, such as blank books, day books, ledgers, journals, cash books, etc., letter, note and bill heads, fine commercial printing, checks, bonds, certificates of stock, lithographic work, stationery, flexible memorandums and letter presses. Mr. Doane makes a specialty of railway, office and bank supplies, and guarantees entire satisfaction. He gives personal attention to the filling of all orders, and quotes prices in all cases very difficult to be equalled elsewhere in the city. Mr. Doane was born in Boston, and is an honorable and able business man, and is well worthy of the liberal patronage, which has rewarded his efforts.

THE METROPOLIS OF NEW ENGLAND.

JOHN POST, JR., & CO., Mechanical Engineers, Mason Building, No. 70 Kilby Street.—New England has no better source of supply in the line of steam engines for its innumerable factories and mills than that offered by Messrs. John Post, Jr., & Company, the well-known mechanical engineers, whose offices are located in the Mason building, No. 70 Kilby Street. This firm have been established in the business here since 1885, and are deservedly prominent and popular as dealers in and agents for the Ide steam engines, the Rollin steam engines, and the Weber centrifugal pump, making a leading specialty of supplying factories and large works with engines of from ten to two thousand horse power. They also contract for supplying entire plants of machinery. The engines furnished by this reliable and responsible house are noted for their simplicity, strength, durability and perfection of operations, and have no superiors in this or any other country. These engines have been furnished by this firm to Messrs. Abbott & Co., Graniteville, N. H.; the Stockinghet mill, at Manchester, N. H.; the Waterbury Watch Company, the Waterbury Clock Company, the American Mill Company, and the Smith-Gregg Manufacturing Company, all at Waterbury, Conn.; the Bridgeport Forge Company, at Bridgeport, Conn.; the P. and F. Corbin Company, at New Britain, Conn., and others. Controlling the sales of these engines throughout New England, this firm are in a position to conduct the business under the most favorable auspices and to place all transactions upon a substantial and satisfactory basis. Contracts and commissions are promptly and carefully fulfilled, and many of the incidental improvements in the engines and machinery supplied are due to the long experience and close observation of Mr. Post, who is determined that perfection shall be as nearly attained as human ingenuity can possibly achieve, in all works set up under his management. Mr. Post is a native of this city, a practical mechanical engineer of large experience and established reputation, formerly employed in that capacity for twelve years in a large cotton mill, and widely prominent as an accomplished and expert master of his profession. He is highly esteemed in the social and business circles of this city, and stands deservedly high in the esteem of the trade throughout New England.

HIRAM W. SMITH, Practical Watch Maker, and Manufacturer of Watch Oil, No. 187 Washington Street.—Mr. Hiram W. Smith, was born in Cornish, N. H., and has been identified with the watch making trade for more than half a century. In 1840 he left his native state to come to Massachusetts, and for thirty-eight years he has been in business on his own account in the locality where he is now located. For office and salesroom he occupies the second floor of the building, which is attentively and appropriately fitted up. Here is displayed a large, fine stock of watches of foreign and domestic manufacture, and the trade which is chiefly of a wholesale character, extends to all parts of the country. Far more than thirty years Mr. Smith has also been engaged in the manufacture of watch oil that, as yet, has met with no equal in the market, and is largely used in the principal watch factories of the country and by the trade generally. This oil is taken from the head of black fish, and is free from acids and glutinous substances, so that it will remain for years perfectly limpid in all climates. As a lubricant for chronometers and watches it has no competitor. The following correspondence will explain itself:—"New York, Jan. 17, 1888. Dear Sir:—Kindly let me know what oil is used on the Waterbury watches at their factory. It is apparently a good one. Yours truly, J. P. Delany." An inquiry in response to above brought the following reply: "The Waterbury Watch Co., Waterbury, Ct., Feb. 1, 1888. Mr. A. Curtis Bond, Editor of The Waterbury—Dear Sir:—For the past two years we have used a watch oil prepared by Hiram W. Smith, No. 187 Washington Street, Boston Mass. Previous to the fall of 1886, we were having trouble with and complaints from the different oils we were then using. From the watchmakers employed in some of the oldest and best-known houses in New York and Boston, we heard such good reports concerning this oil that we concluded to give it a trial, and since then we have used no other. We have put it to the severest test—have found it to stand on our chronometers for over a year and to remain sweet, clear and limpid. As we repair our make of watches we have a good opportunity of witnessing the results on them, and we find that this oil does not gum like most of the other oils which we had previously tried. Mr. Smith is an old and favorably known watch repairer, and experienced the difficulties which all of his craft do in procuring a reliable oil, and solved the problem after years of experimenting. We cheerfully pay the tribute to the product, and trust that the retail dealer who makes the inquiry of you, and all other retail watch dealers who appreciate the need of a good, reliable watch oil, will send to Mr. Smith for a trial bottle as we did. Very truly yours, F. A. Locke, secretary."

CHAS. E. HALL & CO., Manufacturers and Importers of Marble, Nos. 69 to 93 Charlestown Street.—Among the representative and reliable manufacturers and importers of marble in the city of Boston is the old established and successful firm of Messrs. Chas. E. Hall & Co., whose office, salesrooms and works are eligibly situated on Charlestown Street. This business was established a quarter of a century ago by Mr. Chas. E. Hall. In 1868 Mr. M. Moran became a partner, and in 1888 Messrs. W. J. Coogan, F. L. Maguire and M. J. Driscoll were admitted into partnership, the firm being known by the style and title of Chas. E. Hall & Co. The works have an area of 18,000 square feet, and are fully equipped with the latest improved machinery and appliances. Here 250 skilled artisans are employed, and the machinery is driven by a powerful steam engine. Messrs. Chas. E. Hall & Co. import extensively the finest Italian, and deal also in Vermont and Tennessee, and all the other American marbles. They manufacture all kinds of mantels, altars, dados, tiling, plumbers' slabs, soapstone sinks and tubs and all kinds of interior marble and soapstone work. The firm are prepared to furnish any grade of marble work from the plainest to the most elaborate. Their references in Boston are S. S. Pierce's new building, Huntington Avenue; Safe Deposit Vaults, No. 87 Boylston Street; Hermann Building, Tremont Street; The Boston Tavern; Houghton & Dutton's new building; Boston Post Office and Sub-Treasury; Boston Custom House. Elsewhere: Union Railway station, Portland, Me.; State War and Navy Department, Washington, D. C.; United States Court House and Post Office, Nashville, Tenn.; United States Court House and Post Office, Utica, N. Y.; United States Court House and Post Office, Austin, Texas; United States Appraisers Stores, San Francisco, Cal. Estimates are promptly furnished and contracts taken for work of any magnitude, while care, reliability and moderate prices are always guaranteed. The partners are all natives of Massachusetts. They are highly regarded in trade circles for their artistic skill, industry and just methods. Their patronage extends throughout the United States and Canada and is steadily increasing owing to the superiority of their productions.

H. M. BATES & WALLEY, Stock Brokers, No. 53 State Street.—Among the most enterprising and popular firms of stock brokers in Boston are Messrs. H. M. Bates & Walley, whose experience, perfected facilities and influential connections entitle them to the continued confidence and patronage both of operators and investors. The business was established upwards of twenty-two years ago by Mr. H. M. Bates and Henshaw D. Walley. In 1876 Messrs. Bates and Walley formed the existing copartnership and bring to bear every qualification for the carrying on of a stock commission business. They bring to bear the ablest range of practical experience, perfected facilities and influential connections in all the leading financial centres of the country. They transact a general business, promptly filling all orders for the purchase or sale of bonds, stocks, or miscellaneous securities exclusively on commission, and through their correspondents promptly execute all orders in New York, Philadelphia and San Francisco, giving the utmost care and attention to the interests of their customers, who include a number of the leading capitalists and investors of New England and Boston. Mr. Bates has been an active member of the Boston Stock Exchange since 1866, he and Mr. Walley enjoy the confidence and esteem of the leading financial circles and are worthy representatives of the Boston stock market. The firm's offices are centrally located in the Merchants' Exchange Building, and orders and inquiries relating to extended investments receive the immediate personal attention of the partners, and no house is better able to attend to the interests of customers either in the city or in any section of New England than that of this honorable and responsible firm.

NATIONAL MORTGAGE AND DEBENTURE COMPANY, Samuel N. Brown, President; George May, Treasurer; No. 50 State Street.—This company is the only corporation of the kind, having a Massachusetts perpetual charter. It was organized in 1886 with an authorized capital of $500,000, of which $250,000 has been paid in. The following gentlemen, who are widely and favorably known in financial and mercantile circles for their prudence, executive ability and integrity are the officers and directors, viz: Officers, Samuel N. Brown, president; William P. Fowler, vice-president; George May, treasurer; Carroll N. Beal, general manager; Geo. Y. Johnson, general agent. Directors: Samuel N. Brown, of Fairbanks, Brown & Co., No. 83 Milk street, Boston; William P. Fowler, lawyer, No. 50 State Street, Boston; George May, treasurer (formerly cashier First National Bank, St. Johnsbury, Vt.); Carroll N. Beal, manager (president Kansas Mortgage Company); Frank R. Cordley, of Young & Fuller, No. 1-3 Devonshire Street, Boston; Chas. W. Hatch, of Hatch & Woodman, State and Kilby Streets, Boston; Charles A. Rogers, of Rogers & Co., Milk Street, corner Pearl; Samuel B. Heywood, president People's Savings Bank, Worcester, Mass.; Elias S. Beals, of Beals, Torrey & Co., Boston, North Weymouth and Milwaukee; John R. Mulvane, president of Bank of Topeka, Topeka, Kansas; Charles P. Searle, lawyer, No. 70 Kilby Street, Boston; Charles L. James, James & Abbot, No. 97 State Street, Boston; Charles J. Glidden, treasurer Erie Telephone Co., Lowell, Mass. This responsible company has likewise made arrangements, whereby the interests and capital of the Kansas Mortgage Company have been consolidated with those of the National Mortgage and Debenture Company. The Kansas company was one of the earliest pioneers, having begun loaning money upon farms and improved city properties in the west in 1869 as a private firm, and continued actively therein to the date of consolidation two years ago. Its career has been marked by success and conservatism, while the results have been highly satisfactory to all who have had business relations with it. The National Mortgage and Debenture Company is only authorized by its charter. First—To make loans of money secured by first mortgage or deed of trust upon real estate. Second—To sell and dispose of the securities so taken, and guarantee the payment thereof. Third—To issue collateral trust or debenture bonds, and secure the payment of the same by the assignment of the securities owned by it. In the transaction of the business it is authorized to pursue the corporation is required to so conduct its affairs:—First—That no loans be made for a sum greater than half the cash value of the property securing the same. Second—That all moneys loaned shall be secured by mortgages or deeds of trust, which are perfect first liens upon the property covered thereby. Third—That the securities assigned for the benefit of the holders of the company's collateral trust, or debenture bonds, shall exceed the amount of such bonds in the ratio of one hundred to ninety. Fourth—That a guarantee fund, equal to one-fourth of the capital of the company, must be created and kept invested in only such securities as the savings banks of Massachusetts are permitted to invest in. Fifth—That all real estate acquired by the corporation, through enforcing the collection of any loan made, shall be sold within a reasonable time. The corporation is also required by its charter, to make stated returns to the Secretary of the Commonwealth, showing its true condition, and is at any and all times subject to be audited and examined by the Commissioner of Corporations, who is authorized to take proceedings in the interest of the holders of the corporation's securities whenever, in his judgment, it is necessary to do so. Through a complete consolidation of interests, Kansas Mortgage Co., of Topeka has now become the general western department of the National Mortgage and Debenture Co., and its capable and experienced force is now engaged in making loans, which form the basis of the business of both companies, that of furnishing investors with an unusually desirable line of high class securities as follows: first mortgage loans and collateral trust bonds. Trust conditions: As trustee for the bondholders and custodian of the pledged collaterals, an old and favorably known eastern corporation, the Boston Safe Deposit and Trust Company, has been selected, and has entered into a written agreement whereby it undertakes that no bonds shall be certified save those for which collateral deposit has been made; to inspect the mortgages as deposited, and accept none for the trust save those which fully

conform to the standard fixed by the agreement; to maintain the proper ratio between the outstanding certified bonds and the collateral deposit, and, in emergency, to realize upon the deposit, either by sale or collection, and use the proceeds in redemption of the bonds. Each bond issued by the corporation recites the trust conditions on its face, and bears a certificate from the trustees to the effect that it is one of the bonds referred to and that the collateral deposit, to secure payment thereof, has been duly made. The collateral deposit: The mortgage loans which make up the collateral trust deposit are carefully selected by the investing department of the company, and are secured by first mortgage upon choice productive properties in the best agricultural sections of the country. With every possible legislative safeguard thrown around its operations, backed by ample capital, having an extensive acquaintance in, and full information concerning all the desirable fields for investment, and the practical knowledge requisite to the proper management of the interests of its clients, the corporation invites those having funds to place at interest to give the securities which it offers fair consideration, and will cheerfully furnish all who ask, by letter or in person, the fullest information concerning its methods, and the results already attained; and by adhering to those lines, which long experience has clearly proven thoroughly safe and legitimate, and which have uniformly produced the desired results, it can confidently assure all its patrons of the future of such funds as may be committed to its care. Full information regarding the company's bonds will be sent upon application, and all inquiries relative to fields of operation, business methods, etc., are cheerfully replied to. Besides the general offices of the company its securities are on sale at various places throughout the country, notably: L. W. Parker, Rooms Nos. 31 and 32, Clark's Block, Natick, Mass; J. M. Boardman, Belfast, Maine; C. C. Chapman, Oxford Building, Portland, Maine; Warner & Cocks, No. 45 Broadway, New York; Rupert & Philips, Westminster, Pa.; W. A. Stone, No. 27 White's Opera House, Concord, N. H.; James D. Lane, No. 21 Wieting Block, Syracuse, N. Y.; L. B. Tillotson, Cazenovia, N. Y.; Maynard Sumner, Merchants National Bank, Rockland, Maine; Alex. D. Lorie, No. 72 Westminster Street, Providence, R. I.; Blake, Barrows & Brown, No. 9 Central Street, Bangor, Maine; R. L. Scott, Westfield, Mass.; L. L. Keith, Machias, Maine; Frank Nelson, Calais, Maine; N. D. Nutt, Eastport, Maine; John H. Humphreys, Bath-Savings Institution, Bath, Maine; E. W. Swift, First National Bank, Provincetown, Mass.; general western office, Kansas Mortgage Co., No. 109 Sixth Avenue, East Topeka, Kansas.

A. N. REYNOLDS & CO., Manufacturers and Dealers in Fine Oils, No. 202 Atlantic Avenue.—A representative house is that of Messrs. A. N. Reynolds & Co., the well-known manufacturers and dealers in fine oils for all purposes, lubricating compounds and greases, which has been in successful operation for a period of twelve years, and enjoys a large and influential trade, at both wholesale and retail, in this city and throughout all the New England States. The premises occupied comprise a spacious store and basement, and unsurpassed facilities are at hand for handling and storing the immense and valuable stock that is here carried. This stock comprises all kinds of illuminating, engine, spindle, sperm, lubricating, linseed and other oils, compounds and greases, which are of the best quality known to the trade. The oils offered by this firm have from the first been recognized as the best that can be used for cylinder, engine, spindle and general machinery works, and are all guaranteed pure and maintained at the highest standard of excellence. The lubricating compound of this firm is the outcome of the demand of machinery users for a lubricant that would effectually prevent wear and tear and give the best results with the greatest economy. It is warranted not to gum nor to contain any acid or deleterious substance. It requires less attention and lasts many times longer than anything of the kind in the market. The trade of the house in these valuable specialties has developed to great proportions, including among its customers numerous leading mill and factory corporations, railway and steamship companies, steam users and manufacturers all over New England. Mr. Reynolds, the active member of the firm, was born in New York State, and is a member of the Boston Oil Association and stands very high in all circles.

THE QUINCY, Geo. G. Mann, Proprietor.—The Quincy is one of the representative institutions and a feature of Boston, and as a magnificent hotel has no rival anywhere in the United States, combining as it does in the most perfect manner every comfort, elegance and convenience with the refined, quiet atmosphere of the best circles of home life. The Quincy was established seventy years ago and has always been a favorite stopping place for the eminent in every profession, branch of business, and those in public life. Repeated enlargements of this fine hotel have at different periods been necessitated to meet the growing demands of the public, and it is now one of the largest on the continent. Its internal arrangements and furnishings are also of the best, and the house under the able, experienced proprietorship of Mr. George G. Mann, is the best kept, most popular and comfortable hotel in New England. In 1874, Mr. J. W. Johnson and Mr. George G. Mann became sole proprietors under the name and style of J. W. Johnson & Co., and it was under their vigorous, capable régime

hotel of vast dimensions, its seven floors covering an area of 23,000 square feet each, and there are 500 rooms for guests, adapted to every requirement, and many arranged en suite, meeting the wants of families and prominent guests. The utmost care and attention has been bestowed in their fitting up and furnishing, and they offer the most comfortable accommodations in Boston. The Quincy is conducted jointly on the American and European plans, and in either case the house offers substantial inducements not duplicated elsewhere. The cuisine of the Quincy is under the constant study of the most famous of caterers, while a French chef and experienced staff of assistants, meet the demands of the elaborate bills of fare for which this representative house is so renowned. In fact the great feature of this house is the table, which is unsurpassed by any first-class hotel on the continent. Every thing is on the most liberal scale and immense quantities of supplies are used, the beef of the hotel for one year being $25,000, from $400 to $500 per week being spent for poultry, while eighteen to twenty-two bushels

J. W. Johnson, George G. Mann.

THE QUINCY.

AMERICAN AND EUROPEAN PLANS.

500 ROOMS.

J. W. Johnson & Co.

that the Quincy began to make such rapid progress. Both proprietors were exceedingly popular, and both had mastered every detail of the modern art of hotel keeping. The lamented decease of Mr. Johnson occurred in 1886, since which date, Mr. Mann as proprietor has efficiently carried on the business and run the hotel at the same high standard of excellence. The Quincy is a magnificent specimen of architectural achievement, its solid and ornate stone front, rising to a height of seven stories, surmounted by an elegant buttressed clock tower, and having on one side, a series of beautiful bow windows capped by dome and flagstaff, which is 128 feet six inches in length, and one solid piece. No pains or expense have been spared in the fitting up of the interior. Every modern accessory of the decorator, the cabinet maker and the upholsterer have been utilized, and the house is a beautiful and artistic exhibit of the most advanced achievements in the above lines. Marble wainscots and stair-cases, mosaic tiled floors, frescoed ceilings, elaborately decorated walls and furniture in keeping, characterize the public apartments and corridors of the Quincy. It embraces every modern improvement, gas, electric light, safety passenger and freight elevators, which run day and night, and guests coming by late trains, at three and four o'clock in the morning, can take the elevator to the seventh story, electric bells, etc., being a few of the conveniences, while under one roof are gathered all the accessories to complete hotel life. In the basement is the engine room, a large steam laundry, barber shop fitted up at an expense of $20,000, and gents' toilet fitted up at an expense of $10,000, ceiling and walls of solid mirrors, and solid marble, no wood work except door and seat. On the main floor are the office, bar and cafe carrying the choicest stock in Boston; billiard room, smoking room, etc. On the second floor are the magnificently furnished suits of parlors, luxurious in their equipment, likewise handsome club-rooms. The spacious and attractive dining hall is on the first floor, with the finest restaurant in Boston attached. The Quincy is a

of potatoes are used in a day, the potatoes being purchased by the car load of 3,000 bushels. Three tons of butter per month is used and from 100 to 150 dozens of eggs per day. Twenty tons of sugar is bought in one order and canned goods are bought by the car load, the house itself putting up 100 bushels of pears to the table each season. Flour is bought by the 600 barrels or car load, and every thing else is done on the most magnificent scale. All the preserves served here are home made, a specialty being made of strawberry juice for ice cream, of which about 200 gallons is kept on hand in cold storage, (while most hotels use some artificial coloring to produce the same effect,) and which is a delicious fruit for the table. All the beef used in the Quincy is selected by Mr. Geo. G. Mann, who is one of the best judges of meat. This beef is put in cold storage from three to four weeks before being used, they having thirteen immense ice houses in the hotel, which takes from ten to thirty tons of ice per day. Mr. Mann has made a life study of the cuisine, covering a period of over twenty-five years. The wines, liquors and cigars handled are of a superior quality, and in fact everything connected with the house is of the very best. Many notable dinners have been held here in honor of the great men in every branch of public, literary or dramatic life, and the most celebrated statesmen, authors, actors, members of the European aristocracy, clergy, etc., have been and are now guests of the Quincy when in Boston. The registers contain thousands of the prominent names of the age, and under Mr. Mann's able management, the Quincy is, as never before enjoying a patronage of the most extensive and profitable character. Mr. Mann is noted for his superior executive methods and watchful attention to enforcing a thorough system of management, this hotel with upwards of 300 help and servants running smoothly and in perfect order, a fact often spoken of by parties stopping at the house, meeting the wants of the traveling public, and at rates which are extremely moderate, the unrivalled character of the accommodations being considered.

JAMES GOODMAN & CO., Fire Insurance Agency, No. 46 Congress Street.—The city of Boston is one of the principal centres in the United States for fire insurance. This, all agree, can be secured only through the medium of well regulated, honestly conducted and sound fire insurance companies; those that not only issue policies, but adjust and pay losses as soon as they are stated and clearly shown. Many of the leading insurance corporations place their interests in the control of gentlemen who have secured honorable reputations in this important branch of business. Prominent among those in Boston, is the old established and reliable firm of Messrs. James Goodman & Co. This business was originally established in 1848 by Kent & Parsons, who were succeeded by Kent & Goodman. Eventually, in 1872, on the death of Mr. Kent Mr. James Goodman admitted his son, Mr. W. A. Goodman into partnership, the firm being known by the style and title of James Goodman & Co. The firm represents the following first-class and substantial companies, viz:—The Glens Falls, of Glens Falls N. Y., Fire Insurance Company of the County of Philadelphia; Merchants' and Farmers' Mutual, of Worcester, Mass., etc. As practical and experienced underwriters, Messrs. James Goodman & Co. are prepared to offer substantial inducements and advantages to patrons including low rates and liberally drawn policies, while all losses sustained are equitably adjusted and promptly paid through their agency. They undertake the entire charge of the insurance of estates, stores, office blocks, dwellings, merchandise, and business firms, placing and distributing risks among sound, and reliable companies only, renewing policies when expired and generally relieving property owners and merchants of all care and trouble in this important respect. Mr. James Goodman has been a director of the Merchants' & Farmers' Mutual Insurance Company, of Worcester, since 1876. He was for many years special agent of the Merchants' Fire Insurance Company, and for three years was secretary of the Charter Oak Fire Insurance Company, of Hartford, Conn. He is a popular member of the Underwriters' Association of Boston, while his son, Mr. Wm. A. Goodman, is a member of the rate committee of the same association. Mr. James Goodman was born in Springfield, while Mr. W. A. Goodman is a native of New York. The former was for a period of three years connected with the city government as councilman, and during that time never was absent at a meeting, never failed to respond at roll call, and never left the meeting until adjournment.

KENNETH IRVING, Flour and Mill Products, and Millers' and Shippers' Agent, No. 214 State Street.—The activity and progress shown in the Boston flour and grain market is largely due to the enterprise and energy of our leading brokers and commission merchants. Prominent among this number is Mr. Kenneth Irving, flour broker, millers' and shippers' agent, at No. 214 State Street. Mr. Irving established his business in 1884. He transacts a general brokerage and commission business and is especially well known in this market as agent for flour mills and grain shippers in all parts of the west, north-west and New York State. He sells car-lots only and has developed a large and growing trade in the city and throughout the New England States, Maritime Provinces and Canada. He has every facility for doing the business in the best manner possible, and his long experience with and knowledge of the wants of the buyers, makes him a most useful correspondent. Correspondence is desired and consignments are in all cases carefully and profitably handled, and promptly acknowledged. The influence of this house on the trade is steadily on the increase, and those interested in establishing relations with it may depend on receiving prompt and liberal treatment, and other advantages difficult to be secured elsewhere. Mr. Irving, who is a native of Nova Scotia, has also had a long business experience in the west, the benefits of which to the customers who do business through him is manifested in many ways. He is an active member of the Boston Chamber of Commerce, always manifesting a deep interest in all measures conducive to the welfare of that important institution.

FRANKLIN S. PHELPS, Insurance Agent, No. 53 State Street, Room 4 Merchants Exchange.—At the present day the protection afforded by the leading fire insurance companies, is without question one of the most potent influences in the development of trade and commerce. In this connection we desire to make special reference in this commercial review of Boston, to Mr. Franklin S. Phelps, state agent for Massachusetts for the Mutual Fire Insurance Co. of New York, and the Fire Association of New York, whose offices are centrally located at No. 53 State Street. Mr. Phelps established this business in 1885, and has now a number of suburban and local agents under his control. The Mutual Fire Insurance Co. returns the entire profits of its business to policy holders in scrip, without liability to assessment. The scrip issued in 1883 was redeemed August 1st, 1886, at par with 6 per cent. accrued interest. The Fire Association of New York returns to policy holders 80 per cent. of the profits without liability to assessment. In addition to attending to his insurance business, Mr. Phelps deals in Georgia farm and real estate first mortgages, and has always completed loans on hand and for sale at his offices. The terrible shrinkage in nearly all kinds of securities, and the constant and increasing failures of banks, and disasters to railroad and manufacturing companies, have justly created distrust, and careful, far-seeing capitalists of the north are now turning their attention southward where reliable and safe investments in real estate loans can be made at eight per cent. interest. Mr. Phelps is the Boston agent for Mr. C. P. N. Barker, of Atlanta, Georgia, who is not only a wealthy capitalist, but has given his attention for upwards of a quarter of a century to real estate first mortgages. Mr. Phelps is highly esteemed in business circles for his promptness, ability and just methods, fully meeting the influential patronage secured in this growing and valuable enterprise.

C. FOSTER & SON, Provisions and Groceries, Meats, Produce and Fruits, Nos. 336 and 338 Atlantic Avenue, Head of Rowe's Wharf.—An old established and excellent general provision and grocery store is that of C. Foster & Son, located at Nos. 336 and 338 Atlantic Avenue, which for over thirty-six years has maintained an enduring hold on public favor and patronage. It is, in fact, one of the oldest and best known establishments of the kind in this part of the city, and has a very large and growing trade. This flourishing business was started in 1852 by Christopher Foster, the present senior member, who conducted the same alone up to 1882, when he admitted into partnership his son Henry W. Foster. The firm occupy a fine 25x160 foot store and basement. They were formerly located at Liverpool Wharf, where they were burned out in the big fire of 1872. They carry constantly on hand an extensive first class stock, which comprises prime fresh beef, mutton, lamb, and pork, corned, salt and smoked meats of all kinds, lard and provisions, choice creamery butter, cheese and fresh eggs, fruits and vegetables of every variety, fine teas, coffees and spices, canned goods, dried fruit, best brands of western flour, and everything comprehended in staple and fancy groceries; yacht and family supplies being a specialty. About fifteen in help are employed, while several teams are in regular service supplying customers throughout Dorchester, Roxbury and all parts of the South End and Back Bay, and during the summer months keep several teams running to Hull and Nantasket Beach. Orders by telephone (No. 1201) or otherwise receive immediate attention.

G. H. LLOYD, Manufacturing Optician, No. 325 Washington Street.—There is probably no business requiring a greater degree of intelligence than that of the manufacturing optician, and among those in Boston there are probably none more fully conversant therewith, than Mr. G. H. Lloyd who has devoted many years to perfecting himself with all that pertains to it. He commenced operations on his own account in February last, and has since become well known to the medical profession and among oculists, and is doing a large, steadily growing business. His establishment at No. 325 Washington Street, is perfectly fitted up and is well equipped in every particular. Mr. Lloyd, who is an expert optician, manufactures to order, complicated lenses, and has all the latest improvements in spectacles and eyeglasses, and makes to order trial sets of glasses and has a general assortment of many designs in trial frames, and is a practical expert in adjusting glasses to suit the sight of the eye, and also inserts artificial eyes, and repolishes old artificial eyes and makes a fine display of all kinds of optical goods. Mr. G. H. Lloyd, is a native of Nova Scotia, and has lived in Boston many years.

THE METROPOLIS OF NEW ENGLAND.

THE BOSTON TAVERN, No. 347 Washington Street (Within), M. P. Robinson and J. A. Fitzsimmons, Proprietors.—In speaking of the relative merits of New York and Boston hotels, their capacity, management and methods, it must now be stated, as an important and highly creditable fact, that Boston has far the most magnificent and luxurious gentlemen's hotel, there being nothing like it, either in New York or anywhere else on the continent. This splendid consummation of hospitable ideas with practical business methods and marked ability of management is embodied in the already popular and deservedly famous Boston Tavern, located at No. 347 Washington Street (within), which location furnishes quietness, although situated in the very business centre of the city, like the largest banking houses and hotels in London. This hotel is the only one in Boston so located, and first threw open its doors on January 26th, 1889. It is an important event to chronicle in Boston history, as on this historic site is reared one of the finest specimens of architecture in the city, specially planned, arranged and designed throughout its imposing eight stories, as the model bachelor's hostelry of America. Work on the tavern was begun in September, 1887, the owner, deciding to erect here a structure that would fully meet the most advanced requirements of the lessees, Mr. Marvin P. Robinson and Mr. James A. Fitzsimmons, both Boston hotel men of vast practical experience in the highest plane of the business. The building, which cost fully $250,000, is eight lofty stories in height. On the east it fronts on Ordway Place for 85 feet; the north side has a frontage of 66 feet on Province Court, while the other sides have abundance of light and air, rendering it exceptionally desirable for guests. The area of floor space is about 5,000 square feet; the exterior is of brick, with handsome Ohio freestone trimmings, and the height from curb to roof is 102 feet. The architect, Mr. Samuel J. F. Thayer, in planning the Boston Tavern, made a special study to secure to every room windows opening into the outside air, and to insure the house being absolutely fireproof. He has succeeded admirably, and future hotel architects can profitably study the Boston Tavern in detail. The exterior of the first story is of iron columns filled in with brick, while above are thick vaulted walls of brick and freestone. The floors of the building are laid upon iron beams and terra cotta arches, and all interior partitions are of incombustible materials. The floors and walls, being vaulted and deadened, the rooms are practically sound-proof. The interior was planned in consonance with the suggestions of the lessees, whose long practical experience has rendered them recognized authorities. The office, cafe, bar and smoking rooms are situated on the ground floor, and are reached direct from the main entrance. The air of quiet elegance and refined taste that characterizes these apartments has no equal elsewhere in Boston. The walls are finished in light-tinted marble; the wainscots and trimmings are of mahogany, while the floors are paved with marble tiles to match the walls. In the smoking-room is hung Pope's mammoth oil painting, "The Calling of the Hounds," while in the cafe is one of Gallison's marine views. The cafe comfortably seats 100 guests. The kitchen and serving rooms are close adjoining, and models in their line, thoroughly ventilated, so that no odors reach other parts of the house. The magnificent banquet rooms are desirably situated on the second floor. They are the most advanced exponents of architectural skill and decorators' and furnishers' arts. The suite can be thrown into one grand hall, having a seating capacity of over 150. There are 125 elegantly furnished rooms for guests, including many en suite, with toilet room and bath attached, while each floor has a separate bath-room and closets accessible from the corridors. Every modern improvement known to science has been introduced here, including two safety passenger elevators, electric light, electric bells, steam heat, etc. The sanitary appliances are perfect, all pipes being thoroughly trapped and ventilating through the roof. This is the beau ideal home for gentlemen—the most advanced of its kind in America—and which has become instantly popular with and patronized by the leading circles of male society. The cuisine is the most elaborate in Boston; the culinary arrangements are perfect, being under the guidance of the distinguished chef, August Grosselli. A thorough system of organization is enforced and the service of the Tavern is unrivalled. Mr. Marvin P. Robinson has had vast experience in the highest plane of hotel management, and resigned the chief clerkship of the Hotel Brunswick to take the proprietorship with Mr. Fitzsimmons here. He was formerly connected with the Tremont and other first-class hotels, and is noted for the highest order of executive capacity and energy of character. Mr. James A. Fitzsimmons materially contributed to the prosperity of the Parker House during his thirty years' experience therewith, having the advantages of a training under Mr. Harry D. Parker. He resigned from a responsible post in the St. James Hotel, New York, to join forces with Mr. Robinson in conducting the Boston Tavern, and is specially qualified for the post. The proprietors have secured experienced and popular assistants in Mr. S. B. Sabin, cashier, Mr. H. P. Doane, chief clerk, and Mr. C. W. Bickford, chief steward. This harmonious and talented executive force insures the utmost degree of comfort to guests. Messrs. Robinson and Fitzsimmons have thoroughly mastered the difficult art of modern hotel keeping. They are in the front rank of the business, and have a certainty of achieving an international reputation.

BRINE & NORCROSS Reliable Stores, Hosiery, Gloves, Small Wares, Etc., Nos. 17 and 18 Tremont Row, Nos. 7 and 7½ Tremont Street, Nos. 1 and 3 Tremont Street and Nos. 60 and 62 Washington Street.—A house that has been established for ninety years must necessarily engage and attract more than ordinary attention from the compilers of this review of the commerce and industries of the city of Boston. Such an establishment is that of Messrs. Brine & Norcross, whose extensive haberdashery establishments are eligibly located. This widely-known and representative house was established in 1798, by J. Leach, in the old Scollay Building (formerly located where the statue now stands), who was succeeded by J. Holmes & Co. and John Harrington and William H. Brine under the style and title of John Harrington & Co. This firm carried on business with great success for twenty-two years, when Mr. William H. Brine and J. Henry Norcross formed the present co-partnership, Mr. J. Henry Norcross had previously been a member of the firm of Lewis Coleman & Co., for fifteen years. The stores are spacious and as elegantly equipped, and possess every convenience for the accommodation of the extensive and valuable stock, which has no superior in this country for quality, freshness, reliability and general excellence. Two hundred assistants, salesladies, etc., are employed in the various departments, and the stores are the favorite resorts of ladies of every class of society. The stock, which has been carefully selected, includes all kinds of haberdashery goods, small wares, fancy goods, gloves, laces, tapes, pins, needles, thread, hosiery, jewelry, etc. The firm have brought into every-day practice a thoroughly efficient system of organization, which conduces greatly to the successful prosecution of this extensive business. The stock is always complete in every department, and is constantly renewed by fresh importations, and something new, beautiful and useful can always be found upon the shelves and counters, while the prices quoted in all cases are extremely moderate. Messrs. Brine and Norcross are both natives of Boston. They are very popular, socially and commercially, and bear the highest of reputations as business men and private citizens.

INGALLS, BROWN & CO., Leather, No. 137 Summer Street.—In referring to the business transacted in leather in Boston we have particular occasion to note the house of Ingalls, Brown & Co. It was established in 1845. Mr. John B. Ingalls, who has been identified with the trade for more than eighteen years, and Mr. S. H. Brown, Jr., who has also had a long experience in the business, compose the firm. They are both natives of New England, and conduct their operations with that energy and careful attention, which has always distinguished them in their dealings and which have been the means of establishing the prestige and reputation the house enjoys in commercial circles. They represent leading manufacturers of goat, kid and morocco of southern finish, and are well equipped for meeting the demands of the boot and shoe manufacturers, and control a large substantial permanent trade, widely diffused throughout New England. The business connections of the firm are first-class and the goods which they handle are superior in quality and very desirable. The house will be found one of the best with which to form business relations, as the very lowest market prices are always quoted.

YOUNG'S HOTEL, J. Reed Whipple, Esq., Proprietor; Court Square and Court Street.—Boston has of recent years made rapid progress and notably so in the character of her hotel accommodations. She is now, with the enlarged and magnificent Young's Hotel in her midst, fully the equal of New York with its famous old Fifth Avenue Hotel. For what that centre of social resort and of the best classes of the traveling public is to New York, Young's is to Boston. Young's Hotel has an interesting history. It was originally, and that was many years ago, known as Tafts Coffee House, and it was in 1865 that Mr. George Young succeeded to the proprietorship, renaming the establishment Young's Hotel. He then entered upon a lengthy and prosperous career, noted for being a comfortable stopping place and its patronage at times taxing its limited capacity to the utmost. Eventually in 1876, Messrs. Hall & Whipple succeeded to the proprietorship, the house then having but eighty-five rooms. The firm were likewise the proprietors of the Adams House and with the two establishments were doing a business of great magnitude. In 1884 they dissolved partnership, Mr. George H. Hall taking the Adams House, and Mr. J. Reed Whipple becoming sole proprietor of Young's. Mr. Whipple's regime has been one of exceptional ability and remarkably successful. He has made Young's, Boston's social pivot; we say this advisedly, for other places claim consideration, but an examination of the registers of Young's Hotel and a knowledge of the famous clubs and prominent bodies that regularly dine and meet here, it is manifest that this is the social sun round which the lesser social planets revolve. Since 1875, Mr. Whipple has been obliged to enlarge the hotel no less than four times. The alterations and extensions have been effected upon a liberal scale of space, and the hotel is big, broad and roomy every way. There are now 250 rooms, besides magnificent and spacious dining halls, parlors, reading rooms, office, etc. The hotel comprises three connecting buildings, constructed of freestone, one fronting on Court Street and Court Square, and seven stories and basement in height, one on Court Avenue, five stories and basement in height, and opposite which are the new billiard room and bar, the finest and most elaborately fitted up in Boston. Young's Hotel is admirably planned and every portion is convenient of access. On the first floor are four of the largest sized dining rooms, three billiard parlors, etc. The decorations and outfit of the dining halls are most costly and elaborate, and harmonize with the rest of the artistic features of the house. The ladies' parlors and reception rooms, etc., are most richly furnished and everything is modern, stylish and in keeping with the most refined requirements. All the modern improvements have been introduced here, including two passenger elevators, steam heat, electric light, annunciators, repeating call bells, etc. There is a thorough system of organization enforced, and no less than 250 employees are in attendance in the various departments. The service is perfect, and Mr. Whipple in this essential has no rival in the United States. The 250 rooms are all most comfortably and completely furnished, and many arranged en suite are elaborate in their appointments. The house is conducted on the popular European plan, single rooms ranging from $1 to $8 per day, and double rooms or those en suite from $2 to $12 per day. The culinary department has received Mr. Whipple's special attention. He was determined to render the cuisine of Young's the finest in Boston and he has succeeded; nowhere are such elaborate bills of fare served in such perfect form as here, the kitchens being in charge of a distinguished chef, and the dining rooms of a most eminent steward. On an average 2,500 persons dine here daily, and of the most critical classes, who all the more appreciate the excellence and liberality of the table. Among the many leading political and other clubs that dine here weekly or every other week are: the Massachusetts Club, New England Club, Norfolk Club, Middlesex Club, Essex Club, Paint and Oil Trade Club, etc. The registers contain the names of the most eminent politicians and professional men, from all over the country, and the reportorial errand is always first to Young's corridors, where political and other happenings are first heard of. The executive staff of Young's Hotel is composed of the following gentlemen: Mr. W. H. La Pointe, chief clerk; Mr. C. P. Davy, book-keeper; Mr. C. I. Lindsay, room clerk; Mr. H. H. Tirrell, cashier; Mr. Claude M. Hart, book-keeper; Mr. F. E. Tibbets, room cashier; Mr. George H. Newton, cashier; and Mr. Oscar F. Mercer, night clerk. They all being to bear special qualifications for the discharge of their duties, and are deservedly popular. Mr. W H. La Pointe has been with the house for eighteen years. He has been a resident of Boston for twenty years past and for the last fourteen years has ably and faithfully discharged the onerous duties devolving upon him as head clerk. A hotel man from his youth up, he is thoroughly posted and ably supervises the running of this great establishment. Things go smoothly, and every guest is under obligations to Mr. La Pointe and his staff for favors rendered and courteous, prompt attention to every request. Young's Hotel has an equipment that is perfect throughout. It is the leader in this field of enterprise, and under Mr Whipple's skilled proprietorship, has inaugurated a new era in the business. He was born in New Boston, N. H., and has had an experience in hotel management of twenty years duration, having been steward in the Parker House for six years before becoming joint proprietor of Young's. He has made a thorough study of the difficult and complex art of modern hotel keeping, and that he has solved every problem satisfactorily is fully borne out by the marked popularity of Young's under his individual guidance. He resides in his own house on Commonwealth Avenue, and like any other business man, devotes his full day to the personal direction of this magnificent hostelry.

C. A. CAMPBELL & CO, Coal, No. 59 Congress Street.—The commercial interests of Boston are intimately connected with the coal trade, in which not only is large capital invested, but likewise the energy and enterprise of many of our influential citizens. Prominent among the number is the old established and representative firm of Messrs. C. A. Campbell & Co., whose offices are located at No. 59 Congress Street. This business was established twenty-eight years ago by Mr. Campbell, who possesses an intimate knowledge of the wants of the wholesale and retail trade of Boston and the adjacent cities. The yards and wharf are situated at Chelsea, Mass. Messrs. Campbell & Co. deals largely in anthracite and bituminous coal and wood. They promptly load coal steamships from barges, and likewise have a number of first-class barges for lighterage purposes. Orders by mail or telegraph receive immediate attention, and dealers and manufacturers can be promptly supplied with any quantity from a boat load to any smaller lot at the lowest ruling market prices. They deal largely in the finest grades of anthracite, and employ in their yards a large number of workmen. Pine, oak and hickory wood are also sold by the load or cord, sawed and split to order in any size, and delivered to any part of the city. Mr. Campbell is a popular member of the Boston Coal Exchange. Having thus briefly sketched the facilities of this house, it only remains to be added, that its business has ever been conducted on the sound principles of equity, and relations once entered into with it are sure to become not only pleasant but profitable and permanent.

A. FOX & CO., Manufacturers of Cloth Hats and Caps, No. 86 Bedford Street—For enterprise, marked skill and strictly honorable methods, no house has more speedily and permanently attained a position of prominence and popularity than Messrs. A. Fox & Co., the widely-known manufacturers of cloth hats and caps. The business was founded in 1885 by Messrs. A. and B. Fox, gentlemen of a wide range of practical experience in this line, and who early developed influential connections with a trade of great magnitude. They have their factory and salesrooms centrally located at No. 86 Bedford Street, and where they employ upwards of twenty-five skilled hands in the manufacture of all styles and descriptions of cloth hats and caps. Their specialty is children's goods, and in this line the trade recognizes them to be the leaders, whose methods and policy insure perfection in cut, workmanship and finish, and who ever maintain the highest standard of excellence. From their large and comprehensive stock the most critical trade buyers can be suited, and they are doing the largest business of any concern in New England in children's goods. Messrs. Fox have been permanent residents of Boston for the past eight years, and have ever retained the confidence of leading commercial circles. They exercise sound judgment in the selection of materials, and give close personal supervision over all the processes of manufacture, insuring to their patrons the best goods at the lowest prices, and who can promptly fill the largest orders in any special line.

STURTEVANT MILL CO., Manufacturers of the Sturtevant Mill, for Crushing and Pulverizing Ores, Phosphates, Etc., E. C. Huxley, President, No. 53 Mason Building.—This reliable company are the proprietors and sole manufacturers of the famous Sturtevant Mill, which is absolutely unrivalled in the United States or Europe, for crushing and grinding ores, phosphates, cement, and all other hard and refractory materials. The Sturtevant Mill Company was duly incorporated in 1883, under the laws of Maine, with a paid-up capital of $500,000, and since its organization has secured a liberal and influential patronage not only in the United States and Canada, but also in Mexico, Central and South America, Europe, Africa, Australia and New Zealand. The chief executive officers of the company, are E. C. Huxley, president

pies a space of three by ten feet. Receives of some kinds of rock, pieces three inches to five inches through; but for the harder rocks working best to the size of not above four inches square. Speed, 1,200 revolutions. Power, about forty horse power. Twenty-inch heads will crush and grind from two to twenty tons per hour, according to the fineness, and is equal in capacity to a seventy-stamp mill upon the same work. Weight about nine tons. Occupies a space four feet by fourteen feet, and is five and one-half feet in height. This mill is truly a giant grinder. Receives rock from four to eight inches through, but works best on the harder rocks that are not over four inches. Speed, 900 revolutions. Power, about eighty horse-power. These machines are now in operation upon a large scale,

and manager, and W. H. Ellis, treasurer. The Boston office is situated at No. 53 Mason Building. The Sturtevant mill develops an entirely new principle, avoiding the usual wear and tear of machinery, and accomplishing in a much more rapid and thorough manner the work of a crusher and stamp mill combined. The above illustration gives a view of the machine as it appears in operation: the material to be ground is conveyed through the hopper at the top to the case A, filling the case and the revolving cylinders or heads B, B, which, being put in motion, hurl their contents against each other with such power that the rock is at once crushed to atoms. The mill does not grind the materials, but simply furnishes the power that compels the rocks to crush themselves; consequently, the hardness of the rock does not affect the result, as it acts upon itself. The Sturtevant mills are made in three sizes, with heads from eight to twenty inches in diameter and vary in capacity according to size. A mill with eight-inch heads will grind from four hundred to two thousand pounds per hour, according to the fineness. Weight about eighteen hundred pounds, and can be bolted directly to a well-supported floor. Occupies a space three by eight feet, and is built for very heavy work. Will do all that a ten-stamp mill will do upon the same material. Speed, 1800 revolutions per minute. Power, about twenty horse-power. A mill with twelve-inch heads will crush and grind from one to eight tons per hour, and is equal to a thirty stamp battery doing the same class of work. Weighs about three tons. Occu-

doing various forms of grinding, and can be seen at any time at work upon the most difficult material,—ores, mattes, phosphates and cements. It will give the officers much pleasure to show these mills to those who would like to see them at their every day work. The mill has been put to the severest tests. At the Catasauqua Cement Company's Works near Allentown, Pa., in December last, two tons of wet quartz rock were pulverized in the short space of four minutes, a test that was regarded as one of the severest to which the mill could be put. The ease with which it did the work and the fineness to which it reduced the material fairly amazed all who witnessed the test. Still later six and one-half tons of iron ore were sent to the cement mill for the purpose of testing the crushing quality of the Sturtevant mill. The rock was of extraordinary hardness and there were those who doubted the ability of the mill to grind it. Finer screens had to be put in the mill for this purpose and when this was done the machinery was started. The rock was shoveled in and in thirteen minutes the ore was ground and deposited on the second floor of the building, with none of the pieces larger than corn and two-thirds of it as fine as sand and flour. The test far exceeded in its results the anticipations of most of those present and won for the Sturtevant mill the most unqualified praise. Three-quarters of an hour after the test the mill was again fixed for grinding cement and ground it at the rate of eighty barrels per hour. All who witnessed the workings of the mill went away satisfied that it is capable of doing all that is claimed for it. The Sturtevant mills are no toy machines that wear out after a few weeks' run, but giant grinders of unparalleled capacity, whether grinding coarse or fine, while one of their chief merits is the slight wear, which is reduced to a minimum, and their simplicity renders them safe from damage in the hands of a common mechanic. The mills are most highly endorsed by many prominent manufacturers, who have forwarded testimonials of the highest character, and state that after using four years they are in as good condition practically as when first erected. All orders for these splendid mills are promptly filled at extremely low prices, while entire satisfaction is guaranteed in every particular.

WM. DEERING & CO., Grain and Grass-Cutting Machinery, Chicago, Ill.; F. C. Piers, General Agent for New England, No. 80 South Market Street.—In surveying the wide field of manufacturers, in the line of agricultural implements, grain and grass-cutting machinery stand pre-eminent in importance and utility. The largest and best known manufactory in this branch of industry in the United States is that of Messrs. William Deering & Co., of Chicago, Ill., who are represented in Boston by Mr. F. C. Piers, the General Agent for New England. This agency has its office and sample room at Nos. 80 South Market Street, and 71 Clinton Street, and was established in January, 1887. Mr. Piers, the general agent, has been connected with the house for the past ten years, and is thoroughly conversant with all the details of the business and the requirements of the trade. He occupies spacious quarters with the Atlas Warehouse and Storage Company, carrying a large and complete line of Wm. Deering & Co.'s machines, besides a stock of repairs valued at $65,000, operating thirteen transfer houses throughout New England and having three hundred and sixty local agents in the same territory. The reputation of the Deering grain and grass cutting machinery is world wide; the competition among manufacturers of this class of machinery has been and still is very great, stimulating inventions, until more than three thousand patents have been granted in this country that pertain to this line alone. The Deering interest, however, moves steadily on, lengthening and strengthening its stakes, enlarging its commercial relations, increasing its capacities and facilities, and expanding its fame and popularity with coming generations, undisturbed by competition, shining only the brighter by comparison or contrast. It has now but few competitors in the land, and is absolutely without a peer. Six thousand people are employed in the business, and wherever the Deering machinery is introduced, their claim as to its superiority over that manufactured by other concerns, as well as the reputation of the manufacturers, is constantly extended and confirmed. Mr Piers opened the Boston house in January, 1887; previous to that time no sales had been made by William Deering & Co. in New England. During 1887 six hundred and eighty two machines were sold by Mr. Piers and his agents, followed in 1888 by over three thousand five hundred sales. This is the best possible proof of the superiority of the Deering machines when brought into competition with old-established manufacturers who have had the control of this great agricultural territory without serious opposition for many years. Mr. Piers is prepared to offer inducements to agriculturists and dealers as regards terms and quality, which challenge competition, and necessarily command the attention of careful buyers. His house in this city possesses unsurpassed facilities for filling all orders promptly, and attending to the wants of patrons with the greatest care and forethought. Mr. Piers has gained the respect and confidence of a large circle of friends and patrons throughout New England during the past two years, and is certainly the right man in the right place.

ADAMS, TAYLOR & CO., Foreign Commission and Wine Importing Merchants, No. 105 State Street.—The importance of using only the purest and best brands of wines and liquors is generally recognized, and the retail trade and druggists which keep the superior grades of these goods are the ones to retain and build up the heaviest trade in their section. The oldest and leading house engaged in the wholesale branch of this trade in Boston is that of Messrs. Adams, Taylor & Co., located at No. 105 State Street. This firm are widely and deservedly prominent as foreign commission and wine-importing merchants, and have become justly celebrated for their able and honorable business policy. The business was founded by Messrs. Foster & Taylor in 1852, the present firm succeeding to the control in 1874. The business premises comprise four floors, 25x100 feet each, fully supplied with every modern convenience for handling and storing the goods, and giving abundant opportunity for meeting the most extensive demand. This firm are manufacturers' agents for Blue Grass, Royal and G. O. Blake's Bourbon County Kentucky Whiskies, which are accounted among the purest and smoothest whiskies made. They are guaranteed of the finest grade, and are strongly recommended by the medical profession for the use of invalids and consumptives. A leading specialty is also made of Honeysuckle Gin, and cased goods of all kinds are largely handled. They import their fine wines and foreign liquors direct from the most famous European houses, and sell their whiskies free or in bond. They supply a large, first-class and permanent trade throughout New England, both with old rye and bourbon whiskies, old gins and brandies, they specially import champagnes, clarets, ports and sherries, Bordeaux, Burgundy, Moselle and Madeira wines, and offer substantial inducements to customers as regards both reliability of goods and liberality of terms and prices. The house is represented on the road by a corps of talented salesmen, and orders of any magnitude are promptly and satisfactorily filled in all cases. The members of this responsible firm are Messrs. Luther Adams, George W. Taylor and C. A. Barney. Mr. Adams is a native of New Hampshire, and a prominent citizen of the suburban town of Brighton. Mr. Taylor is a native Bostonian, as is also Mr. Barney. All are members of the Massachusetts Liquor Dealers' Association, the National Liquor Dealer' Association and are greatly esteemed in social, financial and trade circles for their ability, integrity and personal worth.

HENRY ATKINS & CO., Wine Merchants, Nos. 8 and 9 South Market Street.—The wholesale house of Messrs. Henry Atkins & Co., at Nos. 8 and 9 south Market Street, has long been recognized by first-class dealers and critical buyers as headquarters for the highest grades of pure wines and liquors. Hundreds of purchasers throughout the United States have long ago discovered that the choicest champagne, ports and sherries can only be obtained through this firm's direct importations. The business of this old and honored house was founded in 1819, by Mr. Henry Atkins, whose lamented demise occurred in the year '70. He was succeeded by his two sons, Messrs. Henry H. and John E. Atkins, the former of whom died in May, 1888, leaving Mr. John E. Atkins sole proprietor. He has been connected with the house for the past thirty-five years, and brings to bear the widest range of practical experience, coupled with ample resources and direct influential connections both at home and abroad. As wholesale wine merchants, importers of foreign wines and spirits, and agents for Pommery & Greno champagne and other choice vintages, this house is justly famed and deservedly popular. The building occupied for trade purposes contains four floors and a basement, 25x60 feet in dimensions, admirably equipped for the storage and preservation of the choice and valuable stock. The house are agents and importers of Pommery & Greno champagne, dog's head bottling of Bass' English ale and Guinness' Doublin Stout, Henkell & Co.'s Rhine wines, Yriarte sherries, clarets, Sauternes and Burgundies, Hennessy's Cognac brandies, the original pine apple and wreath gins, Scotch and Irish whiskies, London dock, Jamaica rum, Philippo & Canard's sardines, etc.; and also have in stock and in bond the choicest old Bourbon and rye whiskies. Every taste of the connoisseur and lover of fine wines and every requirement of a first-class trade can here be met on the spot. We would recommend dealers and critical buyers to sample some of the leading specialties of this house, as they positively are not to be duplicated elsewhere. As authorized agents and extensive importers, this house handles superb vintages of dry, fragrant wines, all the standard goods in fine old Scotch and Irish whiskies, and fine flavored Bourbon and rye, and are in a position to supply club and private cellars with specially selected wines and liquors of unexampled purity and excellence, while they have developed important wholesale connections throughout the country that are very creditable to the energy and intelligence of the management Mr. Atkins is a native of Boston, highly regarded in mercantile and trade circles, and prominent and popular in social life.

THE METROPOLIS OF NEW ENGLAND.

THE NEW ENGLAND WESTON ELECTRIC LIGHT COMPANY, U. S. System, Moses Williams, President, Andrew Robeson, Treasurer, No. 18 Post Office Square.—At the present day it is evident that the electric light has come to stay. The dynamos of the best systems give now over ninety per cent. of efficiency, while the steam engine has only reached fifteen per cent. It is cheaper than gas, where any large number of electric lights are used for any length of time, moreover it gives a better, steadier light, securing also pure air with no heat. In connection with these remarks, special attention is directed in this mercantile review of Boston, to the reliable and successful New England Weston Electric Light Company, whose offices are located at No. 18 Post Office Square. This company was duly incorporated under the laws of Connecticut, in 1886, with a paid up capital of $1,00,000, and since its organization at that date, has secured a liberal and influential patronage in all sections of New England. The chief executive officers of the company are, Moses Williams, president, Andrew Robeson, treasurer, and J. H. Alley, secretary. The New England Weston Electric Light Company contracts for and supplies the following four complete systems: U. S. Incandescent System for isolated plants; U. S. Long Distance System for incandescent lighting of streets and stores from central stations; U. S. Alternating Current System for general distribution of incandescent lights over wide areas; U. S. Arc system for arc lighting, either from central stations or isolated plants. The electric lights produced by the apparatus of this popular company are soft and pleasant to the sight, and are unrivalled for economy, utility and reliability. More than 30,0 0 U. S. incandescent lights are used in textile mills alone; among them are the following: Pacific Mills, cotton, Lawrence, Mass., 2,500; Patterson Mills, cotton, Chester, Pa., 600; Merrimack Manufacturing Company, cotton, Lowell, Mass., 1,350; Boott Mills, cotton, Lowell, Mass., 1,250; Boston Manufacturing Company, cotton, Waltham, Mass., 700; Manville Manufacturing Company, cotton, Manville, R. I., 1,200; Globe Mills, cotton, Woonsocket, R. I., 600; Nourse Mills, cotton, Woonsocket, R. I., 600; Shenandoah Cotton Company, cotton, Utica, N. Y., 400; D. Tainter & Sons, cotton, Trainer, Pa., 400; John Dallas & Sons, cotton, Philadelphia, Pa., 257; Thomas M. Holt, cotton, Haw River, N. C., 350; Natchez Cotton Company, cotton, Natchez, Miss., 250; Nashville Cotton Company, cotton, Nashville, Tenn., 250; Hanover Manufacturing Company, cotton, Hanover, Ill., 250; Washington Mills, woollens, Lawrence, Mass., 600; Lippitt Woollen Company, woollens, Woonsocket, R. I., 600; Alex Smith & Sons, carpets, Yonkers, N. Y., 200; Lowell Manufacturing Company, carpets, Lowell, Mass., 1,250; Rood Manufacturing Company, knitting, Cohoes, N. Y. 400; Luckemeyer & Shefer, silk, Union Hill, N. J., 400; Lipps & Sutton, silk, N. Bethlehem, Pa., 250; Nightingale Bros., silk, Patterson, N. J., 600; Fetwell Bros. & Co., worsteds, Philadelphia, Pa., 600; B. L. Solomons & Sons, Philadelphia, Pa., 375; Dartmouth Spinning Company, Augusta, Ga., 70; Allentown Spinning Company, Allentown, Pa., 20 lights; also The Equitable Building, N. Y., 8,000; The Equitable Building, Boston, 1,500; Massachusetts General Hospital, Boston, 580; Capitol at Albany, N. Y.; All the U. S. Postoffices lighted but two, Boston and N. O.; U. S. S. S. Atlanta; Pennsylvania Railroad System. The electric car fitted up by this company and run on the West End Street Railway with storage batteries has been a complete success, the batteries after eighteen months use being perfect, and the economy of this motive system is beyond question. The patents covering this unsurpassed system will be issued shortly, when the company will be ready to contract for cars. The New England Weston Electric Light Company promptly fills orders for plants for incandescent or arc lights according to the U. S. System, while the prices quoted for all kinds of its apparatus are as low as those of any other contemporary corporation. A large amount of work has already been executed by this responsible company to the entire satisfaction of patrons, and its prospects in the near future are of the most encouraging character.

INTERNATIONAL TRUST COMPANY, John M. Graham, President, No. 45 Milk Street.—This representative Trust Company was duly incorporated in 1879 under the laws of Massachusetts, and since its organization has obtained a liberal and influential patronage. It is ably officered, and its executive committee and board of directors are composed of gentlemen, who are highly regarded in financial circles for their prudence, ability and just methods. The list is as follows: John M. Graham, president; Henry L. Jewett, secretary. Directors:—William Claflin, Robert M. Morse, Jr., William A. Haskell, John C. Paige, William T. Parker, William W. Crapo, John Goldthwait, Patrick A. Collins, John A. Collins, John M. Graham, Thomas F. Temple, Warren B. Potter. The paid up capital of the company is $500,000, which has been further augmented by a surplus of $400,000. By the provisions of the charter the company's stockholders are liable for an additional amount equal to the capital stock. This reliable company is authorized to accept and execute trusts under any will or instrument creating a trust, and to take care and management of property and estates. Trust funds are kept separate and distinct from the general business of the company. The International Trust Company transacts a general banking business, discounts commercial paper, receives deposits subject to check, buys and sells foreign exchange and makes collections on all points throughout the United States and Canada upon favorable terms. It likewise draws its own bills of Sterling Exchange on the London and Westminster Bank (limited), London, England, in amounts to suit customers, and also makes cable transfers. The company, moreover, acts as register, transfer agent and trustees under mortgage of railroad and other corporations. Interest is allowed on deposits subject to check, and special rates when payable at specified dates. All the checks on this company are received through the Boston Clearing House. The following statement of the affairs of the International Trust Company of Boston, to the Commissioners of Banks in Massachusetts, October 31st, 1888, shows its condition to be most substantial and flourishing: Assets—Demand loans, $883,192.34; Time loans, $1,792,560.41; Time loans to corporations in New England, $963,300.00; United States bonds, $125,000.00; Municipal and other bonds, $37,947.50; Railroad bonds and stocks, $44,740.80; Municipal and other securities (special trusts), $75,150.00; Sinking fund bonds (special trust), $30,500.00; Trust funds, $13,825.60; Expenses, $9,504.85; Cash on hand and in banks, $466,753.46; Total, $5,280,200.97. Liabilities—Capital Stock, $500,000.00; Surplus fund, $450,000.00; Undivided profits, $24,738.41; Deposits subject to check, $3,728,188.70; Certificates of deposit, $124,485.17; Trust deposits, $396,355.60; Deposits for coupons, $24,256.32; Sinking funds for corporations, $30,466.79; Dividends unpaid, $450.00; Total, $5,280,200.99. In conclusion we would observe, that the International Trust Company, through an honorable and conservative course has secured a leading position among the solid and responsible institutions of the United States, and fully merits the entire confidence of the community.

THOMAS TODD, Printer, No. 1 Somerset Street.—The industry of the printer in these modern days of enterprise, is of the utmost importance. Not only do our educational institutions depend upon the printing press, but commerce would lose one of her most powerful allies were printing to be suddenly lost to us; the newspaper, that universal educator and friend, would be unknown, and civilization would sink back into the condition from which she was raised at the end of the dark ages. There are but few industries, which have no need of the printing press, and in the great and flourishing city of Boston, those who are engaged in this valuable business have an ample field before them. One of the most popular and reliable printers in the city is Mr. Thomas Todd, whose office is located at No. 1 Somerset Street. This business was established twenty-two years ago by Mr. Todd, who has since built up a liberal and influential patronage in New England, New York and the middle states. He employs thirty expert printers, etc., and his establishment is fully equipped with latest improved printing presses, and all material necessary for turning out work in the best possible manner. All kinds of book, commercial printing and job work are done here at the lowest cash prices, and satisfaction is guaranteed in every particular. Mr. Todd was born in Portland, Maine, and now resides at Concord, Mass. He is highly regarded in trade circles for his energy and just methods, fully meriting the signal success secured in this valuable business. His skill in printing is unsurpassed and is quite equal to anything at home or abroad, and being practical in every department of the art, he has obtained an enviable reputation for the artistic merits of his work.

JOHN A. ANDREWS & CO., Wholesale Grocers, Nos. 5 and 7 Commercial and 8 Commerce Streets.—Representative among the largest and most reliable establishments in the city of Boston, is that of Messrs. John A. Andrews & Co., importers and wholesale grocers, whose offices and salesrooms are centrally located on Commercial and Commerce Streets. This business was established in 1865 by Wadley, Nourse & Raymond, who were succeeded by Wadley, Jones & Co., Wadley, Andrews & Co., and Andrews, Barker & Co. Eventually, in April, 1888, the present firm was organized under the style and title of John A. Andrews & Co., the copartners being Messrs. John A. Andrews, Wm. Y. Wadleigh, B. F. Bullard and William A. Dole. The premises occupied are the best located and most convenient for the business in the city and comprise a superior seven-story building 25x100 feet in area, with a wing 25x75 feet in dimensions. The stock carried is essentially representative of the choicest food products, staple and fancy groceries and sundries from every quarter of the globe. A specialty is made of teas, coffees and molasses, which cannot be excelled anywhere, either as regards prices or quality. In such staples as canned goods, sugars, syrups, spices, farinaceous goods, soaps, tobacco and cigars the firm is prepared to offer substantial inducements to the trade, while all goods are guaranteed to be exactly as represented. In the best selected foreign and domestic dried fruits, condiments, sauces, pickles, and full lines of fancy groceries, their stock challenges comparison with any in the country for purity, quality and general excellence. The firm employ about fifty clerks, assistants, etc., and numerous traveling salesmen. Their trade extends throughout all sections of New England, and the Eastern and Middle states. The partners are popular members of the Board of Trade and Wholesale Grocers Association, and are highly regarded in trade circles for their promptness, business ability and integrity, justly meriting the signal success achieved in this growing and important enterprise.

METROPOLIS LAND COMPANY OF BOSTON, No. 7 Exchange Place, Henry W. Moulton, President.—The rapid development of the real estate market of Boston and the steadily enhancing values of choice property render the financial interests involved of paramount importance. No form of investment has latterly become so popular with the conservative public as judiciously selected real estate, for not only in improved realty is a permanent source of income assured, but there is likewise a reasonable certainty of a prospective increase in value. In this connection we desire to make a special reference to the Metropolis Land Company of Boston, whose offices are located at No. 7 Exchange Place. This business was established in 1869 by Mr. Henry W. Moulton, who conducted it till 1886, when the present company was duly organized under the laws of Massachusetts and succeeded to the management. The capital of the company is $40,000 in shares of $100 each. The following gentlemen, who are widely and favorably known in financial circles for their prudence, sound business principles and integrity, are the trustees, etc.: George D. Wildes, Henry W. Moulton, president; Charles N. Goodrich, Charles J. Patch, Alexander Beal and Frederick W. Marston. This company owns thirty-five lots in the city of Boston. These lots are in the Back Bay District, near the Huntington entrance to the Park, and are rapidly increasing in value. Hotels and stores of high character are being built upon adjoining lots. Also, very large tracts of land in New Hampshire, Vermont and New York State, for development into summer villages or watering places, and large tracts of choice land in Florida and Texas, for development into delightful winter homes. No shares of this company can be bought in open market. Only one or two shares at the most are allowed to any one person; and it is desired that the subscriber be young and active to be eligible to membership. The actual property of the company is far beyond its nominal capital of $40,000, and $100, the par value of shares, is below the real value. Anyone desiring to become a participant in the profits and operations of the company, must be known to the company, and be willing to actively promote its interests, as it contemplates extensive purchases and sales. Mr. Henry W. Moulton, the president, has an excellent reputation as an expert upon the present and prospective values of city and country property, and has often been called on to act officially as an appraiser of all descriptions of realty. His valuations have ever been borne out by subsequent sales, and his just methods have gained for him the confidence and esteem of the entire community. Mr. Moulton is the proprietor of Moulton Hill, generally known as "Moulton Castle," Newburyport, Mass., where the Moulton family has resided for over 200 years. He is the founder and owner of that part of Newburyport called Moultonville. He is a member of the Genealogical Society and various other institutions, both civil and military, and is one of Boston's public-spirited citizens, having laid out, and given to Boston, three public streets, and made many other real estate improvements. During the war he commanded a battalion of troops, under a commission from Governor Andrew, through the Antietam campaign, when he was promoted by President Lincoln, and appointed by him, and by his order commissioned by Secretary of War Stanton, to a high position in the War Department. At the close of the war, after serving in the Massachusetts Legislature, and having the confidence of General Grant, who knew every military man's record, he was appointed by him a marshal of the United States, and commissioned by and with the unanimous consent of the Senate. He discharged the duties of all three positions, with honor and credit to himself, and to those who entrusted him with power.

SULLIVAN CONSOLIDATED GOLD MINING COMPANY, G. E. Yarrington, President; G. W. McKinney Vice-President; C. M Sprague, Treasurer, Offices: No. 27 Doane Street.—There is no section of the mineral regions of the United States where such favorable prospects and results attend the operations of the gold miners as in the famous Black Hills of Dakota. Immense fortunes have already been made in this region and with skilled guidance and sufficient capital to introduce improved machinery, and properly develop the best properties so as to secure abundance of rich ores, the prospects are most favorable to investors. One of the most able and conservatively conducted corporations engaged in mining in the Black Hills, is the Sullivan Consolidated Gold Mining Co., with main office at No. 27 Doane Street, in this city. The Sullivan Mining Company was formed in 1887 to develop certain valuable claims on Castle Creek, Lookout, Pennington County, Dakota, and in September, 1888, its properties, with others adjoining, were consolidated as the property of the present company, and whose capital of $400,000 has been rapidly taken by prominent capitalists and investors of New England. The following are the company's directors: Messrs. G. E. Yarrington, G. W. McKinney, C. M. Sprague, Nathan P. Kidder, F. J. Ayer, J. T. Hooper, Herbert L. Peck. They are all representative and responsible business men of Boston and New York, and whose names are synonymous with integrity and stability. The company's officers are: Messrs. G. E. Yarrington, president; G. W. McKinney, vice-president; C. M. Sprague, treasurer, and Nathan P. Kidder, clerk. Mr. Yarrington is very widely and favorably known in leading railroad circles and is a resident of New York, Mr. McKinney is a respected and influential citizen of Lynn, while Mr. Sprague is a resident of Boston and is a business man of matured executive ability, and who faithfully discharges the onerous duties devolving upon him. Mr. F. J. Ayer, is the company's superintendent, and is a mining expert of wide experience and fully conversant with Black Hill ores and their treatment. The company owns the following mines: Sullivan, Beaver, Elgin, Volunteer, Almont, Aster, Hoosac, Tariff, Revenue and Eclipse, covering 101 acres and forty acres beside of gold placers and claims, notably rich in gold. The company has had Mr. Gilbert E. Bailey E. M., Ph. D., late geologist of Wyoming territory, and a practical authority on the Black Hills gold and tin deposits, make a careful examination of its properties and he reports that they give a greater number and larger grains of gold to the pan than any other mine in the Lookout District. This is saying a great deal and with the efficient management of the company insures a very large return on its capital. The company is erecting a fine sixty stamp mill on its property and has control of a splendid water power on Castle Creek, insuring extraordinarily cheap milling, while the accessibility of the ore and cheapness of handling it, insures the cost of working the mines to average less than $1 per ton of ore mined. Everything points to the company paying big dividends as soon as it starts up and those who desire to fully investigate this opening for legitimate, solid mining investment should send to Treasurer Sprague for a copy of Prof. Bailey's full official report.

BOSTON RUBBER SHOE COMPANY, E. S. Converse, Treasurer; No. 215 Causeway Street.—The Boston Rubber Shoe Company was incorporated in 1853 and has always manufactured rubber boots and shoes. It has been and is one of the most aggressive and enterprising companies in the business, always striving to take the lead in styles and maintaining the best quality regardless of the variations in the prices of its goods. It now has two large factories, one located at Malden, the other at Melrose; both within four to six miles of Boston, possessing the best and largest facilities in the world for the manufacture of rubber boots and shoes. Its very long experience in the business insures

obtain the best wear from a rubber boot or shoe it is absolutely necessary to secure the best fit possible. Many rubbers are rendered worthless the first time worn by the being too small or too large, causing the rubber to break. If careful attention is given to this matter it will often avoid unjust criticism of the manufacturer. Mr. E. S. Converse has been its treasurer for over thirty-five years and it is largely due to his indomitable perseverance and ability that the company has achieved its success; as it has been brought safely through many hard times and trials and the increasing competition in its business. Its general office and ware rooms are located at No. 215 Causeway Street, Boston.

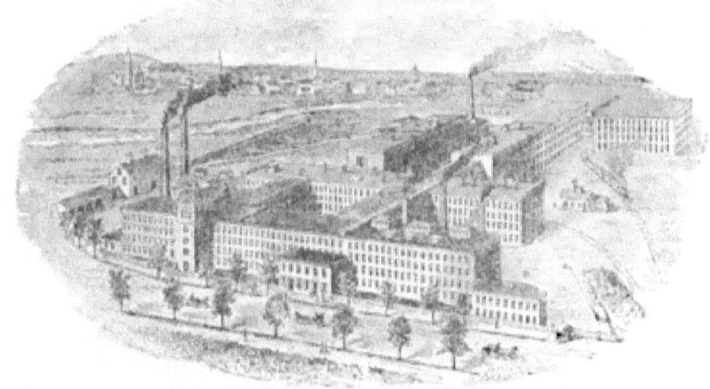

the making of the highest quality of goods which art and experience can produce. It has in its employment about 3,000 persons and its capacity at present is 45,000 pairs per day. Its buildings are all of brick, lighted by electricity and everything is done for the consideration and comfort of its employees. Its name is

JAMES F. DAWSON, Gold Gilder to the Trade, Nos. 30 and 34 Hanover Street.—As a gilder Mr. James F. Dawson has been known in the trade for more than ten years, and is recognized as one of the best in the city. He executes work in all branches of gold leaf gilding, and regilds old pictures and mirror

known throughout the length and breadth of the land, but owing to attempts made from time to time to imitate its name and brand and so confuse the general public, caution should always be taken to see that its full name, Boston Rubber Shoe Company, is stamped upon its goods. It should always be born in mind that in order to

frames which have the appearance of being new after leaving his hands. Frames are also painted, and engraving of all kinds is done to order. Estimates are furnished by Mr. Dawson, who will always be found prompt in his attention to orders. He is a native of England, and came to this country about eighteen years ago.

B. F. BROWN & CO., Manufactures of Blackings and Dressings for Leather, Nos. 154 and 156 Commercial Street.—Boston is headquarters for several great houses which have acquired international celebrity for the superiority of their product. A notable instance of this is afforded in the successful and highly creditable career of the celebrated firm of Messrs. B. F. Brown & Co. Mr. B. F. Brown established this business in 1855 on a comparatively small scale. His blackings and dressings for leather produced upon formulas original and exclusive to himself, speedily attested the attention of the trade as far superior to any others in the market. The demand for them increased at such a rapid ratio that in a short time the facilities of the house were taxed to the utmost, and in 1872 they removed to their present spacious premises, comprising six floors, each 25x100 feet in dimensions, and four others, 50x100 feet. Every foot of the vast floor space is utilized for manufacturing, storage and shipping purposes, and a trade is supplied that practically girdles the earth. Besides the above the house has a factory at No. 41 Banner Street, St. Luke's, London, where fifty hands are employed in manufacturing the same class of goods as are manufactured here and also have another at St. Antoine Street, Montreal. The sole basis of this grand success is MERIT. The late Mr. Brown had made a careful study of the problems involved and invented blackings and dressings that afford the necessary elements to effectually preserve the leather, impart a beautiful polish or gloss at once brilliant and durable. Brown's French Dressing is the finest ever invented. It is entirely free from anything that will shrink, crack or rot the leather and is the only liquid dressing that fulfills all the requirements, leaving the fabric soft and pliable with entire freedom from cracking. No lady's toilet or traveling equipment is complete without the celebrated Brown's Dressing. The introduction of these goods to the Canadian and European markets was followed by as great a demand as in the United States, and now in their Boston and London factories, upwards of 100 hands are employed in the manufacture of French Dressing for ladies' and children's boots and shoes, trunks, harness, carriage tops, etc.; Brown's Satin Polish for ladies' and children's boots and shoes, etc.; and the standard Army and Navy Blacking. These blackings and dressings for leather have been honored with prizes at the great exhibitions of the world, at the Centennial Exposition in Philadelphia in 1876 at Berlin in 1877, at Paris in 1878 where they received the only medal awarded for leather dressings, in Melbourne in 1880, at Frankfort in 1881, at Amsterdam in 1883, and the New Orleans Exposition in 1884 and 1885, Brown's dressings was awarded the highest honors. This is the oldest and leading concern of its kind in America and is a valued factor in the promotion of Boston's commercial prosperity. From its inception the business has been managed carefully and scientifically, using only the best materials in the process of manufacture. The trade of the house is not only extended over every state of the Union and the Canadian provinces, but has reached the most remote countries, including India, Pacific Islands, Australia, New Zealand, Ceylon, Siam, Bengal, Sandwich Islands, etc., with a large trade throughout Europe where Brown's dressing is prized as highly as it is here and where the sales are constantly increasing.

GEO. WINTHROP COFFIN, Agent Atlantic Mutual Insurance Company of New York, No. 29 State Street.—One of the most important departments of insurance is that devoted to mariners' interests, while the first application of the principle of insurance was to marine risks. In this country our early colonists, who were extensively engaged in ship building, commenced to look about for some protection of their capital when disaster overtook their property at sea. Ship-owners and merchants began to combine, and agreed to assume the responsibility for a certain amount of loss, signing their names for the amount of their liability under the list of the ship's cargo, and from this method the name of "underwriter" became applied to marine insurance. The largest and leading marine insurance company in the world at the present day is the Atlantic Mutual Insurance Company of New York. Their last annual statement shows premiums marked off as earned, $3,672,331.21; losses paid, $1,599,468.25; return premiums and expenses, $788,846.58. A dividend of forty per cent. was given to policy holders on terminated premiums during the year. This company do a purely marine and inland business and give to their clients the security of a surplus exceeding ten millions of dollars, and their premiums at cost. As an institution the Atlantic Mutual is recognized as of the highest character and stability in the financial world, having passed through many trying ordeals, having proved by its record in rendering it still stronger and better able to cope with each succeeding difficulty. Its business connections are co-extensive with the civilized world, and its pre-eminence has been honestly won, due to the unremitting care and excellent judgment of its president, Mr. John D. Jones, whose connection with the company dates back to its origin. Mr. Coffin is one of the best-informed insurance men in Boston, having an experience covering thirty-six years in the business, while he has been agent for the company here for a period of thirty-three years, and during that time has developed an extensive and influential connection with all classes of ship and vessel owners, shippers and importers, in this city and all along the Massachusetts coast. He commands all the advantages naturally accumulated by long years of identification with a special line of business, and possesses unequalled facilities for conducting all kinds of marine underwriting on vessels and cargoes. His associate, Mr. William R. Colby, has been twenty years in the business. Both are natives of Boston, and personally are eminently popular with the ship-owners, merchants and the community at large.

J. W. PORTER, Insurance, No. 27 State Street.—Our largest and leading insurance companies invariably place their interests in the control of gentlemen who have secured honorable reputations as insurance agents and brokers, and among the latter in this city is Mr. J. W. Porter, whose office is eligibly located at No. 27 State Street. Mr. J. W. Porter has been prominently identified with the insurance business of this city and vicinity, as agent and broker, ever since 1861, and it is no flattery to say that he occupies a first-class position among our home institutions, and enjoys the entire confidence of the business public by his prompt and equitable methods of adjustment and the liberal and reliable policy that has ever characterized all his transactions. He now represents the following solid and substantial corporations, viz.:—First National Fire Insurance Company, of Worcester; Atlantic Fire and Marine Insurance Company, of Providence; and the Dorchester Mutual Fire Insurance Company, of Boston. Having absolute control of the Boston business of these companies, and also agent for the British and Mercantile Fire Insurance Co., of London, and Providence Washington, of Providence, Mr. Porter is in a position to promptly place the largest risks, quoting the lowest rates of premium, and guaranteeing a sure and liberal adjustment of all losses. He controls the insuring of many of the choicest lines of residential and business properties in this city and its suburbs, and is also prepared to place policies in any company desired at the lowest rates. He is eminently popular with all classes of property-owners, and enjoys a large and influential patronage among leading merchants, manufacturers, ship-owners and steamship companies. Mr. Porter is a Massachusetts man by birth and training, and President of the Boston Board of Fire Underwriters.

PECK BROTHERS, Steam Mercantile Printers and Tag Manufacturers, No. 31 Fulton Street, Cor. Cross.—The business of this concern was organized in 1880 by Messrs. J. A. and H. A. Peck, both of whom had previously had a long practical experience in the trade. In 1884 the latter retired, leaving the former sole proprietor of the business, which he has continued under the original firm style. The premises occupied comprise two floors, each having an area of 25x60 feet. The second floor is utilized as an office and composing room, and the third floor as the press room. The mechanical equipments include the most recently improved cylinder and job presses, which are operated by steam power, and the other accessories of the establishment embrace a vast variety of fonts of fancy, plain, antique and modern types, and all the paraphernalia pertaining to a first-class general mercantile printing establishment. Bill heads, note headings, circulars, cards, price lists, catalogues, memoranda, in fact, everything from a small business card to a book is printed here at short notice and in the highest style of the art. Upwards of a dozen skilled hands are constantly employed. The firm are also manufacturers of tags, and in this department have a brisk trade.

THE METROPOLIS OF NEW ENGLAND 127

DYER, RICE & CO., Hats, Straw Goods, Japanese Robes, and Ladies' Furs, Nos. 36, 38 and 40 Chauncy Street.—The manufacture of specialties in hats, furs and straw goods, has made great progress among the industries of Boston, and a leading factor in the business is the house of Messrs. Dyer, Rice & Co., located at Nos. 36, 38 and 40 Chauncy Street. This firm enjoy a reputation and a trade co-extensive with the entire country as manufacturers of and dealers in hats, straw goods, Japanese robes, buffalo robes, ladies' furs, etc. The business was established in 1836 by Hart, Taylor & Co., and subsequent changes occurred as follows, viz: 1879, Dyer, Taylor & Co.; 1886 Dyer Rice & Co. The building occupied for manufacturing and sales purposes contains five stories and a basement, 75x120 feet in dimensions, and admirably equipped with every convenience for the accommodation and display of the immense and valuable stock carried and for rapid and perfect production. A force numbering from sixty to seventy skilled hands is constantly employed, and the output is one of great magnitude and importance. The necessity of having ladies' fur garments made to order has been reduced to a minimum, as this firm make ample provisions for extreme as well as uniform figures, and can nearly always fit perfectly the most critical and exacting customers from their splendid stock. They make likewise all kinds of fur garments to measure, and employ a corps of highly skilled workmen for this particular branch. Their several departments include seal garments and fancy furs, Japanese robes, rugs, etc.; and straw goods of every description. Only the finest materials manufactured or known in the United States or Europe are utilized, and the goods are sold at the smallest margin of profit. The fur department is a great attraction to the ladies, and is famous far and near. In the manufacture of their sacques, dolmans and other fur garments, only the finest Alaska sealskins, London dyed, are used, so that customers can be absolutely certain of obtaining at this establishment truly first class garments that will last for years, and at prices much lower than those quoted by other noted establishments. Shipments are freely made to all parts of the United States, the mail order department affording a ready means for people throughout the country at large to satisfy their wants. The members of this responsible and representative firm, are Messrs. R. F. Dyer, J. B. Rice, Jr., F. E. Dyer, and N. G. Nickerson, all well-known Bostonians. The two first mentioned partners were previously in business together, and succeeded to control of the present house in 1879. Mr. Nickerson has had large experience in the business as salesman, and was admitted to the firm in 1886, as was also Mr. F. E. Dyer, a son of the senior partner. Those gentlemen are all highly esteemed in business and financial life for their enterprise, business capacity and integrity, and well deserve the brilliant success they have achieved in this field of commerce.

WILLIAM BOND & SON, Chronometer and Watch Makers, No. 112 State Street.—The oldest established and most noted house in the city of Boston actively engaged in the manufacture of chronometers and watches, is that of the Messrs. William Bond & Son, whose store is located at No. 112 State Street. This business after a long existence in England was established in Boston in 1793 by William Bond, who was succeeded by W. C. Bond and his sons. Mr. W. C. Bond was the first director of Harvard College Observatory, which was built by subscriptions of his friends. He retired from business to assume this responsible position in 1856 Mr. Richard F. Bond succeeded to the business, and in 1882 his son Mr. Wm. C. Bond was admitted into partnership; the business, however, is still conducted under the old firm name of William Bond & Son Mr. Wm. C. Bond, the son of the founder made the first chronometer in the United States in 1812, and his son Mr. Richard F. Bond, now dead, introduced many improvements in chronometers, which were at once taken advantage of by European makers. The firm have always received the highest awards wherever they have exhibited their productions in competition with others. They received a medal at the Paris exposition in 1867 for a superior clock invented by Richard F. Bond, and also the Grand Council medal at the London exhibition, 1851, for an astronomical recording apparatus the design of the same gentleman. This last medal was one of the twelve of that grade, which were awarded to inventors in America. The present firm manufacture chronometers, which are unrivalled for accuracy, finish and reliability, and have no superiors in this country or Europe. They are the sole agents in this country for the celebrated watches of Victor Kullberg, and James Poole & Co. of London which are undoubtedly the finest in the world. They likewise sale and loan chronometers and import scientific instruments to order, while their prices in all cases are extremely moderate. The present partners Are highly esteemed for their scientific ability, skill and integrity. Their agents in New York are John Bliss & Co., No. 128 Front Street, and in Philadelphia Wm. E. Harper, No. 10 South Fourth Street.

GEO. F. LOUGEE & CO., Cotton Brokers and Buyers, No. 4 Liberty Square.—One of the most active and enterprising firms engaged as cotton brokers and buyers in this city is that of Messrs. Geo. F. Lougee & Co. who occupy eligible office quarters at No. 4 Liberty Square. The business was originally established in 1868, by Messrs. Gurney & Lougee, who were succeeded by the present firm in 1885. From a comparatively small beginning the business has been steadily developed and increased, its progress being commensurate with the energy and enterprise displayed in its management. The firm buy and sell cotton on commission, supplying mills and dealers throughout New England with all grades desired, through their agents in the South, and are known in trade circles as among the most experienced and successful buyers in the city. Their connections and facilities are of a strictly first class character, enabling them to offer special advantages to customers, and to fill all orders of whatever magnitude in the promptest and most satisfactory manner. Few firms are so highly respected or so universally popular, which result has been attained by years of inflexible integrity and a strict adherence to honorable and legitimate business methods. They carefully consult the best interests of their numerous patrons, and are prepared to offer desirable grades of goods at prices which command the attention of the closest and most prudent buyers. The members of the firm are Messrs. George F. Lougee and Edw R Coleman. Mr. Lougee was born in New Hampshire, is still in the prime of life, and a well known citizen of New Ipswich, N. H. During the war he enlisted in the 23d regiment of Massachusetts volunteers and was distinguished for his bravery and served a term of hardships as a prisoner in both Libby Prison and Belle Isle. Mr Coleman is a native Bostonian and resides in Cambridge. They combine their large practical experience, eminent ability and thorough knowledge of the demands of the trade to form a business firm of commanding influence, wide popularity and solid worth.

LAFORME & FROTHINGHAM, Commission Merchants. Rooms 45 and 46, No. 19 Milk Street.—The city of Boston is ably maintaining her supremacy in every branch of import and export trade. Representative among our leading shipping and commission merchants is the widely known and reliable firm of Messrs. Laforme & Frothingham, whose offices are located at No. 19 Milk Street. This business was established in 1868 by Messrs J A. Laforme and F. G. Frothingham, both of whom are able and enterprising commission merchants, fully conversant with every detail of the shipping trade, and the requirements of foreign and domestic markets. Special attention is given by the firm to vessel business, and to the purchase and shipment of goods on foreign orders. They likewise attend to the chartering and dispatching of vessels, load and discharge cargoes, collect freights and act as agents for the owners of steamships or sailing vessels. Messrs, Laforme & Frothingham own several vessels and export largely petroleum and dry goods to Mediterranean ports. They likewise import opium, figs, dried fruits, wool, rags, etc. and make liberal advances when required on consignments, guaranteeing at all times to patrons quick sales and prompt returns. It will be of direct interest to manufacturers of cotton and dry goods, seeking foreign markets to communicate with this responsible house, which is promoting the expansion of the export trade of the United States in a marked and successful manner. Both Messrs. Laforme & Frothingham are natives of Boston. They are popular members of the Chamber of Commerce and of the Vessel Owners' Association, and are highly esteemed in commercial circles for their business ability, enterprise and integrity.

FISHER'S Restaurant, for Ladies and Gentlemen, No. 202 Tremont Street.—The popular well-known Fisher Restaurant is one of the most prominent in the city of Boston and is liberally patronized by an appreciative public. Mr. Fisher is a native of the city and has the correct idea of what is required by the citizens, and fully understands how to cater to their appetites and please them. He has been established in business since 1880 and for six years was located at No. 202 Tremont Street. In 1886 he removed to No. 7 Hayward Place, but finding his business overgrowing his room to accommodate his increasing patronage he returned to his old stand No. 202 Tremont Street in 1888, which he has had fitted up in a most unexceptionable manner, and made more attractive, comfortable, cosy and inviting by pleasant surroundings. It is elegantly fitted up and finished in artistic woodwork, with mirrors, reflectors, etc. An ample area of 25x100 feet, afford every convenience for the purposes of the business and every attention is given to patrons by courteous assistants. Mr. Fisher is a liberal provider and serves besides the substantials, all the various delicacies and game, poultry, oysters, etc., when in season, at popular prices. In fact all the marine and farm and garden products of our own country and other nations are to be found here. He has been very successful since he commenced business, and has by his enterprise and liberality and serving the choicest, well cooked viands, become well-known as a restaurateur and his establishment is highly commended by business men and citizens generally. Excellent accommodations are provided for ladies with or without escorts, and besides regular meals, delicious lunches are served at all hours. Thorough system and order prevails throughout the establishment, and those who desire to obtain a well cooked, neatly served meal or delicacies, will find just what they want at Fisher's, and a well selected bill of fare to choose from.

H. A. HASKELL, Manufacturer of the Eureka Pipe Bender, No. 38 Chardon Street.—One of the best among the many mechanical appliances that have recently been introduced is that known as the Eureka Pipe Bender which is designed for use among plumbers and house carpenters and builders. It is the first appliance ever devised for bending lead pipe above an inch in diameter for goose necks or other irregular forms and has received the unqualified endorsement of all who have seen or used it. In its construction it is very simple and accomplishes in a very short time all that is claimed for it without flattening or collapsing the pipe. They have only been in use about a year but in that time they have been inquired for and sold in all parts of the United States. Mr. Haskell, who controls the right and is the manufacturer of this bending appliance, occupies the second floor of the building No. 38 Chardon Street which is equipped with special machinery operated by steam power, and is kept constantly busy filling orders. One of the features of this appliance is the low price at which it is sold, averaging from $1.00 to $3.25 according to size. They are made in eight sizes from one to three and a half inches. A sample will be sent to any address on receipt of price, and all information cheerfully furnished by calling or writing to the above address. Mr. Haskell, who was born in Maine and resides in Hyde Park, is an expert practical mechanic and since he introduced the Eureka Pipe Bender he has become widely known and is receiving that reward his skill and ingenuity justly entitle him.

THOMAS O'CALLAGHAN & CO., Wholesale and Retail Dealers in Fine Carpetings, Etc., Nos. 597, 599 and 601 Washington Street.—Handsome carpets and oil-cloths are now properly regarded as but parts of an harmonious whole, in considering the subject of household furnishings and interior decorations, and products of the carpet looms of the present day are works of art, and these indispensable articles for covering our floors are no longer confined to the homes of the opulent, the economy of steam production placing them within the reach of all classes of the community. In this connection special reference is made in this commercial review of Boston, to the progressive and representative house of Messrs. Thomas O'Callaghan & Co., wholesale and retail dealers in carpetings and oil-cloths, whose salesrooms are located at Nos. 597 to 601 Washington Street. This business was established in 1886 by Mr. Thomas O'Callaghan, who is sole proprietor. Mr. O'Callaghan is considered one of the ablest salesmen in the country. The premises occupied comprise a superior four-story and basement building, 60x150 feet in dimensions, fully equipped with all modern conveniences that good taste and enterprise can suggest for the successful prosecution of this steadily growing business. The stock shown here is one of the finest in the United States and comprises all the leading novelties in axminsters, wiltons, Brussels, velvets, ingrains, tapestries, oil-cloths, matwand mattings, rugs, etc., which are unsurpassed for quality, beauty, and excellence, while the prices quoted are extremely moderate. A specialty is made of Lowell and Roxbury carpets. Fifty experienced clerks, assistants, etc., are employed in the various departments, and the attendance upon customers is always prompt, polite, and intelligent. The trade of this popular house is by no means confined to Boston, but extends throughout the principal cities of New England. Mr. O'Callaghan was born in Boston, where he is highly esteemed by the community for his enterprise, energy and integrity. The success which has attended this house since its establishment has caused the proprietor to buy exclusively from the most famous importers and manufacturers, thereby giving patrons the benefits previously acquired by jobbing houses only.

UNION INVESTMENT COMPANY, Kansas City, Mo., W. M. Mick, Manager, Eastern Office Room A No. 31 State Street.—Kansas is now recognized as the most productive agricultural section of the United States. The energetic farmer finds nature at her best in the soil which she gives him, yet he must have capital to enable him to carry on his work successfully. The eastern capitalist supplies him with this, and at the same time the investor places his money where it accomplishes material good, while it yields him a very profitable return in the shape of interest. In connection with these remarks, we desire to make special reference in this commercial review of Boston, to the representative and substantial Union Investment Company of Kansas City, Mo., whose eastern office is located at No. 31 State Street. This company was duly organized under the laws of Missouri in 1886 with a paid up capital of $1,000,000, since which period it has built up a liberal and influential patronage. The following gentlemen, who are highly regarded in financial and business circles for their executive ability, prudence and just methods, are the officers and directors: W. P. Rice, president; H. P. Stimson, vice president; O. F. Page, secretary and treasurer; W. M. Mick, Boston manager; Directors, W. P. Moore, W. M. Mick, W. P. Rice, H. P. Stimson, and O. F. Page. The Union Investment Company confines its loans on improved farms strictly to the corn growing sections of Kansas. The company loans solely on first mortgage, its agents carefully inspecting every security offered, and being centrally located to its field of business, its officers have at all times a thorough knowledge of the values. This corporation not only places sums loaned upon mortgage directly from the investor accompanied by its guarantees, but also issues its debentures based upon farm mortgages, similar in all respects to those it transfers and assigns. These debentures are secured on an average of many mortgages, besides being secured by the company's capital. They are most permanent and reliable forms of investment, can be readily transferred, convenient and amply secured at the ratio of $250,000 security for every $100,000 of debentures. The following statement of the Union Investment Company at the close of business September 19, 1888, shows its affairs to be in a most flourishing and stable condition. Resources: Bills receivable, $275,373.00; accounts receivable, $113,819.00; real estate, $335,042.95; real estate loans, $37,735.00; bonds, stocks and securities, $162,921.40; furniture and fixtures, $5,354.50; cash in Hanover National Bank, New York, $54,444.30; cash in National Bank of Redemption, Boston, $54,912.50; cash in American National Bank, Kansas City, Mo., $12,156.96; due from other banks and bankers, $5,094.01; total, $1,409,678.87. Liabilities: Capital stock, $1,000,000.00; bills payable, $60,000.00; time deposits and accounts payable, $27,3,678.78; debentures, $13,500.00; interest account, $8,723.84; undivided profits, $25,776.61; dividend No. 3, payable October 10, $40,000.00; total, $1,409,678.87. Mr. W. M. Mick, the Boston manager, is a Virginian. He has a large banking experience, is known as a careful and conservative business man, and is highly esteemed in financial circles for his integrity and sound business principles.

THE METROPOLIS OF NEW ENGLAND.

THE BOSTON DAILY GLOBE.—Boston as a central point for distinguished journalistic enterprise and the development of high class newspapers, has long held a prominent position in the United States. In this connection we desire to direct special reference in this commercial review to the representative and progressive Globe Newspaper Company, proprietors of the Daily, Sunday and Weekly Globe, which are the recognized leading newspapers of New England. The Globe Newspaper Company was duly incorporated in 1872 under the laws of Massachusetts. It was

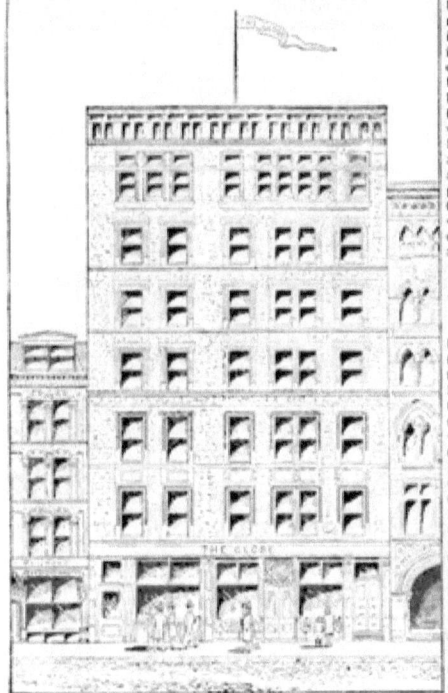

reorganized in 1878, with a paid-up capital of $125,000, and now its Daily and Sunday issues of the Globe have a larger circulation than any other Boston newspaper. The first editor of the Globe was Maturin M. Ballou, and the first paper issued March 4th, 1872, contained eight pages of seven columns, the price being four cents. He was succeeded in August 1873, by Colonel Chas. H. Taylor, who has been the editor and manager of the Globe from that time until the present and the success achieved has been due to his enterprise and industry. The building is one of the finest and largest in Boston, and was built expressly for the Globe; it admirably equipped with all modern appliances, including elevators, electric lights, etc., and no pains or expense have been spared to make this establishment complete in every detail. In the printing rooms are three splendid single and two double Hoe presses, which are able to print 1,100 papers in a minute. The machinery is driven by two superior 125 horse power steam engines, and the total number of persons employed in the various departments is about 500. There are likewise two elevator and electric light engines on the premises, of the latest type. Eight editions of the Globe are turned out daily, which consume fifteen tons of paper. The Daily, Sunday and Weekly Globe are got upon in the highest style of the typographical art. An able and superior staff of editorial writers, reporters and correspondents is employed. It has regular letters from its own correspondents abroad, and carefully covers all political, local and foreign news, while at the same time it gives ample descriptions of races, base ball, and all kinds of manly sports and pastimes. Its editorials are able, crisp, direct to the point, and treat all matters of interest in an impartial and fearless manner. The circulation of the Sunday Globe in November was 127,923, and the Daily Globe 118,219. Its advantages as a splendid advertising medium have been recognized very generally by all classes of the community, and in this line it conducts the largest and most lucrative business in Boston. In consequence of its large size and vast amount of original and able reading matter, it is not only the cheapest but unquestionably the best paper in the city. Col. Chas. H. Taylor, the manager, was born in Charlestown, Mass., and during the civil war was a private in the 38th Mass. Vol. Infantry. He served one year and was seriously wounded at the battle of Port Hudson, Miss., and eventually retired from the service for disability. He was private secretary to Governor Claflin, and was also clerk of the House of Representatives. Col. Taylor is a popular member of the Press, Temple, Central and Algonquin Clubs, etc., and is one of Boston's highly esteemed and public spirited citizens. The circulation of the Globe is steadily increasing not only in Boston but in all sections of New England, and its present prosperous status augurs well for the future.

PARK HOUSE, W. D. Park & Son, Proprietors; European Plan, Bosworth Street—The city of Boston has long been recognized as the centre where unlimited capital, thorough experience and boundless enterprise have combined to make its cafes and restaurants superior to any in the country. As a contributor to the reputation of the city in this regard, and as a model establishment of its kind, the Park House, on Bosworth Street, stands pre-eminent. It is famous the country over for its good cheer and expert management, and is the oldest and best known chop-house in Boston. It was established in 1842 by Mr. T. D. Park, on Devonshire Street, now the site of part of the post office; was removed in 1848 to Morton Place, off Milk Street, where he died in 1865, and was succeeded by his son Hon. W. D. Park, and in 1868 removed to Central Court, off Washington Street, in the rear of Jordan, Marsh & Co.'s; then to present site, off Tremont Street, (formerly known as Montgomery Place,) in 1875. The firm of W. D. Park & Son was organized in 1883, both partners bringing to bear the widest range of practical experience, and giving the business the benefit of their close personal attention and sound judgment. The Park House is an elegant four-story brick building, containing forty-eight guest rooms, conducted on the European plan, while the spacious cafe and restaurant are situated on the ground floor, and cover a floor space of 60x100 feet. The arrangements and appointments are of the best possible character, reflecting the utmost credit upon the enterprise and good taste of the management and perfectly insuring the convenience and comfort of its patrons. The cuisine is in charge of chefs of marked ability and national reputation. The management secures its table supplies from the most varied sources, all the important markets of the country paying tribute to its enterprise. All the delicacies that can possibly be obtained are served in liberal abundance, while the perfect manner in which the viands are served, (having a personal supervision of both proprietors,) make a meal at the Park House a most agreeable experience. While there are larger cafes in the country, there are none which possess such well founded claims upon the public favor or enjoy a more deserved popularity. Any dish is cooked to order in the best manner, and at moderate prices, and a bar and smoking room are located on the same floor. A specialty is made of Park's Musty Ale in pewter mugs, and boiled live lobsters, for which this house has a wide prestige and popularity. The patronage of the Park House is of a character thoroughly complimentary to the firm whose energy, enterprise, discrimination and intelligent enterprise have made the establishment a prime favorite with the best classes the world over. The Messrs. Park are native Bostonians, and are held in universal esteem as accomplished exponents of their business.

THE SUFFOLK NATIONAL BANK of Boston, A. Lawrence Edmands, President, and Edward Tyler, Cashier, No. 60 State Street.—This reliable bank was originally chartered as a State Bank in 1818. Eventually in 1865 it was reorganized under the National Banking laws, as the Suffolk National Bank. The paid up capital of the bank is $1,500,000 which has been further augmented by a surplus of $250,000. The following gentlemen, who are widely and favorably known in financial and business circles for their prudence and just methods are the officers and directors: A. Lawrence Edmands, president, and Edward Tyler, cashier. Directors: Henry Austin Whitney, David R. Whitney, A. Lawrence Edmands, Edmund Dwight, Benjamin W. Crowninshield, Augustus Lowell, Alanson Tucker, and Harcourt Amory. The banking rooms are spacious and elegantly appointed, affording ample accommodations to patrons, and possessing also every convenience for facilitating the dispatch of business. A general banking business is transacted, including the receiving of deposits, the discounting of approved commercial paper, the collection of drafts, and the dealing in government and first-class securities. The bank likewise makes telegraphic transfers of money, and deals in foreign and domestic exchange. This is not only one of the oldest banks in Boston but also one of the best managed and most liberally patronized, and from its foundation has retained the confidence of the public in a marked degree. The investments of the Suffolk National Bank have always been made with care and judgment, and its ventures of capital are at all times well secured. The officers are obliging and efficient in their dealings with the public and are consequently very popular. The president, Mr. Edmands, is a thoroughly capable financier, and a vigorous exponent of the soundest principles governing banking and finance. Mr. Tyler, the cashier, has been in the employment of the bank for the last fifty years—fifteen years discount clerk and thirty-five years cashier. He is an able business man, eminently qualified for his important position. The directors are prominent merchants, manufacturers and capitalists, whose connection with the bank promises a long career of usefulness and prosperity.

REDDING ELECTRICAL COMPANY, Manufacturers of Electrical Supplies; Harvey Redding, President; Jerome Redding, Treasurer; No. 48 Hanover Street.—A representative and successful company in the city of Boston, actively engaged in the manufacture of all kinds of electrical supplies, is that known as the Redding Electrical Company. This business was established in 1868 by Jerome Redding and Harvey Redding, who conducted it till 1883, when it was duly incorporated under the laws of Massachusetts, the officers being Harvey Redding, president, and Jerome Redding, treasurer. The company has a well-equipped workshop and manufactures all descriptions of telegraph and electrical supplies, electrical bells, annunciators, burglar alarms, watch clocks, electric gas lighting apparatus, speaking tubes, and electric lighting and plating machinery. The company makes a specialty of fitting buildings with electrical apparatus of every kind, incandescent lights, etc., and the famous Redding Electric Watchman's Time Register. The Redding Electric Watchman's Time Register is used in buildings where watchmen are employed, and is a guard against fire and thieves, giving an exact report of the faithful, or unfaithful performance of duty of the watchman. It is the only register in the market giving a plain, printed record, which is greatly superior to the ordinary record made by punching small holes through the dial. The punctured record is very hard to read, even when made in the most perfect manner; and in addition to this defect, the needles which make the holes through the dials are very liable to stick and tear the paper dial, thus spoiling the record for the whole night. This usually occurs accidentally, but it is within the power of the watchman to destroy the dial at any time when he wants to neglect his duties, by simply pressing on one of the station buttons for a few minutes, when he can leave his beat for the whole night, and claim that he has performed his duty faithfully. The Redding Electrical Register obviates all these difficulties. Instead of needles to punch holes through the dials, it is provided with steel figures which press against an ink ribbon, and prints the numbers of the stations in plain figures on the face of the dial. These figures cannot tear the dial because they do not stick to it, or against it, even when the circuit is closed, but spring against it mechanically, when the station key is operated in the same manner as the hammer of an electric bell strikes the gong. This register is especially recommended by the Insurance companies, because the record is so plain that the inspector can tell at a glance if the watchman has made every round faithfully, the omission of the record of one station being noticed instantly; whereas the old style of dial has to be very carefully examined all over, in order to see if every minute puncture is in its correct place. This requires such close attention, and takes so much time, that it is sure to be done in a negligent manner, instances having been known where watchmen have for months omitted one station without detection. The company furnishes a burglar-proof Yale lock with every register; but if the watchman succeeded in getting a key to fit it, he could not get at the dial to tamper with it, for one of the printing figures is connected to the lock of the door in such a manner that it prints its number on the dial every time the door is opened, thus effectually preventing any attempt of the watchman to open the door and tamper with the clock without certain detection. The register is placed in the office and connected to iron key-boxes located at every point which it is desired to have the watchman visit, into which he inserts his key (which fits all stations alike), and gives it one full turn; after which the station automatically prints its number on the paper dial in the register. The stations are all independent of each other, and may be visited in any order and number of times. The record of any number of watchmen can be made on the same dial, and each watchman will be obliged to operate his respective beat at the same time the others are operating; therefore, it is impossible for one watchman to relieve the other. The trade of the Redding Electrical Company extends throughout all sections of the United States and Canada, and is steadily increasing. A superior illustrated catalogue and price list is published by the company, which is forwarded promptly upon application.

C. S. KEENE, Eastern Selling Agent, of Buchanan and Lyall's Tobaccos, No. 14 Central Wharf.—New England and Boston form one of the most important fields for the wholesale trade in the highest grades of manufactured tobaccos. As is well known inferior grades have no success in this market. Dealers universally seeking and demanding the best qualities and the most popular brands, more especially those of the famous old house of Buchanan & Lyall, which permanently maintain the lead in the markets of the Middle and Eastern States. They have been selling in Boston since 1863 and have achieved the most enviable of reputations, for every qualification of purity, choice selections of tobaccos, and uniform care in manufacture. In 1881, Mr. C. S. Keene, who from 1878 had been one of the firm's most enterprising and successful traveling salesmen, was appointed the Eastern or New England general agent, and early developed a big increase in the sales. Buchanan & Lyall's tobaccos have only to be brought to the attention of the trade to be bought in the largest quantities, and Mr. Keene in his commodious premises on Central Wharf, carries a heavy stock of Buchanan & Lyall's most popular brands of plug and smoking tobaccos. He employs seven clerks and porters and four men on the road, selling to jobbers and wholesalers all over New England and in the Provinces. His specialties are the celebrated "Planet" brand, admittedly the king of all dark tobaccos, and "Neptune," equally famous, as being by far the finest bright tobacco manufactured. The consumption of the above two brands throughout New England is enormous and constantly growing. Other popular brands handled by Mr. Keene are "Queen Checker Bars," "Sailor's Choice," the standard dark navy," "Flush," the standard light navy, "Rouser Smoking Plug," and Navy Clippings, in two, four, eight and sixteen ounce papers. Mr. Keene is a native of Providence, R. I., and though a young man is old in practical experience, an authority in the wholesale tobacco trade, and universally popular and respected. His energy and enterprise in pushing the sales of the tobaccos he represents have resulted in steady enlargement of trade, and we cannot but urge dealers everywhere who are not already handling Buchanan & Lyall's product to send a trial order to their wholesale merchant. They will find these goods to be the most ready sellers and to give the greatest satisfaction of any in the market.

HATHAWAY, SOULE & HARRINGTON, Manufacturers of Men's Fine Shoes, No. 20 Devonshire Street. New York Branch: Nos. 126 and 128 Duane Street.—One of the most marked records of successful progress and development in the New England boot and shoe manufacturing industry, is that of the celebrated and enterprising house of Messrs. Hathaway, Soule & Harrington. For every essential and every feature of elegance, style and comfort their lines of men's fine shoes are recognized to lead the market, and are in growing demand with the best class of trade throughout the United States. The business was established about twenty years ago by Mr. Savory C. Hathaway, succeeded by the firm of Hathaway & Soule, and who thus continued until 1874, when the present house was organized, composed of Messrs. Savory C. Hathaway, Rufus A. Soule and Herbert A. Harrington. The two former gentlemen are residents of New Bedford, while Mr. Harrington lives in Brookline. They unite every possible qualification, bringing to bear the widest range of practical experience, perfected facilities and influential connections. Their business has grown upon the legitimate basis of supply and demand to proportions of great magnitude, and they now have in active operation, three great factories thoroughly equipped with the latest improved machinery and appliances, and situated respectively at New Bedford, Middleboro and Campello. From six to seven hundred hands are there employed in the manufacture of medium and fine grades of men's shoes, and which embrace every feature of excellence and all the modern improvements rendering them fully the equal of the finest custom work. The copartners give their personal supervision to every branch of the business, selecting their leather and findings with the utmost care, introducing the latest popular styles, employing the most skilful cutters and workmen, and guaranteeing the quality of every pair of shoes leaving their factories. They offer a stock of men's fine hand made shoes, Goodyear welts, and machine sewed, and at their headquarters, No. 20 Devonshire Street, buyers can select from the finest and most comprehensive stock in Boston. The firm's trade extends throughout the United States and the British Provinces, and has necessitated, by reason of its growth, the opening of a branch store in New York City, at Nos. 126 and 128 Duane Street, whence the very finest trade of the metropolis is supplied with these fine shoes, and the demand for which is rapidly enlarging in the metropolis of America, a sure indication of their superiority. Messrs. Hathaway, Soule & Harrington are all natives of Massachusetts, and have here developed a great and growingly important branch of skilled industry, and of the utmost value to Boston as a prominent factor of her commerce. They have ever retained the confidence of leading commercial circles, and are worthy representatives of the boot and shoe manufacturing interests.

SMITH & BLANCHARD, Wholesale Dealers in Lumber, No. 75 State Street.—An old established, progressive and thoroughly representative firm of wholesale lumber merchants, is that of Messrs. Smith & Blanchard, who enjoy unrivalled facilities for the filling of the largest orders of any description of eastern, western or southern lumber both hard and soft. The business, which has now grown to proportions of such magnitude, was originally founded by O. H. Smith, in 1879, thus continuing until 1885, when he and Mr. H. W. Blanchard formed the present copartnership. They have direct and most influential connections with every important lumber region of the country east of the Mississippi. They are direct receivers of southern yellow pine by steamer and in cargo lots from Georgia and Florida; of western hardwoods such as oak, walnut, ash, maple, whitewood, etc., via rail, and of the best growths of New England and Provinces spruce pine, etc. A prominent specialty is their famous Pennsylvania hemlock, in constant and growing demand in the New England markets. They are the sole eastern agents of the Pennsylvania Lumber Storage Company, the largest company ever formed for the handling of hemlock. This company controls over half of the hemlock in Pennsylvania, and expect to handle over two hundred million feet during the ensuing year. The firm is one of the largest shingle concerns in New England, marketing upwards of fifty millions each year. They also furnish large quantities of spruce by rail, controlling the out of several of the best mills in New Hampshire and Vermont. The copartners bring to bear the most practical experience, and thoroughly understand the requirements of every branch of trade. Mr. Smith was born in Maine, and has been a business resident of Boston since 1882. He is largely interested in Maine lumbering operations, and has done much to develop the industries and business of his state. Mr. Blanchard was born in Cambridge, Mass., is a graduate of Harvard College, and is of a race of lumber men. His experience was gained by connections with the western pine yards, and by years of intimate acquaintance with the New England trade. The firm in addition to their long list of customers, who are dealers and manufacturers, sell to exporters for shipment to Europe, West Indies, etc., and are thoroughly representative of the best methods governing the wholesale lumber trade of Boston and New England.

HODGMAN RUBBER COMPANY, Manufacturers of India Rubber Goods, No. 32 School Street.—The extensive enterprise conducted under this heading constitutes the Boston branch of what is unquestionably one of, if not the oldest rubber industries in the country. This industry was founded as far back as 1838, by Mr. Daniel Hodgman, and was incorporated under the present title in 1886. The officers, Geo. F. Hodgman, president, and Charles A. Hodgman, secretary, are sons of the founder, who, from having literally been raised in the business, are familiar with all its details and eminently qualified for its successful conduct. The company has large and well equipped manufactories at Tuckahoe and Mt. Vernon, N. Y., which give employment to a large force of experienced operatives, and the product comprising all descriptions of India rubber goods, has an old established standard reputation in the trade and commands an extensive and profitable market throughout this country and Canada. The Boston branch was established in Jan. 1887, and from its inception has enjoyed an extensive and prosperous business. The spacious premises consisting of a store and basement 25x125 feet in size, are fitted up in a style of modern convenience and attractiveness, every facility being at hand for the advantageous display of goods. The mammoth stock comprises all kinds of rubber clothing and footwear, a specialty being made of gentlemen's mackintosh and plain rubber coats and ladies' gossamers, which are made up in the newest patterns and styles and embody in a notable degree all the advantages and comforts obtainable in these garments. A large force of clerks and salesmen is kept busy in supplying the trade throughout New England with these justly celebrated goods, and the general business is to the highest degree prosperous. Mr. Noyes, the Boston manager, is a gentleman of fifteen years experience in the business, and to his well directed and enterprising management is largely due the signal success achieved.

G. A. SAWYER, Receiver and Dealer in Mutton, Lamb, Veal and Poultry; Basement, No. 3 Quincy Market.—The question of food is one of the first with which the human family in all stages of existence has to grapple, and there is no branch of food supply that attracts more widespread attention, nor one in which more capital is employed than in the meat business, the headquarters of which is this city is Quincy Market. A leader among the commission merchants and wholesale dealers in meat supplies in this central and popular market, is Mr. G. A. Sawyer, who occupies the basement No. 3 Quincy Market. Mr. Sawyer started business twenty-two years ago, and has occupied his present premises for the past five years. The premises are spacious, and are provided with every convenience and facility for the successful prosecution of the business. The latest improvements in the way of refrigerators, etc., can here be found in successful operation. Mr. Sawyer is a practical butcher and brings wide experience to bear on his enterprise. He is quick to recognize and supply the wants of his trade, and there is no better judge of meats in this city. He has a spacious, well equipped slaughter houses at Watertown, and in addition to his supplies therefrom he is in daily receipt of large consignments from the West and elsewhere, so that he has at all times on hand a large stock from which to furnish the wants of his patrons. Mutton, Lamb, veal and poultry form the commodities handled by the enterprising and prosperous house, and the transactions are limited to the fulfilment of wholesale orders. The trade extends throughout the city and New England, and is yearly growing in volume.

METROPOLITAN STEAMSHIP COMPANY'S OUTSIDE LINE OF STEAMERS, H. M. Whitney, Agent, No. 54 Central Wharf.—Boston enjoys superior transportation facilities both by rail and water and has largely increased her commercial and industrial importance and that of the large territory tributary to her, by having direct lines of steamers to important points, competing with and effectually keeping down extortionate railway freight rates. The most important line of coastwise steamships is unquestionably the Metropolitan forming a tri-weekly line direct to New York City by the outside route around Cape Cod, and through Long Island Sound. This line was first established twenty-four years ago, and has had a large measure of patronage from the merchants and shippers of New York and Boston, and also of a large section of the United States, as connected with these cities by lines of steamboats, or railroads. The company is duly incorporated under the laws of Massachusetts, and has a large capital, held in strong hands and is under the ablest executive management. The president of the company is Mr. H. M. Whitney, too widely and favorably known in Boston to require any comment at our hands. Under his guidance, the company is prosperous, its fleet large and of the highest type of modern steamships, and its rates and service deservedly popular. The company's fleet is composed as follows: S.S. "Herman Winter," captain, John M. Hallett; "H. F. Dimock," captain, C. P. Eldridge; "General Whitney," captain, Maynor Bearse, (the above three are of iron); "Glaucus" captain, A. D. Coleman; and the "Neptune" and "Nereus" reserve ships now in commission. The company's steamships are of large size, fine models, carefully built for the outside route, full powered and make regular and speedy voyages in all weather. The rates are lower than by any other line; there are unrivalled wharf accommodations at both ends of the route and no rehandling of goods is required by this line as by all inside routes. Close connection is made at each port with all railroad, steamship and transportation companies, and through rates and bills of lading are a specialty. The company makes a specialty of shipping either from New York or Boston, as rates may favor, all goods for export, granting through bills of lading to London, Liverpool, Havre, Rotterdam, Hamburg, Bremen, West Indies, etc. Mr. Whitney the general manager has his offices at India Wharf, and where all further particulars can be obtained. We recommend the close attention of the merchants and manufacturers of Boston and New England to the unequalled advantages offered by this line for shipping to or from New York and a large portion of the Union. The route is safe, economical and expeditious, and is well worthy of the success attending the company's operations.

J. W. HUNNEWELL & CO., Wholesale Dealers of Refined Petroleum, Etc., Nos. 70 and 72 Commercial Street.—The rapid extension of the use of petroleum is one of the marvels of the present century. It is one of the most prominent articles of export of the United States to foreign countries, over two thousand manufacturing establishments, some of them of vast magnitude, are employed in its refining and purification, and towns and even cities are the outgrowth of its discovery. A prominent and old established house in Boston, engaged in the packing and sale of refined petroleum, is that of Messrs. J. W. Hunnewell & Company, Nos. 70 and 72 Commercial street. This business was established in 1837 by Mr. J. Hunnewell, who conducted it till 1879, when Messrs. George C. Goodhue and Robert D. Archer succeeded to the management, the business being carried on under the old firm name of J. W. Hunnewell & Company. The firm's oil refinery is situated at East Boston. The warehouse is a substantial four story building, fully equipped with every appliance and facility for the successful conducted of the business. The firm deal largely in refined petroleum, spirits of turpentine, lard oil, etc., in patent cans for shipping, also in drugs, paints and oils. The petroleum of this responsible firm has no superior for its entire safety, brilliancy of light and perfection of purification. The other specialities of this house are unrivalled for quality, reliability and general excellence. Messrs. J. W. Hunnewell & Company fill all orders either for the home trade or export at the lowest ruling market prices. They sell largely to ship chandlers in all sections of the United States, and export extensively refined petroleum to Canada, Mexico, South America, the West Indies, Europe, Africa, India and Australia. Messrs. Goodhue & Archer are popular members of the Chamber of Commerce, where they are highly esteemed for their enterprise, promptness and integrity. As exponents of the wholesale refined petroleum trade, we know of no firm more progressive than J. W. Hunnewell & Company, who well merit the large measure of success which has attended their business career.

NESS COUNTY BANK, Ness City, Kansas, A. E. Alvord, Eastern Manager, No. 40 Water Street.—No financial institution of the west has had a more creditable and prosperous career than the Ness County Bank of Ness City, Kan. It was established in 1885 to meet the imperative demand for first-class banking facilities in western Kansas, and on February 23d, 1888, was duly incorporated with an authorized capital of $250,000, and which is held by leading capitalists of Kansas and New England. The board of directors comprises representative men of Ness City, and the following eastern men: A. E. Alvord of Boston; L. Cleaves of Rockport; and L. J. Fosdick of Boston. The officers are as follows: N. C. Merrill, president; J. G. Arnold, vice-president; E. C. Merrill, cashier; A. S. Hazen, asst. cashier; and A. E. Alvord, eastern manager. They possess special qualifications for the discharge of the important duties devolving upon them, and the bank has proved a blessing to Kansas farmers and merchants and affords the safest and most convenient channel for the investment of eastern capital in the finest class of farm and city mortgages; the choicest bonds and county warrants, and a limited amount of gilt edge commercial paper. All loans are taken under the personal supervision and in the name of Mr. Merrill, the president, a pioneer in that section, who is intimately acquainted with both the applicant and his property, and no confidence is placed in local agents in the west to solicit loans. Their $400 and $500 mortgages are on precisely the same class of farms as ordinarily carry $750, $800 and $1,000. The rate of interest offered is the highest possible consistent with absolute safety and ranges from 6 to 7 per cent., according to time and character of the security. Mr. Alvord has most satisfactorily represented the bank's interests in the east. The bank pays twelve per cent. annual dividend and its stock has appreciated rapidly in value. Its last semi-annual statement is of a very flattering character, and indicates not only ability and integrity of management, but also the rapid growth of the western section of the state. Those seeking absolutely safe investments, and of the most remunerative character should apply to Mr. Alvord, at his office, No. 40 Water Street, who always has on hand the best class of farm and city mortgages, and other desirable securities. He is a popular and responsible young business man and gives the closest attention to the interests of all patrons of the bank, and has developed a growing connection of the most desirable character.

C. E. WHITMORE & CO., Brokers, Grain, Stocks and Bonds, No. 131 Devonshire Street.—The centralization of capital in the city of Boston, and the correspondingly marked degree of financial enterprise and activity, inherent in the money and stock markets, are to a great extent due to the conservative methods and ability of our leading bankers and brokers. Prominent among the number, is the reliable and newly established firm of Messrs. C. E. Whitmore & Co., whose offices are centrally located at No. 131 Devonshire Street. The members of this co-partnership are Messrs. C. E. Whitmore and D. W. Coolidge, both of whom possess great practical experience, and an intimate and accurate knowledge of the money and stock markets. The firm purchases and sells for cash or on margin all securities listed on the Boston and New York stock exchanges, likewise grain, provisions and petroleum. Messrs. C. E. Whitmore & Co. are noted for obtaining early and accurate information as to the state of the market, and number among their customers many active operators and wealthy investors. The offices are well equipped and are connected by private wire with New York and Chicago. The partners are popular members of the Boston Stock Exchange, and are highly regarded in financial circles for their prudence, energy and just methods. Their New York correspondent is Mr. W. M. Tewksbury, No. 41 Wall Street and at his hands patrons will ever be treated with courtesy.

RUSSELL COUNTER COMPANY, Manufacturers of Waterproof Moulded Stiffenings, W. H. Russell, President; L. B. Russell, Treasurer; No. 97 Summer Street.—This successful, reliable and representative company was duly incorporated in 1887 under the laws of Maine, with ample capital, and now carries on a trade which extends throughout the entire United States and Canada. This business was originally founded eighteen years ago by Mr. L. B. Russell, who conducted it with great success, till it was incorporated as the Russell Counter Company.

The company's factory is at Woburn, and comprises twelve spacious buildings, which have an area of an acre. The various departments are fully supplied with the latest improved machinery and appliances, necessary for the systematic and successful prosecution of the business. Here 100 operatives are employed, and the machinery is driven by steam power. The waterproof moulded stiffenings manufactured by the Russell Counter Company are unrivalled for durability, quality, strength and excellence, and have no superiors in this or any other market. All orders are promptly and carefully filled, and all goods are fully warranted to be exactly as represented.

E. & A. H. BATCHELLER & CO., Manufacturer of Boots and Shoes; Office No. 106 Summer Street.—Boston has long been noted as being the leading centre of the wholesale boot and shoe trade of the United States, while the command of large capital, coupled with the well-known energy and enterprise of the representative members of this growing industry, has permanently retained the supremacy. Prominent among the largest and most progressive houses, that give tone and character to this trade, is that of Messrs. E. & A. H. Batcheller & Co., whose office and sample rooms are located at No. 106 Summer Street. This extensive business was established sixty years ago by Messrs. Tyler & Ezra Batcheller, who were eventually succeeded in 1852 by Messrs. E. & A. H. Batcheller & Co. Mr. E. Batcheller died in 1870, and the business is now the property of Mr. A. H. Batcheller, who has latterly admitted his son, Mr. Francis Batcheller, into partnership. Both partners are able and experienced shoe manufacturers, fully conversant with every detail and feature of this valuable industry, and the requirements of jobbers, retailers and the general public. The firm's manufactory, which is one of the largest and best equipped in America, and furnishes constant employment to over 1,200 operatives, is situated at North Brookfield, Mass. Messrs. E. & A. H. Batcheller & Co., manufacture extensively brogans, mens', youths' and boys' heavy boots and shoes. Their goods are unrivalled for quality, durability, finish and workmanship and have no superiors in this or any other market, while their prices in all cases necessarily attract the attention of careful and close buyers. The business of this successful and popular house, which is strictly wholesale, extends throughout all sections of the United States and Canada. Messrs. A. H. and Francis Batcheller are both natives of Massachusetts. They are highly esteemed in trade circles for their skill and just methods, and have built up a business and reputation alike creditable to their industry, energy and enterprise.

H. CRINE, Importer and Manufacturer of Fine Fur Garments, Trimmings & Robes, Nos. 15 and 17 Avon Street.—The keen, intelligent public of Boston, and adjoining towns and cities, are quick to perceive and prompt to patronize that tradesman who, by the exercise of skilled experience, sound judgment and untiring industry, facilitates the securing of the choicest honestly-made goods at the lowest prices. In the foremost rank of manufacturing furriers, is Mr. H. Crine, of Nos. 15 and 17 Avon Street, to whom the above remarks strictly apply. His has been a success achieved in the face of extreme competition, and one all the more creditable because, in every case, for every garment turned out by him the public has got the full worth of its money. Mr. Crine was born in Germany, and came to New York in 1857, establishing business there the following year. Subsequently he removed to Georgia, where he enlisted in the 2d Georgia Rifles, serving three and one-half years, and was a portion of the time interpreter at the headquarters of the Army of the Tennessee. After the war he returned to New York and resumed business, and in 1865 settled in this city. Here he occupies a spacious and elegant store, situated in a business portion of the city, absolutely central, and convenient alike to the elite of the city and hotel sojourners. The results have been what might be expected, when we consider the sound judgment of the proprietor and his determination to excel all competition in this direction of trade. As an extensive importer and manufacturer of fine fur garments, trimmings and robes, Mr. Crine is now fast controlling the best American trade. As he selects his skins with the utmost care, the public can rely on securing here the finest sealskin jackets, dolmans, jackets and fur trimmings of all kinds in his showrooms, quoted at prices which cannot be duplicated elsewhere. Making a specialty of the richest seal and fur garments in all standard lengths, we would cordially recommend the public to inspect this splendid stock and get quotations before purchasing elsewhere. The elaborate finish, the perfect cut and symmetry of all Mr. Crine's work has become justly celebrated, confirming the general belief that merit tells, while Mr. Crine is inspired with the laudable ambition to give the best value of any manufacturing furrier in America.

J. P. T. PERCIVAL, City Hall Pharmacy, No. 35 School Street, Cor. City Hall Avenue.—No department of business in Boston is of more direct value and importance to the community at large than that in which the practical pharmacist brings to bear his professional skill and experience. In this connection special attention is directed to the establishment known as the City Hall Pharmacy, and conducted for so many years by Mr. J. P. T. Percival, at No. 35 School Street, corner of City Hall Avenue. This house has been in existence for a period of sixty years, the present proprietor succeeding to the control upward of twenty years ago. The store is located in a new and spacious building, and is one of the most attractive features of this busy and much-frequented thoroughfare. Here is always to be found a complete stock of pure fresh drugs and chemicals, all the reliable and standard medicines and family remedies, and the latest novelties in perfumery, toilet articles and fancy goods of both domestic and foreign production. The goods are selected with scrupulous care and experienced judgment, and can be relied upon as the best that the market affords. The prescription department is perfect in every particular, being fully supplied with the latest improved apparatus and appliances known to this important branch, and is presided over by Mr. A. K. Tilden and a corps of expert pharmacists, whose experience and ability thoroughly qualify them for compounding physicians' prescriptions and family recipes in a careful and accurate manner. This house also handles the following preparations as specialties, viz: nerve tonic, cream of roses, glycerine lotion, tooth powder, extract ginger, Dr. Clarke's cough mixture, sarsaparilla, tomato bitters and calisaya bark. Any articles bearing the name of this house are invariably accepted by the profession and the public as thoroughly genuine, possessing all the qualities claimed for them by the manufacturers. All orders are given prompt attention, and the wants of all classes of patrons are ministered to with eminent success and satisfaction. Mr. Percival is a native of Hanover, Mass., and known and honored in this city as an accomplished pharmacist and a thoroughly responsible and representative business man.

DIAMOND CUTTING.—The art of cutting diamonds originated in Asia at a very early period, but was first introduced into Europe about the middle of the 15th century, the famous Sanci diamond supposed to have been the first one cut. The process was slow and tedious, being entirely done by hand. The Regent of Pitt diamond required two years for its completion. For many years diamonds were imperfectly cut, and the work was done almost entirely in Amsterdam. It was reserved for Boston to show the civilized world to what perfection this most beautiful of all precious stones could be brought. In 1860 Mr. Henry D. Morse opened a small diamond-cutting factory, employing foreign help. He early conceived the idea of teaching Americans, but the secret of how the work was accomplished was jealously guarded by those possessing it. Mr. Morse, however, determined to wrest the coveted knowledge from them, and in order to do so, overcame what would have been to most men insurmountable obstacles. After long and careful examination of the work, he solved the theory by which it was done, and fitting up a place outside his factory, commenced putting the theory into practice. Several hours each day were spent by him in his workshop, and when he came to a part that baffled his efforts, he paid a visit to his workmen, and while engaging them in conversation, carefully observed by what means the desired end was reached. He then retired to his shop and practiced what he had seen, until after a great amount of labor and perseverance he was able to completely polish a diamond. When it is considered that in a perfectly cut stone there are fifty-eight distinct facets, each with a different grain, and that it is impossible to polish a facet except with the grain, some faint idea may be obtained of the difficulties, under which he labored. A man of Mr. Morse's genius was not likely to stop here, and he immediately went to work to improve the art in every possible way. He improved the machines then in use, invented a cutting machine, also a gauge to determine the angles giving the greatest refractive power clearly demonstrating that diamonds could be cut by a system based on scientific principles. Upon learning that Mr. Morse was teaching Americans, his workmen left him and started in business for themselves. They engaged Mr. J. B. Humphrey to build their machines and fit up their factory. The new firm was not very prosperous. In a short time one of the partners fled to Europe with the diamonds, leaving the other with only tools and machinery. Mr. Humphrey, who had gained some insight into the business went to the deserted partner offering to furnish money and start the business anew. The offer was accepted, but in a short time, the Dutchman found that he would be expected to teach Americans. This he refused to do and the partnership was dissolved. Mr. Humphrey was thus left with a factory on his hands, but no workmen, nor could he hire any. But again "Yankee" pluck and intelligence came to the rescue, and after four years of hard labor and indomitable perseverance, he was acknowledged, with the exception of Mr. Morse, the finest diamond cutter in the world. The cleaving of diamonds is by far the most difficult part of the whole operation, requiring superior judgment and very careful manipulation. Indeed there are but three or four cleavers in this country. In this department, however, Mr. Humphrey has also been very successful. About this time Randel, Baremore & Billings of N. Y., offered him such flattering inducements to come there and start a factory for them, that he did so, remaining in their employ nearly two years. After the decease of Mr. Morse he purchased the tools and machines left by him, returned to Boston and again engaged in business for himself. When people began to realize how the value and beauty of a diamond were enhanced by superior cutting, a great demand for Boston cut diamonds sprang up and Mr. Humphrey is constantly in receipt of stones to be recut from many parts of the United States, many of them being heirlooms of more than a local reputation. He is also largely engaged in cutting stones from the rough and is one of the largest importers, making repeated trips to Europe in order to personally select his stock, which he always keeps full and complete. The polishing of a diamond must necessarily be interesting to the artisan. He sees the dull pebbly-looking stone gradually change to a sparkling gem, and feels that here is something over which time has no power, but may be enjoyed by generation after generation for thousands of years, and still shine with the same brilliancy as when it first left his hands.

A. P. FISHER & CO., Brokers in Grain, Stock and Petroleum,—Nos. 28 and 29 Equitable Building, No. 150 Devonshire Street.—There is no more important interest to the financial and mercantile community than that controlled by the several stock exchanges of the country. New York, with its vast interests in railroads, steamship lines, produce and oil, daily transacts an amount of business without parallel in the history of the country. Among the members of the New York Consolidated Stock and Petroleum Exchange engaged in business in Boston is the firm of Messrs. A. P. Fisher & Co., who occupy eligible offices at Nos. 28 and 29 Equitable Building. This firm are brokers in grain, stock and petroleum, having some thirty branches throughout New England, and correspondents in New York and Chicago. The business was originally established in 1881 by Messrs. C. J. Fisher & Co., in New York city, and was removed to Boston in December, 1886, the present firm succeeding to the control in 1888. The facilities here possessed for covering every branch of the business are unsurpassed. This firm are perfectly prepared for the purchase and sale of all kinds of railroad and mining stocks, bonds and investment securities, either for cash or on a margin on commission. Orders are made at once and transfers executed, together with all business of this nature, as readily as could be done by personal attendance at the Exchange. Orders for the purchase or sale of stocks, grain, provisions and petroleum are filled on margins of from one per cent. upward. The members of the firm give their personal attention to every item of business that passes through their office, and the accuracy with which they estimate the value of the various securities has given them a distinction that has merited the confidence of an extensive and influential clientele, and given them a high reputation as financiers. As all business entrusted to them is dealt with promptly and in a manner which secures the greatest possible advantage to customers, their offices are a favorite resort for investors. In this system of business, losses are limited to the amount of margin deposited, while profits are unlimited. Their offices are open alike to the man of wealth and to those of limited means, and each receives the same consideration at the hands of the firm. Full quotations of the different markets are received, as well as the current gossip of Wall street and Chicago, and all sources of information are scanned as a guide to the market. The members of this firm are Messrs. A. P. Fisher, F. H. Tibbitts and L. B. Smith, all practical and expert brokers, of high repute in financial circles.

WEMYSS CONCERT COMPANY, of Boston, Mr. Alex. J. Wemyss, Manager, office No. 82 Canal Street.—The people of the country are naturally fond of amusements and appreciate high class talent and liberally support it. Such being the fact it is only natural that there should be many concert companies and troupes of acknowledged abilities to furnish the entertainment demanded. Among these companies one of the best known hailing from Boston is that of the Wemyss Concert Company, of which Mr. Alex. J. Wemyss, is manager. This company has been before the public several years, and presents talent of acknowledged ability, recognized in their special fortes, the best in the country, all of whom have established reputations at home and abroad as artists of ability and worth. The personnel of the company comprises Miss Nellie Salome Thomas, soprano; Mrs. S. Wemyss Bradbury, reader; Miss Fannie Packard Hoyt, violinist; Mr. Percy J. J. Cooper, late leading tenor o. the C. D. Hess and Nuendorff Grand Opera Company, soloist; Mrs. Alex. J. Wemyss, pianist and accompanist, and Mr. Alex. J. Wemyss, humorist, whose comic songs and droll sayings are one of the features of the entertainments. The programme offered is always varied and well arranged, and wherever the company appears a large and appreciative audience greet the members, and as their repertoire is very extensive the efforts of the artists are sure to give pleasure and satisfaction. Lodges and societies desiring to furnish first-class entertainments for their friends should confer with Mr. Alex. J. Wemyss, the manager, whose office is at No. 82 Canal Street. Mr. Wemyss is a young man, an accomplished musician and humorist and is recognized as one of the best in the country. The Wemyss Concert Company is highly endorsed by the press and commented by all who have had the pleasure of attending the unexcelled entertainments given by the celebrated artists composing it.

THE METROPOLIS OF NEW ENGLAND.

FRINK & HAYES, Contractors and Builders of Gas and Water Works, No. 19 Exchange Place, Room 15.—One of the representative firms of this city, and one controlling a vast business, is that of Messrs. Frink and Hayes, the well-known contractors and builders of gas and water works, who occupy eligibly located offices at No. 19 Exchange Place. The copartners are Messrs. W. B. Frink and A. W. Hayes, both young men of vast practical experience in their business, and of excellent standing in this city. Mr. Frink was born in New Hampshire, and came to Boston in 1871, has had an experience of twenty years in the gas works line, and is thoroughly versed in all the details and requirements of the business. Mr. Hayes is a native of the state of Maine, and has resided in Boston for the past eighteen years. This firm undertake contracts for supplying entire plants for gas or water works in towns, villages and cities, and their services are in constant and influential demand throughout New England. They have supplied the towns of Franklin, N. H., Pittsfield, N. H., Farmington, N. H., and Stoughton, Mass., and in every case their work is of a substantial, permanent and praiseworthy character, forming their best possible recommendation to popular favor and public patronage. Oil gas has a higher illuminating power than any other known substance with one exception (electricity) and contains no impurities such as sulphur, carbonic acid, carbonic oxide, ammonia, etc. And therefore does not require any purification. The gas is produced by the process known as destructive distillation, the oil being introduced into iron retorts five inches in diameter and heated a little above a cherry red heat, each retort contains a current breaking cylinder of wrought or cast iron, having its ends conical or pointed, and having set there in a series of radially projecting pins extending to the inner periphery of the inclosing retort or pipe, said pins being so set in said cylinder as to present effective obstacles to a direct flow of the current of oil through said retort, thereby converting every particle of oil into gas. After the oil has been converted into gas in the retort it passes through a water seal and then through eight scrubbers, which divests the gas of aqueous vapors and tarry matters if any, and from the scrubbers the gas passes into the gas holder and is distributed through the mains. The retorts may be heated with coke, soft coal or wood. Gas plants are supplied by this firm for this gas, and the following is a list of testimonials as to gas plants erected under their supervision. "Farmington, N. H., May 12, 1888. To whom it may concern: This is to certify that I am a consumer of oil gas made by the Farmington Gas Light Company, and find that the light is of a superior character and costs to consumers moderate. It is used in factories, shops, houses, and for streets in this town, and gives perfect satisfaction as I believe generally. Respectfully, F. G. Tebbets & Co., merchants, and one of board of selectmen." "Farmington, N. H., May 12, 1888. To whom it may concern: This is to certify that I am a consumer of oil gas made by the Farmington Gas Light Company, and find that the light is of a superior character and cost to consumer moderate. It is used in factories, shops, houses, and for streets in this town, and gives perfect satisfaction to the best of my knowledge. Respectfully, Chas. W. Talpey, Treas. Farmington Savings Bank." The supplies handled and furnished by this firm have a national reputation for solidity, durability, and perfection of operation, while all contracts are finished in a thorough, workmanlike manner, reflecting the highest credit upon the skill, ability and care of the contractors. Estimates and terms are promptly furnished, and the firm are in a position to defy competition and to place all transactions upon a sound and substantial footing.

ALLAN LINE OF ROYAL MAIL STEAMSHIPS, H. & A. Allan, Agents, Company's Wharf, Pier 6, Hoosac Tunnel Docks; Offices, No. 80 State Street.—The fame of the Allan Line of Royal Mail Line of steamships is world wide. The pioneer in opening regular steam communication between the St. Lawrence and England, it has materially contributed to develop the foreign commerce and prosperity of Boston and Portland, Me. As early as 1873, the company ran several of their steamships to Boston, whose unrivalled through transportation facilities from the west enabled cargoes to be laid down to a direct advantage over New York. The trade steadily enlarged, and in 1880 the Boston agency was duly established by Messrs. H. & A. Allan. The company is the one running a direct line on the important route from Glasgow, Derry and Galway to Boston direct and it is of great importance to passengers to and from the west of Ireland and to and from Scotland that this line of first class steamships include this among their other routes. The full list is as follows: Liverpool and Quebec Service via Londonderry; Liverpool and Baltimore Service via Queenstown, calling at St. Johns and Halifax; Glasgow and Philadelphia service, via Londonderry and Galway; Glasgow, Quebec and Montreal service; London, Quebec and Montreal service, and the one before mentioned from Glasgow to this city. To fully meet the requirements of this list of routes, the company has a fleet of twenty nine of the finest steamships afloat all specially constructed for the North Atlantic trade, having water tight compartments, fitted up in the most admirable manner with all modern improvements, and unsurpassed for strength, speed and comfort. The line has become the most famous for quick passenger service of any on the Atlantic, making the trip from land to land in five days, the distance from Quebec to Liverpool is 500 miles shorter than from New York, while for 1,000 miles, the steamships pursue their course through the magnificent scenery of the lower St. Lawrence, undisturbed by the roughness of the ocean and enabling the passengers to avoid seasickness and enjoy the varied beauties of the trip. This is the favorite route both with tourists and with business men. The fares are as low as by any other first-class line, while the accommodations are unsurpassed. The line is celebrated for liberality of management while the ships are under the command of experienced officers who enforce the strictest discipline. Excursion tickets for first class passage are sold from Boston for from $70 to $150, single cabin passages ranging from $50 to $80. Intermediate and steerage tickets are sold at very low rates. This is the route for steerage passengers, they have superior accommodations, and the best and most liberal of treatment. The wants of female passengers and of children are attended to by stewardesses, and in many other ways, this line's steerage is the best equipped of any in the Transatlantic service. The Allan Line is the popular one in New England. In winter its ships sail from Portland, and in summer the rail trip to Quebec is a short and pleasant one. In every way the Line is worthy of the patronage of the public, and the residents of Boston and New England can obtain full particulars by calling at or communicating with the agents, Messrs. H. & A. Allan at their offices, No. 80 State Street, where Mr. John Bridgewater is the manager in charge of the passenger department, who has had lengthy experience in representing the Allan Line.

BAY STATE HOUSE, George Q. Pattee, Proprietor; No. 382 Hanover Street.—When visiting Boston we would recommend the traveling public to stop at the old established and popular Bay State House in Hanover Street. It is now under new and energetic management and is conducted upon the most approved principles and liberal methods. The house was first opened about thirty years, and after various changes of proprietorship, in October, 1887, passed into the hands of Mr. George Q. Pattee, one of the most widely and favorably known of Boston hotel men, and who was formerly clerk of the St. Nicholas House, Province Court. He has refurnished and renovated the Bay State House throughout, enforces a thorough system of organization and gives that close personal supervision so gratifying to the patrons of a hotel. The house has an excellent location in Hanover Street, and is a substantial brick building, four stories in height, and 50x175 feet in dimensions. All the modern improvements have been introduced, including gas, steam heat, electric bells, etc. On the first floor is the handsome office, and a spacious and well arranged dining room; on the second floor are the parlors, furnished in modern style. There are 106 single and double rooms for guests, light, airy and most comfortably furnished, in a complete manner that invariably gratifies the patrons of the house, and whose interests are so carefully looked after by Mr. Pattee and his popular clerk, Mr. Frank Hardenstett. The Bay State House is conducted on the popular American plan, rooms ranging in price from fifty cents to $3.00 per day; board $1.50 upwards per day. Mr. Pattee is noted for his excellent table. He is a liberal purveyor, and all the delicacies of the season are served here in the best style, the kitchen being in charge of a competent cook and staff of assistants, while the attendance at table is polite and prompt in every particular.

AMERICAN FIRE ALARM COMPANY, C. F. Blackwell, President, J. D. Dexter, Treasurer, No. 71 Kilby Street, Factory No. 570 Atlantic Avenue.—This is emphatically an era of progress, on every hand the ingenious brain of the inventor is constantly at work, and many of our most useful contrivances and discoveries are but a few years old. In this connection, special reference is made in this commercial review of Boston, to the representative and reliable American Fire Alarm Company, whose offices are located at No. 71 Kilby Street, Factory No. 570 Atlantic Avenue. This company was duly incorporated in 1881, under the laws of Maine, with a paid-up capital of $50,000. It has latterly purchased all the patent rights and business for the New England States, of the American Automatic Fire Alarm Association, consequently all correspondence relative to business in said territory, must be directed to the offices of the American Fire Alarm Company. The company's chief executive officers, who are highly esteemed by the community for their enterprise, skill and integrity are as follows: C. F. Blackwell, president; J. D. Dexter, treasurer; A. D. Wheeler, supt. The system of automatic fire alarm, as now carried out by this responsible company has been in practical operation in New England for several years. It has full approval of the various insurance companies, for which they grant a substantial reduction in rates, and is accepted by them as fully equivalent to watchmen and electric clocks. Briefly stated the system is as follows: Thermostats set to give an alarm of fire on the temperature in the room or factory rising thirty degrees above the normal heat of the room, are placed fifteen feet apart on the ceilings, and in all closets and concealed spaces, throughout the building. These sensitive thermostats are connected by wires to an iron case annunciator or indicator, located on outside of building, which indicates the location of an alarm, by doors or other divisions that may be necessary to promptly locate a fire. These wires and thermostats are also connected to a gong on the outside of the building, also to one in the fire engine house, or to places remote from the fire department, two gongs are placed in two different houses adjacent to the premises protected. These gongs ring continually in case of fire. In order that the system may always be in perfect working order, and that owners and insurance companies may be certain of the fact, a recording testing instrument is placed in the office, from which perforated records must be taken daily of the condition of the entire system. These dials are dated and kept for reference. In making this test the batteries, instruments, gongs, and every inch of wire is used; any disarrangement will show the location of trouble on the dial. The batteries used are simple and durable and will last for years. The work is done by contract, and prices vary, according to size and location of factory or building, from $100 and upwards. The following is a partial list of parties, using this unrivalled fire alarm: New York and New England R. R., Boston storage warehouse, Boston art museum, Masonic Temple, Steamer Bristol, Fall River Line, Steamer Puritan, Fall River Line, Steamer Pilgrim, Fall River Line, Boston, Mass.; Eaton & Terry, Emerson Works & Co., F. E. White, H. T. Marshall, James Means, Charles Howard & Co., George G. Snow, I. A. Beals, Burt & Packard, Lilly, Brackett & Co., Brockton, Mass.; Gardner Brothers, John Pilling, Goodrich & Porter, Griffin Brothers, Gage & Johnson, Frst National Bank, W. F. Endicott, Charles W. Arnold, Sanders Leather Company, Perley A. Stone, Field, Thayer & Co., Johnson & Farrar, W. F. & J. A. Blake, Haverhill, Mass.; Bradford Academy, Bradford, Mass.; E. T. Smith & Co., Worcester, M. C. Dizer & Co., East Weymouth, Charles E. Tucker, Abington, Strauss & Kinsley, Braintree, French & Hall, Brocton, Geo. H. Burt & Co., Brookfield, M. F. Thomas, Campello, Churchill & Alden, Campello, Rugg Building, Haverhill, Mass. and C. B. Lancaster & Co., Barnstead, N. H.

BAY STATE BOILER COMPOUND COMPANY, Manufacturers of Bay State Boiler Compound, Etc., E. P. Parsons, President; H. T. Crocker, General Manager; No. 31 Doane Street.—A representative and successful concern in Boston actively engaged in the manufacture of Bay State Boiler Compound, is that known as the Bay State Boiler Compound Company, whose offices are located at No. 31 Doane Street. This business was established in 1884 by Bradshaw, Crocker & Co., and eventually was duly incorporated under the laws of Maine in 1887 with a capital of $80,000, of which $60,000 is paid up. The officers of the company are: E. P. Parsons, president; E. H. Bradshaw, treasurer;

H. T. Crocker, general manager. The company's factory, which is well equipped, is situated at Cambridge. The company manufactures the famous Bay State Boiler Compound, and deals in oils and all kinds of mill and engineers' supplies. They are likewise sales' agents for Mayall's improved packing, and the Ellis cylinder oil cup. The Bay State Compound is unrivalled for utility, reliability and efficiency, and is a general favorite with owners of steam boilers, wherever introduced. The compound is of a soft, mild nature, enters into, softens and goes with the steam throughout the interior of the boilers and all their connecting pipes, preserving the iron by preventing pitting and corrosion, so common to the interior of boilers and pipes. Among the first good results shown will be the softening of incrustation and corrosion, which collects on joints and gauge-cocks. Although it will finally remove all scales, incrustation and rust from interior of boilers and pipes, it is not a quick process, and takes about six weeks to show decided results. Compounds that are sold with results to be shown in from one to three weeks are very liable to contain acids which will have an injurious effect on the iron. It being made from vegetable products, it will not gum or stop up gauge-glasses or valves, and has no injurious effect on dyes, beers, ales or foods. To parties who have never given the matter much thought, we will say, it is an established fact, the conducting power of iron is from 25 to 40 times that of scale, according to the nature of the scale; thus, if a boiler has about an average thickness of 1-20 of an inch scale, it is equivalent to from 1 to 1½ inches of iron to be heated in addition to the thickness of sheets, tubes and flues. This being the case, it will be easily seen that a large amount of fuel must be wasted in keeping steam up to the desired pressure; if the boilers were perfectly clean this could be easily attained. Inasmuch as the company does not claim everything, to parties wishing clean boilers and free connecting pipes, it can show a vast amount of good done and also a large amount of repairs, labor and fuel saved. The company hereby claims for the Bay State Compound: 1. It is a preservative of iron. 2. It can be adapted to any water used for steaming. 3. It will save fuel. 4. It will save labor and repairs. 5. It will save blisters, ruptures and explosions. The Compound is put up in barrels, half and quarter barrel packages. The trade of the company is steadily increasing in all sections of the United States and Canada. The officers are greatly respected for their enterprise and integrity in trade circles.

MERCHANDISE NATIONAL BANK, Offices: Mason Building, No. 79 Kilby Street.—One of Boston's representative financial institutions is the popular Merchandise National Bank. It was duly organized in 1878 in response to the pressing demands of leading mercantile circles for enlarged facilities, and its capital stock of $500,000 was quickly taken by leading capitalists and business men. Their judgment proved correct, for the bank has proved a heavy dividend payer, doing such a large and prosperous business, and maintaining its stock away above par. The directors include Mr. J. G. Whitney, the president; Mr. A. H. Evans, president of the Five Cent Savings Bank; Mr. Nath. F. Truecy retired; Mr. Silas Potter, retired; Mr. Nath. P. Hamlin, commission merchant, and Mr. Thomas Appleton, cotton buyer. A more representative list could not have been gathered together, these gentlemen's names being synonymous with stability and integrity. Mr. J. G. Whitney has retained the presidency since the bank's inception. He is a member of the old and representative house of J. Whitney Brothers, importers, and is a recognized exponent of those great cardinal principles, which underlie the fabric of the commercial world. Mr. Whitney possesses marked executive abilities and regularly and readily discharges a multiplicity of duties that would prove a heavy burden to many. He is a director of the Mercantile & Manufacturers Insurance Co.; of the China Insurance Company.; and of the Boylston Insurance Company. Under his sound practical guidance the Merchandise National Bank is one of the most popular in Boston. He has appreciated support from the cashier, Mr. Charles H. Kilham, who has been with the bank since it first opened, and as an able and clear headed financier. The bank transacts a general business. It is a favorite depository with merchants and has on its ledgers the names of the most eminent houses of Boston and New England and with its capital of $500,000 and large reserve funds, the bank has a handsome surplus of $48,000.

A. T. THOMPSON & CO., Manufacturers and Dealers in Stereopticons, Lenses, Photographic Slides, Etc., No. 13 Tremont Row.—There is probably not one among the many novel and ingenious devices combining the features of utility, instruction and amusement that have taken a firmer hold on popular favor than the stereopticon. And this is true alike as to its application as an effective advertising medium, in street display, as an adjunct to the lecture platform, or stage effects. Keeping pace with the march of progress in science and art, very marked improvement has been effected in these interesting and useful devices of late, a degree of excellence closely akin to perfection itself having been attained in the articles mentioned by some makers, and among those can be named A. T. Thompson & Co., manufacturers of and dealers in stereopticons, lenses, photographic slides, etc., No. 13 Tremont Row, this city, whose productions are articles

of exceptional merit, and, as a consequence, are in wide and growing demand in the trade throughout the entire country. The electric-light stereopticon (which is the leading specialty), patented and made only by this firm, is by common consent the most effective, perfect and altogether superior device ever invented as is amply attested by the extensive sale it is meeting with all over the United States. Mr. Thompson is a man of practical skill and ingenuity, of long and varied experience in this line, and is thoroughly conversant with the business in all its branches. He established this flourishing business in 1851, and from the first has been signally successful in his enterprise. The premises occupied at No. 13 Tremont Row include a neat compact office and salesroom on third floor, with commodious, well equipped factory on fourth floor, while some twenty expert hands are employed. The firm manufactures and deals in stereopticons of every description, lenses, photographic slides and kindred articles, and also makes slides to order in the most prompt and excellent manner, while lectures are illustrated likewise in first-class style, at reasonable rates.

ERNEST F. STEVENS, Artistic Photography, No. 22 Tremont Row.—The reliable and popular photographer, Mr. Ernest F. Stevens, although a young man has had quite an extended experience in the profession, and has achieved an enviable reputation as an artist of undoubted skill and ability. For about six months he was a member of the firm of Stevens & Read whom he succeeded in November last and has since continued the business with marked success, enlarged the facilities and materially added to the reputation of the studio by the superior excellence of his artistic work. The reception parlors which are handsomely furnished occupying the third floor, and the operating room the fourth. In this latter department every modern appliance and improved apparatus known to the business is provided, and the best means are utilized for producing fine work in portraiture and beautiful effects. Two experienced operators are employed, and artistic photography in all its branches is executed with marvelous skill and exactitude. Fine portraits are executed with skill and finished in oil, water colors, pastile, etc.

THE BARBOUR BROTHERS COMPANY, Flax Thread Spinners; Works, Paterson, N. J., Boston Office, No. 21 High Street, F. G. King, Manager.—Boston has long been noted as the centre of the wholesale flax thread trade of New England, while the energy, skill and ability of the prominent merchants engaged in this industry are recognized throughout the length and breadth of the United States. Of such firms it is not necessary to speak any words of praise; their very existence is emphatic evidence of the honorable position they occupy in the commercial world, and the long course of just dealing they have pursued. Such a house is that known as the Barbour Brothers Company, flax thread spinners, whose extensive works are located at Paterson, N. J. The company's Boston office and salesrooms, which is under the able and careful management of Mr. F. G. King, is situated at No. 21 High Street. This business was established 105 years ago in Ireland, and the Boston office was opened in 1876. In Ireland the firm own and operate the extensive Hilden Thread Works, Lisburn, which is carried on by Messrs. William Barbour & Sons. In their factories at Paterson, N. J., and Lisburn, Ireland, and Ottensen, Germany, the firm employ 5,500 operatives, and their trade extends to all parts of the civilized world. The Barbour Brothers Company manufacture in vast quantities all kinds of linen thread for hand work and manufacturing purposes. Their goods have a world-wide reputation, and are unsurpassed for finish, strength, reliability and uniform excellence by those of any other first-class house in America or Europe, while the prices quoted in all cases necessarily attract the attention of close and careful buyers. Mr. King promptly fills New England trade orders, and guarantees entire satisfaction to patrons. Having thus briefly sketched the facilities of this popular and representative company, it only remains to be added, that its business has ever been conducted on the enduring principles of equity, and relations once entered into with it are certain to become not only pleasant for the time being, but profitable and permanent. The headquarters of the Barbour Brothers Company in the United States is at No. 298 Church Street New York.

BOSTON PHOTOGRAVURE COMPANY, Fine Art Publishers, Etc., No. 27 Boylston Street.—The improvements that have been made in the last few years in all that appertains to fine art publishing through the gelatine processes, are nowhere more noticeable than in the work of the Boston Photogravure Company. By means of their various photographic methods, many of them their own invention, paintings, portraits, designs, woodcuts, plans, maps, etc., are reproduced with an accuracy which but a few years ago was absolutely impossible, even by the hand of the most artistic engravers and etchers. This artistic industry is well represented by the Boston Photogravure Company, whose offices and workrooms are located at No. 27 Boylston Street. This business was originally established in 1883 under the title of the Lewis Company, and under that name reproduced some of the best books ever published up to the present day. In 1886 it was reorganized with ample capital, and its name changed as at present. The establishment is one of the largest in the country, and is fully equipped with all the latest improved apparatus and appliances. The specialities of the company are: gelatine printing, or phototypes; half-tone engravings, photo-engravings from line work or prints, photographs on wood, photo-lithographs, as well as designs and drawings of every description. None but the most skilful and careful artists and operators are employed, and the whole establishment is under the direct and critical supervision of the officers, who have earned a wide reputation among the leading publishers and printers for good work.

WILLIAM L. LOCKHART, Manufacturer and Wholesale Dealer in Coffins and Caskets and Undertakers' Supplies, office, No. 149 Stanford Street.—The largest and most reliable establishment in Boston successfully engaged in the manufacture and sale of coffins, caskets and undertakers' supplies, is that of Mr. William L. Lockhart, whose warerooms are centrally located at the junction of Causeway, Stanford and Merrimac Streets. The factories, which are fully equipped with all modern appliances and machinery, and furnish constant employment to 120 skilled operatives, are situated on Bridge Street, East Cambridge. This business was established in 1849 by Mr. Lockhart, who has since built up liberal, influential and permanent patronage in all sections of the United States and Canada. Mr. Lockhart's new warerooms are the largest, finest, best adapted, and most completely equipped of any manufacturer of funeral supplies in this country. Situated in the business portion of Boston, their location is such that they are easily accessible from all parts of the city; being within five minutes' walk of the Northern and Eastern Depots, and ten minutes' car ride of the Southern Depots. The building, six stories in height, at the junction of three streets, is a most imposing structure, as it stands towering above its surroundings. It is most firmly and solidly constructed of brick, redsandstone and iron, and is absolutely fireproof. The interior was designed and finished with the one idea of making this the model funeral furnishing house in America. No pains or expense has been spared in any detail. It will be noted, that light is received from three sides on account of the triangular shape of the building, lighting up the most remote parts of the show rooms. It will readily be seen that this abundance of pure light is absolutely essential for the proper discrimination of the many different shades and qualities of cloths used in the manufacture of the widely known caskets and robes manufactured by this house. The different floors of the building, each containing about five thousand square feet of space, are divided as follows: second floor—offices and salesroom and casket hardware department; third floor—show rooms; fourth floor—packing and shipping; fifth and sixth floors—storage. The second floor is occupied by the offices, salesroom, and casket hardware department. The furniture and fittings are in cherry, while the walls and ceilings are relieved by frescoing in delicate tints, making a rich and artistic effect throughout. On this floor are shown complete lines of robes for ladies, gentlemen and children; casket linings of all qualities, samples of all the leading varieties of casket handles, shrine plates, thumb screws, society emblems, candelabras, Lockhart's embalming board and instruments, undertakers' memorandum books for both desk and pocket, in fact, everything of a miscellaneous nature that is required for a funeral director's use. The show room occupies the whole of the third floor from the street entrance, and contains upwards of two hundred and fifty different and distinct styles of caskets. This room is replete with new ideas and ingenious contrivances, adding much to its beauty and symmetry. Through the whole length and breadth of this vast floor, resting upon gilded frames, may be seen caskets of every variety and color, while about the sides beneath glass cases may be seen many different designs of white broadcloth and plush caskets, many with elegant hand-painted and tufted tops. At the extreme end of the show room, resting beneath a rich catafalque, may be seen one of Lockhart's patent caskets. This casket, which may be completely tufted, lets down upon the sides and ends, giving the appearance of a sofa, when so arranged, thereby relieving the sombreness and box-like effect of the ordinary casket. Here may also be seen casket and floral pedestals of every variety, and Italian wheat in all the latest and most appropriate designs. Mr. Lockhart is confident that all funeral directors will find this room to be the most complete in America. The fourth floor is used as the packing and shipping department, while on the fifth and sixth floors Mr. Lockhart carries a complete duplicate line of all his goods, so that telegraph or telephone orders may be shipped immediately on receipt, day or night. It has been ever his desire to obtain every facility for the prompt execution of all orders that may be entrusted to his care, and he guarantees prompt service in all cases. Funeral directors are cordially invited to an early inspection of these splendid warerooms and to make Mr. Lockhart's offices their headquarters while in the city of Boston. Mr. Lockhart was born in Nova Scotia, but has resided in Boston for the last forty-five years, where he is highly esteemed by the community for his enterprise, geniality of disposition and inflexible integrity, and is one of our progressive and public-spirited citizens.

PERRY YARRINGTON & CO., Manufacturers' and Agents, Representatives of the Automatic Water Gas Company, Office, No. 23 Central Street.—A responsible and able mercantile house of Boston and New England, is that of Messrs. Perry Yarrington & Co., who have now been actively engaged in business for fifteen years as manufacturers' agents, introducing goods and specialties of the most practical, staple value. They are now introducing one of the greatest and most generally useful discoveries of the age, by which every man may have at nominal cost in his own house, factory or store, a complete system, safe and reliable for automatically generating the great essential light, heat and power. These are all obtained by the introduction of the automatic water gas generator, manufactured by Yarrington's patent process, and for which Mr. Yarrington is the owner. These generators can be had of all sizes and to suit all requirements, from a portable cylinder with one light attached, upward. The product is a hydro-carbon gas, intense in the amount of its heat, and the result is the strongest and most brilliant gas light in the world. The cost of making this gas is remarkably small, and merely nominal in use as compared with coal gas or other forms of water gas, being about ⅓ less cost for running gas engines, and ⅔ less for heating purposes. Purity and safety are combined. The processes are all chemical and the insurance underwriters permit its use in all buildings without extra charge for insurance. Mr. Yarrington has remarkable and convincing testimonials in his possession which will be furnished on application. Mr. F. H. Wheeler, Master Mechanic, American Arms Company, Boston, estimated a saving of seventy per cent. cost in running by using water gas. Everybody interested should write to Mr. Yarrington for full particulars and estimates of cost of generators. He is already meeting with a heavy and widely extended demand for the new system, and we predict that it will entirely revolutionize the existing methods of lighting, heating and securing of gas engine motive power. Mr. Yarrington is a native of Connecticut and a prompt honorable business man.

THE AMERICAN LOAN AND TRUST COMPANY, Omaha, Nebraska, J. F. Rogers, Manager, Eastern Office, No. 164 Milk Street.—The judicious and safe investment of capital is a most important question to the capitalist, as well as to the man of moderate means. In all the various openings, that present themselves for the use of surplus funds, there is not one that when prudently and carefully availed of, is so safe, sure and remunerative, as the loaning of money on the first mortgage security of fertile western farms and city property. The superiority of western farm mortgages to most other forms of security is readily apparent. The western farmer borrows to render his farm more productive; he buys implements and stock, builds barns and houses, plants orchards, etc., and thus adds greatly to the original security. In the east money borrowed on bonds and mortgages, very seldom is expended on the security, but goes in some other way. In connection with these remarks, we desire to make special reference in this commercial review, to the reliable and substantial American Loan and Trust Company of Omaha, Nebraska, whose eastern office in Boston is located at No. 164 Milk Street. This progressive company was duly incorporated under the laws of Nebraska in 1883, and already has obtained a liberal and influential patronage in the east and west. Its paid up capital is $400,000, which has been further augmented by a surplus of $42,000. The following gentlemen are the officers: O. M. Carter, president; D. D. Cooley, vice-president; Philip Potter, secretary; A. C. Powell, cashier. The American Loan and Trust Company deals in six per cent. debenture bonds, and six per cent. mortgage loans secured by first lien on improved real estate in Nebraska and Northern Kansas. The principal and interest due to investors are fully guaranteed, and are paid at any local bank in the eastern states. The company has also a savings bank department and pays five per cent. interest on deposits compounded semi-annually. In its loans on improved city and farm property, this responsible company loans only to the extent of forty per cent. of a low valuation by reliable experts.

THE METROPOLIS OF NEW ENGLAND.

A. P. MARTIN & CO., Manufacturers and Commission Dealers in Boots, Shoes and Leather; No. 14 High Street.— The name of Martin has for years been honorably identified with the industrial growth and public interests of Boston, to such a degree, indeed, as to place the house under review in a position far beyond the requirements of any praise which these pages could bestow. It will be sufficient for our purpose, therefore, to merely call the attention of the trade to some of the advantages and benefits accruing from the opening of business relations therewith, together with a brief account of its history and present facilities. The business so successfully conducted at the present day under the name and style of A. P. Martin & Co., was founded some twenty-five years ago, by Messrs. Fay & Stone. The firm name was soon afterwards changed to Martin, Skinner & Fay, which was succeeded by Martin & Skinner, and in 1881, Gen. A. P. Martin, the senior member of the firm for some years, succeeded to the sole control, and has since continued the business under its present firm name, and, by reason of his large experience, commanding ability and business integrity, has built up a trade of enormous magnitude. The house, under his guiding hand, has every essential which can conduce to its permanent prosperity and the steady development of a trade national in its extent. The firm name is widely prominent as representing the extensive manufacture of men's, women's, misses', boys' and children's kip, split, buff and grain polkas and polish boots and shoes. The factory is located at Hudson, Mass., and has had in the past month, a large addition built, and will give constant employment to two hundred skilled hands. The success of the house has been largely due to the great and systematic care used in every detail of manufacture. The goods are not made simply to sell, but, on the contrary, with an idea, that they are to be worn, and must please the consumer. By this course an enviable reputation has been gained upon the policy that goods can be made to sit easily and still have durability and solid worth. The goods go to all parts of the west, south and southwest, and create for themselves a permanent demand wherever once introduced. Hon. Augustus P. Martin, the honored proprietor, was born in the state of Maine, but has resided in Boston since his boyhood. No citizen of the Hub is better known to its people or more universally esteemed in both public and private life. His record as a city official is one of the brightest pages in the history of the municipality. He was elected Mayor of the city by a spontaneous uprising of the people, at a time when his true worth as an executive officer was needed for the maintenance of the good name and fame of the city, and nobly did he respond to the call. As a soldier he was valiant and brave, as a Mayor he won the respect and esteem of all parties and classes, and as a manufacturer he stands in the foremost rank of the trade.

NEW ENGLAND STEAM COOPERAGE COMPANY, Manufacturers of Tanks, Casks and Kegs, Office No. 160 State Street; Factory, East Boston.—One of the recently formed corporations of Boston, and one of the most vital importance to her commercial interests is the New England Steam Cooperage Company. It is the outcome of the honored and successful career of the old house of Hill & Wright, wholesale coopers of East Boston. This firm was established upwards of thirty years ago, and early took the lead in all those important and extensive lines of cooperage for brewers, malters, distillers, sugar houses, exporters and the trade generally. In January, 1888, the important interests involved were duly capitalized under the name and style of the New England Steam Cooperage Company, with Mr. Henry B. Hill as president, and Mr. William N. Hill as treasurer and manager. Both gentlemen bring to bear the widest range of practical experience, coupled with connections of the most influential, widespread character. The company under their able and equitable executive management has made rapid progress and has an equipment, and factory at East Boston covering one and a half acres fitted up with all the latest improved machinery and appliances of all kinds. Here 100 men are employed in the manufacture of ale and beer kegs of all grades. Their facilities are unrivalled by any concern in America. Barrels, halves, quarters and eighths; stock and storage casks; mash and fermenting tubes, beer stills, hop jacks; tanks, cisterns and vats of cedar, cypress, pine or oak for brewers, maltsters, distillers, sugar houses, vinegar works, paper mills, chemical works, railroads, etc. Water casks for shipping, oil casks, reservoirs, etc. Other lines in stock or contracted for at prices difficult of duplication elsewhere, are molasses and rum hogsheads, kegs and pails for white lead, buckets and oyster pails, ships' square tanks; also the best qualities of staves and heading. The company has a capital of $100,000 and controls large tracts of timber lands in the southwest, receiving their staves direct from stump and at lowest cost. The great advantages thus enjoyed by the company are duly appreciated by its customers, to whose prices are quoted that considering the high standard of all the company's work cannot be met elsewhere. The company does a heavy and growing trade, with connections all over the United States and also export shooks, etc. All orders will receive prompt attention at the office, No. 160 State street, which has telephone connections, while the company has first-class arrangements for shipping cooperage to any point.

FURNESS LINE of Steamships, C. Furness, Proprietor; No. 85 Water Street, London Agents; Thomas Ronaldson & Co., Leadenhall Street.—The Furness Line so deservedly popular with the commercial world, and which has developed an enormous freight traffic direct with London, England, to which port the fleet plies from Boston. The line was established six years ago by Mr. C. Furness of Hartlepool, England, one of the leading and most progressive steamship owners in the world. To his spirit of enterprise, Boston is materially indebted for this important feeder to her commerce, and to the popularity of the route to and from London. Mr. Furness removed his Boston headquarters to No. 85 Water Street in March, 1888, and which are in charge of, and the business here generally under the able management of Mr. R. E. Burnett, who brings to bear ample experience and influential connections as a ship and freight broker and steamship agent. The Furness Line fleet of steamships is composed as follows: Wetherby, 2123 tons; Stockholm City, 2086 tons; Ripon City, 2341 tons; Durham City, 3032 tons; Boston City, 2381 tons; Gothenburg City, 2736 tons; Washington City, 226 tons; Damara, 1779 tons, and Ubanda, 1779 tons. These are all A1 at Lloyds, full powered iron steamships, of excellent model and great cargo capacity; speedy, safe and seaworthy, and keep up a regular ten day service between Boston and London, each way, through bills of lading being issued to and from all the principal Baltic, Continental, Mediterranean and Oriental ports, connecting at London with direct steamers. Freight room can be secured from Mr. Burnett at short notice for almost any tonnage required and at low current rates. This is a great convenience not only to our Boston merchants, but also to the thousands all through the west and in Canada, who can import and export on direct through bills of lading via this line and connecting railroads. The Furness ships take eastward full cargoes of grain, provisions, flour, meal, cotton, flax, butter, cheese, apples, etc., and discharge here full lines of merchandise, pig iron, metals, etc. Mr. Furness is doing much to build up Boston's foreign trade and long may his flag continue to be seen flying from steamships in this harbor.

KARL A. RYDINGSVÄRD, Architectural and Artistic Wood Carving, No. 56 Beverly Street.—For exquisite workmanship, or originality and beauty of designs in the line of wood carving, not one in the business in Boston excels Karl A. Rydingsvärd. He was born in Sweden, and has resided in this city about five years. He is a practical wood carver of long and varied experience in the exercise of his art and is a thorough master of the same in all its branches. He started in business on his own account here in 1886, and soon established himself in favor and recognition, acquiring in a short time a very flattering patronage. He occupies ample and well equipped quarters, (with J. W. Clark, manufacturer of desks, wood mantels and interior furnishings) and is prepared to attend to everything in the line of architectural and artistic wood carving, designs being made. Mr. Rydingsvärd has been connected with some of the best firms in Stockholm and Boston, as designer and carver, and has taught in both cities. Mrs. Rydingsvärd has studied under Herr Leonhardt Sturm, Dresden, one of Germany's most celebrated porcelain painters, and for several years has been a teacher in the Mass. Normal Art School.

FOWLE, HIBBARD & CO., Produce Commission Merchants, Butter, Cheese, Beans, Peas, Evaporated Apples, Eggs, Poultry, Etc., Nos. 176 State and 7 Commerce Streets.—The facilities enjoyed by the City of Boston as a distributing point for staple agricultural products have been such as to greatly promote the shipment to this market of general country produce, and the prosecution of the commission business. The enterprise of Messrs. Fowle, Hibbard & Co., of Nos. 176 State and 7 Commerce Streets, in this direction of trade is a prominent one, and deserving of honorable mention in this review. The business was originally established in 1856, by Messrs. L. W. Fowle, S. P. Hibbard and J. W. White, and in 1885 Mr. E. J. Whitman was also admitted as a member of the firm. They occupy spacious and commodious premises, consisting of a salesroom running through the block from State to Commerce Streets, also a basement and five upper floors, thus giving ample accommodations for landing and storing the immense and valuable stock and for supplying the most extensive demand. The firm handle butter, cheese, beans, peas, evaporated apples, eggs, poultry, etc., and are widely known throughout the best producing sections of the country as among the most reliable and successful commission houses in Boston. They receive their supplies direct from producers and first hands, and the facilities possessed by this firm are such that consignments of goods, however large, are quickly placed and prompt returns made in all cases. Sales are made in wholesale lots only, all orders being filled with despatch, while goods are also shipped direct from producers on orders, inducements being offered in this direction unsurpassed by those of any other house in the trade. The firm enjoy a generous patronage from the hands of all who have come in contact with the house in a business way, securing, as they do, the perfect confidence of the trade everywhere, and gaining friends in all their movements. In this way their business is maintained in a promising and healthy condition, and is broadly distributed throughout all the New England States. So much for enterprise, honesty and business push. Messrs. Fowle and White are Massachusetts men by birth and training, Mr. Hibbard is a native of Canada, and Mr. Whitman was born in the State of Maine. They are all gentlemen of high repute and wide acquaintance in commercial and trade circles, and are commended to shippers and dealers alike as worthy of every trust and confidence.

GEO. TYLER & CO., Agricultural Machinery, No. 43 South Market Street.—A progressive and representative house in Boston extensively engaged in the sale of agricultural machinery, is that of Messrs. Geo. Tyler & Co., whose offices and salesrooms are situated at No. 43 South Market Street. This business was established nine years ago by Mr. Geo. Tyler who conducted it till October, 1886, when he admitted his son Mr. F. J. Tyler into partnership under the firm name of Geo. Tyler & Co. The premises occupied comprise four commodious floors 25x60 feet in area, fully equipped with every appliance and facility for the successful prosecution of the business. Messrs. Tyler & Co. keep constantly in stock mowing machines, hay tedders, hayrakes, sulky plows, swivel plows, spring tooth harrows, smoothing harrows, corn planters, ensilage cutters, horse powers, threshers and cleaners. They are agents for the famous Climax Disc Harrow and also keep in stock all kinds of repairs for mowing machines, horse rakes and road machines. Only the best and most reliable agricultural machinery is handled by the firm, and the prices quoted are as low as those of any other contemporary first-class house in the trade. The firm employ three travelling salesmen, and their trade extends throughout all sections of New England and New York. Both Messrs. George and F. J. Tyler are natives of Connecticut. All their dealings are characterized by energy and integrity, and they are highly esteemed in trade circles as able and trustworthy business men.

THE GEO. E. READ Furniture Company, Manufacturers of Chamber Furniture and Sideboards, Nos. 89 to 95 Richmond Street.—The leading representative concern in Boston devoted to the manufacture of the better grades of walnut, mahogany and oak chamber furniture, sideboards, wardrobes, etc., is the George E. Read Furniture Company of Nos. 89 to 95 Richmond Street. The business was established in 1873, and under Mr. George E. Read's skilled and enterprising proprietorship, rapidly developed to proportions of great magnitude, so much so that in 1884, the important interests involved were duly capitalized under the existing title, with Mr. H. Dunning as president, and Mr. G. E. Read as treasurer and general manager. The directors include Messrs. Dunning and Read, and Mr. William E. Litchfield, all prominent citizens, noted for ability and enterprise. Mr. Read is a native of Providence, R. I., and from early life has been actively identified with the manufacture of furniture. He is a leading authority in the line, and brings to bear every qualification, including thorough knowledge of the wants of the trade. The company's main premises are five stories in height, 60x100 feet in dimensions, and in addition the second floor of adjoining building is added. The latest improved machinery and appliances have been introduced, run by seventy-five horse engine with a seventy-five horse boiler. Upwards of sixty hands find steady employment here in the manufacture of the newest and most popular styles of chamber furniture, sideboards, wardrobes, chiffoniers, etc., in the best quality of seasoned walnut, oak, mahogany, cherry, etc. Mr. Read, as general manager enforces a thorough system of organization, and selects materials with the utmost care, only skilled, experienced workmen are employed, the finish is elaborate and the company is justly celebrated throughout the trade as selling the very best goods that can be produced for the money; both as to highest quality and lowest prices. Possessed of sound judgment, marked executive ability, and building up the reputation of this representative concern on the basis of merit, they are worthy of the large measure of success achieved, and have permanently retained in Boston, a most important and valuable branch of trade.

MERCANTILE FIRE & MARINE INSURANCE COMPANY, Geo. R. Rogers, President, James Simpson, Secretary, Office No. 58 State Street.—The Mercantile Fire & Marine Insurance Company, was duly incorporated under the laws of Massachusetts in 1823 with a cash capital of $300,000, which amount was increased to $400,000 in 1877. The executive officers of the company are Geo. R. Rogers, president, and James Simpson, secretary. The company undertakes all kinds of fire, marine and inland risks, also insuring dwellings, stores and furniture in the city and country for one, three and five years at the lowest possible rates, consistent with safety. The present strength of the Mercantile, Fire & Marine Insurance Company is best shown by its annual statement January 1st 1888, which is as follows: Assets—Investments at market value, and secured loans, $606,496.66; cash, notes, interest, and all other items, $8,377.85; total assets, $954,746.01. Liabilities—Unpaid losses, $29,413.05; reinsurance fund, (Massachusetts Standard) $165,564.46; all other liabilities, $8,647.83. Total liabilities $244,625.34. Capital stock paid in, $400,000.00. Net surplus, $320,760.67. We would observe, that the affairs of this responsible company have always been ably and prudently managed, and its surplus as regards policy holders now amounts to $320,760.67.

AARON H. GAY & CO., Account Book Manufacturers, Stationers, Etc., No. 122 State Street.—An old established and representative house in Boston, actively engaged in the manufacture of account books, stationery, etc., is that of Messrs. Aaron H. Gay & Company. This business was established in 1817 by Aaron H. Gay, who conducted it till 1859, when he died, and was succeeded by the present copartners, Messrs. Samuel S. and Edwin W. Gay, who are now conducting the business under the old style and title of Aaron H. Gay & Company. The premises occupied comprise a commodious five-story building 25x42 feet in area. The manufacturing department is fully supplied with the latest modern machinery for the execution of their work. A good force of experienced workmen are employed, and the trade extends throughout the eastern, middle and western states. The firm makes a specialty of all kinds of blank books, such as journals, ledgers, day and invoice books, etc. They likewise furnish promptly to order letter, note and bill paper, checks, drafts, receipts, bonds, certificates of stock, lithographic circulars and cards in the highest style of art at extremely low prices. The blank books manufactured by this responsible firm are unrivalled for quality, finish and excellence, and are used by insurance companies, banks, bankers, etc. Mr. Samuel S. Gay is a native of Roxbury, while Mr. Edwin W. Gay was born in Boston.

THE METROPOLIS OF NEW ENGLAND.

A. E. JEANERET, Watchmaker and Manufacturer, No. 25 Washington Street.—The trade of the watchmaker is well represented in this city by Mr. A. E. Jeaneret, who is a practical mechanician and has acquired a wide reputation for skill and dexterity, and enjoys in a marked degree the implicit confidence of the trade and the public. He is a native of Switzerland, and came to the United States in 1878 and has been established in business since 1876. His patronage is large, and in all his work he exercises the greatest care, and is pronounced one of the best fine watchmakers and repairers in Boston. He occupies a very desirable location, room 14 on the second floor of the building No. 25 Washington Street, and carries in stock a general assort-

ment of gold and silver watches of both foreign and American production, and is conducting a large, prosperous business. Mr. Jeaneret is the president and largest stockholder in the company which was incorporated in 1888 for the manufacture of Diamond Luster for cleaning and polishing gold, silver, plated ware, nickel and glass, which is sold all over the country and is pronounced the finest and best article for the purpose ever before brought to the notice of the public. It is the best selling article of the kind in the market and is far superior to any other preparation and is sold at retail at the low price of 25 cents per box. Many hundreds of testimonials have been received by Mr. Jeaneret all of which highly commend the luster and endorse it as the best preparation ever discovered for polishing metals or glass, and as it is free from grit, acid, or any injurious corrosive substance, will not injure the most delicate surface. It has been in use over six years and has given perfect satisfaction in every case. Jewelers and the trade are supplied by Mr. Jeaneret who will also furnish testimonials and circulars giving full information on application.

GEORGE D. BROWN & CO., Wholesale and Retail Dealers in Mutton, Lamb, Veal and Poultry, Stall No. 15, New Faneuil Hall Market.—Brown's pickled lambs' tongues have attained international celebrity as a great popular nutritious delicacy, and the result of this branch of Boston's skilled industries is that Messrs. Geo. D. Brown & Co. are the second largest bottlers of lambs' tongues in the world. Mr. George D. Brown established in business twenty-five years ago as a wholesale and retail dealer in mutton, lamb, veal and poultry, and early developed a desirable connection and a growing trade in Boston and throughout New England. Upwards of twenty years ago, Mr. Brown, with characteristic enterprise, originated the idea of pickling lambs' tongues by wholesale, and of putting them up in bottles for the trade. He had the necessary energy to carry out his new departure in its every detail, and pickling the tongues by a process that gives them an unrivalled flavor and excellence, he speedily created a new and flourishing branch of industry, and one that has now attained proportions of enormous magnitude. Mr. Brown now sells half a million tongues per annum. The raw tongues are received from Buffalo, Kansas City, Chicago and New England points, at No. 19 Faneuil Hall Square, 30x70 in size, where he has all appliances at command, and employs a number of skilled hands in pickling and bottling. The tongues are put up in pint, quart and two-quart glass jars, and in kegs and barrels. It will reveal no private trade secret by our stating that Mr. Brown puts his lambs' tongues up in white-wine vinegar and boils them to a turn, spicing and specially preparing them before bottling. His is the oldest house engaged in this branch of trade; he sends his tongues to all quarters of the globe, and has made the name of his house, and of Boston, household words at the extremities of the earth. Mr. Brown has by no means neglected to develop his trade in prime mutton, lamb, veal and poultry, and stall No. 15 New Faneuil Hall Market makes one of the finest displays in the city. He supplies numerous large consumers in Boston, such as hotels, restaurants, etc., and sells to the trade within a radius of one hundred miles of the city, his meats giving unqualified satisfaction. He supplies the leading hotels at Narragansett Pier, Newport, Crescent Beach, Magnolia, Cottage City and Martha's Vineyard.

THE CALIFORNIA INSURANCE CO., of San Francisco, Marine Agency for the Eastern States and British Provinces, Nos. 41 and 43 Devonshire Street.—The clientage of this agency is of the best, and few companies in the country have warmer or more steadfast friends. This is owing to its broad and liberal methods and prompt settlements. The officers of the company are of the highest standing and its history is a credit to their management. The company was established in 1864, with a capital of $600,000 in gold. Its present cash assets are $1,250,000. It has received in premiums $6,000,000, and paid in losses over $3,000,000, besides dividends, etc. The stock is largely owned by the directors, a guarantee of safety. The market value of the stock is fifty per cent over par. It was this company, which the Washington Fire and Marine Insurance Co., of Boston, selected to reinsure all its marine risks. This reinsurance was taken by the Boston agents of the California Insurance Co., in this city Messrs. E. Whitney & Co., who adjust and pay all marine losses in Boston. Foreign certificates are issued when required payable in London, Liverpool or Paris.

JEWELL & CO., Bankers and Brokers, No. 175 Washington Street.—One of the leading firms of bankers and brokers in the city is that of Jewell & Co., No. 175 Washington Street. The business was established five years ago and the present elegant offices have been occupied since 1885. Messrs. Jewell & Co. deal in bonds, stocks and securities of every description, either outright or on account, and do a large business in railroad shares as well as in oil, grain and provisions. They have a wire direct from New York, and have correspondents in Chicago and the principal markets of the country enabling them to obtain the latest information on the fluctuations of the market. Mr. Jewell, who is a Massachusetts man, has had a long experience in the stock market and his judgment has been found unerring in important deals. He looks after his customers' interests in the most faithful manner and during the four years he has been established has earned a first-class name as a safe and conservative broker.

THOMAS J. SMITH, Tea Broker; No. 34 Broad Street.—Of all the various articles comprehended in the food supply trade there are none harder to procure in pure, fresh quality than teas, and the greatest care should be exercised by the grocer in selecting his supplies from a reliable source. A representative broker in teas in this city is Mr. Thomas J. Smith, who has been prominent in the business here since 1868, and who occupies eligible office quarters at No. 34 Broad Street. Mr. Smith is a Massachusetts man by birth and training, and has resided in Boston since 1850. He was engaged in the grocery business from 1854 to 1869, and is well and favorably known in Boston business circles. He longs to bear upon his present business the widest range of practical experience and an intimate knowledge of all the needs and requirements of the trade, while his influential connections with the best source of supply enable him to supply the Boston market with teas of every grade and growth in quantities to suit, and at terms and prices which are rarely, if ever, duplicated elsewhere. All goods furnished through him are guaranteed to be strictly pure, fresh and reliable, and all orders of whatever magnitude, are given prompt and careful attention. New season, fresh-crop teas of all grades are handled, including oolong, English, breakfast, Japan, young hyson, gunpowder, Imperial Pekoe, Souchong, and other varieties, and the aim of Mr. Smith has always been to meet every demand of this market.

THE MASSACHUSETTS LOAN AND TRUST COMPANY, Stephen M. Crosby, President; Frank W. Reynolds, Treasurer, No. 18 Post Office Square.—Intimately connected with, and indeed forming an integral part of the commercial and financial interests of the city of Boston, and equal to the largest banks in responsibility and practical necessity, are the various loan and trust companies. Prominent among these is the representative and reliable Massachusetts Loan and Trust Company, whose offices are centrally located at No. 18 Post Office Square. This corporation was duly chartered in 1870, under the laws of Massachusetts, with a paid up capital of $500,000, and with liberty to increase to $1,000,000. The management of this substantial company is in the hands of prudent and experienced business men, whose names are thoroughly familiar throughout financial and commercial circles, as those of honorable and capable citizens. The list is as follows:—President, Stephen M. Crosby; treasurer, Frank W. Reynolds; directors, Samuel Atherton, Cyrus G. Beebe, Stephen M. Crosby, Isaac Fenno, Joseph H. Gray, Lyman Hollingsworth, Henry D. Hyde, Moses Kimball, Frank W. Reynolds, Henry A. Rice, Richard H. Stearns, Edward Whitney. All the usual routine of a large general banking business is carried on, including the receiving of accounts of manufacturers, merchants and others subject to check at sight, while special rates of interest are allowed on money payable on fixed time. The company makes advances on staple merchandise, foreign or domestic, on bills of lading or warehouse receipts. The charter of the company gives authority to receive and hold, collect and disburse money, securities or property in trust or otherwise, from individuals, executors, administrators, guardians, trustees or, by the order of the court. The company likewise acts as trustee for railroad and other corporations, also as financial agent for any persons, societies, corporations or municipal authorities. It is also agent for the payment of bonds, coupons, dividends, etc., and as transfer agent for the stocks and bonds of incorporated companies. The following statement shows the condition of the Massachusetts Loan and Trust Company at close of business Nov. 30, 1888: Assets—Loans on time, $1,751,726.39; loans on demand, $419,072.63; total loan, $2,170,799.02; expenses, $8,351.87; taxes, $6,003.25; cash, $167,632.00; total assets, $2,349,786.23. Liabilities—Capital stock, $500,000; surplus, $110,852.29; profit and loss, $76,530.03; undivided profits, $19,678.29; bills and memo. payable, $847,854.90; deposits subject to check, $902,485.03; dividends unpaid, $318; insurance, $7.50.

WM. GARRISON REED, Fire Insurance Agent and Broker, No. 25 Kilby Street.—Insurance is undoubtedly the right arm and main support of all business enterprises, and as such merits recognition and respect in this work. We have carefully watched the development of insurance ever since the great fires of Boston and Chicago, and especially have we traced the growth and success of the agency business. The insurance agent occupies an important position in the profession. He acts as the agent both of the company or companies he represents, and of the property owner who employs him to place his insurance. Usually he has a number of companies of good standing, and he will take the contract for placing a line of insurance for a client and use his judgment in so doing. The insurance agent must necessarily be a thoroughly posted insurance man, that is, be competent to judge the nature and liability of a risk, and judge what an amount it should pay. The advantage to a property owner in employing such an agent is in the fact that he is relieved of much trouble and expense in placing his own insurance, especially should it be a large line. Among the best known and most experienced insurance agents in Boston, is Mr. William Garrison Reed, of No. 25 Kilby Street. This gentleman, in partnership with his brother, the late Mr. T. Frank Reed, started business in 1868, and, since the death of his brother has continued the business alone. He was formerly located at No. 66 Devonshire Street, and in 1887 removed to his present address, No. 25 Kilby Street. Mr. Reed is a member of the Underwriters' Association and is the representative of the London Assurance Corporation, of England, and the Union Insurance Company of California. He effects insurance at the lowest rates compatible with security, and has a large patronage both in and out of the city. The telephone connection is 1776. Mr. Reed is a native of this city, widely known and universally respected.

WILLIAM W. LOWE, Real Estate, Mortgages and Insurance, Office: No. 31 State Street, Traveller Building.—Prominent among the most responsible and conservative, real estate, loan and insurance brokers of Boston, is Mr. Wm. W. Lowe of No. 31 State Street. He has achieved an enviable reputation for his enterprising yet sound and conservative financial policy. Long active in commercial circles and familiarized with the real estate market of Boston and its suburbs, he is a recognized authority thereon, and since establishing his office ten years ago, has developed an active trade, and a widespread, influential connection. He has carried through many important transactions in the sale and exchange of real estate, and those seeking remunerative investments can secure them to a certainty by negotiating through Mr. Lowe. He secures loans on bond and mortgage at reasonable rates of interest, and at lowest charges, and also offers the mortgages and debentures of the Kansas Mortgage Investment Company of Anthony, Kansas, of which corporation he is the eastern agent. These securities are the most desirable of any offered to New England investors. The Company is managed most conservatively; it loans only to thirty-three per cent. of the value of the best farms and Kansas city property, and offers also the additional security of its own resources. Its investors have never lost a dollar, and it has invested hundreds of thousands of dollars for eastern capitalists in western farm loans in the best corn and wheat sections, saving all trouble, care or danger of loss. Those who seek the most remunerative investment in this market, should write to Mr. Lowe for full details. Mr. Lowe is also prepared to place promptly and to best advantage full lines of fire insurance in the strongest companies. He controls the insuring of important business and residential property, and owners of city and suburban buildings, stocks of merchandise, can obtain lowest rates coupled with absolute security through him. He is a resident of Saugus, and has ever taken a hearty interest in securing public welfare and honest administration of affairs. He was this year nominated for selection as a member of the Legislature from the Essex District, and is a popular and respected citizen, whose honorable methods and sterling integrity, render him specially qualified to conduct the large and growing business in which he is engaged.

CHAPIN, TRULL & CO., Distillers of Pure New England Rum, No. 30 Central Street.—Recent improvements in the processes of distillation assure the production of spirituous liquors, that are of the highest standard both in quality and purity. The representative, oldest and most noted house in Boston, engaged in this growing and important industry, is that of Messrs. Chapin, Trull & Co., distillers of pure New England rum, whose office and salesrooms are located at No. 30 Central Street. The distillery, which is one of the largest and best equipped in the United States, is situated at Charlestown. This reliable house is upwards of 100 years old and was carried on during that period, under the firm names of Trull Brothers, Chase & Trull, and eventually in 1877, the firm of Chapin, Trull & Co., was organized, and succeeded to the management. On April 28th, 1886, Mr. Trull died after a successful and honorable career, and the business is now the property of Mr. Nahum Chapin, who is a thoroughly qualified and practical distiller, fully conversant with every detail of his industry, and the requirements of the trade and a critical public. The capacity of the distillery is about 3000 gallons daily, and the sales for the past year amounted to upwards of 1,000,000 gallons. Messrs. Chapin, Trull & Co., have always distilled their pure New England rum, fire copper,—entirely from superior molasses. In fact, the New England rum distilled by this popular firm is absolutely unrivalled for quality, flavor, purity and uniform excellence, while the prices quoted for it in all cases is regulated by the market. The trade of the firm extends throughout the entire United States and Canada, and large quantities are exported to Europe, South America, Africa and Australia. The trade of this responsible house is steadily increasing, as consumers of this healthful liquor are becoming better acquainted with its merits. Mr. Nahum Chapin was born in Vermont, but has resided in Boston for the last forty-eight years, where he is highly regarded by the community for his energy, business ability and integrity. He is a prominent member of the Distillers' Association, and one of Boston's public spirited and progressive citizens.

THE METROPOLIS OF NEW ENGLAND. 147

MASSACHUSETTS REAL ESTATE CO., Geo. Leonard General Agent, No. 246 Washington Street.—This representative company was duly incorporated in 1885, under the laws of Massachusetts, with an authorized capital of $2,000,000. It was organized for the purpose of investing its capital in the purchase of commercial real estate in the business centres of large and growing cities, not with a view to speculation by selling when a profit can be secured, but for the purpose of holding all property acquired as permanent assets of the corporation from which a steady and increasing income will arise in rentals to be applied to the payment of dividends on the stock. Since its organization this company has earned over ten per cent. per annum on its capital invested up to the present day. The company issues shares of the par value of one hundred dollars each. The shares have coupons bearing interest at the rate of five per cent., payable semi-annually, until Jan. 15, 1891. These coupons are payable on the twenty-fifth day of January and July of each year. The surplus remaining after the payment of the interest due according to the coupons will be accumulated for a period of five years from the time the company was organized (that is, until Jan. 15, 1891), and will be devoted to the purchase of real estate, thus increasing the assets and earning capacity of the company. After this date the full net earnings will be paid out to the stockholders, materially increasing their dividends. As the surplus being accumulated enhances the value of shares, persons purchasing shares must pay their value as adjusted. Adjustments are made on the fifteenth days of January, April, July, and October of each year. The Massachusetts Real Estate Company only purchases commercial real estate, by which is meant blocks and buildings in the centres of rapidly growing cities. It never buys farms, dwelling houses, or property of any kind, outside the business centre of a thriving city. All its buildings are fully insured as taken as the rent rolls, so that in case a building is destroyed by fire the company will continue to receive the rents until the building is repaired or rebuilt. All the titles of the company's real estate are insured in the Massachusetts Title Insurance Company. In carrying out its plans, the company now owns a number of splendid buildings in Boston, Taunton and Providence, which are valued at over a million dollars. These buildings include such properties as the Advertiser Building, No. 246 Washington Street, Boston; the Bertram Building which adjoins the Mutual Life Insurance Company's Building, near Post Office Square, Boston, and the Niles Building, near Dock Square, Boston, occupied by the John P. Lovell Arms Company; the Reed Building, Faneuil Hall Square. The following gentlemen are the officers and directors: President, Porte W. Hewins, treasurer Boston Trust Co.; treasurer, James Y. Anthony, treasurer Anthony & Cushman Tack Co.; directors, Hon. George F. Bemis of Boston; Hon. William S. Greene, ex-mayor of Fall River; Col. Samuel C. Hart, New Bedford, firm of Hart & Akin; Hon. George R. Phillips, chairman committee of finance for the city of Providence, R. I ; Hon. William Reed, jun., pres. Taunton Board of Trade; Judge William H. Fox, Taunton, trustee Bristol County County Savings Bank; George A. Washburn, Esq., treasurer City of Taunton; James Y. Anthony, Esq., Taunton ; Porte W. Hewins, Esq., Taunton; auditors; George A. Washburn, Taunton ; R. C. Pierce, treasurer Presbrey Stove Lining Co.; banks of deposit: Boston Safe Deposit and Trust Co., Boston, Mass.; Machinist National Bank, Taunton, Mass. General Agent, George Leonard, clerk of corporation, Parke W. Hewins. The following is a summary of the financial affairs of the Massachusetts Real Estate Company, June 30, 1888; authorized capital, $2,000,000; capital paid in, $50,000; par value of stock, $100; price per share, $118.50; price of stock July 1, 1888, $114. The company's shares are recommended as an absolutely safe investment for trustees or guardians. Further information and details are cheerfully given on application at the company's office, by Mr. Geo. Leonard, the general agent.

THE AMERICAN INVESTMENT COMPANY of Nashua, N. H., No. 8 Congress Street.—In consequence of the growing scarcity of remunerative and safe investments in the east, capitalists and others are now turning their attention to the desirable and profitable openings afforded by the farm mortgages of the west. The first fact connected with these western farm mortgages is that they are absolutely secure, if the loan is placed through organized and expert hands, and second, that the income is as sure and more than double what can be got from government bonds, eastern loans or savings banks. To those desirous of investing in these western mortgages to advantage, we would specially direct them to the reliable and progressive American Investment Company of Nashua, N. H., whose Boston office is centrally located at No. 8 Congress Street. This Company was duly incorporated June 23d, 1885, under the laws of New Hampshire, with a paid up capital of $500,000, which has been further augmented by a surplus of $50,000. The following gentlemen, are the officers and directors: D. R. Sortwell, president; C. J. Gleason, treasurer; W. M. Upham, assistant treasurer; W. W. Wick, western manager; Finance committee: D. R. Sortwell, Edwin Dresser, C. J. Gleason, Wm. C. Avery. Board of directors: D. R. Sortwell, president of Montpelier & Wells River Rail Road Company, president of Cambridge National Bank, East Cambridge, Mass., firm of Sortwell & Co., East Cambridge, Mass.; Edwin Dresser, president of National City Bank, Cambridgeport, Mass., director of Cambridge Savings Bank, Cambridge, Mass., president of Cambridgeport Diary Company; Wm. C. Avery, firm of Avery & Thayer, Norfolk Mills, Dedham, Mass.; C. J. Gleason, Attorney, Montpelier, Vt., firm of Gloss & Gleason, Vergennes, Vt.; Wm. G. Ward, Lowell, Mass., trustee of Mechanics Savings Bank, of Lowell; Daniel Marcy, Portsmouth, N. H., trustee of Portsmouth Savings Bank, director of New Hampshire National Bank, Portsmouth, director of Portsmouth Trust and Guarantee Company; Fred H. Buttrick, Lowell, Mass., treasurer of City Institution for Savings of Lowell; John H. Goodale, Nashua, N. H., ex-secretary of the state of New Hampshire, vice president of Indian Head Insurance Company of Nashua; J. C. Bullard, East Cambridge, Mass., cashier Cambridge National Bank. The company makes a specialty of western farm mortgages, and also deals in water company, school, county and town bonds. The farm mortgages bear four per cent interest in semi-annual payments, and the principal and interest are always fully guaranteed. The company's loans are on first mortgage only on farms of reputable and thoroughly responsible farmers; the security moreover must be worth three times the amount of the mortgage, while the terms are strict and explicit. The basis of this company are confined to the best sections of the fertile states of Kansas, Nebraska, Missouri and Minnesota, where farms are constantly rising in value. The company is transacting a very safe business.

GENERAL A. YBARRA, Coffee and Cocoa Importer, No. 7 Exchange Place.—The finest cocoa in the world is that grown in the state of Caracas, Venezuela, and from which is manufactured the most delicious chocolate in the market. Among the largest plantation owners in that fertile region, is the family of General A. Ybarra, whose estates are cultivated with the utmost care, and upon the most improved methods. They are some of the largest and most successful growers of coffee and cocoa in Venezuela; and Ybarra coffee and chocolate are eagerly sought for by the best class of trade in the United States, and the General's name has become a veritable trade-mark. The General is now actively engaged in the direct importation of Ybarra coffee and chocolate, from a certain number of plantations. General Ybarra controls the most famous chocolate manufacturers of Caracas. It is made from the best cocoa grown in the world, and with absolute purity, the only ingredients being pure Caracas cocoa and cane sugar, the natural products of the country. This chocolate is not only the purest, but the most fragrant and delicious, it is more economical than any other brand, and is harmless to invalids and children, and can be used continuously as an article of food, producing a mild tonic effect, fattening the body and strengthening the system against fatigue and disease. The General has been established in business in Boston for eight years past, and has developed a trade of great magnitude, selling to wholesale houses, jobbers and dealers, likewise to the trade at far distant points. Both as to price and quality he offers substantial inducements, while his commercial policy is one of honor and integrity. General Ybarra was long a general officer of the Venezuelan army and patriotically led the forces of his native land in defence of liberty. He is an able and popular a merchant as he was a military commander, and has developed a trade of great and growing magnitude, and one of the utmost value to Boston and the United States, where the best and purest food products are always in such demand.

THE WM. H. BRETT ENGRAVING CO., Steel Plate Engravers and Printers, Reuben Carpenter, Manager, No. 30 Bromfield Street.—The steady and marvelous progress made in steel plate engraving and kindred branches during the last quarter of a century is one of the notable features that mark the period in which we live. With the inventions, improvements and other accessories discovered, a degree of excellence akin to perfection has been attained in this industry during the time mentioned. Among the foremost exponents and best known men engaged in the business is Mr. Reuben Carpenter, manager of The Wm. H. Brett Engraving Co., at No. 30 Bromfield Street, who sustains a most excellent and A1. reputation for fine work in this line; and as a consequence is in possession of a very extensive and flattering patronage. Mr. Carpenter is an Englishman by birth, of about fifty years of age, and has been a citizen of the United States, and resident of Boston ever since 1858. This house was established originally under its present title by Mr. Wm. H. Brett in 1879, and soon found its way into popular favor and confidence by the excellent character of its work. Mr. Brett was succeeded in 1884 by Messrs. Frizzell and Carpenter who still retained the large patronage by maintaining the high character of the house's previous productions, and in February, 1887, Mr. Carpenter assumed the entire control and management of the business, which has greatly increased under his direction. The premises utilized comprise two spacious and commodious rooms—office and showroom—which are very neatly and tastefully arranged, and supplied with every convenience and all the latest improved appliances necessary for the production of the very highest class of work known in the profession, also everything in new designs for all kinds of engraved work, and when desired originals are made to order. A number of skilled and first-class artists are kept in constant employment whose operations are conducted under the immediate supervision of the proprietor, who having served a long and faithful apprenticeship and many years of practical experience, permits no work to leave the premises that does not come up to the highest standard of artistic excellence. Mr. Carpenter is prepared to execute everything in the line of commercial steel engraving and printing, such as letter, note, and bill-heads, business and visiting cards, steel plate folders for menus, orders of dancing, wedding invitations, condolence cards, crests, monograms, stamping, vignettes, etc., and no pains are spared to render the fullest satisfaction, while his prices are extremely reasonable, and none but first-class work is turned out from this establishment.

RICE & HOLWAY, Commission Merchants, for the Sale of Butter, Cheese, Eggs, and Beans, Dressed Poultry, Game, Etc.; Domestic Fruit and General Produce; Store and Office, Nos. 15 North Market and 15 Clinton Streets; Butter Department, Basement, No. 15 North Market Street.—For enterprise, drive and success, the firm of Messrs. Rice & Holway take a prominent place among the commission houses doing business in this market. Established in 1872 this house has continued to increase and develop its trade until now it has assumed a very important place in the commission business. The founders were Messrs. Gould, Rice & Co., who continued in partnership until 1876, when the firm was reorganized and became, as now, Rice & Holway, the present partners being Mr. A. Mellen Rice and Mr. Thomas E. Holway. The former is a native of Maine and the latter was born on Cape Cod. Both are active and prominent members of the Boston Fruit and Produce Exchange and also of the Chamber of Commerce, and have had vast experience in their line of trade. The firm handle on commission, dressed poultry, game, domestic fruit and general produce of every description. They occupy commodious and well-appointed premises. As a salesroom and office the store running through from No. 15 North Market Street to No. 15 Clinton Street; and a three-story building at No. 15 Ferry Street is occupied for storage. The establishment is provided with refrigerators and all other necessary appliances for facilitating the handling of the extensive stocks carried and the prompt shipment of all orders. The firm are daily in receipt of fresh consignments, and their favorable relations with producers and shippers enable them to fill the largest orders with dispatch and at the lowest market quotations. The transactions of the house are extensively of a wholesale character, and necessitate the employment of twelve assistants, and the standing of the firm in the trade is A1.

DAVID W. LEWIS, New England Agent for Akron Sewer and Drain Pipe, Boston Office, No. 80 Water Street.—This business was established eighteen years ago by Messrs. Lewis & Millett, who conducted it till 1872, when on the retirement of Mr. Millett, Mr. Lewis became sole proprietor. Mr. Lewis is the New England agent for the famous Akron sewer and drain pipe, land tile, fire clay chimney flue linings, terra cotta chimney tops, wind guards, stove linings mixture, etc. He also deals largely in fire brick, Highland stone vases and cement, and is New England agent for the celebrated "Akron Star Brand Cement." According to official reports a very large per cent. of all fires from known causes, are from defective flues and chimneys. The importance of having a building perfectly safe from fire in connection with the chimneys was never more felt than now. To assure this, attention is called to the fire clay chimney flue lining. It is claimed for this: 1. That it is made of pure fire clay, unglazed, and is warranted to stand the greatest heat, and consequently is as durable as the chimney itself. 2. It effectually protects the building against fires, which so frequently originate from defective flues. 3. It being smooth, the soot does not adhere as to rough mortar surface, and it rarely fails to secure perfect draft. It is easily encased in the brick, and made in size for any ordinary chimney. The cost is trifling compared with the results gained. In unlined chimneys the action of soot and gases will cause the mortar to crumble and fall out from between the bricks, leaving crevices through which the fire is liable to work its way. Where lining is used this great danger is avoided. The Akron sewer pipe is well known by experts to be unrivalled for conducting sewerage, and is so constructed that perfect connection can be made from one pipe to the other, so that no leakage whatever can possibly occur. Mr. Lewis is also agent for Clapp's sewer inlet caps, which have gained an excellent reputation for efficiency and durability. All orders for sewer and drain pipe, etc., are promptly and carefully filled at the lowest possible prices, and the trade of this responsible house, which is both wholesale and retail, now extends throughout all sections of New England. Mr. Lewis' yards, which are spacious and fully stocked, are situated at No. 41 Boylston Avenue, Jamaica Plain, corner Portland and Cambridge Streets, East Cambridge. Mr. Lewis is a native of Walpole, Mass., but has resided in Boston for the last eighteen years, where he is highly regarded in business circles for his promptness, enterprise and just methods. The telephone call of the house is 1878.

BALDERSTON & DAGGETT, Sole Agents for National India Rubber Company, Empire Rubber Shoe Company, Imperial Rubber Company, Nos. 28, 30, 32 and 34 Lincoln Street, near Summer.—As a source of supplies of every kind of manufactured goods the city of Boston possesses advantages and facilities to meet the wants of the country equal, if not superior, to any other city in the union. Numerous and varied as are the industries here carried on they are ever multiplying. Rapidly as the city expands itself and the population increases. One of the enterprises which have gained a permanent establishment in our midst and assumed a leading position in its line, is that conducted by Messrs. Balderston & Daggett, the sole agents for the National India Rubber Company, the Empire Rubber Shoe Company, and the Imperial Rubber Company, located at Nos. 28, 30, 32 and 34 Lincoln Street, near Summer Street. Founded in 1879, this concern has had a remarkably successful career, and vigilance, push and the highest commercial integrity have been its characteristics from the outset. Their premises form one of the most commodious and finest business establishments on the street. They comprise an entire building, containing five floors and basement, the whole standing on an area of 40x60 feet. The fittings and equipments of the establishment are the best that skill and capital can produce, and there is throughout a neatness and method in the general arrangements which cannot escape the attention of a visitor on entering. The stock carried is immense and comprehensive, embracing, as it does, every conceivable article into the manufacture of which rubber enters. The firm, being the sole agents of the producers, and receiving their supplies direct from the manufactories, cannot be undersold in the market, while they are able to offer terms with which no other house can compete. The proprietors are aged respectively 55 and 28 years, both are natives of Boston and as a firm have gained a merited success.

THE METROPOLIS OF NEW ENGLAND.

HARRINGTON & FREEMAN, Watches, Diamonds, Jewelry, Clocks, Silverware and Optical Goods, No. 59 Court Street.—One of the most prominent and popular establishments in the jewelry trade in Boston is that of Messrs. Harrington & Freeman, located at No 59 Court Street, opposite Adams Express. This firm are extensive retail dealers in watches diamonds, jewelry, clocks, silverware and optical goods, and have been established in the business here since 1879. The store is desirably situated for trade purposes, elegantly fitted up, and perfect in convenience of arrangement for inspection and sale. A very large stock is carried in every line and special effort has been made to preserve uniform excellence in quality and make. This has been made fully possible by the splendid connections of the house with manufacturers and importers of the highest repute, and the continual activity of the proprietors in exacting tribute from every source that promises increased usefulness and popularity. In American and foreign watches, French and American

clocks, bronzes, rich jewelry and charms, solid silver and plated ware, gold and silver ornaments, and optical goods, the assortments are rarely equalled in the city. Precious stones of all kinds are kept in abundance, including a choice supply of diamonds, distinguished for purity, beauty and perfect shape. All these goods are selected with care and judgment, exhibiting a wide range in value and calculated to meet the wants of the greatest possible number of buyers. A corps of six assistants is employed, and the house is well prepared to give the best satisfaction in all its operations, being consistent in all its determination to furnish only first-class goods and reliable work on the most advantageous terms that can be afforded. Ample capital is employed in the enterprise, and it is recognized as an important factor in the mercantile activity of the city. The members of the firm, Messrs. L. T. Harrington and Geo. T. Freeman, are both practical jewelers and experienced, progressive and successful merchants. Mr. Harrington is a native of New Hampshire, while Mr. Freeman was born in Roxbury, Mass. They operate a branch store at No. 102 Court Street, and enjoy the respect and esteem of the entire community.

C. H. McKENNEY & CO., Manufacturers of Gas Fixtures, Electroliers, Fine Lamps and Fire Place Goods, Nos. 634 and 636 Washington Street.—The wonderful growth attained by the city of Boston during recent years, as a mercantile and manufacturing centre, is largely due to the energy and intelligent enterprise of the men who conduct our representative houses in every branch of trade, while on every hand is seen the colossal results of their ability and perseverance. In this connection it is a pleasure to record the character and career of a thoroughly representative Boston concern and one which in its particular line has distanced all competitors, and won the proud position of leader of the trade. We refer to the house of Messrs. C. H. McKenney & Co., manufacturers of gas fixtures, electroliers, fine lamps and fire place goods, at Nos. 634 and 636 Washington Street. This house was originally established in 1858, by Messrs. C. H. McKenney and C. H. McKenney, Jr., and from a modest beginning the operations of the firm steadily grew, until it had won in a few short years a national reputation for the artistic and superior excellence of its productions. The lamented death of the senior partner in March, 1888, left his son as the sole proprietor, who now continues this immense business upon the same broad basis of energy and enterprise for which it had become so widely noted. The factory, located on Beach Street, is admirably arranged and equipped in all its departments while employment is furnished in the factory and workshop to seventy five skilled and expert hands. Each department is under the management of a competent head, and the whole is regulated by a system and order that facilitates the transaction of business, and assures the prompt execution of orders. The splendid show rooms on Washington Street, comprising three floors, 25x90 feet each, and two floors of an adjoining building, make a magnificent display, and are a prominent attraction of this busy thoroughfare. No other house in its line is its equal, while in the qualities of adaptability and true art this house possesses facilities in designing and manufacture nowhere else to be found. Artists, both native and foreign, are constantly employed in designing and modelling subjects to be produced in both real and imitation bronze, as also in all ornamental and elegant styles of gas and electric light fixtures. The immense stock here gathered together forms the best exponent of this line of goods ever presented to a discerning public. Business is brisk and lively at all seasons, and the house is an important and still growing factor in maintaining the commercial supremacy of this great metropolis.

ARTHUR YOUNG & CO., Wholesale and Retail Dealers in Masons' Building Materials, Wharf, Albany Street, Corner Lehigh Street, Office No. 54 Kilby Street.—One of the oldest, leading and best known concerns devoted to the handling of masons' materials in this city is that of Arthur Young & Co., (successors to C. Young & Co.,) wholesale and retail dealers in cement, lime, laths, plaster, brick, etc., whose office is located at No. 54 Kilby Street, with wharf on Albany Street, corner Lehigh Street, and which for upward of half a century has maintained a prominent position in its line in Boston. This flourishing business was established in 1838 by C. Young who under the style of C. Young & Co. conducted the same for many years and was succeeded by his sons Arthur and William B., and under the firm name of Arthur Young & Co. it has since been continued with uninterrupted success; the senior partner recently assuming sole control. The wharf and premises at corner Albany and Lehigh streets are spacious and well equipped. Ample and complete facilities being at hand, while a very heavy first-class stock is constantly carried including everything in the line of masons' building supplies—cement, lime, hair, laths, plaster, brick, sand, drain pipe, fire brick, etc., etc. A large number of men are employed, while several teams owned by the firm are in steady service supplying customers. All orders by telephone or otherwise receiving prompt attention, and the trade of the firm, which is of a most substantial character, extends all over the city and surrounding towns. Mr. Arthur Young, who is now the sole proprietor, is a man of entire responsibility in his business transactions, as well as a gentleman of energy and thorough experience in this line, and sustains an excellent reputation in the building trade. Half a dozen schooners or more are employed bringing different materials from the various points where they are manufactured. Messrs. Young and Co. are large importers of English Portland cement, buying direct of the manufacturers in London, England, their principal brand being the "Phoenix," which is well known all over the New England States.

JAMES E. WHITNEY, Importer East India Good, No. 13 Doane Street.—Mr. James E. Whitney, the widely and favorably known importer of East India goods, was born in Newburyport, and early in life became connected with Boston's leading commercial circles, and here made the rapid progress due to his superior qualifications. Over thirty years ago he established in business upon his own account as direct importer of East India products, such as hides, skins, indigo, cutch and other dyestuffs, saltpetre, etc., and early developed important relations throughout the United States. He has ever sustained an enviable reputation for his methods and the superior quality of his goods, which are directly imported from the most famous Calcutta and other houses, and are in staple demand as the best in the market, and concerning whose prices substantial inducements are manifest. Mr. Whitney always has a heavy stock in the public stores, and is prepared to promptly fill the largest orders from dealers, manufacturers, mills, etc.

ILLUSTRATED BOSTON.

BAY STATE MANUFACTURING COMPANY, Egg Beaters, Etc., No. 36 Hanover Street.—The Bay State Manufacturing Company possesses a national reputation and widespread foreign connections as manufacturers of and dealers in wire, metal and glass specialties and novelties. The business was originally established in 1880, by Mr. H. H. Rogers, who was succeeded by Mr. S. H. Dillingham in 1887, under the present title. The manufacturing department is equipped with ample steam power and every modern convenience. Among the leading specialties here manufactured is the Dexter egg beater, which is an exact fac-simile of the Dover, the patent upon which expired May 31st, 1887. For seventeen years past it has been considered by the trade all over the world as the best ever made. The peculiar inter-shearing action of the cutting blades makes it the most effective and perfect egg beater, and probably its superior will never be invented. The Bay State egg beater, another specialty, has been the best seller in the past and will continue to be. It has been greatly improved by a new patent handle, formed flat on top and curved to fit the thumb and fingers. No egg beater has ever before been made with a reasonable handle, and shaped so that a lady can hold it firmly while turning the gear wheel. The Boston egg beater is like the Bay State, except in the cutting device. All the beaters made by this company can be tipped at any angle on the spindle rest, while the Dover strikes and stops if not held straight. The leading features in these beaters are covered by patents and patents applied for, while no other beaters are infringed by them. This company have dropped their prices to meet the low figures caused by recent infringements of some egg beaters. The New England egg beater is a new invention just introduced by this company. It has the handle and spindle ingeniously constructed from one continuous rod of wire, the gear wheel and handle cast in one piece, and is altogether the simplest and best cheap egg beater ever put upon the market. The Bay State towel rack, (patented,) is the most ingenious and taking article recently put upon the market. The Bay State clothes rack, the Bay State two-hook clothes rack with hat hook, the tri-mountain clothes and hat rack, and the Bay State coat hanger are all important and valuable specialties. Special mention should also be made of the Bay State sugars, as being one of the most novel and meritorious specialties lately introduced. Every time the sugarbowl is tipped it will throw exactly a teaspoonful of sugar. The trade for fancy salts, peppers and mustards has been enormous. The electric fruit jar, manufactured by this company, is better than the Mason-Improved or Porcelain-lined, because the cover has an elastic spring lock, and acts equally well under expansion or contraction. Locke's automatic pie turner, lifter and fork combined is another most useful household article sold by this house. The little coffee steeper saves one-fourth in amount of coffee used and greatly improves the quality and flavor. All these specialties, with other novelties introduced by this company, have a large and increasing sale not only in all parts of the United States, but throughout the West Indies, England, Germany, Australia, South America and other foreign countries. Mr. Dillingham is a native of Everett, Mass., and well known by the trade every where as an enterprising, progressive and successful manufacturer.

O. H. ATESHIAN & CO., Direct Importers of Turkish and Persian Goods, Fine Carpets, Rugs and Portiers, Etc., No. 68 Boylston Street.—One of the most attractive among the handsome stores for which Boston is noted, is that of O. H. Ateshian & Co., direct importers of Turkish and Persian goods. The business was established in 1886 at No. 44 Boylston Street, and two years later was removed to the eligible premises now occupied at No. 68 on that thoroughfare, which consist of a store 25x72 feet in dimensions, and a portion of the second floor, and a spacious basement. Throughout the establishment presents a novel and striking appearance, the richness and elegance of the goods at once attracting attention. The assortment is as interesting as it is unique and embraces fine Turkish and Persian carpets and rugs and portiers, and art fabrics of every description, and also fancy goods, choice embroideries for draperies and interior decorations of both antique and modern designs and also a great variety of oriental costumes which are a specialty, and is displayed in great profusion in silk and other fabrics. This firm is one of the largest importers of oriental goods in the country and exhibit many rare beautiful specimens of fancy articles and fabrics to be found in no other establishment. Of course a large business is carried on, the patrons including the best class of cultured and refined citizens. Mr. Ateshian, the head of the establishment, is a native of Constantinople, Turkey, and came here in 1882, and after a four years' course in Amherst, and Boston University, graduated with distinguished honors. He spends his summers in the Orient and visits both Turkey and Persia, where he makes his own selections and is constantly receiving fresh invoices of beautiful goods direct from those places and he and his three assistants will be found courteous and pleasant and take pleasure in displaying the various art fabrics and all the various oriental goods that have been brought together by the firm from those far off countries.

SKILLINGS, WHITNEYS & BARNES LUMBER COMPANY. David Whitney, Jr., President; Henry L. Tibbetts, Treasurer. Eastern Office, No. 5 Kilby Street.—The representative and most enterprising house in the city of Boston in the lumber trade is that known as the Skillings, Whitneys & Barnes Lumber Company. This extensive business was originally established in 1857 by Messrs. Chas. Whitney, D. N. Skillings, L. Barnes, and D. Whitney, Jr., as C. & D. Whitney, Jr., of Ogdensburg, N. Y., and Lowell, Mass.; S. N. Skillings & Co., of Boston; and L. Barnes & Co., of Burlington, Vt. In 1878, these firms were consolidated, and the business was duly incorporated with a paid up capital of $250,000. The present officers of the company are David Whitney, Jr., president; Henry L. Tibbetts, treasurer; W. L. Proctor, Ogdensburg manager; D. W. Robinson, Burlington manager. Mr. D. N. Skillings died in 1880, Mr. L. Barnes in 1884, and Mr. Chas. Whitney in 1887. The company have extensive steam planing mills at Ogdensburg, N. Y., and Burlington, Vt., where several hundred workmen are employed. A specialty is made of dressed and rough pine lumber, of which the company handle immense quantities, its trade extending not only throughout all sections of the Middle and New England States, but also to the West Indies, Mexico, Central and South America, Europe, Africa and Australia. The company have their own vessels on the lakes, and export to foreign parts from Boston and New York. Their facilities and resources are such that the largest orders are promptly and carefully filled at the lowest ruling market prices, an advantage that the trade is quick to appreciate. Mr. David Whitney, Jr., the president, is a resident of Detroit, Mich. He is largely interested in banking, timber lands, etc., and has three large saw mills in Michigan. Mr. Henry L. Tibbetts, the treasurer, manages the Boston business. We would observe in conclusion, that the affairs of the Skillings, Whitneys & Barnes Lumber Company are placed in able and honorable hands, and it worthily maintains a prominent position in this important and valuable industry, reflecting the greatest credit on all concerned.

DWIGHT BRAMAN & CO., Bankers and Brokers, No. 82 Devonshire Street, Corner Water Street.—As a great investment and speculative centre, Boston stands second only to New York, and has of recent years become one of the most active markets in the United States for sound desirable securities. Among the most active and enterprising firms of bankers and brokers in Boston and New England, is that of Messrs. Dwight Braman & Co., of No. 82 Devonshire Street. Mr. Braman is a native of Boston, and though a young man, is old-experienced in banking and the stock market, and very widely and favorably known throughout New York and New England financial circles. He started in business upon his own account in 1879, and has been an active and permanent member of the Boston Stock Exchange ever since that date. He has most desirable connections, and has correspondents on the New York, Philadelphia and Chicago Stock Exchanges. He transacts a general business in receiving deposits subject to check at sight; all securities listed or dealt in on the Boston, New York and Philadelphia Exchanges. Desirable investment securities are a specialty, and he offers stocks and bonds that pay a very handsome and steady income at prices quoted. He numbers among his customers leading capitalists and operators of Boston and New England, and offers every facility, fullest and latest information, prompt filling of all orders, and an honorable, equitable policy. He is a conservative and responsible member of financial circles, universally popular on 'Change, and is a worthy exponent of sound methods and able financial policy.

THE METROPOLIS OF NEW ENGLAND. 151

GEO. D. OTIS & CO., Bonded Truckmen and General Forwarders, No. 173 State Street. Stands: Nos. 61 Chatham Street, 35 and 48 Union Street, Boston, and Continental Sugar Refinery, South Boston.—The commercial supremacy of Boston is greatly aided by the facilities afforded trade by our leading truckmen and forwarders, like the firm of Geo. D. Otis & Co., whose main office is at No. 173 State Street, with stands at Nos. 61 Chatham and 35 and 48 Union Streets, this city; and at the Continental Sugar Refinery, South Boston. This enterprise has been in successful operation for a period of twenty-three years, and is managed by gentlemen who bring to bear the widest range of practical experience and whose connections and facilities are unsurpassed. The firm are prepared to forward goods and merchandise to all portions of the globe, and are in a position to conduct all transactions under the most favorable conditions, to insure entire success and satisfaction to all parties. They transact the leading business of this kind in the city, and have ever retained the confidence of the mercantile community. They give steady employment to thirty skilled and experienced hands to meet the exigencies of their business, and their patronage is especially large and active among leading importers, exporters and jobbers in this city, who confidently place in the hands of this firm goods of great value daily, relying upon the judgment, care and ability of the management to guard their interests safely and securely. The terms are invariably fair and equitable, and perfect satisfaction is assured in all cases. Mr. Otis, the active member of the firm, is a native of Lowell, Mass., and both as regards business ability and true American enterprise his house justly merits the splendid reputation and wide popularity which it has permanently attained.

EDWIN M. FOWLE & CO., Foreign Shipping and Commission Merchants, No. 34 India Wharf.—Boston has ever maintained a front position as a centre for the importation of foreign commerce, and it is here that are found the oldest and most enterprising firms engaged in the foreign shipping and commission trade. One of the oldest established concerns of the kind is that of Messrs. Edwin M. Fowle & Company, of No. 34 India Wharf. The history of this house dates back nearly a third of a century, the business having been founded under its present style in 1856 by Mr. Edwin M. Fowler, the present proprietor, who is one of the best known and most esteemed merchants doing business at this port. Mr. Fowle was born at Jamaica Plains, Mass., fifty-seven years ago, and for the past thirty years has resided at Newton. Since 1875 he has been the consul at this port for San Domingo, an office which he has filled with great credit. Mr. Fowle occupies commodious premises that are in every way admirably adapted for the successful carrying on of his important and extensive business, which consists of the importation of dye woods, sugar, coffee, and merchandise of every description, and of the exportation of lumber, flour, ice, provisions and goods of all kinds. Mr. Fowle buys and sells products and manufactures of all kinds on commission both at home and abroad, and attends to shipments to and from domestic and foreign markets. He is represented by agents in foreign ports, and has the best of facilities for carrying out all orders thoroughly and satisfactorily. He is vigilant and zealous, has his large business systematically regulated and is always at the head of affairs, seeing to the instructions of his patrons being carried out to the letter. In his business career he has won the respect of the mercantile community, and is held in the highest esteem by all.

JORDAN, LOVETT & CO., Insurance, No. 60 State Street.—The development of the insurance interests of the city of Boston have been upon a scale of such magnitude, that the facilities afforded the community by our leading insurance brokers are of an exceptionally favorable character, both as regards low rates of premium, enormous combination of resources and absolute security for all risks taken. In this connection we desire to make suitable reference in this commercial review to the time honored and responsible firm of Messrs. Jordan, Lovett & Company. This business was established in 1849 by W. H. S. Jordan and A. Lovett, fathers of the present members of the firm. They conducted the business till 1867 when they were succeeded by the present firm, the copartners being Messrs. L. S. Jordan and A. S. Lovett. They promptly effect insurance upon hotels, manufactories, mills, etc., carefully renew policies in proper season, and generally relieve the business community of all care and trouble in this important respect, while the rates quoted by them are always as low as those of any other first-class house in the insurance business. The firm are Boston agents of the Greenwich Fire Ins. Co., of New York; Detroit Fire & Marine Ins. Co., of Detroit; Citizens Ins. Co., Cincinnati, Ohio; Fidelity Fire & Marine Ins. Co. Cincinnati, Ohio; and district agents of the Sun Fire Office, of England; Queen Ins. Co., of England; Phenix Ins. Co., of New York; Massachusetts Mutual Ins. Co., of Boston; Ins. Co., of North America, Phila.; Pennsylvania Fire Ins. Co., Phila., and others. Messrs. Jordan & Lovett are both natives of Boston, and her firm will always be found one of the best in the city, through which to advantageously obtain insurance policies of every description, and with the least possible trouble or annoyance on the part of the insured.

CHARLES L. DAVENPORT, Chelsea Salt Company, Salt of all Kinds, No. 170 State and No. 2 Commercial Streets.—A leading house engaged in the wholesale salt trade in Boston is that of Mr. Charles L. Davenport, located at Nos. 170 State Street and 2 Commercial Street. This house was originally established by the Chelsea Salt Company, who were succeeded by the present proprietor in 1874. The premises occupied for the business, consist of an office and salesroom on State Street, large storehouses at Caswell's and Mystic Wharf in Charlestown, and unsurpassed facilities are at hand for conducting the business upon the largest scale. Mr. Davenport has a wide reputation as an extensive importer and wholesale dealer in salt of all kinds, and as the agent for Higgins' Eureka Fine Salt, supplying the trade in boxes, bags and by the ship load. His Caswell's wharf storehouses are connected by rail with all the railroads running out of Boston, thus enabling him to ship to all parts of the country without the expense of cartage. The connections of the house with salt manufacturers of the highest repute places it in a position to command every favorable opportunity of the market and to offer inducements to the trade in quality and prices of goods which challenge comparison and defy successful competition. The business is broadly distributed throughout the New England States, and is annually increasing in volume and importance under enterprising and reliable management. Mr. Davenport is a native and prominent citizen of Malden, Mass., and is well and favorably known in this city as a merchant of rare business tact and ability, possessing a foundation understanding of all the requirements of his trade, and eminently popular and successful in meeting all its demands.

PLUMER & CO., Commission Merchants in Flour, Grain and Hay, No. 173 State Street.—There is probably no single agency that has wielded a more healthful influence in favor, of the commercial advancement of Boston than the flour and grain trade, while the enterprise and activity of the houses engaged therein have been largely instrumental in securing an area of demand co-extensive with the limits of the country, Messrs. Plumer & Co., at No. 173 State Street, operate one of the most prominent commission houses for the sale of flour, grain and hay in the city, presenting a business of heavy proportions, and maintaining a most valuable reputation for adherence to the strictest principles of mercantile integrity in all transactions. The business was founded in 1878 by Mr. Avery Plumer. His son, Charles A. Plumer, came into the concern in 1883, and formed the present firm in connection with Mr. Wm. L. Leavitt in May, 1887. The firm occupy two commodious offices at the above address, and carry a very large and valuable stock of the commodities dealt in at suitable warehouses on the line of the different railways centering in this city. This stock is uniformly superior in quality and is obtained from the most reliable sources of production. Thus orders of any magnitude are readily filled, and, owing to the excellent arrangements that the firm has effected with railroads, shipments are made to the remotest points at the lowest rates of freight. Messrs. Plumer & Co. offer unsurpassed advantages to producers, shippers and others, and consignments are disposed of without delay at the highest current prices. Remittances are made with promptitude and satisfaction. The copartners are both natives of Massachusetts, of wide acquaintance and influential connections throughout New England.

R. R. HIGGINS & CO., Wholesale Dealers and Planters of Oysters, No. 35 Howard Street and Nos. 142 and 144 Atlantic Avenue.—Representative in the wholesale oyster trade of New England is the widely and favorably known firm of Messrs. R. R. Higgins & Co., of No. 35 Howard Street and Nos. 142 and 144 Atlantic Avenue. The public of New England and the provinces are great consumers of oysters and other shell fish, but their tastes are refined and their requirements exacting, and only the choicest growths find an extended market here. Realizing this fact, Messrs. R. R. Higgins & Co. and their predecessors have ever devoted their attention solely to the best grades of Norfolk and Chesapeake, Providence River and native oysters, also clams, quahaugs, little necks and lobsters. This extensive business was founded in 1828 by the late Mr. John S. Higgins, a merchant of marked enterprise and energy, and who was the pioneer in opening up to Boston and New England this highly important branch of trade. He developed it to proportions of great magnitude, and upon his lamented decease, in 1866, he was succeeded by his sons, Messrs. R. R. and John S. Higgins, both of them thoroughly experienced in the business, they having been brought up in it from boyhood. Extending their connections, developing their facilities, and giving their personal attention to the filling of all orders, the firm kept steadily enlarging their business until in 1880 the untimely decease of Mr. John S. Higgins occurred. Mr. R. R. Higgins continued the business upon his own account until in 1887 he admitted into copartnership his nephew, Mr. Alfred S. Higgins, under the existing name and style. The firm supply oysters in bulk, and at wholesale and retail, covering a territory of vast extent, including all New England, Northern New York, Quebec, etc. Their Boston trade is of the greatest magnitude, including leading dealers and large consumers, such as oyster houses, restaurants, hotels, etc. They have largely increased their facilities, and have a large packing house in Norfolk, Va., where they employ fully 125 hands, and open on an average each season, 150,000 gallons. To supply that house they charter eight boats, each with a capacity of over 1,000 bushels. They thus are the leading New England house engaged in the Chesapeake oyster trade; they have another packing house at Brownville, R. I., where they pack the choice fancy oysters grown on their own beds in the Providence River, while at Nos. 142 and 144 Atlantic Avenue, this city, is their local packing house, and whence native oysters can be had in the shell, likewise the choicest hard and soft clams, little necks, and lobsters. The shipping office is at No. 35 Howard Street. The firm ever maintains an enviable reputation for dealing in the best qualities of stock, solid measure, and the lowest market rates; their unflagging energy and enterprise have secured to Boston a highly beneficial branch of wholesale trade, and the partners are worthy of the substantial success attending their ably directed efforts.

WOODBURY, SHAW & CO., Wholesale and Commission Dealers in Lobsters, Oysters and Fish, Nos. 53 and 54 Commercial Wharf.—Recognized leaders in the lobster, oyster and fish trade of the city of Boston are Woodbury, Shaw & Co., whose office and salesrooms are located at Nos. 53 and 54 Commercial Wharf. This business was originally established by L. Richardson, who was succeeded by G. L. Young. In 1868 Woodbury, Shaw & Co. became proprietors. The premises occupied comprise a very commodious five-story and basement building 25x60 feet in dimensions, fully supplied with every appliance and facility for the accommodation and presentation of the extensive stock. Woodbury, Shaw & Co. deal only in the choicest lobsters, oysters and fish, and guarantee the prompt and perfect fulfillment of all orders at the lowest market prices. They make a specialty of lobsters, and their trade now extends throughout all sections of New England and New York. They are also commission merchants in all kinds of country produce, and consignments are solicited, quick returns are guaranteed at the best market prices. Their resources are ample and their facilities for securing supplies are of a perfect character, while the substantial inducements they offer the trade are with difficulty duplicated elsewhere. Mr. Woodbury is a native of Vermont, but has resided in Chelsea for the last forty years. He is in the prime of life, and of excellent reputation and standing in the social and business circles of the city. The telephone call of the house is No. 2176.

BOSTON CONSOLIDATED PRODUCE COMPANY, General Commission; C. H. Kimball, President; Gardner Chapin, Treasurer; No. 97 South Market Street.—This representative and progressive company was duly incorporated under the laws of Maine in 1887 with a capital of $400,000. The company has ten store houses at Aroostook, Maine, a large warehouse at Fitchburg, besides an extensive capacity in Commercial Wharf and six branch stores in Boston. The following are the branch stores and the names of the firms that are managing them: Chas. Kimball & Co., corner Atlantic Avenue and Clinton Street; Chapin Brothers, No. 97 South Market Street; Clark Bros. & Co., No. 112 Clinton Street; McKerver & Hall, Nos. 23, 25 and 27 Richmond Street; J. P. Brown & Co., No. 135 Atlantic Avenue; T. P. Blake, Eastern Railroad. The company deals extensively in potatoes, eggs, beans, apples, onions, turnips, poultry, game, fish, sweet potatoes, Florida oranges, watermelons, berries, and all kinds of southern truck. Special attention is given to all consignments by experienced salesmen, while consignees are at once notified on the arrival of their consignments of the same. Liberal advances are made on receipt of produce when required, while prompt sales and quick returns are guaranteed. The company always fully insures and stores all produce in frost proof warehouses. A full and complete stock is constantly carried in every line, special efforts being made to secure superior and choice produce and to offer only such goods as are fresh and wholesome. The officers of the company are C. Henry Kimball, president, and Gardner Chapin, treasurer, both of whom are highly esteemed in trade circles for their executive ability, energy and integrity. The Boston Consolidated Produce Company refers by permission as to its commercial standing and reliability to the Bunker Hill National Bank, Boston, Fourth National Bank, Boston, Bradstreets' Commercial Agency and Russell's Commercial Agency.

GEORGE H. DICKERMAN & CO., Manufacturers of Paper Boxes, Nos. 32, 34 and 36 Green Street.—This concern is one of the oldest established, having been founded by Mr. Dickerman in 1855. He early achieved an enviable reputation by being the first to introduce to the trade in general the use of the paper box and for the superior character of workmanship, and uniform excellence of materials, and the growing demands of the trade taxed his facilities to the utmost, necessitating repeated enlargements. In 1875, Mr. Joseph L. Becknell was admitted into copartnership under the existing name and style. The firm occupy a very spacious brick six story building on Green Street, 70x80 feet in dimensions. It is equipped throughout with the latest improved machinery and appliances run by steam power from an engine on the premises. Upwards of 200 hands find employment in the manufacture of paper boxes of every description, from the lightest and tiniest for confectioners and bonbons up to the heaviest for stationers, dry goods and furnishing goods. The trade done is almost wholly wholesale on heavy contract orders from leading merchants and manufacturers, not only of Boston, but from all over New England. Anything in the shape of a paper box will be made here strictly to specification and at lowest rates in quantities to suit. Neatness, elegance of finish, strength of materials and lowest prices commensurate with good work, characterize all of Messrs. Dickerman & Co's. transactions. They are both natives of Norfolk County, Mass., and are honorable and respected business men.

CURTIS & MOTLEY, Stock and Bond Brokers. Office: No. 62 State Street.—Among the active and enterprising firms of stock and bond brokers in Boston is that of Messrs. Curtis & Motley. The copartnership was formed three years ago by Mr. Allen Curtis and Mr. E. P. Motley. The firm is represented on the Boston Stock Exchange by Mr. Motley, The earliest information is secured for their customers, and all orders are promptly filled both here and through the firm's correspondents in New York. They transact a general stock and bond brokerage business, buying and selling strictly on commission, for cash or on margin, all securities listed on either Exchange, also miscellaneous unlisted stocks, bonds, and mining shares. Their widespread relations and energetic, prompt, business-like management, making their customers' interest paramount, are securing to them a very large and growing patronage.

THE METROPOLIS OF NEW ENGLAND.

H. C. LITCHFIELD & CO., Manufacturers, Importers and Dealers in Fine Fishing Tackle, No. 302 Washington Street.—Although a comparatively young firm, as such, H. C. Litchfield & Co., manufacturers, importers and dealers in fine fishing tackle, cutlery, skates and dog collars, No. 302 Washington Street, (third door north of old South church) have already established a business second to few engaged in this line in Boston, while their patronage grows apace. The secret of this firm's prosperity is not difficult to discover, either. Making and handling a very superior class of goods, prompt and thoroughly reliable in their dealings, and being withal fully conversant with the business, the results could scarcely have been other than the well merited success they have attained. The premises

occupied as salesrooms are compact, neat, conveniently located and well lighted on the second floor, while an efficient assistant is in attendance also. A large and first-class assortment of everything in the line of fine imported and American fishing tackle, cutlery, etc., is constantly kept on hand, and the trade of the firm, is quite extensive; all orders by mail or otherwise receiving immediate attention. Mr. Litchfield, who is the sole member, is a gentleman of middle age, and a native of Maine and has been in this line of business in Boston for twenty years. He is a man of energy, reliability and ample experience in this line having formerly been a member of the firm of Appleton & Litchfield from 1883 to November, 1887, when he established this thriving business, and prior to that had been for some years with another firm in same line.

J. P. SNOW, Railroad Lands, No. 7 Exchange Place.—At the present day no financial interest is of such paramount importance as that involved in real estate. Investments in real estate under the guidance of the sound judgment of an expert are sure to prove remunerative, as hundreds of persons who have become possessed of realty in Florida and other states for small sums of money have in a few years in consequence of increased values realized a competency. In this connection, special reference is made in this commercial review of Boston to Mr. J. P. Snow, No. 7 Exchange Place, dealer in railroad lands for colonies or investor in large or small tracts. Mr. Snow has been engaged in the land business for the last quarter of a century, and has obtained an excellent reputation with patrons for his honorable methods and correct estimates of the values of all descriptions of country and city lands. He has now on his books 250,000 acres in twenty counties in Florida, and 5,000,000 acres in Mexico on the border below Brownsville, Texas—which are offered in suitable lots to investors and others at nominal prices. He is agent in Boston for the Mexican Development Company, Dyson Land Company of Florida, Florida Land Company, of Florida, Florida Land and Improvement Company, Florida Railway and Navigation Company, etc. Mr. Snow also represents the Mallory Line of steamers to Florida or Texas, and furnishes railroad tickets at special rates to any part of the south or west. He took the first colony to Nebraska in 1856, and also is noted as having been the importer of the first steel pen to the United States from Europe. Mr. Snow is a native of Williamsburg, Mass., but has resided in Boston for the last fifteen years, where he is highly regarded by the community for his energy, enterprise and integrity. Persons wanting a home among the orange groves of Florida can secure a block of ten acres from Mr. Snow near a railroad for $100, payable either ten dollars a month or one dollars a week till paid without interest.

WILLIAM RALPH EMERSON, Architect, No. 85 Water Street.—With the vast increase of population, refinement and wealth in the principal centres of the United States, has arisen a growing demand for the blending of the artistic and the beautiful with the utilitarian in modern architecture. The result has been extremely gratifying to the advocates of progress in this most vitally important profession. Among those who have acquired a national reputation for his great skill and artistic conceptions as an architect is Mr. William Ralph Emerson, whose surname is becoming in architecture a reminder of Ralph Waldo Emerson's name in literature and philosophy. Mr. W. R. Emerson was born at Alton, Ill., and early in life settled in Boston, where he acquired a thorough practical as well as theoretical knowledge of the science of architecture. In 1859 he became copartner with Mr. Jonathan Preston, and in 1874 continued alone the practice of his profession. The steady increase of his commissions and widening field of effort resulted in March, 1883, in his removing to his present commodious offices in Water Street, where he enjoys every facility for draughting, designing, making computations, etc. Mr. Emerson's designs have become deservedly celebrated, his fame rests on a long and successful career, engaged largely in supervising the erection of the most advanced classes of public and private buildings, among which are churches and villas, cottages and mansions at such fashionable centres as Newport, Bar Harbor and such great metropolitan centres as Boston, Philadelphia, Chicago and various large cities. It is needless to particularize in regard to the work of such a nationally famous architect as Mr. Emerson, but we might mention among his creations in this city the beautiful building of the Boston Art Club; several of the handsomest city school buildings and while a very young man assisted in the making of the plans of the old Boston Theatre, etc., Mr. Emerson attends faithfully to details; his plans are well digested and studied and his architectural efforts greatly tended to beautify the urban characteristics of the United States. Mr. Emerson is a member of the Boston Association of Architects and is held in the highest estimation in social and professional circles for his honorable, able methods. He is fully prepared with all the necessary facilities to design and superintend the erection of any building not only promptly, but with that intelligent apprehension of design which has ever caused his efforts to be so highly appreciated.

THE CIGARMAKERS' CO OPERATIVE ASSOCIATION, Salesroom and Factory, No. 276 Atlantic Avenue.—A recently organized enterprise, is the Cigarmakers' Co-operative Association, and from its methods, able guidance and superiority of product is worthy of the patronage and support of all who appreciate pluck, integrity and the honest efforts of an association of skilled workmen to produce the finest grade of handmade cigars now in market. The Cigarmakers' Co-operative Association was duly organized and incorporated under the laws of the state, with a capital of $15,000, in the spring of 1883. The stock was promptly taken by about twenty-five of the most skillful and widely known cigarmakers of New England, and the association has already developed a large and growing trade, under the enterprising and skilled management of Mr. W. H. Batchelor, an old and experienced cigarmaker. The association occupies two floors at No. 276 Atlantic Avenue, where from forty to fifty hands are employed in the manufacture of the choicest grades of 5c. and 10c. goods. The association is sole proprietor of the C. C. A. brand, now the leading 10c. cigar on the market, and which is most carefully made from choicest growths of Connecticut, Havana and Sumatra tobaccos. For delicacy of flavor, true fragrance, perfect workmanship and select leaf, this cigar is rapidly distancing all competition. Their co-operative No. 25, is an equally popular and reliable 5c. brand and cannot be duplicated elsewhere. The association is building up its trade on the basis of fine hand-made goods only, and is a worthy representative of honorable methods and skilled workmanship. We cannot too strongly recommend hotels, restaurants and the trade generally to sample these splendid cigars, which give such universal satisfaction and will be found to sell quickly, hold customers and give a good profit to the retailer. This association is a step in the right direction; its members seek for themselves the benefits of producing the finest goods, and are worthy of confidence and support.

R. A. PATTERSON & CO., Tobacco Manufacturers, Richmond, Va., P. H. Duke, Manager, Boston Office: No. 4 Central Wharf. —One of the largest and leading tobacco manufactories of the United States is that of Messrs. R. A. Patterson & Co., of Richmond, Va. As the natural home of the finest bright leaf tobaccos in the world, Virginia is especially favored as a region to engage in the manufacture of tobaccos for the markets of the country at large. It was in Richmond with its direct water communications to New England and rail connections with all parts of the United States, that in 1856, Messrs. R. A. Patterson & Co., began to manufacture, and with marked success. No house has since the war, developed such a permanently large and flourishing trade north and east as they, and in response to the growing demand from New England they in 1882 opened a branch house in this city, with Mr. P. H. Duke as manager. The results have fully warranted this new departure, as Mr. Duke has developed a trade of great and growing magnitude all over New England. The firm are manufacturers of full lines and numerous styles of plug and twist chewing and smoking tobaccos. All these are carried in the heavy stock in Mr. Duke's salesrooms, No. 4 Central Wharf, and the trade is here offered substantial inducements both as to price and quality. In fact the Patterson brands are pronounced by experts to be the best in this market, and that they are ready sellers is shown by the large increase of orders received. Among the popular brands is the "Lucky Strike," the most famous and popular smoking tobacco in the market. It has received well merited testimonials from all over the United States and is a choice combination of the selected growths of finest Virginia and other tobaccos. Its fragrance and uniform high standard of excellence specially commends this brand to the trade. The firm of Messrs. R. A. Patterson & Co., is composed of Mr. R. A. Patterson, his son, Mr. H. F. Patterson, and Mr. T. M. Rutherford, all gentlemen of ability and experience, of sterling integrity and personal worth and whose factory, one of the most complete in the United States, and affords steady employment to upwards of 600 hands. Mr. Duke is a native of Richmond, Va., and is possessed of a thorough practical knowledge of the tobacco trade. He is a pushing and able business man, universally popular and respected, and is a worthy representative of this great staple branch of trade.

MANNING & BROTHER, Isinglass, Illuminating and Lubricating Oils, No. 105 Fulton Street. —Thirty odd years of unbroken prosperity sums up in brief the history of the widely known firm of Manning & Brother, dealers in isinglass and oils, No. 105 Fulton Street. This thriving business was established in 1856 by Messrs. Charles D. and William H. Manning, and under the same style it has since been conducted with uninterrupted success, although one of the members, (William) was removed by death some five years ago. The business premises at No. 105 Fulton street, occupy a commodious store and cellar, while three in help are employed. The firm handles the entire product of C. Norwood & Son's isinglass factory, Ipswich, Mass., (the oldest concern of the kind in the United States) and sell the same in New York, Mr. Manning & Bro., being general selling agents. They also deal quite largely in illuminating and lubricating oils, the leading specialty, however, being isinglass, and altogether, they do a large and active business; the trade in isinglass extending throughout the entire country, and in oils all over the New England States. Mr. Chas. B. Manning, who is a gentleman in the prime of life, active, energetic and devoted to his business, was born at Waldboro, Maine, but has been a respected resident of this city many years, and is well and favorably known in commercial life.

LENNON & COMPANY, Brass Founders and Finishers, Dealers in Plumbing Materials, No. 292 Washington Street.— Messrs. Lennon & Co. have a deservedly high reputation as brass founders and finishers, and as extensive dealers in plumbing materials, giving particular attention to jobbing on plumbers' brass work in or out of town. The foundation of the business was laid in 1869 by Messrs. Curley and Lennon, and in 1876 Messrs. M. T. F. O'Donnell and John J. Murphy purchased the same and the business has since been continued under the present firm name. The business premises comprise two doors, 25x100 feet each, fitted up in the most approved style with new and improved machinery, operated by steam power, and furnishing steady employment to ten skilled workmen. The supplies here manufactured are highly esteemed by the trade everywhere for their superior quality, thorough durability and uniform excellence and wherever introduced and used they practically supplant all rival productions. Inducements are also offered, as regards reliability of goods and liberality of terms and prices, which are rarely duplicated by rival concerns. The copartners are both Boston men, born and bred, and experienced and accomplished masters of their trade. Mr. Murphy is the first assistant assessor of Boston and has served his fellow citizens as a member of the State Legislature, as City Councilman, and of various other positions of honor and trust.

SAMUEL I. COY, Proprietor of Restaurant, Nos. 243, 245 and 247 Atlantic Avenue.—The multiplication of shipping interests, offices, warehouses, etc., in the neighborhood of Atlantic Avenue has been the means of creating a great demand for all kinds of accommodations and facilities for those whose business relations lie in that part of the city. The spacious and elegantly appointed restaurant of Mr. Samuel I. Coy may be referred to in illustration of what is meant. This establishment has long ranked as one of the best conducted and most popular dining places in this section of the city. The restaurant is very eligibly and conveniently located at Nos. 243, 245 and 247 Atlantic Avenue, and was originally opened some fifteen years ago under the style of Brock & Coy, who dissolved their partnership in 1884, when Mr. Coy took sole control of the business. That he is an accomplished caterer goes without saying, for the extensive patronage he enjoys is a standing permanent proof of that fact. The dining-hall has a seating capacity for two hundred and fifty guests, and is open for the supply of meals from three o'clock in the morning until eight o'clock in the evening. It is a model of cleanliness and order, and so systematized is the business that it runs with the regularity of clockwork. The culinary department is alike highly creditable and will bear the most rigid inspection by the most fastidious. It is furnished with all necessary appliances, and conveniences, and here finest delicacies are cooked and prepared in the most tempting style to order. The tables are liberally provided with the finest edibles, and the service is prompt and courteous, while the charges are of a very reasonable character. Forty-five hands are employed in the various departments. Mr. Coy was born in Cambridge forty-six years ago, and personally is very courteous and popular.

HOUGHTON & COLBY, Grain and Feed Commission, No. 102 State Street.—Its energetic, enterprising and progressive business methods have given the grain and feed commission house of Messrs. Houghton & Colby, at No. 102 State Street, a standing in the great thoroughfares of trade, rarely excelled by its oldest and best known contemporaries. This firm are specially prominent as selling agents for western grain houses, representing large dealers in Chicago, St. Louis, Peoria, Columbus, Burlington and established their business here in 1887. The copartners, Messrs. Chas. W. Houghton and Benjamin L. Colby, are gentlemen of wide acquaintance and large experience, thoroughly posted in all the wants and requirements of the trade, and among the most active and efficient commission merchants and trade representatives of Boston. Messrs. Houghton & Colby command all the best opportunities of the market, and are enabled to render the most valuable service to such as commit their interests to their care. Consignments are disposed of without delay, the market prices are invariably obtained, and remittances are promptly made. The house is responsible in every way, and may be relied upon implicitly. Every facility and convenience is at hand for the transaction of business, and no similar house is more thoroughly prepared to take proper care of its extensive and growing interests. Its resources are ample and abundant, its facilities are complete and perfect, its economical methods are wide-spread and influential, while the substantial inducements it offers to the trade are rarely duplicated elsewhere. Mr. Houghton is a Western man and received his education in Pennsylvania and Chicago, while Mr. Colby was born in Maine, but received his business training in Boston, and both are prominent, public-spirited and popular business men.

THE METROPOLIS OF NEW ENGLAND.

BOSTON & LOCKPORT BLOCK CO., Sole Manufacturers of Self-Lubricating Metaline Tackle Blocks, Etc.; Ambrose S. Beverly, President, No. 162 Commercial street.—The representative and noted establishment in the United States engaged in the manufacture of tackle blocks is that known as the Boston & Lockport Block Company, whose offices and warehouses are located on Commercial and Fulton Streets, Boston. The company's factories are situated in Boston, Mass., and Lockport, N. Y., and two hundred skilled operatives are employed, and the trade of the house now extends not only throughout all sections of the United States, but likewise to Canada, Mexico, the West Indies, Central and South America, Europe, India, Australia and New Zealand. The company has a branch at No. 31 South Street, New York, and its principal agents are C. H. Gurney & Co., No. 267 Lake Street, Chicago, and the Broderick & Bascom Rope Co., St. Louis, Mo. This business was originally established in 1860 by Bagnall & Loud, who were succeeded by the Bagnall & Loud Block Co. Eventually in 1887, it was duly incorporated under the laws of New Jersey, including the Bagnall & Loud Block Co., of Boston, and the Penfield Block Co., of Lockport, N. Y., with a paid up capital of $300,000. The following gentlemen being the officers, viz: Ambrose

S. Beverly, president; E. O. Loud, vice president; Herbert Loud, treasurer; M. H. Tarbox, secretary. The Boston & Lockport Block Co. are the sole manufacturers in the United States of self-lubricating metaline and improved self-adjusting five-roll roller bushed tackle blocks, and star brand. These blocks are absolutely unrivalled for safety, strength, utility, reliability and uniform excellence by those of any other first-class house in America or Europe, while the prices quoted for them in all cases are extremely moderate. The company owns thirty-five patents, which have been duly registered not only here, but also abroad. They are also the sole manufacturers of an improved sanitary lead trap called the Mansfield Compressed Lead Trap, which is the simplest form of a trap in the market, and having a four-inch water seal absolutely prevents the escape of sewer gas into the house, and is highly indorsed by all first-class architects. They also manufacture the best differential hoist in America, being simple in form and far less liable to get out of order. In conclusion we would observe that the affairs of the Boston & Lockport Company are now placed in able and skillful hands, and it worthily maintains the leading position in this valuable and useful industry, reflecting the greatest credit on all concerned.

J. L. KENT & CO., Commission Brokers, Stocks, Bonds, Grain, Provisions and Oil, No. 14 State Street, Room 6.—There is no more important interest to the financial and mercantile community than that controlled by the several stock exchanges of the country. The city of Boston, with its vast interests in railroads, steamship lines, produce and oil, daily transacts an amount of business rarely equalled in the history of any country. A leading firm of commission brokers in this city is that of Messrs. J. L. Kent & Co., whose spacious office quarters are located at Room 6, No. 14 State Street, with entrances also at Nos. 121 Washington and 29 Devonshire streets. The facilities possessed by this firm for covering every branch of the business are unsurpassed. Stocks, bonds, grain, provisions and oil are handled, either for cash or on a margin, on commission, orders are made at once and transfers executed, together with all business of this nature, as readily as could be done on Wall Street or Broadway. The firm give their personal attention to every item of business that passes through their office, and the accuracy with which they estimate the values of the various securities has given them a distinction that has merited the confidence of an extensive clientage and a marked success as brokers and financiers. As all business entrusted to them is dealt with promptly and in a manner which secures the greatest possible advantage to customers, their office is a favorite resort for investors. Quotations are noted by the stock indicator, and every convenience is afforded that customers can desire, including private wires connecting with the various exchanges, and a staff of assistants who contribute to the satisfactory operations of the house. Mr. Kent, the active member of the firm, brings a wide range of practical experience to bear, coupled with superior facilities, in the management of the business, and has a high standing in business and financial circles.

W. F. ROBINSON & CO., Wholesale Dealers in Beef, Pork, Lard, Ham, Etc., Nos. 77 and 79 South Market and 38 Commerce Streets.—The trade in provisions is undoubtedly one of the most important of the industries of Boston, and the New England metropolis is well represented in this respect by a number of responsible and reliable houses, devoted to this branch of commerce. Prominent among the number thus referred to, is that of Messrs. W. F. Robinson & Co., whose offices and salesrooms are situated on South Market and Commerce Streets. This business was established in 1854 by Mr. W. F. Robinson. In 1856 Mr. Charles H. Robinson became a member, and in 1873 Mr. L. G. A. Fanteaux was admitted into partnership. The premises occupied comprise a superior five-story building which is fully equipped with every appliance and facility for the successful prosecution of the business. Messrs. W. F. Robinson & Co. are extensive wholesale dealers in beef, pork, lard, ham, tripe, tallow, dried beef, tongues, beans, cheese, pickles, etc. They are receivers of Geo. C. Napheys & Son's famous pure lead lard, which is carefully put up in pails. The firm handle only the finest qualities of provisions and offer advantages in prices very difficult to be secured elsewhere. They are now prepared to place on the market their Ferguson hams for which they are sole agents for which they claim to be the best quality in the country. They are carefully cured in the most improved manner with granulated sugar, and cannot fail to satisfy the wants of the public who desire a fine and delicately cured ham. Every ham is branded with the name of this firm and none are genuine without it. They are also receivers of Geo. C. Napheys & Son's, gold brand pure leaf lard, which is the finest and purest manufactured. Their trade extends throughout the principal cities and towns of Canada, New England and the Eastern States, and is steadily increasing owing to the superiority and excellence of their provisions, which have no superiors in this or any other market. Messrs. W. F. Robinson & Co. make liberal advancements on consignments of first-class provisions, and guarantee entire satisfaction to shippers and packers. The partners are members of the Chamber of Commerce, where they are highly esteemed for their sound business principles and integrity. Messrs. W. F. and Chas. H. Robinson were born in Vermont, while Mr. L. G. A. Fanteaux is a native of Boston. Their long experience in the provision trade gives them excellent advantages, and their high character is a sufficient assurance, that all orders will receive faithful attention and will prove satisfactory to patrons in every instance.

COMMONWEALTH LOAN & TRUST COMPANY, Eastern Office: No. 131 Devonshire Street, Boston; Western Office: Commonwealth Building, Kansas City. C. A. Parks, President and Western Manager; W. W. Mason, Eastern Manager.—At the present day in all the vast array of openings, which present themselves for the use of surplus funds, there is not one that when prudently availed of through the best channels is so sure, remunerative and legitimate, as the loaning of money on the mortgage security of productive western improved farms. The rapid growth of the fertile north-west in population and wealth would have been greatly hindered without the free borrowing of Eastern capital, which has enabled farmers and stock raisers to improve their farms, to purchase blooded stock, new and improved tools and implements, and to erect larger barns, stronger fences and set out orchards. These are all legitimate improvements, and for every dollar thus expended add two to the value of the farm. The loans on western farm mortgages are thus in the nature of things, the most secure of any that can be made. In connection with these remarks, we desire to make special reference in this commercial review of Boston, to the substantial and reliable Commonwealth Loan & Trust Company, whose Eastern office is located at No. 131 Devonshire Street. The company's western office is situated in the Commonwealth Building, Kansas City. This company was duly incorporated under the laws of Kansas with a cash capital of $100,000, and since its organization has obtained a liberal and influential patronage. The following gentlemen are the officers and directors, viz: C. A. Parks, president and western manager; W. W. Mason, treasurer and eastern manager; E. I. Parks, secretary; E. W. Mason, assistant secretary; F. M. Hayward, attorney. Directors, Oscar B. Bradley, Geo. M. Woodward, G. T. Baker, A. C. Stiphen, Ed. B. Rogers, L. H. Smith, W. D. Smith, and George E. Thayer. Loans are only made to the extent of one third the value of the farm, subject to independent and critical appraisement, and the mortgages are drawn so as in every case to fully protect the mortgagee. These guaranteed first mortgage western farm and city loans are absolutely safe, and yield always 7 per cent. net to the investor. The company also offers to the public its secured 6 per cent. debenture bonds, interest and principal payable at the company's Boston office. The following is the statement of the condition of the Commonwealth Loan & Trust Company, at the close of business, July 31, 1888: Resources, first mortgages on real estate, $357,374.03; fixtures and furniture, $3,941.59; stocks in corporations, $2,000.00; cash on hand and in banks, $50,021.51; bills receivable, $4,415.00; total, $295,754.33. Liabilities, capital stock, $100,000.00; six per cent. debenture bonds, $86,000.00; accrued interest on same, $434.50; bills payable, $25,000.00; funds and deposits held for customers, $46,115.01; Kansas City office, $9,066.53; undivided profits, $14,951.29. Further details as to the operations and methods of this substantial corporation may be obtained at the company's offices in Boston and Kansas City.

J. MORRILL, JR., & CO., Manufacturers of Soap and Candles, No. 8 Commercial Street.—There is no branch of manufacture of more vital importance to a community than that of soap and candles; in this line the oldest house in New England is that of Messrs. J. Morrill, Jr., & Co., of Roxbury and Boston, and whose product is pronounced the purest and the best by the trade and consumers. It is now ninety-two years since the grandfather of Mr. Morrill started the industry of soap manufacturing upon a comparatively small scale. He achieved marked success, and was succeeded by his son, father of the present proprietor. It is now forty-four years ago since Mr. Morrill was taken into copartnership by his father, under the name and style of Morrill & Son, and after a lengthy career, he eventually became sole proprietor and has been doing business for many years past under the existing name and style. He brings to bear the widest range of practical experience, coupled with perfected facilities, and has in operation at Roxbury a large and fully equipped soap and candle factory. He is a resident of Roxbury, and exercises close supervision over the processes of manufacture, having the reputation of being the most skillful soap manufacturer in the U. S. His product is absolutely pure and of the highest standard. Mr. Morrill selects his materials with the utmost care; only the best of tallow and all chemicals, etc., are permitted in these works, while skilled hands attend to the various processes. The candles produced have also become internationally celebrated. The firm permanently maintain their enviable reputation and have a heavy trade of the most desirable character. Their depot and warehouse is at No. 8 Commercial Street, where is carried a large and complete stock. The firm sell strictly at wholesale to the grocery and export trade. Their brands of soap and candles are deservedly popular and are largely consumed in Boston and New England, while they find a market in New York and elsewhere; in the provinces, with a heavy export trade to the West Indies and Central and South America. The Morrill soaps are the most effectual detergents of dirt known. They are strong and effectual, yet do not harm the most delicate fabric, and are the most economical and reliable soaps in existence. Mr. Morrill is a popular and respected manufacturer, and his concern is a valued factor in promoting Boston's commercial supremacy.

RITCHIE & BROWN, Auctioneers, Real Estate and Commercial Brokers, No. 172 Washington Street.—The firm of Ritchie & Brown, No. 172 Washington Street, are well-known in Boston in connection with the business of real estate, while as auctioneers and commercial brokers they have come to the front within a comparatively recent period and shown an enterprise and ability which mark them as one of the most successful houses in the city of the kind. The business was established twenty years ago by the senior partner of the house, W. K. Ritchie, who is a justice of the peace and has always enjoyed the respect of the trading community. A little over a year ago the present firm was formed by the admission of Mr. J. L. Brown, who had much experience in the different branches of the business, and was well qualified in every way to advance the interests of the house. Messrs. Ritchie & Brown as auctioneers, real estate and commercial brokers, do a large business in buying, selling and exchanging all kinds of real estate, improved and unimproved, in town and country, disposing of all kinds of property at auction or private sale, sales being attended in all parts of the country, negotiating business properties, securing partners and capital, and having stocks, stores, markets, saloons and boarding houses on their list. Legal papers are drawn by Mr. Ritchie of the firm, and only the most moderate commissions are charged by the house in every case. Both gentlemen are natives of Boston, and are admittedly fine representatives of the commercial ability of the city.

F. P. ADAMS & CO., Proprietors of Kellogg's Flavoring Extracts, Salad Cream, Etc., Manufactory and Salesroom, No. 280 Dover Street.—The steady and growing demand that has become so manifest of late years for choice flavoring extracts, sauces and kinds of table relishes has resulted, in the very nature of things, in placing upon the market some especially fine goods of condiments manufactured in this city. And while it is gratifying to note that very marked improvement has been effected in these palatable articles, special mention ought here be made of the productions of F. P. Adams, proprietor of "Kelloggs" flavoring extracts, olives, catsup, salad creams, etc., manufactory and salesrooms at No. 280 Dover Street, which are goods of exceptional merit. The articles put up by this widely known firm are noted for their purity, quality and flavor, and for general excellence are not surpassed by anything of the kind produced in the country, having taken an enduring hold on popular favor throughout the land, and as a consequence they are in wide and increasing demand in the trade all over the United States. The business premises occupy the whole of a 40x125 foot floor, which is supplied with ample and complete facilities, while some ten to twelve in help are employed, besides several traveling salesmen. The productions included besides "Kellog's" flavoring extracts (which are the leading specialty), also olives, maple syrup, catsup, salad cream, bay rum, French mustard, lemon and lime juice, and a full line of choice condiments; a large and complete assortment being carried constantly in stock, and all orders for the trade are promptly and reliably filled. They are the largest packers of olives in the northeast. Mr. F. P. Adams, who is the sole proprietor, is a man of middle age, active and energetic, and prior to embarking in this flourishing enterprise in 1884 had been engaged in the grocery business for about fifteen years.

THE METROPOLIS OF NEW ENGLAND.

HASKINS BROTHERS, Manufacturers and Dealers in American Isinglass, Irish Moss, Cod Liver Oil, Curriers Oil, Fish Roe for Export, No. 176 Atlantic Avenue; Factories, Rockport, Jeffries Point; Cable Address, "Haskins, Boston."—Prominent among the representative manufacturers of specialties peculiar to their respective establishments in this city is the firm of Haskins Brothers, widely and favorably known as extensive manufacturers of and dealers in American isinglass, Irish moss, cod liver oil, curriers oil, and fish roe for export, whose main offices are at No. 176 Atlantic Avenue, in this city, with factories at Rockport and Jeffries Point. This important enterprise has been in successful operation for a period of twenty years, and its influence and connections have become widely extended over all portions of the civilized globe. Their factory at Jeffries Point is used for preparing salt fish and fish roe for export, and for the manufacture of cod liver oil and curriers oil; while their Rockport factory is devoted exclusively to the manufacture of their celebrated American isinglass. They import fish sounds direct from Europe, Asia and South America for the manufacture of their isinglass, and produce an article unequalled for durability and general excellence by any other house on this continent. Wherever introduced and tested it is preferred above all other makes, and is in permanent and increasing demand throughout the United States and the Canadas. Employment is provided for some fifty skilled hands, and the output is of great magnitude and importance. In all branches of their business the Messrs. Haskins exercise the utmost care that all products shall be maintained at the highest standard of excellence, and as a result their oils are widely preferred on account of their salability and solid merits, and their trade is constantly increasing in its proportions. Orders are filled with promptness and care in all cases, and goods are placed on the trade at prices difficult to be duplicated elsewhere. The copartners, Messrs. Moses W. and Leander M. Haskins, are natives of Rockport, Mass., and, in addition to their business as here briefly sketched, they are also active and prominent in this market as members of the firm of Haskins Bros. & Co., wholesale fish dealers, with headquarters at No. 18 T wharf. They are energetic and enterprising in all their business methods, and have won success in all their undertakings by honestly deserving it.

COMER'S COMMERCIAL COLLEGE, No. 666 Washington Street.—We desire to direct special attention in this review of the commerce and industries of Boston to that well-known and popular institution, famed far and wide under the name of Comer's Commercial College, which is situated at No. 666 Washington Street, corner of Beach street. This splendid institution was founded in 1840, and was the first commercial college established in America. Its founder was Mr. George N. Comer, who laid the foundations strong and deep for the good of coming generations, giving it the benefit of his wisdom and sound management until 1877, when he was succeeded by his son, Mr. Charles E. Comer, the present efficient educator and scholarly principal. That Mr. Comer, by long training under his father in all the departments of the college, was peculiarly fitted for the position, is shown by the remarkable success of the institution under his principalship. Since its foundation Comer's Commercial College has graduated hundreds of young men who owe their success in life to the instructions here imparted, while the leading merchants, brokers and business men of this city and throughout the country manifest their approval of its educational course and system by sending their sons and daughters to it. The building occupied has been fitted up with an especial view to its permanent occupancy as a business college. Here will be found the theoretical and the practical departments in full swing; the banks, with all the paraphernalia for conducting a legitimate banking business, and other departments, all in charge of successful educators. It is the aim of the theory department to make the student thoroughly familiar with the principles of arithmetic, writing, spelling, grammar, correspondence and book-keeping, thus to establish a solid foundation upon which to build his subsequent knowledge, and which shall make him a thorough accountant, competent to properly dispose of any transaction, no matter how complicated it may be, or how different from anything which he has before had to do. In the actual business department may be found the college bank, merchandise emporium, transportation department, and offices for conducting retail, commission and jobbing business. Through these houses, arranged after the best models, with necessary appointments and equipments unsurpassed by any similar institution in the country, business is conducted as in the great world of commerce and trade. Every young man should take a course of study here after leaving the public schools, and before going into business. It will prove of inestimable value to him. That this course of study meets the demands of the times for a business education is proved by the ability and success of its graduates in business and by the demand for them by the business men of this and other cities. A worthy graduate of Comer's is always sure of employment. It had in attendance last year over 450 students; and the enrollment for the forty-eight years past amounts to over 25,000 students. The faculty is one of the best qualified ever brought together in the various departments of a business college. Mr. Comer and his corps of assistants are gentlemen of the highest culture and training, and possess skill and experience in educating the youth of this country not excelled, and rarely equalled.

L. B. SMITH & CO., Manufacturer of Small Machine Screws in Steel, Iron, or Brass, Screw Machine Work to Order, No. 59 Hanover Street.—The increased attention given of late years to the production of an improved grade of machine screws and kindred articles has resulted, as it is needless to mention, in marked progress being made in this direction. A Boston firm that has been notably successful in this line is that of L. B. Smith & Co., manufacturers of small machine screws in steel, iron and brass, whose office and works are located at No. 59 Hanover Street, and whose products are in steady and growing demand in the trade, owing to the general excellence of the same. The articles turned out in this concern are of a very superior character in every respect, alike in design, strength and efficacy, and taken altogether, are not surpassed by anything of the kind produced in or around this city. This thriving enterprise was started about fourteen years ago, and from its inception the venture proved a highly gratifying success. The office and salesroom of the firm are located on the second floor with commodious and well equipped factory on the fifth, while some dozen or more expert hands are employed on the premises. The productions include machine screws of every size, style and variety, in steel, iron and brass; also studs, rolls, taper pins, etc., while odd designs are produced, and screw machine work of every description is executed to order in the most prompt and excellent manner, and the trade of the firm which extends throughout the city and state is of a very substantial character. The copartnership consists of Messrs. L. B. Smith and W. E. Thomas, natives of New Hampshire and Maine, respectively, and are men of energy, experience and practical skill.

CHAPIN BROTHERS, Wholesale Produce Commission Merchants, No. 97 South Market Street.—Among the widely known and reliable produce commission merchants of this city, there are none having a better representation or controlling a more substantial business than Messrs. Chapin Brothers, whose office and salesrooms are located at No. 97 South Market Street. This business was established in 1874 by Messrs. Gardner and Ira Chapman, both of whom have had great experience in the wholesale produce trade. Mr. Ira Chapin continued in the business until January 1, 1882, and in 1882 Mr. Preston V. Chapin, who has been with the concern since its inception, was admitted a partner. Their premises are commodious and are arranged with a due regard for storage purposes and for business operations. The firm have influential connections in the best producing sections of the country, and are constantly receiving in season potatoes, eggs, beans, apples, onions, poultry, game, sweet potatoes, Florida oranges, watermelons, berries, and all kinds of fruit and produce, which are offered to customers at the ruling market prices. Liberal advances are made on consignments of first-class grades of fruit and produce, and shippers can always find a ready sale for their products through the medium of this concern, and at the same time prompt and satisfactory settlements. Messrs. G. and P. V. Chapin are natives of Ogdensburgh, N. Y. They are highly esteemed in trade circles for their promptness and integrity, and are popular members of the Boston Fruit & Produce Exchange and Chamber of Commerce.

CHICAGO, MILWAUKEE & ST. PAUL RAILWAY, General offices, Milwaukee, Charles A. Brown, New England Passenger Agent, H. D. Corbett New England Freight Agent, Office, Old State House, No. 210 Washington Street.—The great trunk route and fashionable line to the north-west is the famous and deservedly popular Chicago, Milwaukee & St. Paul railway. The country tributary to it is the richest and most prosperous agricultural region in the world, with a vast and constantly enlarging population, and in spite of numerous lines of railroad which here and there exercise a competitive influence, the mighty St. Paul permanently maintains the lead as the great artery of inter communication between the fertile north-west including the continental regions across to the Pacific slope, and the east, south and seaboard. This is the favorite route with eastern travelers and shippers, and the most direct connections, fastest trains and lowest rates give it the lead and permanent supremacy over all other routes. A general eastern agency has for many years been maintained in Boston, and since 1885 the offices have been centrally located in the Old State House. The New England passenger agent is Mr. Charles A. Brown, who has been in charge since 1880, while Mr. H. D. Corbett is the New England freight agent. Both gentlemen bring to bear the widest range of practical experience, coupled with influential connections, and abundant energy and enterprise. Mr. Brown is a native of Maine and has from early youth been closely identified with the railroad business. He was formerly with the Wabash railroad, and by reason of his qualifications, urbanity, and close attention to the promotion of the welfare and comfort of the traveling public, has become one of the most popular passenger agents in the United States. Mr. Corbett was born in Hingham, Mass., and has been with the company for four years. He has been actively engaged in the railroad business for the past thirteen years, and has achieved an enviable reputation for the efficient manner in which he discharges the important duties devolving upon him. The Chicago, Milwaukee and St. Paul railway has through the energetic and ably directed efforts of Messrs. Brown and Corbett very greatly increased its New England business, and the substantial inducements offered cannot be duplicated elsewhere. Among the advantages are its direct lines to all the principal cities of the north-west and west; the choice of four routes either going from or returning to Chicago; splendid vestibuled trains free of extra charge between Chicago and Milwaukee, St. Paul and Minneapolis; the finest dining cars in the world are run on this line; its short line to Omaha is the favorite route between the great lakes and the Pacific railroads; it gives the best and most direct route to Sioux City and Yankton; and is also the great connection between Dakota and Nebraska, etc.; it has a new, easy grade line to Kansas City and St. Joseph; it carries its emigrants on regular express trains in comfortable cars, and stop-over checks are issued to all first-class passengers, enabling them to stop at any number of way points for fifteen days each; the track, rolling stock and equipment generally are kept up to the highest standard; the conductors and station agents are courteous and intelligent, the service is frequent and fast, and all who travel to and through the north-west will consult their best interests and comfort generally by purchasing tickets via the old, reliable and popular Chicago, Milwaukee & St. Paul railway.

WISE, HARRIS & CO., Importers and Manufacturers of Fine Cigars, Dealers in Pipes, Tobaccos and Smokers' Articles, Sole Proprietors of the Celebrated Rising Sun Cigar, Nos. 119 and 121 Hanover Street.—The manufacture of cigars and the trade in tobacco form a prominent feature in the commercial enterprise of Boston. Among those manufacturers of fine cigars who are noted for the superiority of their output is the firm of Messrs. Wise, Harris & Co., at Nos. 119 and 121 Hanover Street. This firm established their business here two years ago, and are fast acquiring a national reputation as extensive importers and manufacturers of fine cigars, dealers in pipes, tobaccos and smokers' articles, and as sole proprietors of the celebrated Rising Sun cigar, which they sell at $60 per thousand to the trade. Their facilities for rapid and perfect production are of the finest and most complete character, their resources are ample and abundant, and their experience as manufacturers has given them a foundation understanding of all the wants and requirements of the trade. In their manufacturing department only thoroughly seasoned and carefully selected tobaccos are used and the best processes are employed, the result being that the cigars here produced are widely preferred for their absolute purity, fine flavor, and even combustion. The Rising Sun is the best ten cent cigar in the market to-day, while Cumberland and the P. Q., both five cent brands made by this house, are in great demand among dealers on account of their salability and solid merits. A complete stock of these specialties is kept in store, and orders of any magnitude are filled with promptitude and satisfaction on terms that are invariably fair and satisfactory to the trade. A fine retail trade is also enjoyed in cigars, tobaccos and smokers' goods, while the wholesale trade extends to all parts of New England and the west, and is rapidly increasing under enterprising and reliable management. The members of this popular firm are Messrs. Albert Wise and Henry D. Harris, both natives of Boston, and gentlemen of wide acquaintance, eminent popularity and high standing in the social and business circles of this city.

E. B. BARNES & CO., Manufacturers of Fine Gold and Bronze Frames, Ornamenters and Gilders, No. 127 Court Street.—Among the leading and best known firms engaged in the production of ornamental and gilt work that have come to the front within recent years in Boston, may be mentioned the popular and prosperous firm of E. B. Barnes & Co., manufacturers of gold and bronze frames, etc., No. 127 Court Street. The work turned out by this firm is of a very superior character, alike as to beauty of design, execution and finish, and as a consequence, their productions are in steady and growing demand all over the New England States, with some trade also throughout other sections of the country. This thriving enterprise was started about three years ago, and the unequivocal success that has attended it from the first abundantly attests the excellence of the work produced. The premises occupied are ample and well equipped, a commodious workshop being maintained also at No. 100 Sudbury Street, while from a dozen to fifteen expert hands are employed. Gold and bronze frames in every size, design and variety are manufactured; also mirror and looking-glass frames, while old frames are regilded in the most prompt and excellent manner at very reasonable rates, everything in the line of gilding and kindred artistic work being executed in the very highest style of the art. Mr. Barnes, who is the sole member, the "Co." being nominal, is a native of England, but has resided in the United States for over twenty years. He is a practical and expert gilder himself of many years' experience in the exercise of his art, and is thoroughly conversant with the business in all its branches.

S. S. WOODCOCK, Architect and Landscape Gardener, No. 40 State Street.—The important and exacting profession of an architect is ably represented in Boston by Mr. S. S. Woodcock, whose office and draughting rooms are eligibly located at No. 40 State Street. Mr. Woodcock commenced the practice of his profession in 1854, and is widely known as an accomplished and expert architect and landscape gardener. He has designed and built upwards of forty churches, also a number of public buildings in Boston and the neighboring cities. His buildings are greatly admired for their stability, finish and elegance, while the elaboration of detail and care bestowed upon every department of his work reflect the utmost credit upon his honorable and business-like methods. Mr. Woodcock is now superintending the construction of the Free Public Library, Kittery, Maine. His patronage extends throughout the entire United States and Canada, and he has also designed several extensive and important buildings for the Sandwich Islands. Mr. Woodcock is at all times prepared to furnish plans, specifications and estimates for churches, chapels, houses, stores, cemetery enclosures, monuments, and the improvement of estates, and likewise to superintend the construction of the most elaborate and expensive buildings. He is a native of Sidney, Kennebec County, Maine, but has resided in Boston the greater part of his life, where he is highly regarded by the community for his skill, ability and integrity. Mr. Woodcock is practically conversant with the growth and wants of Boston, and is fully competent to carry to successful completion all work pertaining to his profession a proof of which is the constant and constantly increasing demand for his services.

THE METROPOLIS OF NEW ENGLAND.

WHITAKER BROTHERS, Ecclesiastical Decorative Painters, Etc., No. 650 Washington Street.—A representative and prominent firm in the city of Boston actively engaged as ecclesiastical decorative painters, and manufacturers of stained glass, altars, etc., is that of Messrs. Whitaker Brothers, whose office, salesrooms and workshops are located at No. 650 Washington street. This business was established in 1878 by the present copartners, Messrs. Frank and William Whitaker. Both partners after many years of experience have learned, that in order to have perfect harmony in interior decorations, the various parts of the work usually let out to a number of contracts, should be dealt with as a whole under one contract, thus saving the clergy a great deal of annoyance, which of necessity must be endured by different contracts. Messrs. Whitaker Brothers make a speciality of furnishing under one contract the frescoing, altars, vestment cases, confessionals, pews, windows, etc. The firm also keeps in stock altars and paschal candlesticks, candle holders, vases, stations of the Cross

paintings, engravings, chromos, representing religious subjects, religious statues of oil composition, gas and kerosene fixtures, artificial flowers, baptismal and holy water fonts, crucifixes for altars, processional crosses, etc., and all kinds of church goods. The firm have done a large amount of work for many prominent Catholic churches, Convents and Protestant churches in New England, in every case giving entire satisfaction. All church goods handled by this reliable firm are unrivalled for elegance of design, quality of materials and uniform excellence, and have no superiors in America or Europe, while the prices quoted in all cases are exceedingly moderate. Both Messrs. Frank and William Whitaker are natives of Boston, where they are highly esteemed by the community for their artistic skill, ability and just methods. They give special attention to the fitting up chapels, in Convents, and promptly furnish estimates and drawings upon application.

NATHAN SAWYER & SON, Book and Job Printers, No. 79 State Street.—In "the art preservative of all arts" it is safe to say that the firm of Messrs. Nathan Sawyer & Son, of No. 79 State street, stands unexcelled in the city of Boston as an enterprising, practical and progressive house. The senior partner, Mr. Nathan Sawyer, was born in Boston, Mass., in August, 1819, and began to learn his trade in Portland, Me., in 1832. In 1853, he came to Boston, and served his apprenticeship with Samuel N. Dickinson, at No. 52 Washington street. January 1st, 1866, the present firm was organized by Mr. Sawyer and his son, Henry N. Sawyer, and they are seen recognized as one of the oldest houses in this line of Boston. No house has been more successful in book and job printing, or produced a better class of work than that of Nathan Sawyer & Son. Their premises are admirably arranged and equipped for the business with all necessary presses, type and modern facilities with which to expedite the work in hand with wonderful ease and rapidity of execution. Work in book and commercial printing, both plain and ornamental, is performed with true artistic conception and with fine effect. The patronage of the house is large, influential and permanent in this city and throughout all the New England States, and a competent force of expert printers are kept constantly busy. The prices which prevail are invariably fair and reasonable, and the judgment displayed in designing new and appropriate styles, commend this firm to the favor and confidence of all. The Messrs. Sawyer are both practical printers of ripe experience and established reputation. The senior partner is known far and wide as one of the oldest printers in the state and one of Boston's solid and substantial business men. The junior partner was born in this city, and is a member of the Masonic Order.

B. F. LAMB & CO., Lumber Merchants, No. 130 State Street.—It is an admitted fact that the lumbering interests of the United States form a very important item in the general aggregate of our country's business. The most important and essential branch of the lumber trade is that carried on by the firm of Messrs. B. F. Lamb & Co., the well-known lumber merchants. This firm deal in Michigan pine and hard woods from South Tennessee and Indiana, and have been established in the business here since 1882. They ship direct to buyers, carry stock at different railroad sheds—and the connections of the firm are of so important and influential a character that all orders and commissions, of whatever magnitude, are promptly and satisfactorily filled. They have an immense permanent trade in this city, and are continually lengthening and strengthening their stakes, expanding their commercial relations and increasing their facilities, so that they are becoming widely recognized as leaders in the trade. But few houses in this line have had the active experience, or possess the comprehensive knowledge with regard to the wants of contractors, builders and dealers as the case with the management of this house. The policy upon which the business is carried on has ever been characterized by liberality and a careful fostering of the interests of all patrons, so that transactions once begun are such as prove both pleasant, profitable and lasting. The copartners, Messrs. Geo. A. Heywood and B. F. Lamb, are well and favorably known in this city as energetic, enterprising and representative business men. Mr. Heywood is a native of Athol, Mass., while Mr. Lamb was born in New London, Conn., and both are gentlemen of high social and business standing in this community.

J. HENRY SEARS & CO., Shipping Commission Merchants, No. 92 State Street.—The business of the shipping and commission merchant, when properly conducted, is an essential benefit to every commercial centre. In Boston there are a number of extensive and influential houses engaged in this line, and a leading and representative one is that of J. Henry Sears & Co., located at No. 92 State Street. This house was established twenty-five years ago by Messrs. J. Henry Sears and A. Nickerson. The latter gentleman retired in 1877, since which time Mr. Sears has continued the business under the original firm name. He owns his own vessels, and transacts an extensive business in California, East Indies, Europe and all parts of the world. He deals in merchandise of all kinds, shipping direct to the export trade, and receiving important consignments daily, fresh from the hands of the manufacturer and producer, which are promptly disposed of at his hands. He has acquired a high reputation and the entire confidence of all who have been brought into business contact with his house. Honorable dealing, push and enterprise are the means that have effected this result, and have served to give this house a prestige on both sides the water that could not be acquired in any other way. Mr. Sears is a native of Cape Cod, and has long been recognized in this city as a leader in his line of commercial activity. He gives his business the benefit of his large experience and close personal application, and is a thorough and complete master of all its details and various phases, besides being an able and intelligent business man, fully competent to maintain and increase the splendid record of this distinguished establishment, and standing high in business, financial and shipping, as well as in social circles.

162   ILLUSTRATED BOSTON.

STEPHEN TILTON & CO., Sole Agents for P. H. Mayo & Bro's, Manufactured Tobaccos, No. 90 Central Wharf.—There are no manufactured tobaccos in the world which have attained the popularity and deserved pre-eminence of those of P. H. Mayo & Brothers. These goods are the standards in the New England market and as such their sales have attained proportions of enormous magnitude. The sole agents and representatives are Messrs. Stephen Tilton & Co., one of the oldest established firms in Boston and New England, and the most prominent in the wholesale tobacco trade. It was founded fully fifty years ago by the late Mr. Stephen Tilton, one of Boston's old-time merchants and whose decease occurred in 1852. He was succeeded by his sons, Messrs. Stephen, Joseph B., and Charles T. Tilton. Their energy and enterprise resulted in a greatly increased development of the trade. Mr. Stephen Tilton died in 1871; Mr. Joseph B. in 1882, and Mr. Charles T. in 1877, being succeeded by Mr. Charles H. Tilton, son of Mr. Charles T. and by Mr. George B. Tilton, a son of the founder. As thus constituted the firm brings to bear every possible qualification, including vast practical experience, perfected facilities and influential connections. They have established most desirable relations with leading jobbers, retailers, etc., and also do considerable export trade in the world-famous Mayo tobaccos. Their establishment at No. 90 Central Wharf, comprises four entire floors, 25x75 feet in dimensions, and where is carried a very heavy stock of the choicest Virginia chewing and smoking tobaccos, including among others, the following brands: Mayo's genuine U. S. Navy, the great favorite for chewing and whose sales are as steady and staple as wheat; Clarence smoking, a brand that needs no praise here, for all lovers of the weed have personal knowledge of it; Holly, a delicious sweet chewing tobacco; Figlantine, a bright brand, and Ivy, a standard dark brand. Other brands equally well known and all favorites are: Mayo's cut plug, Royal, and Boston Ideal. Tobacconists carry Mayo's tobaccos as their leading line and a standard product that competition fails to keep up to. The partners are members of the Chamber of Commerce, merchants of sterling integrity, who have ever retained the confidence of leading commercial circles, and are worthy representatives of one of the great staple branches of trade and have largely contributed to Boston's mercantile supremacy.

GOSLER & CO., Bankers and Importers, No. 70 State Street.—A representative firm and one of the most important factors in affording necessary facilities for the carrying on of an enormous foreign trade, are Messrs. Goosler & Co., the widely and favorably known firm of bankers and general commission exporters and importers. The house here is a branch of the great Hamburg house of Messrs. John Berenberg Gossler & Co., of Hamburg, Germany. The concern here is one of Boston's oldest commercial establishments, dating away back to 1870. Throughout a series of copartnership changes the name and style of Gosler & Co., has remained unchanged, and is synonymous with integrity and stability. The present partners, Messrs. Arthur Donner and J. B. Schroeder, assumed control in 1882 and are too prominent and widely known in Boston's and New England's social and commercial circles to require any explanatory comment at our hands. Mr. Donner is the Consul here for the Empire of Austria-Hungary, and worthily performs the exacting duties of his office. Mr. Schroeder holds the equally responsible post of Consul for the Empire of Germany, and faithfully performs the onerous duties devolving upon him. Messrs. Gossler & Co., have direct trade and monetary relations with Europe of enormous magnitude. They annually ship and receive a long series of cargoes of natural products, and manufactured articles on commission account and numerous vessels are consigned to them from Hamburg, Bremen, Liverpool and other great European seaports. The firm's State Street offices are commodious and handsomely furnished in the most perfect manner, and every facility attends the transaction of business. Though young men, Messrs. Donner & Schroeder are old in practical experience and have achieved an enviable reputation for the thorough and honorable manner in which they carry through and conclude all transactions. Their trade is principally with South America and the West Indies and is constantly increasing extending in all directions and promises in the near future to be of immense proportions.

C. L. PERKINS, Manufacturer of Choice Chicago Caramels, and Fine Candies, No. 90 Court Street. Branches: No. 639 Washington Street, and in New Haven.—For the highest grades of pure confectionery, there is no establishment in Boston or New England, where they are manufactured so carefully or can be so advantageously obtained, as that of Mr. C. L. Perkin's, of Nos. 90 Court Street, and 639 Washington Street. The reputation of Mr. Perkin's Chicago Caramels is international in character; they are not duplicated for their delicious qualities elsewhere, and their consumption here in Boston has attained proportions of enormous magnitude. The business was founded by Messrs. Perkins & McDonald about ten years ago, and in 1882, Mr. Perkins and McDonald dissolved. His trade grew rapidly, and to adequately meet it he opened a second and elegant establishment at No. 639 Washington Street. Both are handsomely fitted up and decorated, reflecting the highest credit upon Mr. Perkin's sound judgment and good taste. He has a large soda fountain in each, and makes a specialty of mineral waters of superior quality. For years Mr. Perkins manufactured nothing but his "Chicago Caramels," and had all he could do to cope with his orders, selling them not only all over the United States, but in England as well. His facilities were taxed to the utmost, and in enlarging he introduced the manufacture of other choice lines of pure confections. Marked success attended his efforts, and he is to-day the leading confectioner here catering to fine trade, and makes the largest variety of bon bons or dip goods in the city, and has ready call at retail for all he can make, employing a large force of skilled hands, and personally superintending the work of manufacturing. He caters to Boston's best citizens, and his fine candies have a reputation of their own. Mr. Perkins also does some jobbing trade in fancy confectionery throughout the United States, and dealers will find his fine and fancy confections to excel their most exacting standard. He holds the same prominent position in the fine confectionery trade of New Haven, as he does of Boston, and is an enterprising, able and honorable representative of the high class confectionery trade.

CHARLES D. ELLIOTT, General Civil Engineer and Surveyor. Room 5, No. 31 Exchange Street.—One of the best known, experienced civil engineers and surveyors in the city is Charles D. Elliott, whose office is room 5, No. 31 Exchange Street. Mr. Elliott has been established for the long period of twenty-five years or more, and during that time has executed work of an important kind in the city and immediate neighborhood, his services having been in large demand, both in a public and private way. For a considerable period he held the important position of city engineer of Somerville, and gave general satisfaction. In private undertakings, he has been no less successful as an engineer and surveyor, having carried out many important enterprises and laid out estates in a manner to elicit the highest praise from those who commissioned him to do the work. Mr. Elliott, apart from his eminent professional skill, is a gentleman of first-class scientific and general attainments, and takes a lively interest in the current questions of the day. He resides in Somerville and socially is held in the greatest esteem.

HAZELTINE & CO., Butter, Cheese and Eggs, No. 16 Blackstone Street.—Although a comparatively young firm, H. Hazeltine & Co., receivers of and dealers in butter, cheese and eggs, have already attained a commercial standing and built up a business connection vouchsafed to but few among the older handlers of these staple food products in this vicinity. This pushing and popular firm was established something over two years ago. They handle nothing but prime goods, and all orders are promptly and reliably filled, the concern being conducted on strict business principles, while its management is characterized by energy, sagacity and integrity. The premises occupied are ample, neatly kept and well equipped, while several efficient salesmen are in attendance, and the trade, which is of a wholesale nature exclusively, is large and active, extending all over the city and surrounding cities and towns. Mr. Hazeltine, who is the sole member, the "Co." being nominal, was born in Vermont, and has lived in Boston since 1870.

THE METROPOLIS OF NEW ENGLAND.

WAVERLY MANUFACTURING COMPANY, Confectioners' specialties, for Chocolate Coverings, Oxyline Chocolate Butter, Chocolin, Albarine, Etc., Nos. 23 and 25 Fulton Street.—The leading representative of the trade in confectioners' supplies is generally recognized as the Waverly Manufacturing Company of Nos. 23 and 25 Fulton street. As manufacturers of specialties peculiar to their house, this company occupies a unique position in the industrial world, and it is safe to say that it has no successful imitators and no peers in this or any other country. The company has a reputation and a trade coextensive with the civilized world, as manufacturers of confectioners' specialties, patented by them in 1874 and 1881, and endorsed by the best confectioners and chemists in this country and England. The business has been in successful operation since 1874, and is conducted exclusively at wholesale with connections and patrons in every part of the world. The premises occupied for manufacturing and sales purposes comprise three spacious floors, equipped with new and improved machinery, operated by steam power, and steady employment is given to a large force of skilled and expert hands. The most prominent specialties produced by this company are oxyline, chocolate butter, chocolin and albarine, for chocolate coverings; and caramel butter for the manufacture of caramels, butter scotch, butter cups, chewing candy, molasses candy, cocoanut taffy, corn sheets and balls. These goods are guaranteed as having no deleterious substances used in their manufacture, and are for sale by all confectioners' supply houses. The largest caramel and butter scotch specialty houses in this country and Europe have adopted the caramel butter made by this company, and it may be safely asserted that there is no formula, process or compound that can compare with it. This company also manufactures the Orange County Creamery Butter Color, indubitably the best and most perfect butter color made. Dealers selling it are authorized by this company to guarantee it the best on the market, perfectly harmless, will never grow rancid, and will do just what we say for it. The receivers of butter in this city are recommending shippers to encourage, among creameries and dairymen, the use of this color in preference to all others. This company also manufactures Waverly Slab Dressing for confectioners' use, endorsed by the largest and finest confectioners in the country. Both as to quality and price, the goods offered by this house present superior inducements to the trade, and in every case give entire satisfaction. Orders are filled promptly and carefully, and the best interests of patrons are closely watched and intelligently promoted. Mr. John Hobbs, the moving spirit of this deserving enterprise, is a Boston man by birth and training, a practical chemist of large experience and high reputation, and a sound, reliable business man. He is treasurer of the Standard Gas and Electric Light Company, of this city, and prominently identified with the growth and prosperity of the community in the broadest sense of the term, promoting the commerce of this great metropolis with enterprise, discrimination and success.

SWAIN, EARLE & CO., Teas and Coffees, Importers and Manufacturers, No. 65 Commercial Street.—The leading representative firm of coffee roasters, and importers of teas and coffees in Boston, is that of Messrs. Swain, Earle & Co., of No. 65 Commercial Street. The business is very old established, having been founded by Messrs. Swain, Platt & Earle in 1868. They early developed an active and growing trade, and thus continued until in 1881, Mr. Platt retired, and Mr. T. S. Swain, Mr. F. B. Earle, and Mr. R. T. Thayer formed the existing copartnership. They possess numerous qualifications not found in combination elsewhere; these are long practical experience, thorough knowledge of the best methods of roasting coffees, and the best plant at command to do it; ample resources and facilities in the importation of full lines of teas and coffees. Messrs. Swain, Earle & Co. occupy an entire six story building, No. 65 Commercial Street, 25x80 feet in dimensions, and containing a splendid outfit of coffee roasting and grinding machinery, also spice mills, etc. The firm are heavy importers of Rio, Santos, Java, Mocha, Jamaican, and Central American coffees, handling select Peaberry grades, which produce in the usual combinations the finest and strongest fragrant coffee in this market. Their brands of coffees deservedly maintain the lead, and should be handled by every firm desirous of securing and retaining the best trade. Their stock of fresh crop teas is also worthy of special mention, and commands a large share of the best grocery trade of New England. The firm employ forty hands in their various departments, and require the services of twelve travelers on the road. They generically towery punt in New England and their goods are as widely known as they are justly appreciated all over the west, etc. Mr. Swain is a native of this state, and has long been prominent in the import and wholesale trade in teas and coffees; Mr. Earle is a native of New York, and has been a resident here and active in business for many years past. Mr. Thayer is a native of Massachusetts and a resident of Chelsea. He is an authority in this branch of trade. There are no better judges of the great staples of tea and coffee than the above gentlemen. They handle only the best and purest of every grade and in their long and honorable career have achieved a success as substantial as it is legitimate in character.

CROCKER & ELDRIDGE, Wholesale Grocers, Nos. 84 and 86 South Market Street.—Among the most active and enterprising of the wholesale grocery, flour and provision houses of Boston, is that of Messrs. Crocker & Eldridge of Nos. 84 and 86 South Market Street. The copartners, Mr. John F. Crocker and Mr. Eldric Eldridge, though young men are old in experience in their line of trade while their facilities are perfect, and their connections of the most influential wide-spread character. They formed the present copartnership and started in business in January, 1884, as wholesale grocers and wholesale dealers in the best brands of western flour, also produce and provisions. They early developed a desirable, growing trade. They occupy a spacious four-story building, appropriately fitted up, and where is carried the choicest line of staple as well as fancy groceries. This firm are also the sole proprietors of the famous "Brunswick" brand of canned goods. Carefully put up under their special supervision a full line of fruits and vegetables, packed in the most careful manner, and sold at prices which, quality considered, cannot be duplicated elsewhere. The firm do a heavy trade throughout New England and the Provinces, employing fifteen hands in their establishment and five travelers on the road. In this connection special mention should be made of their celebrated brands of cigars and tobaccos. Their ten-cent "La Colona," and five-cent "Bains Best" are the leaders, being hand-made by skilled workmen from choicest seed leaf tobacco. Their sales are growing at a gratifying ratio, as also of their "Boss Chew" and "Boss Smoke" brands of tobaccos. These goods meet with ready sale, and have few equals and no superiors. The firm are active and popular members of the Chamber of Commerce and of the Wholesale Grocers Association. They have ever retained the confidence of leading commercial circles, and are worthy representatives of one of the most important branches of Boston's wholesale trade, a position which under the present management they are sure to maintain.

W. A. BATTEY, Commission Merchant and Wholesale Dealer in Flour, Etc., No. 218 State Street.—The house of Mr. W. A. Battey is justly accounted one of the most substantial and successful establishments in the wholesale commission trade in flour in this city. The proprietor established his business here twenty years ago. He occupies two floors at the above address, and every facility is provided for handling stock, while the transportation arrangements are unsurpassed. Extensive storage accommodations are furnished in State Street Block, and an immense stock is constantly carried, comprising the best brands of western flour, toilet meal, corn flour, wheat meal, pearl meal and kindred specialties. The proprietor has special arrangements in force with leading millers and producers in all parts of the country, for the procurement of supplies, and is thus enabled to secure the finest goods in every grade and to fill the heaviest orders without delay. The house represents a large share of the milling industry interested in Boston as a point of distribution for its products. The high reputation acquired by Mr. Battey among those identified with the flour interest everywhere within the scope of its trade, is the best and most satisfactory recommendation that could be given his establishment. He is a native of Attleboro, Mass., and is known as one of the most capable exponents of the flour trade in this section of the city.

M. T. QUIMBY & CO., Manufacturing Jewelers, Importers and Wholesale Dealers in Watches and Clocks, No. 14 Hanover Street.—One of the oldest established and leading firms of manufacturing jewelers in Boston is that of Messrs. M. T. Quimby & Co., of No. 14 Hanover Street. This extensive business was founded in 1846 by Mr. M. T. Quimby, a native of Vermont, and who early in life learned the jewelry trade in its every detail. He early developed an active trade, and in 1862 admitted Mr. L. V. Quimby into copartnership. The firm thus continued until 1881, when Mr. L. V. Quimby died, deeply regretted by the trade and the public. Since then Mr. M. T. Quimby has continued the business and has greatly enlarged it. His factory is at Providence, R. I., where he manufactures full lines of solid and plated cuff and collar buttons, rings, chains, bracelets, and general lines of gold and silver jewelry in sets, half sets and individual articles. His designs are among the most popular known to the trade. His jewelry is rich and elegant, and commands a heavy sale all through New England and the British Provinces. An equally important department of Mr. Quimby's business is his direct importations of fine Swiss watches, renowned for the excellence of their movements and being reliable timekeepers. He also deals in Waltham and other fine American movements, and can supply the trade with watches of any style in nickel, silver or gold cases at prices which cannot be duplicated elsewhere. The attention of jewelers is directed to the substantial inducements offered here to secure a stock of fashionable and readily salable jewelry and the best makes of watches. Mr. Quimby is a respected business man, and has ever retained the confidence of leading commercial circles—a worthy representative of a most important branch of trade.

F. A. SMITH & CO., Commission and Wholesale Paper Warehouse, Nos. 37 and 39 John Street.—The enormous consumption of paper in all departments of trade, as well as in the private affairs of life, has led not only to the foundation of many huge paper manufactories in all parts of the country, but to the establishment of extensive houses in most of the principal cities of the Union having for their object the diffusion of the products of the mills in wholesale quantities. The concern of Messrs. F. A. Smith & Co., at Nos. 37 and 39 John Street, is one of this class, and in its line of trade has gained a prominence unsurpassed by but few other establishments. The business was first organized some twenty years ago by Mr. F. C. Bacon, Jr., who subsequently formed a partnership with Mr. F. A. Smith, under the style of Bacon & Smith. In 1885 Mr. Smith purchased his partner's interest, and assumed entire control of the business under the style of F. A. Smith & Co. The premises occupied comprise a building containing four floors and basement, and 25x60 feet in dimensions. The business is of a commission and wholesale character, and the firm are the selling agents for the Rensselaer Mills, Central Mills, Keuka Mills and sundry paper bag manufacturers. The firm make a specialty of handling all kinds of wrapping and straw paper and paper bags of all strengths and sizes, and receiving supplies direct from the mills and offering them at manufacturers' prices, they have a very extensive and growing trade throughout the whole of the New England States. Mr. Smith is a native of Massachusetts, and a member of the Paper Trade Association. He is widely known in mercantile circles, and as much esteemed as he is well known.

J. A. STUBBS, Wholesale Dealer and Shipper of Extra and Common Oysters, Clams, Quahaugs, Etc., No. 154 Atlantic Avenue, Head of T Wharf.—Among the leading and oldest established wholesale oyster merchants and shippers of Boston is Mr. J. A. Stubbs, whose business card with its big gilt shell, and the men with their tongs fast to a mammoth oyster is typical of his sterling enterprise, and big growing trade. Mr. Stubbs was born in Wellfleet, Cape Cod, Mass., and early in life became identified with the branch of trade in which he has achieved such success. He learned it thoroughly in every detail, and about twenty-five years ago, established in business upon his own account. He devoted himself energetically to the various branches of the business and early became noted for the superiority of the oysters he delivered. He has enlarged his facilities and they are now second to none in the wholesale oyster trade of New England. Mr. Stubbs removed to his present directly convenient premises, No. 154 Atlantic Avenue, head of T Wharf in 1886, and here receives fresh every day direct from his own beds. He owns very extensive beds at Warren, R. I., also at Pocasset, Mass., planting a very select seed oyster, and securing a quality of extras that are renowned in this market. Mr. Stubbs is also a regular receiver of cargoes of extra and common Virginia oysters, and ships by the package and in the shell all over New England, while in Boston he supplies retail dealers and leading restaurants, oyster houses, hotels, etc. He employs upwards of 100 hands in getting the oysters from the beds, opening, sorting and shipping. He has his own fleet, including some of the fastest sloops in the business, and permanently maintains the lead for desirable, strictly fresh and select shell fish, including large quantities of hard and soft clams, lobsters, shrimp, etc. His trade is annually enlarging, and he ships hundreds of miles out of Boston to numerous customers along every line of railroad and by steamer.

C. N. CARTER, Cloaks, Suits and Furs, No. 406 Washington Street.—One of the best known houses in the city engaged in the manufacture and sale of cloaks, suits and furs is that of C. N. Carter at No. 406 Washington Street. Mr. Carter has been engaged in this business for twenty-seven years, and was located on Winter Street until last year when he removed to the premises now occupied, which consists of two spacious floors, each having an area of 25x60 feet, affording ample opportunities for display and convenience of the patrons. Throughout, the establishment is very attractive and contains a large and valuable assortment of the latest styles of ladies' cloaks and handsome suits and costumes in silk, velvet and other fabrics, and also seal sacks, pelisses and fashionable furs of the very highest quality. Mr. Carter is not only one of the oldest and most reliable dealers in this line of goods, but is also a leader in introducing the new styles and fashions, and always has the first to introduce the new styles and fashions before the public. In the assortment, which is perfect and complete in every department, is exhibited everything that is new and desirable and in accord with the fashionable ideas of the day, and in such variety that no one, and even the most fastidious, need find any difficulty in making a selection. The patronage of the house is large and fashionable, and Mr. Carter and his dozen lady assistants give their special attention and are prompt in looking after the wants of the customers who are afforded every facility and advantage for inspecting the elegant goods that have been brought together expressly for their examination. Mr. Carter is a native Bostonian and is an authority upon the styles and fashions of ladies' cloaks, costumes and furs, and can offer the very best goods and unsurpassed inducements at all times.

WILLIAM H. EDMANDS, Optician, No. 47 West Street.—Keeping pace with the march of progress in science and art, very notable improvement has been effected of recent years in the devices intended to increase the power of vision and restore impaired sight. What with invention, discovery and the marked development of skill, a comparative degree of perfection has been reached in optical goods. A gentleman who has won an A1 reputation for judgment and skill in this line is William H. Edmands, the well-known optician of No. 47 West Street, who has attained a position in the front rank in his profession. Mr. Edmands who is a man of middle age and a native of this city, is a thoroughly practical and expert optician of many years' experience in the exercise of his profession, and a thorough master of the art in all its branches. He was formerly with the firm of Thaxter & Brother, and in May, 1888, succeeded to H. Roth, who had conducted the business here since 1874. The store is compact, ample and very tastefully appointed—an elegant display being made—while competent assistants are employed. A large and first-class assortment is constantly kept on hand, comprising telescopes, microscopes, lenses, opera-glasses, field and marine-glasses, philosophical and scientific instruments, spectacles, eye-glasses and optical goods in great variety, while repairing and adjusting in all their branches are promptly and reliably executed at reasonable rates, all work being fully warranted, and, altogether, Mr. Edmands has a very fine and constantly increasing patronage.

THE METROPOLIS OF NEW ENGLAND.

THE BOSTON TYPE-WRITER COMPANY, Nos. 180 and 186 Washington Street.—It can be stated without fear of successful contradiction that the type-writer has done more to revolutionize the details of daily business life than any other one improvement, and as a result almost every house of any importance has one or more of the instruments in use. Being an accepted fact, it is only necessary to select always what is deemed to be the best, and ranking at the head for both efficiency and economy is the Boston Type-Writer, manufactured by the Boston Type-Writer Company. This company was incorporated in 1886, with Benjamin Bore, president; James H. Currier, treasurer and general manager; and are manufacturers of typewriters, copying presses, and dealers in general supplies. There has long been needed a good, cheap type-writer that would do all the work that could be done on the high-priced machines. There are thousands of persons who have wanted a type-writer but could not afford one on account of the price, or could not operate it should it be purchased, and not having a business that would require the continuous employment of an operator have had to do without one. The Boston type-writer exactly fills the bill. It will do all kinds of work that can be done on any writer, and more than can be accomplished on some. It is simple in construction, easy of action and does good work, while it is easier to learn to operate than other writers and any one can write with it without practice. The alignment is perfect and straight as print; it cannot get out of alignment by use, mistakes can be easily corrected, and several copies can be written at one time. It has a stationary index plate, which does not tire the eyes as do those on other writers, which are constantly moving up and down. The letters and characters are large and plain, and those used most frequently are nearest the centre, and many words frequently used are already formed as shown in diagram of index.

Familiarity with the position of the letters on the index is all that is necessary to produce rapid work. Metal and interchangeable type are important features of the Boston writer, as the operator can use a variety of styles, if desired, at a trifling expense. It takes but a few minutes' time to change type, as they are fastened upon the type wheel with a set screw which can be easily turned. Should a type get injured it can be readily removed and another replaced at a trifling cost without trouble or inconvenience. The type can be cleaned with a stiff brush without being removed from the machine, as they are always accessible. It writes on a flat surface, the paper lying in the same position as though using the pen, and on this account is superior to other writers in which the paper is wound around a roll as envelopes, cards, etc., can be written on as well as any kind of paper. The operator can at any time inspect all that has been written, correct any mistake, or insert omissions without removing paper from the machine. It is made with such accuracy that any part can be duplicated if worn or broken. It is light, strong and portable; is less complicated than any practical writer in the market, while the price places it within the reach of all who desire a type-writer. It is the best writer for the money, and in quality of work equals the highest priced writers. The latest improvement in copying presses is the Boston wall copying press, manufactured by this company. It is a combination press, table, water receptacle and brush holder, made to fasten upon the wall, thus leaving as much room on the floor for a chair or table as there would be if there was no press in the room. It can be adjusted to suit any thickness of book, and all the parts are interchangeable and can readily be duplicated. They are in use in many of the largest mercantile houses, hotels, offices, markets, etc., throughout the country, and is universally acknowledged to be the most convenient and best working letter press extant, and far superior to the old style. The Boston Type-Write Company is in a position to guarantee the prompt and perfect fulfillment of all orders for these important improvements, and offer inducements to purchasers that cannot be duplicated elsewhere. Their trade is large, influential and steadily increasing throughout the United States, the Canadas and England, and agencies are established in all the principal cities. The officers of the company are gentlemen of large experience and thorough knowledge of the business; are enterprising, progressive and practical in all their methods of manufacture.

W. PORTER & CO., Agents of Quincy Mutual Fire Insurance Company, of Quincy, Traders and Mechanics Insurance Company, of Lowell, and General Insurance Brokers, Office, No. 27 State Street.—One of the best channels through which to effect fire insurance in this city is that afforded by Messrs. W. Porter & Co., the agents of Quincy Mutual Fire Insurance Company, of Quincy, Mass., and Traders and Mechanics Insurance Company, of Lowell, Mass., and prominent as Insurance Brokers, at No. 27 State Street. This agency was founded forty years ago by Mr. W. Porter, who died October 20, 1882, and was succeeded by Chas. H. Porter, his son, and W. P. Butler, who have continued the business under the original firm name. Without in any way reflecting on others' offices, it is but justice to say that these gentlemen have secured the leading position in their line, and have developed a connection and patronage of a most influential and permanent character. This firm are placing risks with the above-named companies, and with all responsible fire insurance corporations in the world, at remarkably low rates; their policies are clearly worded, explicit and devoid of technicalities, and all losses are promptly paid on adjustment. They control the insurance of important lines of business, residential and manufacturing property, stocks of merchandise, boxes, rents, yachts and household effects, etc., and are steadily extending their patronage and influence. The partners are recognized authorities in their line, and have an unrivalled knowledge of the principal risks offering, rendering them safe as agents for conservative companies like those they represent. Mr. Porter is a prominent citizen of Quincy, and a director of the Quincy Mutual Fire Insurance Company. Mr. Butler resides in Cambridge, and has been connected with this house for thirty-two years. Both gentlemen are members of the Board of Underwriters and the Insurance Brokers' Board, and are noted for their excellent business methods and liberal policy, ever retaining the confidence of leading commercial and financial circles.

F. P. TRICKEY, Boarding, Baiting, and Sale Stable, No. 255 Atlantic Avenue.—The well conducted boarding, baiting and sale stable at No. 255 Atlantic Avenue, is an important and essential convenience to this community. It occupies a fine location for the business, being close to pleasure boats landings, and also close to other steamer landings. It has been established the past fifteen years and under the able management of Mr. F. P. Trickey, the proprietor, it has become widely known and is liberally patronized. The premises have an area of 80x100 feet, containing stalls and accommodations for 160 head of horses, every convenience being provided for their care, and only those who are familiar with the duties of stablemen are employed about the place. The accommodations provided for boarding horses, of which there are a large number in the stable, are of a superior character, and for baiting horses, every convenience is at hand. The whole establishment is kept neat and clean and every provision is made for proper ventilation. Mr. Trickey also conducts a large business, buying and selling horses, and always has a number of fine animals suitable for driving or heavy draughting purposes. He is a correct, upright, honorable gentleman to deal with and can always be relied upon in all transactions. A native of Dover, N. H., where he was born forty years ago, Mr. Trickey has since 1869 been a resident of Boston where he has made many friends and is well known as a popular horse dealer and the proprietor of an establishment which is admirably suited for the purposes for which it is maintained.

SEARS' PEOPLE'S DRUG STORE, No. 136 Hanover Street. —An old established and excellent Hanover Street pharmacy is Sears' People's Drug Store, which is eligibly located in the Blackstone Bank Building, corner of Union Street, and which for forty odd years has maintained an enduring hold on popular favor and confidence. It is one of the oldest and leading establishments of the kind in this part of the city; and has a large and flourishing trade. Physicians' prescriptions and family recipes are here compounded from absolutely pure and best quality ingredients, and in the most careful and accurate manner by thoroughly competent pharmacists, while bottom prices likewise prevail at all times. The store, which is open from 7 a. m. to 12 midnight, is commodious, handsomely appointed and complete in every respect, an elegant soda fountain, beautiful plate glass show cases and attractive fixtures imparting to the place a very inviting appearance. A large and first-class stock is always carried, embracing besides fresh and pure drugs, medicines and chemicals of all kinds, all the standard proprietary remedies, alcohol, spirits, acids, extracts, essences, flavors and druggists' sundries in great variety; also pure medicinal wines, liquors, and mineral waters, and a fine assortment of toilet articles, perfumery, fancy soaps, sponges, chamois, choice cigars, etc., while four experienced assistants are in attendance, the proprietor exercising close personal supervision over the prescription department. Mr. G. T. Sears, who is a man in the full prime of life and a native of this state, is a gentleman of agreeable manners and the highest personal integrity, as well as a pharmacist of judgment and skill, with long and varied experience in the laboratory, and is a prominent member of the Druggists' Alliance, the Massachusetts Pharmaceutical Association and the Massachusetts College of Pharmacy.

STEDMAN & KELLOGG, Bankers and Brokers, No. 8 Congress Street.—A widely known and representative house in Boston, dealing largely in investment securities, stocks, bonds, etc., is that of Messrs. Stedman & Kellogg, whose offices are located at No. 8 Congress street. This business was established in 1872 by Charles F. Emery, who was succeeded in 1883 by the present firm. The copartners, Messrs. C. L. T. Stedman and Geo. G. Kellogg, have long been identified with the leading financial circles of Boston, and are recognized authorities on the most reliable classes of investment securities and guaranteed dividend paying bonds. The firm buy and sell all kinds of investment securities, and make a specialty of guaranteed realestate mortgages. Messrs. Stedman & Kellogg are agents in Boston for the sale of bonds and mortgages of the Central Kansas Loan & Trust Co., of Russell, Kansas, also of the Charles T. Emery Real Estate Loan Co., of Kansas City, and the Union Investment Co., of Kansas City. They devote close attention to this branch of finance, and have an influential circle of permanent customers, numbering many wealthy capitalists and investors. Both Messrs. Stedman and Kellogg are natives of Boston. Mr. Stedman was for several years with the National Eagle Bank, and the American Loan & Trust Company of Boston. Mr. Kellogg was also connected with the American Loan & Trust Co., of Boston, and the Montpelier National Bank of Montpelier, Vermont. The firm of Stedman & Kellogg have ever conducted their business on the enduring principles of integrity, and are also always cognizant of the true position of a house, that holds the interests of its patrons in its hands.

FOGG BROTHERS & CO., Bankers and Dealers in Commercial Paper, No. 68 Congress Street.—The banking interests of Boston are of the greatest importance, not only to the city, but also to all sections of New England. Capital naturally seeks this city for investment, and here are found some of the most wealthy and enterprising financiers in the United States. Prominent among the number thus referred to, is the reliable and widely known firm of Messrs. Fogg Brothers & Co., bankers and dealers in commercial paper, No. 68 Congress street. This business was established in 1865 by Fogg Brothers & Dates, who were eventually succeeded by Fogg Brothers & Co. In 1871 Mr. T. S. Fogg died after a successful and honorable career. The business is now the property of Messrs. John S. Fogg, E. S. Bristol, A. S. Austin and A. D. Vining, all of whom are able financiers and recognized authorities with regard to the values of stocks, bonds and first-class investment securities. They transact a general banking business in all its branches, and make a specialty of dealing in high class commercial paper. Possessing a large capital, this responsible firm is well able to handle all business in a prompt and satisfactory manner, while their standing in financial circles gives the utmost confidence to their numerous patrons. Messrs. J. S. Fogg and A. D. Vining are natives of Weymouth, Mass., Mr. Bristol of Winthrop, and Mr. Austin of Salem. They have ever conducted their business on the enduring principles of integrity, and are always cognizant of the true position of a house that holds the interests of others in its hands. The firm's New York correspondent is Mr. H. L. Horton.

EDWARD SAWYER, Civil and Mechanical Engineer, No. 60 Congress Street.—The profession of a civil engineer is one of great responsibility, requiring the highest order of ability, skill and experience to secure success. One of the best-known and most popular and civil and mechanical engineers in Boston is Mr. Edward Sawyer, of No. 60 Congress Street. This gentleman established himself in the practice of his profession here in 1865, and has devoted his time and talents during all these years to manufacturing plants, mill work and sanitary engineering, securing a reputation and a patronage that early placed him in the front rank of enterprise, popularity and success. The fidelity and accuracy of all his plans and engineering designs have been widely recognized and appreciated, and he has been entrusted with many important public and private commissions that have materially added to his prestige as an engineer and master workman. Among the works executed by him may be named two mills for the Chicopee Manufacturing Company, at Chicopee Falls, Mass.; several mills for the Arlington Company at Lawrence, Mass.; and other large cotton and worsted mills throughout New England. Mr. Sawyer was born in New Hampshire, and has resided in Boston for the past thirty years; is treasurer of the Sawyer Spindle Company of this city; a member of the Boston Society of Civil Engineers, and is widely and prominently known to the trade and public as an eminent leader in his profession and a gentleman of large business capacity and thorough reliability, with whom it is always a pleasure to meet socially, professionally or in a business way.

BALLANCE & SORRELL, Manufacturers of Boots and Shoes, No. 42 Lincoln Street.—Frequently have we spoken of the steady progress Boston has made in almost every branch of industry and department of trade, but probably in none has that progress been more visible than in the sale and manufacture of boots and shoes. For half a century this city has been recognized as the great boot and shoe mart of the Union. The quality of goods handled here is constantly growing in popular favor; consequently every portion of the country draws its supplies from Boston. This is in part, no doubt, due to the enterprise and energy of our wholesale houses. We have in Boston many firms engaged in the trade, that for wealth, standing and reliability, no city in the land can duplicate the same. Worthy of mention among such is the concern of Ballance & Sorrell, with commodious quarters at No. 42 Lincoln Street. The firm are manufacturers of men's and women's machine and hand sewed boots and shoes at wholesale only. The business was organized in 1885 by Messrs. W. P. Ballance, I. W. Ballance and M. W. Sorrell. Mr. Ballance is a native of North Carolina and has always been identified with the boot and shoe trade, in which he was formerly a salesman. Mr. Sorrell, in 1887, disposed of his interest in the business to Mr. J. M. Dunwoody, who is a native of Georgia, where he was formerly in the shoe trade, and subsequently was located for a time in New York City. The original style of the firm, that of Ballance & Sorrell, has been retained, and the firm has gained a high reputation and a trade which extends to every section of the country. The premises occupied comprise the first floor and basement of the building which is 20x75 feet in dimensions, and are admirably fitted up and arranged. A very heavy stock is carried, and the firm control the products of factories in Lynn and Brockton, thus enabling them to fill all orders promptly and at the lowest prices ruling in the trade. Shipments are made to all sections of the country and the standing of the firm in the trade is of the highest, a position which they have gained by straightforward methods and first-class goods.

FARMER'S LOAN & TRUST CO., T. O. Moffett, President; A. C. Goss, General Eastern Agent; Western office, Anthony, Kansas; Boston Offices, No. 54 Devonshire and 29 Water Streets.—The State of Kansas is the heart of the American Continent. In a few years the face of the land has been transformed with orchards and osage hedge rows. Everywhere in this splendid and fertile state are evidences of culture, thrift and enterprise; everywhere the promise of prosperity and greatness. City lots which five years ago sold in Anthony, Harper County, for seventy-five dollars, are worth to-day $5,000. In connection with these remarks, we desire to make special mention in this commercial review of Boston to the successful and progressive Farmer's Loan & Trust Co. of Kansas, whose office in this city is located at No. 54 Devonshire and No. 29 Water streets. The company's Western office is situated in Anthony, Kansas, and its Philadelphia branch at No. 205 Walnut Street. This company was duly incorporated under the laws of Kansas in 1883 with a capital of $500,000, of which $300,000 has already been paid in; $100,000 of the above capital has not yet been issued, but is reserved as treasury stock. All who desire absolutely safe and profitable investments should investigate and compare the merits and records of this reliable company with the best corporations in the same business. The company has been remarkably successful, and maintained its reputation for careful, conservative management, because its western members are composed of men whose reputation for integrity and business ability is well known throughout Kansas. Most of them have been in this business from ten to twenty years, and are thoroughly familiar with real estate values. Being well known and trusted, farmers would naturally select them to place a mortgage on their homes. Among the eastern members are some of the strongest, most successful, and best known business men of Boston and other parts of New England, New York, and Philadelphia, who keep a careful supervision over all the affairs of the company, and send from their number each year one or more committees to make a thorough examination of all the affairs of the company. This commends the company to careful investors. Able counsel with a thorough knowledge of Kansas law and the loan business have been retained by the company, to attend to all legal matters. The company's examiners are each paid a salary; their compensation does not depend on the number of loans made, as it does where commissions are paid. The company issues seven per cent. guaranteed mortgages, and six per cent. debenture bonds, based upon real estate mortgages, on the following plan: A series of $100,000 six per cent. coupon bonds are issued in sums of $500 and $1,000, payable in six years after date, coupons being payable quarterly. Principal and interest payable at office of Boston Safe Deposit and Trust Company. Bonds of $500 and $300 to meet the requirements of small investors are also issued. Each series of these debentures is secured by $100,000 of this company's first mortgages on property valued at not less than two and one half times the amount of the loan, by a pledge and assignment of the mortgages by this company to the Boston Safe Deposit and Trust Company, of Boston, Trustee. Each bond bears the certificate of the Boston Safe Deposit and Trust Company, which holds the securities, setting forth plainly the terms of the trust. No bond can be issued until the mortgages required to secure it are duly assigned to the trustee, and no bond will be certified by the trustee until such security has been delivered to it by the company. This is rapidly becoming the most popular form of investment in western securities. The following gentlemen, who are highly regarded in financial and commercial circles for their prudence, executive ability and just methods are the officers and directors: T. O. Moffett, president; Col. Wm. H. Long, vice-president; J. K. Wilson, 2d vice-president; J. M. Bent, secretary; W. R. Stivers, assistant secretary; S. A. Darrough, treasurer; E. H. Goss, assistant treasurer. Directors: T. O. Moffett, president of Ashland Bank, Kan.; J. M. Bent, capitalist, Anthony, Kan.; S. A. Darrough, president of First National Bank, Anthony, Kan.; John F. Reese, real estate, Wichita, Kan.; Frank Evans, Wichita, Kan. (Examiner for Co.); J. K. Wilson, Anthony, Kan. (Ass't examiner for Co.); Jas. G. Woods, Bluff City, Kan.; O. F. Casteen, treasurer Harper Co., Kan.; J. M. Pollock, capitalist, Wichita, Kan.; W. R. Tucker, retired merchant, Wichita, Kan.; J. M. Russell, director of First National Bank, Anthony, Kan.; Max Tandler, merchant, Anthony, Kan.; J. P. Pancoast, M.D., treasurer Insane Asylum, Concord, N. H.; also director N. H. Savings Bank; J. A. Wright, of Peter Wright & Sons, Philadelphia, Pa.; Albert Poomer, clothing manuf., Schwenksville, Pa.; J. L. H. Cobb, capitalist, and trustee Bates College, Lewiston, Me.; Col. Wm. H. Long, Jordan, Marsh & Co., Boston; Herbert Nash, of Nash & Co., tea importers; Moses S. Page, of Moses S. Page & Co., Boston; Levi S. Gould, of F. M. Holmes Furniture Co., Boston; A. C. Goss, Gen. Eastern Agent of the company, Boston; Chas. H. Bond, of Waitt & Bond, Boston. Mr. A. C. Goss, the General Eastern Agent of the company has control of the Boston offices, and will be glad to give any information relative to the real estate mortgages and securities of this successful corporation.

C. BLAKE FURNITURE CO., Manufacturers of Desks, Hall Stands, Etc., Office and Warerooms, No. 100 North street.— Prominent among the numerous houses of enterprise and refinement in the city of Boston, extensively engaged in the manufacture of desks and fancy cabinet ware, is that known as the C. Blake Furniture Company, whose offices and warerooms are located at No. 100 North Street. This business was established in 1856 by Mr. C. Blake, who conducted it till April, 1887, when he retired, and was succeeded by his son Mr. J. M. Blake, and Mr. C. F. W. Schlinger, the business being carried on under the style and title of the C. Blake Furniture Company. The factory of the company which is fully supplied with latest improved wood working machinery, tools and appliances, and furnishes constant employment to 100 skilled cabinet makers and operatives, is situated on Dorchester Avenue, South Boston. The C. Blake Furniture Company manufacture to order or otherwise desks, hall stands, book cases and fancy cabinet furniture of every description. Many of the rarest woods are utilized, and the furniture is carved in the most workmanlike and artistic manner from unique and original designs and patterns. Their goods are unrivaled for elegance, finish, quality of materials and workmanship and have no superiors in this country, while the prices quoted in all cases are as low as those of any other contemporary first class house in the trade. The company's resources and facilities are such, that the largest orders are promptly filled, and its trade now extends throughout all sections of the United States. Messrs. Schlinger & Blake are natives of Boston. They are highly esteemed for their integrity and sound business principles, the exercise of which in all transactions has won for them an excellent reputation with the trade, and been instrumental in the achievement of their business success.

J. T. DYER & CO., Gents' Furnishers, No. 12 Bowdoin Square.— The firm of J. T. Dyer & Company has been for the past eighteen years prominently identified with the trade in the finest grades of gentlemen's furnishing goods. They established their business originally in 1870, at No. 19 Green Street, and in 1880 they opened their present main headquarters at No. 12 Bowdoin Square, under the Revere House, which has since continued as a leading representative of all that is stylish, original and refined in gentlemen's furnishings. Both stores are now operated on a large scale, maintaining the early reputation of the firm, and controlling the very best class of fashionable trade. The stock displayed is the most complete and comprehensive in its character, embracing a magnificent line of the newest shades and patterns in fall and winter hosiery; a most beautiful assortment of stylish ties and cravats possessing the most tasteful and correct combinations of colors; white and ornamental colored linen handkerchiefs; silk, merino and lamb's wool underwear; shirts and collars, gloves and suspenders, canes and sticks, the best makes of imported and domestic umbrellas, and all the choicest importations in fine furnishings and outfittings. These goods have been selected with an experienced eye and a keen appreciation of the popular want, and are calculated to meet the tastes and the demands of the greatest possible number of patrons. They are placed to customers at prices which are eminently fair and equitable, and competition is challenged as regards both quality and novelty of goods and liberality of terms and prices. Mr. J. T. Dyer, the senior partner of this firm, is a native of Cape Cod, Mass., while Mr. R. H. Gardner, the junior member, was born in Maine. Both are well and favorably known in the social and business circles of this city, and have won their large measure of success by honestly deserving it.

BOSTON ICE COMPANY, No. 76 State Street, H. O. Bright, President; James H. Reed, Treasurer.—Ice, which was formerly but little used for any purpose, has become within recent years a staple commodity and an indispensable necessity. There are few families so poor in the great cities of the United States, that they do not patronize the ice man, during the heated term at least, and in a great city like Boston, the quantity used for various purposes is simply immense. Among the enterprising firms and corporations engaged in the ice trade of this city, the Boston Ice Company, which was duly incorporated in 1866, is in all respects the leading company. The operations of this popular company are extensive, requiring the services of 400 operatives and eighty teams. They own immense ice houses, and draw their supplies of ice from various large lakes in the state, so in case one location fails to furnish it, a larger quantity can be cut and housed where it is thick, clear and free from snow. The company controls 500 acres of surface, and its ice is absolutely unrivalled for quality, purity and uniform excellence. During the ice cutting season, the company often employs 1200 hands. The headquarters of the company is at No. 76 State Street, Telephone 563, while its sub-offices and depots are in East Cambridge at Prison Point Bridge, Telephone 6453, and in Charlestown on Front Street, Telephone 634. The chief executive offices of the company are Mr. H. O. Bright, president, and Mr. James H. Reed, treasurer. The company makes a specialty of supplying the retail trade with the best ice at lowest rates, also families, hotels, stores, etc. The charges for supplies of ice are reasonable, as shown by the subjoined tariff of rates: May to October 1st, twelve pounds daily, six dollars; eighteen pounds daily, nine dollars; twenty four pounds daily, twelve dollars; thirty-six pounds daily, seventeen dollars. By weight, fifty pounds for fifteen cents; twenty-five pounds for ten cents. Monthly prices (for other than season time): twelve pounds daily, per month, one dollar and fifty cents; eighteen pounds daily, per month, two dollars and twenty-five cents; twenty-four pounds daily, per month, three dollars; thirty-six pounds daily, per month, four dollars and twenty-five cents. Customers are supplied before and after the season at proportionate rates, and the company can always be relied upon for prompt and effective service. The trade of the Boston Ice Company extends throughout all sections of the city and its vicinity, and it also transacts an extensive wholesale trade. Mr. Bright, the president, is a native of Belmont, Mass., while Mr. Reed, the treasurer, was born in Boston. Mr. Reed is also president of the National Wax Thread Sewing Company.

ROBERT F. CLARK, Stock Broker, No. 40 State Street.—The importance of Boston as a great financial centre is generally recognized. She is in fact the most prominent point for the disposal of desirable investment securities, and the purchase and sale of active stocks and bonds, and the Stock Exchange of this city ranks second only to that of New York in point of volume of trade and number of members. Representative among the number is Mr. Robert F. Clark, the widely and favorably known banker and broker, of No. 40 State Street. Mr. Clark was born in Boston, and has long been actively identified with the interests of investors, having been established in business since 1865, and has developed an excellent reputation for executive ability, and accurate knowledge of every phase and feature of the stock and money markets. He has long been an influential member of the Boston Stock Exchange, ever according a conscientious support to all measures and regulations for the benefit of this useful institution, and to secure increased facilities to the public. He has been repeatedly called on to serve in executive capacities, and is now the vice president of the Exchange. The responsibilities and duties of the Vice Presidency are onerous, and no one could more ably and faithfully perform same than Mr. Clark who has filled the office several times and is universally popular and respected and spoken of in the highest terms on 'Change and in the street. He conducts a general commission business in the purchase and sale, for cash or on margin, of all stocks, bonds and miscellaneous securities as listed by this Board, or listed on the New York Exchange. His New York correspondents are Messrs. Hallgarten & Co., of No. 78 Broad Street. He occupies two central and commodious offices fitted up in the most thorough manner, with tickers, one for Boston stock quotations and news, the other for New York quotations. Every convenience is afforded customers, who include leading capitalists and active operators. His facilities for obtaining the latest reliable information as to the course of the market, are of the most perfect kind; and no one is better qualified to fill orders for country capitalists or city operators and investors, either for investment or speculative purposes. He is a recognized authority on the market, intimate with the records of railroads and other corporations, while his methods are truly conservative, his standing and reputation are of the highest character, and he is a faithful exponent of the enduring principles of equity which are the substantial foundations of the business and influence of the Boston Stock Exchange.

ALBION MILLING COMPANY, Merchant Millers and Shippers of Mill Feed, Corn, Oats, and Choice Michigan Produce, Beans, Butter, Eggs, Etc., No. 130 State Street.—There is not, as it goes without saying, among the great staple food products entering into general consumption, any one that comes within measurable distance of flour in point of interest and importance, and it is in the nature of things, therefore, that the production and sale of this and kindred articles should constitute one of the principal branches in commercial activity in every centre of trade and commerce. Among the flourishing concerns in this line that have come into prominence of recent years in Boston can be named that of the Albion Milling Company, merchant flour millers and shippers of mill feed, grain, and choice Michigan produce, with mills and warehouse at Albion, Mich., and Eastern headquarters at No. 130 State Street, this city. This widely known and responsible concern was established some fifteen years ago, at Albion, Mich., the Boston office being opened in May, 1888, and from its inception the enterprise has proved a highly gratifying venture. Producing and handling a very superior line of goods, liberal and honorable in their dealings, and being withal men of energy, sagacity and excellent business ability, Messrs. W. B. Knickerbocker and Joshua S. Ingalls, the proprietors, have been enabled to secure the hold on public favor and to build up the extensive connections they enjoy. Besides a fine and very superior grade of family flour of their own production, they also handle corn, oats, and everything in the line of mill-feed; also prime creamery butter, eggs, beans, and choice Michigan produce of all kinds, and transact a wholesale business exclusively. The office and salesroom in this city, which are under the efficient management of Mr. Ingalls (Mr. Knickerbocker being the resident partner at Albion), are ample and commodious, all orders for home or export trade (cable address "Bates") being promptly and reliably filled, and the business of the Boston branch, which is chiefly with the New England States, is of a most substantial character, and grows apace.

B. F. GREEN & CO., Tailors, No. 190 Court Street.—For a period extending over twenty-eight years the well-known firm of B. F. Green & Co., merchant tailors, No. 190 Court Street, have maintained an enduring hold on popular favor. They are, in fact, among the oldest and foremost exponents of the tailoring art in this quarter of the city, and fully sustain today their well earned reputation for fine work, promptness and reliability. The business was formerly located on Washington Street, whence it was moved to the present commodious quarters some three years ago, and has here been conducted since with uninterrupted success. The premises here occupied are spacious, neatly appointed and well ordered, a large and A1 assortment of imported and domestic suitings being constantly carried, including the latest novelties in cassimeres, cloths, checks, cheviots, serges, meltons, stripes, plaids and fashionable woolens and worsted in quite a variety, while as many as twenty first-class hands are employed in the busy season. Fine tailoring is the specialty, the garments leaving this reliable establishment being noted for their general excellence, alike as to design, cut, fit, finish and fabric, and the patronage which extends throughout the city and environs is of a very substantial and influential character. Mr. Green, who is the sole member, is a gentleman in the prime of life and a native of England, but has resided in Boston some thirty odd years. He is a practical and expert cutter and general workman himself, of long and varied experience in the exercise of his art, and is conversant with the business in all its branches.

THE METROPOLIS OF NEW ENGLAND.

CHARLES C. BEALE, Author, Publisher and Teacher of Simplified Phonography, Nos. 180 and 186 Washington Street.—The Beale School of shorthand, type-writing and business correspondence was formed five years ago, by Messrs. Charles C. Beale and L. E. Lovejoy, but soon merged into the control of Prof. Beale, under whose management it has ever since remained. From its inception it met with almost phenomenal success, thus proving the need of a reliable and well conducted institution of the kind. It has accomplished a great work in training young men and women for the duties of the stenographic amanuensis and reporters, and to-day its graduates filling responsible and lucrative positions, probably outnumber those of all the similar schools in Boston combined. Nearly two hundred and fifty of its working graduates attest the thorough and practical manner of instruction. Much of this success is owing to the fact that Prof. Beale, after long study and research in stenographic literature, as well as after preparing himself by long actual practice in every branch of the profession, succeeded in evolving a system of shorthand, preserving the salient features of the previous systems, but so harmoniz-

Very truly, Charles C. Beale

ing and simplifying the details as to make it comparatively simple of acquisition. The school has been constantly growing until now it has probably the largest and best appointed quarters of any shorthand school in the country. It is centrally located at Nos. 180 and 186 Washington Street, and visitors, who are always welcome, are impressed by the quiet elegance of its appointments. On account of its superior facilities, simplicity of system taught, thoroughness of instruction, and moderate price, this school offers unrivalled inducements to the intending student of these most useful studies. The unprecedented success which his improvements in stenography met, induced Professor Beale to publish a complete series of works on shorthand and kindred subjects, necessitating a large and well fitted printing office, which forms a by no means small department of his business. He is the author and publisher of the complete series of works on Simplified Phonography, the name appropriately given to his system of shorthand, as well as being editor and publisher of stenography, now in its third year, the most influential journal of its class in the world. Professor Beale became deeply interested in Volapük, the international commercial language, so useful to business men throughout the world, and was one of the pioneers in its introduction in this country. He is publisher of a series of text-books on the subject and editor and publisher of "Volapük," the first magazine published in this country devoted to this wonderful language. He has also published various other educational works. We append herewith a complete list of his publications, with prices: Phonographic.—All about stenography, 10 cents; advantages of Simplified Phonography, 5 cents; Manual of Simplified Phonography, $1.00; Text Book of Simplified Phonography, $3.00; Reading Book of Simplified Phonography, 25 cents; Pocket Reading Book of Simplified Phonography, 25 cents; Book of Wordsigns and Contractions, 5 cents; Book of Business Letters, 5 cents; Stenography, Vol. I, bound, $1.50; Stenography, Vol. II, bound, $1.50; Stenography, monthly, per year, $1.00; Annual catalogues, 1885, 1886, 1887 1888, 1889, free; Complete catalogue of publication, free; Shorthand in a Nutshell, 10 cents. Nutshell Series.—Typewriting in a Nutshell, Spelling in a Nutshell, Shorthand in a Nutshell, Punctuation in a Nutshell, Volapük in a Nutshell, Memory Culture in a Nutshell, 10 cents each. Volapük.—All About Volapük, 5 cents; Volapük in a Nutshell, 10 cents; Sitwell's Volapük Grammar, 35 cents; Volapük Dictionary, $2.00; "Volapük," a monthly magazine, per year, $1.00. Miscellaneous.—Sylvester's Cipher Code, 50 cents. Mr. Beale, is well known by the business community, and highly esteemed for his ability, professional skill and integrity, justly meriting the signal success achieved by him in his school and publishing business, as well as for the efforts he has made to place art of stenography on a higher plane, and to smooth the difficulties and obstacles formerly abounding in the study of this profession, while hundreds of his graduates thank him for the aid he has given them towards securing a livelihood.

N. K. FAIRBANK & CO., Lard Refiners, Chicago; S. W. Andrews, Wholesale Agent for New England; Office, No. 5 Central Wharf.—The largest and oldest established lard manufacturers in the world are Messrs. N. K. Fairbank & Co. It was in 1863 that Mr. N. K. Fairbank began the manufacture of the purest, highest grade of refined lard known. He had mastered every problem attending the production of a perfect quality of a lard for general use, that would remain sweet and good in any climate and stand transportation to any part of the world. From small beginnings the business has grown to proportions of colossal magnitude, upwards of 1,500 tierces a day now being manufactured, rendering it the largest industry of the kind on the globe. In addition the firm manufacture a pure, edible refined substance for culinary purposes from cotton seed oil, known as Cottolene and which has every desirable quality of pure leaf lard, coupled with a flavor and uniformity of strength and quality that is rendering it a great popular favorite. The evidence of the most eminent chemists and experts goes to show that cotton seed oil is a healthful and nutritious article, and when duly refined by the elaborate methods in the Fairbank refinery, and the product known as Cottolene is prepared, it is absolutely the most healthful, wholesome and desirable article in existence for culinary use. The firm also manufacture immense quantities of lard oil, neat foot's oil, tallow, gold dust, the famous washing powder, and Santa Claus soap, the best and most economical laundry and bath soap in the world. The firm has extended its trade relations all over the world and has its own depots and branches throughout the United States. Here in Boston is the headquarters for Massachusetts, the agency having been established here in 1877 by Mr. S. W. Andrews, who came direct from Chicago in that year to take charge of this branch house. He is the recognized authority on lard and its kindred products, is an active member of the Chamber of Commerce. Mr. Andrews' office is at No. 5 Central Wharf, where all wholesale orders are promptly filled, shipments being made direct from Chicago to wholesale grocers, jobbers, oil men, etc. We advise the people of New England to secure the interesting pamphlet, entitled "Facts About Lard," demonstrating and proving that Fairbank's lard is made strictly from the choicest of the hog product, with sufficient refined cotton seed oil and beef suet added to place it far ahead of all other lards, etc., as regards the essentials of positive purity, freedom from anything deleterious or unwholesome, sweetness, richness and economy as the best article for cooking in the known world.

J. F. HUTCHINSON & CO., Wholesale & Commission Dealers in Butter, Cheese, Eggs, Poultry, Game, Beans, Etc., Nos. 103, 105, and 107 South Market Street.—The character and magnitude of the wholesale produce commission trade of Boston is forcibly illustrated by a review of the leading houses engaged therein, representative among the number being that of Messrs. J. F. Hutchinson & Co., of Nos. 103, 105 and 107 South Market Street. It was in 1875 that Mr. Hutchinson founded the present business, and which under wise and honorable management has been developed to proportions of such magnitude. In 1878 to secure increased accommodation, the firm removed to their present eligible premises, Nos. 103 to 107 South Market Street, 40x90 feet in dimensions, carefully fitted up to meet their requirements, and which is crowded to its utmost capacity with high grade butter, cheese, eggs, poultry and country produce generally. The firm ranks among leading receivers of dairy butter, and best makers of New York State and western creamery, and are also extensive buyers of same in open market, thus rendering their stock specially attractive both to the city and New England trades, as also to exporters. Their annual sales of butter alone have attained extended proportions. In eggs they are also large receivers and buyers of the freshest lots, direct from shippers and packers in Ohio, Pennsylvania, New Jersey and New England, while they handle the best brands of New York State and western cheese. Liberal advances are made on consignments, and prompt account sales are rendered the firm's high standard being practically demonstrated by reference to its influential trade connections. Mr. J. F. Hutchinson is a native of Brookline, and has been a permanent resident of Boston since boyhood. He is still a young man, though old in experience, and has ever retained the confidence of leading commercial circles. He is an active and respected member of the Boston Chamber of Commerce, and of the Fruit and Produce Exchanges, affording his customers the facilities enjoyed by meeting all the leading dealers on the floors of these institutions, and ever according a hearty support to all measures best calculated to advance the welfare of Boston Produce trade. Mr. J. F. Hutchinson has just been elected a member of Legislature.

NEW ENGLAND & SAVANNAH STEAMSHIP COMPANY, Boston Agents; Richardson & Barnard, North Side Lewis Wharf.—One of the most reliable and comfortable line of steamers plying from Boston to the Gulf States and Cuba, is the famous New England & Savannah Steamship Company, in connection with the Ocean Steamship Company's vessels. Average passage by these steamers from Boston is seventy-two hours, and from New York fifty-five hours. These steamers being provided with electric head-lights, during the night can be navigated in the Savannah River, avoiding all delay. Close connections are made at Savannah with the various routes diverging from that city. A steamer leaves north side of Lewis Wharf, Boston, every Thursday at 3.00 P.M. First-class tickets include berth in state-room and meals on all steamers, except on St. Johns River and Tampa Bay. Intermediate ticket entitles holder to all the privileges of regular first-class ticket, except location of state-room and first table. Intermediate accommodations being limited berths should be engaged when ticket is purchased. Children under four years, free; between four and twelve, half rate, unless requiring accommodations wanted for adults. Rates named are limited and include transportation of 150 pounds of baggage. Richard & Barnard, agents, North side Lewis Wharf, Boston; A. DeW. Sampson, agent, C. H. R., No. 20 Washington Street, Boston; O. G. Pearson, agent, Sav., Fla. & W. R'y., No. 211 Washington Street, Boston. The steamers of the New England & Savannah Steamship Company are fitted with every possible convenience and luxury. The table is equal to that of any hotel, and what is far more importance than this, everything that is possible is done to insure the safety of the ships and passengers. The officers are among our best known navigators, selected for their particular fitness for their positions. The passages of the company's steamers are speedy, and the line is very popular both in Boston and the South. This is now the favorite route from New England to Florida, Georgia, Alabama, Mississippi, Louisiana, Texas and Cuba. Messrs. Richardson & Barnard were previously the company's agents in Savannah, and assumed the management of the Boston branch in 1886, and since then have materially increased the patronage of the line.

DAVID LEVY, Manufacturer of Clothing, No. 735 Washington Street.—One of the most popular and successful concerns in the city engaged in the wholesale manufacture of custom and ready-made clothing, and one deserving of special mention in these pages, is that of Mr. David Levy, whose establishment is very centrally located at No. 735 Washington street. This enterprise was started in 1878 by Messrs. Levy Brothers, and on the dissolution of their partnership in 1885 Mr. David Levy took control of the business, and by bringing to bear upon it energy, ability and integrity, has developed a trade of great magnitude and a most desirable and wide-spread connection. It is needless to add that Mr. Levy has an intimate practical knowledge of the clothing trade, and vast practical experience in every detail. Thus constituted the house is the most competent to afford the fullest satisfaction to the numerous wholesale clothiers who now form the patrons of the establishment. For the purposes of the business the third floor of the building is occupied, and this has an area of 5x9,100 feet. It is admirably equipped with all necessary appliances and conveniences for the business and permanent employment is provided for some sixty skilled and expert hands. The house has from its inception enjoyed a steady run of business, and undertakes the making of every necessary description of male attire, a specialty being made of fine custom order work. Style, make and fit are guaranteed, and the charges are warranted to be as low as those of any other house in the trade. Mr. Levy is a native of Germany, and a gentleman of fine business ability and honorable methods.

SCANLON & DILLON, Wholesale and Retail Dealers in Fruit, Vegetables, Poultry, Eggs, Etc., No. 78 Blackstone Street.—Few among the many prosperous fruit and produce firms that have come to the front of recent years in this vicinity have been more fortunate than that of Scanlon & Dillon, wholesale and retail dealers in domestic fruit, vegetables, poultry, eggs, etc., whose commodious and well-kept stand is located at No. 78 Blackstone Street. This popular and responsible firm was established in 1884 and from its inception the business has been conducted with uniform and gratifying success. Handling a reliable and excellent line of goods, upright and straightforward in all their dealings, and withal prompt and courteous in attending to the wants of customers, Messrs. Scanlon and Dillon have been enabled to gain the hold on public favor and to build up the substantial patronage they deservedly enjoy. They occupy a spacious and nicely ordered basement store, with ample and excellent storage facilities, and carry constantly on hand a large and carefully assorted stock, including domestic fruits, nuts, berries and vegetables of every variety in their season; also poultry and game, fresh eggs, and country produce generally, while several capable assistants are employed likewise; all orders both wholesale and retail, receiving immediate and satisfactory attention. The individual members of the firm are E. Scanlon and James J. Dillon, natives respectively of Ireland and Nova Scotia, but residents each of the United States many years.

CHAS. H. MORE & CO., Importers and Manufacturers of Granites, Main office, No. 14 State Street.—This business was established many years ago, the copartners being Messrs. Chas. H. More and A. L. Rhinehart, both of whom are practical and experienced granite manufacturers, fully conversant with every detail of this growing and important industry and the requirements of patrons. The firm have branch offices and works in Aberdeen, Scotland; Barre, Vermont and Quincy, Mass. At Barre they employ sixty experienced and skilled stone cutters in their own sheds besides giving employment to fully as many more by subletting contracts to other manufacturers. The same is true in Quincy, Mass., where they have lately purchased a plant and are thus in position to take advantage of the market in regard to time and class of work that others in the same line cannot who have no sheds, and their trade covers the whole of the United States and Canada. Messrs. Chas. H. More & Company import and deal largely at wholesale in Scotch, Swedish, German and American granites, which are offered to customers at the lowest possible prices. They keep constantly in stock granite suitable for monumental and cemetery work and promptly furnish estimates. Messrs. More & Rhinehart were born in Roxbury, N. Y.

THE METROPOLIS OF NEW ENGLAND. 171

THE MERCHANTS NATIONAL BANK of Boston, No. 28 State Street, Franklin Haven, President; Alonzo P. Weeks, Cashier.—In no respect has the City of Boston developed a greater degree of influence and progress than in that of her banking facilities, which are in every way of a thoroughly representative and conservative character. In this connection we desire to make special reference to this commercial review to the old established and reliable Merchants National Bank, whose banking offices are centrally located at No. 28 State Street. It was originally organized as the Merchants Bank in 1831, and eventually became a National Bank in 1864. The paid up capital of the bank is $3,000,000, which is further augmented by a surplus of $1,000,000. Its management has always been signally prudent and sagacious, and the financial crises that have smitten the country from time to time since its organization, have never affected its strength or overshadowed its standing and reliability. Its board of directors is composed of gentlemen, who are prominent and influential in commercial and social circles, whose names are synonymous with strict probity and stability, and there is no fiscal institution in Boston, which challenges and enjoys a greater confidence with its numerous customers. The Merchants National Bank transacts a general banking business, receiving the accounts of banks, bankers, corporations, manufacturers, merchants and others upon favorable terms, and affords every possible facility and convenience for monetary transactions. The bank has always paid semi-annual dividends, and has based no bill for less than five dollars since 1865. The present building is the property of the bank, and was purchased by it in 1875 from the United States Bank. The area of the site is 9,000 square feet. The president, Mr. Franklin Haven, Jr., is confessedly one of our most able financiers, and an energetic exponent of the soundest principles governing banking and finance. He is treasurer of the Massachusetts General Hospital, a director of the Bay State Trust Company, and also of the New England Trust Company, and other institutions. From 1868 to 1879 Mr. Haven was assistant treasurer of the United States at Boston. Mr. Alonzo P. Weeks, the cashier, is highly esteemed as a prompt and faithful bank officer, with every qualification for his responsible position.

H. S. McKAY, Architect, No. 28 Beacon Street.—A rising and popular young Boston architect is H. S. McKay, who by skill and reliability is rapidly pushing his way to the front ranks in his profession. Mr. McKay was born in Canada, but has resided in this city a number of years. He is a thoroughly practical and expert draughtsman and general architect, of ample experience, and is a complete master of the art in all its branches. Mr. McKay was formerly a member of the firm of Silloway & McKay, established in 1883, and about three years ago assumed sole control. Plans for all classes of buildings are executed in the most reliable and excellent manner, and designs and estimates are cheerfully furnished on any proposed work, while construction is judiciously superintended always in person. Among the more notable pieces of work executed on Mr. McKay's plans may be mentioned the Prospect Hill church at Somerville, the Medford Opera House, Worthen Street, Baptist church, Lowell, and the Methodist church at Marion, Ohio.

E. H. WAKEFIELD, Real Estate, Mortgages, Etc., No. 194 Washington Street.—The house of Mr. E. H. Wakefield, dealer in real estate and mortgages, at No. 194 Washington Street, is one of the oldest and best-known in its line in the city. The proprietor has been engaged in the business here for the past thirty years, and has developed a solid business connection in all branches of realty. He negotiates mortgage loans and business paper of all kinds, buys, sells, rents and leases property, invests money, collects rents, and takes the entire management of estates. He has the fullest confidence and esteem of leading capitalists, investors and property owners, and owing to the wide range and superior character of his connections he is prepared to promptly dispose of realty at fair values, while offering to conservative investors the best possible bargains that are guaranteed to produce a steady income and a prospective increase in values. His varied experience, keen appreciation of value, and large acquaintance with business men, combine to render his services peculiarly valuable to parties dealing in realties and those in need of loans, and any business entrusted to his care is always faithfully and honorably attended to in every particular. Mr. Wakefield is a native of New Hampshire, a resident of Boston for many years, in high standing in the real estate circles of the city, and commands the confidence of all with whom he comes in contact in a business way.

R. WARNER & CO., Manufacturers and Wholesale Dealers in Wooden Ware, Brooms, Brushes, Baskets, Mats, Etc., Nos. 26 and 28 Commercial Street.—Boston is a most important centre for the wholesale woodenware business, willowware, basket, broom and brush trade, and in the above lines the oldest, most enterprising and one of the largest firms in Boston is that of Messrs. R. Warner & Co., of Nos. 26 and 28 Commercial Street. The business was established in 1843 by Mr. R. Warner, a native of Massachusetts, and one of the representative members of Boston's financial and commercial circles. From its inception, under his able management the business rapidly grew, and in 1846 he permanently removed to his present central stand, and here has continued a trade of the highest importance, both domestic and export. The premises comprise two buildings each five stories in height, 25x100 feet in dimensions, and where is carried the most complete stock of woodenware, willowware, etc., in Boston. Messrs. Warner & Co. are manufacturers on the most extensive scale, owning and operating a large factory in Concord, Mass. They began manufacturing fully thirty years ago, and have ever maintained the reputation of producing the most reliable and handsomest goods of this kind on the market. Their factory is fitted up with the latest improved machinery and appliances, run by steam power and where upwards of forty hands are employed in the manufacture of full lines of woodenware. The firm's stock includes all standard sizes of tubs, pails and buckets, washboards, clothes horses, stepladders, meat safes, refrigerators, etc.; all kinds of baskets, painted tubs, brooms and brushes for all purposes, mats, etc. Manufacturing themselves so extensively and contracting direct with many factories for special lines in the largest quantities; also selling extensively to jobbers, exporters, etc., this house positively quotes prices that are not duplicated elsewhere. Both as to styles, quality and finish its goods compare favorably with any others, and the concern is thoroughly representative in every respect. Mr. Warner is a respected and public spirited citizen. He has been a director of the Faneuil Hall National Bank for thirty-five years past, and has ever pursued a policy of equity and honor, likewise ever according a hearty support to all measures best calculated to advance the permanent welfare and prosperity of the city of Boston.

SNOW & HIGGINS, Provisions, Groceries, and General Ship Stores, No. 253 Atlantic Avenue.—The establishment of Messrs. Snow & Higgins, dealers in provisions, groceries and general ship stores is one of the most prominent in the section of the city in which it is located. Mr. J. M. Snow and Mr. R. S. Higgins, the copartners, have quite an extended experience in this line of trade, the former having been engaged in it eighteen years and the latter fifteen years previous to their becoming associated in 1876. Their business connections are of the most satisfactory character and have established a trade and a reputation for integrity and fair dealing which has given their house a wide-spread prominence. The dimensions of the premises are 25x75 feet and complete in their arrangements and here purchases may be made under the most advantageous circumstances both with reference to quality and price. The stock embraces everything in the line of provisions and staple and fancy groceries and general ship stores and to assist them in the business the firm employ two clerks and supply a large demand derived from the city and from vessels and make a special business of furnishing ships, for large or short voyages and also coasting and fishing vessels with supplies. They also furnish yachts with their supplies during the summer season and do a larger business in this line than any other house in Boston. Both members of the firm are natives of the old Bay State, are middle-aged gentlemen and as popular representative citizens enjoy the confidence and esteem of all who have dealings with their house and connections once established with them are sure to continue and always prove profitable and pleasant to all concerned.

CLARK & HALEY, Commission Merchants, Flour and Produce, Cheese, Butter, Etc., Nos. 78 and 80 Commercial Street.—As a centre of the wholesale commission produce trade, Boston is second to no other point in the United States, and offers one of the finest markets in the world for all kinds of fruits, vegetables, poultry, game, butter, cheese, etc. Among the leading firms and one of the most active and enterprising of those devoted to flour, butter and cheese, is that of Messrs. Clark & Haley, with warehouse centrally located at Nos. 78 and 80 Commercial Street. The business was founded by Mr. J. Foster Clark and Mr. Charles B. Haley in 1885, both partners bringing to bear the widest range of practical experience, coupled with perfected facilities, and influential connections. They speedily developed a desirable and growing trade, and have during the intervening period manifested special abilities in the securing of the choicest of all kinds of supplies for the New England market. They make a specialty of western flour, receiving direct from several of the most famous roller mills, and handling our standard and other brands of fancy patent flour, which are specially popular with the New England public. They also are regular receivers of large consignments of butter, cheese, eggs and poultry. They are the receivers of the justly celebrated Cloverdale Creamery butter in demand with the choicest trade; also Franklin County Dairies. They handle the finest factory brands of cheese direct from the New York State and Canada markets, fresh eggs and poultry in season. They are prepared to promptly dispose of the largest consignments of first-class produce, rendering account sales at the earliest possible moment, they are are a responsible, honorable and one of the most desirable with which buyers and shippers can enter into commercial relations with. Mr. Clark is a native of Chester, Vt. He has had a varied and successful career. For a period of fifteen years he was actively engaged in the Pennsylvania oil trade, and since 1876 has been a resident of Boston. He is a popular member of the Chamber of Commerce and a bulwark of Boston produce trade. Mr. Haley was born in Cambridge, Mass., and from early in life has been actively identified with this branch of trade. He was for four years member of the firm of C. L. Cotton & Co., and is an able exponent of this branch of commerce. The house is conducted on the principles of equity; its stock is worthy the attention of the best class of trade, and it has before it a wide sphere of activity and usefulness.

CAPE ANN GRANITE COMPANY, Granite, Building and Monumental Work. Offices: No. 40 Water Street. Quarries: Bay View, Gloucester.—The finest veined granites in the world, and the best adapted for building and monumental work, flagging, paving, etc., is that furnished by the nationally celebrated Cape Ann Granite Company, of Boston. The business is very old established, having been founded many years ago by citizens of Boston and Gloucester. In 1869 the important interests involved were duly capitalized at $400,000, and the company incorporated, with increased resources and facilities and the business has attained proportions of enormous magnitude, and the company not only supplies thousands of tons annually throughout Boston and New England, but ships to New York, Philadelphia, and other large centres in the middle states. The quarries are situated at Bay View, Gloucester, and are operated upon the most extensive scale, having steam cranes and every improvement, also large shops for the sawing to dimensions and for polishing of blocks, slabs, and shafts. This granite from its fineness of texture, hardness and susceptibility to polish, is specially adapted to secure the finest architectural effects, and for monumental purposes. It has the endorsement of leading architects and builders, proprietors of monument works, etc., and those seeking a building material alike of great strength and beauty should place orders for Cape Ann granite. It is likewise unrivalled for flagging and paving purposes, and is the popular stone for the broad pavements in front of new buildings. Mr. Jonas H. French, the president of the company, is a capitalist and business man of the highest standing, both in Gloucester and Boston, and all over the country. He is a director of the Maverick National Bank, an energetic exponent of the soundest business principles, and has ably guided the company in its career of usefulness and prosperity. Mr. H. H. Bennett is the company's treasurer, and resides at Bay View. He is an experienced business man, possessed of the highest order of executive abilities, and faithfully discharges the onerous duties devolving upon him. The superintendent is Mr. Chas. W. Foster, practically experienced in the most advanced methods of quarrying, and who enforces a thorough system of organization. The Cape Ann Granite Company is the leading exponent of this important branch of industry, and they are fully prepared to enter into the heaviest contracts for the supply of granite by the cargo for public buildings, private structures, and to manufacturers of, or dealers in all kinds of monumental work.

JAMES HALL & SON, Fine Carriages, Etc., No. 21 Hawkins Street.—This business was established thirty-five years ago by Mr. James Hall, who eventually in 1866 admitted his son Mr. James Hall, Jr., into partnership. In August, 1885, Mr. James Hall, Sr., died after a successful and honorable career. He was succeeded by his son, who is now conducting the business under the old firm name of James Hall & Son. The premises occupied comprise a spacious five-story brick building, fully supplied with every facility and convenience for the successful prosecution of this useful industry. Mr. Hall manufactures to order or otherwise all kinds of fine carriages, buggies, etc., from a coach down to a trotting wagon. He employs thirty-five skilled workmen, and turns out nothing except first-class hand work, while the prices quoted for them are extremely moderate. Mr. Hall obtained medals at the centennial, Philadelphia, and at the Massachusetts Charitable Mechanics Association for the superiority and excellence of his vehicles. He is a native of Boston.

FRANCIS FRENCH, Proprietor of The Old Original Nova Scotia Employment Company, No. 298 Washington Street.—The largest and leading employment agency in the city is the widely and favorably known old original Nova Scotia Employment Company of No. 298 Washington Street. Both by reason of its facilities in securing the best class of help and success in placing applicants, is is thoroughly representative and enjoys the confidence and patronage of the best families of Boston and New England. The business was established in 1804 by Mr. A. W. Winkfield, to whom Mr. Francis French succeeded as sole proprietor in 1876. He is possessed of vast practical experience and influential connections and has achieved an enviable reputation for the accuracy of all statements and the thorough good character of all servants and employees hired through him. The steady growth of patronage resulted in 1888 in the removal of his office to its present most central stand in Washington Street, where he has splendid accommodations both for male and female help, and for the public to call and make engagements. The enormous amount of business done here indicates the popularity of Mr. French's office. A large number of persons, male and female, secure situations through his agency, which is by far the best place in town to get good, reliable help just from the Provinces, also the best class of help of all nationalities, including skilled and experienced hands for every branch of employment. Mr. French is a native of Massachusetts, a business man of the highest standing and responsibility and is ably and faithfully discharging his duty to the community in supplying it with honest, efficient help at reasonable rates of wages.

CHAS. D. BLAKE & CO., Music Publishers, No. 488 Washington Street.—One of the best known houses in the music publishing trade is that of Chas. D. Blake & Co., No. 488 Washington Street. This popular firm was established in 1881, Mr. Charles D. Blake, the sole partner has been identified with the business for many years and is generally acknowledged to have no superior in his line. The firm occupy a commodious store and show room, 30x60 feet in dimensions in which they carry an excellent line of upright, square and grand pianos of the leading makers, handling chiefly however the celebrated Schubert Piano Company's elegant upright pianos for which they are the New England agents. These instruments are conceded to be the most perfectioned instruments made and are in wide demand all over the country. As music publishers the firm of Chas. D. Blake has a reputation second to none, as a glance at the catalogue of their publications sent on application will convince anyone. Mr. Blake who is a Boston man, in the prime of life, has built up a splendid business by the exercise of ability and energy.

THE METROPOLIS OF NEW ENGLAND.

J. SMITH & CO., Manufacturers of Fine Harness, Interfering Boots, and Horse Clothing, No. 26 Sudbury Street.— For strictly the finest grade and most skillfully made lines of fine carriage harness, gentlemen's road and sulky interfering boots and horse clothing, the American public as well as many foreign customers have learned to place their orders with the old responsible house of Messrs. J. Smith & Co., of No. 26 Sudbury street. He established in business upon his own account in

1857 and bringing to bear natural inventive ability, sound judgment, keen observation and marked enterprise, he speedily created for his work the reputation of being the best on market. He has the distinguished honor of being the first to make horse boots, and has introduced to the horsemen of the world the most improved and perfect lines of interfering boots, toe weights, etc. Mr. Smith has been at his present location for twenty-seven years past, and has every facility at command. He employs a numerous force of skilled hands, and turns out by far the finest track, road and carriage harness in the market at lowest prices, quality considered. Selecting his materials with the utmost care, Mr. Smith personally supervises all the work, the trimmings and mountings are the best obtainable, and the harness of his make are renowned alike for elegance and symmetry, and strength and durability. He manufactures every description of horse boots for elbows, breasts, arms, knees, shin and ankle, elastic supporting boots, quarter boots, and toe weights and full lines of horse clothing, muzzler bandages, scrapers, brushes, etc., of the finest materials and most skillful design. Mr. Smith's interfering boots are the neatest and most perfect fitting of any. The original introducer of these goods, he is the leading maker and fully maintains the lead of all competitors. He sells to fine trade and leading horse owners all over the United States and Canada, and has customers in all parts of the world.

GILLETTE & HENNIGAN, Receivers of and Wholesale Dealers in Apples, Oranges, Lemons, Bananas, Domestic Fruits and Produce, No. 135 Clinton Street.— Among the leading and most enterprising produce commission houses of New England is that of Messrs. Gillette & Hennigan. They are direct commission receivers from every section of the continent that in the season contributes vegetables, fruits, etc., to the markets, while their connections in the line of sales are equally influential. The business was founded in 1877 by the present proprietors, Mr. George A. Gillette and Mr. F. Frank Hennigan. Both gentlemen being to bear the widest range of practical experience. Their spacious warehouse on the wharf has seven floors, suitably fitted up for the firm's purposes, and where they always carry a heavy and comprehensive stock of sweet potatoes, apples, and all domestic fruits and vegetables in season, while a specialty is made of tropical fruits such as oranges, lemons and bananas direct from the West Indies, Central America, Florida and the Mediterranean. Quality is their first consideration. They ship no fruit or green stuff not in prime condition and can be fully relied on by parties at a distance to fill all orders promptly and at lowest rates. They now do a trade that covers a vast area, including New England, Nova Scotia, New Brunswick, and west and south. They employ a number of hands and are in daily receipt of consignments and handling promptly and to best advantage and make prompt returns. Mr. Gillette was born in New York State, and has resided in Boston for twenty-three years. Mr. Hennigan was born in Massachusetts and has resided here for fully twenty-two years past. They are popular and influential members of the trade and we strongly recommend both consignees of fruits and produce, and dealers and retailers to order through this able and responsible old house.

THOS. W. EMERSON & CO., Growers and Jobbers in Garden, Field and Grass Seeds, Nos. 74 and 76 South Market Street. — A representative and old established house in Boston, extensively engaged in growing and jobbing garden, field and grass seeds, is that of Messrs. Thos. Emerson & Co., whose office and warehouse are located at Nos. 74 and 76 South Market street. This business was established in 1859 by H. Blanchard, who was succeeded in 1861 by Blanchard & Emerson. Eventually in 1864 Mr. Thos. W. Emerson became sole proprietor, and is now conducting the business under the firm name of Thos. W. Emerson & Co. The premises occupied comprise a spacious five-story building 25x100 feet in area, equipped with every facility and appliance for the systematic conduct of this growing and important business. Mr. Emerson grows and deals largely in garden, field and grass seeds, also in beans and peas of every description for cooking purposes. His seeds are always carefully prepared for the market, and are absolutely unrivalled for reliability and uniform excellence and have no superiors in this country. He constantly keeps on hand an immense stock, and quotes prices that necessarily attract the attention of close and prudent buyers. Mr. Emerson employs a number of agents in New England, the Eastern States and Provinces, and his patronage is steadily increasing owing to the superiority of his productions and seeds, which are general favorites with intelligent farmers and agriculturists. Forty employees, assistants, etc., are required in his warehouse to attend to his extensive trade. Mr. Emerson was born in New Hampshire. He is a popular member of the Boston Chamber of Commerce and has served on several of the committees with credit. He is highly esteemed in business circles as a liberal, able and honorable merchant, fully meriting the signal success achieved in this useful and valuable industry.

H. E. WOODWARD & CO., Wholesale Dealers in Salt and Pickled Fish, Fort Hill Wharf, Nos. 116 to 454 Atlantic Avenue.—One of the oldest, if not the oldest house in Boston, devoted to the wholesale trade in all kinds of salt and pickled fish is that of Messrs. H. E. Woodward & Co., of Fort Hill Wharf. The firm has ever been a leading representative in this branch of commerce, and has contributed very materially to the development of Boston's export and southern coastwise trade. It is about fifty years ago that Mr. W. R. Clark started this business, Mr. Harrison E. Woodward coming into copartnership in 1848, under the name and style of Clark & Woodward. It thus continued, a steadily enlarging trade being developed until in 1873 the present firm was formed by Mr. Woodward, and who brings to bear the widest range of practical experience, perfected facilities and influential connections. His extensive premises are centrally located on Fort Hill Wharf, and where they have maintained their identical location for over fifty years past. Here in their warehouse, 30x150 feet and two stories in height, the firm carry a large and complete stock of all kinds of salt and pickled fish packed in every style of package, as specially adapted to the wants of southern and foreign trade. Many cargoes each season leave Fort Hill Wharf, shipped by them to West Indies, Baltimore, New Orleans, Mobile, Galveston, etc. They also do a heavy New England trade with wholesalers and fish dealers. Mr. Woodward has an active member of the Fish Association and a popular, respected merchant, who has ever retained the confidence of leading commercial circles.

MERCHANTS & MINERS TRANSPORTATION CO., Boston, Baltimore and Norfolk Steamship Line, George E. Smalley, Agent, Central Wharf.—The leading and largest coastwise steamship line, making Boston its eastern terminus is that of the Merchants and Miners Transportation Co., which was duly incorporated in 1856 by leading capitalists of Boston, Baltimore and Norfolk. The line has ever been ably managed and a public spirited policy has characterized its operations, its fleet being composed of some of the fastest, strongest and most seaworthy iron steamships afloat. The line is equally popular for passengers and on every trip there is a long list inward and outward from Boston. The annually increasing travel to the southern states can find no such comfortable and pleasant a route as this, which takes passengers direct via the Atlantic Ocean and Chesapeake Bay to Norfolk, Baltimore and by connecting river steamer direct to Washington. The fare is much lower than by rail, being only nine dollars first-class to Norfolk, and ten dollars first-class to Baltimore, including meals and berths, second-class tickets to above points are only seven dollars and also include meals and berth. The steamers connect with the splendid railroad systems of the south and west via Baltimore and Ohio Railroad from Baltimore, and Norfolk and Western and Chesapeake and Ohio from Norfolk. There is sleeping car and palace car service to Cincinnati, Louisville, Memphis, Baton Rouge, New Orleans and West. The company's steamships make sure connections, and both going and returning offer most substantial inducements to the traveling public of New England and the British provinces. The company enjoys an enviable reputation for its successful and efficient service during the past thirty years and it has built up an enormous and steadily enlarging traffic. It now has a fleet of ten first-class steamships of which the following are devoted to the regular tri-weekly passenger service between Boston and Norfolk and Baltimore: "Chatham," 2,800 tons, captain, F. M. Howes; "D. H. Miller," 2,276 tons, captain, J. C. Taylor; "Berkshire," 2,300 tons, captain, J. S. March, Jr.; and "Allegheny," 2,300 tons, captain, D. P. W. Parker. These ships have large and roomy saloons and cabins, elegantly furnished, light and airy state rooms, and every convenience and accommodation for first and second-class passengers. They are the equal of any steamships afloat as regards coastwise Atlantic service, are under the commands of able, experienced captains and have had immunity alike from accident and detention. The public cannot do better than travel by this line when bound south on business or pleasure, and thus secure the invigorating breezes and pleasure of an ocean voyage, instead of the cramped seats or stuffed berths of the cars on the dusty and tedious railroad route from New England to Virginia. The company's officers are, George J. Appold, of Baltimore, president, and Henry A. Whitney, of Boston, vice-president. Both are possessed of vast practical experience, and manifest marked executive ability in the management of the line. The Boston agent is Mr. George E. Smalley, who has energetically and efficiently represented the company here for four years past, he is a popular member of Boston's business circles, and is a genial and courteous representative of the company, of whom all information can be obtained as to rates, time of sailing, length of voyage, connections, etc. The company has largely contributed to the prosperity of Boston and has opened the most direct and popular route for shipments of iron, cotton and tobacco from the south, and of New England manufactured goods from the east.

BOYCE BROTHERS, Wholesale and Retail Dealers in Furniture, Carpets, Etc., No. 739 Washington Street.—There is no branch of industry in which such rapid progress and improvement have been made in recent years, as in the production of artistic household furniture and upholstery goods. One of the oldest established and representative houses in Boston actively engaged in this important trade is that of Messrs. Boyce Brothers, wholesale and retail dealers, No. 739 Washington Street. This business was established in 1848 by Boyce Brothers and Squire, and after some changes in the firm, in 1882 Messrs. C. B. and Wm. Boyce succeeded to the management under the style and title of Boyce Brothers. The salesrooms of the firm are spacious, and are fully stocked with a superior assortment of parlor, library, dining room, drawing room, hall, chamber and kitchen furniture, carpets, mirrors, bedding, upholstery goods, etc. The specialty of the house is fashionable furniture, much of which is made from mahogany, cherry, French walnut, rosewood and ebony, which, from the fineness of grain and richness of color maintain always such a fine finish. The upholsterers of this popular house are the admiration of experts, the richest stuffs of all desirable shades and textures being used. In the carpet department, the firm keep constantly in stock the latest patterns in Wiltons, body Brussels, velvets, tapestries, ingrains, also oil cloths, linoleums, mats and matting, all quoted at extremely low prices. Messrs. Boyce Brothers promptly furnish estimates for furnishing completely all sizes of houses and flats, and guarantee entire satisfaction to patrons. They sell either for cash or on the installment plan, which latter method permits those of moderate circumstances to obtain what they want for housekeeping safely and easily. Messrs. C. B. and Wm. Boyce are natives of Vermont, but have resided in Boston since boyhood. They are highly esteemed by the community for their enterprise and just methods, and are among Boston's substantial and public-spirited citizens.

BARNES & CUNNINGHAM, Bankers and Brokers. Offices: No. 60 State Street.—Among the solid financial houses of Boston, and recognized as a leading representative firm of bankers and brokers is that of Messrs. Barnes and Cunningham. The partners, Mr. W. Howard Barnes and Mr. Stanley Cunningham are very widely and favorably known in financial circles, and are valued factors in promoting the importance of Boston as an active market for the purchase and sale of all descriptions of securities. The business was established in 1878 by Messrs. Barnes, McBirney & Co., succeeded in 1883 by the present firm. Mr. Barnes is an active member of the Boston Stock Exchange, while Mr. Cunningham is a member of the New York Stock Exchange. The house by this double connection affords unexcelled facilities to its customers for the filling of all orders direct on the floors of the two leading exchanges on the continent. The firm transact a general business as bankers and brokers, receiving deposits and allowing interest on daily balances; buying and selling on commission, for cash or on margin, all descriptions of stocks, bonds, and miscellaneous securities, making a specialty of those listed on the Boston and New York Exchanges. Their connections are influential and wide-spread; they have the most perfect facilities for the receipt of the earliest information as to the course of the market, having in their offices the tickers of the Boston and New York Exchanges, also a private wire direct to New York, Philadelphia and Chicago. They number among their customers leading capitalists and operators, and have carried through to a successful issue many important transactions. No firm offers better facilities to corporations for the placing of their bonds, and none have a more enviable reputation with the public as to sales of remunerative and safe investment securities. Messrs. Barnes & Cunningham are prominent and popular in the leading financial and social circles of Boston, New York and elsewhere.

TAMARACK MINING COMPANY, No. 246 Washington Street.—This representative and successful copper mining corporation was duly incorporated under the laws of Michigan in 1882, and has a capital stock of $1,250,000 in 50,000 shares of $25 each, 40,000 shares issued, 10,000 shares in the treasury. The following gentlemen are the officers and directors: President, Joseph W. Clark; Secretary and treasurer, A. S. Bigelow. Directors, John N. Denison, Franklin Fairbanks, Joseph W. Clark, Nathaniel Thayer, Edward S. Grew, George F. Demis, and John Daniell, of Michigan. The result of last year's mining relative to cost, has never before been equalled by any copper mine in the world. The promise made by the management of producing copper at a cost of six cents a pound has been realized. The company owns 1,160 acres of rich copper lands and last year its mine yielded 10,780,867 pounds of refined copper for which it realized $1,418,263.88. The works of the Tamarack Mining Company are equal in all modern appliances and machinery to anything in the United States or Europe. This extensive property is now held by the company without debt or incumbrance, and is now paying dividends at the rate of $20 per share annually. The officers and directors are able business men, and experts in mining matters. The company's Boston office is centrally located at No. 246 Washington Street.

BROWN, RILEY & CO., Bankers and Brokers, Nos. 9 Congress Street, and 4 Congress Square.—One of the best known representative houses which has materially contributed to the importance and stability of the Boston stock and money markets is that of Messrs. Brown, Riley & Co., of No. 9 Congress Street, and No. 4 Congress Square. Messrs. A. L. Brown and W. J. Riley formed the existing copartnership in 1882 and have developed a trade of great magnitude, coupled with a wide-spread, influential connection. They transact a general business as bankers and brokers, deposits are received, and interest allowed on balances; collections are made and exchange bought and sold. The firm make a specialty of the purchase and sale on commission for cash or margin, of all securities dealt in at the Boston and New York Stock Exchange including petroleum; also cotton futures and spot cotton, grain, lard, pork, etc. They enjoy unsurpassed facilities, bringing to bear ample resources, vast practical experience and influential connections. Mr. Brown is an active member both of the Boston Stock Exchange and the New York Stock Exchange; while Mr. Riley is a member of the Boston Stock Exchange, and of the New York Cotton Exchange. The latter connection affords unusual opportunities to Boston capitalists for direct dealings and quick turns in the cotton market. The firm have a private wire to New York, their correspondents there being Messrs. Edward Sweet & Co., of Broad Street. They have elegantly fitted up and most centrally located offices with every convenience for customers, and receive the earliest accurate information as to the course of the market. They number among their customers leading capitalists and operators of this city and New England, and have conducted several of the most important movements in this market. Both gentlemen have ever extended a hearty and valued support to all measures best calculated to advance the welfare and prosperity of the Boston Stock Exchange, and rank among the most conservative houses, whose advice and judgment can at all times be relied on, so that their extensive business is the result of the exercise of legitimate commercial principles based on sterling integrity and the highest order of executive ability.

R. H. EDDY, Former Associate and now Successors, W. H. Singleton and S. N. Piper, Solicitor of Patents, No. Stgate Street.—The first regular solicitor to appear before the United States Patent office in behalf of an inventor, was Mr. R. H. Eddy, who established himself in the practice of his profession in Boston in 1832. He steadily and successfully followed the practice of patent law until his death, which occurred in May, 1887. The business has since been continued by Mr. W. H. Singleton, Counsellor-at-law, and Mr. S. N. Piper, mechanical expert, former associates of Mr. Eddy and now his successors, at No. 76 State Street, in this city, with an office also in the St. Cloud Building, opposite the Patent office, Washington, D. C. Mr. Singleton had been the Washington correspondent for Mr. Eddy for many years, and still resides in that city and personally attends to the business of this office before the Bureau of Patents. His reputation has long been firmly established as an able, scientific and successful solicitor, and as a clear-headed, reliable counsellor in patent causes. No attorney is better known at the Patent Office, and none can secure fairer treatment or more prompt consideration of their cases. Mr. Piper had been an assistant in Mr. Eddy's office since 1865, and is now the resident manager of the business in this city. He is an experienced solicitor of patents, accomplished and practical as a mechanical expert, and his papers, filed in the interest of his clients, are models of accuracy, wisdom and perfect understanding of the case in hand. The facilities here possessed for securing patents are unsurpassed by those of any office in the country. The practice here relates to the preparation and prosecution of applications for patents, including the making out of specifications, drawings, caveats, assignments, releases, designs, trade marks, labels and copyrights; the making of preliminary examinations as to the patentability of an invention, and to examinations as to the scope and validity of patents; to cases in interference, upon appeal and before the courts, and to every other item of service necessary to the complete success of the application down to the time the patent is granted and tested by the commissioner of patents, and patents are also procured in all foreign countries for citizens here. Messrs. Singleton and Piper are both gentlemen of the highest personal integrity.

A. PORTER, Optician, No. 333 Washington Street.—Among the well-known and prominent opticians in this city there are none more thoroughly competent than Mr. A. Porter, whose experience extends over forty years in the profession, and in 1871 he established business on his own account, fully conversant and equipped in every particular, and familiar with all the details connected therewith. He occupies a very handsome store 30x40 feet in area, at No. 333 Washington Street, and keeps in stock a general assortment of all kinds of spectacles, and eye-glasses and optical goods. Mr. Porter is highly recommended for his skill and knowledge as an optician, and he is very careful with oculists' prescriptions which are correctly set and every attention is given to all orders. Spectacles and eye-glasses are manufactured in the very best manner, and in fitting glasses to suit the sight of the eye, he is probably the most practical expert in the city. Particular attention is given to repairing spectacles, eye-glasses, opera glasses and optical goods generally, and everything coming from the establishment is fully guaranteed to be as represented. Two skilled assistants are employed and those who have dealings with Mr. Porter, will not only receive the very best class of goods and satisfactory work but manifest advantages in prices. He is a native of the state of New Hampshire, where he was born about sixty five years ago. He however has passed most of his life in this city where he has not only become well known as one of the best among the leading opticians, but is held in high esteem in professional and in social circles.

J. F. AMSDEN & SON, Bankers, No. 50 Congress Street.—One of the most favorably known, substantial and enterprising firms of bankers in the city of Boston, is that of Messrs. J. F. Amsden & Son, whose handsome offices are centrally located at No. 50 Congress Street. This business was established twelve years ago by Mr. J. F. Amsden, who admitted his son, Mr. H. F. Amsden, into partnership. This house has long held an honorable position in financial circles, and numbers among its permanent customers many wealthy capitalists, operators, and investors. Messrs. J. F. Amsden & Son transact a general banking business, receiving deposits subject to check at sight, making collections on all available points, and acting as correspondents for a number of banks and bankers. As brokers, they promptly fill all orders for the purchase or sale of all stocks, bonds, Government and miscellaneous securities available on the Boston and New York Stock Exchanges, strictly on commission. They likewise make a specialty of the purchase of municipal bonds, western mortgages and other dividend paying securities. Mr. H. F. Amsden represents the house on the floor of the Boston Stock Exchange. Their correspondents in New York are Messrs. H. L. Horton & Co. Both partners are highly regarded in financial life for their integrity, promptness and ability, as well as social worth, and have made themselves prominent in a field of monetary business of the greatest importance to all who desire a good and safe income with absolute security for their investments.

FRANCIS H. LINCOLN, Real Estate and Insurance, No. 60 Devonshire Street.—Mr. Francis H. Lincoln, the well-known real estate broker and insurance agent, is a prominent citizen of Hingham, Mass., his native town, and opened his office in this city in 1875. He has proven his thorough knowledge of the various details embraced in real estate and insurance, and gives his attention to the purchase, sale and renting of properties, both improved and unimproved, in the city and country; collects rents, manages estates, and negotiates loans on bond and mortgage. Special attention is given to fire insurance, and Mr. Lincoln is especially prominent as agent for the Hingham Mutual Fire Insurance Co. for Boston and vicinity. This company was incorporated in 1826, and its sixty-second annual statement, made April 1, 1888, shows the following facts and figures, viz: amount at risk, $23,758,735.00; cash assets, $348,201.86; liabilities, $186,692.27; surplus over liabilities, $159,509.39. Seventy thousand dollars in dividends have been paid back to policy-holders the past year. Mr. Lincoln is also prepared to place the largest risks in any of the desirable companies, quoting the lowest rates of premium, and guaranteeing a prompt and liberal adjustment of all losses. Mr. Lincoln is highly esteemed in insurance circles.

BROWN, DeLORIEA & CO., Commission Merchants, and Dealers in Butter, Cheese, Eggs, Etc., Nos. 89 and 91 South Market Street, and No. 60 Commerce Street.—Among the most active and enterprising firms of produce commission merchants in Boston is that of Messrs. Brown, DeLoriea & Co. whose establishment is so centrally located at Nos. 89 and 91 South Market Street, and No. 60 Commerce Street. The business was founded in 1880 by the present proprietors, Messrs. A. C. Brown and J. F. DeLoriea. They brought to bear perfected facilities, ample resources and wide experience. Every element essential to the advancement of the interests of consignees and the public has been controlled by this popular house, and whose trade is enlarging at such a rapid ratio. The premises occupied are unusually extensive, comprising five floors each 25x100 feet, and suitably fitted up for trade purposes. They are direct and regular receivers of staple lines of produce, including the choicest of western and New York State creamery and dairy butter; New York and Western cheese, fresh eggs, peas, beans, dried apples and peaches, lard, etc., etc. The firm offer substantial inducements to buyers, growers and shippers all over the country, and handle the largest consignments quickly, rendering prompt account sales. Their selling trade is heavy and one of a very desirable character, as they cater to the leading houses of Boston and all the cities and towns of New England. The co-partners are very widely and favorably known. Mr. Brown is a native of Winslow, Maine, and has been a permanent resident of Boston for twenty-three years past. He is an active member of the Chamber of Commerce, and a popular member of the trade; so is Mr. DeLoriea, who was born in Woburn, Mass., and though a young man is old in experience. He also is a popular member of the Chamber of Commerce.

B. S. MOULTON & CO., Art Gallery, Engravings, Water Colors, Etchings, Paintings, Etc., No. 42 Hanover Street.—For strictly high class works of art, engravings, paintings, water colors, etchings, etc., we strongly recommend an appreciative public to inspect the magnificent display in the art gallery of Messrs. B. S. Moulton & Co., so centrally located at No. 42 Hanover Street, near the American House. The business was established about twenty years, by Mr. B. S. Moulton, a gentleman who both by tastes, direct practical experience and skill was qualified to cater to the wants of the public in this branch of trade. He has had his gallery in its present location for fifteen years. It is 20x110 feet, handsomely furnished and fully stocked with the highest class of steel engravings, water colors and oil paintings by artists of renown; etchings, photographs and art goods. There is here the widest range for selection while the prices are remarkably reasonable. Mr. Moulton has a large picture frame depot and gilding room up-stairs, and is prepared to promptly fill all orders for any style of frame; old frames are also here regilt in the highest style of the art, and at moderate prices. Mr. Moulton does a heavy trade in Boston and all over New England, also has many customers in nearly every section of the Union. He has even filled orders from as far away as Buenos Ayres, and those living at a distance, seeking adornments for the house, cannot do better than communicate with Mr. Moulton, who has all the facilities and the ability to suit them. He employs nine salesmen and assistants, and is doing one of the finest trades in this line in Boston. He is an honorable business man, and is a worthy member of art circles.

STORY & STEVENS, Wholesale and Commission Dealers in Fresh and Frozen Fish, Nos. 35 and 36 Commercial Wharf. —Boston justly feels a sense of pride in her wholesale fish trade, the most prominent and extensive of any in the United States, and which reflects such credit on the leading houses engaged therein. There is none more representative than that of Messrs. Story and Stevens, of Nos. 35 and 36 Commercial Wharf. They deal in fresh and frozen fish at wholesale and retail, and started in business about ten years ago, bringing to bear the widest range of practical experience, perfected facilities and influential connections. From the start they offered to the trade superior qualities of carefully selected fresh and frozen fish, and have always made a specialty of the famous Phillips beach cod, pronounced the finest in the world by competent experts. The demand for this catch of cod is always active, and the firm's facilities are taxed to the utmost. They occupy most centrally located and admirably fitted up premises at Nos. 35 and 36 Commercial Wharf, where they are daily receivers of all fish in season, including Phillips beach cod, halibut, herring, mackerel, smelts, salmon, blue fish, etc. They also handle lake and southern fish, and are prepared to promptly fill the largest orders. They sell all through Boston and suburbs, Massachusetts, Connecticut, New York City and State, Philadelphia, etc., and offer substantial inducements to proprietors of fish markets to place orders here. They handle and ship several tons of fish a day, and are authorities in the market. Both partners are natives of Rockport, Mass., and have long been identified with the wholesale fish trade of Boston. Their policy is an equitable one. They have ever retained the confidence of leading commercial circles, and are worthy of the large measure of success attending their ably directed efforts.

WHITON, BROTHER & CO., Agents for the Woodberry Cotton Duck Mills, Nos. 91 and 93 Commercial Street.— Prominent among the great manufacturing establishments of the United States, which have by permanently locating a branch in Boston, added so materially to the city's influence as a source of supply, are the Woodbury Cotton Duck Mills, of which Messrs. Whiton, Brother & Co., Nos. 91 and 93 Commercial Street, are the popular agents. This agency was established originally in 1859 by A. Fearing & Co., who were succeeded in 1875 by Fearing, Thatcher & Whiton. In 1881 Mr. Whiton retired and organized the present firm of Whiton, Brother & Co. The present partners are Messrs. E. J. Whiton and Walton Hall, both of whom became members of the firm in 1879 on the death of Mr. L. C. Whiton. The Woodberry Cotton Duck Mills are situated in Baltimore, Md. They are among the largest and best equipped in the country, and one-third of their product is handled by the Boston agents, Messrs. Whiton, Brother & Co. The firm occupy spacious premises and always keep in stock full supplies of the famous Woodberry Cotton Duck, which is absolutely unrivalled for quality, durability, strength, finish and excellence, and has no superior in the American or European markets. They give special attention to packing the cotton duck in waterproof packages for export, and promptly fill all orders at the lowest possible prices and their trade now extends not only throughout the United States and Canada, but also to Europe, South America, India, China and Australia. Mr. Whiton was born in Boston, while Mr. Hall is a native of Marshfield, Mass. They are popular members of the Cotton Duck Dealers' Association, and are highly esteemed in trade circles for their enterprise and integrity, and are accounted among Boston's public spirited citizens.

CASWELL, LIVERMORE & CO., Wholesale Dealers in Smoked, Salt and Pickled Fish; Store, Snow's Arch Wharf; Nos. 416 to 428 Atlantic Avenue; Smoked Fish Works, Wales Wharf.—One of the oldest established and most important concerns in the wholesale fish trade of Boston is that of Messrs. Caswell, Livermore & Company, of Nos. 416 to 428 Atlantic Avenue (Snow's Arch Wharf). The extensive business conducted here was founded nearly sixty years ago by James Perkins, and after various firm changes, in 1866, Messrs. Caswell, Livermore & Company bought out the heirs of K. and S. A. Freeman, actively continuing the trade, and making a specialty of high grade smoked fish of their own preparation. Mr. G. K. Livermore retired in 1887, and since then Mr. A. S. Caswell has actively carried on the business and with marked success. He is a native of Maine, and a practical man, having from boyhood been identified with the curing and smoking of fish. His premises here are extensive, comprising three floors, 60x100 feet each, and large smoke house attached, where French cod, mackerel, herring, salmon, halibut, etc., are smoked, boned and packed upon the most approved methods. Upwards of twenty-five hands are employed, and the product is in constantly growing demand both with the New England and shipping trade. Mr. Caswell deals in full lines of salt and pickled fish, and offer substantial inducements both as to price and quality, and his is the only house here dealing in French cod fish, in which they have a large trade. It is to such ably and honorably conducted houses as these that Boston owes her supremacy in the wholesale trade in salt and smoked fish, and Mr. Caswell, is to be congratulated upon the success rewarding his efforts.

W. P. PHILLIPS, Manufacturer of Lubricators, Boiler Trimmings and General Brass Work; No. 71 Sudbury Street.—In the vitally important lines of lubricators for steam engines, shafting, etc., and in the manufacture of the best grades of improved steam users' supplies, Mr. W. P. Phillips, of Boston, has achieved a national reputation. He started in business upon his own account about six years ago and is developing a large trade in steam users' supplies, and in the specialties of great magnitude. His lubricators are the best in the world, remedying the inherent defects of old style methods for the bearings of high speed engines, continuous service and providing automatic and perfected methods that have secured the heartiest endorsement of steam users. Mr. Phillips has a large and fully equipped machine shop largely devoted to the manufacture of the best class of brass fittings and various lines of steam users' supplies. One of his prominent specialties is an improved water gauge, of which large numbers are now in use. It is a vast improvement over old style gauges, and couples the easiest and most securely of any in the world. To all interested in the best type of boiler trimmings—and nowhere are they so needful and such a safeguard as in the boiler room—send to Mr. Phillips for his elegant illustrated circular describing his various devices. Mr. Phillips is unremitting in his attention to business and gives conscientious care to accurate filling of all orders. He has a deservedly high reputation with builders and engineers.

EYELET TOOL CO., G. W. Robbins, Agent, No. 49 Lincoln Street.—The founder of this concern, Mr. G. W. Robbins, is an old, well-known, popular Bostonian, who was born in this city in 1836. His business career has been an extended one. In 1840 he established a music and umbrella store on Court street, and continued this until he founded his present enterprise, the manufacture of tools, in 1864. The enterprise has been attended by the most marked success, and the premises now in use have been occupied since 1878. The workshop has an area of 3,800 feet, and is equipped with all necessary steam power machinery and other appliances, while constant employment is afforded to from six to eight skilled artisans. The tools made here include eyelet punch and set combined, 6-inch eyelet set, paper punch, burr set, drive or belt punch, simple tubes for spring punches, 6 inch spring punch, 6 inch and other sizes of spring punches, etc. These tools are regarded as standard goods in the trade, because of their being always in working condition and thoroughly reliable. The house has a fine business connection with all sections of the United States, and has an excellent financial standing.

F. G. BARNES & SON, Auctioneers, Real Estate, Mortgage and Insurance Brokers, No. 27 State street.—This firm have long been prominent both as auctioneers, real estate, mortgage and insurance brokers, and have largely contributed to the development of the real estate interests of the city and its suburbs. The business was originally established in 1857, by Mr. F. G. Barnes, the present style being adopted in 1874. The founder of the business died May 31, 1888, the son continuing the business under the same firm name. Mr. Barnes conducts an extensive real estate business in all its branches; buying, selling, renting and exchanging properties of all kinds; negotiating loans on bond and mortgage, taking the entire management of estates, collecting rents, and selling private city and country property at auction. He has made the study of real estate a specialty, and can be engaged with implicit confidence in all matters pertaining thereto. He handles a class of houses and lots in Newton and other suburban towns, such as the average buyer wants, either for a home or investment. He is also prepared to place insurance risks in any of the leading companies, securing payment for all losses promptly and without litigation, and quoting the lowest rates of premium. By the careful and able manner in which he conducts his affairs, Mr. Barnes has established a reputation and developed a clientele in this city and elsewhere that assures his continued success and permanent prosperity. He is a Massachusetts man by birth and training.

F. J. O'HARA & CO., Wholesale and Commission Dealers in Fresh Fish and Lobsters, Oysters, Clams, Etc., Nos. 112 and 116 Atlantic Avenue.—A representative house in its special line of trade, is that of F. J. O'Hara & Co., the well-known wholesale and commission dealers in fresh fish and lobsters, cod liver oil for medicinal purposes, oysters, clams, etc. This house is one of the largest of its kind in the city, and has been in successful operation since 1877. Mr. O'Hara, the active member of the firm, is a merchant of large experience and established reputation, and has long enjoyed a national reputation in the sale of live and boiled lobsters, fresh fish, oysters and clams. He occupies two spacious and commodious stores, thoroughly equipped in every particular. The trade is carried on at both wholesale and retail, and orders are filled with the utmost despatch, coming from all parts of the United States. As a commission merchant, Mr. O'Hara has a wide and influential connection with fishermen along the coast, and is daily in receipt of the choicest lobsters, fish, oysters and clams to be found in this market, while quick sales and prompt returns are the invariable rule with this establishment. Employment is furnished to twelve skilled and expert hands. Mr. O'Hara has resided in Boston since his boyhood.

ARCHER & PANCOAST MANUFACTURING CO., Gas Fixtures, Warren D. Kinny, Manager; No. 12 West Street.—In 1880 this widely known company opened an establishment in Boston, located at No. 12 West Street. This house is under the experienced management of Mr. Warren D. Kinny, who has been connected with the company in New York for a number of years, and succeeded to the control of this establishment in October, 1887. He is intimately conversant with every requirement of the public in this direction of trade, and has proved himself eminently popular and successful in meeting promptly all its demands. The spacious show rooms at the above address are models of elegance, taste and beauty, the goods shown making a magnificent display, and forming one of the most attractive features of this fashionable thoroughfare. Here can be seen all that inventive genius and mechanical skill have been able to produce in the way of artistic illuminating apparatus, while the assortment of fine metal work is unsurpassed in the city. This house has fitted up with gas fixtures and electric light apparatus some of the largest and finest public edifices in this section of the country. Hundreds of Boston's palatial private residences and extensive commercial buildings also bear evidence of their artistic products. It is such concerns as the Archer & Pancoast Manufacturing Company that are the acknowledged exponents of our capacity and enterprise as a manufacturing and commercial centre, and there is none more deserving of special mention. Mr. Kinny, the manager, has made many friends in this city by his promptness and reliable business policy.

THE GREAT ATLANTIC AND PACIFIC TEA COMPANY, Importers, Coffee Roasters and Retailers of Teas and Coffees, No. 92 Court Street, and Five Branch Stores.—The people of the United States are under great obligations to the spirited and honorable policy of The Great Atlantic and Pacific Tea Company, the largest concern of its kind in the world and the pioneer in importing direct for the benefit of retail customers. The company import teas and coffees by the ship load, and holding in great warehouses in New York and Boston millions of pounds of the choicest fresh crop teas and select coffees in order to meet the wants of its hundreds of thousands of consumers, and who are served in the company's chain of 200 branch stores. The first store was opened in Boston in 1875 and there are now four others in this city and one in Chelsea so great has the increase of trade. The headquarters for the enormous business done in Boston and New England is at No. 92 Court Street, where is a splendid store and salesroom, 30x90 feet in dimensions, fitted up in most elaborate manner. Here are a series of mammoth pictures illustrating the growing of teas and coffees, etc. There is every modern convenience here, including the cash railway system, two large coffee grinders run by a gas engine, etc. A large staff of experienced and courteous clerks are employed and the store is thronged with customers. On a Saturday night the stores of The Great Atlantic & Pacific Tea Co. are brilliant with light and full of the bustle and activity incident to thousands purchasing their weekly supplies of teas, coffees, sugars, etc. The company's interests have been rapidly advanced in Boston and New England and the public have come to realize that nowhere can such pure choice and fresh teas and coffees be purchased at such remarkably low prices as in The Great Atlantic and Pacific Tea Co.'s chain of stores and the location of which are as follows: Headquarters, No. 92 Court Street, Branches, No. 29 Eliot Street, and No. 107s Tremont Street; No. 292 Broadway, Chelsea; No. 109 Meridian Street, East Boston; No. 395 West Broadway, South Boston.

GEO. B. APPLETON & CO., Importers and Dealers in Cutlery, Fancy Hardware, Skates and Fishing Tackle, No. 304 Washington Street.—The most progressive firm engaged in the importation and sale of cutlery, leather goods, fancy hardware, fishing tackle and skates, in this city, is that of Messrs. Geo. B. Appleton & Co. Their methods, character and quality of stock bear no comparison with the average dealer in this line. Every class in the community finds it pleasant and profitable to buy here, where is carried the finest assortment in this line in town. The business of this enterprising house was originally established January 1, 1883, by Messrs. Appleton & Litchfield, who were succeeded by the present firm on November 15, 1887. The store is spacious and attractive, and the proprietors bring to bear ample resources and perfected facilities in collecting together from the four corners of the earth such a bewildering, yet charming display of the unique and the useful, the novel and the beautiful, in the lines of cutlery, fancy hardware, fishing tackle, etc. The stock embraces the products of the most celebrated makers both in Europe and America. In cutlery the assortments include the best ivory handled knives, forks, carvers, slicers, steels, knife-rests, spoons of solid silver and heaviest electro plate ; also, beautiful sets of knives, forks and spoons in satin lined cases, admirably suited for wedding and holiday presents. In fancy hardware Messrs. Appleton & Co. show one of the largest and most serviceable varieties in America, while as regards fishing tackle the assortment is unequalled anywhere for material, design and novelty. It is simply impossible to particularize, or to attempt an enumeration of the goods in stock. It is safe to say they keep everything. The copartners, Messrs. Geo. B. Appleton and Charles Z. Bassett, are both natives of Boston and gentlemen of large experience, eminent business ability and strict integrity.

J. W. TUTTLE & SONS, Wholesale Commission Merchants for the sale of all kinds of Country Produce, Nos. 16 and 18 Clinton Street.—An honorable and successful career of forty-five years has given the house of Messrs. J. W. Tuttle & Sons, the well-known wholesale commission merchants, a high standing in the great thoroughfares of trade. The business was founded in 1843, by Mr. J. W. Tuttle. In 1848 Mr. Geo. W. Tuttle was admitted to partnership, followed in 1874 by the admission of Mr. Charles Jones and in 1875 by the admission of Mr. Chas. H. Tuttle, and in 1883 Mr. Herbert A. Tuttle, who had been connected with the house five years, also became a member of the firm. The founder of the house retired from active business in 1885, and the remaining partners have since continued the enterprise under the present firm name. These gentlemen are recognized as merchants of wide and mature experience; thoroughly posted in all the wants and requirements of the commission interest, and as among the most active and efficient trade representatives of Boston. They command all the advantages naturally accumulated by long years of identification with a particular industry, and are in a position to render the most valuable service to such as commit their interests to their care. The lines handled embrace butter, cheese and eggs, beans, apples and potatoes, poultry, fresh meat and dressed hogs, maple sugar and syrup, and all kinds of country produce. The populous and fertile section of which this city is the centre gives her great importance as a point of distribution for these products, and the commission merchant and dealer is the recognized medium through which such goods are placed upon the market. Every facility and convenience is at hand here for the transaction of a large and active trade. Consignments are received daily in vast quantities, fresh from the hands of the producer, and are disposed of without delay, the highest prices being invariably obtained, and remittances are promptly made. A large and complete stock is always kept on hand, from which orders are filled with the utmost satisfaction. The house is responsible in every way, and can be relied upon implicitly. The copartners are all Massachusetts men, born and bred, members of the Chamber of Commerce and the Fruit and Produce Exchange, and highly esteemed in social, business and financial circles.

J. DOOLING, Caterer and Confectioner, Nos. 11 and 13 Temple Place.—The business of the caterer and confectioner is an important one and is well represented by Mr. J. Dooling who has had many years' practical experience and enjoys the distinction of being one of the most proficient in the city. He has been established in the business since 1861 and was formerly on Washington Street—south end—but during the past four years he has occupied the very eligible and commodious premises at Nos. 11-13 Temple Place which have dimensions of 30x90 feet and are attractively fitted up in modern style with ornamental fixtures, plate glass cases and marble tile flooring. Mr. Dooling furnishes parties, weddings and dinners with all the delicacies and dainties, fancy cake, ices and ice cream and confections of every kind and also table ornaments and personally looks after all orders himself. His establishment is well equipped for meeting all demands promptly and he numbers among his patrons many of the leading families in the city and vicinity and throughout the New England States. Lunches, dainties and delicacies are furnished to the public and patrons in the commodious saloon parlors adjoining the store and ladies and gentlemen will find here a great variety from which to make a selection of something delicious and appetizing. Mr. Dooling was born and brought up in this city and is one of the most expert and we may say "prince of caterers" whose skill in preparing tempting dishes and choice confections is not surpassed by any other in Boston.

ROBERT JUDGE, Merchant Tailor, Boylston Building, Washington and Boylston Streets.—The merchant tailoring trade has many and able representatives in Boston but none better known or more popular than the gentleman whose name appears in the above heading. Mr. Judge is a native of Boston where he early served his apprenticeship and became an expert tailor. As far back as 1860 he began business for himself and in the interval has built up an enviable reputation and secured the substantial regard of the local trade. The present premises which have been occupied for the past four years are very desirably located in the Boylston building, Washington and Boylston Streets. In the attractive salesroom is shown a carefully selected line of imported and domestic suitings, trouserings, overcoatings, etc., which are made up in the highest degree of artistic and mechanical excellence by a corps of experienced tailors. Mr. Judge counts among his many patrons some of the leading society and business men of the town and is generally respected as one of the ablest city exponents of his art.

J. F. BUMSTEAD & CO., Importers of Paper Hangings and Textile Fabrics for Interior Decoration, No. 148 Tremont Street and Nos. 63 and 66 West Street.—By far the oldest established in its line, and one of the oldest in New England is the famous house of Messrs. J. F. Bumstead & Co., the leading importers and dealers in high art paper hangings. The business was founded by the late Mr. Josiah Bumstead, grandfather of the present proprietor, in 1790. It was the pioneer and exponent of the most advanced skill of old world manufacturers, and continued ever in the van of progress. About 1830, Mr. Bumstead took his son, Mr. Josiah F. Bumstead, into copartnership under the style of J. Bumstead & Son, the junior partner being the father of the present proprietor. In 1845 Mr. Josiah Bumstead retired, and in 1859 Mr. J. F. Bumstead formed a copartnership with Mr. N. Willis Bumstead, his son, under the existing name and style of J. F. Bumstead & Co. The lamented decease of the senior partner occurred in 1868, since which date Mr. N. Willis Bumstead has remained sole proprietor. The concern's original location was in Cornhill, later on having been removed to the site of the present Herald building on Washington Street. In 1845 it was removed to the large store corner of Spring Lane and Washington street. Steady growth of trade necessitated further enlargement and in 1878 they removed to their present splendid premises on Tremont and West Streets, having an area of 50 feet by 160 by 60, extending through an L into West Street. Mr. N. Willis Bumstead is the leading authority on foreign and the best of domestic paperhangings and also on curtains, and the rich and beautiful textile fabrics used for interior decorations. Here he carries the largest, most elaborate and artistic stock of paperhangings in the city; he is an expert in regard to shades and effects, and to the patterns which will best serve the purposes of harmonious designs in household decoration. In rich draperies he is in regular receipt of the latest novelties, and from his immense stock the most exacting taste can be satisfied and secure shades and patterns of papers and fabrics adapted to any of the numerous styles of interior decorative treatment. He numbers among his customers the leading families of Boston and New England. Mr. Bumstead was born in Boston and is a veteran officer of the war of the rebellion, having gone to the front as captain of the Forty-Fifth Massachusetts volunteers, gallantly leading them during numerous battles and engagements throughout the war. He is a director of the Louisville, Evansville and St. Louis Railroad; and of the Pueblo Refining and Smelting Company, ever ably and faithfully discharging the onerous duties thus devolving upon him.

J. L. BROCKWAY & CO., Wholesale Grocers, Country Produce, Etc., No. 29 Norman Street. Branches: Harvard Square, Brookline, and No. 350 Broadway, Chelsea.—One of the most popular, ably conducted and largely patronized firms of wholesale grocers in Boston and suburbs is that of Messrs. J. L. Brockway & Co., with main warehouse at No. 29 Norman Street. The business was established about twenty years ago by Mr. J. L. Brockway who brings to bear perfected facilities, influential connections and the widest range of practical experience. In his extensive Norman Street establishment he carries a heavy and comprehensive stock of staple and fancy groceries, including the choicest of teas and coffees, pure sugars, spices and condiments, all farinaceous products, and the most desirable stock of canned goods in Boston. This is evidenced by reference to the brands, being those only of old established responsible packers. Messrs. Brockway & Co. are direct receivers of country produce, including choicest creamery butter, high grade cheese, strictly fresh eggs, and choice cured hams, bacon, etc. So great became the demand for the firm's superior lines of groceries and produce that to meet it Mr. Brockway in 1879 opened a large retail branch at No. 350 Broadway, Chelsea, and in 1885, a still more extensive establishment in Harvard Square, Brookline. Both places are under able management, and afford to the residents of those sections, unrivalled and duly appreciated opportunities for the purchase of the best and purest food products in the market. Mr. Brockway's laudable ambition is to excel in quality and reasonable prices, and his heavy and constantly growing trade all over New England shows how ably and satisfactorily he is purveying to the wants of the public.

J. L. HAMMETT, Dealer in School Furniture and School Apparatus, No. 24 Cornhill.—Mr. Hammett established this business twenty-four years ago in Brattle Street, and eventually in 1871 removed to his present convenient premises. He occupies a commodious five-story building and two floors of the adjacent warehouse. These are completely stocked with a well selected and valuable assortment of school furniture and apparatus, blackboards, maps, charts, globes, slates and school supplies, also Bradley's kindergarten gifts and occupation material. He handles only the finest and most reliable grades of goods, while his prices in all cases are as reasonable as those of any other first-class house in the trade. The business is both wholesale and retail, extending not only throughout all sections of the United States and Canada, but also to Turkey, China, India, Japan, Ceylon and Sandwich Islands, in which countries Mr. Hammett supplies a number of missionary stations. Mr. Hammett is the New England agent for the Albemarle Slate Pencil Company, Va., and the Hyatt Slate Company, Bethlehem, Penna., manufacturers of superior school slates and slate black-boards. The proprietor is a native of Rhode Island, but has resided in Boston for the last twenty-seven years. There is no better authority on school furniture and supplies than Mr. Hammett, and those of our readers who enter into business relations with him, can always rely on securing advantages in goods and prices not obtainable elsewhere. Mr. Hammett issues annually a very superior illustrated catalogue and price list of school furniture and apparatus.

PATTERSON & LAVENDER, Manufacturers of Show Cases, Counters, Desks, Etc., Nos. 43 and 45 Cornhill Street.—The most justly celebrated manufacturers in the United States of high class show cases, store and office counters, desks, and fixtures are Messrs. Patterson & Lavender. The extensive business conducted here is very old established, having been founded upwards of thirty years ago by the present proprietors, Mr. J. Patterson and Mr. S. Lavender. They early developed an active trade, since developed to proportions of great magnitude, and bring to bear special qualifications including marked skill and originality, vast practical experience, coupled with perfect facilities and influential connections. Their factory is situated in Roxbury, and is of large size, equipped with the latest improved machinery and appliances, and where an average force of from twenty to thirty skilled cabinet-makers are steadily employed. The firm are the designers and manufacturers of the most stylish and elaborate show cases in the market, among the woods used being black walnut, mahogany, cherry, ebony, rosewood, etc., etc. All work is guaranteed, while the trimmings, plating, glass, etc., are strictly first-class. They also make all popular styles of counters, desks and fixtures, and enjoy the perfect facilities, that enable them to promptly fill the largest and most difficult orders for the fitting up of stores and offices. Many of the finest establishments in Washington and Tremont Streets have secured their outfit here, while their customers are found in every city and town throughout New England and here and there all over the United states. The firm occupy an entire five-story and basement building, 30x60 feet in dimensions, as warerooms and office.

L. BEEBE & CO., Cotton, No. 9 Merchants Row.—This business was established forty years ago by Mr. L. Beebe who eventually admitted his sons Messrs. Cyrus G. and Frederic Beebe into partnership, the firm being known by the style and title of L. Beebe & Co. In 1884 Mr. L. Beebe, the founder died after an honorable and successful career, the business, however, is still conducted by his sons under the old firm name. Both partners are recognized authorities relative to the qualities and grades of all kinds of cotton and a test by them is always sufficient to definitely determine the value of any particular lot. They buy largely in the South, and make liberal advances on consignments, and at the same time always secure the highest market quotations, while the firm have ever been noted for their promptness in making returns. Messrs. L. Beebe & Co. own and operate cotton mills in Taunton and Fall River, Mass., where they manufacture print cloths. They supply several of the largest New England mills with cotton. Both Messrs. Cyrus G. and Fred S. Beebe are natives of Boston.

J. WHITNEY BEALS, Jr., Timber Land Investments, No. 4 Post Office Square, Room No. 15.—The great and growing importance of the product of the forest, as a commercial factor, together with the steady and materially increasing demand therefor, imparts to the timber lands of the United States a peculiar interest. Especially so as a field of financial investment. And right here it may be observed, that there are few, if any, features of realty that offer more certain or substantial returns for capital; and none, toward which the shrewd and sagacious investor is so steadily leaning, as to timber lands located in the south and southwest. The sales of Alabama and Mississippi timber lands in Boston are conducted on an extensive scale, while the transactions afford evidence of constant and notable increase annually; and in this connection special mention ought here to be made of J. Whitney Beals, Jr., with office at No. 4 Post Office Square (Room No. 15), who carries an extensive and very desirable line of investment property of the kind referred to, and none engaged in this particular sphere of activity in this city is more widely or honorably known, or enjoys a larger measure of public favor and confidence. Mr. Beals, who also has a branch office in Chicago, (No. 125 La Salle Street,) is agent for and dealer in Alabama and Mississippi timber lands of which he has for sale upwards of 500,000 acres; and does a large and active business, numbering among his clientage some of the most solid citizens in the community. He has been engaged in this line some three years, and by strict integrity, energy and sagacity has built up the excellent patronage he deservedly enjoys. Mr. Beals, who is a young man, and a native of this city, is well and favorably known alike, in commercial and social life, and is a member of the old Beals' family, whose name has long been associated with the Boston *Post*.

BANGS & HORTON, Agents for the Lehigh and Wilkes-barre Coal Co., Maryland Coal Co., and Despard Gas Coal Co., No. 60 Congress Street, Howe Building.—The excellent position of Boston as regards economical transportation facilities, render it the most convenient distributing point in New England, for that important element in the commercial and manufacturing greatness of the country—coal. In this connection special reference is made to the old established and reliable firm of Messrs. Bangs & Horton, No. 60 Congress street, agents for the Lehigh and Wilkes-barre Coal Co., Maryland Coal Co., and the Despard Gas Coal Co. This agency was established a quarter of a century ago by Messrs. Geo. P. Bangs & Chas. P. Horton; the present members of the firm being George P. Bangs, Charles P. Horton and Robt. C. Heaton. The firm have superior facilities for the prompt delivery of the above-named companies' coals in cargo lots, shipments being made direct from Philadelphia, Baltimore, Port Johnston, etc. They also have packets at Mystic Wharf, Charlestown, and Boston and Maine Wharf, Somerville, with facilities for storage and the delivery of coal in car load lots or greater quantities to manufacturers and dealers on the lines of the eastern and western and Lowell divisions of the Boston and Maine railroad. The prices quoted are always regulated by the market. All coals handled by Messrs. Bangs & Horton are extremely rich in the elements producing the most intense heat and complete combustion, and are universally recognized as of very superior quality, being great favorites with manufacturers, railroad companies and dealers. They are guaranteed to maintain in every respect the highest standard of excellence as regards care in their preparation for the market, coming as they do from some of the best equipped collieries in America. Messrs. Bangs & Horton are natives of Boston, while Mr. Heaton was born in Philadelphia. The partners are highly regarded in business circles for their promptness and integrity, and their patronage now extends throughout the principal cities of New England.

SIMPSON BROTHERS, Asphalt Floors, Concrete Walks and Driveways; Offices, No. 22 Milk street.—The famous Swiss and French rock asphalts have manifested their superiority to all other materials for smooth, hard, dry, fire and water proof floors and linings that have rapidly come into use all over the United States, and to a very great extent in Boston and New England, where the public is so appreciative of the most improved and reliable materials and methods. It was in 1870 that Messrs. Frederick and James Simpson commenced the importation and application of Neuchatel and Seyssel rock asphalt. They early developed a lively trade, as the merits of these natural asphalts became known to owners, architects and builders, and have filled large orders for leading citizens and corporations all over Boston and New England. They carry a heavy stock of the pure rock asphalt specially intended for their trade, and employ upward of forty skilled hands in the work of preparation and application. It is specially popular for the floors of basements, kitchens, laundries, stables, water-closets, dwelling-houses, cellars, breweries, manufactories, warehouses, hospitals, courtyards, walks, driveways, etc.,—in fact any and every place where a hard, smooth, clean, dry, fire and water proof, odorless and durable covering is required in basement or upper stories, laid either over cement, concrete, brick or wood, in one sheet without seams; it is also the best coating for roofs. As a sanitary agent nothing is so valuable as this impervious rock asphalt, which permanently excludes all dampness, odors, malarious exhalations and vermin. As a material for public and private driveways, walks, plazas, squares, etc., it is unquestionably far superior to any other article in the world, and has long been so recognized by architects and engineers. The firm use only the natural rock asphalt, free from coal tar and all artificial substances; it hardens immediately, and is ready for use within a few hours after being laid. Messrs. Simpson Brothers are prepared to promptly estimate for the covering of any surface, large or small, and refer to work done in the largest buildings in Boston, including Institute of Technology, Wells Memorial Institute, Harvard Medical School, Bay State and Standard Sugar Refineries, Masonic Temple, Young's Hotel, Mutual Insurance Building, United States Hotel, Boston Advertiser Building, and many others too numerous to mention. Work has also been done for F. L. Ames, H. H. Hunnewell, and others. Those contemplating building operations or repairs should investigate the superiority of natural rock asphalt, samples of which will be shown and prices quoted at the firm's office, No. 22 Milk Street, while work in use can be readily seen in almost every quarter of the city. The Messrs. Simpson are members of the Master Builders' Exchange, and of the Mechanics' Exchange.

COLLINS & CO., Real Estate Agents and Agents for the Florida Fruit and Investment Company, No. 15 Kilby Street.—The consumption of fruit grows apace with the ever increasing population, and the demand for southern fruit in all parts of the country has developed fruit growing into a very profitable business, and opens the way for the lucrative investment of capital. Facilities for this are afforded by the Florida Fruit and Investment Company, of Mayfield, Alachua County, Florida, through its agents, Messrs. Collins & Co., the well known real estate firm of No. 15 Kilby Street, Boston. This company was incorporated under the laws of New Hampshire, and its president is Dr. J. A. McDonald, No. 116 Main Street, Charlestown, Mass., and the treasurer is Mr. G. H. Sutherland, of Gainesville, Florida. The company has a capital of $100,000, and its purpose is to raise on a scientific plan, fruits for which Florida has become famous. They have 640 acres of land at Mayfield, five miles northwest of Gainesville, and through this the line of the Florida, Savannah and Western Railroad runs. The company's land is very fertile, and fertilizers of only known merit are used, and a class of fruits are to be raised, such as oranges, peaches, pears, plumbs, persimmons, grapes, etc., as will mature in rapid succession so as to secure continuous crops of fruits from early spring until the oranges are marketed in November, December and January. The cost of maturing an acre of trees to four years old and having everything in the best working condition is $250, and the value of each acre will then be $1,000, while in ten years' time the value will be $2,000, thus paying 100 per cent. yearly on the outlay. Fifty-thousand fruit trees have already been planted. The company's stock is issued at a par value of $50 per share, the first payment being $5, the balance being spread over two or three years. A profitable field of enterprise is here offered to investors, who can obtain the most detailed information from Messrs. Collins & Co. They conduct a general real estate business, buying and selling, exchanging and leasing properties in town and country, collecting rents, negotiating loans, and taking management of estates. Mr. W. P. Collins, the head of the firm, is a native of New York State and has resided in Boston for the past eighteen years.

THE METROPOLIS OF NEW ENGLAND.

W. S. HIXON & CO., Manufacturers of Soapstone, No. 14 Marshall Street.—The old soapstone works of W. S. Hixon & Co., manufacturers of soapstone articles of every description, has long maintained a hold on popular favor throughout the country, owing to the general excellence of its productions. The goods turned out in this widely known concern are of a very superior character, being all hand made and first-class in every feature of merit—in design, workmanship, finish and durability—and, as a consequence, are in steady and extensive demand in the trade all over the United States. This thriving enterprise was established in 1860 by O. W. Cushing & Co., who conducted it up to about five years ago, when they were succeeded by the present proprietors, who have since carried on

the business with uninterrupted success. The works and warerooms occupy commodious and well equipped premises, ample manufacturing and storage facilities being at hand, while sixteen skilled workmen are employed. The productions include sinks and wash trays, register and funnel stones, griddles, fire places and soapstone stoves; also soapstone slabs and in short, everything that can be manufactured from soapstone, a large and first-class assortment being constantly carried on hand, and, altogether, the firm does a flourishing business. Mr. Hixon, who is the sole proprietor, was born in New York State, and has resided in this city some twenty-two years. He is a man of experience, energy and skill in this line, and is thoroughly conversant with the business in all its branches.

JOSEPH W. HOMER, Real Estate Broker, No. 27 Kilby Street, and No. 26 Exchange Place.—Among the young representative real estate and insurance brokers in this community, there are none more prominent than Mr. Joseph W. Homer, who is well known in business circles, and enjoys a wide reputation for promptness and reliability in his transactions. He has been established in the business the past seven years, and has a large influential connection in this city and vicinity, numbering among his clients many of the substantial citizens. He is familiar with the valuation of real estate in this section, and during his business career has been conspicuous as a broker in many of the operations that have been going on. Mr. Homer also makes a leading specialty of the negotiations of mortgage loans, and effects insurance in the leading substantial companies at the lowest rates of premium. He is a native Bostonian and a gentleman of experience, high standing and popularity.

A. S. MITCHELL, Auctioneer and Appraiser, Real Estate and Mortgages, No. 113 Devonshire Street (Room 54).—Of the many successful real estate brokers that have come to the front in this city of recent years, few have been more fortunate in establishing a reputation for integrity and reliability than Mr. A. S. Mitchell, who is a native and a respected resident of the historic town of Lexington, Mass., where he fills the office of constable with efficiency. He is a gentleman of entire probity in his dealings, and is thoroughly conversant with everything connected with the handling, transfer and management of realty. Mr. Mitchell has been actively engaged in this line since 1883, and from the first he has enjoyed a very flattering measure of merited recognition, numbering among his clientele some of the solid citizens of Boston and environs. Mr. Mitchell, whose office is at No. 113 Devonshire Street (Room 54), conducts a general real estate business, buying, selling and exchanging city and country property of all kinds on commission, and gives personal attention also to the collection of rents and the care of estates, real estate sales at auction being a specialty, and loans are negotiated likewise, and investments judiciously placed, while insurance is effected in first-class fire companies at the lowest rates compatible with absolute security.

GEO. A. KENDALL, Feathers and Mattresses, Curled Hair Ticking, Etc., No. 14 Friend Street.—The attention that has been directed of late years to the production of mattresses and bedding of every description in this country has developed the fact that American skill and inventive genius are quite as successful in this branch of enterprise as they have proved in many others. Of the marked improvement made in this department of industrial activity no more convincing proof is to be found in the city of Boston than by visiting the establishment of Mr. Geo. A. Kendall, the well-known manufacturer and dealer in feathers and mattresses, curled hair, ticking, etc., located at No. 14 Friend Street. The enterprising proprietor has been engaged in the business since 1870, and established his present house in January, 1887. He occupies four floors, 30x120 feet each, and possesses the best possible facilities for conducting the enterprise under the most favorable conditions and upon the largest scale. The methods of manufacture in vogue are the most enterprising and progressive character, resulting in the production of a class of specialties that are rarely equalled in this country embracing utility, reliability, elegance and uniform excellence. The house bears the unmistakable marks of judicious and conscientious management, and exercises an influence that extends far beyond the limits of this city, its trade being broadly distributed throughout New England and New York, and annually increasing in volume and value. A force of fifteen skilled hands contribute to the satisfactory operations of the house, while all the details of the business are conducted under the personal supervision of the proprietor, thus insuring to the trade only such products as will withstand the most critical tests, both as regards materials used in their construction and the workmanship employed. A splendid stock is constantly carried and orders are filled with promptness and care in all cases. Mr. Kendall is a native of Boston, a practical leader in his line of trade, and occupying a position in the business circles of this city only accorded to those whose operations are conducted on the enduring principles of equity and honorable dealings.

BEALS & CO., Wholesale Dealers and Exporters of All Kinds of Leather Remnants, and Manufacturers of Leather Shoe Laces and Sheep Skins; Boston Office; Nos. 31 and 33 South Street.—Among the many flourishing industries developed by the vast growth of the boot and shoe interests in the United States during the past quarter of a century, not the least important is the branch devoted to the production of leather shoe laces and kindred articles for the trade. Engaged in this line are some really noteworthy firms, the oldest and largest of which is that of Beals & Co., wholesale dealers in all kinds of leather remnants, and manufacturers of leather shoe laces, whose Boston office and salesroom are located at Nos. 31 and 33 South Street, with factory within ten miles from Boston, and whose business extends throughout the entire country. This enterprising and widely known firm was established twenty years ago, and they operate a commodious, well equipped factory, and employ a large force of hands, and in 1873 opened an office in this city, on Federal Street, whence they subsequently moved to No. 79 South Street, occupying the present commodious quarters since 1885. They occupy here a 30x100 foot floor and carry constantly on hand an extensive and first class assortment of leather remnants and shoe laces; all orders being promptly and reliably attended to, and the trade of the firm, which extends to all parts of the United States, besides having a large export trade to foreign countries, is large and active. Messrs. J. M. Beals and J. O. Guild, who compose the firm, are both men of energy, enterprise and practical skill in this line, and are thoroughly conversant with the wants of the trade.

A. M. BATES, Dealer in Carriages, Harness and Sleighs Nos. 25 and 27 Haverhill Street.—The leading headquarters in Boston for carriages, harness, sleighs, blankets, and robes of all kinds, is the establishment of Mr. A. M. Bates. This is one of the widely known and justly famous business houses that have added so much to the name and fame of this city, both at home and abroad, as a great commercial centre. It has been in successful operation since 1862, and well deserves the title of "leader of the trade." Mr. Bates deals very extensively at both wholesale and retail, in both new and second-hand carriages and kindred articles, and also sells on commission. His large double building, four stories high and 60x80 feet in dimensions, is completely filled at all times with a class of vehicles suited to the requirements of all sorts and conditions of buyers. A general line of fine carriages for pleasure and family use is noticed, besides sleighs of new and original designs; carriages in many styles, shapes and patterns, from an ordinary no-top road wagon to an elegantly finished coach, besides coupes, victorias, landaus, phaetons, rockaways, etc., while a leading specialty is made of the Timkin spring carriages, which are unexcelled in this or any other market for strength, lightness, durability, ease of draft and elegance of finish. The line of harness is also worthy of the attention of close and careful buyers, being kept up to the highest standard of excellence, and are placed upon the market at prices which are safe from successful competition. The trade of this responsible house is large and influential not only throughout the entire United States, but also in Africa, South America and other foreign countries. Mr. Bates is a native of Sutton, Mass.

J. JOHN N. ROBERTS, Collateral Banking Rooms, No. 666 Washington Street.—One of the prominent and well-known city business men in his important branch of commercial activity is Mr. John N. Roberts, proprietor of the collateral banking rooms at No. 666 Washington Street. Mr. Roberts has been engaged in his present enterprise since 1868, eleven years at the present site—and in the interval has reared what may well be termed a representative business in his line. The commodious and attractive business offices are fitted up in bank style and all requisite facilities are supplied for the advantageous prosecution of the enterprise. A general collateral banking business is done, money being advanced upon bonds, mortgages and other collateral security, funds are also placed by the same methods, care being exercised to insure the customer a safe as well as profitable investment. Mr. Roberts by his sound financial judgment and upright, honorable dealing has won the substantial regard of local capitalists and investors generally and secured a clientele which distinguishes him as one of the foremost exponents of his line of business in his native town.

H. HARRISON ALDRICH & CO., Wholesalers and Jobbers in Eggs, Butter and Cheese, Nos. 28 State and 47 Commerce Streets. —Among the most enterprising and popular commission merchants and wholesale dealers in eggs, butter and cheese in this city is the firm of Messrs. Harrison Aldrich & Co. The business was originally established in 1878 by Mr. Harrison Aldrich, and in 1887 Mr. Charles B. Osgood was admitted to partnership. The business premises comprise a fine six-story building, 25x80 feet in dimensions, fronting on both State and Commerce Streets, supplied with every modern facility for the preservation of perishable articles and for the convenient handling of the large and valuable stock here carried. This firm are possessed of every qualification for the business, including vast practical experience, influential connections and perfected facilities. Consignments of goods are arriving daily from the dairies of Vermont and the best producing sections of New England, and the most substantial inducements are offered to shippers, including quick sales at highest rates and prompt returns. It has become fully recognized among shippers, jobbers and leading retailers that this firm deliver the choicest butter, cheese and eggs in prime condition, and readily command the highest market prices. Their egg department is well worth a visit, where many egg-chandlers are constantly employed in examining and assorting eggs. The credit of the house is A1 in the trade, ample capital being employed therein. Mr. Aldrich is a native of Vermont, while Mr. Osgood was born in Boston, Mass.

C. CHAS. E. EAMES, Druggist and Apothecary, No. 396 Hanover Street.—The popular establishment of Mr. Chas. E. Eames, the well-known druggist and apothecary is probably the oldest of the kind in the city and as we have been reliably informed its foundation dates back over a hundred years. It has been under the control of Mr. Eames since 1871 and conducted by him with rare tact, skill and ability. The store is of ample dimensions and the interior fittings and fixtures are of a character which reflects the greatest credit upon the taste of the proprietor. Drugs and chemicals and proprietary preparations of the highest standard quality are kept in stock, also a great variety of toilet articles and all the specialties pertaining to the business. Mr. Eames is a practical apothecary and peculiarly well qualified to compound and dispense medicines and exercises that intelligent care necessary and requisite in this special department. He employs two skilled assistants who are under his immediate supervision and every attention is given to filling physicians' prescriptions and difficult formulas. A native of Wakefield in this State Mr. Eames has lived in Boston many years and is held in high estimation in professional and social circles as an accomplished druggist and apothecary, and as a useful popular citizen.

E. E. F. RITZ, Photographic Artist, No. 56 Temple Place.—In no department of the arts are the improvements of the past quarter century so conspicuous as in photography and one need only contrast the exquisite productions of our modern artists with the crude portraiture in vogue even twenty years since to fully comprehend the great progress that has been made in this direction. In this connection as a leading and representative Boston photo-artist is mentioned the gentleman whose name appears in the caption of this sketch. Mr. E. F. Ritz, was born in Sweden, although has lived nearly all his life in this country. At an early age he served his time and acquired the degree of knowledge then attainable in his profession, and in 1865 opened a photographic establishment in Boston with a copartner under the firm name of Ritz & Hastings, and thus continued for many years, building up in the meantime a reputation for superior work, second to none in his profession. Since 1884, Mr. Ritz has been alone, and for a like period has occupied the present eligible site at No. 56 Temple Place. The premises consist of two floors, one fitted up in the most sumptuous and tasteful style, and occupied as a reception parlor—while above are the operating and ante-rooms. The studio is supplied with all the newest and best improved photographic methods and appliances; several experienced assistants are employed and everything pertaining to modern portraiture is executed in the highest degree of artistic and mechanical excellence. Mr. Ritz counts among his numerous patronage the high class town and suburban custom and has long been reflected as a leading and prominent city photo-artist whose success is but a just tribute to his indefatigable and able efforts in its promotion.

B. BARRELLE & CO., Auctioneers, Real Estate, Collection and Business Agents, No. 157 Washington Street.—In reviewing the real estate and kindred interests of Boston and environs, more than passing notice should be given the popular and responsible firm of Barrelle & Co., auctioneers, real estate, collection and business agents, who numbers among its extensive clientele some of the most solid citizens and wealthy property owners in the community. A general real estate business is transacted, city and suburban property of every description, improved and unimproved, being handled on commission, while rents are collected and estates judiciously managed also; special attention being given sales at auction, leasing and business chances. Loans are effected and mortgages negotiated likewise, while investments are desirably placed also; in short, everything appertaining to the purchase, sale and transfer of realty is attended to in the most reliable and satisfactory manner. Mr. T. W. Barrelle, who is the sole member, is a gentleman of middle age, and a native of this state, having his residence now at South Framingham. He is a capable and experienced attorney-at-law and was formerly engaged in the practice of law in Iowa. Returning to Boston in 1872, he established himself in his profession here, and devoted his attention exclusively to the same for about three years, when he added the real estate business in which he has been signally successful from the first.

THE METROPOLIS OF NEW ENGLAND.

AMERICAN MANUFACTURING COMPANY, Manufacturers of the Allen Fertilizer and Bedding, Robert C. Wiggin, General Agent, No. 19 Exchange Place.—A representative house in Boston, engaged in the manufacture of fertilizers, etc., is that known as American Manufacturing Company, whose office is located at No. 19 Exchange Place. This business was established in 1881 by Mr. L. Allen, and eventually was duly incorporated in 1885 with a capital stock of $20,000. The works of the company which are spacious and fully equipped with the latest improved machinery, apparatus and appliances, are situated at Westville, N. H. The company makes a specialty of manufacturing the Allen fertilizer, a complete high grade fertilizer for all crops, also the Allen special fertilizers for potatoes and corn, and Allen's top dressing and lawn dressing. They also deal in nitrate soda, sulphate ammonia, ammonia, muriate potash, dried blood, etc., at the lowest market prices, compounded from the very best chemicals, and prepared with the greatest care and with the most improved machinery. The Allen fertilizer will be found to be rich in all the elements of plant food in an available form, and the chemical analysis appears upon each package and the percentages of ammonia, phosphoric acid and potash contained in this fertilizer are derived from the very best sources which supply these three great requisites for satisfactory crops. On most farms the success of the crop depends largely upon the yearly use of manures, and it is of the greatest importance that the distribution should be even. This is especially true of a manufactured fertilizer where the small amount used cannot be evenly applied unless it is in good mechanical condition. The Allen fertilizer is in the very best condition as to fineness and dryness, so that it will work to the very best advantage in the drill. In bulk the Allen fertilizer will be found to go much farther than any high grade fertilizer in the market. It is a general fertilizer for all crops, and it may be used in connection with stable manure or alone, and will be found to be a valuable help to the growth of crops throughout the season, since its fertilizing ingredients are in a soluble condition and are ready to act at once, and continue with the growth of the plant. The Allen fertilizer contains fifteen times the amount of available plant food contained in one ton of fresh stable manure. A better crop of potatoes can be raised on a good fertilizer than on stable manure. The crop will ripen earlier, will be free from disease, and will be of better quality. The Allen fertilizer for potatoes will give these results, as it contains not only the ammonia and phosphoric acid but a large percentage of potash. The American Manufacturing company has latterly introduced "Bedding," a very superior article for bedding in stables, for horses, cows, etc. It is cheaper than straw and much better, and is packed in medium sized bales of 250 pounds each being free in the bale and not hard, hence it is as available as straw. Bedding makes a soft and elastic bed, giving an easy bed to horses with sore feet. It absorbs all urine and will not burn, hence it is a safeguard against fire. When thoroughly used up it becomes a valuable fertilizer, containing from three to eight per cent ammonia, making it worth to the farmer at least $10.00 per ton. The officers of this reliable company are highly esteemed in trade circles for their enterprise, energy and just methods, and their patronage now extends throughout the entire eastern and middle states, owing to the superiority, reliability and excellence of their productions, which are general favorites with farmers wherever introduced.

BRUNSWICK-BALKE-COLLENDER CO., Manufacturers of Billiard and Pool Tables, Nos. 44 to 48 Hanover street.—The world-wide renowned concern of the Brunswick-Balke-Collender Co., which manufactures more billiard and pool tables than any other establishment on the face of the globe, had its beginning in 1860 at Cincinnati, when it was established by Brunswick Brothers. The firm afterwards became J. M. Brunswick & Co., and in 1872 this firm amalgamated with Julius Balke of Cincinnati, who had then been in the business some years. The style was then changed to J. M. Brunswick & Balke Co. In the same year the concern consolidated with the Collender Manufacturing Co., of New York, and then the present title of the Brunswick-Balke-Collender Co. was adopted. The company was incorporated in 1882 under the laws of Ohio with a capital stock of $1,500,000. Mr. John M. Brunswick died in 1886 at Cincinnati, and his interest in the business is represented by Mr. Ben M. Brunswick. Since Mr. Brunswick's death, Mr. H. W. Collender, of New York, has been the president, and Mr. A. F. Troescher, of New York, secretary and Treasurer. The directors are Messrs. M. Bensinger and Leo Schmidt, of Chicago. The company have factories in New York, Cincinnati, Chicago, St. Louis and San Francisco, and branch establishments in Boston and all the principal cities in the country. They manufacture billiard and pool tables, billiard merchandise of every description, saloon fixtures and beer coolers, ten pin alleys, office, bank and drug store fixtures, mirrors, bar tables, chairs, etc., in the production of which many hundreds of workmen are employed. The Boston branch was founded in 1882 and has proved eminently successful. The premises occupied here comprise a fine office and show room 6x80 feet in dimensions, and here a splendid showing is made of samples of the manufactures of the company. Through this branch the whole of the New England trade is controlled and the business is under the efficient management of Mr. Henry Bercy, Jr., who is a native of New York City.

G. A. WALKER MACHINE COMPANY, Manufacturers of Band, Jig and Circular Saw Machinery, Cabinet Bench Vises, Etc., No. 35 Sudbury Street.—This concern was founded twenty-five years ago by the late Mr. G. A. Walker, and are making marked advances in the manufacture of band, jig and circular machinery, cabinet bench vises, etc. Upon his decease in July, 1888, he was succeeded by the following: Messrs. I. S. Craig, S. F. Gould, J. P. Craig, C. G. Smith, and C. W. Brown, gentlemen who had previously carried on the work of manufacturing in Mr. Walker's shops, and who had become recognized authorities in every detail of piano forte and general machinist work. They began operations as the G. A. Walker Machine Company, in September, 1888, and have retained the patronage and wide-spread connections of the old concern. They have a first-class shop on Sudbury street, 4000 feet in dimensions, well equipped with lathes and other machinery, run by steam power, and where they carry in stock and are prepared to promptly manufacture to special order all styles and sizes of the most improved and reliable band, jig and circular saw machines. The reputation of the Walker Sawing machinery is too well known to require comment here. They are not only in use in the leading and largest piano-forte shops of New England, but have been introduced all over the United States, as also the improved cabinet bench vises. The company also executes general machine work of every description and is the representative in its line. Mr. Craig is a native of New Hampshire, Mr. Gould was born in Boston, Mr. J. P. Craig in New Hampshire, Mr. Smith in Waltham, and Mr. Brown in New Hampshire, and they are all able and respected business men.

L. B. GATCOMB & CO., Manufacturers of Banjos and Guitars, Music Publishers, Etc., No. 39 Hanover Street.—Very marked improvement has been effected in banjos of recent years, a degree of excellence akin to perfection having been attained by L. B. Gatcomb & Co., manufacturer of banjos and guitars. The productions of this firm are articles of exceptional merit, being All in every respect—in fullness and sweetness of tone, beauty of design, construction and finish—and for general excellence are unsurpassed by any instruments of the kind produced today in this country, as is amply attested by the steady and increasing demand that has grown up for them all over the United States. This enterprising and widely known firm was established about five years ago, and the positive and permanent success that attended the venture from the start abundantly attests the superiority of the instruments manufactured as well as the energy and ability displayed in the management of the business. The premises occupied, including neat office, salesroom and factory, are commodious and well equipped in all respects, while eight or more expert hands are employed. The firm also publish and deal quite extensively in music and general musical merchandise, and are prepared to furnish anything in this line in the most prompt and satisfactory manner at lowest rates. Lessons are given on the banjo, guitar, etc., by such competent and experienced instructors as Messrs. B. E. Shattuck and A. A. Babb; banjos and banjo instruction being specialties and their goods have always given satisfaction to customers.

LABAN HEATH & CO., Importers & Manufacturing Opticians, No. 48 Hanover Street, Room 35.—One of the most valuable specialties here manufactured is Heath's patent adjustable microscope, designed for the use of bankers, botanists, mineralogists, geologists, physicians, jewelers, miners, mechanics and others. This microscope has two double convex lenses, 1¾ inches in diameter, embracing a very large field of vision; handsomely nickel plated and embossed and having the patent adjustment of focus which admits of use at any angle. They are substantially built, neat in design, and easy of comprehension; they can always be at hand and ready for immediate use; their great simplicity preventing them being put out of order except by extreme violence. They are admirably adapted for examining bank notes, engravings, photographs, minerals, or any object where a high power is not required. The focus is easily adjusted to any point or angle, by simply opening or closing the frame. As an aid in detecting counterfeit money these microscopes are peculiarly adapted; the lenses being of the correct power for that purpose, and the mechanism of the frames is such as to make them exceedingly convenient to use. The Practical Microscope, or No. 14, has two double convex lenses, each 1⅞ inches in diameter, giving a large, clear field of vision, and magnifying 125 times. This microscope is intended to accommodate that large class of people who are desirous of possessing an instrument having a wide range of vision, easily managed, of good reliable power, and at a moderate price. It will be found very useful in the various branches of trade and agriculture, in determining the quality and composition of various articles, and detecting adulteration, while in solving the practical day wants of society this microscope is unrivalled. The Botanical Microscope, No. 16, for botanists, mineralogists, geologists, physicians, jewelers and others, magnifies 200 times, and meets a want long felt by that large class of investigators who wish to possess a really good and reliable microscope at a moderate price. This instrument has two double convex lenses, 1 5-16 inches in diameter, admitting of wide application. Its portability admits of being carried in the pocket, and the botanist will find it an indispensable companion. The Vest Pocket Microscope, No. 18, meets a growing demand for a good pocket microscope, of high power, and affording a large field of vision. It embraces all the qualities of a first-class microscope, and is simply invaluable to handlers of cloth and other textile fabrics, being regarded as the best linen prover in the market. The Bankers' Microscope, No. 24, is used for examining bank notes, engravings, photographs, etc. A great feature of this microscope is the large size of the lenses, giving a field of vision covering nearly the whole face of a bank note. It is also a very useful ornament for the parlor table, for examining photographs, engravings, paintings, etc. This firm are also especially well known as publishers of "Heath's Infallible Government Counterfeit Detector at Sight," twenty-five years on the market and issued by authority from the U. S. Treasury Department, and the only reliable text-book for the student who desires to become an expert in the art of detecting, at sight, counterfeit bank and treasury notes. A new set of plates, of both United States and National bank notes, from the original dies engraved at the United States Treasury Department, have been made expressly for this work. It is recognized as the most elegant and complete work of the kind ever before offered to the world. Mr. Heath, the active member of the firm and moving spirit of this enterprise, eminent as an author, inventor and manufacturing optician, was born in the state of New Hampshire.

ROBERT M. DIAZ & CO., Importers and Wholesale Dealers in Cutlery and Fancy Hardware, No. 292 Washington Street.—The leading headquarters in this city for cutlery and fancy hardware is the establishment of Messrs. Robert M. Diaz & Co. This firm are widely prominent as wholesale dealers and extensive importers of this class of goods, and have been established in the business here since 1882. They occupy spacious and attractive quarters in the very heart of the city, and possess unequalled facilities for conducting the business under the most favorable auspices. The firm is given a prestige in this special line of trade as the New England agents for the following celebrated manufacturing concerns, viz: Ulster Knife Company, American pocket knives; J. Wiss & Son, shears, dental and tinners' snips, tailors' paper and pruning shears, straight and bent trimmers, ladies' and pocket scissors; Jos. Barnard & Sons, pocket knives and scissors; Benj. F. Badger, genuine Emerson razor strops; Medford Fancy Goods Company, dog collars; J. Russell Cutlery Company, table cutlery, etc.; Tuck Manufacturing Company, fine steel tools, knives and tempered springs; Rogers Bros. A1 silver plated ware; and, in addition to these goods, the firm also carry a full and complete line of Jona. Crookes & Son's pocket knives; Geo. Wostenholm & Son's and Joseph Rodgers & Son's pocket knives, razors, etc.; Wade & Butcher's, Frederick Reynolds' and Bengal razors, Engstrom's Swedish razors and hunting knives, and Robert Murphy's corkscrews and steel goods. The razors carried are of the firm's own importation, each of which is thoroughly tested before being sent out, and are fully warranted, besides barbers' shears and strops, toilet clippers, and all kinds of cutlery and fancy hardware, and a splendid line of dog collars. Fine goods are handled exclusively. The trade is immense and influential throughout New England and the west. Mr. Diaz, the active member of the firm, was born in Plymouth, Mass., was trained in this line of business as a clerk for Messrs. Bradford & Anthony for a period of eighteen years.

HINCKLEY BROS. & CO., Cordage, Chains, Anchors, Chandlery and Stores, Nos. 56, 58 and 60 Commercial street.—One of the oldest established and representative houses in Boston, extensively engaged in the sale of ship chandlery and stores, is that of Messrs. Hinckley Bros. & Co., whose office and store are located at Nos. 56 to 60 Commercial Street. This business was established in 1839 by Howland, Hinckley & Co., who were succeeded in 1866 by the present firm of Hinckley Bros. & Co. The copartners, Messrs. Gustavus Hyder and S. B. and D. F. Hinckley have had great experience, and possess a thorough knowledge of the ship chandlery trade and the requirements of captains and ship owners. They have a well equipped oar factory at Claire, N. Y., where they employ forty skilled workmen. The Boston warehouse is a spacious four-story building 25x100 feet in area, fully supplied with every appliance and facility for the successful conduct of their steadily increasing business. Messrs. Hinckley Bros. & Co. deal largely in chandlery and stores, cordage, chains, anchors, oakum, duck, wire rope, boats and skiffs, ash and spruce oars and sculls and English sheathing felt. They are agents in Boston for the Mount Vernon Cotton duck, Suffolk Cordage Company and the Broderick Bascome Manufacturing Company, St. Louis, (wire rope), and are part owners of several vessels, trading to the New England ports and all over the world. The firm handle only the best grades of ship chandlery and stores, and fill orders promptly at the lowest possible prices. Mr. S. B. Hinckley was born in Cape Cod, Mr. D. F. Hinckley in Boston, and Mr. Hyder in Chatham, Mass. The partners are popular members of the Vessels Owners' Association, and are highly regarded in trade circles for their promptness, enterprise and integrity, fully meriting the liberal and permanent patronage secured in this valuable industry.

DYKE, SHUTE & CO., Weighers, No. 4 Central Wharf.—The leading representatives of the weighing trade in Boston is the firm of Messrs. Dyke, Shute & Co. The business so successfully prosecuted by this firm was established nearly fifty years ago, by Mr. J. W. Livret, and in 1868 Mr. George E. Dyke became a member of the firm of Livret & Dyke, who were succeeded by the present firm in 1882. The members of this firm all bring special qualifications to bear upon the management, and have established wide and influential connections on change and among shippers, exporters and dealers in all descriptions of merchandise. They give steady employment to a large force of skilled assistants, and place their tariff of charges at the lowest point of moderation. Possessed of superior and perfected facilities, this firm are in a position to guarantee satisfaction in all their transactions and thorough accuracy in all weights. The copartners are Messrs. George E. Dyke, Henry L. Shute and George D. Dyke. The Messrs. Dyke, father and son, are natives of this city, while Mr. Shute was born in South Scituate, Mass. All are gentlemen of large experience and tried ability, and are regarded as valuable and responsible members of the field of mercantile and commercial activity named and their names are synonymous with honorable, straightforward business matters.

THE METROPOLIS OF NEW ENGLAND.

CHARLES H. NORTH & CO., Packers and Curers of Pork, Beef, Lard, Hams, Etc., Nos. 33 and 34 North Market Street.—An historical review of Boston's principal commercial and manufacturing interests would be incomplete without special mention of the old established and representative house of Messrs. Charles H. North & Co., packers and curers of pork, beef, hams, bacon and manufacturers of strictly pure lard, etc., and whose office and salesrooms are centrally located at Nos. 33 and 34 North Market Street. Their slaughtering, curing and packing houses are among the largest and best equipped in the United States, and are situated at Medford Street, Somerville, Mass., covering about eight acres of ground. Here 150 men are employed, and the machinery is driven by steam power. The number of hogs slaughtered and packed daily is 1,500 to 2,000 and upwards. This business was established thirty years ago by North, Merriman & Co., who conducted it till 1874, when the present firm succeeded to the management. The copartners, Messrs. Charles H. North and S. Henry Skilton, have had great practical

experience in the packing business, coupled with an intimate knowledge of the requirements of the home and export trade. Only the best stock is handled and the greatest care and attention are given in the packing house to the meat, while being prepared for the market. Messrs. Charles H. North & Co. deal extensively in pork, beef, lard, hams and bacon, live and dressed hogs, etc., while the prices quoted in all cases are always regulated by the market. The hams and bacon of this popular house are packed and cured by a process which adds greatly to the flavor of the meat, and renders them free from all injurious substances and unpleasant taste of excessive salt. The trade of the firm not only extends throughout all sections of the United States and Canada, but they likewise export largely to Great Britain, Germany, France and South America. Messrs. North and Skilton are popular members of the Chamber of Commerce, where they are highly regarded for their enterprise, sound business principles and integrity. Mr. North is a native of Vermont, while Mr. Skilton was born in Burlington, Mass.

LEONARD L. HODGES, Ornamental and Plain Japanner, No. 105 Haverhill Street.—In the steady advancement of the arts and industrial undertakings, the ornamental and fancy decorative effects are more sought after, and the leading firms engaged in the manufacture of metal goods are specially solicitous to secure the highest results of the japanners' art. In this line the leading representative is Mr. Leonard L. Hodges. The present extensive business was founded by the firm of Hodges & Coleman on Sudbury Street, upwards of twenty-five years ago. Eighteen years ago, Mr. Hodges became sole proprietor, and the growth of his trade was so great that in 1875 he removed to his present spacious premises, comprising four entire floors, 22x60 feet in dimensions. Here he employs a large force of skilled hands in both plain and ornamental japanning, and kindred branches of the trade. He has all the most perfect appliances, and follows the most approved methods, turning out the most elaborate and perfect class of work known to the trade. He is prepared to fill the largest orders for ornamental and plain japanning, ornamental painting and bronzing of all kinds, pearl inlaying, wood enameling, etc., etc. He numbers among his customers the leading New England manufacturers of all kinds of machinery—ornamental castings, articles of metal, wood enameling, etc., etc. He offers substantial inducements both as to price and quality of work.

H. W. BERRY, Sole General Agent for the celebrated Kranich & Bach's Grand, Square and Upright Pianos, and the Prescott Parlor Organs, No. 592 Washington Street.—A good piano is the great desideratum of every American household. There are numerous instruments in the market which it is claimed, meet this want, but the palm for general excellence is now freely given to the celebrated Kranich & Bach make, which are now superseding all others in the line of superior quality. Mr. H. W. Berry, of 592 Washington Street, is the agent for these first-class instruments. He began selling them in 1870 and two years later opened an establishment of his own, removing in 1880 to his present commodious premises, 30x90 feet in dimensions, which enable him to display to the best advantage the magnificent stock of grand, square and upright pianos of the Kranich & Bach make which he keeps on hand. He is also sole agent for the Prescott Parlor Organs which are constantly meeting with the highest approval from musicians who have tested their merits. Mr. Berry is an indefatigable worker and has built up a splendid trade both in pianos and organs throughout the city. He is a native of Boston, forty-five years of age, and is highly popular in business and social circles.

HATHEWAY & CO., Ship and Freight Brokers, No. 22 Central Wharf.—This business was established in 1873 by Mr. Geo. F. Hatheway, who conducted it till 1884, when Mr. D. W. Simpson became a partner. Both partners bring great practical experience to bear, and possess an accurate knowledge of all details, and at the same time are well qualified to represent shipping interests in the port of Boston. Special attention is paid to vessel business, and to the purchase and shipment of goods on foreign orders. Messrs. Hatheway & Co., attend promptly and carefully to the chartering and dispatching of vessels, load and discharge cargoes, collect freights and act as agents for the owners of steamships or sailing vessels. They likewise buy and sell steamers, sailing vessels and tugs, and carry on an extensive trade with Nova Scotia, New Brunswick, Prince Edwards' Island, New foundland, etc., in flour, produce, lumber, fish and other products. The firm occupy a commodious five-story building, and makes advances on merchandise when required. Mr. Hatheway was born in St. Johns, N. B., while his partner, Mr. Simpson, is a native of East Boston. Both are popular members of the Chamber of Commerce.

MAZEPPA SIGN COMPANY, F. F. Applequist, Manager, No. 15 Water Street.—For originality, beauty and variety of design, or for really artistic workmanship in the line of sign and ornamental painting, none in the business in Boston surpass the "Mazeppa Sign Company," F. F. Applequist, manager. The work turned out here is A1 in every feature of merit, while the prices prevailing are maintained at the very lowest figures consistent therewith, and all orders are executed in the most expeditious and excellent manner, satisfaction being guaranteed in every instance. This thriving enterprise was started in 1879 by J. L. Gannon and the present proprietor, who conducted it up to about one year ago, when they were succeeded by the present proprietor. The premises occupied as shop, etc., are commodious and well equipped and half a dozen or more expert hands are employed. Sign and ornamental painting of every description is done in the highest style of the art at short notice, special attention being given to hall and interior decorating. Mr. Applequist, who is sole proprietor and manager, is of Swedish birth but has lived in this city since early childhood. He is a practical and skillful workman himself, of many years' experience.

BUNKER LAUNDRY & TOWEL SUPPLY, Monroe & Conley, Proprietors, No. 34 Hawkins Street.—Boston is the centre of manufacturing and commercial industries which characterize New England, and here new enterprises, unique and useful, are continually arising and contributing to the sum total of the conveniences and comforts of the people. An apt illustration of this is furnished by the Bunker Laundry & Towel Supply concern doing business at No. 34 Hawkins Street, and of which Messrs. Monroe & Conley are the proprietors. This enterprising and prosperous house was founded in 1886 by Mr. George W. Bunker, hence its title; and in 1887 he was succeeded in the business by the present proprietors. The business is a novel one, and is one of usefulness to workingmen. The firm laundry overalls and jumpers and furnish one clean towel for fifteen cents per week, or a jumper and apron with one clean towel for ten cents per week. They also furnish one suit of overalls and one clean towel for twenty-five cents per week, or one jumper and apron, with towel, for twenty cents per week. The firm keep all articles in reasonable repair, put on buckles and buttons and sew up all rips free of charge. They have an excellent system for collecting and delivering, and one that does not interfere with the men's time or make it objectionable to their employers. The firm have two teams and seven hands in service, and a roomy laundry, equipped with the newest and most improved laundry machinery, and provided with steam power. The business is conducted with energy, push and reliability, and a large trade connection has been established not only in Boston, but in Providence, Lynn, Hyde Park and other suburban towns. Mr. George A Munroe is a native of New Hampshire and Mr. Conley was born in Maine. They are to be congratulated upon the success of their commercial venture.

C. D. STONE & COMPANY, Grocers, Nos. 95 and 97 Chambers Street.—For fine groceries at moderate prices we would strongly recommend the public to patronize the large and fully stocked store of Messrs. C. D. Stone & Co. Mr. Stone is a native of New Hampshire who early in life became connected with this important branch of trade, and about fifteen years ago embarked in business upon his own account. He was located at Nos. 99 to 105 Chambers Street but has recently removed to Nos. 95 and 97, a splendid modern plate glass front store, 38x85 feet in dimensions, and which he has furnished in a bright and attractive manner, rendering it without exception one of the finest in the city. Messrs. Stone & Co. make a specialty of fresh crop teas, select coffees, pure sugars, spices and condiments, the best grades of fancy patent flour, all kinds of farinaceous goods, green and dried fruits, and one of the choicest stocks of canned fruits, vegetables, fish, meats, etc., in Boston. Mr. Stone handles those brands only which are put up by honorable and responsible packers, and guarantees quality. In all his immense stock, the prices compare favorably with those quoted elsewhere. He buys direct in large lots from producers, packers and importers and doing such a heavy trade, can put prices where they are a positive attraction to the public.

FISHER & FAIRBANKS, Importers, Proprietors of Fairbanks' Rock Cordials, Etc., No. 19 Exchange Street.—Messrs. R. B. Fisher and C. A. Fairbanks bring a wide range of practical experience to bear, and since they established this house fifteen years ago, have developed an extensive and influential patronage. The premises occupied comprise a spacious store and basement about 25x100 feet in area, fully fitted up with every appliance and convenience for the systematic conduct of the business. They also have offices in New York at No. 79 Warren Street, and in Chicago at No. 51 Wabash Avenue. Messrs. Fisher and Fairbanks are proprietors of the famous Fairbanks' rock cordials, and deal largely in imported and domestic champagnes, Renault & Co.'s Cognac brandies, Geneva and Gold Seal gin, Misa and Amontillado sherries, imported and domestic bay rum, case goods of every kind, and foreign and domestic cigars. They make a specialty of Hermitage and Old Crow whiskies in bond or free. They import direct from the most celebrated European houses, and offer advantages in prices very difficult to be secured elsewhere. Mr. Fisher is a native of Vermont, while Mr. Fairbanks was born in Mass. Their trade now extends throughout all sections of the United States and Canada and is constantly increasing.

TRACEY, Photographer, No. 913 Washington Street.—The steady and remarkable progress made in photography is one of the notable features that mark this age of progress in which we live. The improvement and advance made in this direction since daguerre introduced the process of retaining likenesses by chemical action on sensitive plates, half a century ago, is nothing less than marvelous. And now even moving objects, and it is understood, are reproduced to the life instantaneously. A South End artist who has won an excellent reputation for skill in this line is Thomas Tracey, whose finely appointed and well equipped studio is located at No. 913 Washington Street, corner Pleasant, and who ranks among the foremost exponents of the photographic art in this section of the city. Mr. Tracey, who is yet a young man, was born at Halifax, N. S., whence he moved to New York and learned his profession in the Metropolis under the tutelage of the best artists. He is a practical and expert photographer, of ten years' experience, and is a thorough master of his art in all its branches. He established himself in business here in October, 1887, and by the superiority of his work, soon acquired recognition and patronage, gaining in a short time a large and flattering trade. Mr. Tracey occupies commodious, handsome and well ordered quarters, and has in service all the latest improved apparatus, appliances and general appurtenances to a first-class photo-gallery, including the instantaneous process, while seven competent assistants are employed. Everything in the line of photography is executed in the highest style of the art at popular prices, fine portrait work being a specialty, while portraits are copied in oil, water-color, India ink, crayon and pastelle in the most expeditious and excellent manner, the pictures leaving this establishment being A1 in every feature of merit, in fidelity to original or copy, in design, execution, shading and finish.

BOYLE BROTHERS, South End Furniture and Carpet House, Nos. 851 to 855 Washington Street.—This business was established in 1878 by Messrs. T. F. Boyle and E. J. Boyle both of whom are thoroughly practical men, fully conversant with every detail of the furniture trade and the requirements of patrons. The premises occupied comprise a spacious three-story and basement building 40x125 feet in area. The various salesrooms are fully stocked with a superior assortment of parlor, chamber, dining-room, hall, drawing-room and kitchen furniture, the parlor sets being obtainable in all the latest and choicest styles of upholstery. In the carpet department are the finest patterns in Axminsters, Wiltons, velvets, Brussels, ingrains, etc., which are offered to customers at the lowest possible prices. Various patterns of oil cloths, linoleum, cocoa mats and matting can always be found here, all quoted at astonishingly low figures. Purchasers intending to buy for cash or desiring a liberal credit can always at this establishment obtain the lowest prices and the best terms. Messrs. Boyle Brothers make a specialty of completely furnishing any sizes of houses or flats, and promptly furnish estimates when required. Both partners were born in Boston. They have a branch store and employ upwards of 500 men who carry their merchandise throughout New England and sell their goods on the installment plan.

WILLIAM P. CHASE, Book-Lettering and Stamping a Specialty, No. 383 Washington Street.—Mr. Chase has been engaged in this business for the past twenty years and has achieved a fine reputation for the artistic skill he has invariably displayed in all the work he has turned out. He has occupied his present commodious premises for the past ten years, comprising office and workroom on the second floor, 25x40 feet in dimensions, finely equipped with every appliance in the trade. Five to ten men are employed in the establishment in book lettering and stamping of every description, a specialty of the house being the marking of names on books, albums, traveling bags, pocket books, trusses, silks, satins, ribbons, society badges, etc. The trade in this line is very extensive extending all over New England, while in Boston a large portion of the work is executed for the various book stores of the city. No one can claim superior skill in this branch of trade with Mr. Chase who has devoted nearly all his life to its pursuit and who was the recipient of a medals and diplomas at the fair of the Massachusetts Mechanic Association for book lettering and stamping.

THE METROPOLIS OF NEW ENGLAND.

S. M. SPENCER, Stencil and Stamp Works, No. 112 Washington Street.—There is perhaps not one among the many well equipped and flourishing stencil and stamp works in this city that is more widely known than the popular and prosperous concern of S. M. Spencer, No. 112 Washington Street, whose productions are in steady and increasing demand, not only throughout the New England States, but also in the West and South, with some export also to the South American countries. It is, in all respects, one of the leading, largest and most responsible establishments devoted to this particular branch of industrial activity in Boston, and has a large, active and growing business. The articles produced here are of exceptional merit, and for efficacy, reliability and general excellence are unsurpassed by any device of the kind yet placed on the market. As is amply attested by the enduring hold the stamps, stencils, presses, etc., manufactured in this concern have gained on public favor everywhere. Mr. Spencer who is a gentleman in the prime of life, active and energetic, is a practical and expert workman himself, of many years' experience, and is a thorough master of the art in all its branches. He established in business in Vermont his native state) upward of a quarter of a century ago, moving to Boston in 1872, and has occupied the present commodious quarters about ten years. The business premises occupy an office and salesroom on second floor, with five rooms used as shops on the third floor, while a dozen or so skilled hands are employed. The productions include everything in the line of steel and rubber stamps, seal presses, dies, stencil, brass labels, automatic numbering machines, check protectors, key tags, checks, badges, gilding, etc., a large and complete assortment being constantly kept in stock, while stamps, stencil, presses, dies, letters and kindred devices are made to order likewise in the most expeditious and excellent manner. A fine seventy-six page illustrated catalogue is published, giving exact cuts and price list, the same being sent free to any address on application.

COTTON & HALEY, Commission Merchants, and General Importers, No. 138 State Street.—This firm are widely known as Commission Merchants and General Importers, receiving sugar, molasses and West India goods from producers and shippers in the West Indies, and exporting ice and general merchandise to various foreign ports. The foundation of this business was laid some fifty years ago, by Mr. D. P. Cotton in the West Indies. In 1870 he came to Boston with Mr. Chas. L. Haley, and founded the house here, still retaining an extensive business connection at Barbadoes and Trinidad, which has been continued down to the present time. The original founders have both been dead for a number of years, and the house is now controlled by Messrs. W. D. and N. H. Cotton, sons of the original senior partner. These gentlemen have been trained in the business from their youth up, and their name is an honored and familiar one on both sides the water. As commission merchants their connections are wide-spread and influential, their resources are ample and abundant, and their facilities are unsurpassed, enabling them to fill the largest export orders for merchandise of all kinds, and affording the best possible market for the prompt disposal of consignments of sugar, molasses and other West India products. They are one of the best and most favorably known Boston firms trading between this city and the West Indies, and have built up an influential and prosperous trade throughout New England, New York and other portions of the Union. The Messrs. Cotton were born in Boston.

P. D. WHEATLAND, Stock Broker, No. 40 State Street.—Among the prominent and popular stock brokers of Boston is Mr. P. D. Wheatland, who occupies spacious and well-equipped quarters at No. 40 State Street. This gentleman is a member of the Boston Stock Exchange, and has been established as a broker here since early in 1887. He handles stocks of all kinds, and represents the interests of S. Morris Pryor & Company, of New York, in this city. He has built up an extensive and influential connection with the principal cities throughout the Union, and is entrusted by many parties with important commissions for investment which receive at all times the most careful consideration. Mr. Wheatland buys and sells all securities dealt in at the Boston, New York and Chicago Stock Exchanges at lowest rates of commission permitted by those organizations, obtains continuous reports of the markets, executes all orders promptly, and placing all transactions upon a thoroughly substantial and satisfactory basis. His office is connected by private wire with New York and Chicago, and orders for the purchase or sale of stocks are filled by him in quantities to suit purchasers, from ten to five thousand shares. In this system of business houses are limited to the amount of margin deposited, while profits are unlimited, and all the advantages of the market obtainable by members of the different exchanges are here offered to clients as though they were present on the floor of the exchange themselves. Full quotations are received by ticker, and all sources of information are searched as a guide to the market. This office is open alike to the man of wealth and to the man of limited means, and each receives the same consideration at the hands of the management. Mr. Wheatland is a native of Boston, and a young man of large experience on change, of high reputation and standing in financial circles, and has built up a business in this and other leading cities of the Union that clearly shows his energy, ability and influence.

NORRIS & CORTHELL, Insurance Agents and Brokers, No. 25 Congress Street.—Of the numerous responsible insurance firms in the city of Boston, none stands higher in public confidence, or has received a larger measure of recognition from the leading merchants, manufacturers and property owners of this community, than that of Messrs. Norris & Corthell. This business was established in 1859 by Mr. W. H. Norris, who conducted it till 1861, when on the breaking out of the Civil War he enlisted in the Union Army. He continued in the service till the capture of General Lee's army at Richmond in 1865, when he returned to Boston, and bought his brother's insurance business, which had been founded in 1858. In 1878 Mr. J. K. Corthell became a partner, the firm being known by the style and title of "Norris & Corthell." This reliable firm represents the following first-class American and British companies, viz: Niagara of New York; American of Newark, N. J.; London & Lancashire of London; Commercial Union of London; Traders of Chicago; Providence Washington of Providence, R. I.; Union of Philadelphia; Williamsburg City of Brooklyn, N. Y.; Sun of London; Standard Accident of Detroit, and several others. As practical and experienced underwriters Messrs. Norris & Corthell offer substantial inducements to the public, including low rates and liberally drawn policies, while all losses sustained are equitably adjusted and promptly paid through this popular agency. The firm are prepared to take entire charge of the insurance of large mill, factory and warehouse properties, dwellings, stores, etc., placing and distributing risks among sound companies only, renewing policies when expired, and generally relieving the business community of all care and trouble in this important respect. Mr. Norris was born in New Hampshire, while his partner Mr. Corthell is a native of Hingham, Mass. Their long experience in insurance matters is a guarantee that they fully understand every detail, and offer the best possible indemnity to patrons furnished by the most responsible insurance companies in existence.

C. EDWARD FRENCH, Distiller of N. E. Rum, Copper Distilled, No. 154 State Street.—The oldest established and most noted house in the city of Boston actually engaged in distillation of New England Rum, is that of Mr. C. Edward French. This business originated upwards of a century ago was founded by one of the French family. In 1845 Mr. Wm. E. French became sole proprietor, and was succeeded in 1878 by Mr. James H. French. Eventually in 1885 Mr. C. Edward French assumed the management. The distillery, which is admirably equipped with the latest improved apparatus and appliances is in Essex Street. The capacity of the distillery is upwards of 600,000 gallons annually. The New England Copper Distilled Rum produced at this famous distillery is unrivaled for purity, quality, flavor and uniform excellence, and is a general favorite with the trade and public. Mr. French fills orders promptly and carefully at the lowest ruling prices, and his trade is by no means confined to the United States, but extends to Europe, Africa and Australia. Personally, Mr. French is a native of Boston, where he is too widely known in the trade to require any comments at our hands.

REVERSIBLE COLLAR CO., Manufacturers of "Linene" Collars and Cuffs, and all kinds of Cloth-backed Paper, coffee, No. 27 Kilby Street, Factory, Cambridge.—One of the most practical, useful, and highly appreciated inventions of the age is that of the methods of manufacturing the world famous "Linene" collars and cuffs, the handsomest, most durable and economical articles of their kind in existence. The late Mr. George K. Snow was the inventor of the process of making "Linene" collars and all kinds of cloth-backed paper, and in 1862, in partnership with several capitalists he began the manufacture of the above goods. They were an instant success and the demand of the trade grew so rapidly as to tax their facilities to the utmost. Eventually in 1866, the important interests involved were duly capitalized under the appropriate title of the Reversible Collar Company, with a capital that is now $250,000. A large factory was erected in Cambridge, fitted up with special machinery and appliances and where the manufacture of "Linene" collars and cuffs, Gray's moulded collars, and collars and cuffs for the ladies are produced upon the most extensive scale, upwards of seventy-five hands being employed. The decease of Mr. Snow occurred in 1885, and he was succeeded in the presidency by Mr. Phineas Pierce, a capitalist and merchant of the highest standing and who is of the old and widely known house of Messrs. Marsh Bros. & Pierce, wholesale dry goods. Under his able guidance the company has made substantial progress and achieved a great success. Mr. Eben Denton is the treasurer, and general manager. A business man of sound judgment and marked executive ability, he brings ripe experience to bear in this line, and in the faithful discharge of his duties has permanently maintained the high standard of excellence of the company's product. "Linene" collars cannot be distinguished from the finest linen collars. They are of the highest finish, never wilt in warm weather, are easy, handsome and stylish, and being reversible wear so long that it is to the economical advantage of every one to wear them in preference to linen. Every traveler and all residents in the country prefer these collars and city people find them a great saving in laundry bills and annoyance. The company sell all over the world and have a resident wholesale agent in Liverpool, whence the goods find their way all over Great Britain and Europe. The company manufacture cloth-backed paper for lithographers, draughtsmen, printers, etc.

PETER McINTYRE & CO., Wholesale Grocers, and Dealers in Flour and Provisions, Nos. 196 Commercial and 171 Fulton Streets.—One of the oldest established and most reliable houses in Boston, actively engaged in the wholesale grocery trade, is that of Messrs. Peter McIntyre & Co. This business was established seventy-five years ago. After various changes the present firm was organized, the copartners being Messrs. Peter McIntyre and J. Harvey McIntyre. Mr. Peter McIntyre, who is now seventy years old, has been connected with this house for the last forty-eight years. The premises occupied comprise a spacious floor and basement 20x125 feet in dimensions, fully stocked with a well selected and choice assortment of teas, coffees, spices, dried fruits, canned goods of every description, sugars, syrups, and everything pertaining to the staple and fancy grocery trade. The firm make a specialty of dealing in flour and provisions and of supplying steamships, sailing vessels, yachts, etc., with stores. Only the purest and best goods are handled, and the trade of the house now extends throughout all sections of New England, while the prices quoted in all cases are as low as those of any other first-class house in the trade. Mr. Peter McIntyre was born in Scotland, but has resided in the United States the greater part of his life—his son Mr. J. Harvey McIntyre, however, is a native of Boston.

DANIEL FRANK & CO., Imported and Domestic Cigars, No. 10 Post Office Square.—The initials "N. S." constitute the most valuable trade-mark known to the cigar trade, and the vast demand for these reliable and fragrant goods has resulted in the development of one of the greatest manufacturing interests of the kind in the world, while Boston is materially benefited as being the depot of supplies for these popular cigars. Their manufacture was begun by Mr. N. Samuel, who established his business here in 1869 and was succeeded in 1884 by Messrs. Daniel Frank & Co., the present proprietors, who occupy spacious quarters at No. 10 Post Office Square. This firm are widely prominent and popular as wholesale and retail dealers in imported and domestic cigars, and their house is known and honored by the trade and the public in this city and throughout New England as the depot for the genuine N. S. cigars. They also handle the Sublime. And a number of private brands of known excellence, besides Key West cigars in vast quantities, and fine Havanas which they import direct and supply to the trade and the public at terms and prices which defy successful competition. The management has made a close study of the public want, and has in stock by far the most varied and comprehensive assortment of fine goods, in all styles, sorts and makes, to be found in this city, so as to be prepared to satisfactorily meet the most exacting requirements. In a word, this firm make their customers' interests their own, and dealers feel safe in buying from such an honorable, responsible house realizing that they best meet the wants of their own trade, and can in that way permanently develop a profitable business in their section against all odds; while consumers patronize this place because they are made happier by so doing. Mr. Frank, the active member of this firm and moving spirit of the enterprise, is a native of the City of Baltimore, a resident of Boston for the past ten years, still in the early prime of life, and a true type of American pluck, enterprise, true grit and thoroughly reliability.

WM. G. ANDERSON, Manufacturer of Metallic Swivel Window Screens, Automatic Window Sash Balances, Etc., No. 178 Washington Street.—Mr. Anderson is the inventor and patentee of Anderson's metallic swivel window screens, automatic window sash balances, sash starter, combining lifter, closer and lock and patent combined felt and rubber weather strips. Mr. Anderson's automatic window sash balance and combined felt and rubber parting beads, acting as weather strips, prevent any binding or shaking of the sashes, keeping out wind, dust, etc. By pressing a spring lock the sash immediately opens to the top, and by drawing down will stay, and when closed is self-locking and burglar-proof, and will last for years. It does away with weights, cords, pulleys, lifts, sash-fasts, and weather strips, and costs less than the old method. Needs only to be seen to be appreciated. These sash balances are fitted with patent steel spiral springs (three-eighths to one-half inch in diameter), which will last indefinitely and are guaranteed in every case. The heavier the sash the better. Price, from $1 to $5 per window. Anderson's sash starter, combining lifter, closer, and lock, combines with a window sash a simple starting lever of great power, that will enable any person, with but slight exertion, to start and lift a heavy sash, or to start a sash that has become wedged or frozen in,—it being well known to housekeepers and others that window sashes will, from a great number of causes, bind after having been closed. This device may also be used as part of sash-fastener. Mr. Anderson has been awarded medals for his inventions at the Massachusetts Charitable Mechanic Association. Mr. Anderson originally founded this business in Worcester, Mass. In 1880 he removed to Boston.

F. H. SUMNER & CO., Bankers and Brokers, No. 7 Exchange Place.—One of the most staunch and sagacious among the younger firms engaged in financial and stock transactions in Boston is that of F. H. Sumner & Co., bankers and brokers and members of the Consolidated Stock and Petroleum Exchange, at No. 7 Exchange Place, who by close study of the market coupled with energy, ability and thoroughly honorable business methods, have succeeded in establishing an excellent standing, and acquiring a large, active and highly gratifying patronage numbering among their clientele many of the solid citizens of Boston and vicinity. This prosperous business was established in 1885 by the present senior member. They occupy finely appointed and well equipped offices, having in service all necessary appurtenances, including private wire to New York while Purcell, Hagaman & Co., of the latter city, represent the firm as correspondents. A general banking and brokerage business is transacted, stocks, bonds, securities, grain and provisions being bought and sold on commission, and carried on margin, and orders are executed both on the Boston and New York markets.

MASON & CO., Coin Dealers, No. 255 Washington street.— The oldest coin dealers and publishers in the United States are Messrs. Mason & Co., who occupy spacious and commodious quarters at No. 255 Washington Street, in this city. The active member of the firm and moving spirit of the enterprise, Mr. E. L. Mason, established the business originally in 1860, in the city of Philadelphia, removing to Boston in 1883. He is widely known as an authority on coins, and as the publisher of the first coin price catalogue and coin collectors' magazine in the United States; also a beautifully bound and complete illustrated history of the coins of the world, containing ancient Greek, Roman and Jewish coinages; early and modern coins of Asia and Africa; Anglo-American, American Colonial, and continental issues; pattern pieces, experimental issues, and coinages of the United States; 120 pages, illustrated with over 1700 fac similes, collated and arranged by Mason & Co.; to which is added an appendix by E. L. Mason, (numismatist,) presenting an authenticated statement of the coinage of the late Southern Confederacy at New Orleans, in 1861, with copies of papers on file in the confederate archives at Washington, and fac-similes of the coins

issued. Price $5.00; to subscribers of Mason's Illustrated Coin Collectors' Magazine, $3.50. The magazine mentioned was established by Mr. Mason in 1867, is published monthly, price twenty-five cents per copy, or two dollars per annum. A splendid assortment of coins are here exhibited, including ancient Greek and examples in all metals from Athens, Thebes, Argos, Agrigentium, Syracuse, Crotona, Illyria, Egypt, Macedonia, Syria, Judea, etc.; some issued under republican, others imperial and regal governments, with historical tyrants everywhere, and the coins varying

in sizes from the Hemi-obolus to Tetradrachm in silver, one fourth to four staters in gold, and from the most minute to the largest size in bronze. The prices are the most surprising part of the exhibition, for coins, so many centuries old, many of them can be had for ten cents to one dollar each, and seldom do any but the gold coins call for more than ten dollars. The "tribute penny" of the Bible (a Denarius of Tiberius Cæsar) which was offered to test the Saviour's loyalty, can be bought here in fine condition at two dollars to three dollars almost as perfect as when coined nearly 1900 years ago. The bronze coins of the Roman emperors from Augustus Cæsar to Constantine the Great and his family, can be bought at fifteen cents to fifty cents each; in fact, they are cheaper here than when found, as a rule. The rare coins of the ancient Hebrews are also shown. The Pine-tree and Oak-tree shillings are the most common of the Massachusetts silver coins, while the Willow-tree is the rarest of the series. Many interesting coins of the colonial period are shown, including the famous gold doubloon of New York, the "King of the Colonials." The coin price book of sixteen pages, showing buying and selling prices of this firm for coins, is sent to any address on receipt of twenty-five cents in stamps.

H. E. ABBOTT, Insurance Agency; offices, No. 2 Advertiser Building.—One of the most popular, ablest and successful general insurance agents in Boston and New England is Mr. H. E. Abbott, of No. 2 Advertiser Building. The extensive business conducted by him was founded in 1868, and has had a rapid and substantial growth. As agent, Mr. Abbott represents the most desirable fire, life, accident and marine insurance companies with which to do business. He is the authorized agent for the Royal Queen, Southern and Sun Fire Office, all of London, England; British America, of Canada; the Hanover and Niagara, of New York; the Fire Association and Pennsylvania, of Philadelphia; the National Fire, of Hartford; the Traders, of Chicago; the Dorchester Mutual, of Boston, the Quincy Mutual (both paying dividends of sixty per cent.); and the old Worcester and Middlesex Mutuals (paying dividends of seventy per cent.). These companies present an admirable array, and policy holders in any of them feel an absolute security. Mr. Abbott is prepared to promptly place the largest lines of insurance at lowest rates, the risks being well distributed among responsible companies. He controls the insuring of desirable lines of business and residential property in Boston and vicinity, and has become deservedly popular with our leading property owners. As a matter of fact, Mr. Abbott brings good fortune both to the companies he represents, as well as the insured. He had the agency of the Royal, Hanover and Pennsylvania companies for over ten years, writing hundreds of policies annually, with premiums from thirty to forty thousand dollars during the time, without a single loss in either company. Such an enviable record is, we believe, unparalleled in the history of New England fire insurance. Mr. Abbott represents the Equitable Life Assurance Company of New York, the most powerful in the world, which writes the most liberal policies in all schemes, from the old-time life to ten and twenty years tontine, and whose heavy dividends practically give a man insurance on his life for next to nothing. The company's popularity is deservedly very great among the shrewd and conservative citizens of Boston. Mr. Abbott is an active and respected member of the Board of Fire Insurance Underwriters and of the Board of Insurance Brokers, and is a responsible, popular agent, of the highest standing, and who refers to leading firms as to his ability, and honorable and efficient methods in the vitally important fields of fire and life insurance. Mr. Abbott also transacts a large and successful real estate business in Brookline, where he has resided for the last fifteen years.

E. A. BOARDMAN, Wine Merchant, No. 2 Post Office Avenue (rear of No. 22 Congress Street).—A carefully prepared review of the general business interests of Boston, reveals the existence of some noteworthy establishments many of which, although not widely known outside of the city and environs, have been in prosperous existence long enough to merit the distinctive, veritable landmarks. Among the places referred to may be named the time-honored and deservedly popular store of E. A. Boardman, the well known wine merchant, which is eligibly located at No. 2 Post Office Avenue (rear of No. 22 Congress street), and which, for nearly sixty years, has maintained an enduring hold on public favor. It is one of the oldest and best-kept establishments of the kind in this city, and fully sustains to-day its old-time reputation for fine goods and reliability—none better in Boston—while its patronage grows apace with years. Only A1 goods are handled, and patrons can rely upon getting a very superior article, courteous attention and satisfactory treatment in every instance here. The business was established in 1871 by E. A. Boardman, the elder, who conducted the same up to 1868, when, owing to his death, which occurred at this period, it passed into the hands of his son and successor, who has since continued it with uninterrupted success. The store is compact, ample and neatly appointed, several competent assistants being employed, while a large first-class stock is constantly carried, including the choicest brandy of imported and native wines, brandies, champagnes gins, liquors, cordials, rums, whiskies and bottled goods of every description, Mr. Boardman, being a direct importer. The establishment maintains both a wholesale and retail department, club and family trade being a specialty, and altogether, a large and influential patronage is received.

J. H. FLITNER & CO., General Commission Merchants, Ship Brokers, Etc., Nos. 290 Commercial and 175 Fulton Streets.—An old established and prominent firm in Boston, engaged as general commission merchants, ship-brokers and dealers in ship stores and chandlery is that of Messrs. J. H. Flitner & Co., whose offices and salesrooms are located at Nos. 290 Commercial and 175 Fulton Streets. Mr. Flitner engaged in this business in 1862 at his present stand as clerk with Mr. Jos. J. Durham who sold out to Messrs. Pitcher, Fuller & Co. in 1864. Mr. Flitner being admitted to the firm as junior member, in 1867. Mr. Fuller retiring from the firm, the new firm was organized under the style of Pitcher, Flitner & Co., which continued until 1876, when J. H. Flitner became sole proprietor, conducting the business under the style and title of J. H. Flitner & Co. Mr. Flitner is well qualified to represent shipping interests in the port of Boston, of both vessels and merchandise and to make advances on the latter, when required. He attends promptly and carefully to the chartering and dispatching of vessels, collects freights, and acts as agent for the owners, and deals largely in ship stores and chandlery. Mr. Flitner was born in Maine, but has resided in Boston for the last twenty-five years. He is a member of the Chamber of Commerce, and is highly regarded in business circles for his energy, promptness and integrity. The liberal methods of this house render it a desirable one with which to deal, and those forming business relations with them will obtain all the advantages of their experience.

GEORGE E. LITTLEFIELD, Dealer in Old, Rare, and Curious Books, Genealogies, Etc., No. 67 Cornhill Street.—Mr. George E. Littlefield has become nationally celebrated as one of the leading and most enterprising dealers in old, rare and curious books. Since establishing in business in 1868, he has bought and sold many thousands of the most valuable works treating of American history and genealogy, biography, travels, theology, science, etc., and his store is a veritable treasure house to students, collectors and librarians. Mr. Littlefield is a recognized authority as to the values of old Americana, and has handled more of these cherished old products of the press than any other dealer. In genealogies and histories he is specially strong, and the attention of all interested is directed to his most interesting and very complete priced catalogues, which contain descriptions of hundreds of the rarest and most curious books now in the market. Mr. Littlefield purchases libraries or smaller collections of books, appraises values, etc., and secures for his patrons almost any book in existence. Thousands of volumes, long out of print, can be had through him, and he does a large trade with the great libraries throughout the United States, also leading private collectors. He likewise sells to the trade. He enjoys special facilities for filling difficult orders and for picking up rare and valuable old books. Mr. Littlefield is a native of Boston, a graduate of Harvard University, and has here developed the leading business in his line. This store is the daily resort of old students, and of men interested in the collection of old books of all descriptions.

GEORGE W. HAWES, Manufacturer of the Paris Adjustable Suspender, Shoulder Braces, and all kinds of Elastic Goods, No. 71 Sudbury Street.—The leading manufacturer in New England of fine webbing and all elastic goods for ladies' and gentlemen's wear, is Mr. George W. Hawes. The business was established by him in 1875. Mr. Hawes, a native of Randolph, Mass., and long a respected resident of Boston, brings to bear every possible qualification. He has fitted up his factory with the latest improved machinery and employs an average force of twelve hands in the manufacture of his justly celebrated Paris adjustable suspender, ladies' and gents' London and Crown shoulder braces, and all kinds of elastic goods for ladies' and gentlemen's wear. The materials used are the best, while the workmanship is of the most skilled and perfect character, finish elaborate, and his brands of suspenders and shoulder braces are handled and eagerly sought by the best class of men's furnishing and fancy goods stores in our large cities. Mr. Hawes manufactures largely for the trade, producing from sample in any quantity, the exact style of suspenders, braces, abdominal supporters, etc., at prices which quality considered cannot be duplicated elsewhere. Suspenders are mounted for the trade in the most careful and substantial manner. Mr. Hawes is a worthy member of Boston industrial circles.

J. W. BAILEY & SONS, Wholesale and Retail Dealers in Mouldings, Brackets, Stair Rails and Posts, and Building Trimmings of all Kinds, No. 14 Charlestown Street.—This firm have a wide reputation as extensive wholesale and retail dealers in mouldings, brackets, wood mantels, stair rails and posts, newels, balusters, gutters, conductors and building trimmings of all kinds. The business was originally established in 1873, by Messrs. E. W. Bailey & Co., who were succeeded by Messrs. Jotham W. and Edward S. Bailey, under the firm name of J. W. Bailey & Son, in January, 1875. The firm of J. W. Bailey & Sons was organized January 1, 1886, by the admission of Mr. Willard L. Bailey to partnership. The honored senior partner, Mr. Jotham W. Bailey, died on November 4th last, at his home in North Scituate, where he was born May 5, 1832, and where he was known as a prominent and useful citizen. His two sons have since continued the business under the old firm name. The business premises consist of a substantial building containing six floors and a basement, 25x85 feet in dimensions, giving ample accommodations for handling and storing the immense and diversified stock that is here carried. This firm are Boston agents for the Mankey Decorative Company, manufacturers of fancy wood carving, of Williamsport, Pa.; and also for the Fred A. Taft Company, manufacturers of wood ornaments, of Hartford, Ct. The stock includes also pressed corner blocks and ornaments which, while possessing the attractiveness of carved wood, are much less expensive, and have a standard reputation in the market; also, marbleoid mantel shelves, metallic conductors and other specialties which bear such a character for utility and usefulness as to command universal attention and general patronage. These goods are in heavy and permanent demand wherever once introduced, and the trade of the house is large, first-class and influential in New England, and throughout the west and south, while a fine growing export trade is enjoyed with England and other foreign countries. The Messrs. Bailey are Massachusetts men by birth and training, standing deservedly high in business and trade circles.

CHARLES W. HOLDEN, General Insurance Agent, No. 42 Congress Street.—Mr. Holden established this business in 1867, and during the intervening period has developed a connection of a very influential and superior character. He conducts a general life, fire, marine, accident, plate glass, and boiler insurance business, and represents the following first-class companies, viz:—The Merchants' Insurance Company, of Newark, N. J.; Washington Life, Fidelity and Casualty Company, of New York, etc. Persons about to cross the ocean and travel abroad, whether for business or pleasure, should not fail to secure an accident policy in the Fidelity before starting, it being but a trifling addition to the cost of the trip. A policy issued by this company insures against death or disabling injury, and is as effectual against the dangers of ocean or railway travel as a policy for same amount issued by a life insurance company, while it costs only about one-tenth as much. No medical examination is required. In fire insurance Mr. Holden offers substantial inducements and advantages to the public including low rates and liberally drawn policies, while all losses sustained are equitably adjusted and promptly paid through his agency. Mr. Holden is a popular member of the Boston Underwriters' Association.

NEW ENGLAND LOBSTER COMPANY, Nos. 268 and 270 Atlantic Avenue, G. L. Young, Manager.—Boston is the most important fish market in the country, and the business is conducted on an extensive scale by the New England Lobster Company. Mr. Lorenzo Richards established the business in April, 1887, and in September 1888, the present company was formed, which is under the immediate management of Mr. G. L. Young, whose experience as a dealer in sea food, extends over many years. Ample facilities are provided for the purposes of the business and all kinds of deep sea fish, lobsters, oysters and frozen herring and smelts are received daily and a large wholesale trade supplied. The company also smoke and pack for the trade, the celebrated Youngs' Finnen Haddies which have a standard reputation and are always in demand throughout the country. The business carried on is very extensive and Mr. Young who is a native of St. Johns, New Brunswick, holds a high position among those engaged in his special line of trade.

THE METROPOLIS OF NEW ENGLAND.

H. P. WEBSTER, Tea and Coffee, No. 90 Blackstone Street.—This is the headquarters for pulverized coffee and tea, and the only house putting up coffee hot from the roaster, ground to snuff like powder; also for Webster's Earthen Coffee and Tea Pot Combined, patented June 3, 1884; and for the finest grades of tea and coffee at both wholesale and retail. This deserving enterprise was inaugurated here in 1882, by Mr. Webster, who had been engaged for many years in the grocery trade and was thoroughly posted as to all its requirements and demands. He occupies a spacious and attractive salesroom, with a large storeroom in the rear, and carries a very extensive stock of tea and coffee at all times, which is always of standard excellence, guaranteed purity and direct from the importers, including the choicest selections of oolong, Japan, English breakfast and China green teas, old Government Java, Malt and Java, and Maltava coffees, which for strength, delicacy of aroma and purity, are unexcelled. The latest and leading specialty handled by Mr. Webster is Maltava coffee, a perfect liquid food and delicious table beverage combined, produced by skilfully blending the purest malt and the finest Java coffee, which is put up for Mr. Webster by Messrs. Chase & Sanborn, the well known coffee importers and roasters of this city, who placed it upon the market in June, 1888. Webster's compound Malt and Java coffee is another specialty of this house, which was copyrighted in 1888 by Mr. Webster, and is put up in two pound cans and for sale by first-class grocers everywhere. Webster's improved earthen coffee and tea pot, patented June 3, 1884, is made from Rockingham ware, has two percolators, one each for tea and coffee, no rust, and is just as clean as a glass tumbler. Coffee contains six per cent. tannaic acid; tea, fourteen per cent., and should not be made in tin or metal pots, but in earthen, to obtain its proper flavor. There is no doubt that, for bankers, lawyers, bookkeepers, and all who live by mental labor, coffee made by the percolating process is the best. There is also no doubt that the best way to make this is by the use of the Webster earthen percolating coffee pot, and the fine ground Java coffee. All goods sold by Mr. Webster are warranted pure. Mr. Webster was born in Plymouth, Mass., and settled in Boston in 1868. He is an eminently popular merchant, and enjoys a national reputation as the foremost representative of the tea and coffee trade at the Hub.

DAMM & PENKERT, Manufacturers of Clarinets, Flutes, Piccolos and Oboes, Nos. 39 and 48 Hanover Street.—Among those who are prominently identified with the manufacture of reed instruments, no firm in the city enjoy a higher reputation than that of Messrs. Damm & Penkert, successors to Messrs. Enders & Co., who established and had carried on the business for a period of five years previous to March last, the time it came under the control of the present firm. Messrs. Damm & Penkert are experienced, practical men and are doing a large business, manufacturing to order clarinets, flutes, piccolos and oboes, and have achieved a high reputation for the standard character of the instruments of their production, which are used extensively in bands and orchestras throughout all parts of the New England States, and are highly endorsed by musicians wherever introduced. The firm occupy a well equipped workshop and give special attention to repairing, and fully warrant their work which is done in the best manner at reasonable prices. Mr. August Damm and Mr. Fr. Penkert, the copartners, are Germans by birth. The former has been a resident of this country sixteen, and the latter eight years. They are both skilled musicians.

CHARLES F. McCARTHY, Manufacturing Jeweler, No. 75 Hanover Street.—The manufacture of jewelry is carried on quite extensively in Boston by a number of expert practical artisans, among whom will be found Mr. Charles F. McCarthy. He is an experienced, practical workman, and, during the two years he has been established in the business his success has been well merited. He has introduced many new, novel and unique designs in rings, watch chains, lodges, seals and various articles of jewelry, and manufactures for the trade and to order goods of any design or pattern. He occupies a very desirable location and is well equipped for doing all kinds of work and repairing in his line of business and has won an enviable reputation. He is a native of Charlestown.

P. CANNY, Importer and Dealer in West India Goods and Groceries, also Foreign and Domestic Liquors, Nos. 439, 441, 443 and 374 Hanover Street.—The establishments conducted by Mr. P. Canny, have long been celebrated as true representatives of what the possibilities of the modern grocery and liquor trade are. The enterprising proprietor has been established in business for a period of twenty-eight years, and has become widely known as an extensive importer and wholesale and retail dealer in West India goods and groceries, foreign and domestic liquors, tobaccos and cigars, and agent for XX and XXXX Amber and Pale ales and porter. His main headquarters are at Nos. 441 and 443 Hanover Street, where he occupies a spacious and commodious store and basement fitted up with an attractive sample room and well stocked with choice and desirable goods. There is nothing in either hemisphere that comes under the head of staple groceries or choice liquors that is not to be found here in its most attractive form, and pure, fresh and reliable as to quality. Mr. Canny's sound judgment in selecting his goods is well demonstrated by his choice importations of champagnes, clarets, ports, sherries and other desirable wines; besides liquors, cordials, cognac brandies, etc. As regards domestic staple groceries, the stock is comprehensive, covering the entire wide range, and including everything in its best quality. Such staples as teas, coffees and spices, so hard to obtain of the desired standard, are prominent specialties of this house. In the choicest brands of imported Havana cigars this house has an established reputation, and a fine hotel and private trade throughout the city. Sample rooms are also operated at Nos. 445 and 374 Hanover Street. Twelve clerks and salesmen contribute to the satisfactory operations of this extensive business. All orders are promptly and carefully filled; goods are delivered to any part of the city free of charge, and prices are placed at the lowest point of moderation.

FRANCIS SARGENT & CO., Manufacturers and Dealers in Carriages, Sleighs, Harness, Etc., No. 72 Sudbury Street.—One of the most noted and old established houses in Boston, successfully engaged in the manufacture and sale of carriages, sleighs, etc., is that of Messrs. Francis Sargent & Co., which was established fifty-six years ago by Francis Sargent, who sold carriages all over the United States, traveling with a team with a number of carriages hitched behind. He would often sell out his stock and return on horseback. In 1852 he opened his Boston Repository, and in 1862 admitted his son Mr. Elmer P. Sargent into partnership, the firm being known by the style and title of Francis Sargent & Co. In 1868 Mr. Elmer P. Sargent established a carriage factory at West Amesbury, and eventually in 1883 returned to his father's house, of which in 1887 he became sole proprietor, carrying on the business under the old firm name of Francis Sargent & Co. Mr. Francis Sargent, the founder, who has now retired from business, though seventy-eight years old is still hale and hearty. He is a strong republican and was born in West Amesbury, which is now called Merrimac. Mr. Elmer P. Sargent is now conducting the business with energy, and occupies a commodious store and basement which are fully stocked with a superior assortment of carriages, buggies, sleighs, harness, robes, mats and whips. He makes a specialty of the "Goddard Buggy" and deals only in the finest carriages and goods, while his prices in all cases are extremely moderate. Mr. Elmer P. Sargent is a native of Merrimac.

WILLIAM T. MURPHY, Watchmaker, Jeweler and Optician, No. 8 Washington Street.—Among the practical, expert watchmakers, jewelers and opticians in this city there are none more proficient in those branches than Mr. William T. Murphy, whose experience extends over many years. He occupies a very neatly, tastefully fitted up store and keeps on sale a general assortment of all kinds of American and foreign gold and silver watches, and also new style jewelry in rich elegant designs, and also clock-and-eye glasses and spectacles and optical goods generally. Mr. Murphy carefully cleans, repairs and regulates watches and clocks and repairs jewelry and spectacles and eye glasses, executing the work with the best manner with remarkable skill and judgment. He also lets glasses to suit the sight of the eye, and as an optician is pronounced one among the best in the city. He is a Bostonian by birth and well known to the community, where he has always lived until the past few years when he removed to Everett, an adjoining suburb.

READ, HAWKINS & CO., Flour and Produce, No. 148 State Street.—Few houses are so well equipped for successful and satisfactory service as that of Messrs. Read, Hawkins & Co., the well-known commission merchants in flour and produce, at No. 148 State Street, above State Street Block. The foundation of this business was laid in 1865 by Mr. Joseph Hawkins, who was succeeded by Messrs. Hawkins & Read, and in 1879 the present firm was organized by Messrs. E. M. Read, Joseph Hawkins and John M. Hawkins, all thoroughly experienced merchants, commanding a wide and valuable acquaintance in trade circles, and active, enterprising and capable to a marked degree. The result of their union has been the development of an extensive and important trade, broadly distributed throughout the entire New England States. The business premises comprise three spacious floors, admirably arrayed for handling and storing the choice and valuable stock here carried. The advantages possessed by the firm are of the best possible character, and their transactions are marked by prompt attention to every detail. The facilities and resources of the firm are admirable for reaching a desirable class of buyers, and the distinguishing policy of the house is the activity displayed in placing its consignments on the market and in making prompt and satisfactory returns. Every grade of flour is handled, including the best brands from Minnesota, Ohio, Indiana and Illinois, spring wheat and winter wheat flour being prominent specialties, while the best dairy and creamery butter from Vermont and other New England points is given special attention. In fact, in every department of the business the most perfect system prevails for insuring the highest returns, while the reputation of the house for fair and honorable dealing is an additional inducement to those requiring such service. Mr. Joseph Hawkins is a native of Vermont, while the other members of the firm are Massachusetts men by birth and training, and are all well and favorably known in the mercantile and trade circles of the city and throughout New England, as earnestly devoted to the interests of their patrons, and promoting the commerce of Boston and its good name abroad with activity, discrimination and success.

JAMES EMERY, JR., & CO., Wholesale Dealers in Fresh, Salt, Pickled and Smoked Fish, Nos. 17, 18, 20 and 34 Commercial Wharf.—Prominent among the most reliable and old established houses actively engaged in this growing trade, is that of Messrs. James Emery, Jr., & Co. The salting house of the firm is at Kittery Point, Maine, and the factory at Bunker's Wharf, East Boston. This business was established forty years ago by Brown, Seavey & Co., and was continued by them till July, 1887, when the present firm succeeded to the management. The premises occupied are spacious, and are fitted up with every appliance and convenience for the successful prosecution of the business. The firm deal largely in all kinds of fresh, salt, pickled and smoked fish, their goods being unrivalled for quality, reliability and uniform excellence, while the prices quoted are always regulated by the market. They make a specialty of fresh salmon. No firm offers more substantial inducements to the trade, and they number among their customers the principal fish mongers and dealers in all the chief cities of the country.

EASTERN LOBSTER CO., S. S. Poole, Manager, No. 42 Lewis Wharf.—The Eastern Lobster Company, S. S. Poole, manager, wholesale dealers in live, boiled and canned lobsters, is one of the largest establishments devoted to this particular branch of commercial activity in the city. This widely known and flourishing concern was established about ten years ago, and from the inception of the enterprise the business has grown apace, until now it is exceedingly large, extending to all parts of the United States. The business premises occupy two 25x75 feet floors and are well ordered and equipped with every facility and convenience for receiving, storage and shipping, while ten or more in help are employed. A carefully assorted and immense stock is constantly carried, including lobsters of every description, live, boiled, pickled and canned, receiving in barrels, boxes and bulk, and the trade of the concern, which is of a wholesale character exclusively, is fully commensurate with the name and standing of the house. Mr. Poole, who is the sole proprietor, is a native of Nova Scotia, but has resided in Boston for many years.

D. S. BURNHAM, Real Estate and Broker in Mortgages, Notes, Stocks, Etc., No. 267 Washington street.—But few conducting transactions in the realm of realty in Boston are more widely or honorably known than D. S. Burnham, the popular and responsible dealer in real estate, and broker in mortgages, notes and securities, whose office is conveniently situated at No. 267 Washington Street, opposite Water Street, Room 5. Mr. Burnham has been engaged in this line for more than twenty years, and by energy and judicious enterprise, coupled with strict integrity in all his dealings, he has built up a large and substantial connection, numbering among his extensive clientele some of the staunchest citizens in the community. He transacts a general real estate business, buying, selling and exchanging city and suburban property of all kinds, while mortgages are negotiated, and notes, stocks, bonds and other securities handled, also rents are collected likewise, and estates taken in charge, special attention being paid to the leasing, transfer and care of realty, while titles, deeds, leases, etc., are carefully and thoroughly examined and attested; in short, everything connected with the sale, purchase, conveyance and management of real estate is judiciously and reliably attended to. Mr. Burnham is a man in the prime of life, and a native of Ipswich, Mass., but has resided in this city many years. A gentleman of entire probity in his business relations, as well as sound judgment and thorough experience in all that appertains to real estate and kindred interests he enjoys the confidence and esteem of a wide circle of patrons throughout Boston and environs. Mr. Burnham is connected with a large number of charitable institutions, and has been overseer of the poor for the city of Boston for six years, and was chairman of the committee on the report on outdoor relief, a pamphlet which has been largely circulated throughout the country.

THE ALDEN FURNITURE SPRING CO., No. 53 Charlestown Street.—The Alden Furniture Spring Company is not only a prominent, but an old established enterprise, having been founded thirty years back by Mr. W. E. Alden, who is an expert spring maker of extended experience. In 1884 the concern assumed its present title, and the business is still under the able direction of Mr. Alden, whose reputation for producing the most elastic and durable springs put upon the market is of the highest in the trade. The premises occupied for business comprises three upper floors of a four-story building, 25x36 feet in dimensions. The manufacturing department is provided with the most efficient modern machinery and tools pertaining to the trade, and a number of experienced and skilled artisans are permanently employed. The company are also extensive dealers in excelsior, burlaps, casters, twine, tacks, moss, tow and other furniture makers' and upholsterers' supplies; and of these goods have at all times on hand heavy stocks, from which all orders can be immediately supplied at the lowest current rates. The trade is a brisk and growing one, and the business relations of the concern are of a most influential character. The leading manufacturers in the city and its surroundings are the patrons of the concern, whose standing in mercantile circles is an enviable one. Mr. Alden is a native and resident of the city.

CHARLES RUSSELL & CO., Wholesale Dealers in Boston and Kennebec River Ice, No. 92 State Street.—This firm have a national reputation as wholesale dealers in Boston and Kennebec River ice, and have been prominently established in the business since 1860. They operate extensive ice houses all through the state, also one on the Kennebec River. The firm gathers its crop of ice from the best sources of supply, and the stock can invariably be relied upon as being pure and free from all foreign matter. The ample and abundant resources, superior facilities for securing supplies, and intimate knowledge of the wants of the trade, possessed by this firm enable them to conduct the business under the most favorable auspices and upon the largest scale. They ship by cargo and car lots to all the principal points on the coast, and are in a position to offer inducements to the trade, as regards both superiority of stock and liberality of terms and prices, that challenge comparison and defy successful competition. Mr. Charles Russell, the active member of the firm, is a Massachusetts man by birth and training, of large practical experience and of deserved popularity in business circles.

J. HUBBARD & CO., Manufacturers and Proprietors of Hubbard's Deodorizer, and Germicide, No. 23 Court Street.— At last a long felt want has been filled by the inventive skill and ably directed investigations of Mr. J. Hubbard, who has in his wonderful Germicide, brought within reach of the world and of suffering humanity a sovereign preventative and remedy for a long chain of diseases, and the microbic and pestilential causes thereof. It was in 1885 that Mr. Hubbard perfected and first put his Germicide on the market. Its sales have rapidly grown and wherever introduced it is its own best advertisement. Hubbard's Vegetable Compound is the most powerful, yet benign and pleasant antiseptic known. It is absolutely free from poisonous substances, and is in its effects and results a marvelous power over disease and the causes thereof. It is in a word, the annihilator of the insidious and offensive emanations and germs, which everywhere infest the air and under certain favorable conditions seize hold of the system causing disease and death. Cleanliness of person, house and contents is powerless to stop the ravages of these disease germs as evidenced in the recent yellow fever epidemic, but with the invincible powers of Hubbard's compound, as thoroughly sprayed by Mr. Hubbard's improved Atomizer, the destruction of these germs is assured. In a sick-room, or for the purifying of sinks, waste pipes, urinals, washbasins, its marvelous powers instantly destroy all offensive odors, and germs, due to the active affinity of the ingredients forming the compound for atmospheric oxygen converting it into per-oxide of hydrogen, similar in character to ozone. Recollect this compound neutralizes that deadly enemy of the household and school—sewer gas; it purifies the air alike in private houses, schools and public institutions, hotels, restaurants and boarding houses, hospitals, etc. It is an absolute necessity in every house, and those interested should send to Mr. Hubbard for his descriptive circular, containing numerous testimonials from physicians and prominent citizens of Boston and New England. Here are a few of its special uses; invaluable to undertakers; in the operating and dissecting room; deodorizing offensive wounds and ulcers; driving out mosquitoes; for storage warehouse exterminating moths and bugs; for protecting furs, feathers, blankets, clothing, etc., from moths. As a remedy it promptly relieves and cures catarrh, hay fever, colds, sore throat, diphtheria, croup, whooping cough, bronchial pulmonary complaints, for rheumatism, neuralgia, headache, toothache, earache, cuts, wounds, scalds, burns, sores, bruises, bites of insects, etc., it has no equal, while it is the best eye water, when diluted, in existence. This remedy is sprayed on the parts affected; it supersedes all stomach drugging and painful applications and is at once a merciful remedy and a boon to humanity. It has the most enviable of reputations and the sincerest form of recognition of its sovereign merits is shown in the efforts of unscrupulous dealers to sell inferior and worthless compounds by declaring they are just like Hubbard's. The public should beware of imitations and use only the genuine. Mr. Hubbard was born in New Hampshire and has long been a popular and respected resident of Boston, a business man of integrity and energy and a keen and successful investigator in nature's storehouse of knowledge.

NATIONAL SUPPLY COMPANY, J. Brodie, Manager, Clothing, Dry Goods, Etc., on the credit system, No. 45 Temple Place.—The establishment of the National Supply Company at No. 15 Temple Place, is not only a credit to the intelligent enterprise of its management, but as the first of its kind marks an era in the business history of the city. In supplying the public with clothing, dry goods, etc., on the installment system this company is the recognized leader. The enterprising and popular manager, Mr. J. Brodie, early in life embarked in business in England, and on coming to Boston and foreseeing the advantages which such a system would afford to the great mass of the working classes, in 1885 inaugurated his present enterprise under the name of the National Supply Company. His premises, situated in the very business heart of the city, are spacious in size and perfect in convenience of arrangement. A choice stock of gentlemen's and youths' ready-made clothing of substantial make, in latest styles and patterns, is constantly kept on hand, and sold at current cash prices, and, in many cases, at lower prices than can be purchased elsewhere. To those who prefer custom made clothing this house offers the services of first-class tailors, who make goods on their order. A novel part of the system is the arrangement made with the leading business houses of the city in different lines of trade to furnish their patrons with anything they may select from their varied stocks, thus practically placing almost everything within the reach of those who choose to make use of their credit system, which requires a small payment down at the time of purchase, and a still smaller payment each week until the account is paid. The purchaser is thus enabled to get the best, at the time most needed, in the beginning of the season and to make payment in such a way that the expense is not felt as a burden or inconvenience. An immense business is done, the store being kept open evenings till eight o'clock for the benefit of its large number of patrons, who are found in every profession and vocation in life, and who reside not in the city only, but in all the suburban districts. Mr. Brodie is a gentleman who possesses all the elements necessary to the successful direction of the affairs of this progressive and popular house. His experience has made him intimately acquainted with the wants of the public in this direction. He follows a liberal, vigorous and pushing policy that insures his continued success and prosperity.

BEN. LEVY & CO., French Perfumers, No. 31 West Street.— Perfumery preparations have become a very important auxiliary to our present civilization and society, and no refined individuals at the present day, consider their toilet complete without the use of some standard preparation in the shape of a perfume. The house of Ben. Levy & Co., No. 31 West Street, has gained a wide-spread and excellent reputation for manufacturing and dealing only in the purest and most lasting perfumes, their goods and specialities being in great demand in all sections of the United States and Canada. Mr. Ben. Levy, who is sole proprietor, established this business in 1871. He makes a specialty of manufacturing at his laboratory, Levy's Parisian Cream, Levy's perline or liquid pearl and Levy's French cream. He makes a specialty of the Sublache face powder, which has received the highest testimonials from the prominent celebrities of the stage both in America and Europe. Levy's French Cream is a scientific beautifier. It is the result of long observation, careful experiments, has had the aid of the best French chemist and of a skillful skin doctor of Paris. This is stated that the ladies may have no fear of bad results following its use, as is the case of cheap catchpenny preparations, which have been forced upon the market. Levy's French Cream is not only harmless, but is positively beneficial. Mr. Levy has letters from Marie Roze Mapleson, the celebrated vocalist, Sarah Bernhardt, and other prominent artistes of the lyric and dramatic professions, endorsing its claims for recognition in the warmest terms. They do not consider their toilet complete without this article. The price is only $2.00 per bottle, or three bottles for $5.00. Sent by express to any part of the country upon receipt of price. Levy's Parisian Cream, (Creme Therapeutique.) A delightful preparation for purifying, refreshing and renovating the complexion. Its capability of soothing irritation and removing all roughness of the skin render it indispensable to every toilet. It is perfectly innocent, and can be used on the most delicate skin with the greatest safety. Jars forty and seventy-five cents. Levy's Perline, or Liquid Pearl. A very fine preparation for imparting a delicate and youthful bloom to the complexion. White, pink, and cream tinted for brunettes. Price, only seventy-five cents per bottle. Mr. Levy's store is elegantly equipped, and completely stocked with the finest extracts, colognes, soaps, lotions, cosmetics, powders, etc., which have been imported direct from the most celebrated Paris and London houses. All these splendid goods are fully warranted, and are offered to customers and the trade at the lowest possible prices. New perfumes are constantly added to the stock by every invoice. Mr. Levy was born in France. He is highly regarded by the community for his skill, enterprise and integrity, justly meriting the influential patronage secured in this unique industry.

CANNING & PATCH, Manufacturing and Dispensing Pharmacists, No. 109 Green Street.—No department of commercial enterprise in Boston is of more direct value and importance to the community than that in which the practical manufacturing and dispensing pharmacist brings to bear his professional skill and experience. The representative and progressive firm of Messrs Canning & Patch was established in 1880 by Messrs. Henry Canning and Edgar L. Patch, both of whom are able and highly qualified chemists, fully conversant with every detail and feature of the wholesale and retail drug trade and the requirements of the most critical customers. The premises occupied are spacious, convenient and elegant and contain a large and choice stock of the finest drugs and chemicals, proprietary medicines of acknowledged merit and reputation, fancy toilet articles, perfumery, mineral waters, surgeons' and physicians' requisites, and, indeed, every article that may be thought of in connection with a first-class pharmacy. There is no branch of the drug business so important as the careful, conscientious and intelligent compounding of physicians' prescriptions and family recipes, and this branch holds a paramount position in this establishment. All modern appliances have been provided to secure accuracy, and no persons more fully appreciate the responsibility that rests upon them than Messrs. Canning & Patch. For this purpose they are supplied with the purest possible drugs and chemicals, and duly qualified druggists and assistants who have graduated at our pharmaceutical colleges. As manufacturing and dispensing chemists Messrs. Canning & Patch manufacture in their well equipped laboratory many fine officinals, medicines and preparations for the trade. They are proprietors and manufacturers of Patch's improved pill coater, patented Dec. 10th, 1884, Patch's pharmaceutical boiler, Patch's pharmaceutical still, C. & P.'s fluid extract of malt, C. & P.'s pepsinated emulsion of cod liver oil with hypophosphites, etc. Any preparation bearing the name and stamp of Messrs Canning & Patch is invariably accepted by the medical profession as a genuine article possessing all the qualities claimed for it by the manufacturers. The trade of this reliable firm is by no means confined to Boston, but extends throughout all sections of New England and New York. Mr. Canning is a native of Boston, while Mr. Patch was born in Worcester, Mass. Mr. Canning has for the last seven years been president of the Massachusetts College of Pharmacy, and Mr. Patch is now professor of the theory and practice of pharmacy, and director of the Pharmaceutical Laboratory in that popular institution.

MYERS BROS. & CO., Tobacco Manufacturers, A. D. Barnes, Eastern Agent, No. 5 Central Wharf.—Among the foremost houses in the tobacco trade in this city is that so successfully conducted by Mr. A. D. Barnes, as New England agent for the old dominion tobacco works of Messrs. Myers Bros. & Co., at Richmond, Va. Mr. Barnes occupies spacious and commodious quarters and has been engaged in his present enterprise here since 1883. The parent house at Richmond is one of the oldest and largest tobacco manufactories in the United States, employing from five hundred to nine hundred hands, and producing a superior line of plug and fine cut smoking and chewing tobaccos, which have a wide and permanent sale all over the country. Mr Barnes is a native of Lynchburg, Va., and a practical exponent of the tobacco trade, possessing a foundation understanding of all its details and requirements. The interests of the house are represented upon the road by a corps of talented salesmen, and the Boston house is in a position to grant advantages to customers in this line that are readily appreciated and rarely duplicated elsewhere. Orders of any magnitude are filled with the utmost dispatch, and all transactions are placed on the most substantial and satisfactory footing.

F. E. WEBER, Confectioner and Caterer, Nos. 23 to 27 Temple Place and 34 West Street.—A representative and highly popular confectioner and caterer in Boston is Mr. F. E. Weber, whose elegant and well appointed lunch rooms and restaurant are located at Nos. 23-27 Temple Place and 73 West Street. This business was established by Mr. Weber in 1870 and was the first establishment of its kind in Temple Place, since which period he has built up an extensive and influential patronage with the best classes of society in Boston and its vicinity. His premises are spacious and commodious, luxuriously and handsomely arranged in all their appointments, and fully stocked with a large and varied assortment of the most delicious confections,—creams, ices, fancy cakes, etc. Mr. Weber is prepared at all times to serve in the very best style to order all the delicacies and luxuries of the seasons afforded by the marine and farm and garden products of this country and Europe, and all kinds of meats, game, etc., in season. An important specialty is the attention which he gives to the preparation of wedding breakfasts, lunch, dinner, receptions, parties, private dinners, and all such varieties of entertainment which can be held at private homes and halls. Accommodation can be given at Weber's for large or small parties, while the menu provided are unrivalled for quality and excellence. Mr. Weber was born in Germany, but has resided in Boston since boyhood. He is highly regarded by the community for his energy, promptness and just methods, and as a confectioner and caterer has no superior in New England. The business is managed at the store by Mr. D. F. Wise who has had many years' experience and is a gentleman of polite and courteous manners.

LEWANDO'S FRENCH DYEING AND CLEANSING ESTABLISHMENT AND LAUNDRY, W. Lincoln Crosby, Manager, Main Office, No 17 Temple Place.—The largest and best equipped dyeing and cleansing establishment in the United States, is that known as Lewando's French dyeing and cleansing establishment, whose principal offices are located at No. 17 Temple Place, Boston, and Fifth Avenue corner West Fourteenth Street, New York. The following are the branch offices and works: New York City, 731 Sixth Avenue, near Forty-second Street, 276 Eighth Avenue, opposite Grand Opera House; Philadelphia, Pa., 1607 Chestnut Street; Baltimore, Md., 16 North Charles Street; Providence, R. I., 275 Westminster Street; Newport, R. I., 227 Thames Street; Boston (Highlands), 2206 Washington Street; Boston (South), 765 Broadway; Lynn, Mass., 3 Market Street; Watertown, Mass., Galen Street. Works: New York City, and Watertown, Mass. This business has been established for sixty years, and the company has now fifteen offices and over a thousand agents. The company dyes, cleanses and presses in a very superior manner, all articles of clothing worn by men or women, in fact, everything from the finest laces to carpets. In dyeing, every color is matched, while a speciality is made of the fashionable shades. The company gives nothing but the best dyes, and has given for a number of years entire satisfaction to the most critical customers, as is evidenced by the remarkable increase in its business. Mourning orders always receive special attention, clothing is dyed or cleansed whole, while the greatest care is paid to feather dyeing, laces, ladies' garments, lace curtains, etc., which are turned out equal to new. In laundry work the same care is taken as in all other departments, while the prices quoted in all cases are as low as the lowest. In the French dry cleansing department the work is done exactly as in Paris. The most of the workmen in this department have served their time in France. Goods are called for and delivered in the City Proper, Boston Highlands, South Boston, Longwood, Brookline, Cambridge, Charlestown and Dorchester. The telephone call of this office is No. 1393.

JOHN E. MARSHALL, Manufacturer of Saratoga Potato Chips, No. 44 Clinton Street.—This gentleman inaugurated his enterprise here in 1882, and conducts a large and influential wholesale trade throughout New England and the west. His business premises are spacious in size, thoroughly equipped with every modern facility for insuring rapid and perfect production, and employment is constantly provided for a dozen or more skilled and expert hands. The product is put up in cases of two dozen half pound boxes, in kegs and barrels, and the goods can be ordered through wholesale grocers or direct from the factory. The demands upon the resources of the house are such that a large stock is necessarily carried at all times, to the end that no delay may be experienced in the filling of orders, while the fine facilities here possessed enable the proprietor to place his goods upon the market at lower prices than can be afforded by competitive concerns. Mr. Marshall is a native of the state of New Hampshire, and reliable in catering to the demands of a first-class custom of which he is the recipient.

THE METROPOLIS OF NEW ENGLAND.

BOSTON DYEWOOD & CHEMICAL COMPANY, Nos. 103 and 105 Milk Street, Corner Kilby Street.—The importance of the trade in dyewoods and chemicals to New England as the greatest manufacturing centre on the continent in the lines of textile fabrics, leather, paper, etc., cannot be overestimated. Likewise throughout every section of the United States, there exists an increasing demand for nearly everything dealt in, in this branch of commerce; it is thus a matter for congratulation that Boston is the headquarters for the leading and most thoroughly representative concern devoted to this trade, viz: the Boston Dyewood and Chemical Company. It was duly incorporated under the laws of Massachusetts, in 1868, with a capital of $200,000, the stock being taken by leading capitalists and members of the trade. It has been ably managed from its inception, and has extended its commercial relations all over the world. The company exports and imports upon the most extensive scale, and likewise manufactures full lines of dyewood liquors and extracts, of superior quality. It imports logwood, fustic, camwood, redwood, etc., deals in acids of all kinds, soda, ash, borax, brimstone, etc., etc. It is a leading importer of cochineal, cutch, gambier, madder, indigo, sumac, etc., likewise scores of other necessities and accessories to the dyeing and chemical trades. They also manufacture logwood, fustic, bark, hypernic and sapan liquors and extracts. Quality has ever been the first consideration, while substantial inducements are offered as to prices. They settle the trade of the United States and largest cotton, woolen, paper and leather manufacturers, while they have direct commercial relations with the leading countries in Europe, Canada, China, South America, Australia, Mexico, and the East Indies. The officers of the company, are merchants of sound judgment and vast practical experience, and faithfully perform the responsible duties devolving upon them, and have placed the company upon a basis of strength and efficiency, that renders it paramount in the dyewood and chemicals trade of the United States.

WILLIAM HASKINS & SON, Southern Pine and Cypress Timber and Lumber, No. 75 State Street.—In the old established and most enterprising house of William Haskins & Son, Boston has a concern that stands second to none in the United States as regards the direct facilities enjoyed and development of the trade in southern hard pine and cypress lumber, spruce and Oregon pine. The well nigh universal demand for these woods, has resulted in the growth of the trade to proportions of enormous magnitude, and no firm has more permanently maintained a representative position therein, than the one under discussion. The business dates its inception back to 1856, when the late Mr. William Haskins began cargo shipments of yellow pine from Georgia and Florida, to this port. His methods were able and honorable and his trade grew rapidly. In 1867 his son Mr. W. C. Haskins was taken into copartnership under the existing name and style. The firm has ever had the reputation of handling the best and clearest growths of yellow pine timber and flooring, and cypress lumber, and its relations have grown into international importance, as the concern is a direct exporter by the ship load to South America, Mexico, Africa, Australia, China, Great Britain and Europe. The lamented decease of Mr. William Haskins, occurred in 1871, since which date Mr. Wm. C. Haskins has continued the business under the old and honored name and style. The house owns and controls the product of large and valuable timber regions in Georgia, Florida, South Carolina, etc., and ships direct from southern ports to New England and New York manufacturers and dealers, and to foreign parts. The firm have also developed an important trade in northern spruce and Oregon pine including superior spars and mast stuff. In every department, Mr. W. C. Haskins exercises a close personal supervision. He is a lumber merchant of vast practical experience and perfected facilities and has ever retained the confidence of leading commercial circles, recognized as a representative factor in securing to Boston such a prominent position in the wholesale lumber trade.

EDWARD F. EVERETT, Insurance Adjuster of Fire Losses, No. 5 Doane Street.—In reviewing the commercial interests of Boston we find no branch of business of more importance than that of insurance. In it are engaged men of great ability, and the capital represented is something enormous. Boston may well feel proud of many representatives who give their attention to this branch of commercial activity. The subject of this sketch, Mr. Edward F. Everett, has been identified with the insurance business since 1866, from a period when this city was in its infancy as compared with its present growth and population. Mercantile business since that date has assumed proportions in the same ratio with the growth of the city until now a very extensive insurance business is annually transacted. For many years Mr. Everett was the New England representative of the Fire Insurance Association of England, and, since 1878, has been a general fire insurance broker and an adjuster of fire losses. Mr. Everett effects insurance on all kinds of insurable property in any and all of the leading substantial insurance companies, home and foreign, at the lowest rates compatible with security. He makes a special feature of the adjustment of losses by fire where insurance companies are concerned, and in this capacity is frequently called upon by the most prominent insurance corporations to determine damages. His ability and long experience well qualify him for these important duties, which are invariably discharged to the entire satisfaction of all concerned. Mr. Everett has a neat, well appointed office at No. 5 Doane Street, first door from Kilby Street. The success he enjoys has been brought about by the exercise of commercial ability and financial integrity, combined with a straightforward system of honorable dealing. He is a native of Massachusetts, and is a life member of the New England Historic Geological Society, and was formerly its recording secretary.

W. S. LAWSON & CO., Bankers and Brokers, No. 44 Exchange Place.—The influential position held by Boston in the financial world, is chiefly due to the enterprise and ability of her leading bankers and brokers, who have procured the capital and freely used the same for the development of the great railway, mining and manufacturing interests of the country. In this connection it is a pleasure to make prominent mention in this commercial review of the city, of the widely known and reliable firm of Messrs. W. S. Lawson & Co., bankers and brokers, No. 44 Exchange Place. The firm's headquarters are in New York, at No. 49 Exchange Place. The New York office was established in 1876, and the Boston office in 1881. The individual members of this firm are Messrs. William Sheldon Lawson, member of the New York and Philadelphia Stock Exchanges, Harry A. Day, member of the New York Stock Exchange, Fisher Howe, Jr., member of the Boston Stock Exchange, and Bennet H. Preston. The firm occupy in Boston well equipped offices, with private wires to New York, Philadelphia and Chicago, and their facilities for transacting business are of a very complete character. Messrs. W. S. Lawson & Co., purchase and sell for cash or on margin all stocks, bonds, government and miscellaneous securities as listed on the various Stock Exchanges, also grain, provisions, petroleum, mining stocks, cotton, etc. This firm has been noted for obtaining early and accurate information as to the state of the different markets, and numbers among its permanent customers many active operators and wealthy investors. The Chicago correspondents of the firm are Messrs. Counselman, Day, Schwartz and Dupee.

J. R. GROSE, Paper Box Factory, No. 13 Kingston Street.—Among the best known paper-box manufacturers of Boston can be named J. R. Grose, whose commodious and well equipped factory is located at No. 13 Kingston Street, and whose productions are in steady and extensive demand all over the New England States owing to the general excellence of the goods. Mr. Grose, who is a man of about 55, and a native of this city, is a gentleman of long practical experience in this line, and prior to starting in business on his own account, in 1878, had worked at his trade as a paper-box maker for several years. The factory was originally located on Court Street, and was subsequently to Chauncey Street, whence the business was removed to the present quarters in 1881. Mr. Grose occupies here four 30x100 foot floors, supplied with ample steam power and completely equipped with the latest improved machinery, while upward of twenty-five in help are regularly employed. The productions include paper boxes of every size, style and variety, both plain and fancy; and, altogether a large and flourishing business is carried on.

WM. LINCOLN & SON, Brookline Insurance Agency, No. 43 Devonshire Street, Near State Street.—Among the leading insurance agents of Boston is the firm of Messrs. Wm. Lincoln & Son. This firm have been established in the business here since 1872, and bring a wide range of practical experience to bear, acquired from many years' personal identification with the most important insurance interests of Boston and its suburban towns. They now represent some of the leading insurance companies in the world, including the following, viz: the Liverpool and London, the Commercial Union, the North British, the Fire Insurance Association, the Norfolk Mutual, the Boylston, the Home, the Phœnix, the Massachusetts Mutual, the Springfield, the Connecticut, the New Hampshire, the Dwelling House, and the Holyoke Mutual. Their connections, as is shown by the above list, are of the most superior character, and they insure some of the choicest property. Their methods are of the most equitable character, and they offer undoubted security to policy holders at the lowest rates, while they have also achieved a high reputation for the promptitude with which they settle and adjust all losses. This firm are also deservedly prominent as real estate agents and brokers, and have contributed materially to the development of the interests of the city and its suburbs in this important line, and include among their customers many of our leading capitalists and investors. They are prepared to transact a general real estate business, buying, selling and exchanging property, collecting rents, managing estates, and negotiating loans on bond and mortgage. All transactions are placed upon a substantial and satisfactory basis. The Messrs. Lincoln are Massachusetts men by birth and education, members of the Board of Underwriters, and gentlemen of the highest reputation and standing in social, business and financial circles.

JOHN P. DALE & CO., Publishers and Bookbinders, No. 17 Boylston Street.—One of the best known among the business houses in this city is that of the firm of John P. Dale & Co., publishers and bookbinders, which is located at No. 17 Boylston Street. It was established in 1872 by Jackson Dale & Co., who continued it about a year when the present firm was formed, and the business has since been vigorously prosecuted, the facilities increased and the operations extended. The premises are 50,000 feet in extent and thoroughly adapted for the business, and in mechanical equipment cannot be excelled. Besides twelve presses operated by steam power, there are cutting and ruling machines, and all the essentials necessary for executing the finest book and general work by the accessories of all the arts, identified with bookbinding, and also special machines and appliances required for the purposes of binding books. From thirty to forty practical bookbinders are employed about the establishment, which we may safely say, is one of the largest and most complete of the kind in the city, and that the facilities and conveniences for the prompt and accurate execution of work are unequalled and the position it occupies is such as to require no comment. Mr. John P. Dale who is at the head of the business, is a native of England and an old-time citizen of Boston, and has been identified with the business of the publisher and bookbinder for more than thirty years.

WARNER & JARVIS, Importers and Dealers in all kinds of Salt, Nos. 214 State Street, and 57 Commerce Street.—The wholesale salt trade of Boston owes very much of its important character and growing magnitude to the enterprise and ably directed efforts of the house of Messrs. Warner & Jarvis and their predecessors. The senior partner, Mr. B. H. Warner, went as salesman with Messrs. Clark & Baker, one of the oldest houses in the trade, in 1853. Mr. Baker retired in 1857, subsequently Mr. Warner was admitted into copartnership under the name and style of Messrs. A. P. Clark & Co. He continued thus until 1876, when he retired, and embarked in business upon his own account. The following year, Mr. Freeman, who had been senior of the firm of Freeman & Sears entered into copartnership with him, thus continuing up to the spring of 1888, when the decease of Freeman occurred. Mr. T. Jarvis, who had been connected with the firm from 1867 and had been partner in the house of Warner & Freeman, continued with Mr. Warner since May, 1888, under the style of Warner & Jarvis, and have a trade developed of the most desirable character. They are direct importers of Liverpool dairy salt; Turks Island salt and all other foreign qualities. They also handle Onondaga and western salt and other substantial inducements to purchasers and the trade in cargo and round lots. They are leading manufacturers of double refined dairy and table salt in constant demand with the grocery and dairy trade and of exceptional purity and high quality. Any salt bearing the brand of Messrs. Warner & Jarvis can be relied on to give entire satisfaction and prove profitable to keep in stock. The firm occupy an entire five-story brick building at No. 214 State Street, extending through the block to No. 57 Commerce Street, and here at all times is carried full lines of their fine salt for domestic and dairy use. They have large warehouse facilities elsewhere, including 22,000 feet of floor space at Mystic Wharf, and employ from twenty to eighty hands according to season and demands of trade. The firm are in every way thoroughly representative of Boston's best commercial interests. Mr. Warner is a native of this city and has from his youth been actively identified with the trade in which he has achieved such success. Mr. Jarvis was born in Brewster, Mass.

WILLIAM C. FRENCH, Ash and Maple Bedsteads, Folding Cribs, Etc., Nos. 80 to 84 Fulton Street.—This business was established twenty-six years ago by the present proprietor, who has since built up one of the largest industries of the kind in New England. The premises occupied comprise two spacious five-story and basement buildings, with well equipped and commodious salesrooms. The factories are equipped with the latest improved machinery and appliances, and furnish constant employment to 120 skilled workmen. Mr. French manufactures extensively a very popular line of ash, maple, black walnut and birch bedsteads, platform rocking cribs, folding cribs, rocking and swing cradles. These goods are unrivalled for quality of materials, finish, elegance and uniform excellence by those of any other contemporary house in the trade, while the prices quoted in all cases necessarily attract the attention of close and careful buyers. Mr. French keeps constantly on hand an immense stock and can fill the largest orders quicker than any other house in the trade in New England. This trade now extends throughout all sections of the United States, and he also exports largely to Canada, Mexico, the West Indies, Central and South America, Europe and South Africa. Mr. French was born in Lowell, Mass. Dealers and large buyers who are desirous of obtaining the most desirable bedsteads, etc., should and fail to examine carefully the stock at this establishment, which offers advantages in goods and prices, very difficult to be duplicated elsewhere.

C. N. HOLLIS, Commission Merchant, Mutton, Lamb and Veal, No. 54 North Market Street.—The commission trade in meat supplies in Boston is an industry of very large and superior importance. Few, except those actually engaged in it, or connected with it, are aware of the immense aggregate value invested or the number of prominent merchants engaged in it. A leading house in this line of enterprise deserving of special recognition in this work on the city's commercial and manufacturing industries, is that of Mr. C. N. Hollis, of No. 54 North Market Street. This business was organized in 1874, by the present proprietor's father, the late Mr. E. A. Hollis, who died in 1885. Mr. C. N. Hollis, who then succeeded to the business, has developed a trade of large volume both in the city and its suburbs. The premises occupied comprise a basement, 20x60 feet in dimensions, and this is equipped with cold storage for perishable goods and with all other appliances and conveniences essential to the facilitating of business. Mr. Hollis conducts a general commission trade in mutton, lamb and veal, and is in daily receipt of consignments from the most reliable sources of supply. The stock is consequently always kept fresh and choice, and the prices are put at a point to ensure quick sales. Prompt returns are made to consignors, and Mr. Hollis has a reputation second to that of no other commission merchant in the trade. The sales are exclusively wholesale, and retailers find it to their interest to place their orders with this enterprising house. Mr. Hollis is a native of Brighton, Mass., and is held in the highest repute for his business activity and honorable methods which have won for him fame in mercantile circles.

THE METROPOLIS OF NEW ENGLAND.

GEO. V. YENETCHI, Importer and Wholesale Dealer in Wines and Liquors, Nos. 142 and 144 Blackstone Street.—In Boston, throughout New England, and a wide-spread connection elsewhere, the name of Yenetchi is looked upon as a veritable trade mark—a guarantee of quality, that is so fully borne out by the experience of consumers, that the trade conducted by Mr. George V. Yenetchi has upon the legitimate basis of supply and demand attained proportions of enormous magnitude. This is an old and honored concern. It was founded away back in 1830 by Mr. Horatio Hammond, one of the old and respected school of New England merchants. He was succeeded by the firm of

Messrs. Ralph Smith & Sons, able and enterprising merchants and with whom, Mr. George V. Yenetchi, a native of that cradle of nations, the ancient Hellas, or modern Greece, and which has produced so many distinguished merchants, became their confidential book-keeper and eventually business manager. In 1850 he became sole proprietor and has during the intervening period greatly enlarged and extended the business. The fine four-story and basement building, Nos. 142 and 144 Blackstone Street is occupied, and where purchasers at wholesale can best satisfy their requirements. Mr. Yenetchi carries constantly in stock the oldest and choicest vintages of sherries, ports, madeiras, Piper Heidsieck, Roederer and other dry, superb champagnes; also cordials and liquors, gins and brandies, including such famous brands as Anchor and Schiedam gins, and Martelle and Hennessy brandies. In all the above this stock is not limited (like so many) to a few vintages but is a wide and comprehensive one, containing many old and mellowed wines and brandies, difficult to obtain. This is recognized headquarters for pure old bourbon and rye whiskies. Mr. Yenetchi carries the best brands, including from his lengthy lists, such standards as old crow, Ashland, old crown and Keller's old superior bourbon, monticello, hermitage, and astor sour mash rye whiskies; he also carries the most celebrated brands of New England and Jamaica rums, California wines, etc. These goods are popular for medicinal purposes and sell largely to druggists, as well as to hotels, restaurants and retailers. Mr. Yenetchi also does a heavy case trade with families, shipping, etc. In cigars, he carries the fine hand made Magnolia brand, and the justly famous Voretta luxury, the finest clear Havana filled cigar found on this market—at $50 per 1,000.

CITIZENS' MUTUAL INSURANCE CO., H. C. Bigelow, President, J. W. Peabody, Secretary, Office, No. 8 Exchange Place. —The history of the rise and progress of the leading life insurance companies, doing business in the City of Boston is one of the most interesting topics to merchants and property owners, and thus a careful effort is made in this commercial review to give accurate information in regard to the substantial and reliable corporations, which have so long afforded complete protection to their policy holders. Prominent among the number thus referred to is the Citizens' Mutual Insurance Company, whose principal offices are situated at No. 8 Exchange Place. This company was duly incorporated under the laws of Massachusetts in 1867, since which period it has secured a liberal and permanent patronage in all sections of the state. It is ably officered, and its directors are gentlemen, who are highly regarded in commercial and financial circles for their prudence and just methods. The list is as follows: H. C. Bigelow, president, J. W. Peabody, secretary. Directors: H. C. Bigelow, Dedham; Granville Fuller, Boston; J. S. Bacon, Newton; Life Baldwin, Boston; Henry Baldwin, Boston; Herman Bird, Cambridge; S. N. Davenport, Boston; E. C. Sparhawk, Boston; Jessie Gould, Chelsea; Leonard Huntress, Jr., Lowell; Arthur Anthony, Fall River; Leonard Winch, Natick. The company's semi-annual statement June 30th, 1888, shows its affairs to be in a most flourishing condition: Number of policies in force, $1,727$; amount of property insured thereby, $22,692,98.08$, Cash assets, $62,150.00$; contingent liability, $50,377.57$; available assets, $32,18.03$. Reserved for reinsurance, $74,188.78$; uncollected losses, 500.00; total, $64,8.77.78$. Cash surplus over all liabilities, $109,512.31$. Increase of each fund during last six months, $9,611.05$. Its condition is a guarantee of its ability to meet promptly all claims, and at the same time to carry its policies upon terms most favorable to the insured. One class of property only,—viz., dwellings, private barns, and contents of each,—is insured; and an equality of risk is thereby maintained among its policy holders. Promptness and courtesy to both agent and insured are practiced in the conduct of its business, and a careful attention paid to the selection of its risks. This company pays for damages caused by lightning, though no marks of fire are visible. The following dividends are now being paid: on five years' policies, sixty per cent., on all other policies, forty per cent. Mr. H. C. Bigelow, the president, has held office since 1878. He is one of our best known insurance men, and is highly esteemed in business circles for his energy, ability and integrity. Mr. J. W. Peabody, the secretary, has held his important position for the last eighteen years.

CHARLES F. RAND, Auctioneer, Appraiser, Insurance and Real Estate Agent; Boston Office, Room 23, No. 113 Devonshire Street; Newton Office, No. 417 Centre Street. —The real estate agent in Boston and its suburban towns has, at the present day, opened before him an ample field for enterprise and usefulness, and many of the most influential and energetic citizens are engaged in this important business. Prominent among the number thus referred to is Mr. Charles F. Rand, the well known auctioneer, appraiser and real estate agent, who makes a specialty of Newton property, and whose Boston office is located at No. 113 Devonshire Street, Room 23, where he is to be found from 10 to 11.30 a. m. This gentleman has been established in the business since 1852, and by faithful, conscientious zeal for the best interest of his customers, has long enjoyed the confidence of the community and secured a very superior clientele. He is familiar with both present and prospective values of realty in and around the city, and has always on his books many desirable bargains, including business, residential and manufacturing sites, for sale, to let or exchange. The large line of property in Newton, which he handles, is absolutely perfect as regards its title and all realty dealt in through him may be relied upon as a safe investment. Both Boston and suburban property is offered for cash or on instalments to suit the purchaser. Mr. Rand possesses unsurpassed facilities for the prompt negotiation of loans on bond or mortgage, and is, in this branch of his business of the utmost service to both borrower and lender, securing to the one ample funds with which to extend his enterprise, and to the other a profitable and perfectly safe investment. His Newton office, at No. 417 Centre Street, opposite the Public Library is one of the finest in New England. It is supplied with all modern appliances for the prosecution of his business, including a stenographer and type writer, also has telephone connections with Boston and suburban places; his telephone call is, Newton 263. The walls of his office are hung with maps and photographs of estates for sale, while his table is loaded with atlases of Boston, Brookline, Newton, and other places in the vicinity, making this one of the most complete offices for the business in New England.

AMERICAN LOAN & TRUST COMPANY, S. E. Peabody, President pro tem, E. A. Coffin, Treasurer, No. 55 Congress Street. — This company was duly incorporated in 1881 under the laws of Massachusetts with a paid up capital of $500,000, and its surplus fund and undivided profits now amount to $774,856.7. This institution is one that affords the most complete protection and security to its patrons, and for safety, solidity and a perfect system of responsibility is a peer of any similar corporation in the United States. The management of the American Loan & Trust Company is in the hands of prudent and experienced business men, whose names are thoroughly familiar throughout financial and commercial circles, as those of honorable and capable citizens. They are as follows: Directors, Oliver Ames, Elisha Atkins, Isaac T. Burr, B. P. Cheney, F. Gordon Dexter, D. F. Kimball, Thomas Nickerson, R. S. Robbins, Fred. L. Ames, John Q. Adams, A. L. Coolidge, Henry D. Hyde, George C. Lord, Wm. Minot, Jr., S. E. Peabody, and Alexander H. Rice. Officers, S. E. Peabody, president pro tem.; N. W. Jordan, actuary; E. A. Coffin, treasurer. This company receives deposits subject to check, allowing interest thereon, and is prepared to extend to its patrons all the facilities for business that may be required of a banking corporation. It receives money payable at fixed times, and allows interest at special rates, while it loans money upon approved collateral; is a legal depository for administrators, executors, assignees, trustees and guardians; acts as trustee under mortgages for railroads and other corporations; transfer agent and register of stocks and bonds; financial or other agent for municipalities and corporations, paying bonds, coupons, dividends, etc. Mr. E. A. Coffin, the treasurer, and Mr. N. W. Jordan, the actuary, have been with the company since 1881. They are able and experienced officers with every necessary qualification for their important and responsible positions. Mr. S. E. Peabody, the president pro tem, is a gentleman whose ability and integrity is widely known in the financial world. The statement of the condition of the American Loan & Trust Company, rendered October 21, 1888, shows its affairs to be in a most substantial and favorable state.

BICKNELL & ROBINSON, Fire Insurance Agents and Brokers, No. 82 Water Street.—This deservedly popular and reliable firm was established 1883, and at once bounded into prominence and prosperity, numbering among their extensive clientele many of Boston's leading business men, merchants, manufacturers and property owners, while they direct attention, by permission, to the following unexceptionable list of references: Hon. Moses Kimball, Boston Museum; Sam'l Johnson, Esq., of C. F. Hovey & Co., No. 33 Summer Street; E. A. Stearns, Esq., of R. H. Stearns & Co., Nos. 139 and 140 Tremont Street; Wm. G. Webb, Esq., Nos. 42 Congress Street and 6 Commonwealth Avenue; Isaac T. Burr, Esq., president National Bank of North America; Chas. Carruth, Esq., formerly of N. & C. Carruth; Joseph H. Gray, Esq., No. 1634 Congress Street; Joel Goldthwait, Esq., of Joel Goldthwait & Co., No. 160 Washington Street; Henry D. Hyde, Esq., of Hyde, Dickinson & Howe, Equitable building; Elbed S. Ripley, Esq., of Rhodes & Ripley, No. 99 Summer Street; Sam'l Carr, Esq., cashier Shoe and Leather National Bank; Hon. John E. Sanford, Taunton, Mass.; Geo. W. Pope, Esq., No. 469 Columbus Avenue; Joseph F. Paul, Esq., Albany Street, cor. Dover Street; Solomon Hovey, Esq., Hyde Park, Mass.; George Sowell, Esq., No. 14 83. James Avenue; John J. McNult, Esq., Wareham Street; Cyrus T. Clark, Esq., Wareham Street. Messrs. Bicknell & Robinson conduct a general fire insurance business, placing all classes of desirable risks with first-class companies at lowest rates consistent with absolute security; and also represent these stanch and sound institutions: Scottish Union and National of Edinburgh, Scotland; Sun Fire office of London, England; Niagara of New York; Dwelling House Insurance Company of Boston; Worcester Mutual of Worcester, Mass., and New Hampshire of Manchester, N. H., and Continental of New York. Alfred Bicknell and John H. Robinson are gentlemen of the highest integrity as well as men of excellent business qualities and thorough experience, and were formerly actively connected with both the old and new Mechanics' Mutual Insurance Company, Mr. Robinson having been secretary of the new company, while Mr. Bicknell who had been the surveyor of the old "Mechanics" was the president of the new organization. Both gentlemen are members of the Underwriters Association.

O. L. STORY, Scenic Artist, Scenery Made, Painted to Order and to Let, No. 109 Haverhill Street.—In these days of advanced culture, refinement and improved tastes among all classes of the people the scenic artist, if he is to succeed in his calling, must have a thorough training, and, more than all be possessed of great natural ability and an aptitude for the business. That these attributes are possessed in an eminent degree by Mr. O. L. Story, of No. 109 Haverhill Street, all acquainted with him and his work readily acknowledge, and he has won, not only fame, but a wide-spread patronage. He was born and reared in the business, his father before him enjoying an unsurpassed reputation for talented and conscientious work and a large clientele in the same line. Mr. Story was born twenty-eight years ago in Charlestown, and is now a resident of Somerville. In 1882 he embarked in business on his own account on Beverly Street and in the following year removed to his present premises at No. 109 Haverhill Street where he occupies the fourth and fifth floors, each of which have an area of 9x50 feet. Every facility is at hand for the successful prosecution of the business, and every description of scenic work is carefully executed with thorough fidelity to detail and brilliancy of touch. Scenery is not only made and painted to order, but a large variety is kept on hand for hire at reasonable rates. Four experienced and talented artists are in constant service, and in the management of his business Mr. Story is animated with but one aim, to excel in his chosen profession. He has a fine patronage throughout the whole of New England, and this, each year grows in extent.

JAMES BLISS & CO., Grocers & Ship Chandlers, Dealers in Cordage, Etc., No. 328 Atlantic Avenue, Head Rowe's Wharf. —The name of James Bliss & Co., the well-known grocers and ship chandlers, has become a veritable trade mark. The business of this widely-known and representative house was founded nearly fifty years ago by Mr. James Bliss, who continued in control until his death in 1875, when his son, Mr. James F. Bliss, and Mr. Israel E. Decrow succeeded as proprietors under the original firm name. They deal both at wholesale and retail in all kinds of supplies for vessels, and are also largely interested in vessels and the shipping trade. They occupy spacious and commodious quarters, and possess every facility for conducting the business under the most favorable auspices and upon the largest scale. The demands upon the resources of the house are such that a very large and comprehensive stock is necessarily carried, to the end that no delay may be experienced in the filling of orders. Each in its special line is the best and purest in the market. Vessels out of port in New York, Portland, Philadelphia, Baltimore and other places, are supplied by this house with promptness and satisfaction with reliable goods in quantities to suit, and at prices which preclude successful competition. The marked success attending the operations of this house is due to the superior mercantile connections enjoyed by the firm, as well as to the permanent maintenance of the highest standard of excellence in all goods sold. The copartners are prominent members of the Vessel Owners' Association and of the Chamber of Commerce.

A. LEAVITT, Manufacturer of Church Organ Keys, No. 63 Charlestown Street.—Boston has long been the home for the manufacture of musical instruments. One of the most prominent and extensive manufacturers in this line is that of Mr. A. Leavitt, who started in business eighteen years ago on Tremont street, where he remained until June, 1888, when he removed to his present quarters, at No. 63 Charlestown Street. Here he occupies a floor, 30x40 feet in dimensions, and this is thoroughly equipped with all the best mechanical equipments known to the trade for securing the best results. Several hands are employed, and keys are promptly made to order from the cheapest to the most costly materials, as desired. Mr. Leavitt has built up a very extensive trade with organ builders in all parts of the New England and western states, and his facilities for promptly and satisfactorily meeting all orders with the most reliable goods at reasonable charges are of the most ample kind. Mr. Leavitt has had vast experience in the business, and gives his close personal attention to the filling of all orders. He was born in Maine and thirty-five years ago came to Boston to learn his trade. He is now a resident of Lexington.

THE METROPOLIS OF NEW ENGLAND. 199

COOLIDGE HOUSE, Bowdoin Square, Wm. P. Comee, Proprietor.—Among the most popular first-class family hotels is the Coolidge, centrally located on Bowdoin Square. This house is architecturally an ornament to the city, and is constructed in modern style with due regard to the comfort, convenience and safety of its guests. It is five stories in height, what frontage of eighty and a depth of one hundred feet, and contains one hundred rooms, many of them *en suite*, so that the requirements of families, so seldom met in a proper manner in fashionable hotel accommodations, are here provided on the most elaborate scale, and at rates cheaper than would be quoted in houses and flats for the same class of accommodations. On the first floor is one of the finest cafés in the city, the culinary department being presided over by an experienced chef. The hall and stairs are of solid marble, and the upper floors are reached by means of a hydraulic elevator. The rooms are all airy and pleasantly situated, elegantly furnished. In location the Coolidge is directly central to the most fashionable sections of the city, to the best shore theatres and churches, and is the place above all others for our wealthy and out-of-town people to make a home while in the city. With regard to sanitary arrangements and means of escape in case of fire, the Coolidge is absolutely unrivalled. Guests will find here every convenience and all modern improvements, while the rates of the house are $3.00 per day for transient guests, with special rates for boarders by the week or month. The proprietor, Mr. Wm. P. Comee, is one of the best known hotel men in New England, with a well-earned reputation for enterprise, managerial skill and executive ability.

ALFRED F. CHAPMAN, Editor and Publisher of *The Liberal Freemason*, General Fire and Life Insurance Broker, No. 221 Washington Street.—Boston has always enjoyed the reputation of being one of the great intellectual centers of the world, and prominent among its literary productions is the *Liberal Freemason*, of which Mr. Alfred F. Chapman is the editor and proprietor. This publication is a monthly magazine of thirty-two pages, octavo, and was founded originally in 1872 since which date it has increased steadily in circulation throughout the entire United States, and has become one of the standard publications of the order. It is edited with marked ability and its contents comprise the writings of some of the brightest members of the mystic tie in this country. It is unusually bright, newsy, and full of information for the craft, while its entire typographical appearance is most commendable. To those belonging to the order it will prove most interesting and instructive, and as the price is only two dollars per year, it should be in the hands of every member seeking light. In addition to publishing this interesting magazine, Mr. Chapman also conducts a general life and fire insurance brokerage business, in which he established himself in this city many years ago. He is prepared to effect insurance in all lines to any amount according to risks in the most reliable and reputable companies in the country and at the lowest rates. His many years of experience in this line of business has given him great popularity among those desirous of placing risks in companies which are known to be of the very best character. Mr. Chapman was born in Nova Scotia in 1829, but has been a resident of Boston since 1854.

ISAAC WASHBURN, General Insurance, Mortgage and Real Estate Agent, No. 270 Washington Street.—Mr. Isaac Washburn, the well-known general insurance, mortgage and real estate agent, has been established in business here since 1856, and, in addition to conducting a general real estate and insurance agency, he is the agent of the Massachusetts Real Estate Company, which owns many valuable properties; he also represents the Sun Fire Insurance Company, of London, England; is a notary public and justice of the peace, and is also licensed to procure fire insurance in foreign companies not authorized to do business in this state. He has a large and influential clientele in this city and throughout the New England States, and also does business for parties in New York, Pennsylvania, Missouri and other states. He invests money on mortgages, possessing unsurpassed facilities for the negotiation of loans; takes the entire management of estates, collects rents, pays taxes and acts as agent for the purchase, sale, lease or exchange of properties of every description. He has a thorough knowledge of real estate matters in this city and vicinity, is an accepted authority upon present and prospective values, and can be engaged with implicit confidence in his ability and sound judgement. Mr. Washburn pays particular attention to the placing of insurance, and has ever been eminently successful in this line, securing payment for all losses arising from fire promptly and without litigation, and discharging the important trusts committed to his care with fidelity and conscientious regard for the welfare of his patrons. Mr. Washburn was born in Taunton, Mass., and is highly respected in this city.

MEKELBURG & COBE, Manufacturers of Fine Cigars, No. 280 State Street.—Producing nothing but reliable and A1 goods, Mekelburg & Cobe's productions have secured a firm hold on popular favor throughout Boston and environs owing to the uniformly high standard of excellence at which the same was maintained. The cigars turned out by this firm are of a very superior character in every respect, being made from carefully selected stock, of choice flavor and quality, while none but expert hands are employed in their manufacture; their favorite brands, "M. & M." and "67," 10 and 5 cent cigars respectively, being articles of exceptional merit, and as a consequence are in steady and growing demand in the trade. This thriving concern was established in September, 1887, by Murphy & Mekelburg, who were succeeded in August, 1887, by Mekelburg & Cobe, and under this style the business has since been conducted with uninterrupted success. They occupy as factory a fine third floor in the building at 280 State Street, and have at hand ample and complete facilities, while some eight to ten experienced cigar-makers are employed. The productions include fine cigars exclusively, a large and first-class assortment being always kept in stock, and the trade of the firm, which is of a wholesale character entirely, is quite extensive, and grows steadily apace. Messrs. Abraham Mekelburg and Andrew Cobe, who compose the firm, are both natives of this city.

S. VORENBERG & CO., Gents' Fine Clothing, No. 67 Washington Street and Nos. 87 to 93 Hanover Street.—Prominent among the retail clothing establishments of Boston, is that of S. Vorenberg & Co., who are extensive dealers in gents' fine clothing and furnishing goods, and have been established in the business here since 1874. The store is spacious in size, attractive in all its arrangements, and stocked to repletion with new, choice and desirable goods. The line of ready made clothing embraces all the desirable grades and the latest styles and patterns in the market, while the finer grades are equal in every respect to the best custom work, in fit, finish, elegance and fashion. The goods have all been selected with rare judgment, while the plainest as well as the most costly possess special points of superiority. Their assortment of gentlemen's furnishing goods embraces the latest novelties in neckwear, and all the standard supplies in white and colored shirts, underwear, hosiery and gloves, collars and cuffs, umbrellas and canes, and general outfittings. The lowest prices invariably prevail, and the patronage is large, first-class and influential in city and country. Mr. Vorenberg, the active member of the firm, is a native of Germany, and a resident of this country since his boyhood.

BOSTON WATCH COMPANY, No. 16 Green Street.—For genuine bargains in watches, clocks, jewelry, etc., no establishment of the kind in this part of the city compares with the neat and well-kept store of the Boston Watch Company. W. W. Farr, proprietor. Nothing but reliable and excellent goods are handled, the Boston Watch Company watch being a specialty, and watches are cleaned and adjusted in the most prompt and superior manner at from $1.00 to $3.00; while clocks, jewelry and spectacles also are repaired in the very best style of the art at reasonable prices. The store is compact and tastefully appointed, and a first-class stock is constantly carried, including watches, clocks and jewelry of every description; also, solid silver and plated ware, art novelties, opera glasses, spectacles, eye-glasses, and kindred articles; special attention being given to fine watch repairing, and, altogether, Mr. Farr has a very nice trade. This business was established about six years ago by Messrs. W. W. Farr & Co., who has since conducted it with uniform success, under the original style of the "Boston Watch Company."

ROYAL B. LEIGHTON, Insurance, Real Estate, and Mortgages, Boston Office, No. 27 Kilby Street, Room 29.—The placing of risks on property and the handling of realty constitutes, as it is needless to observe, one of the most important branches of business, contributing to the sum of activity in every centre of industry, commerce and trade. And, it may be added, in this connection, that it is a sphere of usefulness that occupies the attention of some of the most solid and sagacious citizens in every community. Among those engaged in this line in Boston, there are few better known, or enjoy a larger measure of popularity and confidence, than the gentleman whose name stands at the head of this sketch. Mr. Royal B. Leighton, who is a native of Boston, and resides at No. 161 Emerson Street, Melrose, is a gentleman of the highest personal integrity, as well as a man of energy and judicious enterprise, with thorough experience in all features connected with insurance and real estate. He has been actively engaged in business during the past fifteen years, and has acquired a large and flourishing patronage. Mr. Leighton conducts a general insurance brokerage business, and is the authorized local agent, also, in Melrose, representing the following first-class companies: —North British and Mercantile Insurance Company, Liverpool and London and Globe Insurance Company, Hamburg Bremen Fire Insurance Company, Hartford Fire Insurance Company, American Fire Insurance Company, Niagara Fire Insurance Company, London and Lancashire Insurance Company, Western Insurance Company, Anglo-Nevada Assurance Corporation. Mr. Leighton, whose office is located at No. 27 Kilby Street, also transacts a general real estate business, buying, selling and leasing city and suburban property, and also negotiates mortgages and loans. He makes a speciality of handling Melrose property, while rents are collected and estates taken in charge and judiciously managed.

S. W. DEWEY & CO., Cotton Buyers, Offices, No. 85 Water Street.—One of the oldest established and leading firms of cotton buyers in the southern, foreign and New England markets is that of Messrs. S. W. Dewey & Co. The business was founded in 1837, though for a number of years prior to that the late Mr. S. W. Dewey, Sr. had been actively and extensively engaged in the imported woolens trade. In 1857 his son, Mr. S. W. Dewey, Jr., came into copartnership, under the existing name and style, and from that date devoted their attention to the wholesale foreign and domestic cotton buying trade. They early became celebrated for their sound judgment, marked enterprise and sterling integrity, and developed an active trade and influential connection with leading New England mills and exporters. The decease of Mr. Dewey, Sr., occurred in 1873, deeply regretted by the large circle of friends and acquaintances, who had learned to esteem him during his long and honorable career. In 1874 he took into copartnership his brother, Mr. Arthur W. Dewey, and the firm is thus composed to-day. They were for a period of sixteen years located at No. 45 Kilby Street, and in May, 1888, removed to their present commodious offices at No. 85 Water Street. Here they have the facilities at command necessitated by the enormous magnitude of their trade. No firm in the United States has such desirable international connections in the cotton markets of the world as they. They are direct importers of the finest long staple Egyptian cotton from Alexandria, and of the choicest Peruvian growths from Lima. These desirable qualities are a prominent speciality of the house, while it also purchases the best growths of the famous Sea Island, and other desirable southern growths. The Messrs. Dewey are the recognized authorities in their line; no more so thoroughly understands the needs of the New England mills as they, and none have such perfected facilities for meeting same.

E. P. SARGENT, JR. & CO., Manufacturing Stationers and Mercantile Printers, No. 38 Central Street.—Prominent among the representative firms in this trade is the well known and popular house of Messrs. E. P. Sargent, Jr. & Co., the well known manufacturing stationers and mercantile printers, No. 38 Central Street. The business of this concern was first organized in 1880 by Mr. R. Davis, who was succeeded by the present firm in March, 1888. The members of the firm are Messrs. E. P. and F. P. Sargent, Jr., who are brothers, and have had a long practical experience in the trade, with every detail of which they are thoroughly familiar. They have, since they took hold of the enterprise, developed the trade of their establishment very considerably, and have attained a liberal and influential patronage from the trade and the public, owing to the unsurpassed quality and excellence of their various manufactures and to the artistic character of their printing. The firm occupy the third floor of the building and their premises are equipped with all the latest improved machinery and appliances, by means of which the work produced is accomplished with dispatch and in the best manner, employment being furnished to a large number of skilled and experienced operatives. There is a full assortment of types for every description of printing, two of the most modern printing presses operated by electric power, and in the book-binding department every mechanical requisite of a superior order. The firm make a speciality of the manufacture of all kinds of blank books, ledgers, journals, day books, check books, drafts, etc., which in mechanical execution cannot be excelled by any contemporary house in or out of the city. Throughout the establishment there prevades a system of order that facilitates the transaction of business, and makes the house a pleasant one with which to establish business relations. Both partners are natives of Merrimac, Mass., and we take pleasure in giving them just mention in this work.

THOMAS L. O'BRION, Insurance Agent and Broker, Office; No. 75 Central Street.—One of the most popular and responsible fire insurance agents and brokers of Boston, is Mr. Thomas L. O'Brion, whose wide-spread influential connections and ample practical experience render him a recognized authority in fire underwriting throughout New England. The extensive business now conducted by Mr. O'Brion was founded in 1873 by Mr. Richard Page, who was succeeded by Mr. O'Brion in 1880. He has occupied his present offices since 1885, and is one of the best known agents in the city. Mr. O'Brion is the New England agent for the Reliance Fire Insurance Company, of Philadelphia, and the local agent for the Insurance Company of the State of Pennsylvania, of Philadelphia, of the United Firemen's Insurance Company, of Philadelphia; the Commercial of California; the Marine, of St. Louis, and the Jersey City, of Jersey City. These are large and powerful companies, ably conducted, honorably managed and whose policies are clear, positive contracts, without ambiguous clauses. They all have the enviable reputation of promptly paying all claims as soon as adjusted, and under Mr. O'Brion's guidance do a flourishing business in Boston. There is no more reliable authority on the principal risks of Boston and vicinity than he, and none more conversant with the character of mill and factory risks, etc., throughout New England. He controls the insuring of large lines of residential and business property and offers substantial inducements as to low rates and absolute security. Mr. O'Brion was born in Portland, Maine, and has been actively engaged in the fire insurance business for twenty-two years past. He is a popular member of the Underwriters' Association, and a valued representative of a business of direct vital importance to every property owner and householder in Boston and New England.

GEO. S. PARKER, Real Estate and Mortgages No. 27 Kilby Street.—A successful and well conducted real estate agency is that carried on by Mr. Geo. S. Parker, at No. 27 Kilby Street. Mr. Parker, who is a young man and comes from Washington, D. C., has been a resident of Boston for the past five years and been identified with the real estate business most of that time. In February, 1888, he established his present flourishing agency, and has succeeded in a comparatively short time in making first-class business connections throughout the city. Mr. Parker does a general real estate business, negotiating for the sale and purchase of city and country property of all kinds, effecting exchanges, procuring loans on bond and mortgage and taking charge of property, looking after repairs, collecting rents, paying taxes, etc. His clients are numerous and repose the greatest confidence in his judgment and energy which he has displayed on the various transactions he has carried out. Mr. Parker is a good judge of Boston realty, and will be found a safe man to deal with in the purchase, sale or negotiation of real estate.

THE METROPOLIS OF NEW ENGLAND.

GEO. E. MESSER & CO., Manufacturers of and Dealers in all kinds of Black Walnut and Amber Fancy Work, No. 73 Haverhill Street.—Not in many of the industrial arts has there been made more progress of late years than in the sphere of activity devoted to the production of fancy work in black walnut

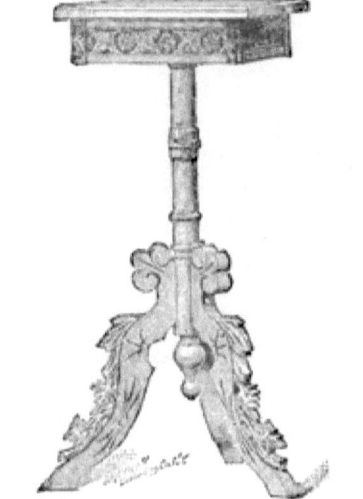

and amber. The parlor brackets, toilet cases, bouquet tables, hat racks and kindred articles of household use, turned out in a lead

ing concern in this line in these days are marvels of artistic skill and things of beauty, truly. A noteworthy Boston firm engaged in this branch of industrial activity is that of Geo. E. Messer & Co., (successor to Messer & Higgins) manufacturers of and dealers in all kinds of black walnut and amber fancy work, No. 73 Haverhill street, whose productions have secured an enduring hold on popular favor throughout the entire country, owing to their general excellence. The articles produced here are of exceptional merit, being noted for their beauty of design, exquisite workmanship and elegant finish and as a consequence, they are in steady and extensive demand in the trade all over the United States. This thriving enterprise was started in 1870 by Eldrige Walcott, who was succeeded by Messer & Higgins, who were in turn succeeded by Geo. E. Messer & Co., by whom the business is conducted at the present time. They occupy as factory and salesroom a 40x80 foot (second) floor, with ample steam power and complete manufacturing facilities, while twelve expert workmen are employed. The firm manufacture everything in the line of black walnut and amber fancy work, including artistic parlor brackets in all sizes and designs, superb book and toilet cases, exquisite slipper racks and pockets, handsome bouquet and marble-top tables, whatnots, coat and hat rack, towel racks, paper and music racks, view holders, comb cases and a great variety of ornamental articles of interior decoration, while a large and complete assortment is kept in stock always; and all orders for the trade are promptly and reliably filled. Mr. Messer, who is the sole proprietor, is a man of long, practical experience and skill in this line, and ranks among the foremost in his business in the country. All these goods are shipped, knocked down, and can be packed in a small compass, making freight charges very light.

J. B. DIXON & CO., Wholesale and Commission Dealers in Lumber and Shingles, No. 11 Central Street.—Few among the varied and vast business interests in this city at the present day are of greater importance than the great branch of trade devoted to the wholesale handling of lumber. The transactions in this product of the forest, both rough and dressed, in Boston, in the course of a year, aggregate immense magnitude, and represent hundreds of millions of dollars. Among the young firms contributing most extensively to the sum of commercial activity in this line in the city can be named that of J. B. Dixon & Co., wholesale and commission dealers in lumber, shingles, etc., No. 11 Central Street, and which, although a comparatively new concern—having been established in 1883—has already attained a degree of prominence and achieved a measure of success vouchsafed to very few among the lumber firms that have come to the front within a decade or two in Boston. They handle everything in the line of Michigan and Canada pine, also oak, plain and quartered; sycamore, plain and quartered; pine shingles, sixteen and eighteen inches, cedar shingles, sixteen and eighteen inches, brown ash, grey ash, white ash, basswood, beech, red birch, butternut, cherry, cottonwood, rock elm, soft elm, white, wood and all kinds of lumber cut to order. The firm do a wholesale business exclusively, shipping direct to dealers and large consumers from the mills, and their trade, which extends to all parts of the New England States, is of a very substantial character. Mr. Dixon is a young man of energy, enterprise and ample experience.

W. E. WOODWARD, Architect, No. 82 Water Street.—One of Boston's oldest and foremost architects, is W. E. Woodward, who enjoys a high reputation for skill and reliability. Mr. Woodward is a Bostonian by birth and residence. He is a thoroughly competent architect, of long and varied experience in his profession, and is a complete master of the art in all its branches, and is a well-known member of the Architects Association of Boston. He has been established upwards of thirty-five years, and during this entire period has maintained an excellent standing in his profession, having many noteworthy pieces of work to his credit in and around the city; one of the last structures of note erected by him, being the Quincy House. Plans for all classes of buildings, dwellings, churches, institutions, hotels, business blocks, etc., are made in the most reliable and superior manner, in every instance, designs, specifications, etc., being promptly furnished, while construction is superintended personally, when desired.

EDWIN MORSE, Billiard Table Manufacturer, Salesroom, Room 8, No. 3 Tremont Row.—The increased attention given to the production of an improved class of work in the line of billiard and pool tables has, in the nature of things, resulted in notable progress being made in this direction of late years. What with inventions, improvements and the development of mechanical skill, something akin to perfection itself has been attained by some of our billiard-table manufacturers. Among those referred to may be mentioned the name of Edwin Morse, of this city, whose salesroom is located at No. 3 (Room 8) Tremont Row, with factory at Athol, Mass., and whose productions have secured an enduring hold on popular favor owing to the uniformly high standard of excellence at which the same are maintained. The tables manufactured by this gentleman are of a very superior character alike in beauty of design, construction, durability and finish; being all furnished with Samuel May's celebrated patent steel spring cushion (the best made, and warranted for ten years), and for general excellence are unsurpassed by any articles of the kind to-day upon the market. This flourishing business was established in 1878 and no better evidence of the superiority of the work turned out could be offered than the unequivocal success that has attended this enterprise from its inception. The factory is a commodious well equipped concern, where some fifteen expert workmen are employed, while at the salesroom, at No. 3 Tremont Row, an efficient corps of salesmen are in attendance. The productions include billiard and pool tables in every size, style and variety, a complete and elegant assortment being always carried on hand, and the trade, which is large and constantly growing, extends throughout New England and also to New York State, Pennsylvania and Florida. Mr. Morse, who is a gentleman in the prime of life, and of long practical experience and skill, was born in Nova Scotia, but has resided in Boston for over thirty years.

CHICAGO LUMBER COMPANY, Manufacturers of Sash, Doors, Blinds, Etc., Albany Street, near East Dedham Street.— A successful and representative house largely engaged in the manufacture of sash, doors, blinds and mouldings is that known as the Chicago Lumber Company, for whom Messrs. A. H. Bolton & Co. are the wholesale agents for eastern New England, with offices located on Albany Street at the foot of East Dedham Street. The Boston branch was established in 1889, since which period it has secured a liberal and permanent patronage, not only in this city and its vicinity but in all sections of New England. The Chicago Lumber Company are wholesale manufacturers of white pine, poplar and yellow pine lumber of all kinds, having recently, in addition to their immense white pine interests in the west, erected large saw and planing mills at Ironton, Ohio, where they are turning out about thirty million feet per annum of poplar lumber. They have also perfected arrangements which enable them to place long leaf yellow pine from Georgia and Alabama at the lowest prices. In a word, the company are prepared at all times to furnish anything in the way of building material. They make a specialty of thick finishing lumber of all grades—dressed flooring, siding and ceiling, and have at all times a large stock of shingles of different grades, kiln dried for shipment to points where freight is an object. A. H. Bolton & Co. promptly fill orders for car load or cargo lots, and guarantee entire satisfaction to patrons. All sash, doors, blinds and mouldings manufactured by this responsible company are unsurpassed for quality, finish and excellence, and the reputation thus acquired is maintained by carefully keeping the grading and finish of their goods to the same high standard; while the prices quoted for his stock is always regulated by the market. We bespeak for the Chicago Lumber Company an increasing trade, as they are prompt in filling orders, reliable in their representations, and honorable in all their dealings.

W. H. & S. L. EMERY, Hard and Soft Coal and Wood, Wharf, No. 298 Federal Street.—One of the most powerful factors in the remarkable development of the commercial and manufacturing interests of Boston is the coal trade. Prominent among the old established and representative houses engaged in this business is that of Messrs. W. H. & S. L. Emery, the well known dealers in hard and soft coal and wood, whose wharf is located at No. 298 Federal Street, opposite Beach. This house was founded in 1860 by Mr. Isaac Emery, and, in 1883, his son, Mr. W. H. Emery, was admitted to partnership. The present firm was organized in 1878. Both partners have had a vast range of practical experience and possess an intimate knowledge of the coal business and the requirements of this market. Their premises are spacious and conveniently arranged, and every modern facility is afforded for the receipt and shipment of supplies, and for the storage of the immense stock that is constantly carried. The firm conduct an extensive trade in the leading brands of anthracite and bituminous coals, including the best from the Lehigh, Lackawanna and Cumberland regions, and the resources of the house are such that the largest orders can be filled with the utmost promptness, an advantage that the trade and the public are quick to appreciate. All coal purchased of this responsible house is guaranteed to maintain in every respect the highest standard of excellence and holds the front rank as regards the care in its preparation for the market, coming, as it does, from some of the best equipped collieries in America. The patronage is large, first-class and influential in the city and throughout the surrounding country, requiring the constant employment of from twelve to twenty men, and inducements are offered, as regards both excellence of stock and economy of prices, which challenge competition. The Messrs. Emery are natives and prominent citizens of Boston. Mr. Stephen L. Emery has served with credit as a member of the city council and as school committee, and has been a Justice of the Peace for many years. Both gentlemen are known and honored in commercial circles for their business ability and sterling probity, and have attained a prominence in trade which is accorded only to those whose transactions are based on principles of equity and honor.

DESK EXCHANGE, Office and Library Furniture, Etc. No. 78 Portland Street, Benjamin James, Jr., Proprietor.—The perfection that has been attained in the furnishing business houses during recent years has been of the most gratifying character, and in one branch in particular has marked advancement been achieved, and that is in the manufacture of office desks. The most popular desk exchange, and a leading source of supply for this class of furniture in Boston, is that so admirably conducted at No. 78 Portland Street. This house is headquarters for office and library furniture, roll top desks and sales, chairs, book cases and copying presses; also, for the purchase, sale and exchange of second hand desks, safes and fixtures, and for securing special office fittings to order. The enterprise was inaugurated in 1886, the present proprietor succeeding to the control April 12, 1888. The premises occupied for the business are spacious in size, thoroughly equipped for display, inspection and sale, and stocked to repletion with new, choice and desirable goods. The roll top desks and other specialties of this house are unrivalled for originality and beauty of design, fine finish and artistic workmanship, and recommend their own peculiar merits to the confidence and patronage of critical and discriminating buyers by reason of their mechanical excellence, while bargains are constantly offered as regards terms and prices, which cannot be duplicated elsewhere. The trade is brisk and lively in this city, and a heavy and influential demand is ministered to.

R. F. NAYLOR, Real Estate and Insurance, No. 23 Pemberton Square.—Among the many engaged in the handling of realty and the placing of risks on property in this city, there are few better known, or enjoy a larger measure of public confidence and favor, than R. F. Naylor, the popular and responsible real estate and insurance agent. Mr. Naylor was born in Taunton, Mass., but has lived in Boston thirty odd years. He has been actively and successfully engaged in this line for over twenty years, and has built up a large and steadily improving business. Mr. Naylor carries on a general real estate and insurance business, buying, selling and exchanging houses, lots and city or suburban property of every description; and attends, also, to leasing, renting and collecting. Special attention is given to auction sales of real estate and general merchandise, likewise, and estates are taken in charge and judiciously managed, while insurance is placed with first-class companies at lowest rates. Mortgages are negotiated, and loans effected, and, in short, everything appertaining to real estate and kindred interests is attended to in the most reliable and satisfactory manner.

N. C. LOMBARD, Mechanical Engineer, and Solicitor of Patents, Room No. 41, No. 40 State Street.—This gentleman is an expert mechanical engineer of large experience and high reputation, and gives skillful attention to perfecting new inventions and to superintending the construction of machinery, when desired. His time is, however, mostly taken up with his patent law practice. Possessing a foundation understanding of the principles of patent law, a complete and thorough knowledge of the rules and practice governing the administration of the United States Patent office, and an experience of twenty years as a patent attorney, has eminently fitted him for success in every branch of his profession. He is a native of the state of Maine, a resident of Boston and Cambridge for the past thirty years, and established himself in practice here as a mechanical engineer and solicitor of patents in 1868. His reputation has long been firmly established as an able, scientific and successful solicitor, and a clear-headed, reliable counsellor in patent law. His practice before the U. S. Patent Office relates to the preparation and prosecution of applications for patents, including the making out of specifications, drawings, caveats, assignments, reissues, designs, trademarks and labels; the making of preliminary examinations as to the patentability of an invention, attending to cases in interference, on appeal, and as an expert before the courts, and to every other item of service necessary to the complete success of the application up to the time the patent is granted and issued by the office. No attorney is better known at the patent office, and none can secure fairer treatment or more prompt consideration of their cases. His papers, filed in the interest of his clients, are models of accuracy, wisdom and perfect understanding of the case in hand, while the facilities possessed by him for securing patents are unsurpassed by any practitioner in the country. His patronage is large, first-class and influential in this city and throughout the New England States, and his standing is of the highest.

J. FRENCH & SONS, Real Estate, Mortgages, Etc., No. 160 State Street.—There is no feature of progress in our country that assumes an importance equivalent with that of real estate. Desirable and eligibly located parcels of real property are more than ever in demand with conservative capitalists and prudent investors, who, in making these investments, rely to a large degree upon the superior knowledge, advice and assistance of reputable brokers and agents. One of the oldest and best-known real estate firms in Boston is that of Messrs. Jonathan French & Sons, whose offices are eligibly located at No. 160 State Street. Messrs. John D. W. and A. D. Weld French, his two sons, are associated with him and are all natives of Boston, and prominent and popular in financial and real estate circles. The firm do a general real estate business, and a safe packed with powers of attorney tells its character. The house is recognized as one of the best authorities on present and prospective values of realty in the city and suburbs, taking the entire management of estates while the owners are enjoying European life for years at a time. In fact their principal business is the care of large trust properties.

McPHERSON BROTHERS, Commission Merchants, and Wholesale Dealers in Flour and Produce, Nos. 204 State and 39 Commerce Streets.—The activity and predominance of the Boston flour and produce market is largely due to the sterling enterprise and business push manifested by our leading commission houses. One of the most widely and favorably known is that of Messrs. McPherson Brothers, whose splendid establishment is located at Nos. 204 State and 39 Commerce Streets. This firm are commission merchants and wholesale dealers in flour and produce, and have been established in the business here since 1873. The premises occupied are spacious and convenient, finely fitted up and admirably equipped for handling and storing the immense stock that is constantly carried. The building contains seven floors, 25x80 feet each, and extends through the block from State to Commerce Street. The firm carries on an extensive business in the best brands of flour and in general country produce, and have built up a large and influential trade that extends throughout all the New England States. Liberal advances are made on consignments when desired, while quick sales and prompt returns have always been the characteristic of this reliable and trustworthy house. The firm is in a position to offer every facility and advantage as regards the sale of these staple commodities, and number among their customers many large shippers in the best-producing districts of the country, and prominent dealers and buyers throughout New England. The influence exerted by this house on the flour and produce commission trade of Boston has been of the most salutary and useful character, and those interested in establishing relations with it can depend on receiving prompt and liberal treatment and other advantages difficult to be secured elsewhere. The copartners Messrs. E. B. and John McPherson, are well and widely known as enterprising merchants and solid, substantial business men.

OSCAR F. HOWE, Wooden and Willow Ware, Nos. 4 and 5 South Market, and 41 and 42 Chatham Streets.—One of the indispensable branches of trade in all cities, is that of wooden and willow ware. A representative and one of the oldest established houses in Boston actively engaged in this useful and growing trade, is that of Mr. Oscar F. Howe, whose office and salesrooms are situated on South Market and Chatham Streets. This business was established in 1850 by Daniel Cummings & Co., who were succeeded in 1853 by Wakefield & Howe, and in 1877 by N. & J. Howe, and in 1864 by Nelson Howe & Son. Eventually in 1868 Mr. Oscar F. Howe became sole proprietor, and in 1877 purchased the present business house, which had for many years been engaged in the wooden and willow ware trade. The premises occupied comprise a spacious four-story and basement building, having frontages on South Market and Chatham Streets. The warerooms are fully stocked with a superior assortment of all kinds of wooden and willow ware, including pails, tubs, washboards clothes wringers, brooms, baskets, brushes, mats, churns, kegs, snow shovels, twine, cordage, clothes dryers, etc. All goods are purchased direct from the most famous manufacturers, and are supplied to the trade in quantities to suit at the lowest possible wholesale prices. The trade of the house extends throughout all sections of New England, Australia, California and South America, and is steadily increasing owing to the reliability and superiority of its productions. Mr. Oscar F. Howe was born in New Hampshire, but has resided in Boston for the last thirty-five years, where he is greatly respected in trade circles for his enterprise and integrity. This popular house fully merits the confidence it enjoys, and the pronounced success it has acquired and held for so many years.

H. & R. ATWOOD, Planters and Wholesale Dealers in Providence River and Virginia Oysters, Nos. 43 Commercial and 56 Clinton Streets, and Nos. 146 and 148 Atlantic Avenue.—An important factor in the wholesale and retail oyster trade of Boston is the establishment of Messrs. H. & R. Atwood, whose offices and stores are centrally located on Commercial and Clinton Streets and Atlantic Avenue. This business which is the oldest and largest in the city, was established seventy-six years ago by David Atwood, who retired and was succeeded by his sons Messrs. H. & R. Atwood. In 1888 Mr. H. Atwood retired in consequence of ill-health, and the business is now the property of Mr. R. K. Atwood. The premises occupied are spacious, and are fitted with every modern convenience and facility for the rapid handling and perfect preservation of the extensive stock, that is here at all times on hand. In the various departments of his business as a planter, wholesale and retail dealer, Mr. Atwood gives employment to 200 hands and possesses the best possible facilities for the prompt fulfillment of all orders. He deals extensively in Providence River and Virginia oysters, and all varieties of native oysters, also in clams, little necks and quahaugs. Only the freshest and finest stock is handled, and the trade of the house now extends throughout all sections of New England and New York. The prices are always regulated by the market, and the partners of this old established and reliable house are unanimous in the praise of the liberality and enterprise of its management. Mr. Atwood was born in Cape Cod, but has resided in Boston the greater part of his life. His long experience in the oyster trade gives him peculiar advantages, which he freely shares with his patrons, while his high character is a sufficient guarantee of the reliability of all transactions. The firm still continues under the name of H. & R. Atwood, as heretofore.

GLEASON & KIMBALL, Commission Dealers in Foreign and Domestic Fruits, and Produce of all Kinds, No. 19 Faneuil Hall Market, South Side.—The special department of commerce devoted to the wholesale handling of fruits, domestic and foreign, and to all kinds of country produce, constitutes, as it is needless to remark, one of the great branches of commercial activity in the United States at the present day. The transactions in these products in Boston alone reach enormous proportions annually, while the volume of business affords evidence of steady and material increase. Among the firms contributing most largely to the aggregate of trade and commerce in this line in the city may be mentioned that of Messrs. Gleason & Kimball, commission merchants and jobbers in foreign and domestic fruits and produce of all kinds, doing business at No. 19 Faneuil Hall Market (south side). Although this firm was founded so recently as January, 1888, the co-partners are by no means new to the business, but being a long practical experience to bear upon their enterprise, and already they have become one of the most prominent and responsible engaged in this important branch of business in the city, while their connections, which extend throughout the country, are of a most substantial and gratifying character. The premises occupied by the firm are commodious and well-equipped, and they carry constantly on hand an extensive and carefully assorted stock of native and foreign fruits of every variety and the finest quality, a specialty being made of Florida oranges, lemons, pears and grapes; while particular attention is given to the handling of all kinds of country produce. The firm are in daily receipt of heavy consignments, for which they find a ready and remunerative market, and they make a special feature of furnishing immediate returns to shippers. The individual members of the firm are E. W. Gleason and Mr. A. W. Kimball. The former was born in Boston, and the latter in New Hampshire.

THE MILLER Boot and Shoe Trees, O. A. Miller, Sole Proprietor and Manufacturer, Office and Factory at Brockton, Mass.; Boston Office, No. 89 Bedford Street.—Like all the other devices connected with the footwear industry, very notable improvement has been effected in boot trees of late years in this country. What with invention, improvements and the marked development of mechanical skill, a degree of excellence akin to perfection itself has been attained in these useful and indispensable appliances within the past decade or so. And while on this subject, it may not be amiss to the readers of this volume to direct attention here to the widely known Miller Boot and Shoe Trees, O. A. Miller, sole proprietor and manufacturer, with factory at Brockton, Mass., and Boston office at No. 89 Bedford Street, which are articles of exceptional merit; and as a consequence have secured an enduring hold on favor among shoe manufacturers throughout the whole of the United States. They are by common consent the ne plus ultra in boot and shoe trees; being, in all respects, the most complete, perfect, effective, and, altogether, superior devices for the purposes intended produced to-day in this country; and are in steady and growing demand in the centers of the footwear industry all over the land, the sales being especially large in New England. Mr. Miller, who is a comparatively young man, and a native of New York State, has been established in the manufacture of these trees in Brockton since 1878, and the unequivocal success that has attended the enterprise from its inception abundantly attests the merits of the productions. The Miller Boot and Shoe Trees are made with patent side-expansion tree leg, and also with patent split or sectional tree feet, while eighteen expert workmen are employed in their manufacture; every facility and mechanical contrivance necessary to the business being at hand, and all work is executed under the close personal supervision of the proprietor. All communications pertaining thereto, addressed to O. A. Miller, Brockton, Mass., or No. 89 Bedford Street, Boston, will receive prompt response, descriptive circulars, price-list and references being cheerfully mailed to any part of the country upon application for the same.

S. S. LEARNARD, Beef, Pork, Lard, Hams, Bacon, Tallow, Etc., Nos. 50 and 52 Faneuil Hall Market.—One of the oldest and best known and most popular concerns engaged in the beef and provision trade in Faneuil Hall Market is that of Mr. S. S. Learnard, of stalls Nos. 50 and 52. Mr. Learnard was born in Brighton, Mass., and fifty-four years have elapsed since he founded the business conducted here, and in the management of which he still takes an active part. He is, however, ably assisted by three active partners. One of these is his son, Mr. E. B. Learnard, who was born in Brighton, and has been a partner for the past twenty years. Mr. C. S. Hapgood, a native of Concord, Mass., has also been connected with the firm for a like period; and Mr. R. A. Pettigrew, who was born in Ludlow, Vt., has been a partner since 1883. The firm have an abbatoir at Brighton, where they slaughter all their own cattle, etc., and conduct a trade of great and growing magnitude. The two stalls occupied by the firm in the market are spacious and commodious, and are provided with all appliances and conveniences for facilitating the transaction of business, which is of both a wholesale and retail character, but chiefly wholesale. The patronage of the firm both in the city and suburbs is as influential as it is extensive and substantial. The firm include among their permanent customers the leading hotels, such as the Vendome, Brunswick, etc., and the stock carried is always kept up to the highest standard of excellence. It embraces the choicest cuts of beef and pork, also hams, bacon, lard, tallow, etc. The stalls are connected by telephone, and all orders are filled promptly and satisfactorily, and the firm, while handling the best class of goods to be found in the market, always keep their prices at the lowest point.

CHAS. NOWELL, Real Estate and Mortgages, No. 31 Milk Street (Room 18).—Prominent among the most successful and reliable real estate agents in this city, is Mr. Chas. Nowell. This gentleman makes a specialty of the care of real estate and the collection of rents. Some of the largest estates in the city and vicinity, are placed entirely in the hands of Mr. Nowell, while the owners go to enjoy travel and European life for years at a time. Having been a builder and contractor for forty years, and a First Assistant Assessor for six years in the Back-Bay District, he is specially competent to estimate the value of real estate, and to give advice in the purchase and sale of the same. He has also acquired an enviable reputation as a negotiator of loans on bond and mortgage, his thorough knowledge of city realty, and facilities as regards capital, enabling him to promptly loan to the utmost limit at current rates and lowest charges. He also gives prompt and skillful attention to orders for the repairing and remodelling of houses and stores, including carpentry, mason-work, plumbing, painting, etc., exercising his personal supervision over all the details of the work, and guaranteeing satisfaction in all operations. There is a considerable line of selling done by Mr. Nowell, of both city and suburban property, every ward in the city being represented on his books as well as every class of property, while he is justly recognized as one of the best renting judges in the city. He has a large amount of property to sell, rent or exchange on easy terms, and is in a position to suit the needs and requirements of all classes of investors and house hunters.

J. McGRATH, Real Estate and Business Broker, No. 28 School Street, Room 48.—Among the fraternity of real estate and business brokers, Mr. J. McGrath, at No. 28 School Street, is widely known, since his settlement among them in 1887, as having introduced the quickest known methods of handling investments in real estate and business chances. By his system of obtaining the fullest information in regard to all property placed in his hands for sale, thoroughly investigating everything with his keen knowledge of values, and assuming responsibility for his statements, he has made his office a trustworthy directory, whose merit is rapidly making itself known to investors, and his large and rapidly increasing patronage, which enables him to dispose of property without delay, of course, induces owners who desire quick transactions to engage his services. As a bright example of the fact that, in this progressive age, business enterprise, when backed by sound financial judgment, rare executive ability, and upright principles, need not grow old waiting for appreciation, the success of this gentleman furnishes an inspiring lesson to the young men of Boston. His motto when advising any of his customers to engage in business of any kind is, "the right man in the right place;" and many whom he has directed into that path of fortune best fitted to their abilities, have for him a high regard, which is the best evidence of the permanence of his already enviable reputation.

THE METROPOLIS OF NEW ENGLAND.

M. S. PAGE & CO., Merchandise and Money Brokers, No. 1 Salem Street, Corner Endicott Street.—Among the old business landmarks in this old section of the city stands the busy and popular store of Messrs. M. S. Page & Company, on the corner of Salem and Endicott streets. The firm are general merchandise and money brokers, watchmakers and jewelers, and dealers in diamonds and other precious stones, gold and silver watches of every description, guns, pistols, clocks, etc. It is thirty years since this business was organized, and it has during the whole of its long career been a noted business centre and commanded a patronage that has been the envy and admiration of others in the same line of trade. In 1858 the firm of Felch & Page was organized and began business at this spot, where it has ever since been continued. For eighteen years or more Mr. Page has been the sole proprietor, and has conducted the enter-

prise under the style of M. S. Page & Co. The premises occupied comprise two connecting stores, with upper room and basement, and ample accommodation is afforded for the display and storage of stock and transaction of business, in which six assistants are engaged. The firm buy, sell and exchange, or loan money on, watches, diamonds and other personal property, and have always on hand for disposal precious stones of all kinds, watches, clocks, jewelry of every description, guns, pistols, musical instruments in great variety. Specialties are made of diamonds, watches and guns, in which a brisk and extensive trade is done, a sale being made of over 800 watches a year. Particular attention is given to the repairing of watches and jewelry by experienced workmen. Mr. Page is a native of New Hampshire, is a pushing, energetic and straightforward business man, and is esteemed by all who have had dealings with him or acquainted with him in social life.

NIAGARA FIRE INSURANCE COMPANY, Henry R. Turner, General Agent, No. 5 Doane Street.—Among the leading fire insurance men of Boston, is Mr. Henry R. Turner, of No. 5 Doane Street, a gentleman who has spent all of his life in this important department of our business interests. His thorough knowledge of fire insurance has made him an authority on the subject, and he is considered as one of the best informed underwriters in the city. He has been identified with the insurance business for the past twenty-five years, and for a long period was secretary of the Fairfield Fire Insurance Company of Norwalk, Conn. He is now president of the New England Insurance Exchange, and for the past eight years or more he has been the general agent of the Niagara Fire Insurance Company of New York, for the states of Massachusetts, Maine, Vermont and Rhode Island. The company, whose representative he is, is one of the largest and most responsible insurance corporations in the east, and is extremely popular with business men and property owners throughout both the eastern, middle and western states. The seventy-second semi-annual statement given to the public on January 1st, 1888, shows the finances of the company to be in a most gratifying condition, showing assets of $3,277,491.50, a cash capital of $500,000; reinsurance reserve, $1,1824,6.28; reserve for all other liabilities, $218,746.05, and a net surplus, $575,974.19. From its very inception the business of the company has increased with each succeeding year, until it to-day occupies a prominent position among our home institutions, and has secured the entire confidence of the business public by its prompt and equitable methods of adjustment, and the liberal yet conservative policy which has ever characterized its transactions. In Mr. Turner, the company have a diligent and valuable representative. He controls a large number of sub-agencies throughout the four states named, and cheerfully affords all necessary information on insurance matters to those who apply for it. He is a native of Norfolk, Conn., and resides at Auburndale. Personally, he is a gentleman widely known throughout all circles, and merits the high esteem with which he is regarded.

WAIT & CUTTER, Architects, Mason Building, No. 70 Kilby Street.—These gentlemen established their business here in 1879, and have since steadily devoted themselves to solving the complex problems of how best to utilize the minimum of building space with the maximum of accommodation, coupled with architectural beauty of design and with a conscientious regard for the excellence and perfection of every detail. Their recognized standing in professional circles is proven by their large and influential patronage throughout New England and other sections of the country, while their worth as architects and builders is easily pointed out in our midst and confirmed wherever they have been engaged. They have erected, among other fine specimens of architecture, the armory in this city, the court house at Cambridge, Mass.; the library buildings at Brookfield, Mass., and Tilburn, N. H., and elegant and elaborate church edifices at Nashua, N. H., Easton, Mass., and other points, besides numerous private residences, offices and public buildings of their own designing. Orders and commissions receive their prompt personal attention, and a corps of skilled assistants is employed. The co-partners, Messrs. R. Pote, Wait and Otis W. Cutter, are both Massachusetts men by birth and education, and are recognized as thoroughgoing and accomplished exponents of those measures best calculated to embellish this metropolis with an architecture worthy of its commercial fame.

CHARLES BABSON, JR., American & Foreign Patents, No. 24 Congress Street.—One of the best known and most reliable patent agents in Boston, is Mr. Charles Babson, Jr., whose office is at No. 24 Congress Street. Mr. Babson has been identified with the business since 1872, and has been a close observer of the mechanical, scientific and industrial inventions which have marked our history during the period that has elapsed since then. In 1886 he established his present agency, opening up connections with the principal centres both at home and abroad, and having his agents at Washington to carry out his orders in a prompt and reliable way. He deals in patents of all kinds, both American and foreign, handling all meritorious inventions, securing patents for them without unnecessary delay at the lowest rates, negotiating for their purchase and sale and generally acting in the most varied manner for the best interests of his clients. He has put through a vast number of inventions since he undertook the business, and has given the greatest satisfaction to those who have employed his services. His knowledge of patent law is unusually thorough, and enables him to advise his clients to the advantage both of their time and pocket.

WINN, RICKER & CO., Commission Merchants, and Dealers in Fruit, Vegetables and Pickles, Nos. 93 and 95 Faneuil Hall Market, and Cellar No. 17, under the Market. (South Side.)—No branch of commerce in Boston is more important and representative in character than the commission trade in fruits and vegetables. Prominent among the number and one of the oldest houses engaged therein is that of Messrs. Winn, Ricker & Co., located at Nos. 93 and 95 Faneuil Hall Market. This firm have long been widely known as commission merchants and wholesale and retail dealers in fruit, vegetables and pickles. The business was founded some forty years ago, under the firm name of Winn, Ricker & Co., which has been continued down to the present time. Mr. Winn died in 1876, and Mr. Ricker had retired from business three years previously. Mr. J. W. Hill was admitted to partnership about 1868, and in company with Mr. W. Craig, who was admitted to the firm in 1885, now conducts the business without change in the firm name. Both these gentlemen bring large practical experience to bear, coupled with an intimate knowledge of the requirements of the trade. They occupy large and commodious quarters, fully supplied with every modern convenience for the storage and preservation of the choice and valuable stock. The firm deal extensively in the commodities named, and number among their permanent patrons many of our wealthy dealers and largest shippers. They are in daily receipt of fine foreign and domestic fruits, including the choice of the markets in Florida, California, Curacoa and Jamaica; also early vegetables from the leading market gardeners of Massachusetts and other rich producing sections of New England, besides pickles and preserves of every description suited to the requirements of a first-class family trade. They are always ready to make liberal cash advances on consignments, and are in a position to guarantee quick sales and prompt returns. The policy on which the business is conducted is such as to meet with the hearty commendations of the trade and general public, and those forming relations with this trustworthy firm may be assured of receiving that just and equitable treatment which has ever characterized the operations of this house. Mr. Hill is a native of Massachusetts, while Mr. Craig was born in Vermont, and both gentlemen sustain an excellent status in social and business life.

GEORGE F. BROWNE, Insurance Broker and Dealer in Real Estate and Mortgages, No. 79 Milk Street, Room 2 A.—The insurance interests of this great city is most ably represented by Mr. George F. Browne, insurance broker and dealer in real estate and mortgages. Having had an extensive experience in these lines of business, Mr. Browne, who is a native Bostonian inaugurated this enterprise originally in 1868, and making a specialty of insurance in all its branches, coupled with an intimate knowledge of real estate, he developed an extensive connection of a strictly first-class character within a comparatively brief period, and is still increasing to proportions of great magnitude. He occupies a finely furnished office, most conveniently located, and which is supplied with every facility for the transaction of the business in hand, embracing the fullest and most reliable information concerning the insurance and real estate interests of Boston and the surrounding vicinity, and with these adjuncts to his business, which are absolutely unsurpassed he is enabled to place the largest risks at low rates, with a line of our most responsible and popular companies, while on favorably located parcels of real estate, he can quote prices and terms that are unrivalled in the market. His long experience with special talents for the business, coupled with executive abilities of the highest order have given him a high prestige in the real estate market, and possessing, as he does, an intimate knowledge of the various residential and business sections of the city and its environs, investors can rely at all times upon his judgment and advice. Mr. Browne also possesses every facility for the negotiation of loans on bond and mortgage upon the most favorable terms.

S. F. WOODBRIDGE & CO., Wholesale Dealers in Dressed Beef, Pork, Lard, Hams, Tallow, Etc., Nos. 65 and 67 Faneuil Hall Market, and No. 111 Clinton Street.—Few houses, if any, engaged in the trade in dressed beef, pork, lard, hams, tallow, etc., in this city, enjoy a more honorable name, or cleaner record, than that of Messrs. S. F. Woodbridge & Co., located at Nos. 65 and 67 Faneuil Hall Market. Since this house was started here in 1874, it may be said to have reaped uninterrupted prosperity, and in 1886 a wholesale department, at No. 111 Clinton Street, was added to the business. Built upon a solid foundation, undisturbed by the periodical seasons of depressions which have crippled many others, carried not away by currents of surrounding entering speculation, this firm have gone steadily ahead, until now it takes a leading place in the trade. The premises occupied for trade purposes are well supplied with the necessary cold storage and refrigerating rooms for the storage and perfect preservation of the beef, pork and perishable articles, while the stock is replenished daily from the most reputable sources, and is kept at the highest point of excellence and efficiency. The business is carried on at both wholesale and retail, and the firm pride themselves upon their ability to fill orders in any part of the New England States with the utmost despatch and with entire satisfaction. The reputation of this house for handling the choicest stock of dressed beef, pork and other kindred specialties, is absolutely unexcelled, and this prestige has resulted in the development of a trade of large volume and far reaching influence. Inducements are also offered in regard to terms and prices which challenge competition, and tend to add materially to the popularity of the house among all classes of buyers. The firm is composed of S. F. Woodbridge and his son, W. F. Woodbridge, both natives of Cambridge, Mass., eminently popular in this city and throughout New England, and have always borne an unblemished name in society and business circles.

WHITMAN E. SMITH, (Successor to W. B. Smith & Son,) Wholesale and Retail Dealer in Fruits and Vegetables, also, Canned Goods, Stalls, Nos. 103 and 105 Faneuil Hall Market.—Mr. Whitman E. Smith by his ability, enterprise and energy has maintained a front rank in the best class of Boston's wholesale fruit and produce trade. His stalls in Faneuil Hall Market are always the most attractive of any, with the choicest and best, not only of what is in season, but also of hot house goods during the winter and spring. It is here that Boston's leading caterers can best obtain supplies. The business was established by the late Mr. W. B. Smith, upwards of thirty-five years ago, the firm of Hiland, Smith & Co. succeeded, and about ten years ago, the firm of Smith, Avery & Maynard was formed. In 1883 it dissolved and was succeeded by Messrs. W. B. Smith & Son. The lamented decease of Mr. W. B. Smith occurred about eighteen months ago, since which date his son, Mr. Whitman E. Smith, has remained sole proprietor and has ever maintained the high standard of his stock for which it has always been so celebrated. His stalls are a most attractive spectacle, with their complete array of all fruits and vegetables in and out of season. Mr. Smith handles whatever is choice and desirable; he has the trade which demands the best, and he has the ability to supply it. Fine fruits are a specialty, including the product of the large hot houses, such as grapes, strawberries, green stuff, etc., which can be had in midwinter. Associated in the business with Mr. Whitman E. Smith is Mr. C. W. Smith, his brother, a young merchant of ability and experience. They do a heavy wholesale and retail trade, supplying hotels and Back Bay residents, and have achieved a most enviable reputation both as to character and quality of product, and prompt, liberal business methods.

OSCAR LOW, Real Estate and Mortgages, No. 75 Equitable Building.—Prominent among the leading and popular real estate agents in this city and well worthy of mention is Mr. Oscar Low, real estate agent and broker, negotiator of loans, etc. Mr. Low is a native Bostonian and at present resides in Dorchester. He is a gentleman of about middle age, and established himself in this line of business originally in 1882. He brings years of practical experience to bear, besides an intimate knowledge of the value of improved and unimproved real estate in the city and the entire surrounding city. He occupies a very neatly and handsomely appointed office in which will be found every facility for the transaction of business together with accurate information regarding all lines of properties with which he is connected. His connections are of a first class character, and he numbers among his permanent customers many of Boston's capitalists and property-owners.

THE METROPOLIS OF NEW ENGLAND. 207

BOSTON & GLOUCESTER STEAMBOAT COMPANY, E. S. Merchant, Treasurer and Agent; Office, North Side, Central Wharf.—This enterprising and progressive company was duly incorporated in 1870 under the laws of Massachusetts with ample capital. It has obtained a generous and permanent support from all classes, and excursionists desirous of visiting Annisquam, Bay View, Lanesville, Bass Rock, East Gloucester, Rockport and Pigeon Cove, will always find this line the most pleasant way of traveling, avoiding heat and dust. The company's steamers which are among the finest and best equipped in New England are the "City of Gloucester," captain, E. S. Young, and the "Geo. A. Chafey," captain, N. Proctor. The steamers of this line leave North Side of Central Wharf, Boston, daily (Sundays excepted). This route affords to tourists one of the finest ocean trips along the North Shore, a distance of thirty miles, with scenery unsurpassed. Some of the points of interest along the North Shore to the city of Gloucester are the beautiful islands of Boston Harbor, including Forts Independence and Winthrop, and Deer Island, and also a view of all the lighthouses of the bay. Passing out of the harbor, the first sight of interest is the renowned summer resort of Nahant, its shores and beaches lined with cottages and summer residences on the one side, and the broad Atlantic on the other. Next comes the shores of Swampscott and the quaint old town of Marblehead; then passing near Halfway Rock, where the crews of the fishing fleets cast their pennies on their outward trips for good luck and safe return. Next in view come Lowell and Baker's Islands, off the shores of Beverly. Lowell Island, with its large hotel, makes one of the many beautiful spots of the coast. On Baker's Island are the Twin Lights, so well known to mariners entering Salem and Beverly harbors. Then comes Manchester-by-the-Sea, one of the most fashionable watering places of these shores, and one of the many beautiful suburban drives of Gloucester. Then we have Magnolia, noted for its fine and numerous hotels, filled to overflowing with guests during the summer season, —with its walks to Rafe's chasm and Norman's Woe Rock, made famous by Longfellow's poem, "The Wreck of the Hesperus." Entering the harbor gives one a fine view of the City of Gloucester, the most renowned fishing port of the world, also noted for its drives and beautiful summer resorts for pleasure seekers. The harbor is noted for its beautiful beaches for sea-bathing, as well as for its boating and fishing. Single fare, 50 cents; consultation tickets of six trips, $2.40; round trip, 50 cents. The following gentlemen, who are widely known in business circles for their energy and integrity are the executive officers: Henry W. Whitney, president; E. S. Merchant, treasurer and agent, Boston; Abbott Coffin, agent, Gloucester.

H. C. WAINWRIGHT & CO., Stock Brokers, No. 40 State Street.—The financial firms of Boston are justly recognized as substantial and reliable as those of any city in the United States. Among the enterprising and representative firms of stock brokers in the city may be named that of Messrs. H. C. Wainwright & Co., whose office is located at No. 40 State Street. This firm have had a long experience in financial life and their reputation is one of conservatism and integrity. They do a general commission brokerage business, and have every facility for its prompt execution, and number among their clients many wealthy investors and large operators. They have correspondents in New York and other cities with private telegraph wire to the former. Both members of the firm are members of the Boston Stock Exchange.

DOWNER & CO., Bankers and Brokers, No. 28 State Street.— The development of the Boston Stock Exchange is in no small degree due to those old established and reliable business houses, that have for so many years not only created its volume of trade, but have originated and enforced a code of regulations which has permanently placed this institution on an enduring basis of equity. Among the popular and old established houses thus identified with the Stock Exchange, is the responsible firm of Messrs. Downer & Co., bankers and brokers, whose offices are centrally located at No. 28 State Street. This business was established in 1842. Ten years ago the present copartners, Messrs. Frank W. Downer, G. Fred. Gibbley and Edward C. Fletcher succeeded to the management. They possess an intimate knowledge of every phase and feature of the stock and money markets, and customers can always rely on their experience and facilities for securing the earliest official information relative to the value of all kinds of securities. The offices are spacious, and afford every convenience to patrons, who number many wealthy investors and active operators. The firm conduct an extensive business in the purchase and sale strictly on commission of all stocks, bonds, Government and miscellaneous securities as listed by the board for cash or on margin, and are at all times prepared to render their customers every possible advantage. They likewise sell drafts and telegraphic exchange on San Francisco, New York, Washington, Montreal, Halifax, N. S., St. John, N. B., and Prince Edward Island. Messrs. Downer & Co., likewise draw sight exchange on England, Ireland, Germany, France, Switzerland, Italy, Norway, Sweden and all other European countries. The partners are popular members of the Boston and New York Stock Exchange, and have a private wire to New York. During the Civil War Messrs. Downer & Co. conducted an extensive business in gold. The firm points with pride to a record of honorable dealing from its establishment up to the present time.

R. W. TURNER, Real Estate and Insurance, No. 194 Washington Street.—The varied and vast interests involved in real estate and insurance transactions in every important centre of activity in this country have in the nature of things, attracted to this branch of business some of the most enterprising and far-seeing men in every community, and, it is scarcely necessary to state, Boston is no exception to the rule. One of the leaders in this line of business activity is Mr. R. W. Turner, whose office is centrally located at No. 194 Washington Street. This gentleman has been engaged in business here since 1876, and enjoys a deservedly high reputation for business ability, sound judgment and thorough reliability. He transacts a general real estate business in the city and vicinity, buying, selling, leasing and exchanging property of all kinds; attending to the management of estates, the collection of rents, the negotiation of loans on bond and mortgage, and effecting insurance in reliable companies. He is prepared to place risks in any insurance company desired, quoting the lowest rates of premium, and guaranteeing a prompt and liberal adjustment of all losses. His business has been conducted from the outset with growing and gratifying success, and his connections are of the most substantial and desirable character, numbering, as he does, among his permanent customers many of the solid and wealthiest capitalists, investors and property owners in Boston and its vicinity. He is a recognized authority as to the present and prospective values of realty in this city and its suburban towns, and all advice given or transactions effected through him can be relied upon as absolutely safe. His services are promptly and conscientiously rendered, and his charges are invariably moderate. Mr. Turner is a native of Lynn, N. H., resides at No. 14 Jerome Street, Dorchester district, and refers by permission to Messrs. Samuel A. Carleton, president National Security Bank; and H. W. Paine, No. 209 Washington Street, as to his reliability and personal worth.

C. WRIGHT & CO., Lard Refiners, No. 72 Market Street.—An important adjunct to the lard refinery industry of Boston is that of Messrs. C. Wright & Company. The firm's refinery, which is fully equipped with modern apparatus and appliances, is situated on Norfolk Avenue. This business was established twenty years ago by Mr. Chandler Wright, who conducted it till 1872, when Mr. Edward E. Baldwin became a partner, the firm being known by the style and title of C. Wright & Company. The firm refine extensively pure and compounded lard, and pack lard in tierces, pails, etc., expressly for the English, German and South American markets. They handle only first-class stock and produce lard, which is absolutely unrivalled in this or any other market. In fact their brands of lard are everywhere recognized and appreciated by the trade as standard productions. Messrs. C. Wright & Company fill all orders promptly and carefully for either the home or foreign trade at the lowest ruling market prices. Mr. Wright is a native of Arlington, Mass., and Mr. Baldwin of Cambridge, Mass. They are active members of the Chamber of Commerce, and are highly esteemed in trade circles for their enterprise, business ability and integrity.

C. T. DERRY & CO., Dealers in Granite, Bridge Abutments, Sea Wall and Wharf Builders, Office, No. 68 Devonshire street.—The leading builders and contractors of Boston in the line of sea walls, wharf walls, stone piers, abutments, etc., are Messrs. C. T. Derry & Co., of No. 68 Devonshire Street, and Mechanics' Exchange. The business conducted by them is as long established as it is widely extended. It was founded thirty-five years ago by Mr. C. T. Derry, a native of Quincy and a practical master mason, quarry proprietor, and granite contractor, of the highest standing, and widest range of experience. He early developed an active trade, and in the year 1868, took into copartnership, Mr. C. H. Edwards under the name and style of C. T. Derry & Co. In 1880, Mr. Edwards withdrawing, Mr James Burr came into the firm under the same style, and the house has since permanently maintained the lead in its line. Its facilities are unrivalled, its resources ample, and its connections most influential. Having had experience in the performance of the heaviest contracts in the building of sea walls, piers, bridge abutments, etc., the firm is called on to perform the most important engagements in this line. Their first contract was in 1856 for William Evans, contractor with the city of Boston, on Albany Street, it being a wall over a mile in length, of heavy dimensions, thirteen feet wide at bottom, four feet wide at top, and fourteen feet high. They built a portion of the splendid Long Wharf, the substantial wharf and piling for the Standard Sugar refinery at South Boston; the wharf for the Franklin Coal Co. of South Boston, owned by Francis B. Hayes. In 1883 they built the great sea wall on Beacon Street, 2700 feet long and one of the most substantial of its class. They are now engaged on the heaviest contract of the kind ever let, viz:—for the Boston & Maine Railroad, the wall being 4000 feet long, of the most durable and substantial character. This contract is the largest of the kind ever accomplished in the same length of time, (from June 1, to December 1,) it being thirty feet wide at the base, three feet wide at top, and twenty feet high, built in seven feet of water at low tide, and requiring about one hundred thousand tons of stone. To give some idea of the magnitude of their business, we may state that they paid out for labor and stone from eighteen to twenty thousand dollars per month last summer, employing a large number of men and vessels in freighting and laying stone. Among their customers are the United States Government, for which they handled all the twenty-five ton guns with their appurtenances, during the war, landing them at all the different forts from New York Harbor north; leading railroads, such as the Fitchburg, for which the Hoosac Tunnel Dock and Elevator was built, at which three of the largest foreign steamship lines running into Boston discharge; they also furnished the foundation for the large freight house of the Boston & Providence Railroad, and the new bridge at Dedham and the one at Hyde Park for them; Manufacturing corporations—the Boston Gas Light Co., for whom they built about 1700 feet of heavy sea wall and foundation for their works at Commercial Point, and the Bradley Fertilizing Works at Weymouth where they furnished about 500 feet of sea wall. They have filled many contracts in public competition and in the most satisfactory manner, and are thoroughly responsible, honorable contractors. Their stone is supplied from the quarries at Rockport and Quincy, and they employ as many as twenty vessels in the work of transporting it from there to Boston. The removal and rebuilding of old sea walls and wharves is a speciality and in this line they challenge competition. They are also owners of strongly built, able, and seaworthy lighters of large capacity, specially adapted for the transportation of heavy merchandise, granite, etc., to all parts of the harbor; builders, S. S. agents, and others should apply to them when in need of superior lighterage facilities. Mr. Derry is one of the oldest members of the Mechanics' Exchange, having been connected therewith for fully thirty-five years past, and has ever accorded a hearty support to all measures best calculated to advance its permanent welfare and prosperity and that of the trade. Mr. James Burr is also a practical man, for eight years past connected with the house, a native of Quincy; he also is a popular and active member of the Mechanics' Exchange. In conclusion we would state, that Capt. C. T. Derry, is one of the prominent citizens of Sharon, Mass., being a large real estate owner, and takes an active interest in all improvements tending to the benefit of this most healthful town. He bought the property and formed the company, that constructed the Massapoag Hotel, situated on the border of Massapoag Lake, well known to all Boston people who are in the habit of residing in the country during the summer months. Mr. Burr is also a prominent man in the town of Quincy, and, so far as his standing there is concerned, need only state, that the people have chosen him as a representative of their new city government.

M. T. DENHAM, Treasurer and Agent of Eastern Forge Co., of Portland, Me., Rooms 78 and 79 Mason Building.—The most advanced and perfect industrial plant in New England to-day is that of the Eastern Forge Company of Portland, Me., of which Mr. M. T. Denham of Boston is the treasurer and general agent. It represents a heavy outlay most judiciously applied and has secured to New England, the credit of having a steam forge plant second to none in the country. The site of these great works has long been devoted to iron manufacturing, the business having been started by the Casco Iron Works in 1878. They were succeeded by the Presumpscot Iron Co., and after some years of activity, the concern laid idle for two years preceding September, 1885, when the Eastern Forge Company was organized by Mr. M. T. Denham and others, and vigorous measures were taken to develop an establishment that should have full capacity for the largest and all kinds of forgings. They bought the old plant, effecting extensive alterations therein, and making important additions, with the result that when they started up they were prepared to execute all orders from marine engine builders, founders, locomotive works, shipbuilders etc. They ran steadily and with a steadily increasing business until fire destroyed the works in December, 1887. With characteristic energy and enterprise Mr. Denham and his associates speedily set to work to rebuild, this time, taking every precaution to avoid all future dangers from fire, erecting their works entirely of iron, and which is the only forge building so constructed in the country. They spared neither pains nor expense in fitting it up with the most powerful and perfect machinery of every description specially made to meet their requirements. The trade interested has not been slow to mark its hearty appreciation of such well directed enterprise on the part of the Eastern Forge Co., and it has since starting up afresh been running night and day, employing a large force of hands in the manufacture of all classes of heavy forgings for marine engine builders, machinists, shipbuilders, railroads, and making a prominent speciality of forgings for locomotives, such as frames, driving axles, connecting rods, crank pins, etc. Quality is ever the first consideration, which fact, coupled with the high finish and moderate prices at which contracts are taken, has resulted in a rapid growth of trade, the volume of business now representing over $200,000 per annum. The works consume 500 tons of best No. 1 wrought scrap iron and open hearth steel per month and are the leading industry of the kind in New England. Every facility is at command, including deep water frontage for receiving of iron and coal and shipping of heavy forgings, also side track railroad connections at the rear. This is a modern plant run under the most approved and skilled methods, and, under the able executive guidance of the treasurer the works are achieving a great and permanent success. Mr. Denham is also contracting agent for the famous Cape Ann Anchor Works, and, as the representative of the above leading concerns, renders Boston the centre of a highly valuable branch of commerce. He is a respected member of business circles, and is worthy of the substantial success achieved.

W. A. WATERHOUSE, Lumber, Wholesale and Commission, No. 11 Central Street.—Among the younger lumber merchants of this city there is perhaps none that has been more fortunate in establishing a business connection or attaining a standing in the trade than W. A. Waterhouse, Mr. Waterhouse, who is a Bostonian by birth, and has been in business on his own account about eight and a half years, and from the first his efforts have been attended with uniform success. Mr. Waterhouse does a strictly wholesale and commission business and handles northern, southern and western lumber of all kinds, shipping direct from the mills in car and cargo lots. All orders receive immediate attention, shipments being made from all points in the most expeditious and reliable manner; and his trade which is large and active, extends throughout the whole of the New England states.

VAN DERVEER & HOLMES BISCUIT COMPANY, Sole Manufacturers of the Æ Crackers, etc., F. A. Scranton, Manager, No. 50 Merrimac Street.—The representative and most noted house in the United States, extensively engaged in the manufacture of the famous Æ crackers and biscuits, is that known as the VanDerveer & Holmes Biscuit Company, whose office and salesrooms in Boston are located at No. 50 Merrimac Street. The principal offices and manufactory of the company are situated at Nos. 200 to 206 Washington Street and Nos. 25 to 45 Hubert Street, New York. This extensive business was originally incorporated as the Aerated Bread Company, and eventually in 1876 was succeeded by the VanDerveer & Holmes Biscuit Company. The factory is admirably equipped with the latest improved machinery, ovens and appliances, operated by steam power, while employment is given in the various departments to 350 skilled operatives. The most perfect cleanliness and neatness pervade every nook of this establishment, and it would be well for con-

sumers of crackers and biscuits if there were more like it. The variety of goods produced by this progressive company is almost interminable, and being the principal manufactory in the United States, it has originated the popular new styles now in general demand, and at the same time it still continues the introduction of desirable novelties in rapid succession, and in advance of all competitors. The company now manufactures upwards of five hundred varieties of crackers, biscuits, wafers, etc., which are absolutely unrivalled in this country or Europe for quality, purity, flavor, finish and uniform excellence, while the prices quoted for them are as low as any other contemporary house in the trade. The company's goods are put up in handsomely labelled glass front cans, with the newly invented polished brass helms, patented October 9, 1888, and exclusively used by the VanDerveer & Holmes Biscuit Company. The beautiful appearance of this glass front cans adds greatly to the sale of the celebrated Æ crackers and biscuits. The trade of the company now extends not only throughout the entire United States and Canada, but also to the West Indies, Central and South America and Europe, where the well-known trade-mark Æ is a household word. The executive officers of the company, who are highly regarded in trade circles for their enterprise, business ability and just methods, are J. R. VanDerveer, president; L. C. Fuller, vice-president, and B. B. VanDerveer, secretary. The Boston branch is under the able and careful management of Mr. F. A. Scranton, who is noted for his promptness and also honorable manner in which he attends to the interests and requirements of patrons.

L. A. ROGERS & CO., Commission Merchants and Dealers in Butter, Cheese, Eggs, Etc., Nos. 61 and 63 Clinton Street, and No. 81 Faneuil Hall Market.—This enterprising and prosperous firm was established about six years ago, and its career from the start has been a history of steady progress. They occupy spacious and commodious premises and carry con-

stantly on hand a heavy and excellent stock, which includes butter, cheese, eggs, lard, beans, peas and country produce generally; butter, cheese and eggs being specialities. Some half a dozen salesmen are employed, all orders placed with the house being promptly and reliably filled, and the trade of the firm which extends throughout the New England states, with a flourishing patronage also, is very large. Mr. Rogers, who is the sole member, was born in the state of Maine, but has lived in the vicinity of Boston for some time, having his residence at Malden. He is a young man of push, enterprise and good business qualities, thoroughly honorable in his dealings, and is a popular member of the Produce Exhange.

THOMAS TURTON & SONS (Limited), Successors to William Greaves & Sons, Manufacturers of Wm. Greaves & Sons' Celebrated Coach Spring Steel, Shear Steel and Cast Steel of all kinds, Sheffield, England, Boston Office: No. 61 Kilby Street, Alan Arthur, Agent.—The leading headquarters in this country for coach spring steel and locomotive and railroad car springs is the establishment of Thomas Turton & Sons (Limited), the well known manufacturers of Sheffield, England, located at No. 49 Kilby street, in this city. This house controls the trade of the above corporation in the United States and Canada, and was established in New York for a period of seventy years, when the office was removed to Boston in 1879. The management is placed in the experienced hands of Mr. Alan Arthur, as the American Agent of the manufacturers, who has a foundation understanding of all the details and requirements of the trade, and has proved himself eminently popular and successful in meeting all its demands. The works of Thomas Turton & Sons (limited), are the largest of their kind in Great Britain. As successors to William Greaves & Sons, they are noted throughout the civilized world as manufacturers of Wm. Greaves & Sons' celebrated coach spring steel, shear steel, and cast steel of all kinds; best warranted cast steel files, engineers' tools, locomotive and railroad car springs of all descriptions. The house has been in existence for over one hundred and fifty years, and stands by common consent at the head of its particular line of trade throughout the world. It is a well known fact that steel made from the purest brands of charcoal iron is the most reliable for carriage springs. The best iron for this purpose is the Swedish iron. The coach spring steel of this representative house is made entirely from Swedish iron, and the same quality of stock has been used for one hundred and fifty years. Greaves' steel is the only best, and is known as such amongst the carriage trade throughout the world. Some carriage builders use cheaper steel, still professing to use the best, but Greaves is the only perfect and it can easily be ascertained if one is getting the genuine article. Greaves is the easiest riding and most elastic steel made; lasts longer than any other steel, and never sets. This steel is used entirely by Brewster & Co., New York, and by the best carriage-makers in the United States, England, France and Russia. Another important specialty of this house is Wm. Greaves & Sons' toe calk steel for horses. It is known to the horse-shoe trade generally that the calking steel bearing the above firm name is the best ever made for toe calks, and, if owners of horses and horse-shoers would keep their own best interests in the front, this steel alone would be used. It will outwear any other make, and will retain its edge under the severest and most lengthened tests. In addition to manufacturing the above named specialties, this firm has a world-wide reputation for the superiority of its warranted cast steel files, engineers' tools, and crucible cast steel made expressly for mill picks, rock drills, dies, hammers, taps, cups, cutters and fine-edge tools. The productions in these important lines are unequalled for quality, finish and temper, and are supplied to the trade at prices which are safe from successful competition. The firm also supply all the leading railways in England, India and Australia with springs and spring steel. They supplied the steel that was used in that wonderful work of engineering skill, the Mount Cenis tunnel, as their steel was found to be superior to all others when brought to test and comparison. Mr. Arthur is a young man of large business experience.

WM. HIGHTON & SONS, Manufacturers of Hot Air Registers and Patent Indicator Ventilators, Etc., No. 55 Charlestown Street.—Mr. Wm. Highton & Sons have become nationally celebrated for their improved hot air registers and patent indicator ventilators. The business was established in 1877 by the late Mr. William Highton and his late sons, Messrs. Marshall and James Highton. They early developed a trade of great magnitude, and maintained the lead in their line. The lamented decease of Mr. William Highton occurred in July, 1877, while the deaths of his two sons preceded his own, James dying in March, 1878 and Marshall in April, 1887. The business has since been actively carried on by Mr. Enoch Shenton, as general manager, on behalf of the widow and daughters, heirs to, and proprietors of the concern. The factory occupies two floors at Nos. 55 and 63 Charlestown Street, 30x90 feet, and fully fitted up with the latest machinery and appliances. Here seventeen hands are employed under Mr. Shenton's personal supervision, and moulders to the number of thirty men are employed at the foundry at Nashua, N. H., on this work. In the manufacture of all styles, plain and or-

namental registers and ventilators, with vertical wheel, lock out, and adjustable end pieces; round two valve ventilators, smoke pipe, round revolving registers and hot air grates; also circular top fire-place registers and adjustable summer piece borders. They are produced in the most elaborate patterns, elegant in appearance and beautiful in various styles of finish, such as Japanned bronzed, nickle-plated, etc., brass and bronzed metal registers. Not only are they the finest goods known to the trade, but include many valuable improvements, for instance a register can be changed to a ventilator, by simply replacing two of the screws holding the face. The firm carry a large stock of soapstone borders of the very best make, and Mr. Shenton is always in the van of progress, evidenced by the fact that he is now getting out new designs for all sizes of registers and ventilators specially adapted to the wants of architects and builders. They and the stove, range and furnace trade should send for the firm's catalogue and price list. Mr. Shenton is a native of England, and has been a permanent resident of the United States since 1867.

B. S. PRAY, Importer and General Commission Merchant, India Building, No. 80 State Street.—The importance of Boston as a great commercial centre, is forcibly demonstrated by her extensive import, export and general commission trade. Representative among the principal houses, which have materially the volume of this trade, is that of Mr. B. S. Pray, importer and general commission merchant. This business was established in 1863 by Mr. Pray who transacts a general commission business, both as regards imports and exports. His resources are large, his connections in financial and his facilities unrivalled. He exports provisions, breadstuffs, petroleum, machinery and manufactured goods, and is also a receiver of merchandise and produce of every description, chiefly from Africa, Central and South America, etc. Mr. Pray's intimate knowledge of the requirements of foreign countries, coupled with his high mercantile standing, affords ample assurance that business intrusted to him will receive careful and faithful attention.

THOMAS DANA & CO., Importers and Wholesale Grocers Nos. 41 to 47 Commercial and Nos. 55 to 59 Clinton Streets.—No branch of commercial enterprise in the city of Boston is more important or representative in character than that of the wholesale grocery trade. Prominent among the number is the old established and reliable house of Messrs. Thomas Dana & Co., importers and wholesale grocers. This business was established originally in 1830 by Messrs. Thomas Dana and Thomas Hastings. Eventually after several changes in the constitution of the firm, the present copartners assumed the management, the members being Messrs. Thomas Dana, William M. Raymond, William O. Delano and Herbert F. Brooks. Mr. Thomas Dana has been a member of the firm since 1855, and Mr. W. H. Raymond since 1872. The founder, Mr. Thomas Dana, died in 1878 after a long, honorable and successful career. The premises occupied comprise a superior seven story building 125x60 feet in area, fully equipped with all modern appliances, elevators, etc. The stock carried is extensive, well selected, and complete in every department and includes everything pertaining to the staple and fancy grocery trade. Messrs. Thomas Dana & Co., make a specialty of teas, coffees, spices, molasses, etc., the choicest Mocha and Java coffees, fresh crop Oolongs, Japans, English breakfast, Young Hyson and other standard teas are always to be found here all quoted at the firm's usually low prices. In flour, farinaceous goods, sugars, syrups, canned goods, foreign and domestic dried fruits, tobacco, cigars, soaps, etc., they are prepared to offer substantial inducements to jobbers and retailers. The firm import direct, and handle goods which are absolutely unrivalled for quality, purity, freshness and general excellence, while the prices quoted in all cases necessarily attract the attention of close and careful buyers. They are agents for the sale of the famous American Milling Company's flour, and their trade now extends throughout all sections of New England, the eastern, middle and western states. The partners are popular members of the Board of Trade, the Produce Exchange, and the Wholesale Grocers' Association. Mr. Dana is one of Boston's public spirited citizens. He is a director of the Maverick National Bank, the Union Glass Co., the Boston Marine Insurance Co., the Beacon Publishing Co., and several other prominent corporations. Mr. W. H. Raymond is president of the Electric Lustre Starch Co. The influence exercised by this responsible firm in the wholesale grocery trade of Boston has been of the most salutary and useful character, and those interested establishing relations with it, will obtain advantages very difficult to be duplicated elsewhere in this country.

F. W. TODD & CO., Real Estate and Insurance Brokers, No. 186 Washington Street.—This firm are deservedly prominent as Real Estate and Insurance Brokers and Conveyancers, and make a leading specialty of the negotiation of mortgages. The business was originally established in 1873, by Mr. F. W. Todd, and in 1886 the present firm was organized by the admission of Mr. Francis Todd to partnership. Both gentlemen are natives and well-known residents of Roxbury, and have an intimate knowledge of property values in all sections of the city and its various suburban towns, and a wide acquaintance with men and things. They give special attention to the purchase, sale, leasing, care and improvement of real estate, collection of rents and examination of titles, and to all other matters that come within the legitimate sphere of their usefulness. Their books contain at all times a great number of desirable houses and lots for sale and lease, including many choice business sites, and special advantages are possessed for rendering very valuable service. No house in the city is better equipped for its specialty of negotiation of mortgages, in which a list of permanent customers are secured, embracing many of the best-known property-owners, investors and business men in the city. Insurance is effected in the best fire companies at the lowest rates of premium, and a speedy and satisfactory adjustment is guaranteed in all cases of loss. This firm are agents in West Roxbury for the City of London Fire Insurance Company, which is widely known for its solidity and reliability. They refer by permission to the following well-known citizens of Boston, viz: Elisha Atkins, No. 35 Broad Street; Alpheus H. Hardy, Sears Building; Geo. E. Bullard, Agent for Brown Bros. & Co., No. 68 State Street; Wm. F. Day, President of Sewell & Day Cordage Company.

THE METROPOLIS OF NEW ENGLAND.

RICHARDS & CO., Importers and Dealers in Tin Plates, Sheet Iron and Metals, No. 60 Union, and No. 47 Friend street.— A house established upwards of seventy-six years, must necessarily engage more than ordinary attention, from the compilers of this review of the commerce and industries of the city of Boston. Such an establishment is that of Messrs. Richards & Co., importers and dealers, in tin plates, sheet iron and metals, whose offices and ware-house, are situated on Union and Friend streets. Mr. Reuben Richards, founder of the metal business in Boston, was born in Dedham, Mass., in 1812, where he received an excellent academic education. He came to Boston at fourteen years of age, and entered the hardware store of John Odin, where he obtained several years of mercantile training, which laid the foundation for his future successful career. In 1842, Mr. Richards established in Dock Square, the metal importing business, in which he was eminently successful. In 1855 he removed to South Market Street, and continued there in business until 1876, when he retired from active business with an ample fortune. Mr. Richards had purchased a summer home, in his native town, several years before, and the fine house on Summer Street, Boston, was his winter residence. It was here that he lived, in the enjoyment of friends, and among his books for which he had a cultivated taste, until his death in May 5, 1885. Messrs. William Richards and Reuben Richards succeeded their father in the metal business, on South Market Street, and formed, a seven years' copartnership with Mr. Daniel Farrar, with whom they had been former clerks of Mr. Reuben Richards. In 1855 Mr. Farrar retired, the brothers then removed to Commercial Street. In 1858 Mr. William Richards retired from active business, leaving his brother sole proprietor of this well-established house. In 1862 Reuben Richards removed to the large granite store on North Street, which he erected on the estate inherited from his father, here he continued an extensive and profitable business. After the great Boston fire, he built a large store on Milk street, to which Richards & Co., removed, since 1877 the present and spacious store has been occupied; it is fully equipped with every facility and appliance for storage and prompt shipping of metals. Messrs. Richards & Co. import direct from the most noted foreign houses, large quantities of metals, they have constantly in stock a full line of sheet iron, pig tin, tin plates, Russia sheet iron, spelter, copper, antimony, lead, sheet copper, etc., which are offered at the lowest market price. Their trade extends, not only throughout New England, but also, to the principal cities of the west and south. The policy of this well-known, and popular house, has been one of liberality and fair dealing, to this is due the profitable, permanent and honorable commercial relations established with their customers. Several of the leading metal dealers, owe their knowledge of the business to their experience gained in the employ of this firm. Mr. Reuben Richards has formed several limited copartnerships in his long business career, and in 1886, he admitted his son Mr. Reuben Richards as partner. Both father and son were born in Boston, the former on Hancock Street, the latter at No. 14 Arlington Street, which was for many years the home. Their present residence is in Cambridge, Mass.

WESTON LUMBER COMPANY, Harold Weston, Treasurer; Office: No. 71 Kilby Street; Mills: Groveton, N. H.; Easton, N. H., and Lanesboro, Vermont.—The importance of the New England and Middle states as a market for spruce, hemlock and hard-wood lumber is forcibly demonstrated by the great concerns and large capital enlisted in the cutting and sale of the best grades of the above lumber. In this line one of the leading representatives in New England is the Weston Lumber Company, with headquarters at No. 71 Kilby Street. The company was duly incorporated in 1888, with a capital stock of $100,000 to acquire valuable timber lands and engage in lumbering and milling operations upon an extensive scale. The president is Mr. H. G. White, of Boston, a well-known and respected business man. The treasurer is Mr. Harold Weston, a native of Boston, and who, though a young man, is old experienced as a practical lumber operator, and the organization of the present company is due to his ability, foresight and sound judgment. He is its principal stockholder and faithfully discharges the onerous duties devolving upon him. The company has no less than 22,000 acres of the choicest spruce and hemlock birch and maple timber lands in New Hampshire and Vermont. The value of such a body of timber so close to market, cannot be over estimated, and the company is vigorously at work this winter getting out millions of feet of logs to keep its mills busy next summer. Its mills are situated in Groveton, N. H.; Easton, N. H., and Lanesboro, Vermont. They are equipped with best machinery and saws, and have an aggregate capacity of 85,000 feet per day The company has direct railroad communications and every possible facility at command for supplying the markets of Boston and Massachusetts, Rhode Island, and Connecticut with the best grades of hemlock, spruce, birch and maple lumber of all dimensions. Mr. Weston also does a very heavy wholesale business, shipping in car lots, or by season or other contracts to our leading jobbers and retail lumber merchants manufacturers and exporters. His policy is one of integrity. Quality is the first consideration, while there are substantial inducements offered as to prices, direct and prompt delivery. Bills of stuff are sawed to dimensions that cannot readily be duplicated elsewhere. The management of the company is in Mr. Weston's charge as their only representative, and whose operations will prove of material advantage in promoting Boston's commercial prosperity.

H. L. LAWRENCE & CO., Wholesale and Retail Dealers in Poultry, Wild Game, Pigs Feet, Tongues, Etc.; stalls, Nos. 46 and 48 Faneuil Hall Market.—The leading and oldest established house in Boston and New England devoted to the trade in poultry and game, is that of Messrs. H. L. Lawrence & Co. The business was established forty-six years ago by Mr. H. L. Lawrence, one of the ablest and most enterprising merchants of the city. In 1878 his brother, Mr. J. P. Lawrence came into copartnership, and the firm thus formed continued to do a steadily growing and desirable traffic, permanently maintaining the lead in their line. In October, 1887, Messrs. W. H. Jones and F. H. Hosmer became copartners under the existing name and style, and the house permanently enjoys the reputation of handling the choicest consignments of poultry, game, etc., of any in the trade. The largest game dealers in Boston, the firm have trade relations extending all over the United States, England, Canada, etc. In season, every description of game can be had here, while at all seasons the firm carry a heavy stock of the choicest poultry, smoked tongues, pigs feet, tripe, etc. Twelve hands are employed in the various departments, and the firm supply the leading families of Back Bay and prominent localities, our principal hotels, restaurants, steamboats, etc. Both as to quality and lowest range of prices, the firm carry a heavy stock of the reputation; their prompt, liberal methods, and ability to supply the largest wholesale orders, render them the favorites with the trade of New England, while they secure to retail purchasers the choicest of everything in their lines. The Messrs. Lawrence are natives of Lexington, Mass., and have long been active and influential members of Boston's commercial circles. Their partners, Messrs. Jones and Hosmer are natives respectively of South Boston and Framingham, respected and capable members of the mercantile community, and the house, as thus constituted, is a worthy exponent of the commerce of Boston.

J. Q. NEWHALL, Pattern Maker, No. 65 Haverhill Street.— This enterprising and reliable business man opened his doors to the business world in 1854, and from the first his establishment has been attended with remarkable success. His motto from the outset has been honest work and square dealing. During the whole thirty-four years Mr. Newhall has been in business he has been located at No. 65 Haverhill Street, where he occupies the third and fourth floors, each containing an area of 25x70 feet. They are provided with steam power and the best modern wood-working machinery, tools, etc, identified with the trade. As a pattern-maker Mr. Newhall is the most experienced man in the business in the city, and is known far and wide as an expert in his vocation, and as a prompt reliable man of business. Employing an adequate staff of skilled artisans, he is at all times prepared to make at short notice the most accurate patterns for all kinds of machinery, stoves, steam-fittings, globe valves, cocks, and for castings of every description.

DOLL & RICHARDS, Fine Arts, No. 2 Park Street.—The leading house in Boston devoted to the fine arts is that of Messrs. Doll & Richards, whose gallery and studio are so desirably located at No. 2 Park Street. Nowhere, as in Boston, has such a sound and critical taste developed the highest achievements of the painter, etcher, photographer, etc. Nowhere can these tastes be so thoroughly gratified as in this firm's establishment. The business is a very old one, having been founded by Messrs. Hendrickson, Doll & Richards in 1866. In 1870 Messrs. Doll & Richards became sole proprietors, and thus continued throughout a long, honored and markedly beneficial career, until the lamented decease of Mr. Doll in 1880. Since that date, Mr. J. Dudley Richards has remained sole proprietor, retaining the old and familiar firm name. In 1878, the concern removed to its present location in Park Street, consisting of an elegantly decorated office and display room for etchings, engravings, paintings, etc., 25x50 feet in dimensions; while in the rear, and advantageously situated to secure the best light, is a large, fully-appointed studio, the patronage coming from the leading social circles of Boston and New England. The establishment is a veritable treasure house of valuable paintings, etchings and other works of arts. At intervals the firm issue a catalogue of the works of art for sale in their galleries, and there are now to be secured such chef d'œuvres as Haig's etchings, proofs on parchment and on Japan, after J. F. Millett; very choice examples after Rembrandt, and a large miscellaneous collection of etchings from celebrated pictures by Titian, Rosa Bonheur, Meissonier, Dickens, Constable, Corot, Breton, Munkacsy, etc., by the most noted etchers, including Rajon, Titian's Bacchus and Ariadne, by Macbeth; Munkacsy's Christ Before Pilate, by Waltner, etc. The finest photographs are a specialty, including A. Braun's carbon photographs; the collection consisting over 600 subjects, taken principally from the galleries and collections of old masters in Europe; also photographs from Italian ruins and, from many important pictures in Florence, Rome, Venice, etc. All the Arundel Society publications are kept on hand, and also many pictures by local artists in oils and water colors. This is headquarters for unique cabinet photograph frames and framing generally and the leading business of the kind is done. Mr. Richards personally superintends the various departments of the concern, and is a recognized leading authority on the fine arts in Boston.

M. D. JONES & CO., Manufacturers of Ornamental Iron Work, for Decorating Lawns, Cemeteries, Residences, Etc., No. 76 Washington Street.—In this age of utilitarian refinement, when the most prosaic surroundings are rendered artistic, bright and beautiful by the introduction of the wonderful achievements of skilled artisans, it is natural that a trade of great magnitude should be developed in ornamental ironwork. The leading American house in one of the most important departments of this line is that of Messrs. M. D. Jones & Co., of No. 76 Washington Street. The business was founded by Mr. Jones in 1870 and has had a steady growth and an ever widening area of connections. The house is specially devoted to ornamental iron work for the decoration of lawns, cemeteries, residences, public edifices, etc. Mr. Jones, who is a native of Boston, is the leading authority in this line, and has gathered here a magnificent sample stock, among which we might specialize, elegant iron vases and fountains, for gardens, lawns and cemeteries; iron chairs and settees, artificial plants and foliage; metal wreaths and crosses for cemeteries; lawn sprinklers of ornate patterns, with four, six, and eight arms; ornamental fountains and drinking fountains, as novel in design as useful and beautiful; also, all kinds of iron stable fittings, hay racks, oat mangers, iron crestings and finials. Jones' improved stall floors and partitions admirably constructed and vastly superior to all other styles; also flower pot and shelf-brackets, wire railings, flower stands, etc. The iron used is of the best quality; the castings are of the most perfect character, and give evidence of having been designed and moulded by experts. Mr. Jones' factory and finishing shop is at No. 38 Chardon Street, and all orders in his line whether from the trade or individuals will receive prompt attention, and prove in every way satisfactory. To all who are now improving and beautifying their grounds or houses or realize the need of doing so, we would strongly recommend to inspect this thoroughly representative stock of ornamental iron work.

FRED I. CLAYTON, Merchant Tailor, No. 8 City Hall Avenue.—For a very superior article in custom-made clothing we commend our readers to the establishment of Mr. Fred I. Clayton, the well-known merchant tailor, at No. 8, City Hall Avenue, between School Street and Court Square. This gentleman has been established in the business for a period of twenty years, and has built up a high reputation and a large and steadily increasing trade. His store is very handsomely fitted up and furnished, and a stock is displayed of foreign and domestic fabrics, embracing always the latest styles and most fashionable novelties for each incoming season. A force of twenty-five skilled hands is constantly employed, and garments are made to measure of unsurpassable excellence, both as regards style, fit and artistic workmanship. The reputation of the house is so high that the proprietor cannot afford to allow inferior or imperfect work to leave the establishment, and nothing is delivered to customers but what can be guaranteed to be perfect in every respect. The special rule of the house is to make no mistakes in fitting, and to have all orders finished at the time desired, while the prices which prevail are eminently fair and equitable. The patronage is very large and influential in the city, and also extends to all parts of New England and as far as California, and is annually increasing in volume and importance under enterprising and reliable management. Mr. Clayton is a native of the state of Maine, a resident of Charlestown, and in business in Boston since 1862. He is thoroughly accomplished as a practical master of the tailor's art, entirely reliable and responsible in all his dealings, and a young man of high social and business standing.

DR. E. S. TAYLOR, Dentist, No. 23 Tremont Street.—One of Boston's foremost dental practitioners is Dr. E. S. Taylor, the popular and well patronized dentist, at No. 23 Tremont Street, who has established a first-class reputation for judgment and skill in his profession. Dr. Taylor, who is a comparatively young man, and a gentleman of pleasing manners and the highest personal integrity, was born in Vermont, but has resided in this city many years. He is a thoroughly practical and expert dentist, of ample experience in all branches of the art, and is a graduate of the University of the State of Iowa. He has been in practice here since 1878, and from the first has steadily increased his hold on popular favor and confidence, owing to the general satisfaction rendered to those availing themselves of his professional services. Dr. Taylor occupies neatly furnished and well equipped parlors, having in service all the latest appliances and appurtenances, both mechanical and scientific, and is prepared to attend to all branches of the profession. Teeth are extracted, inserted, filled and adjusted in the most superior and reliable manner, special attention being given to extracting and gold filling, while gas or ether is administered likewise, when desired, with absolute safety, and altogether Dr. Taylor, whose terms are most reasonable, has a fine city and out of town patronage.

ELIAS BLOCK & SONS, Distillers, Cincinnati, W. D. Ellis, Eastern Agent, Boston Office, No. 20 Broad Street.—A representative and widely known house in Boston extensively engaged in the wholesale liquor trade, is that of Messrs. Elias Block & Sons. The firm own and operate three distilleries —Carroll Co. Distilling Co., Wide Awake, Ky.; Darling Distilling Co., Prestonville, Ky., and the Mercantile Club Distillery Co., Wide Awake, Ky. The firm's re-distilling and rectifying are done on Sycamore Street, Cincinnati. This business was originally founded in 1849, by Mr. Elias Block, who eventually in 1867 admitted his sons Messrs. Louis, Samuel and Joseph Block, and his son-in-law, Mr. E. J. Mack into partnership, the firm being known by the style and title of Elias Block & Sons. For excellence, purity and evenness of quality, the whiskies of this responsible firm are unsurpassed by any in the market. The Darling Bourbon is the special brand of this popular house, and is thoroughly appreciated by the trade and public wherever introduced. These whiskies are entirely free from any adulteration, and possess a natural flavor.

INGERSOLL ROCK DRILL COMPANY, Mellen S. Harlow, Manager New England Office; Nos. 159 Friend and 66 Canal Streets.—The Ingersoll Rock Drill Company, of New York and Boston, is known the world over as builders of first-class machinery for mining, tunneling and quarrying. Their Ingersoll Eclipse and the Sergeant rock drills are now recognized by all large contractors as by far the best in the market. The extent of their use in the United States may be seen by the following taken from a leading engineering journal, viz: "Seventy-five per cent. of the metal produced from machine mined ore in the United States

during 1888 was mined by the Ingersoll and Sergeant drills. Four-fifths of the rock on the new Croton Aqueduct was removed by Ingersoll drills where the average record of tunnel progress shown by engineer's tables was twenty per cent. in advance of others. Twenty-four of the twenty-eight large tunnels which have been driven with machine drills in this country have employed the Ingersoll drill." The new Ingersoll-Sergeant air compressor, in design, material and workmanship is the best in the market. Automatic and adjustable regulation for air and steam—cooling by water circulation thorough and automatic lubrication; accomplishing the most economical production of compressed air power. The air compressors, built by this company, probably equal in number those of all others combined, and by their patent cooling process, only about four to six per cent. is lost by heat in compressing the air, while the old process lost twenty-five per cent. and over. With the new automatic regulator there is no loss of air through the safety valve when compressor is running, whether air is being consumed or not, therefore no loss of power as by all other regulators. The New England office which has been established two years is at Nos. 159 Friend and 66 Canal Streets, Boston,

where a full line of sizes of Ingersoll and Sergeant rock drills, hoisting engines, boilers and other machinery is kept in stock. The manager of the New England office, Mr. Mellen S. Harlow, is an engineer of several years experience with this special class of machinery and is well fitted for the place as is shown by the large amount of machinery sold, not only in New England but also in Canada where they are fitting out several gold mines with their improved mining drills, air compressors, etc. It will be for the interest of all parties to call and examine the machinery.

FRANKLIN RUBBER COMPANY, Fuller, Leonard & Small, Proprietors, No. 13 Franklin Street.— There is no substance now in use that is capable of subserving so many and varied purposes of man as India Rubber. Not only are water-proof garments, boots and shoes made of this material, but a great number of fabrics and articles especially adapted for mechanical purposes. Each year but enlarges the sphere of its usefulness, and its manufacture is increasing in enormous proportions. A leading headquarters in this city for india rubber goods of every description is the establishment of the Franklin Rubber Company, located at No. 13 Franklin Street, near Washington. The proprietors, Messrs. Fuller, Leonard & Small, are widely prominent as wholesale and retail dealers in india rubber goods, and have been established in the business here since 1862. They occupy spacious and attractive salesrooms, and display at all times a large and elegant stock of goods. The assortments are thoroughly complete and comprehensive, and include rubber clothing, boots and shoes, ladies' and gent's gossamer clothing, druggists' sundries, elastic bands and rings, syringes of all kinds, endless belts and machine belting in large assortment, rubber and cotton hose, including every description of fire, steam, oil, tanners' and garden hose; felt mats in various colors and rubber door mats, pails, buckets, and steam packing of all kinds; carpeting, stair plates, door springs, wagon springs, weather strips, umbrellas, toys, gloves, drinking cups, dolls, chair tips, brushes and a thousand and one things both useful and ornamental. Special attention is given to the character and quality of the productions, the aim of the proprietors being not only to meet every want in that line, but to offer the very best in every case that the market afford. The goods handled are received direct from the most reputable manufacturers, and are absolutely unrivalled for utility durability and uniform excellence, in this or any market in the country. They are shipped in large quantities throughout the New England States, while a fine export trade is enjoyed with England, France, Italy and Spain. The prices quoted are as low as those of any contemporary house in the trade.

ALLEN & WHITNEY, Marine Insurance Brokers, No. 41 Devonshire Street.—The firm of Allen & Whitney is the oldest marine brokerage house in Boston having been established over thirty years. Their clients are the leading merchants and shipowners in this country, and their connections with other cities in the United States, as well as with London and Liverpool, give them facilities for placing large lines on all kinds of marine hazards. A long experience enables them to make clear contracts, and thus avoid questions and complications. Their correspondents in this country and abroad, are among the most expert in the marine insurance business.

THEODORE W. GORE, Average Adjuster, No. 30 Kilby Street. — A specialty little known to the general business world, yet, within its proper sphere, of great usefulness, is the profession of the average adjuster, or stater of marine losses, as he is often called. It arose from the necessity of our maritime commerce, since the complicated, delicate, and perplexing questions daily arising, required some dispassionate and impartial authority to dispose of them; and so the average adjuster came into the exercise of a distinct and independent calling by a natural or necessary division of our commercial industry. His place has not been created by any act of the state nor has his authority been enforced by official position; he is the development of a mercantile want, and his influence depends on, indeed his very reason for existence, consists in his fitness, his experience, his impartiality, and his moral character; neither an accountant nor a lawyer yet of necessity sufficiently skillful in accounts, to clearly arrange and simplify the countless complications to which maritime affairs give rise, and at the same time not only the depositary of the traditional lore, usages and customs of maritime and insurance settlements, but resorted to as a dictionary or digest of all the litigation and decisions bearing upon marine insurance and average matters. The profession requires a peculiar combination of talents, a liking for the law, skill in the management of accounts and a willingness to submit to the drudgery which an intricate statement of general average, or the correct solution of the many points constantly arising necessarily involves. The head of this profession in Boston, by common consent, is Mr. Theodore W. Gore, of No. 30 Kilby Street. This gentleman is a native Bostonian, educated in the public schools and graduating from the English High School in this city. He entered at an early age the office of General John S. Tyler, the distinguished adjuster of marine losses, remaining there until the General's death in 1856, when the firm of Winship Bros. & Gore was formed to continue the business. This firm was dissolved in 1884, and Mr. Gore has since conducted the practice of his profession in his own name with eminent and uninterrupted success. Mr. Gore's long and varied experience, thorough proficiency and perfect understanding of intricate and complicated points in insurance law are such as to give to his evidence in courts of law the value of an expert. In marine causes, he is often referred to as an arbiter, whose decisions are readily acquiesced in by both contending parties, and he thus prevents much costly litigation. His services are in important request in this city, and are rendered in a manner to increase his reputation, as a sound arbiter and expert adjuster, and to commend him to the confidence of all who need the aid and counsel of a reliable expert in insurance matters.

HERMAN ZOHRLAUT LEATHER COMPANY, Manufacturers of the Celebrated Milwaukee Oil Grain, Boston Store; Nos. 181 and 183 Summer Street, Leavitt & Libbey, Managers. — It is a well known fact that Boston leads the United States in regard to the manufacture of leather and boots and shoes, and that every year her products in this line show a decided tendency to increase. Hence it is that outside manufactories find it advantageous, if not essential, to have branch representative houses here and to compete for the trade which has for so long centred in the capital of the Old Bay State. Manufacturers of leather goods of every description in all parts of the country look to Boston for supplies, and where the demand is most felt there are sure to gather those who make it the business of their lives to meet the demand. Hence it is that the leather industry in Boston continues to grow. Among the most active and successful competitors in this market to-day is the Herman Zohrlaut Leather Company, an old established, highly reputable concern, whose headquarters are located at Nos. 809 to 825 North Water Street, Milwaukee, Wis. The business was founded there in 1857, and in 1879 the concern became an incorporated company, the proprietors being Herman Zohrlaut, Edward Zohrlaut and Henry Eskuche. They have an immense tannery, employing hundreds of hands, and manufacture the celebrated Milwaukee Oil Grain, warranted to hold black and not to crack; also kool grain, wax, upper, finished splits, kip, calf, russet and oiled skirting, harness leather, etc. In 1885 the company established their Boston branch house, and have occupied their present store at Nos. 181 and 183 Summer Street for a year or more. This has an area of 40x72 feet, is finely fitted up, and contains a very heavy, carefully selected stock that is fully representative of the company's high class goods. The business here is under the management of Messrs. Leavitt & Libbey, both of whom are Bostonians, and who have developed a fine trade throughout the New England States.

L. FACCINI & CO., Agents for Wines, Brandies, Whiskies, Etc., No. 45 North Market Street, Room 16. — The pure and unadulterated wines of California are now consumed in large quantities by Americans and Europeans, and as the latter, especially the French and Germans, are considered to be the best judges of wines in the world, the approval of the vintages from the Pacific Slope is a convincing proof of their purity, excellence and superiority. The leading source of supply for these wines in Boston is the agency conducted by Messrs. L. Faccini & Co., at No. 45 North Market Street. This firm are the Boston agents for the well-known New York house of Messrs. C. Carpy & Co., controlling the trade for the entire New England states. As agents for the best California wines, brandies, whiskies, etc., making a specialty of Italian wines, Chianti of 1881, and Italian maccaroni, cheese, etc., they are in a position to conduct all operations in their line under the most favorable auspices and upon the largest scale. They pride themselves upon offering the trade a perfectly pure and reliable wine at a moderate price, and it is therefore not surprising that this popular house stands at the head of the business in this flourishing commercial center. The goods are shipped direct from the vineyards of California, all orders being guaranteed prompt and perfect fulfillment, and inducements being offered as regards superiority of stock and liberality of terms and prices which challenge comparison and defy successful competition. The copartners, Messrs. L. Faccini and Ilario Bruno, are natives of Italy, experienced merchants in this line, and gentlemen of high repute in trade circles.

J. GARDNER CURTIS & CO., Importers of Coffees and Spices, No. 50 Central Street. — The house of J. Gardner Curtis & Co., at No. 50 Central Street, enjoys a national reputation in the importation of coffees and spices, having direct trade relations upon the most extensive scale with the far east, the spice Islands, West Indies, and other noted producing sections, and a home trade co-extensive with the limits of the country. The house has been in successful operation for a period of twenty years. Mr. Curtis, the enterprising proprietor, is held in universal esteem by the trade throughout the country. Bringing ample resources to bear, importing direct from the centres of growth, and controlling cargoes of the choicest products, he is enabled to supply the trade promptly with the choicest grades and brands of coffees and spices, in quantities to suit, and at prices which are rarely duplicated by rival concerns. He handles the finest spices brought to the United States, including Singapore, Sumatra and white pepper; Cayenne pepper, China and Saigon cassia, Pimento, Amboynia and Zanzibar cloves; African, Calcutta and Cochin ginger, unbleached Jamaica ginger, nutmegs, mace, etc. The trade is strictly of a wholesale character, and the house numbers among its permanent customers the leading spice mills, jobbers and wholesale grocers in Boston and the principal cities and towns of the United States. Mr. Curtis is a native Bostonian and a recognized authority in this branch of trade.

ANDREW L. McCLEERY, Sawing, Planing and Moulding, Nos. 20 and 22 Lancaster Street. — This business was established here in 1883, and has been prosecuted with marked ability and steadily increasing popularity. The premises occupied are spacious in size, and the appointments are of the most complete and finished character. The outfit of machinery is perfect, including every late and valuable invention calculated to promote production, together with ample steam power, while a competent force of skilled assistants contribute to the satisfactory operations of the house. Skilful attention is given to every description of sawing, planing and turning, and estimates are promptly furnished for the execution of all orders and commissions for any part of wood-work for buildings, materials, mouldings or interior finish. The best of skilled labor is employed in every case, and the several stages of completion are guarded with scrupulous vigilance and care. The house is at all times prepared to fill its current orders with promptness and thorough satisfaction.

WALKER & PRATT MANUFACTURING COMPANY, Manufacturers of Heating and Cooking Apparatus, Nos. 31 to 35 Union Street.—In the production of heating and cooking apparatus, American manufacturers are a long way ahead of those of other countries. Great improvements have also been made latterly in all kinds of stoves and ranges by our manufacturers, which increase their efficiency and capacity without a proportionate addition in the consumption of fuel. In this connection, special reference is made in this commercial review of Boston to the representative and progressive Walker & Pratt Manufacturing Company, who manufacture extensively a complete assortment of hotel and family cooking apparatus, furnaces, ranges, laundry stoves, sectional steam boilers, radiators, water heaters, etc. The company's stoves and ranges are unequalled for economy in the consumption of fuel, durability, quality and elegance, and are the embodiments of mechanical workmanship of the highest order of perfection. The company's office and salesrooms are located at Nos. 31 to 35 Union Street. This business was established in 1858 by Mr. Geo. W. Walker, who in 1864 admitted into partnership Mr. Horace E. Walker, the firm being known by the style and title of Geo. W. Walker & Co. In 1874 the firms of Geo. W. Walker & Co. and Miles, Pratt & Co., an old and well-established firm, manufacturers of furnaces, ranges and stoves, at Watertown, Mass., amalgamated under the title of Walker, Pratt & Co. Eventually, in 1877, the business was duly incorporated under the laws of Massachusetts with a paid up capital of $500,000 The following were the officers: Geo. W. Walker, president; Miles Pratt, treasurer; Geo. W. Walker, Miles Pratt, Horace E. Walker and W. G. Lincoln, directors, all of whom are now dead with the exception of Mr. Geo. W. Walker, who is now president and owner of one-third the stock. Mr. Walker came to Boston forty years ago with but six dollars in his pocket. He worked both in Boston and Troy, N. Y., where by energy and industry he acquired the necessary experience and capital for the success of the growing and important industry of which he is now the president. Mr. Walker resides at Malden, where he was chairman of the selectmen two years prior to its incorporation as a city. He was a Republican representative in 1885 and 1886 to the Massachusetts legislature, and has also filled several other important offices. The foundry and works of the Walker & Pratt Manufacturing Company are situated at Watertown Mass. These are equipped with the latest improved machinery, apparatus and appliances, and furnish employment in their several departments to some 270 men. Everything connected with the works of this reliable company reflects the greatest credit upon its management for ingenuity, skill and attention to details, while the executive ability displayed in carrying on such an extensive establishment merits the commendation of the public. The Boston store is a spacious five story warehouse 50x84 feet in area. It is fully stocked with a complete assortment of the company's goods and specialties, large quantities of which are also exported to South America, Europe, Africa and Australia through the medium of several of our noted commission houses. In conclusion, we would observe that the affairs of the Walker and Pratt Manufacturing Company are now under the care and management of able and responsible officers.

P. E. EDDY, Insurance Agency, No. 44 Kilby Street.—The fire insurance companies of the United States must always take a prominent position in the business world as institutions, practical, beneficent and indispensable. These companies invariably place their interests in the control of gentlemen who have earned an honorable reputation as this important branch of business. Among the most prominent insurance agents of Boston is Mr. P. E. Eddy, of No. 44 Kilby Street. This gentleman has been an insurance agent and broker for a period of twenty-five years, and now represents the following well known and thoroughly responsible corporations, viz: the Merchants Insurance Company, of Providence, R. I.; the Firemans' Fund Insurance Company, of San Francisco, Cal.; the Commerce Insurance Company, of Albany, N. Y.; the Albany Insurance Company, of Albany, N. Y.; and the Packers and Provision Dealers' Insurance Company, of Chicago, Ill., whose combined net cash assets of nearly $3,000,000 furnish attractive and undoubted security to policy holders. As a thoroughly conscientious and experienced underwriter, Mr. Eddy offers the most substantial inducements and advantages to the public, including lowest market rates and carefully drawn policies, while all losses sustained are equitably adjusted and promptly paid through this agency. Mr. Eddy is at all times prepared to take entire charge of the insurance of properties, placing and distributing risks among sound companies only and giving careful attention to the insurance interests placed in his hands. As a responsible and painstaking agent and broker, Mr. Eddy enjoys the confidence of his patrons.

L. B. WHELDON & CO., Real Estate Brokers, Room No. 62, No 85 Water Street.—The superiority of mortgages on improved real estate in the west to all other forms of security is readily apparent. Among the prominent dealers in first-class mortgages of this class in Boston none possess better facilities for prosecuting a safe and reliable business than the firm of Messrs. L. B. Wheldon & Co., the well-known real estate brokers, whose office is eligibly located at No. 85 Water Street, in the Cushing Building. This firm are engaged extensively in bonding securities on St. Paul and Minneapolis improved real estate, representing the firm of Gage & Whitney, bankers and brokers of St. Paul. The members of the firm, Messrs. L. B. Wheldon and L. A. Whitney, are both gentlemen of large experience in the real estate business, and have started operations under the most favorable circumstances for ultimate and permanent success. The western property holder invariably borrows to extend his enterprise and enlarge his field of operations, thus aiding in all cases to the original security. In the east, money borrowed on bond and mortgage is very seldom expended on the security, but goes some other way. Hence the advantage to the lender in the one case over the other western cities pay a much larger percentage if of equal value than eastern securities, or than can be given on eastern investments. Investigation of the securities dealt in by Messrs. Wheldon & Co., will convince the most credulous of the safety and profit afforded by an investment therein, and we advise all who desire greater interest with the utmost security to communicate with this firm, believing, as we have reason to, that all interests entrusted to their management and care will be scrupulously guarded and intelligently promoted. Mr. Wheldon is a native of Boston, was formerly connected with the house of Dwight, Braman & Co., brokers, of this city, and stands well in business, financial and real estate circles. Mr. Whitney is a member of the banking firm of Gage & Whitney, of St. Paul, and is well and favorably known in that thriving city.

KNOWLES & CO., Grain Shippers, No. 75 State Street.—In making suitable reference to those representative concerns that are materially contributing to the commercial growth and prosperity of this city, prominence should be given to the house of Knowles & Co., the well-known grain shippers, at No. 75 State Street. The proprietor, Mr. Geo. H. Knowles, is an extensive buyer and shipper of grain, by car and cargo lots, supplying millers, jobbers and dealers throughout New England in quantities to suit, and at the shortest possible notice. He has been engaged in the business for a period of twenty years, being formerly a member of the firm of Knowles & Coon, and opened his present office in 1886. He has developed a connection of a very superior character, bringing a wide range of experience to bear, and is a recognized authority on grain shipping circles. He numbers among his permanent customers many leading millers and merchants throughout the different New England states, and has built up a large and influential patronage, which is of a character to form the best possible assurance of his continued success and increasing prosperity in the future. He makes a specialty of car and cargo lots of grain of every kind, and is in a position to promptly fill the largest orders to the letter, while his facilities on 'change enable him to offer the most substantial inducements to buyers, whose interests are sedulously protected by his vigilance and care. Mr. Knowles is a native of Nashua, N. H., a well-known citizen of Boston, a member of the Chamber of Commerce, still in the prime of life, and thoroughly enterprising, liberal and reliable in all his business methods and dealings. Mr. Knowles owns the larger part and has control of the Nashua Street Railway of Nashua, New Hampshire and devotes considerable time to that enterprise.

GEO. F. ROACH & CO., Manufacturers and Dealers in Chamber Furniture, Chairs of Every Variety, Etc., Nos. 107 to 135 Fulton Street, and Nos. 13 to 144 Commercial Street. —The leading exponent of the wholesale home and export trade in the staple grades of chamber and dining furniture in Boston, New England, etc., is the popular and enterprising house of Messrs. George F. Roach & Co., of Fulton and Commercial Streets, and for the accommodation of whose enormous stock, no less than an acre of floor space is required. This is an old as well as solid and ably conducted business. It was founded by Mr. Otis W. Merriam over forty years ago, succeeded by Otis W. Merriam & Co., and followed about fifteen years ago by Geo. F. Roach & Co. Mr. Roach having a wide range of practical experience at command and the entire confidence of the commercial world. Three years after, Mr. Roach reorganized the firm of Roach, Bradbury & Co., and eventually, after it dissolved, carried on the business alone, until four years ago when Mr. Samuel H. Mayo was admitted under the existing name and style. The house is now the largest in the United States devoted to the trade in medium grades of chamber furniture. The partners are pushing business men, experienced and exercising superior executive abilities. They know exactly what the home and foreign trade want, and making quality their first consideration, are enabled to retain old customers while constantly making new ones. A glance at their facilities and extent of establishment will indicate the importance of this great concern to Boston's commerce. They occupy seven buildings on Fulton Street, all connecting, each four stories in height, and 25x60 feet in dimensions. Here are the offices (No. 121 Fulton Street,) vast salesrooms and furnishing rooms. On Commercial Street are three additional buildings, each four stories in height, devoted to storage, with finishing shops, etc. An average force of thirty-five hands are here employed in the manufacture, finishing and packing of the finest quality of chestnut, ash and painted chamber furniture, cane and wood seat chairs of every variety, tables, etc. Carefully boxed furniture for shipping is a speciality, and the firm do a most extensive export trade to the British Provinces, Africa, South and Central America, West Indies, etc. They have permanently maintained the lead as to prices and quality and their connections include the leading retail furniture dealers of New England. Mr. Roach has been a permanent resident of Boston for forty years past, and is one of our self-made men, coming here with only $1.50 in cash, but an abundant capital of physical vigor, mental ability, energy and enterprise, and he soon made himself useful and popular and is now in the furniture trade truly representative of its best and most equitable methods. He is a respected member of the Masonic Order, being in the thirty-third degree, and a valued member of commercial circles. Mr. Samuel H. Mayo is an authority in the furniture trade, and the house of Messrs. George F. Roach & Co., is in every way, a most valuable factor in promoting Boston's prosperity.

HEATH & COMPANY, Apothecaries, No. 635 Washington Street.—One of Boston's oldest and finest drug stores is the well-equipped and elegant pharmacy, of Heath & Co., Apothecaries, (successors to A. Littlefield, and John I. Brown & Son,) which is desirably located at No. 635 Washington Street, opposite Essex Street. It is a commodious, attractive and in all respects, first-class establishment, where physicians' prescriptions and family recipes are compounded in the most accurate and reliable manner, to every instance from absolutely pure and best quality ingredients, while bottom prices also prevail here. This time honored and excellent pharmacy was originally established in 1820, by John I. Brown, the style subsequently changing to John I. Brown & Son, who were in turn succeeded by O. Littlefield & Co., by whom it was conducted up to 1882, when W. B. Heath assumed control, and under the firm name of Heath & Company, has since continued the business with uninterrupted success. The store which is 20x90 feet in dimensions, with beautiful tile flooring, is very tastefully appointed, and well ordered in every respect, while three competent assistants are in attendance; the firm have recently added to its attractiveness by the introduction of one of Tuft's modern soda water fountains, and they now make a specialty of all kinds of choice temperance drinks. A large and carefully selected stock is constantly kept on hand, including besides pure and fresh drugs, medicines, chemicals,

acids, extracts, essences, alcohol, spirits, pure medicinal wines and liquors, mineral waters, herbs, barks and kindred pharmaceutical specialties of every description, also a complete and fine line of perfumes, fancy soaps, toilet articles, sponges, chamois and druggists' sundries in great variety; special attention being given to prescriptions, and, altogether, a large and influential patronage is received. Mr. Heath, who is a comparatively young man and a native of this city, is a gentleman of courteous manners and the highest personal integrity, as well as a thoroughly practical and responsible apothecary, with ample experience in the laboratory

INGALLS, BROWN & CO., Leather, No. 137 Summer Street.— In referring to the business transacted in leather in Boston, we have particular occasion to note the house of Ingalls, Brown & Co., as being prominent for the enterprise and energy with which its operations are conducted. It was established in 1861 by Mr. John B. Ingalls, who has been identified with the trade for more than eighteen years, and Mr. S. H. Brown Jr., who has also had a long experience in the business, compose the firm. They are both natives of New England, and conducted their operations with that energy and careful attention, which has always distinguished them in their dealings and which have been the means of establishing the prestige and reputation the house enjoys in commercial circles. They represent some of the leading manufacturers of goat, kid and morocco of southern finish, and are well equipped for meeting the demands of the boot and shoe manufacturers, and control a large substantial permanent trade, widely diffused throughout New England. The business connections of the firm are first-class and the goods handled are superior in quality and very desirable, and the house will be found one of the best with which to form business relations, as the very lowest market prices are always quoted.

SEWELL & DAY CORDAGE COMPANY, Nos. 83 and 85 Commercial Street.—The production of cordage and oakum in large quantities occupies an important place in the list of prominent manufacturing industries, that have reached a high state of development and growth in New England. In this connection, we desire to make special reference in this commercial review of the trade and industries of Boston, to the old established and representative Sewell & Day Cordage Company, whose office and store are located at Nos. 83 and 85 Commercial Street. This business was established many years ago by Messrs. Sewell & Day, the firm name changing from time to time, until 1880, when it was duly incorporated under the laws of Mass., with a capital stock of $600,000. The factory, which is one of the largest in New England is equipped with improved machinery, and furnishes constant employment from 100 to 500 operatives. The company manufactures largely all kinds of manilla, sisal, and tarred cordage also lines and oakums. The cordage turned out by this company is unrivaled in quality. A large stock of all their manufactured goods is kept on hand by the company, and the trade of the house extends throughout all sections of New England and the western states, as well as foreign countries.

D. M. OLIVER & CO., Pork, Lard, Hams, Bacon, Sausages, Tripe, Dried Beef, Beef, Tongues, Bolognas, Etc., No. 26 Faneuil Hall Market.—Among those prominently identified with the trade in provisions in this city there is no firm enjoying a wider reputation than that of Messrs. D. M. Oliver & Co., of No. 26 Faneuil Hall Market. The business was established in 1860 by Oliver & Stetson and afterwards continued by Mr. Oliver, and then by Oliver & Woodbridge, who carried it on for three years and were succeeded by the present firm. The operations have always been ably managed and conducted and the business continued to enlarge from year to year, capital and facilities expanding together until to-day the firm ranks equal with any other in the market. All kinds of provisions are dealt in, a specialty being made of pork, lard, hams, bacon, sausages, tripe, dried beef, tongues, bolognas, etc., and a business transacted extending throughout Boston and vicinity, and the State of Massachusetts. Mr. Oliver, who is a native of Maine, has been a member of this community twenty eight years, and earnestly engaged promoting such measures as seemed best calculated to encourage trade and advance the commercial prosperity.

THE METROPOLIS OF NEW ENGLAND.

C. F. APPLETON, Gent's Fine Boots and Shoes, No. 238 Washington street.—Boston, as the great centre for the boot and shoe trade of the country, contains not only numerous wholesale, but many retail establishments engaged in this line, and some of these devote themselves exclusively to the handling of special lines of footwear. The house of Mr. C. F. Appleton, located at No. 238 Washington Street, furnishes an illustration of this. The house confines itself entirely to dealing at retail in gentlemen's boots and shoes of fine and medium grades, and in this department has built up a very large and substantial trade and won wide-spread popularity by its enterprising and honorable business methods. Mr. Appleton founded his business ten years ago, and from the outset his career has been a most prosperous and progressive one. The store presents a bright, tasteful and inviting appearance, the arrangements and furnishings being of a superior

billiard tables at each place are available at a moderate charge for games, and smoking is allowed in that part of the room. It is found that these attractions draw in the floating population, the patronage is large every evening, and the best order invariably prevails. On Sunday the billiard hall is closed, and the day is kept quiet as possible. Both houses are kept open all night and meals are served at all hours. There is no question that a vast amount of good is accomplished by this company. Christian men are behind the enterprise, and it enjoys deservedly the confidence of the public. Mr. Farnsworth, the president of the company, was the principal founder of this enterprise, and is a gentleman known and honored throughout New England for his philanthropy, sound judgment and broad liberality, to whom the success and prosperity of the movement is largely due. Mr. Ybarra, the treasurer, is a native of Venezuela, and formerly a general in the Venezuelan

character for securing the convenience of customers and the ample and effective display of the stock carried. The stock is a large, carefully selected and comprehensive one, and embraces every description of men's footwear—boots, shoes, slippers, rubbers, gaiters and shoe dealers' findings of all kinds. All the latest and most popular novelties are comprehended in the stock, and the prices are fixed at a point to insure quick sales, the policy of the proprietor being to do a brisk trade with small profits rather than have large profits and few sales. He numbers among his patrons many of our leading merchants and professional men, and is personally very popular with his customers. Mr. Appleton is a native of Boston and resides at Cambridge.

ORIENTAL COFFEE HOUSE COMPANY, A. Ybarra, Treasurer, Office, No. 7 Exchange Place.—One of the most deserving and beneficial enterprises ever inaugurated pro bono publico in Boston was that established by the Oriental Coffee House Company in 1881. This company was incorporated under the laws of the state of Massachusetts, during the year named, with a capital of $20,000, and with Mr. Ezra Farnsworth, as president, and Mr. A. Ybarra, as treasurer. They started a small place at Washington Street and Floral Place for the entertainment of the public, and in 1883 had opened two establishments, one at No. 285 Washington Street, and the other at No. 11 Green Street. These houses are now on a thoroughly satisfactory financial basis, feeding some fifteen hundred guests per day, and paying about six per cent. annually to the two hundred stockholders. They furnish the best of coffee for a very few cents, while edibles of all kinds likely to be found in a good restaurant are provided at rates some twenty per cent below the prices elsewhere. Each of these houses occupies a large room on the street floor, and has a seating capacity at the small tables for one hundred; while a lunch counter, with steaming tanks of coffee, is ranged on one side. The rooms are made attractive with mirrors and pictures; are well-lighted and neatly kept, and the aim is to furnish all the entertainment which the saloons offer, minus the liquors. To that end, half-a-dozen

army. He is a practical coffee-planter of large and valuable experience, and receives his supplies of that beverage and chocolate direct from the fields of his native country.

WM. TURNBULL & CO., Dry Goods Commission Merchants, Nos. 57 and 59 Worth Street, No. 239 Devonshire Street, Ebenr. Dale, Agent.—The commission merchant and manufacturers agent occupies a very important position in the industries of the present day. A prominent agent for one of the most conspicuous and reliable dry goods commission houses in the United States, is Mr. Ebenezer Dale. Mr. Dale is a native of this state and has been a resident of Boston many years, who having had many years' experience in the handling of dry goods, became thoroughly familiar with that trade in all its branches, and was made the agent or representative of the old and substantially established dry goods commission concern of Messrs. Wm. Turnbull & Co., of Nos. 57 and 59 Worth Street, New York City, in 1879, and since the date of his becoming such has met with the most gratifying and uniform success. The house Mr. Dale represents was founded originally in 1851 in New York, and is considered one of the most reliable of its kind in that great metropolis. They are the selling agents for the celebrated Pranker Manufacturing Company, of Saugus, Mass., and the Iredale, whose productions of flannels and kindred articles have an excellent and extensive reputation for superiority, also agents for the Dexter Woolen Mills of Dexter, Maine, and sole agents of the Pontoosuc Woolen Manufacturing Company, of Pittsfield, Mass., whose goods have a wide celebrity for fine quality also, and many other manufacturing companies. Mr. Dale's office contains a full and complete line of samples of the products of these famous concerns. The entire Boston and New England trade is supplied from this agency; all orders being shipped direct from the mills at manufacturer's prices, by which means, a large saving of freight, traveling and incidental expenses is saved to jobbers, and retailers. All orders by mail or telegraph are promptly filled at lowest possible terms.

SIMMONS, AMSDEN & CO., Fruit and Vegetables, Stalls Nos. 96, 97 and 98; Cellar, No. 17, North Side, Faneuil Hall Market.—Among the articles of food which the people of Boston have superior facilities for procuring, and which they highly appreciate, are fruits, native and foreign, at all seasons of the year. One of the oldest and leading houses engaged in handling fruits and vegetables at both wholesale and retail, is that of Messrs. Simmons, Amsden & Co., in Faneuil Hall Market. This firm occupy Stalls Nos. 94, 96 and 98, and Cellar No. 17, north side. The facilities here at hand for the transaction of a large business are unexcelled in the city, embracing, as they do, excellent cold storage and ripening rooms for foreign fruits, and every convenience for the receipt and delivery of fruit with the least possible handling. The business of this house was originally established in 1844, by Messrs. Harrison Porter and A. B. Simmons. In 1855 Mr. Porter died, and Mr. T. J. Amsden was admitted as a partner under the firm name of A. B Simmons & Co. In 1864 Mr. D. E. Butterfield became a partner, and the firm name became as at present. Mr. Simmons died in 1872 and the business has since been continued by the surviving partners without a change in the firm's style. The stock of this house is a large and fresh one, green and ripe fruits and vegetables of all kinds arriving daily, and sales are made at both wholesale and retail in this city and throughout all parts of New England and the British Provinces. Shipments of fruit are received direct from Florida, including, in their season, oranges, lemons, bananas, peaches, apples, pears, grapes, figs, dates, citrons, nuts, sweet potatoes, onions, and rare fruits from Baracoa and Jamaica, while California also contributed largely to the domestic fruit, and generally commands attention and admiration for its good qualities. The trade is brisk and lively at all times, requiring in its transactions the service of a dozen or more clerks and salesmen. Mr. Amsden is a native of New Hampshire, while Mr. Butterfield was born in Boston. Both gentlemen are closely allied to the advancement of the commercial prosperity of this city, and are in a position to offer advantages in goods and prices rarely equalled by any of their contemporaries.

W. H. PRIOR, Successor to Hiscock & Prior, Mutton, Lamb and Veal, Nos. 9 and 11 Faneuil Hall Market.—Among the individual business enterprises carried on in Faneuil Hall Market there is none which enjoys a more deservedly high reputation than that conducted by Mr. W. H. Prior, the occupant of Stalls Nos. 9 and 11. The business here had its beginning as far back as forty-five years ago, and was founded then by Mr. Sewell Hiscock. This gentleman subsequently admitted at different dates his two sons, Sewell and Lowell B. Hiscock, as partners. After the founder had retired from the business the style of the firm was changed to Hiscock & Winslow, and, later, Mr. Lowell B. Hiscock bought his partner's interest, and then ran the business alone for about fifteen years. Then he formed a partnership with Mr. W. H. Prior, under the style of Hiscock & Prior. This partnership subsisted for about eight years, and until January, 1887, when Mr. Hiscock retired. Since then Mr. Prior has had the sole direction of the business, which has attained large proportions. Mr. Prior brings great experience to bear upon his enterprise, and is quick to recognize and supply the wants of his trade, hence his patronage is drawn from the best people in the city, is large and steadily increasing. Here at all times can be found the best mutton, lamb and veal, which are offered at prices not to be surpassed in the trade. The stock carried is necessarily an extensive one, and the trade is both wholesale and retail in its character. Four assistants and a delivery wagon are kept busy in filling orders, and prompt and courteous attention is accorded to all patrons. Mr. Prior is a native of Boston, and a most pleasant gentleman with whom to establish business relations.

QUINCY CLUB STABLE, Boarding, Hack and Livery; H. W. Miller, Manager, No. 23 Chardon Street.—One of the most important and popular boarding, hack and livery establishments in Boston is that known as the Quincy Club Stable, No. 23 Chardon Street, of which Mr. H. W. Miller is the enterprising and energetic manager. Mr. Miller established this business two years ago and now commands a liberal and influential patronage. The stables are spacious, well drained, ventilated and lighted, and are in charge of careful grooms and stablemen. They have first-class accommodations for 250 horses, and every care and attention are given to the animals entrusted to the proprietor. Mr. Miller has some of the most stylish and finest equipages to be seen in the city, and a stock of superior thoroughbred driving horses, which can be hired night or day for business purposes or pleasure on very moderate terms. Among the carriages are included some elegant hacks, coupes, landaus, barouches, etc., for drives, calls, shopping or weddings. In the stock of horses will be found some suitable for ladies to drive, and also some famous goers for those who desire to make lively movements on the road. Mr. Miller is an authority on the noble animal, and has in his stables some of the crack horses of gentlemen residing in this vicinity. He conducts an extensive business in the livery department and also in boarding and taking care of horses, while he likewise disposes of a number of animals by private sales. Orders left at the office of the Quincy House or No. 23 Chardon Street will receive prompt attention. Mr. Miller is agent in Boston for the celebrated Merchants' Gargling Oil Liniment, which was introduced in 1833. It is the oldest and best liniment in the United States, and is invaluable for curing diseases in man and beast. Mr. Miller in addition to his extensive Quincy Club Stable, is also proprietor of the Washington House, Howard Street.

TURNER & KAUPP, Silver Platers, and Repairers of Silver and Plated Ware, No. 378 Washington Street, Room 2.—After working at their trade many years, and becoming thoroughly competent in all its various branches Messrs. Turner & Kaupp founded this concern originally on Spring Lane in 1867, and owing to the increase of patronage they were obliged to seek more commodious quarters and moved to Bromfield Street, where they remained until 1882 when they removed to their present location. The premises occupied are of ample size 30x35 feet in dimensions, of easy access and situated in the very centre of all lines in their business. They are admirably arranged and adapted for the purpose and equipped with all the latest and best improved machinery and tools operated by steam and manual labor both as occasion requires, and a corps of skilful and experienced workmen are employed constantly in filling the orders, of which they are in daily receipt. The firm is prepared to execute all kinds of silver, gold and nickel plating for the trade, also electro bronzing and oxydizing, cyprus, copper and other colors at the shortest notice and in the most satisfactory manner. Everything in the line of silver-plating is most successfully accomplished, particular attention being given to repolishing and replating hotel, restaurant and private wares, also plumbers' materials, car, coach, and harness trimmings, house builders' hardware, etc., and in fact everything included in the line of plated ware. The individual members of this concern are Mr. John B. Turner an Englishman by birth, but a resident of Boston for many years having served a faithful apprenticeship and learned his trade here, and his partner Mr. Andrew Kaupp is a native of Germany, who also came to the United States when quite young and likewise acquired his knowledge of the business in this city.

J. H. OSGOOD & CO., Printers' Rollers, No. 100 Milk Street.—This business was established twenty-one years ago by Mr. J. H. Osgood, who eventually in 1878 admitted his brother into partnership. In 1883 on the retirement of his brother, Mr. Osgood became sole proprietor. The premises occupied comprise a spacious floor 25x100 feet in area, fully supplied with every appliance and facility for the successful prosecution of the business. Mr. Osgood manufactures to order or otherwise all sizes of printers' rollers. These specialties are unrivalled for finish, quality, durability and excellence, and have no superiors in this or any other market, while the prices quoted are as low as the lowest. Mr. Osgood is sole proprietor of Osgood's Patent Composition, which is unsurpassed for durability, strength and utility, and is a general favorite with the trade wherever introduced. The trade of this progressive house extends throughout New England and the provinces and is steadily increasing. Mr. Osgood was born in Danvers, and has been a resident of Peabody, Mass., for the last fifteen years, and is well known in his special line of industry throughout this vicinity.

BRIGHAM & PILLSBURY, General Commission Merchants, Ship and steamship Agents, Boston Agents, Beaver Line of Steamers, to Liverpool, No. 58 Central Street.—An important factor in the importing and commission trade of Boston is the widely-known house of Messrs. Brigham & Pillsbury, general commission merchants, ship and steamship agents, at No. 58 Central Street. The business of this house was originally established in 1851, by J. R. Brigham & Co., who were succeeded by the present firm in 1888. They are extensive commission merchants in general merchandise and produce for European local merchants, receiving consignments daily from the best manufacturing and producing sources, and conducting their immense business on the most liberal and enterprising methods. As steamship agents, they represent in Boston the Beaver Line of steamers to Liverpool, and are prepared to make custom entries at the most reasonable rates. Consignments are solicited, promptly acknowledged and carefully handled, with profit to the shipper in all cases. They have an extensive and influential connection with the best sources of supply in Venezuela, Mexico and the West Indies, and in all matters relating to the shipping trade from those countries they are prepared to transact business after the most approved modern methods. In the ship brokerage Mr. Pillsbury has an extensive acquaintance and large correspondence with the leading shippers and ship owners in the United States, Canada, West Indies, South America and Europe, and is making a specialty of this branch. The experience enjoyed by the proprietors in these regions gives them peculiar advantages in this market, while their high character for business reliability and personal worth is a sufficient assurance that all orders will receive prompt and satisfactory attention. Mr. Brigham, the senior partner and founder of the business, is a native Bostonian, a member of the Chamber of Commerce, Trustee of the Penny Savings Bank, and prominently identified with the commercial growth and material prosperity of this city in many ways. Mr. A. F. Pillsbury, the junior member of the firm, was born in Rockland, Me., and was formerly a master of a vessel. Both are highly regarded in shipping and trade circles, and have won success and popularity by honest, enterprising and legitimate methods of dealing.

L. M. DYER, Commission Dealer in Mutton, Lamb and Veal, Nos. 2 and 4 Quincy Market.—The house of L. M. Dyer, at Nos. 2 and 4 Quincy Market, has long been prominent in this city, and has achieved a well merited reputation both at home and abroad as a leader in the commission trade in mutton, lamb and veal. This house was founded in 1861 by Mr. L. M. Dyer, who is well and favorably known in this city and throughout New England as an experienced merchant and a solid and substantial business man. In 1882 he admitted his son, Mr. F. W. Dyer, to partnership, without change in firm name. This house slaughters its own meats, handling mutton, lamb and veal exclusively, and conducting their business principally at wholesale. They exercise great care in the selection of their stock and in preparing it for market, and can make good the claim for offering the trade and consumers a line of meat products that cannot be excelled. They are prepared to supply hotels, restaurants, steamers, sailing vessels, dealers and families with these meats in quantity to suit, fresh killed and guaranteed perfect in wholesomeness and preservation, at prices which challenge competition. Orders from patrons are filled with promptness and care, and a force of sixteen skilled hands contribute to the satisfactory operations of the house. Having always been earnest in their endeavors to please, the Messrs. Dyer have established a reputation and a trade throughout New England that few of their contemporaries can equal. The Messrs. Dyer are natives of Boston, highly esteemed in both social and commercial circles for their strict probity and personal worth, and eminently popular with their host of permanent patrons.

S. C. TRYON, Wholesale and Retail Dealer in Beef, Pork, Lard, Hams, Bacon, Etc., stalls, Nos. 12 and 13 New Faneuil Hall Market.—There are few business places in the city which can show a larger congregation of old established and reputable business men than New Faneuil Hall Market. Here are located merchants who have been engaged in the trade of supplying the people with food products for periods ranging from over half a century downwards. Mr. S. C. Tryon has for the past thirty-two years been the occupant of stalls Nos. 12 and 13, and is one of the best known among the old established business men in the market. His stall is a commodious one, is neatly fitted up, and is a model of cleanliness and order. Here is daily displayed a splendid stock of choice cuts of beef and pork, and also hams, bacon, lard, tripe, sausages, pigs' feet, etc., in great variety. The stock, too, is renewed daily, and is kept fresh and wholesome. The supplies are drawn from the most reliable sources, and is selected with great care and excellent judgment to meet the requirements of a first-class trade. The prices ruling here will compare favorably with those of any other concern in the same line, the policy pursued by the proprietor being that of relying on small profits to secure a brisk and active trade. This is the secret of his success, and he now controls a business which has its ramifications throughout the whole of New England, the trade being of both a wholesale and retail character. Particular attention is given to family orders, and special rates are quoted for hotels, restaurants and boarding houses. Mr. Tryon is a native of Maine, and during his long residence in Boston has earned the reputation of being a straightforward business man.

GEO. H. CHESSMAN & CO., (Successors to Hiland, Chessman & Co.), General Commission and Produce Dealers, Basement, No. 23 South Side Faneuil Hall Market.—There is no branch of trade in this great commercial community of more direct value and importance to people than that of produce commission. One of the most enterprising and oldest established houses in this line is that of Messrs. George H. Chessman & Co., whose office and salesroom are located in Basement No. 23 Faneuil Hall Market (South Side). This business was founded forty-four years ago under the firm style of Hall & Chessman. In 1871 this firm was re-organized and became Hiland, Chessman & Co., who dissolved partnership in 1886. In June of that year the present firm of George H. Chessman & Co. was formed, the members of the concern being Mr. George H. Chessman, Mr. S. B. Elwell and Mr. J. M. Sullivan. The latter is a native of Canada, and the two former were born in Boston. Mr. Chessman has been identified with the produce trade in Faneuil Hall Market for the past forty-seven years, and is one of the most experienced, best known and most popular men in the business. The present firm since its inauguration has earned an excellent reputation for the prompt and careful manner in which the disposal of all consignments are attended to, the extensive and influential connections of the concern enabling the proprietors to do full justice to the largest wholesale invoices. The business premises are commodious and are fully supplied with cold storage, etc. Messrs. George H. Chessman & Co. handle large quantities of country produce of every description, including foreign as well as domestic fruits and vegetables consigned to them by producers. The transactions of the firm are entirely of a wholesale character, and the house numbers among its customers many of the best known shippers, jobbers, grocers, etc., not only of Boston, but of New England and Canada.

GEORGE B. WILCOX, Book, Job and Programme Printer, Electrotyping and Stereotyping, No. 29 Washington Street.—Among the well conducted establishments in the commercial or job printing line in this city will be found that of Mr. George B. Wilcox, located at No. 29 Washington Street. Mr. Wilcox began business at the present site in 1886 and in the interval by superior work and prompt and satisfactory execution of orders has secured a large and liberal patronage made up of the best local custom. The spacious premises are fitted up in a manner appropriate to the business, the presses—four in number, are of the newest and best improved type, operated by steam power and a competent force of experienced printers is employed. Everything in the line of book and job printing is executed in the highest degree of artistic and mechanical excellence, a specialty being made of fine programme work. Electrotyping and stereotyping are also done in the most skillful manner, estimates are furnished on all work when desired and the prices are the lowest possible for first-class service. Mr. Wilcox, is thoroughly conversant with and experienced in the business in hand and popularly regarded among his many patrons as one of the oldest city job printers.

A. T. FOGG, Art Embroideries and Materials for Interior Decorations, No. 5 Hamilton Place.—Among the industrial occupations of American trade and commerce, we find the manufacture of ladies' and children's underwear, in its distinctive character, to be one of vast importance and magnitude in every large community. No house has been so successful in concentrating this trade and in directing attention to the city of Boston as a source of supply as that of A T. Fogg, located at No. 5 Hamilton Place. The proprietress of this establishment has introduced a system of improved under garments for ladies and children which takes a front rank in this line in the esteem and popularity of every community wherever it has been tested, and deserves more than ordinary mention in this review. The object of improved under-clothing for ladies and children is to reduce as much as possible the number of articles worn, by combination, to equalize the temperature of the body by clothing all parts alike, and to suspend all clothing from the shoulders. Many ladies have been discouraged from wearing the combination suits because of having been unsuccessful in procuring a satisfactory article. Attention is called in this connection, to the fact that these combination suits, both cotton and flannel, are cut from measure in a style peculiar to this house, and a good-fitting, comfortable garment is always warranted. While recommending the improved style, and making a specialty of its manufacture, this house will make any article of underwear for ladies or children, from patterns furnished by the customer or cut here. The proprietress also recommends for infants an improved style of underclothing upon the same plan as that for grown people, and having the same objects in view. The pinning blanket is made with waist and skirt in one piece. The flannel skirt is also made with waist and skirt in one piece, and all tight bands around the body are avoided, leaving the limbs and muscles perfect freedom. Slips and dresses are made in the usual manner, and for any price. Among the specialties made by this house are the knit suit, or union under-flannel, which is made for ladies and children, and can be made of any thickness desired, furnished ready-made or to order; the chemiloon, suited for misses as well as ladies, combining chemise, drawers, and corset cover in one piece; the Gabrielle or Princess skirt, combining skirt and corset cover; the Sanitas or Absorbent Pad, extremely soft and comfortable; Gray & Foster's Abdominal Supporter, the cheapest thing in the market; the Emancipation Waist, intended to take the place of corset, corset cover and chemise, ready made for ladies or to order for ladies and children; the Cordial Corset, intended to take the place of the ordinary stiff corset, cords being used in place of bones; also, drawers, Tampico bosom forms, ladies' skirt supporters, dress drawers, hose supporters, ladies' safety suspenders, and union under flannels in Scotch wool, and heavy merino. This house also makes a specialty of imported wash silks, and handles art embroideries and materials of the finest description for interior decorations. The business has been successfully conducted here since 1876, and is recognized as an important and valuable factor in the mercantile activity of this great metropolis.

GEO. R. CLARKE & CO., Interior Decorations, No. 48 Boylston Street.—The art furnishing rooms of Geo. R. Clarke & Co., No. 48 Boylston Street, are well known to every one in Boston, who has had occasion to think of beautifying a home. Mr. Clarke combines, with an educated and refined taste, a great power of absorbing and realizing the individual wants of his customers and embodying them in furniture and decoration. His long experience as an architect gives an artistic value and harmony to his work which places it above that of the general decorator. The firm make a specialty of stained glass, both ecclesiastical and domestic, and their rooms are full of the latest conceits in tiling of all kinds, from all parts of the world. Their wood mantels are fine in design and execution, and difficult indeed must be the taste that could not find something to satisfy it among the numerous samples presented. The firm also carry a full line of fire-place fittings. They will soon leave their present quarters and move to the fine building now in process of construction which they expect will be ready for them in the fall. Any one desiring furnishings from a single room to an entire house may rest assured of being served with the best workmanship and the most refined taste, if they leave their affairs in the hands of this firm.

J. NEWMAN & SONS, Floral Artists, No. 51 Tremont Street, Suffolk Bank Building.—There is not perhaps within the entire range of activity in the United States any branch of industry, science or art in which more steady and remarkable progress has been made of late years than floriculture, what with invention, improved facilities and the development of artistic skill, the advance made in this direction during the past quarter of a century has been among the notable features of the times; and now the shrine of flora need never lack gifts both fresh and green any season of the year. And while on this subject special mention ought here be given to J. Newman & Sons, the well and favorably known floral artists, of No. 51 Tremont Street, who rank among the very foremost exponents of the art in Boston. For variety, originality and novelty in designs, or for exquisite workmanship, promptness and reliability in executing orders, Messrs. Newman maintain a reputation second to none in their line in this city, while their patronage, which is large and influential, is fully commensurate with the name and standing of the firm, extending all over the New England States. This flourishing business was established in 1870 by Mr. J. Newman, who continued alone up to 1876, when he admitted to partnership his sons J. K., and A. H. Newman, and under the style of J. Newman & Sons, it has since been conducted with uninterrupted success, the senior member, however, retiring from active connection three years ago. The nurseries and conservatory of the firm, which are located at Winchester, cover an acre and a half of ground, are supplied with every facility and completely equipped with all the latest improved appliances and general appurtenances, while a large force of help—some fifteen, all told—is employed. The store on Tremont Street is eligibly situated in the Suffolk Bank building, and is ample, compact and tastefully appointed, several competent assistants being in attendance. An exceedingly fine assortment is constantly carried on hand including choice cut flowers, roses and bouquets, (fresh and fragrant daily,), wreaths, rustic work, baskets, crosses, pillows, anchors, harps and emblematic floral designs in great variety, also plants, bulbs, mosses, grasses, etc., special attention being given to artistic funeral designs, and all orders are executed in the most expeditious and excellent manner, at reasonable rates.

SAMUEL HANO COMPANY, Manufacturers exclusively of Manifold Books, Factories at Allston, Mass., No. 105 Summer Street.—The earliest record of the invention and use of manifold paper dates back to the year 1806, when Ralph Wedgewood, of London, recorded his claim for a patent. But it was not until seventy years after, when Samuel Hano & Co., established their business in Massachusetts, that manifold books became generally known and used throughout the United States. To the efforts of this reliable house is due the fact that manifold books have become regarded as a necessity in many branches of business, and that at the present day there are one hundred people using them where there was one ten years ago. The firm of Samuel Hano & Co., continued to expand and prosper until 1887, when the Samuel Hano Company was incorporated, with Louis Hano, president; J. L. Hano, vice-president; J. W. Sanders, secretary; Samuel Hano, treasurer and general manager. This company now enjoy a reputation and a trade that is practically world-wide, as manufacturers exclusively of manifold books, with factories at Allston, Mass., and salesrooms at No. 105 Summer Street in this city. The factory at Allston is the largest and best-equipped institution of its kind in the country, supplied with every modern improvement and appliance tending to facilitate rapid and perfect production, while constant employment is given to a force of one hundred and twenty-five skilled hands. The output is one of great magnitude and importance, and heavy shipments are continually made to all parts of the United States, while a fine growing export trade is enjoyed with England and other foreign countries. The manifold books bearing the imprint of the Samuel Hano Company can be recommended to all who have occasion to write in duplicate as the simplest, cheapest and best process ever offered to the public, and are so regarded by all who have used them. A complete stock is constantly carried at the Boston salesrooms, where orders of any magnitude are filled at the shortest possible notice, at terms and prices which are invariably satisfactory to the trade. The founder of the business and its present manager, Mr. Samuel Hano, held in the highest esteem by the business community.

THE METROPOLIS OF NEW ENGLAND.

CHESTER MANUFACTURING COMPANY, Suspenders, Braces, Etc., No. 84 Bedford Street.—Among the many prosperous enterprises located upon this great business avenue of the city will be found that which is made the immediate subject of the present sketch. The Chester Manufacturing Company, was organized and began business at the present site in the latter part of 1887, and from the start the enterprise has had a substantial and rapid growth. The spacious premises are conveniently arranged, and all requisite business facilities are supplied in the generally complete equipment of the establishment. The manufactured product comprises a large and varied assortment of suspenders, braces, etc., a specialty being made of the Chester Brace, which deserves more than a passing mention. The brace is the invention of the proprietor, Mr. A. A. Mandell, who has had a wide experience in the business, having been for a number of years in charge of superintending the same line of manufacture. In the Chester Brace are embodied all the advantages of former braces, with a total absence of some of their most striking objectionable features.

In this brace, the elastic is in a link connecting the buckles and back piece with the straps or parts attaching to the trousers, thus leaving the main portion of the suspender to be made of a light but strong web, an arrangement which does away entirely with the discomfort experienced by wearers of an all elastic brace which is at all times liable to absorb perspiration, and while losing its elastic strength, increase in weight. The link mentioned is made of strands of pure rubber neatly encased in a knitted web, and while giving an abundance of elasticity—gives it in the right place. The Chester Brace, although hardly introduced to the trade as yet already has a wide sale and is bound to soon supersede all the old style productions in this line to which it is decidedly superior in every respect. This company also manufactures many elegant and tasteful styles of suspenders and braces, the production of which gives employment to a goodly number of hands, and the trade which reaches throughout New England, and is still spreading—as of prosperous, general aggregate. Mr. Mandell is a gentleman in the prime of life, active, enterprising and able, and under his supervision the business is fast assuming prosperous proportions.

A. D. PERKINS, Dealer in Mutton, Lamb and Veal, No. 1½ Basement, Faneuil Hall Market.—The popular and well patronized meat store in No. 1½ Basement of Faneuil Hall Market was established over six years ago, by the present proprietor, Mr. A. D. Perkins, who has achieved a marked degree of success in his undertaking, and numbers among his permanent patrons many of the best known residents and dealers, not only in the city, but throughout the state of Massachusetts. The store is desirable and convenient in location, is roomy, is equipped with refrigerators for the preservation of the food handled, and is possessed of all needed facilities for the prompt and accurate execution of all orders. A heavy stock of choice, fresh mutton, lamb and veal is always kept on hand, and these are warranted to be fresh and wholesome in quality when offered for sale. The stock is renewed daily from the most reliable sources of supply, and Mr. Perkins, who has had vast experience in the trade and is an excellent judge, exercises great care in keeping his stock up to the highest standard of quality, while his prices compare favorably with those of any other house in the trade. The business is a very active and progressive one, and is of both a wholesale and retail character. Three assistants are employed in the service of patrons and all goods are delivered free of charge to any address in the city. Particular attention is given to family orders, and special rates are quoted for supplies to hotels, restaurants and boarding houses. Mr. Perkins is a native of Kennebunk, Me., but has long resided in the Hub. He is widely known and is respected alike by his competitors in the trade, and by his patrons for his integrity, enterprise and honorable dealings.

HALL & COLE, Commission Merchants, and Wholesale Dealers in Cranberries, Fruit and Vegetables and Produce of All Kinds, Nos. 100 and 102 Faneuil Hall Market.—In considering the relative value of commercial interests those which contribute most largely to the supply of the retail necessities of mankind are entitled to be regarded as the most important; and we know of no branch or department which can justly claim such pre-eminence as that of the fruit and produce trade, for it deals exclusively with the necessities of every day life. A well-known, old established and highly respected house in this line is that of Messrs. Hall & Cole, Nos. 100 and 102 Faneuil Hall Market. The business of this flourishing concern was started originally by Messrs. Highland & Hall some forty years ago. Subsequently the firm was changed to Hall & Haynes, and about a quarter of a century ago, it became, as now, Hall & Cole, the co-partners being Mr. Stacy Hall and Mr. H. G. Cole both of whom are natives of Maine. The firm occupy two spacious stalls and tenement and here they have at command the best of facilities for the successful carrying on of their large and important trade. The firm are general commission merchants and jobbers and wholesale dealers in cranberries, fruit and vegetables and produce of all kinds, and they are daily in receipt of consignments from the best producing districts in all sections of the country. By means of their large connection amongst dealers in the city and in all parts of the New England States the firm have unusual facilities for disposing speedily and to the best possible advantage, of all consignments, for which they make prompt and satisfactory returns. The long practical experience of the members of the firm, coupled with their abundant energy and unimpeachable integrity, render them in every way worthy of the confidence of producers and shippers and of the trade generally. To both buyers and sellers, who form business relations with them, they offer many advantages not easily obtained elsewhere.

W. A. HOLMES & CO., Wholesale and Retail Grocers, No. 91 Causeway, and Nos. 25 and 26 Portland Street. — The old established house of Wm. A. Holmes & Co., has long been justly celebrated for the superior character and comprehensive variety of its stock of staple and fancy groceries. Mr. W. A. Holmes is a recognized authority in every branch of the trade, and brings to bear not only vast practical experience but also perfected facilities and judicial connections. He is a native of Maine and early in life became connected with the grocery trade, in he establishing his present home, and laying the foundation for his markedly prosperous and efficient career. His large store is 30x130 feet in dimensions and most centrally located directly opposite the Lowell and Eastern depots, on Causeway and Portland Streets. It is most handsomely fitted up, with all the modern improvements, including the cash system, etc. Here is one of the largest and the most carefully selected stocks of staple and fancy groceries in New England. To those seeking the best and purest of everything, we say, you will find it here, from the choicest growths of coffees, fresh crop teas, pure sugars, spices, etc., up to full lines of canned goods, bearing the brands of the most responsible packers, delicacies of all kinds, and extra fine cigars, renowned for the excellence of the leaf tobacco used, and for the skilful workmanship. He employs an average force of eighteen hands in the various departments, and sells and delivers to customers all over Boston and vicinity, and along the lines of railroad leading out into New England. Mr. Holmes is possessed of superior executive abilities and has ever maintained the highest of standing for sterling integrity, and to whom great credit is due for having built up in the face of strong competition, the finest business of its kind in the city.

PALMER, PARKER & CO., Mahogany and Veneers, Mills and Wharf, Medford Street, Charlestown District; Office and Salesrooms, Corner Portland and Travers Streets.—Boston is one of the most important centres in the United States for the trade in foreign and domestic cabinet woods, such as mahogany, rosewood, walnut, etc. The leading house engaged in the preparation of these woods for market, and the manufacture of veneers, is that of Messrs. Palmer, Parker & Co. The extensive business conducted here was established in 1857 by Mr. Harrison Parker, succeeded by the firm of Parker & Sleeper, and thus continuing until 1871, when Mr. Sleeper retired, and the business was conducted under the firm name of H. Parker & Co., till 1875 when the present firm was formed, composed of Mr. J. S. Palmer and Mr. H. Palmer. Both gentlemen bring to bear the widest range of practical experience, while their house enjoys the most perfect facilities of any in the trade. Their mahogany mills and veneer sawing establishments are centrally and conveniently located in Medford Street, Charlestown, having superior wharfage, where vessels arriving with cargoes of mahogany can discharge direct into the yards of the firm. The mills are three stories in height, and fully equipped with the latest improved machinery and appliances. Here the firm carry a heavy stock and are prepared to promptly fill the largest wholesale orders. A large force of hands are here employed in the manufacture of cabinet woods into every variety of size and thickness. Among the woods sawed into veneers and cabinet sizes here are mahogany, rose wood, French walnut, plain and figured ash and oak, black walnut, plain and figured maple, white holly, etc. Special attention is given to dimension orders, and the firm fill important contracts for leading furniture manufacturers, cabinet makers and lumber dealers, not only over New England, but throughout every section of the United States and Canada, with a heavy and growing export trade in holly, maple and other native woods specially adapted to the leading circles of the piano case and cabinet makers trade; likewise, for furniture manufacturers and house finish. Mr. Palmer is a native of New Hampshire, and Mr. Parker, of New York city. Both gentlemen are universally popular in trade circles.

E. I. MORRISON & CO., Commission Merchants and Dealers in Fruits and Produce of All Kinds, Basement No. 16, South Side Faneuil Hall Market.—An honorable and successful career of upwards of forty years has given the well-known commission house of Messrs. E. I. Morrison & Co. a high standing in the great thoroughfares of commerce and trade in New England's metropolis. The business of this concern was founded in 1848, and throughout the whole of the long career of this successful concern, the business has been conducted on business principles which have earned for it the position it now holds. The premises occupied, comprise the basement store, No. 16, on the south side of Faneuil Hall Market, and here every convenience and facility are at hand for the storage and effective handling of the heavy stock of fruits and produce of every description necessarily carried to meet the immediate wants of the firm's numerous patrons, scattered over all parts of the New England States. Messrs. E. I. Morrison & Co. command all the advantages naturally accumulated through long years of identification with an industry. They are gentlemen of wide experience, and thoroughly posted in all the wants and requirements of the commission interest. Consignments are received daily from all the best producing sections of the country and from the most noted foreign fruit-growing countries. The firm have the most advantageous arrangements with growers for securing supplies, and are enabled to offer to the trade terms of an exceptionally favorable character. The transactions of the firm are exclusively of a wholesale character, and the business is of such extent as to require the constant services of ten assistants in filling orders. The proprietors are prominent, public spirited and progressive business men, who have done much to sustain and enhance the commercial name of the city. The senior member of the firm is a native of New Hampshire.

HORACE W. TAYLOR, Mortgages Negotiated and Real Estate Purchased, Sold and Leased, No. 87 Equitable Building.—The city of Boston has no financial interests of greater importance than that of real estate, and the course of financial investments in other lines of securities during the last few years, has directed the attention of capitalists to the purchase of well located city real estate. In order to attain the greatest measure of security and the best prospective results, the services of an experienced broker are always necessary, and prominent among those engaged in this business in this city, is Mr. Horace W. Taylor, whose office is centrally located at Nos. 87 and 88 Equitable Building. Mr. Taylor is a native of New York and at present resides in Newton, near this city. Having had a number of years experience in all branches of the real estate business, he founded this house on his own account originally in 1884, and from the start has been the recipient of a very flattering and remunerative patronage, which is constantly increasing to proportions of great magnitude, and at present includes among his permanent customers many of our leading capitalists and investors. He occupies a very neatly equipped office which is furnished with every convenience for the speedy transaction of business and reliable information for investors. Mr. Taylor is a recognized authority in regard to value of residential and business property throughout the city, and has brought to a successful issue many important transactions, and intending investors, who rely upon his sound judgment and judicious advice in purchasing property will secure not only a steady income, but likewise, a prospective increase of value. He also makes a speciality of negotiating loans on bonds and mortgages, and is very popular with those property owners in need of financial assistance, as his methods accord the most honorable character.

T. C. SAVORY, Banner Painter, No. 14 Tremont Row.—The oldest and leading house in Boston engaged in designing, painting and manufacturing military and society banners to order, is that conducted by Mr. T. C. Savory, at No. 14 Tremont Row. This gentleman established himself in business here in 1844, having been twenty-seven years in his present stand and has long enjoyed a liberal, influential and permanent patronage from all sections of the United States. He makes a prominent speciality of silk flags, excelling all his contemporaries in careful attention to details as well as in the superior quality of materials used. His house is the favorite headquarters for the finest work in this line, and his services are in constant requisition by leading societies in this and other cities throughout the Union. Among the special orders filled by him may be mentioned the banner presented by the city of Boston to the city New Orleans in 1884; also, a banner for the Grand Commandery Knights Templar of Mass.; and is now making a fine Masonic banner for the Consistory of Boston. His productions in this line are rarely equalled and never excelled in this country for beauty of design, artistic workmanship and elegance of finish, and have served to give him a prestige and a popularity of which he has every reason to be proud. A visit to his workrooms and an inspection of his methods will satisfy the most critical that his work well merits the praises bestowed upon it. His son, Mr. Walter Savory, is an expert in water colors, and his services are in demand in making scenes for decorative purposes which are highly regarded by connoisseurs for their artistic merit. Mr. Savory is a native of this city, a reliable and accomplished master of his art, fair and conscientious in all his dealings and enduringly popular with his host of friends and patrons in this city and throughout the country.

SHEDD & CRANE, Leather, Nos. 98 and 100 South Street.—The firm of Shedd & Crane, Nos. 98 and 100 South Street, has, in a comparatively brief period, taken a leading rank in the leather trade, and now ranks with the largest concerns in the line. The firm is composed of Wm. E. Shedd and Charles R. Crane, who have long been identified with the business in their capacity as salesmen. In February 1888 they established their present flourishing house, occupying a fine, commodious, three-story building, in dimensions 30x72 feet. Here they carry an immense stock of leather of every description, which they handle on commission, having the best facilities for placing large lots owing to their intimate acquaintance with the leading buyers throughout the country. Their principal trade is in upper leather, and in this branch they can compete with any other house both in regard to price and quality. Both gentlemen are natives of Massachusetts, and in the prime of life. They are highly esteemed in business circles for their energy and the first-class reputation they have always borne.

THE METROPOLIS OF NEW ENGLAND.

WILLARD H. DUNBAR & CO., Merchant Tailors, Nos. 165 and 167 Court Street.—The firm of Messrs. Willard H. Dunbar & Co., at Nos. 165 and 167 Court Street, are recognized as leading exponents of the tailor's art in Boston, and stand in the front rank of popularity and success. This business was originally established in 1852, by Messrs. Morgan, Clarke & Co., who were succeeded by Dunbar, Clarke & Co., and in February, 1888, the present firm was organized as Willard H. Dunbar & Co., Mr. Dunbar being sole proprietor. This gentleman is a practical and experienced master of his art, and is rapidly pushing his way to public favor and prosperity by the general excellence and thorough reliability of his work, and the uniform satisfaction rendered to patrons. He occupies a fine double store, handsomely arranged with heavy plate glass show windows, marble top tables and attractive fixtures, and containing one of the finest assortments of cloths and trimmings ever brought to this city. It is complete in material, design and novelty, and the very best sources of American and European production have contributed to its wealth. The firm devote their entire attention to fine custom work, and the garments here turned out are perfect in every feature—in cut, fit, style and finish. A very large and flourishing trade is enjoyed, requiring in its transaction the constant services of a large force of skilled assistants, while among the permanent patrons of the house are very many of the best-dressed citizens of Boston and its suburban towns, the business during certain years aggregating as high as $60,000. Mr. Dunbar is a resident of Chelsea, and is a gentleman of the highest repute and standing in society, liberal and conscientious in all his dealings and eminently popular with his host of friends and patrons.

KIMBALL'S FINE CONFECTIONERY, R. H. Kimball, Proprietor, No. 78 Tremont Street.—The fine confectionery of Mr. R. H. Kimball, at No. 78 Tremont Street, has since its establishment become a favorite resort for consumers of fine confectionery. Mr. Kimball was born in Maine, but has been a resident of this city since 1870. He first embarked in the produce business on Blackstone Street, and was quite successful in that line of trade, but having a preference for his present occupation he embarked in it in 1886, and although not so long established as some others in the same line of trade he has been the recipient of a patronage, which is not often accorded to older houses. His store is centrally located and is of ample dimensions, handsomely and neatly appointed with elegant fixtures consisting of large and attractive display windows, elaborate counters, show cases, etc., in fact everything pertaining to the outfit of a first class confectionery house. Here will always be found an almost inexhaustible supply of everything in the confectionery line, all of which are the freshest, purest and best that can be obtained in the market, and comprise bon-bons, gloves, candied fruits and nuts, caramels, chocolates in all styles, dragee candies, lozenges, Boston chips, mottoes, gum drops, jellies, etc. It is well-known to every intelligent person that purity is the main essential with all kinds of confectionery. This necessary quality is the great feature with all goods sold at this establishment, and as it is very difficult in these days to obtain candies and confectionery devoid of adulteration and deleterious substances, the advantage of dealing with a house whose reputation is so high for selling none but the purest and best goods is at once manifest.

MRS. S. A. MacDONNELL, Importer and Retailer of Kid, Suede and Fabric Gloves, No. 86 Tremont street, Under Tremont Temple.—Mrs. S. A. MacDonnell, importer and retailer of kid, Suede and fabric gloves, is a native of New York State where she was engaged in the mercantile business for several years, but came to Boston and established this enterprise in March, 1888, and by handling only first-class goods, carefully attending to the wants of her customers, and liberal dealing has made her establishment the centre of a first-class trade, which has few if any successful rivals in this section of the city. The store is of ample size having a frontage of twelve feet and a depth of over three times that distance, and is very elegantly fitted up, having a fine display window, show-cases and handsome counters, together with other conveniences for the exhibition of her fine stock of goods and the comfort of patrons. The assortment to be found here constantly is full and complete and embraces a full line of kid, Suede and fabric gloves, which have been imported direct and comprise the very best and highest grades produced by the most eminent and reliable manufacturers in Paris, Vienna, Berlin and London. These goods are in all colors and sizes, shapes and styles, and an examination of them cannot fail to supply the wants of the most fastidious, as they are offered at prices that absolutely defy successful competition. In addition to the excellent line of gloves carried by Mrs. MacDonnell, she has the agency for the celebrated Big al Stainless Fast Black Hosiery for ladies, gents and children. These goods are guaranteed absolutely fast black, prices from 37½ cents up. Ladies understand that it is a very difficult thing to get a black stocking that will not crock, but on buying this particular make, they will find them just as represented. All goods are purchased direct from manufacturers in large quantities for cash, which enables her to offer superior inducements to patrons.

D. W. STARRATT & CO., Tailors, No. 11 Hamilton Place.—The history of prominent representatives of the tailor's art in this city must make conspicuous mention of the firm of Messrs. D. W. Starratt & Co., whose establishment is very eligibly located at No. 11 Hamilton Place. This house has long been recognized as a tower of strength in the merchant tailoring trade, and a popular source of supply for well-made and perfectly fitting garments. The business was originally established in 1876, by Messrs. Putnam & Starratt, who were succeeded by Starratt & Trench, and in February, 1887, the present firm was organized by Messrs. D. W. Starratt and J. B. Mason. They occupy spacious and elegantly appointed quarters for manufacturing and sales purposes, and are in a position to guarantee the prompt and perfect fulfilment of all orders and commissions. Here is exhibited one of the finest stocks of cloths and trimmings to be found in the city. It is complete in material, design and novelty, and the very best sources of American and European production have contributed to its wealth. The proprietors devote their entire time and talents to fine custom work, and the garments made by them to measure are recognized as simply perfection in style, fit and artistic workmanship. To seek their services once is to be their patron always. Among their permanent customers are very many of Boston's best-dressed citizens, gentlemen old and young, who understand the merits of a thoroughly first-class tailor, and who find in Messrs. Starratt & Co.'s establishment not only a line of goods that is at all times superior, but a place where the general make-up, fit and trimming of a garment is a matter of careful consideration and study. The co-partners are both well known Bostonians, accomplished masters of their art, fair, liberal and conscientious in all their dealings, and young men of high social standing, whole popularity and thorough reliability, who have won success by honestly deserving it.

TIGHE & BURKE, Grocers, No. 3 Charles Street.—The house so long and so successfully conducted by Messrs. Tighe & Burke, was founded in 1862 by Messrs. John Tighe and William Burke, and on the death of Mr. Burke in January 1882, Mr. Tighe succeeded to the sole control, continuing the business under the original firm name. There is nothing in either hemisphere that comes under the definition of a food product or grocer's sundries that is not to be found here in its most attractive form, and pure, fresh and reliable as to quality. As regards domestic staple groceries and food products the stock is thoroughly comprehensive, covering the entire wide range and including everything in its best quality as demanded by the refined tastes of the people of this city, while a leading specialty is made of fancy groceries, such as canned and preserved meats, fruits and vegetables; peas, mushrooms and capers; preserves, pickles and sauces; table delicacies, condiments and luxuries of both domestic and foreign production, and including only those brands that experience and test have shown to be perfect and wholesome. Such staples as teas, coffees and spices, flour, sugar and butter, so difficult to be obtained of the desired standard, are received direct from the most reputable producing sources, and recommend their own superior merits to the confidence and patronage of critical and discriminating buyers. Not alone the rich but also the poor patronize this store, for they are sure of finding here the best and freshest goods at lowest current prices. Mr. Tighe is a foreigner by birth, but a resident here for the past thirty years.

JOHN EARLE & CO., Civil and Military Tailors, No. 370 Washington Street.—The most famous firm of tailors in the United States is that of Messrs. John Earle & Co., of No. 370 Washington Street. They are the oldest established, the business having been founded by Mr. John Earle, away back in 1849. He early developed an enviable reputation for the superior character of his work, and the business rapidly came to the front, the leader in its line. The existing copartnership was formed in 1887, the old and honored name and style being retained. The partners are Mr. Walter Earle, born in Boston and son of the founder of the house. He was in the old firm for twenty-eight years, and connected with the business for a total of thirty years. He is the leading authority on gentlemen's fashionable attire both civil and military, and gives close attention to the guidance of the heavy business transacted. Mr. Benjamin Parker is a native of New Hampshire, who has been a resident of Boston thirty-five years past. He also has been with the house for a period of thirty years, and in copartnership since 1887, and no one better than he is qualified to extend advice to customers and to take charge of the work of production of the elegant garments for which the concern is so famed. Mr. Frederick E. Poole was born in Worcester, and has resided in Boston for thirty-five years past. He has been with the house since 1858, and is in the firm since 1887. He is a skilled and accomplished master tailor, and the firm is thus the strongest possible both as to skill, experience, facilities, resources and connections. They import direct, full lines of the choicest fabrics including all the newest shades, textures and patterns, and the most fastidious can be suited from their magnificent display. Fashionable tailoring is done here on correct principles, all the niceties of gentlemen's attire are given strict attention to, while the styles are absolutely correct, and the work of the cutter, fitter etc., of the most perfect, skilled character. Each figure is made a study and treated as to its needs, and garments made here are faultless. The firm employ upwards of 100 of the most skilful journeymen obtainable, and are driven with orders from the best circles of civil and military society. Military uniforms have ever been a specialty, and the firm have supplied same to officers of many of the crack regiments both volunteer and regular in every section of the United States. The importance of accuracy in making uniforms cannot be over-estimated, and the wide experience of the firm in this line, measuring all ranks from general to non-commissioned officer, it is manifest that nowhere can such absolute satisfaction be attained as here. Though the firm has so long maintained the lead for quality, elegance and style, yet its prices are remarkably moderate and the fashionable world gets what it wants here at prices to suit the times. To those who appreciate the importance of perfect fitting garments from new goods, we strongly recommend to patronize this old and honorable house which built up its trade and reputation strictly on the basis of enterprise, equity, skill and integrity.

NEW ENGLAND GRIP COMPANY, No 144 State Street.—Boston has long held a pre-eminent reputation as a manufacturing centre, and there are certain enterprises which deserve special mention in this review. Among these may be named that conducted by the New England Grip Company. This company are the manufacturers of the celebrated Hand Power Test Machine, and has acquired by purchase of patent rights the exclusive right to operate in the states of Massachusetts, Maine, New Hampshire and Vermont. It was incorporated in December, 1887, with a capital stock of $150,000, and is officered as follows, viz: president, Robert J. Edwards, treasurer, Henry E. Russell; directors, R. J. Edwards, W. E. Cox, H. E. Russell, Schuyler Walden, Augustus Nickerson, H. E. Swasey and E. Bridge. The use of this machine is to test the grip of the hand, and it is placed in all places of public resort and interest. The principle upon which it is worked is this: Upon a person dropping a nickel five-cent piece into a slit in the top of the machine, it is set ready for use, and by gripping the handles the number of pounds gripped will be registered upon the dial of the machine. The earnings of the company will depend upon the number of times the machine is used in the course of a year. Machines of this kind already set up have proved to be extremely profitable. They have several advantages over the weighing machines: Their original cost is less; they are not apt to get out of repair; accuracy is not essential to their successful operation; and they appeal to two traits of human nature found in every American—personal vanity and competitive spirit—both of which are apt to induce the person who grips once to repeat the test, especially if a friend has beaten his record. Experience has shown that two or three persons will drop a half-dozen nickels into a machine in a very few minutes, something that would never occur with a weighing machine. The company propose to put these machines up in the most advantageous places, and on the most favorable terms possible. They will be placed, when proper arrangements can be made, in such places as college and other gymnasiums, fairs, hotels, summer resorts, depots, excursion steamers, and in all other places where people are accustomed to congregate. Parties desiring to have these machines placed in their establishments, or to acquire the sole right to certain cities, towns or counties, should apply to the office of the company in this city, or they will be visited by an agent on sending notice to the company.

WATERS & LITCHFIELD, Dealers in Beef, Pork, Lard, Hams, Tripe, Pigs' Feet, Etc., Nos. 41 and 43 Faneuil Hall Market.—Among the substantial and reliable meat and provision dealers in Faneuil Hall Market are Messrs. Waters & Litchfield, whose long, practical experience amply qualifies them to carry on their enterprise in the most approved manner and to supply the needs of the public with the choicest goods to be had in all seasons. The business now controlled by this progressive firm was inaugurated on August 26, 1856, by Mr. J. G. Sanderson, at stall No. 53. In 1859 he removed to stalls Nos. 41 and 43, and here the business has ever since been successfully conducted. In 1874 a partnership was formed under the style of Sanderson, Neese & Waters. Mr. Sanderson died about a month after, and a copartnership was formed under the firm name of Sanderson, Morse & Waters, the former being the son of the late Mr. Sanderson. Two years later Mr. Sanderson also died, and in 1879 the present firm was formed. Mr. Waters has had a large experience in this line, dating back to 1863, when he first entered the house as a clerk and was admitted to partnership eleven years later. Mr. Litchfield has been a member of the firm since 1879, the copartners being Messrs. J. A. Waters and A. S. Litchfield. The latter was born in Maine and the former is a native of Massachusetts. They are rated among the most popular, successful and substantial business men in the market, and they have under control a wholesale and retail trade of considerable magnitude, and one which extends throughout the city and New England. Their two stalls are commodious, neatly and appropriately fitted up, and provided with all necessary appliances for the successful prosecution of the business. The firm select the articles of food dealt in with great care, and they carry at all times a large stock of the choicest meats, including beef, pork, lard, hams, tripe, pigs' feet, etc., all of which are warranted to be first-class in every particular, and may be purchased at the lowest market prices. The trade is of both a wholesale and retail character, and is yearly increasing in volume. Three assistants are employed, and all orders are promptly and satisfactorily filled.

T. C. PAZOLT & SON, Furs, No. 92 Chauncy Street.—An old established house well known in this community is that of T. C. Pazolt & Son, importers, manufacturers and dealers in furs. It was established as long ago as 1849, by Mr. Pazolt, and has always occupied a conspicuous position in the trade and received a liberal patronage and is very popular. In 1880 his son Lewis Pazolt was given an interest in the business, and since that time it has been continued under the present firm name. The premises occupy a three-story building 25x60 feet in area affords ample space for manufacturing purposes and displaying the stock, the salesroom being particularly neatly fitted up in which is exhibited an elegant assortment of rich, elegant cloaks, dolmans, paletots and seal sacks and ladies furs of every description, also everything suitable for men's wear, gloves, etc. These goods are in every respect first-class and very desirable, and have been carefully made and trimmed, and are in perfect accord with the prevailing fashions. Mr. Pazolt is an authority upon the different kinds of furs and was brought up to the business in Austria, his native country. He came to the United States many years ago, and during his long residence in Boston, has become widely known as one of the best practical experts in the fur trade in the city. His son and copartner was born in Boston.

N. SCHLOSS, Wholesale Dealer in Cigars and Tobaccos, Pipes, Etc., No. 167 Hanover Street, Corner North Centre Street.—A leading representative house devoted to the wholesale trade in cigars and tobaccos, pipes and smokers' articles generally, is that of which Mr. N. Schloss is the enterprising and popular proprietor. He established in business ten years ago, bringing to bear the widest range of practical experience, perfected facilities and influential connections. He makes a speciality of the direct importation of pipes and smokers articles generally and carries the largest stock in Boston and New England. He has manifested marked enterprise in this line, and in his spacious establishment can always be found full lines of pipes, from the ordinary T. D. Clay to the finest, most elaborate and artistic meerschaum pipes. In fine meerschaums he has no rival, and the trade in search of choice, salable goods will consult their best interests by making their selections here. Mr. Schloss shows many novelties in smoking sets, and also carries a full stock of the choicest hand made Havana, key west and domestic cigars, and chewing and smoking tobaccos, snuff, etc. He quotes the lowest prices for the best goods and has ever pursued an equitable policy toward the trade. His business has had a rapid growth and six years ago he was obliged to move to his present spacious store. He has three salesmen on the road, a staff of clerks in the store, and is doing one of the largest and best trades of the kind. He has ever retained the confidence of leading commercial circles, and his familiar trade-mark, A pipe, stamped C. S., is a sure guarantee of the highest standard of excellence.

GEO. A. CLARK, Broker in Chemicals; Room No. 4, No. 79 Milk Street.—The immense quantities of bleaching powders, soda ash, caustic soda and kindred rough chemicals used in the United States impart to the trade in these useful and indispensable products an importance that places it among the principal departments of commercial activity in our great seaboard cities. The transactions in the articles referred to here in Boston annually through the medium of the broker and commission merchant reach enormous proportions, while the volume of business grows apace with years. Among those engaged in this line in this city there is perhaps no one known or who receives a larger measure of recognition than Geo. A. Clark, broker in heavy chemicals, whose office is located at No. 79 Milk Street, (Room 4,) and who for some twenty-four years, during which he has been established in business has maintained an excellent standing in the trade. He makes a leading specialty of handling English chemicals, such as bleaching powder, soda ash, etc., selling the same on commission for Boston importers, and is prepared to execute all orders for anything in this line in the most expeditious and reliable manner, while his business connection, which is of a most substantial character, extends throughout the whole of the New England States and the principal portion of the west. Mr. Clark, who is a gentleman in the prime of life, and a native of Boston, is a man of entire responsibility in all his dealings, as well as of energy and ample experience, and is thoroughly conversant with the wants of the trade.

KIMBALL BROTHERS, Beef, Pork, Lard, Hams, Tripe, Sausages, Pigs' Feet, Etc., Nos. 54 and 56 Faneuil Hall Market.—Stalls Nos. 54 and 56 are among the most largely patronized of those in the far-famed Faneuil Hall Market, the opening of which carries the mind back to generations that have passed. Since 1862 the business at the stalls named has been conducted under the style of Kimball Brothers. The founders were Messrs. J. W. & W. H. Kimball, whose partnership was terminated by the death of the latter in 1885. The surviving partner has continued the business under the old firm name, and he has fully sustained the high reputation the firm gained in years gone by for liberal and straightforward dealing, and for handling superior grades of meats at reasonable prices. The two stalls occupied for the business are commodious, and these are neatly and orderly kept, while they are provided with refrigerators and other necessary accessories for keeping the stock fresh and sweet. The stock on hand is at all times an essentially large one to meet the requirements of the numerous patrons of the establishment. It is renewed daily from the most reliable sources of supply, and consists of the choicest cuts of beef and pork, also lard, hams, tripe, sausages, pigs' feet, etc. Besides having a large family trade, the firm caters to an extensive and growing wholesale trade. The distributing trade of the firm extends throughout the city and beyond it, and two competent and experienced assistants and a delivery wagon are kept in constant service. Mr. Kimball was born in Vermont, and is an old resident of Boston, where he is widely known and esteemed for his business energy and rectitude.

SANDERSON & SON, General Agents; Wilson Line of Steamers, Between London, Hull, Newcastle, Boston and New York; No. 4 Liberty Square; New York Office: Nos. 21 and 22 State Street.—Boston has of recent years secured valued accessions to her facilities for handling the enormous growth of her foreign trade, one of the most important being the placing of a line of powerful and roomy steamships on the route between this city and London, Hull, and all other ports of importance by the famous firm of Messrs. Thomas Wilson Sons & Co., of Hull, Eng. Their agents in America are Messrs. Sanderson & Son, quite as widely and favorably known for their success in securing the cargoes and passengers for the steamships consigned to their houses. Mr. B. Sanderson, the head of this old and influential house is resident in Liverpool, Mr. L. B. Sanderson is resident in Boston, Mr. Harold Sanderson is the resident New York agent, while Mr. Oswald Sanderson is at the head of the firm's branch house in St. Petersburg, Russia. The Wilson Line is steadily enlarging its volume of traffic between Boston and New York and Europe. The line is the largest one privately owned in the world. It comprises upwards of eighty of the best style of modern ocean steamships, and of varying sizes, with regard to special routes and lines of trade. The house flag and funnels of this line are seen every week in nearly 100 great ports of the world, as they pursue their commercial voyages, and millions of tons of freight are thus transported to their destination. The service is a weekly one to New York from Hull and London, and a fortnightly one to Boston from Hull. The saloon passage to London or Hull is only $75 return, $40. Intermediate, $30. Steerage to London only $15. Those intending to visit Europe should note these new rates and visit Messrs. Sanderson & Son's office, No. 4 Liberty Square, where full information can be obtained. The firm offer equally fine facilities to merchants quoting lowest rates to London Hull or Newcastle issuing through bills of lading to all ports on the Mediterranean, Baltic and Black Seas, India, China and Japan, thus enabling Boston shippers to at any time ship via steam to every port of importance in Europe or the east.

MILLS & GIBB, Importers of Lace Curtains, Embroideries, White Goods, Etc., Room 46 Phillips Building, Hamilton Place; Wm. Byers, Agent.—This is an old established New York concern, and in its line of trade is one of the most extensive and most widely known in the country. The Boston branch of the house was handed in 1887 for the more efficient service of the wants of customers in the New England States. The firm are importers of lace curtains, embroideries, trimmings, novelties and white goods of all kinds, and these goods are shipped direct from the European factories, and in quantities so great that terms and prices are secured impossible to be obtained by small dealers; by this means the firm are in a position to confer advantages and benefits that few of their competers can accord. In their Boston office the firm carry a fine sample stock that is being constantly renewed and maintained as representative of all the newest designs in lace curtains, embroideries, white goods, etc., and orders are filled direct from the New York house. Since 1887, Mr. William Byers has been the firm's representative in Boston. He is a native of New York, was raised in the firm's business house there, and was for a long time traveling salesman. He is a wide awake, energetic and courteous business man, and in him the dealers in New England have a straightforward, honorable representative of a house, whose record is of the highest, to deal with.

HERBERT SEAVERNS, Representing Russian Hair Felt Company; S. Stroock & Co. Felts and Velours, No. 115 Summer Street.—The different industries engaged in the manufacture of wearing apparel, whose principal headquarters are in Boston, have opened up a very extensive field in the way of making and furnishing necessary articles used in those various manufactures. Among these kindred industries to the boot and shoe, also cap making, is the well-known house of Mr. Herbert Seaverns, at No. 115 Summer Street, who represents the Russian Hair Felt Company and the felt and velours house of Messrs. S. Stroock & Co., of No. 62 Walker Street, New York City. Mr. Seaverns is a native of Boston, and has had a very large experience as a salesman and handler of these goods, and established himself in the business on his own account in 1887. He occupies a very neatly fitted-up office, together with sample room, in which will be found a full and complete assortment of samples and stock of all goods in his line of trade required in the boot and shoe, also cap manufacturing business. Although not so long in the business as many other houses in the same line, Mr. Seaverns has built up a very large and substantial patronage, such as is not often accorded to many older in the trade. He receives his goods direct from the manufacturers and importers, which enables him to offer special inducements to purchasers, while the lines which he handles are well-known as to excellence of quality and reliability by the entire trade. His trade extends not only throughout the city and vicinity, but to the entire New England States. The hair felt manufactured by the Russian Hair Felt Company has long held a very prominent place among the requirements of manufacturers, and its reputation is consequently increasing, as is also the goods coming from the house of S. Stroock & Co., and especially so is it with their line of velours of all grades. By their selection of Mr. H. Seaverns as their representative in this city they have placed their goods in closer relations with purchasers in Boston and surrounding country. Mr. Seaverns is a wide awake, energetic and reliable business man, who fully understands the needs of the trade, and the success he has already attained is justly merited by his honorable and fair business methods.

ROBERT T. ALMY & CO., Clothiers, No. 622 Washington Street.—One of the most popular among the leading clothing houses in this city, is that of the firm of Robert T. Almy & Co., which is located at No. 622 Washington Street. In endeavoring to draw a brief sketch by which at least a partial impression may be obtained of the character and magnitude of the business carried on we must necessarily be compelled to omit many interesting features and confine ourselves to the few salient points most readily suggested. It was originated by L. P. Bennett & Co. in 1860, who were succeeded by the Eagle Clothing Company, and in 1880 by Edward C. Almy & Co., who continued its direction until 1888, when Robert T. Almy & Co. succeeded to it and have since conducted the business vigorously upon the same liberal, honorable methods that have always characterized the operations of the house. The location is a very desirable one, the premises embracing two floors of the ample area of 50x90 feet, with handsome plate glass front. The interior arrangements are neat, elegant and attractive, and in every respect adapted to the necessities of the business, and are highly ornamental in general appearance. The store is carpeted throughout, and no exertions have been spared to render the stock of goods it contains unapproachable either in extent or elegance from the medium to the finest fabrics. It is replete with everything fashionable and seasonable in every size and style for men, boys and children, cut by skilled designers and made and trimmed in the very best manner by practical tailors, the whole assortment being of uniform excellence, and highly creditable to the judgment, good taste and sagacity of Mr. Robert T. Almy, the head of the firm, who superintends and manages the entire establishment, in which he is assisted by fifteen clerks and salesmen. The house enjoys a large and steadily growing trade, and is certainly a very desirable one to deal with, as customers will find the prices such as to defy successful competition. Mr. Almy is a gentleman of thorough enterprise and large experience, and can always offer the best goods and guarantee perfect-fitting clothing and full satisfaction and meet the requirements of a critical and exacting public in every instance.

REED & BROTHER, Fire Insurance; Office, No. 50 Kilby Street.—One of the leading representative firms of fire insurance agents and brokers in New England is that of Messrs. Reed & Brother, of No. 50 Kilby Street. The business is one of the oldest of its line, and has been continuously in the hands of Mr. George M. Reed and his associates ever since he first opened his office in 1848. The firm of Reed & Hastings was subsequently formed, succeeded by Reed & Brother in 1856, Mr. J. H. Reed coming into copartnership. The lamented decease of the latter occurred in 1880, since which date the honored and widely known name has remained unchanged, while the present firm was formed in 1882 as follows: Mr. George W. Reed, Mr. Geo. C. Boyson, Mr. Eugene M. Smith, and Mr. W. Herbert Boynton. Mr. Reed was born in Danvers, and from early youth has been a resident of Boston. He is a recognized authority on the fire risks of this city and vicinity and on the manufacturing risks of New England, and has long commanded the friendship and patronage of leading firms and corporations. Mr. Boyson, who came into the firm in 1882, is a widely-experienced underwriter and an able and popular business man. Mr. Smith is a Bostonian of long experience in fire insurance, having been with the house twenty years, and in partnership six. He is universally popular and respected, and so also Mr. Boynton, who is a native of Boston, with the house eighteen years and a partner for six. As thus constituted, the firm has the facilities, knowledge and experience essential to conducting the most extensive business upon the most approved basis. They have won, and retain, the confidence of the public by pursuing a strictly honorable, liberal policy, and represent as agents the following old and powerful corporations: Springfield Fire and Marine Insurance Company, with a cash capital of $1,250,000; Meriden Fire Insurance Company, of Connecticut, with a cash capital of $200,000; Security Insurance Company of New Haven, with a cash capital of $250,000, and the Liberty Insurance Company, of New York, with a cash capital of $400,000. They all have large surplus and reserve funds, and are among the most popular in the field. Their policies are clear and liberally worded, their rates the lowest consistent with security, while all losses are promptly paid when adjusted. The firm control the insuring of desirable lines of business and residential property, and also of large mills and factories throughout Massachusetts, and those seeking full security, low rates, and fair, honorable treatment, can have same by insuring here. The firm is universally popular and respected, and is as to character a leading factor and exponent in New England.

T. WHITE'S SONS, Truckmen and Forwarders, No. 44 Kilby Street.—For expeditious and reliable handling and transferring of heavy freights, or for promptness and despatch in the forwarding of general merchandise, no firm engaged in the business in this city enjoys a better reputation, as few receive a larger measure of merited recognition, than that of T. White's Sons, the well-known and responsible truckmen and forwarders, whose office is located at No. 44 Kilby street. They are in all respects one of the leading and best equipped concerns in this important branch of business in Boston, and have a very large, permanent patronage. They have in service thirty horses, and a corresponding number of trucks, wagons, etc., while twenty experienced drivers and others are employed, the proprietors exercising close personal supervision over every feature and detail of the business. Trucking of every description is promptly and reliably attended to, special attention being given to lumber and heavy freight, while goods are forwarded to all parts of the United States, by rail and water, with despatch, every facility being at hand for handling steam engines, boilers, machinery, etc.; and all business entrusted to these gentlemen is certain to be attended to in the most expeditious and satisfactory manner. This flourishing enterprise was originally started some twenty years ago by T. White (deceased), who conducted the same up to 1880 when owing to his death, the business passed into the hands of his sons and successors, F. J. and J. J. White. In January 1886, one of the brothers—J. J. White—was also removed by death, and E. K. Houghton was admitted into partnership, and under the style of T. White's Sons the business has since been continued with uninterrupted success. Messrs. White and Houghton are both young men of energy and untiring industry, thoroughly reliable in their business relations, and fully merit the large measure of public favor they enjoy.

AMERICAN GRIP MACHINE COMPANY, No 114 State Street. — Among the many remarkable productions of American inventive genius which have appeared within recent years, and which have challenged praise and won the appreciation of the public, is that ingenious device known as the hand-power grip machine. A leading concern engaged in the manufacture of this production is the American Grip Machine Company, whose headquarters are located at No. 114 State Street, this city. The organization of this company was effected in November, 1888, the capital being $25,000. With a good article to place upon the market, and energy and ability to direct its affairs, the company has already met with flattering success, and over two hundred of their hand-power grip machines are now in use in various sections of the United States and Canada, while the demand for them is constantly on the increase. The machines are fully protected by patents owned by the company, and it is well worth while to make an examination of their merits. The machine is operated by dropping a nickel into a slit in the top of the apparatus, and then gripping the handle of the machine, the number of pounds gripped being registered on a dial. Constant practice will strengthen the muscles of the hand and arm, so that physical benefit is received, while there is a continual opening for friendly bouts of strength between friends who may meet where the machines are placed. The company dispose of the machines on ninety-nine year leases, which is a practical ownership to the party who takes the lease, and they are also willing to sell the sale rights to any undisposed of territory. In every place where the machines have been put they have been a source of much profit. The officers of the company are the following well-known gentlemen: President, Walter P. Clarke; treasurer, Henry E. Russell; Directors, R. J. Edwards, H. E. Russel, Walter P. Clark, Thornton N. Motley, Schuyler Walden. Interested persons will obtain further information by addressing the company at their office in this city. The following parties have their grip machine in use, and recommend it highly: Beckman & Pinchard, proprietors of the Parker House; machine in one year took in $275. J. H. Whipple, proprietor Young's Hotel; machine in one year took in $125. H. M. Hartshorn & Co, proprietors of the Tremont House; machine in one year took in $270. M. Englehardt, No. 20 Avery Street, machine in nine months took in $87.35. Hollis & Cobb, Washington Street, machine in one year took in $152.65.

IRVING A. HOWE, Manufacturer of the Hub Shirt, the Hub Wraps and Hub Drawers; salesroom, No. 384 Washington Street, Room 10.—The manufacture of novelties in shirts, wraps and drawers has in this city grown to an extent of great importance, affording employment to vast capital and many thousands of operatives. It is a business peculiarly adapted to the female sex, who find in it a lucrative employment both at their homes and elsewhere. For more than thirty years Mr. Irving A. Howe has been one of the most noted manufacturers in this line in the city, and has won, through the real merits of his productions, a leading place in the front rank of American manufacturers of shirts, wraps, bath robes, drawers, etc. He founded the business in 1852, and its history from the first has been one of continuous success. His salesroom is at No. 384 Washington Street, room 10, and this is appropriately fitted up and arranged for the business. It is heavily stocked with materials and manufactured goods, and every facility is at hand for promptly and satisfactorily meeting all orders. Fourteen hands are employed here, and this number includes several experienced cutters of garments. All the manufacturing is done outside, Mr. Howe having in service a large number of women, who make up goods at their homes. These goods include smoking coffee and breakfast jackets, bath robes, shirts, drawers, wraps, etc., and a brisk wholesale and retail trade is done throughout the United States. The Hub Wraps and Hub Drawers, with suspensory gore, are made under patent, granted August 8, 1893. These wraps and drawers are made from non-shrinking goods, manufactured expressly for Mr. Howe, and they have a freedom which cannot be obtained in any other pattern. The Hub Shirt, noted for being stylish, easy and perfect fitting are made to order as desired but a liberal stock of ready made goods is always kept on hand ready for shipment. Mr. Howe is a native of Rutland, and is universally esteemed for his business ability.

THOS. HOLLIS, Drugs, Medicines, and Chemicals, No. 23 Union Street.—In many respects the wholesale and retail drug establishment of Thomas Hollis, at No. 23 Union Street, is the most eminently representative in its line of any in this city. To its splendid facilities as dealers and manufacturers, it adds old-established, influential connections, while the management is in the hands of young men full of zeal and vigor and possessed at the same time of vast practical experience. The business was founded in 1826 by Mr. Thomas Hollis, who died in 1876, and was succeeded by his two sons, Messrs. Thomas and Francis Hollis, who continue the business under the honored name of its originator and founder. They occupy the whole building at the above number, which is utilized for the extensive business transacted. Both partners are skilled workers, their eyes supervise every detail, and their guarantee as to purity, freshness and accuracy, means exactly what it says. This old stand at sign of the golden mortar, has long been recognized as a land-mark in the history of the past and a prime factor in the commerce of the present. The proprietors deal at both wholesale and retail in drugs, medicines and chemicals of all kinds, and are also widely pronounced as extensive manufacturers, and keep all valuable patent medicinals. They carry a full supply of all these specialties, besides a great variety of other articles needed for mechanical, chemical and culinary purposes, not usually kept by druggists. Their goods are in heavy and permanent demand, not only through out the entire United States, but in Turkey, the Sandwich Islands and other foreign countries. The stock recommends its own peculiar merits to the confidence and patronage of critical and discriminating purchasers, while a corps of skilled assistants give prompt attention to the demands of the trade. The Messrs. Hollis are members of the Wholesale Druggists' Association, and stand high in trade circles, and it is to such houses that Boston owes her supremacy in the drug trade.

J. M. JELLISON & CO., Boston and Maine Drug Company, Haymarket Square.—One of the leading houses in the drug trade in Boston and one of the oldest established, is that of J. M. Jellison & Co., the Boston and Maine Drug Company. The establishment of this business dates back to 1844 when Messrs. Wise and Ellis Miller opened it in the same place, carrying it on for over a quarter of a century with marked success. They were succeeded by Riley & Stebbins and the latter five years ago by the present firm. The store is one of the most attractive on the street and is 25x90 feet in dimensions. A full line of the purest drugs and chemicals is carried as well as all the leading proprietary remedies, fancy articles, surgical goods etc., while the preparations of the house are numerous, including Jellison's Honey of Horehound Cough Cure, Jellison's Diarrhoea Cure, Jellison's Diabetes Water, which are standard remedies of their kind and are in great demand all over the city. A large wholesale and retail trade is carried on, four clerks being employed in the establishment which is also a favorite place for the filing of physicians' prescriptions. Mr. Jellison is a native of Lyman, York County, Maine. He has had fifteen years experience in the drug trade is a regular licensed pharmacist and is regarded as one of the safest and most capable men in his line.

L. B. FRAZIER, Stock Broker, No 19 Exchange Place, Room 7.—Among the most popular and responsible stock brokers of Boston may be mentioned the name of L. B. Frazier, whose office is at Room 7, No. 19 Exchange Place. Mr. Frazier, who is a gentleman of middle age, was born at Lynn, Mass., and has his residence at Lynn. He is a man of strict probity in all his dealing and business relations, and also of energy, sagacity and thorough experience in stock operations, enjoying a creditable reputation in the financial circles of the city. Establishing himself in business here in 1875, Mr. Frazier has, during the fourteen years since intervening, by judicious transactions, close study of the market and unfailing devotion to the interests of his clients, steadily increased his hold on public confidence and favor until his patronage has grown to quite substantial proportions. He buys and sells stocks, bonds and securities and also deals in western cattle roads, etc., doing a strictly commission business, special attention being given to negotiating corporation and municipal loans.

SHATTUCK & JONES, Dealers in all kinds of Fresh Fish, Lobsters and Pickled Fish, Green Turtle and Terrapin, No. 128 Faneuil Hall Market.—A leading and one of the oldest firms engaged in the handling and shipping of sea food, in the Faneuil Hall Market, is that of Shattuck & Jones, dealers in all kinds of fresh fish, pickled fish, lobsters, terrapin etc., whose commodious and well equipped stall is centrally situated at No. 128, Faneuil Hall Market, and which is one of the oldest stalls in the market, having been opened in 1826. It is one of the oldest, foremost and most responsible firms devoted to this branch of business in Boston, and fully sustains to-day its well-earned reputation for choice goods and reliable dealing, none better in this city. This flourishing business was established in 1854 by Messrs. George Shattuck and Allan H. Jones, under the firm name of Shattuck & Jones, and by these gentleman it was conducted up to 1856, when Mr. Shattuck was removed by death; Mr. Jones, the surviving partner, continuing alone for some years and then admitted into partnership his son Chas. A. Jones. In 1881, on the occasion of the death of Mr Jones, E. B. Newton became a member of the firm, and under the original style of Shattuck & Jones, which has endured from the start, the business has since been carried on with uninterrupted success. The premises occupied in the market are spacious, well-ordered and completely equipped with all the latest improved appurtenances for the storage, display and preserving of fish etc., including a capacious aquarium, while eighteen efficient assistants are employed. An extensive and varied stock is constantly carried on hand to meet the requirements of a steady and wide demand, and includes everything in the line of ocean, lake and river fish, both fresh and pickled; also lobsters, green turtle and terrapin, and also pure cod liver oil, and the trade of the firm which is both wholesale and retail, is exceedingly large, extending throughout the New England States and to New York, Philadelphia and other sections of the country. Messrs. Jones and Newton, who are natives respectively of Boston and Weymouth, Mass., are both gentlemen of entire probity in their dealings.

PETTEE MACHINE WORKS, Manufacturers of Cotton Mill Machinery. Office, No 70 Kilby Street.—Among other machine shops that have lately brought out some improvements in cotton machinery, special mention should be made of the Pettee Machine Works, which is the first shop in America to undertake the building of the Revolving Flat Carding Engine. The manufacture of carding machinery was begun by the late Mr. Otis Pettee, in 1831, and who, from small beginnings developed a large trade in various kinds of cotton machinery. He was considered an authority on cotton mill machinery for many years, and even now his speeders may be found in mills all over the country, doing excellent work when their age is considered. Eventually, in 1882, the important interests involved were duly capitalized, with ample resources and improved facilities at command, a number of leading capitalists of Boston and New England becoming interested in the enterprise. The aim of the new company has been to improve the works in every way and to build nothing but the best machinery, and it is now devoting its entire attention to its specialty—carding machinery—and is manufacturing a class of machinery unequalled elsewhere in America. To meet the rapid increase of orders the company has built a new shop, and its works at Newton Upper Falls are now the best equipped in their line of any on the continent, having special machine tools, etc., and affording employment to upwards of 250 hands. The works are now largely engaged in the manufacture of the Revolving Flat Carding Engine, which is the best system for producing coarse, medium and fine counts, the yarn being stronger, with less waste and labor, coupled with a great saving of floor space. These engines are being made interchangeable in all their parts, and finished with the greatest accuracy. Every machine is tested before leaving the establishment, all appliances and accessories are the best of their kind, and the machines are now rapidly being introduced into the finest cotton mills of New England and the Middle States. They also manufacture combination and top-flat cards; English and American drawing frames and railway heads, with or without Ryley's double-reversing motion; and patent chain-eveners; also furnish all repairs for Haggans' roving frames and Pettee speeders and looms.

EUSTIS & ALDRICH, General Commission Merchants and Dealers in Starch and Flour, Nos. 55 Kilby and 92 Water Streets.—A representative and widely known firm in Boston, actively engaged as general commission merchants and dealers in flour and starch, is that of Messrs. Eustis & Aldrich. This extensive business was established ten years ago by Messrs. A. S. Eustis and Frank Aldrich, both of whom being ample resources to bear and possess influential connections in all sections of the United States. They deal largely in potato, corn and wheat starch and flour in car-load lots. Messrs. Eustis & Aldrich make a specialty of handling potato starch, and are selling agents for the famous Aroostook Starch Company and also for other choice brands of Maine, New York and New Hampshire potato starch. They promptly fill the largest orders for flour or starch at the lowest ruling market prices, and their trade now extends throughout all sections of the country. The firm makes liberal advances when required on consignments of first-class flour and starch, and guarantees at all times quick sales and prompt returns. The characteristics which regulate the business policy of this responsible firm are such as to entitle it to every consideration, while the extent of its business has made it the most prominent one in its line in Boston, and the inducements offered to customers are of the most substantial character. Mr A. S. Eustis was born in Maine, while Mr. Frank Aldrich is a native of New Hampshire. Both partners are popular members of the Boston Chamber of Commerce, where they are highly esteemed for their promptness, enterprise and integrity. Mr. Eustis is also a director of the Fourth National Bank, and one of our progressive and public spirited citizens.

BEAMAN BROTHERS, Commission Merchants, No. 234 State Street.—Of the many responsible firms engaged in handling the products of the British Provinces here in Boston, few, if any, are more widely or honorably known in the trade than that of Beaman Bros., commission merchants, No 234 State Street. The house was established in 1869 by Messrs. Nathaniel P. and George H. Beaman, who conducted the same with uninterrupted prosperity up to November, 1887, when the last named member of the firm retired, Mr. Nathaniel Beaman since continuing the business alone with uniform success. The house is conducted on strict business principles, and its management characterized by energy, sagacity and honorable methods, while all orders placed with the concern are filled in the most expeditious and excellent manner. The firm handles Nova Scotia canned lobsters, salt and smoked fish, potatoes, eggs, butter, lard and general produce; also lumber, receiving consignments regularly from Nova Scotia, New Brunswick and Prince Edward's Island, and does a commission business entirely; and, altogether the trade of the house is of a very substantial character. Mr. Beaman, who is a man of middle age and a native of this state, is a gentleman of the highest personal integrity as well as of push, enterprise and thorough experience in this line of trade, and maintains an excellent standing in commercial life.

I. M. GEORGE & CO., Commission Merchants. Foreign and Domestic Fruits, Butter, Cheese, Eggs. Beans, Poultry and Lard, No. 114 South Market Street.—Messrs. I. M. George & Co., as commission merchants are constantly in receipt of consignments, and supply a widespread wholesale trade. The operations of the firm are very extensive, and ample premises are provided for storage purposes. While foreign and domestic fruits are handled in large quantities, a specialty is made of prime creamery and dairy butter, and cheese, poultry, beans, lard and country produce generally. This house which is reckoned one of the most substantial in this line of trade in the city, was established in 1880, by Baldwin & George who continued it for seven years, when I. M. George & Co, succeeded to it, and have since enlarged the facilities and extended the operations. Consignments are solicited and quick sales and prompt returns are made, and as an evidence of the character and standing of the house, it is only necessary to state that among the references offered are The Traders' National Bank of Boston, and any produce house in the city, and Mr. J. R. George of Barre, Vermont. Mr. George who is a young man, is a native of Vermont. He has full charge of the management of the business of the house, and conducts it in a manner to make it popular.

THE METROPOLIS OF NEW ENGLAND.

W. E. NICKERSON, Patentee of Nickerson's Hydraulic Elevator Safety, No. 62 Sudbury Street.—An invention destined to come into universal use is the unique device invented and patented by Mr. W. E. Nickerson for preventing the falling of elevators, thereby avoiding accidents and danger to property, life and limb. Eleven patents have been allowed and several more are pending and it is endorsed by elevator manufacturers, architects and mechanics, and is pronounced the most positive, substantial, secure and perfect device yet introduced. It is designed to increase the safety of elevators and guard against their falling from any cause, and combines great strength with simplicity and can be applied to any style of elevator and never fails to act under any circumstances, or gets out of order. The machine or device is practically double, either side alone being sufficient to prevent a fall, and converts the ropes usually supporting the counter balance weight only into regular suspension ropes thus increasing the safety a thousand fold, and is certainly the most perfect safety device ever before brought to the notice of the public. Old or unsound elevators are made safe by applying it, thereby obviating the necessity of expense of a new one. The Nickerson hydraulic elevator safety will soon be introduced in Boston and in all the large cities, and all who have witnessed its operation uniformly agree in saying that it is the best device for the purpose, and is pre-eminently superior to any other device for the purpose to which it is designed, and wherever used is giving perfect satisfaction. Mr. Nickerson will soon be prepared to manufacture this unexcelled machine on an extensive scale, and will be pleased to answer all inquiries and send circulars giving full particulars to any address on application. Mr. Nickerson is an ingenious mechanic, and was born at Provincetown, in this state, and resides in Cambridge. He is well known in this

community, and since he introduced the elevator safety he is receiving many inquiries concerning it and is kept constantly busy filling orders from various sections of the United States.

CHARLES CARR, Consulting Mechanical Engineer, No. 7 Exchange Place.—For thoroughly reliable and expert work in the line of mechanical drawings and designs, or for skill and reliability in machine construction, there is not to-day in this city a man that sustains a higher reputation than the gentleman whose name stands at the head of this sketch. He is, by general consent, one of the foremost exponents of mechanical engineering in Boston; and prior to establishing himself in the exercise of his art here in 1888, had been for twenty years the efficient general manager of the Boston Machine Company; and is still their contractor for specialties. Mr. Carr, occupies as offices two well equipped rooms at No. 7 Exchange Place, is a middle-aged gentleman, active and energetic, and was born in Maine, but has resided in Boston some thirty odd years. He is a practical and expert machinist, as well as an experienced and successful consulting mechanical engineer, and is master of his profession in all its features and details. Machinery is designed, and detailed drawings furnished in the most expeditious and excellent manner, while construction is personally superintended, and the same also contracted for. Mr. Carr likewise being prepared to give consultations and render professional advice at reasonable terms. Attention is given also to outside work; in short, everything comprehended in mechanical engineering is executed in the most superior and reliable manner at short notice.

W. C. DEMAIN & SON, Blank Book Manufacturers and Steam Paper Rulers, Nos. 31 Milk, 8 Hawley and 9 Arch Streets.—The leading manufacturers of blank books in this city are Messrs. W. C. Demain & Son, who are widely prominent as patentees of various attachments on paper ruling machines. The business was established in 1855 by Mr. W. C. Demain, the present head being organized in 1885 by the admission of Mr. W. C. Demain, Jr., to partnership. The business premises are spacious in size, thoroughly equipped with new and improved machinery and appliances, including twelve ruling and two cutting machines, and ample steam power, and steady employment is given to from twenty to twenty-five skilled hands. The co-partners have no peers in their vocation, the senior partner being the patentee of the first paging and numbering machine ever introduced, and both being to bear the widest range of practical experience in every department of the business. The firm personally superintend all the work performed, and carry on a general line of transactions as manufacturers of blank books of every description, and as steam paper rulers. Ample resources are possessed for promptly meeting all orders at the shortest possible notice. Their patronage is large, first-class and permanent in this city and throughout the New England states. The Messrs. Demain are natives of Liverpool, England.

THE LEARNARD & BIRD OIL COMPANY, Manufacturers and Wholesalers of Oleomargarine Oil, Tallow and Stearine, Office, Nos. 38 and 50 Faneuil Hall Market.—Few, if any, of the scientific discoveries in the domain of chemistry in late years have been more wonderful and more useful to the general masses of the public than oleomargarine, or butterine, as it is sometimes called, and oleomargarine oil, tallow and stearine. The process of manufacturing butter from beef suet was invented by Mr. Mege, a progressive and accomplished French chemist and scientist about twenty years ago. Notwithstanding the opposition cries which have been raised to oleomargarine hundreds of analyses have shown it to be as pure, clean, palatable and healthful as the best products of the dairy, and that it is nothing more nor less than good wholesome butter, differing, it is true, from the dairy product in the manner of its preparation, but not in its constituent parts or molecular formation. It is as much a beef and farm product as dairy butter, and has the advantage over the old article of uniformity in taste, color and general appearance. The Learnard & Bird Oil Company, whose factory is at Brighton, and whose city office is at Nos. 38 and 50 Faneuil Hall Market, are largely engaged in the manufacture of this oleomargarine oil, tallow and stearine. The concern was formed in 1886 by Mr. S. S. Learnard and Mr. H. Bird. The latter died in 1887, and the business has since been conducted by Mr. Learnard alone. He is a native of Brighton, and has been connected with the meat business in Faneuil Hall Market for the past fifty-four years. The factory is provided with the most modern and efficient mechanical appliances, and twenty hands are employed in the business. About two hundred cattle are weekly slaughtered to supply meat to the market, and the fat of beasts is used in the factory for the manufacture of oleomargarine oil, muchof which is shipped to Rotterdam, and the rest sold for that purpose and converted into butterine. Tallow and stearine are also made in large quantities. The products of the establishment are noted for their purity and excellence, and the trade, which is exclusively wholesale, has attained large dimensions, and is constantly expanding. In trade circles no man is better known or more highly esteemed for business ability and probity than Mr. Learnard.

F. H. JOHNSON & CO., Wholesale, Retail and Commission Dealers in all kinds of Fresh Fish, Stall No. 114 Faneuil Hall Market.—The growth which has attended the fish trade of Boston is illustrative, in no small degree, of that general development which has characterized the commerce and manufactures of the city, during the past quarter of a century. The demand for fish now includes, not only for home consumption, but also heavy cargoes for foreign shipment, certain brands of goods, packed in Boston having gained a great reputation abroad. When it is stated that nearly $9,000,000 worth of salt and fresh fish is disposed of annually in Boston, some idea of the extent to which the trade has grown may be formed. Ever since Faneuil Hall Market was built, Stall No. 114 has been a noted one among fish consumers and dealers. For a score of years the proprietors at this stall have been Messrs. F. H. Johnson & Co., and they have and do conduct a trade of great magnitude. The stall is a spacious one, and is provided with all necessary appliances and conveniences essential to the successful carrying on of the business. It is at all times heavily stocked with an endless variety of fresh fish of every description, and the trade is of a commission, wholesale and retail character. The facilities of the firm in every department are unsurpassed, and it has always been a strict rule with them to sell everything exactly as represented, hence dealers and consumers everywhere know that the goods offered by this concern may be implicitly relied upon. A large and growing city and out of town trade is enjoyed, and twelve hands are necessarily constantly employed in supplying the wants of customers. The business is carried on upon a basis of liberal and honorable dealing, and the firm merit the prominence and success enjoyed. Mr. F. H. Johnson is the sole proprietor. He is a native of Nahant, Mass., and a merchant of the highest repute.

CHARLES POLLOCK, Art and Landscape Photographs, No. 2 Hamilton Place.—The charming repository of art conducted by Mr. Charles Pollock, at No. 2 Hamilton Place, was first opened to the public in 1877, on Washington Street. The increasing demands of the public necessitated larger quarters, and the present spacious and elegant premises were occupied in 1887. The store is thoroughly modern and attractive in all its arrangements and appointments, handsomely fitted up with plate-glass windows, cherry fixtures and elaborate interior decorations, and perfect in convenience of arrangement for display, inspection and sale. Devoting exclusive attention to those artistic novelties by which the home is enriched and the charm of domestic life is heightened, there is no order of goods of such character that may not here be found in the greatest prodigality. Special attention is given to these three departments. Studies for artists, illustrations of architecture, imported mainly from France and Italy, and life portraits of the most distinguished individuals in Europe and America. The products of all nations and all climes, here find their way. The magnificent stock, carefully selected under the trained eye and artistic tastes of the proprietor, by which the house seeks to deserve and maintain its high position, are ably supplemented by a corps of assistants, each chosen with special reference, to ability and experience ready at all times to assist the purchaser by their fine technical knowledge. The patronage is large, first-class and influential in city and country, and the specialties here offered in art and landscape photographs, are recognized as the finest specimens in their line to be found in the city. Popular prices prevail, and the most critical and fastidious tastes are readily suited and promptly met through the enterprise and judgment of the talented proprietor. Mr. Pollock is a Bostonian by birth and education, for thirty years an exponent of this branch of mercantile activity, and a gentleman of great popularity in social, business and art circles.

G. L. TURNBULL, Ready Made Clothing, Hats and Furnishing Goods, Nos. 29 and 31 Meridian Street.—It may not be uninteresting to the masculine reader of this volume to receive some information pertaining to the matters of attire, for the apparel oft claims the man, which may result in future advantage. As the caption of this sketch indicates we refer to the house of Mr. G. L. Turnbull, the popular and widely known dealer in ready-made clothing, hats and furnishing goods, Nos. 29 and 31 Meridian Street. The business was originally established by Mr. Turnbull at No 26 Maverick Square, where it continued to be conducted until August, 1886, when it was removed to its present eligible location. The premises occupied consist of a most attractive store with a frontage of fifty feet and a depth of thirty-five feet, and this is most elegant and attractive in its fittings and appointments. The stock shown embraces a full and complete assortment of ready-made clothing of the best materials and workmanship and in all the leading popular styles; also hats and caps representing the latest fashions, and all the newest styles of gentlemen's furnishing goods, including fine imported and domestic hosiery, shirts, underwear, neckwear, gloves, etc. In fact, the stock in all departments quite equals in quality and variety any that may be found in the metropolis of New England. A special feature is made of Carter & Churchill's Lebanon overalls, of which a large assortment is kept on hand. While the stock is large the prices are low, and the result is a brisk and extensive trade. Mr. Turnbull is a native of Massachusetts and resides at Winthrop. He is a wide-awake, energetic, courteous business man.

SOULE, DILLINGHAM & CO., Pavers and Street Railway Contractors, No. 4 Liberty Square.—This firm are widely prominent as practical pavers and street railway contractors, and have been established in business here since 1884. They are thoroughly equipped for promptly executing all kinds of plain and fancy paving on streets, sidewalks and avenues, and for setting of curbstones and supplying all kinds of materials for paving and railway stock. Particular attention is given to the construction of street railways, and they have carried through to a successful completion many important contracts, including the horse railroads at Lawrence, Mass.; Cambridge, Mass.; Portland, Me.; Waterville, Me.; Haverhill, Amesbury, Newburyport, East Salisbury and Lowell, Mass.; Plum Island, Black Rocks, and other places through out New England, besides many private contracts in this city and vicinity. They furnish all kinds of paving and railway stock, and give steady employment to a large force of skilled hands, and their resources and facilities are such as enable them to fill all orders and commissions with the utmost promptness.

THE METROPOLIS OF NEW ENGLAND. 231

H. BIRD & CO., Dealers in Beef, Pork, Lard and Tallow, Smoked Beef, Hams, Pigs' Feet, Tripe, Etc., also Learnard and Bird Oil Co.'s Product, Tallow, Olio Oil, Etc., Nos. 28 and 40 Faneuil Hall Market.—Boston is not behind any city in the world in the extent and magnitude of its provision trade, and the enterprise which characterizes her representative firms is not excelled in any other branch of commerce. One of the leading and best-known houses in this line is that of Messrs. H. Bird & Co., at Nos. 28 and 40 Faneuil Hall Market. This firm are widely prominent as wholesale and retail dealers in beef, pork, lard and tallow, smoked beef, hams, pigs' feet, tripe, etc.; also, Learnard & Bird Oil Co.'s product, tallow, olio oil, and packers of the celebrated India mess beef. The business was founded in 1836, by Mr. Harrison Bird, and in 1879 the present firm was organized by the admission of Mr. A. H. Bird—a son of the founder—and Mr. R. H. Sturtevant to partnership. Mr. Harrison Bird died in 1887, deeply lamented as one of Boston's oldest and most honored merchants. This firm slaughter their own meats, and are also largely interested in the manufacture of oil from beef fats, made for use in making oleomargarine, by Learnard & Bird, at Brighton, Mass., and ship the product in immense quantities to Rotterdam, Holland. As packers of India mess beef, they have an extensive trade in London and Liverpool, shipping the beef in tierces—300 pounds to a tierce—for use in the English army and navy. Their trade in fresh beef, pork and other meat products is immense and influential in this city and its suburban towns, and extends, during the summer months, to the mountains and seaside resorts throughout New England. This firm supplies many of the largest and leading hotels and club houses in this city with all their beef and pork, including the Tremont Hotel and the Quincy Hotel; also Wellesley College, and other noted public institutions and resorts. No firm of the present day recognizes more fully than the partners the essential importance of absolute purity, quality and freshness in this class of goods, and their patrons have the satisfaction of knowing that nothing inferior or adulterated will be offered them. Orders by telephone, or otherwise, will be given prompt and careful attention, and every advantage is granted to patrons that is embraced in reliable goods and economy of prices. Employment is given to a force of fourteen skilled hands, and the trade is brisk and lively at all seasons of the year. Mr. Bird was born in Brookline, Mass., while Mr. Sturtevant is a native of Centre Harbor, N. H., and both are gentlemen of large business experience, high social repute and eminent popularity and are gentlemen with whom it is a pleasure to do business.

D. A. DUNBAR, Poultry and Game of all kinds, Nos. 10, 12, 14 and 16 Quincy Market.—Boston and its surroundings contain a population reaching far on towards a million, to say nothing of the large number of strangers who daily visit the city. As a consequence our public markets are all constantly drawn upon more or less for the food supplies necessary to feed the multitude, but nowhere in the city is a larger number of people provided with the daily necessities of life than at Quincy Market, and no inconsiderable portion of the trade done here is in the line of poultry and game. Among the old established and successful dealers we may mention Mr. D. A. Dunbar, whose neatly fitted up and commodious stalls are Nos. 10, 12, 14 and 16. This business now controlled by this gentleman was originally established by his brother, the late Mr. Curtis S. Dunbar, about sixty years ago, and about thirty years since the present proprietor succeeded to the control of it. He makes a specialty of poultry and of all kinds of game in season, and supplies dealers, hotels, restaurants and boarding houses as well as private families. He also does an extensive shipping trade to all points in the New England States. Being a good judge of poultry and game, and having proper facilities for handling the best, which is supplied at reasonable rates, his trade, as would naturally be inferred, is constantly being enlarged. Mr. Dunbar draws his supplies from the most reliable sources, and carrying at all times a very extensive stock is prepared to fill all orders, large and small, promptly and satisfactorily. Seven assistants are needed to cope with the demands upon the house and liberal and courteous treatment is accorded to all patrons. Mr. Dunbar is a native of Easton, Mass., and both as a merchant and private citizen is held in high estimation.

S PALDING, ELMS & CO., Importers and Jobbers of Tailors' Trimmings, No. 27 Franklin street.—A leading firm of importers and jobbers of tailors' trimmings in this city is that of Messrs. Spalding, Elms & Co., whose establishment is located at No. 27 Franklin street. The members of this firm, Messrs. Chas. E. Spalding and Jos. D. Elms, are gentlemen of large and valuable experience in this branch of trade, and combined their abilities and talents to form the present firm in 1884. They occupy spacious and commodious salesrooms in the business heart of the city, and are in a position to conduct their extensive trade under the most favorable conditions. They import their supplies direct from the most reputable foreign sources, and are prepared to minister to every requirement of the trade with unexampled promptness and universal satisfaction. An immense stock is carried at all times to supply the best of permanent patrons of the firm throughout New England and New York, while every advantage is granted to customers in liberality of terms and prices that is known to the trade. Their magnificent stock is celebrated for original novelties and shades, textures, patterns and combinations, and as suited to meet the best classes of American trade, recommending its own superior merits to the confidence and patronage of critical and discriminating purchasers. The house is a strong one, both by reason of the talents of the partners and their unrivalled connections abroad, while their interests are represented on the road by a corps of talented and experienced salesmen. Both members of the firm are Massachusetts men by birth and training, of high repute and standing in trade circles throughout New England and New York, and evidently deserving of the success and prosperity they have achieved as enterprising merchants and representative business men.

B. JOHNSON, Mutton, Lamb and Veal, Wholesale and Retail, Nos. 1 and 3 Faneuil Hall Market.—The trade in fresh meats is one of the most important branches of business in the city, and, as a rule, is conducted by men of capital and ability of a high order. In Faneuil Hall Market there are to be found some of the finest stands devoted to this business to be seen in any market in the country, notably those of Mr. B. Johnson, Nos. 1 and 3, which are eligibly located at the entrance to the market. They are fitted up in a first-class manner, and provided with all the latest improved appliances for the preservation of meats and the speedy handling of supplies and the filling of orders. Mr. Johnson is one of the best known men doing business in this far famed market. It is now more than twenty-eight years since he founded his enterprise here, and his long career has been a most honorable and successful one. Liberality and straightforwardness have ever characterized his transactions, while his prompt and obliging manner have gained him his present circle of customers, together with the respect of his competitors. His stall is a model of cleanliness and order, and always presents an inviting appearance. A very heavy stock of choice mutton, lamb and veal is carried at all times, and can be relied upon for freshness and wholesomeness. A very active and extensive trade is done both in the city and suburbs, and is of both a wholesale and retail character. The exigencies of the business call for the constant employment of from four to five hands and a delivery wagon, and orders by mail, telephone or telegraph are promptly and satisfactorily filled at the lowest rates.

F RED. N. LEMAN, Sign Painter, No. 75 Portland Street.—Mr. Fred. N. Leman, the widely known and skillful sign painter, has established something like a national reputation for meritorious work. He is, in all respects, one of the leading exponents of the art in Boston, while his patronage extends to all parts of the United States. Mr. Leman, who has a branch at No. 45 Eliot Street, also, is a gentleman of middle age, and a native of this city. He is a thoroughly practical and expert workman himself, of long and varied experience in the excesses of his art, and is, in short, a genuine artist in his line. He has been established in business for the past twenty years, and has built up a large and flourishing trade. Sign and ornamental painting in all its branches is executed in the highest style of the art and in the most expeditious manner, some half a dozen competent assistants being employed, and no orders are too large and none too small, while all work done by this gentleman is performed under his supervision.

WM. S. BUTLER & CO., Importers and Retailers of Millinery Goods, Hosiery, Etc., Nos. 90 to 98 Tremont Street.—In every branch of mercantile activity in a large community, there is one house that is justly and popularly spoken of as the representative of its class. In the metropolitan city of Boston in the line of the finest imported millinery, hosiery, gloves, small wares, etc., the position of supremacy is held by the firm of Messrs. Wm. S. Butler & Co., whose extensive and attractive establishment is located at Nos. 90 to 98 Tremont Street. This business was established originally in 1844, by Cushman & Brooks, who were succeeded by E. F. Cushman in 1852, Seligman, Macy & Butler in 1866, and Butler & Norwood in 1870. Eventually in 1873 Mr. Wm. S. Butler became sole proprietor, and is now conducting the business under the firm name of Wm. S. Butler & Co. The premises occupied comprise a very superior five-story and basement building, 80x125 feet in dimensions, fully equipped with every appliance, which capital and science can devise, including electric lights, elevator, automatic cash system, etc., for the comfort and convenience of patrons. The wood work and splendid plate glass front, and interior fittings convey a substantial yet highly luxurious aspect of elegance and beauty to the establishment. On the first floor will be found an extensive and choice assortment of hosiery, gloves, laces and ribbons, flowers and feathers, untrimmed hats, millinery goods of every description and small wares. The second floor is fully stocked with cloaks, jerseys, jackets, corsets, bustles, ladies' and children's underwear, yarns, stamped linens, etc., also china, bric-a-brac, vases, china dolls, tea sets, etc. On the third floor is the upholstery department, which contains a superior selection of high art fabrics of every description including silk damasks, velours and rich silks in vast variety, brocatels, sateens, plushes, satins, etc., and all kinds of upholstery trimmings of the latest styles and fashions. The fourth and fifth floors are utilized for the wholesale trade, and contain a full and complete stock of all goods handled or imported by the house. The basement contains the packing and shipping departments, and the electric light plant, also a spacious lunch room for clerks. Two hundred salesladies, clerks, assistants, etc., are employed in the various departments, who are very popular with customers, owing to their kind and obliging manners, promptness and efficiency. All the finest millinery goods are imported direct from the most celebrated Paris and London houses, and the imported hats and bonnets of this establishment are seen every day worn by the most fashionable members of society. In fact all the goods handled by Wm. S. Butler & Co., are absolutely unrivalled for quality, elegance, freshness and uniform excellence, and have no superiors in this country, while the prices quoted in all cases are as low as the lowest. A thorough system of organization is observable in all departments, Mr. Butler gives close personal attention to every detail, and is noted for his executive ability and honorable methods. Mr. Butler was born in Connecticut and when a youth came to Malden, and served his apprenticeship. Subsequently he was employed in New York as a salesman by Seligman & Macy. Mr. Butler is a type of the self-made man, who has risen by his own exertions, frugality and industry from a modest position to a prominent place in commercial circles. His establishment is a lasting source of credit to Boston, and a monument to his energy and enterprise.

HENRY COWAN, Importer of Fine Swiss Watch Materials, and Manufacturer of Jewelers' Trimmings and Finest Quality Silk Guards, Studio Building, No. 110 Tremont Street.— Keeping pace with the never-ceasing march of progress in science and art, very perceptible are the advances which have been made during recent years in the watch-making and jewelry industries in all their branches, which is observant to every person giving the matter the slightest attention. A well-known and reliable house engaged in some of the branches of the watch making and jewelry business in the city of Boston, and worthy of more than passing notice in these pages, is that of Mr. Henry Cowan, located in the studio building, No. 110 Tremont Street. This enterprise was inaugurated originally in 1881 by Mr. Henry Cowan, and was conducted by him with the most encouraging results. Mr. Cowan is a native of Australia, about twenty-seven years of age, and has been a resident of this city ever since 1870. He is a thoroughly practical man in the business and gives it his entire attention. The premises occupied are spacious and commodious, and are fitted up in a very attractive manner, with every convenience for the transaction of the trade. He conducts a very large business as an importer of fine Swiss watch materials, direct from the most famous and reliable establishments in Switzerland, whose reputations are known throughout the entire civilized world. He also manufactures all kinds of jewelers' trimmings for the trade and the finest quality of silk watch guards, a specialty with this house unsurpassed by any other in the United States. In his store will be found at all times a full and complete assortment of all materials belonging to a watch, also other lines of goods pertaining to his business. His trade extends throughout the United States, and is constantly increasing in consequence of the splendid and unsurpassed inducements he is enabled to offer customers. The advantages he derives by his superior connection with his correspondents in Switzerland, and manufacturing his own specialties he is prepared to execute all orders promptly and satisfactorily, and at prices which cannot be duplicated elsewhere.

GLEN SHIRT & COLLAR CO., Glen's Falls, N. Y., A. B. Rice, Manager, Boston Store, No. 121 Tremont Street.—The manufacture of shirts, collars and cuffs has grown, as a distinct branch of industrial enterprise, to one of vast proportions in late years. The largest manufactory in the country in this line is that of the Glen Shirt and Collar Company, located at Glen's Falls, N. Y. Since 1885 this company has had a branch house in Boston, for the sale of its manufactures. It was at first located on Essex Street, but in April, 1887, a removal was effected to the store now occupied at No. 121 Tremont Street, opposite Park Street church. It is now the leading establishment of its kind in Boston, and is under the management of Mr. A. B. Rice, who is a Bostonian by birth, and a graduate of Brown University class of '81, a gentleman of large practical business experience. The store is a spacious one having a capacity of 30x100 feet, and is very elegantly and attractively fitted up. A very heavy stock of fine shirts, ladies' and gentlemen's collars and cuffs of the "Glen" brand, and made at the company's Glen Falls factories, together with a full assortment of gentlemen's furnishing goods of all kinds, and representative of all the latest novelties, is kept on hand. The business here is both wholesale and retail, and the trade has under the management of Mr. A. B. Rice, grown to large volume. The "Glen" shirts, collars and cuffs are recognized by the trade as the most perfect fitting, durable and handsomest goods made for the money. They are the product of skilled workmanship, judicious and careful selection of materials, and nice discrimination in styles. The company aims to produce the best goods in the market for the least money, and to keep abreast of all competitors in bringing forward new and popular styles. That it has succeeded is generally admitted, the "Glen" goods being acknowledged leaders in the collar and cuff and shirt market. The company employ 500 hands, have in use the most improved machinery, and, buying raw materials in vast quantities at advantageous rates, are enabled to offer their manufactured goods at prices which defy competition. At the Boston house from eight to twelve assistants are employed, and customers can rely upon prompt and courteous attention.

ALFRED CLAPP & CO., Wholesale Lumber; Room No. 13, No. 11 Central Street.—Few, if any, among the many prosperous lumber firms that have come to the front in this city of recent years have been more fortunate in attaining a standing in the trade or building up a business connection than that of Alfred Clapp & Co., whose office is located at No. 11 Central Street, (Room 13.) Established in 1884, this responsible and well known firm has from the first enjoyed an uninterrupted career of prosperity. The house is conducted on strict business principles, and its management characterized by energy and sagacity; and all orders placed with this firm are promptly and reliably attended to. They are commission merchants and wholesale dealers, and handle hard and soft lumber of every description, the transactions being by car and cargo lots entirely, and the trade of the firm, which is at once large and active, extends all over the New England States. Mr. Alfred Clapp is the sole member, the company being nominal. He is a gentleman of entire responsibility in his dealings, as well as of experience and judicious enterprise, and is a member of the Bay State Lumber Dealers' Association.

THE METROPOLIS OF NEW ENGLAND.

HORACE E. WALKER & CO., Manufacturers and Dealers in Stoves Ranges, Furnaces and Hotel Cooking Apparatus, Nos. 17 and 19 Union Street.—A most important new departure in the stove, range and furnace trade, was taken by the organization on June 1 1888, of the new of Messrs. Horace E. Walker & Co. The copartners, Mr. Horace E. Walker and Mr. F. Volney Streeter, bring to bear the widest range of practical experience. Both gentlemen were for many years actively identified with the old Walker & Pratt manufacturing company, and are authorities in their line, making a prominent specialty of hotel cooking and heating apparatus and of the Walker Furnaces. They have every facility at command, coupled with influential connections, and have developed an active and far-reaching trade with bright prospect in the near future. Their premises in Union

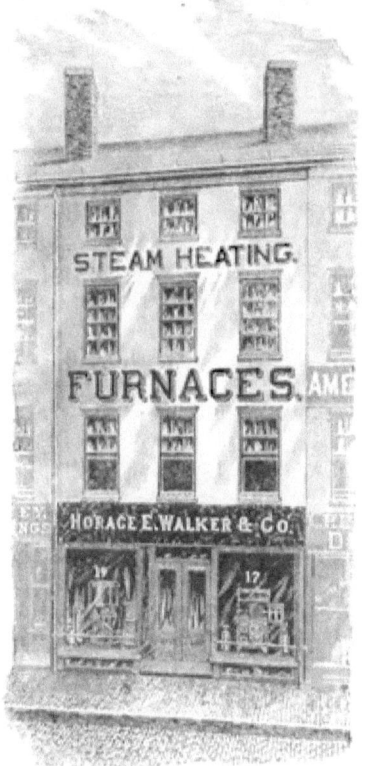

Street are extensive and compose four floors, 25x130 feet in dimensions, with work shops for fitting and manufacturing in a three story building in the rear. Their factory and foundry are located at Haverhill, Mass., and where they are producing new and improved styles of stoves, ranges and furnaces, embracing all the modern improvements, and many specially desirable features nowhere else duplicated. An inspection of their fine salesrooms, so bright and attractive will prove conclusively that this stock is the best for the trade, both as regards heavy castings, careful design, perfect finish and fittings, while for both cooking and heating on lines of stoves and ranges are so economical on fuel, yet producing such effectual results. They are prepared to contract for and introduce the most perfect and extensive heating and cooking apparatus for hotels, restaurants, clubs, etc., and having vast practical experience in this line, the special attention of hotel men and restaurant proprietors is directed thereto. The firms' system of steam and hot-water heating is pronounced the best, safest and most economical of any by experts and an even temperature is maintained in the largest buildings at a minimum cost for fuel and attendance. Thorough ventilation is provided for, and the firm have filled many important contracts. Having made a careful practical study of all the problems involved the firm is fully prepared to give absolute satisfaction, and both in regard to their lines of stoves and ranges and their system of heating, they are the representative house in Boston.

HENRY H. CLARK & CO., Printers of School and College Text-Books, Educational Scientific and Miscellaneous Books Etc., No. 77 Kilby Street.—The advance made in the typographic branches is one of the notable features that mark this age of progress in which we live. What with invention, improvements and discovery, a high degree of perfection has been reached in the art preservative within a decade or two. Among the noteworthy printing establishments of Boston may be named the well-equipped concern conducted under the style of Henry H. Clark & Co., book and job printers, No. 77 Kilby Street, who sustain a well earned reputation for excellent work, as well as promptness and reliability in executing orders—none better in the city. They occupy two 25x100 foot floors supplied with ample steam power and all the latest improved machinery, appliances and general appurtenances to a leading printing house, including three capacious power presses, a first-class outfit of type and kindred devices, while ten to a dozen expert hands are employed. Book and general job printing in all its branches is done in the most expeditious and superior manner at bottom prices, special attention being given to school and college text books, educational, scientific and miscellaneous books, catalogues, pamphlets and fine commercial printing, all work executed here being fully warranted to render satisfaction; and all orders receive immediate attention. This flourishing business was established about four years ago by Henry H. Clark (deceased) who under the firm name (that heads this sketch conducted the same up to spring of 1888, when, owing to his death, which occurred at this period, the business passed into control of his son E. W. Clark, who, as manager for the estate of his father, has since continued it under the original style with uninterrupted success. Mr. Clark, Jr., is a gentleman of excellent business qualities, as well as a young man of energy and several years practical experience, and, unless all signs fail, he possesses all the necessary qualifications to keep the concern in the position it has from the first occupied in its line.

MARK FISK, Cigars, No. 14 Central Street, Near Kilby.—Whether smoking be wholesome or deleterious is a matter upon which there are many diverse opinions, and it is a subject upon which medical men venture to differ; and while they are differing the habit of smoking goes on increasingly and the consumption of the favorite "weed" grows apace. If any change at all has been noted in the ways of those who apply themselves to the smoking habit it is the steady and persistent demand that has set in for a higher and purer grade of cigars; and to meet this demand satisfactorily is Mr. Mark Fisk's great object in life. That he is doing it successfully at his popular store No. 14 Central Street, near Kilby, is evidenced by the large and increasing patronage which is accorded him. Mr. Fisk started in this line of business in 1882, and conducted it with remarkable success until 1885, when sickness compelled him to relinquish it for a time. On recovering his health he resumed business at his present stand in September, 1888, and he soon drew about him a very liberal and substantial, as well as an influential, patronage. The store is very elegant in its appointments and arrangements, and is heavily stocked with a splendid assortment of choice cigars of both foreign and domestic manufacture, and carefully selected to meet the requirements of a first-class trade. Mr. Fisk conducts his operations exclusively to the retail trade in cigars, of which he has gained the reputation of being an expert judge.

GEORGE R. McFARLIN, Dealer in China, Glass and Pottery of all Countries; No. 39 Franklin Street.—The importance of Boston as a great commercial centre is forcibly illustrated in every branch of trade, and in none more than the import trade in china, glass and pottery. A representative and thoroughly progressive house engaged therein is that of Mr. George R. McFarlin, located at No. 39 Franklin Street, corner of Hawley. The proprietor has been connected with this line of business for a period of twenty-eight years, and opened the present house in January, 1888. He occupies two floors and a basement, 40x60 feet each, giving ample accommodation for supplying the most extensive demand, and conducts the business at both wholesale and retail. The trade has been developed to proportions of gratifying magnitude and importance, and strictly upon the legitimate basis of supply and demand. The large practical experience of the proprietor is supported by sound judgment and close attention to detail, so that in the essentials of texture, elegant and symmetrical designs, beauty of pictorial ornamentation, coupled with richness and harmony of coloring, and artistic effects, the selections here displayed are recognized as pre-eminent in the trade. Such splendid styles of goods have rarely been imported to this country. The attractiveness of the stock and its artistic arrangement bespeak the taste and systematic methods of the proprietor, and in the show rooms can be seen the most delicate china sets, decorated mantel and table ware, baccarat glass ware, porcelain, cut glass and the charming Bohemian glass ware in vast variety; bisque statuettes of exquisite beauty, bric-a-brac in bewildering array, articles of vertu, and thousands of ornaments, all displayed in a manner befitting the proprietor's distinguished enterprise and ample resources. The stock is a criterion of all that is new, serviceable, beautiful and ornate in the china, glass and pottery trade, and the products include every feature of elegance and excellence brought from manufacturers whose reputation is worldwide. Inducements are here offered to dealers and consumers, in both reliability of goods and liberality of terms and prices, which challenge comparison and preclude successful competition, while the house is in a position to guarantee the prompt and perfect fulfillment of all orders, of whatever magnitude. Mr. McFarlin is a native of New Bedford, Mass., and was formerly manager of the house of Clark, Adams & Clark, in the same line. He is eminently popular in social, business and trade circles, and is affording the American public unexampled opportunities for securing the most beautiful wares known to civilization.

HEWINS & HOLLIS, Outfitters, No. 4 Hamilton Place.—For more than a third of a century the name of this firm has been prominently identified with the men's outfitting trade of this city, and to-day there is no more popular house in the "Hub" in its line than that of Hewins & Hollis, No. 4 Hamilton Place. They have occupied this handsome and spacious store (which was planned and built expressly for them) about five years. The business was originally founded in 1843 by the senior member of the firm, Mr. C. A. Hewins. Mr. Wm. H. Hollis became his associate and partner in 1855, and since their removal to Hamilton Place, Mr. Frank A. Hewins, the son of the senior member, has been admitted to the firm. There is an established stability about these old Boston houses that is noteworthy and refreshing in this age of changes, and the good English custom of continuing a business by the incoming of the younger members of the family is the best evidence of continued growth and prosperity. Mr. Hewins informs us that on the books of the firm to-day are the names of customers who have never left them since the beginning of the business; that there are many names of sons and even of grandsons of such customers, and, in one case, at least, a great grandson, his name on the order book, making four generations who have supplied themselves from this establishment. As the firm has numbered among its customers in the last thirty years nearly all the prominent men, not only of Boston, but of all New England, it now admittedly stands at the head of this branch of trade. Their new store has a frontage of forty feet and is admirably lighted both in front and rear. It is plainly but elegantly fitted in hard wood interior finish, and was planned and adapted for the strictly first-class line of trade by which they have gained their peculiar reputation. In the rear is a large cutting room, and here the fine dress shirts, the superior excellence of which is so well known, are "carefully made to order." This manufacture has grown to large proportions and is a very important and prominent part of the business. Of the stock of fine furnishing goods, (the largest retail stock in this line in New England), it is only necessary to say that it is intended to be complete in all its departments and to exhibit the best goods of the best manufacturers of every nation. All the members of the firm are Bostonians.

N. F. McCARTHY & CO., Commission Dealers in Cut Flowers, Florists' Supplies, No. 1 Music Hall Place, off Winter Street, also entrance through Music Hall from Hamilton Place.—In this city of culture and refinement the demand for floral decorations is naturally large and the business of supplying the requisites in the premises is proportionately extensive and prosperous. Prominent among the well-known and popular establishments in this line of trade will be found that of Messrs. N. F. McCarthy & Co. commission dealers in cut flowers and importers and jobbers in florists' supplies of every description at No. 1 Music Hall Place, off Winter Street. This enterprising young firm composed of Messrs. N. F. McCarthy and W. F. Mollay after an extensive experience as employees began business for themselves at No. 9 Park Street in September, 1885. Later they removed to No. 63 Bromfield Street and finally in August last to the present site. From its inception the business has been characterized by a substantial and steady growth indicative of an active and able management and the present status is that of a prosperous and representative enterprise in its line. Mr. McCartay represented the firm of Wm. J. Stewart, No. 1548 Chestnut Street, Philadelphia, in the same line for three years before he was twenty-one years of age. He conducts auction sales on Wednesday and Saturday during spring and fall, disposing of enormous quantities of bedding plants, nursery stock, etc., at very low prices. The selection being large, varied and choice. The spacious and well arranged premises are fitted up in a manner convenient to and supplied with all requisite facilities for the advantageous conduct of the business. The firm are in daily receipt of large consignments of choice cut flowers fresh from the suburban greeneries and keep constantly on hand a large, comprehensive and complete stock of baskets, and, in short, all embraced in the general term of florists' supplies. Several experienced assistants are employed in the transactions of the extensive and fast increasing business and the patronage received represents the most desirable city custom.

J. Y. BAKER & CO., Wholesale and Retail Dealers in Oysters, North East cor. F. H. Market, and Nos. 120 and 122 Atlantic Avenue, opp. Richmond Street.—Boston has, from the first settlement of the city, more than two hundred and fifty years ago, been the great centre for all kinds of sea and river food, and this distinction the city occupies to-day. In the oyster branch of the trade, the leading and oldest concern now actively engaged in it, is that of Messrs. J. Y. Baker & Co., who have two busy and prosperous establishments, one of these being located on the northeast corner of Faneuil Hall Market, and the other at Nos. 120 and 122 Atlantic Avenue, opposite Richmond Street. This concern was founded under its present style as far back as 1827 by the late Mr. J. Y. Baker. Subsequently, he was joined in the enterprise by his brothers, Simeon and William S. Baker. The founder retired from the business in 1880, and both he and his brothers are now dead. The business is still carried on under the original style by Marcellus G. Baker (son of Simeon,) and Charles W. Badger, who succeeded to the control of the enterprise in 1881. Mr. Baker is a native of Wellfleet, Mass., and Mr. Badger was born at Woburn, Mass. In the north-east corner of Faneuil Hall Market the firm have a spacious stand, always stocked with a liberal supply of choice, fresh oysters. Their packing house and salesroom on Atlantic Avenue is a spacious establishment, and provided with all necessary appliances for the handling of the extensive stock carried, the packing and pickling of oysters for shipping, and the prompt filling of all orders, whether at wholesale or retail. The bulk of their supplies are from Virginia waters, and the distributing trade of the firm extends throughout New England and the British Provinces, and necessitates the constant employment of a large force of hands. This old house is as honorable as it is old, and as vigorous and progressive as any in the trade.

THE METROPOLIS OF NEW ENGLAND. 235

WHIDDEN, CURTIN & CO., Parlor and Chamber Furniture, Carpets, Rugs, Etc., Nos. 1-9 Washington Street.— A great representative concern is that of Messrs. Whidden, Curtin & Co., whose enterprise has secured to them a trade of enormous magnitude in the better grades of furniture and in that incomparable folding bed, the Windsor. The business was established about twenty-five years ago by Messrs. Beale & Hooker, they were succeeded by Mr. T. M. Whidden, whose view of the rapid growth of the trade formed the firm of T. M. Whidden & Co. The firm of Whidden & Curtin followed, and in 1889 was finally succeeded by the present copartnership, composed of Messrs. Thomas M. Whidden, John Curtin and A. H. Seaver. The premises occupied are unusually extensive, comprising two entire buildings, of five stories and basement, Nos. 1-9 Washington Street, fronting on Friend Street from Nos. 95 to 107, and on Haymarket Square at Nos. 7 and 8. The warerooms are very handsomely furnished, spacious and finely lighted, while the immense stock is displayed to admirable advantage, and is the admiration of the throngs of customers, who daily visit the store. Here are carried full lines of parlor and chamber furniture in the new styles of artistic workmanship and elaborate finish. Here are parlor sets in mahogany, walnut, oak, etc., upholstered in the richest manner, and quoted at prices that render them the best value in town. The firm are also leaders in chamber sets, dining room and library furniture and are the exclusive dealers in the celebrated Windsor folding bed which is the only perfect bed of the kind. Its utility is apparent. It covers all the good features of other beds and has none of their defects, but instead many marked advantages and improvements. It is got up in a variety of styles adapted to the pockets of all, and is emphatically the folding bed of the age. As only three firms handle this bed, the public should call at Messrs. Whidden, Curtin & Co.'s when in search of one and thus make sure of seeing it. The firm also have a very large carpet department, where are carried full lines of the best makes of Axminsters, Moquettes, Wiltons, Brussels, Ingrain, etc., likewise rugs, mattings and oil cloth. This is headquarters for the furnishings of houses of a quality and at prices, impossible of duplication elsewhere. They not only number among their customers leading citizens of Boston and New England, but also do a trade of importance in such far off points as Florida and California. Mr. Whidden was born in Boston, Mr. Curtin in Beverly, and Mr. Seaver in Worcester.

EDMUND W. MILLER, Manufacturer of Miller's Reform Boot, No. 5½ Hamilton Place.—Miller's reform boot is deserving of special notice in this review, being made on anatomical principles and needs no breaking in. The manufacturer, Mr. Edmund W. Miller, occupies spacious salesrooms at No. 5½ Hamilton Place, with a factory on South Grand Street, and is in a position to conduct the enterprise under the most favorable conditions for success. The business was originally established in 1870 by Mr. Robert A. Miller, who died in 1884, and was succeeded by his son, the present proprietor. The reform boot, in the production of which this house is so widely noted, is a combination of perfect ease and comfort, and meets the long looked for want, and is the annihilator of corns, bunions, ingrowing nails, and the various feet distortions which are the woes of mankind. It copies nature, the great artist, so nearly that miles of walking, or hours of standing, instead of tiring and agonizing the whole body, finds it unaffected by weariness after exertion of any kind. The combinations utilized by manufacturer and inventor of this boot tend to place the foot in just the same position as if a plaster of Paris cast was taken of a natural foot. Satisfaction is guaranteed in all cases. The work is all hand-made and of the best and finest imported stock. No house in the country has made so systematic and successful a study of this subject, or is so well prepared to meet promptly the various needs of humanity in this important line. The large and still increasing patronage of this house, extending not only to all parts of the United States, but throughout Europe and numerous foreign countries, is due not only to the peculiar merits of the goods produced, but also to the honorable spirit of equity and fair dealing that pervades the management, and which is a surety that the house will continue to prosper and be a potent instrumentality in the growth and importance of this city as a great purchasing centre. Mr. Miller is well known and highly respected in this, his native city, and was trained to the business in which he is now so successfully engaged from his youth up; is enterprising, reliable and progressive in all his business methods, and a young man of high social and commercial standing.

A. R. MITCHELL & CO., Cigars and Tobacco, Manufacturers and Manufacturers' Agents, Nos. 33 to 37 Broad Street and No. 132 Water Street.—One of the great representative houses devoted to the trade in cigars and tobaccos throughout New England, is that of Messrs. A. R. Mitchell & Co. with salesrooms and offices at Nos. 33 to 37 Broad Street, and No. 132 Water Street. The business was founded about twenty-five years ago by Mr. A. R. Mitchell, who is a leading authority in this branch of trade. In 1882, Mr. J. L. Richards came into copartnership under the existing name and style, and the house has made rapid and substantial progress. They are both manufacturers of fine cigars, and also New England agents for the most famous brands of tobaccos, conceded by all who understand the trade or consume the weed, such for instance as D. H. McAlpin & Co's. tobaccos, N. Y.; Force Tobacco Co., Louisville, Ky.; Weyman, Bros., Copenhagen Snuff, Pittsburgh, Pa.; Kenney Bros. Tobacco Co's. cigarettes, and Blackwells Genuine Bull Durham Tobacco. These are grades and brands which have no equal, and ever maintain the same high standard of excellence. The firm have developed a trade of enormous magnitude in their smoking and chewing tobaccos, and are annually enlarging their sales. They are also manufacturers of fine cigars, employing only skilled hands, and the very choicest of imported and domestic leaf tobaccos. Their goods ever command the best class of trade and are in ever increasing consumption. Messrs. A. R. Mitchell & Co., sell to the leading jobbers and dealers of Boston and New England. Mr. Mitchell was born in Cummington, Mass., and has all his active life been in business here. He is universally respected for his sound judgment, and integrity, and is president of the West Newton Savings Bank, and vice president of West Newton National Bank. Mr. Richards was born in Springfield, Mass., and has been with the house twelve years, evincing marked energy and ability. His acquaintance in the trade like that of Mr. Mitchell, is extensive and influential, and we know of no house so thoroughly representative of the New England tobacco trade.

SECURITY INVESTMENT COMPANY, Thomas M. Babson, President; Francis I. Meston, Secretary; Western office, Yankton, Dakota; Eastern Office, No. 17 Milk Street, Post Building.—The judicious and absolutely safe investment of capital is one of vital importance not only to capitalists, but also men of moderate means. In all the vast array of openings for the use of surplus funds there is not one so sure, legitimate and remunerative, as the loaning of money on first mortgage security of productive western farms. In this connection, special reference is made in this commercial review to the representative and reliable Security Investment Company, whose eastern office in Boston is located in the Post Building, No. 17 Milk Street. The company's western office under the able and careful management of Mr. E. T. White, is in the First National Bank Building, Yankton, Dakota. The Security Investment Company was duly incorporated in 1886, with a paid-up capital of $100,000, and is under the supervision of the Savings Bank Commissioners of Connecticut. In fact it is owned and controlled by a number of representative business men and capitalists of New England. The company confines its loans on first mortgage to textile farms in Dakota, Nebraska, Kansas and Texas. The mortgages are made under the supervision of the western manager, Mr. E. T. White, who has resided in the west for sixteen years, engaged in loaning eastern money with excellent judgment and success. The company deals in debenture bonds, farm mortgages and first-class western securities. Its seven per cent guaranteed gold real estate first mortgages are unrivalled for security. The interest on these loans is payable semi-annually at the office of the American Loan and Trust Company, Boston, or can be collected through local banks free of expense. The Security Investment Company to meet the wants of men of very moderate means has latterly issued six per cent. specially secured ten year gold debenture bonds in amounts of $50 and upwards, the American Loan and Trust Company of Boston, being the trustee. These securities are confidently recommended to the most conservative.

WM. R. SCHAEFER & SON, Manufacturers, Agents, Importers and Dealers in Fire Arms, Sporting Goods, and Fishing Tackle, at Wholesale and Retail, No 61 Elm Street.—The leading headquarters in this city for firearms, sporting goods and fishing tackle, at both wholesale and retail, is the splendid establishment of Messrs. Wm. R. Schaefer & Son, located at 61 Elm Street, corner of Dock Square. The business of this house was founded in 1853 by Mr. Wm. R. Schaefer, the present firm being organized in 1880 by the admission of Mr. J. F. H. Schaefer to partnership. The business premises comprises three floors 25x100 feet each, giving ample accommodations for handling and storing the immense and valuable stock, and for the systematic and successful prosecution of the business in all its departments. The firm are widely prominent both as manufacturers, importers, dealers and manufacturers' agents in the above named goods, and also make a leading specialty of fine gun repairing and engraving. They do not aim to transact a clap-trap business, advertising goods with fancy brands and fraudulent and misleading descriptions, but to do a square business, buying their goods in very large quantities and at the lowest cash prices, and giving their customers the benefit of their large experience and wide connections in the trade. This firm are given a deserved prestige in the trade as agents for the sale of goods manufactured by Chas. Daly, breech loading hammer and hammerless shot guns, the National, Colts, L. C. Smith, Lefever, Ithaca, and Pieper hammer and hammerless breech loading shot guns, the F. Wessons, Marlins, Ballards, and Winchester repeating and single shot rifles, the Union Metallic Cartridge Company, Winchester Repeating Arms Company, United States Cartridge Company, annual, lions, hunting boots and shoes, coats, vests, hats and sportsmen's wearing apparel, imported Finland leather jackets, Smith & Wesson, Marlin, Standard, Merwin & Hulbert, Stevens and F. Wesson target and pocket revolvers, Spratt's English Dog Food, Medicines, chains, leaders and whips for dogs, Belchers' automatic rapid shell loaders, American, Hazard, Duponts, and Oriental Mills gun powders, Blue Rock Pigeons and traps, Ligowsky clay birds and traps. They imported number of thousands guns the past year to meet the demands of their business, and in every department make a specialty of handling the finest goods manufactured either in America or Europe. They guarantee every article as represented, and have unsurpassed facilities for executing all orders with promptness and dispatch. Their experience in the gun manufacturing of the finest guns warrants every sportsman that their new improved hammerless and hammer breech loading shot guns in point of excellence of material, mechanism, simplicity and shooting qualities, are not to be excelled; their custom made guns are made by the most expert and experienced workmen that this firm are able to obtain in Europe. Their trade extends to all parts of New England, to the west and south, and inducements are constantly offered to the trade, as regards terms and prices, which are safe from successful competition. The senior partner was born in Germany and came to this city forty years ago, after having learned his trade as a gun-maker in Germany, beginning at the young age of thirteen years. The son is a native of Cambridge, Mass., and combines his energy and talent with the ripe experience of his father, having worked at the bench to obtain a thorough knowledge of firearms in their various branches, beginning when twelve years of age, hence they form a firm of wide popularity, commanding influence and solid worth.

B. NOYES, Mortgages, Room 32, No. 31 Milk Street.—There is no financial interest of this great and important business centre than that of real estate, and the present condition of the stock market and other forms of investment has given stronger assurances than ever of the reliability and safety in placing surplus resources in improved or unimproved real estate, in well selected localities. This line of business has enlisted the services of many of the most responsible and enterprising of Boston's business men, and prominent among the number is Mr. B. Noyes, whose office is so centrally located at No. 31 Milk Street, (Room 32.) Mr. B. Noyes is a Bostonian by birth, and brings to bear in his business a long and intimate knowledge of the values of real estate through all the different sections of the city and its environs, and a thorough familiarity with all legal matters pertaining to transactions in that line of business. Although having founded his establishment in this line on his own account, having commenced late in 1880, he has been the recipient of a very liberal and permanent clientage, which includes many of our leading capitalists and investors, and in fact the patronage he now enjoys is of such a character in influence and magnitude, that it surpasses many older houses in the same line of industry. Mr. Noyes occupies a very neat and tastefully arranged office, which is easy of access, and is fitted up in a first-class manner, and supplied with every facility for the proper transaction of business. He is prepared to execute all commissions in the real estate trade, such as buying, selling, leasing and exchanging, collecting rents, managing estates, paying taxes, effecting judicious repairs and keeping the same up to the highest point of productive efficiency, also appraising and valuing, searching titles, conveyancing, etc. Mr. Noyes makes a specialty of lending money on bond and mortgage, and forecloses mortgages when directed by clients in the most efficient manner, and in this particular department of his business he has acquired a very enviable and noteworthy reputation, in consequence of his thorough knowledge of all its details and legal conditions existing between mortgagee and mortgagor. Assignments and transfers of liens, mortgages and other legal real estate transactions receive prompt care and attention and in fact all matters pertaining to the entire business are transacted in their entirety, and without vexations annoyance to patrons.

H. LOCKE, Wholesale and Retail Dealer in Beef, Nos. 42 and 44 Faneuil Hall Market.—Among the oldest merchants still successfully conducting a vigorous and extensive trade in Faneuil Hall Market, Mr. H. Locke, the occupant of Stalls Nos. 42 and 44, merits special mention in this work. Forty long years mark the business career of this gentleman in this time-honored market, and from first to last he has sustained a reputation as a straightforward and vigilant business man of the highest character. He started business alone here in 1848, and for about seven years in the 60's, he had a partner, the style of the firm during this period being Locke & Woodbridge. Since the retirement of Mr. Woodbridge, Mr. Locke has managed the business alone, and it has grown and prospered under his experienced direction. His stalls are neatly arranged and of fine dimensions, and are fitted up in a very attractive manner and provided with all modern appliances, including the latest and best improved refrigerators for the preservation of perishable articles during hot weather. Mr. Locke spares no expense nor trouble to provide the choicest of every thing, and his facilities for doing this are not surpassed by those of any competitor. He makes a specialty of the very primest and choicest beef, and, carrying at all times a very large stock, he is enabled to fill orders with the utmost promptitude, both at wholesale and retail. Four assistants and a delivery wagon are kept constantly busy, and a large city patronage is enjoyed. Mr. Locke was born in Arlington, Mass., and is to-day one of the best known and most deservedly popular business men of Boston.

ESSEX BOOT and SHOE CO., L. F. Keene, Proprietor, No. 28 Essex Street.—The Essex Boot and Shoe Co., No. 28 Essex Street, is a new acquisition to the commercial industries of Boston and its operations are being prosecuted with unabated vigor by Mr. Leslie F. Keene, the proprietor, who is a young man of business experience and practical in his special line of trade, having had fifteen years experience in manufacturing. The store, which is 20x80 feet in area is very neatly and attractively fitted up and very handsome in its fittings and appointments, and is well stocked with a new, full and complete assortment of everything pertaining to the boot and shoe trade, including fine and medium grade boots, shoes and gaiters for men, youths, and boys, and an almost endless variety of everything desirable and seasonable for ladies, misses and children, together with rubbers and slippers of every description. The assortment has been selected with care and as Mr. Keene possesses all the facilities enjoyed by his older competitors, he is in every respect capable of furnishing the best class of goods of the highest standard quality, and make the prices as advantageous to customers as any kindred establishment in the city. Boots and shoes are also made to measure of the best material and every attention is given to perfection of fit and ease and comfort to the wearer. Mr. Keene is a native of Maine.

THE METROPOLIS OF NEW ENGLAND. 241

LOUIS COHN & CO., Wholesale Manufacturers of Picture Frames, Mouldings, Etc., No. 4 Charlestown Street.—Among the various lines of business represented in Boston, in which a considerably increased amount of activity is now observable, may be mentioned that of manufacturing picture frames, mouldings, etc., and the handling of backing, glass, mats, chromos, screw eyes, nails, cords, etc., upon a wholesale scale. This is one of the most encouraging signs of the time, for, as the intelligent reader will readily understand the volume of the consumption of these classes of manufactures, constitutes an excellent criterion as to the condition of trade in general. An enterprising and deservedly prosperous concern engaged in this branch of trade is that of Messrs. Louis Cohn & Co., of No. 4 Charlestown Street, Haymarket

Square, opposite the Boston & Maine depot. The business was organized in 1881 by the present proprietor, Mr. L. Cohn, and the venture has been attended with the most satisfactory results— a very extensive and substantial city and suburban trade having been established, and one necessitating the permanent employment of ten hands. The premises occupied are commodious and admirably equipped with the best mechanical contrivances pertaining to the trade. Picture frames and mouldings in any and every style desired are made to order from the best materials obtainable and at prices which defy successful competition. To meet the orders of dealers a heavy stock of frames, mouldings, backing, glass, mats, chromos, screw eyes, nails, cord, etc., is kept always on hand, and the service in all cases is prompt and reliable. Mr. Cohn is a native of Germany but has long resided in Boston, and has acquired wide-spread esteem by his industry and integrity.

WILSON, CASSELS & CO., New England Representatives of Hall's Safe and Lock Company's Standard Fire and Burglar-Proof Safes, Dove-Tailed Burglar-Proof Bank and Vault Work, and Infallible Time Locks, No. 66 Sudbury Street.—Modern safe construction has attained a degree of perfection that seems marvelous to the public. It is not every so called safe which, when subjected to the severe test of use, the in roads of fire, or attacks of burglars, prove to be in reality, a safe. The Hall Safe and Lock Company, of Cincinnati, was organized in 1849, and has had a remarkable growth of success. Its facilities have been repeatedly tasked to the utmost to supply the growing demand. In 1881 the Boston branch was opened under the proprietorship of Messrs. Wilson, Cassels & Co., gentlemen conversant and long experienced in the manufacture and sale of these celebrated safes. They have developed very influential connections, and have sold the Hall safes to the leading houses of New England, also supplying the majority of banks with their celebrated dove-tailed burglar-proof vault and safe work. Their sales room and office are at No. 66 Sudbury Street, where they carry a full stock and complete assortment of these safes, adapted to the needs of all business, large and small. These safes are absolutely fire-proof; they are made upon the latest and most improved principle, embodying all recent improvements; the workmanship is of the best, while the locks are models of ingenuity. The record of these safes for nearly half a century is an unbroken one of perfect security, either against fire or burglars, and they are to-day the popular and leading safe in the market. More than 200,000 of them are in use. The company has branch houses in all the principal cities and centres of the Union. Their capital and facilities are unlimited, and though any of their numerous branches they are prepared to furnish safes, at reasonable prices, that cannot be duplicated elsewhere, and also to contract for their celebrated dove-tailed bank and vault work. Their time lock is considered the best and most modern in operation. Those requiring any work in their line would do well to obtain estimates and prices from the Messrs. Wilson, Cassels & Co.

NATHAN ROBBINS, Dealer in Poultry and Wild Game, Stalls, Nos. 33 and 35 Faneuil Hall Market.—The oldest established and most widely known concern in this section of Boston is that of Nathan Robbins, dealer in poultry and wild game, whose stalls, Nos. 33 and 35, are located in Faneuil Hall Market. This business was established sixty-two years ago by Mr. Nathan Robbins, who conducted it till Sept. 4th, 1888, when he died after a long, honorable and successful career, deeply lamented by a host of friends and acquaintances, owing to his generosity and integrity. His grandson, Mr. Olny Robbins, is now managing the business under the old name of his grandfather Nathan Robbins. The following is a short sketch from the Boston Record, Sept. 5th, 1888, of the life of Nathan Robbins, the veteran of Faneuil Hall Market. Nathan Robbins, for more than fifty years a Faneuil Hall marketman, died at his residence in Arlington last evening, after an illness of several months. Nathan Robbins was born in Arlington, formerly West Cambridge, Mass., September 7, 1805. At an early age he found employment with Jabez Fisher, later of Fisher & Chapin, dealer in pork and provisions in Boston. He remained in Mr. Fisher's employ but a short time, when he began business for himself, having only such funds as he had accumulated from his small trading and the savings of his youth ful ventures in business. On the 26th day of August, 1826, Mr. Robbins took possession of stalls 33 and 35 Quincy market, being one of the very first occupants of that structure. Very few of the stalls were then, and for some time after the market opened, occupied the whole scheme of the market being at the time regarded as a chimerical one, and sure to come to grief. His business at the time he opened in the market was that of a dealer in poultry, wild game and live pigs for shipment. Mr. Robbins was a shrewd business man, and always had a pleasant word for everybody. By his enterprise and honorable dealing he soon built up a large business, supplying the leading hotels and private families of the city and vicinity with game and poultry. Among his private customers were many of the best Boston families—the Lawrences, Adamses, Websters, R. G. Shaw and the Williamses being among the number, their children and grandchildren being still his customers. He indulged in no outside speculations, and could always be found at his place of business. He was one of the founders of the Faneuil Hall National Bank in 1864, since which time Mr. Robbins had either been a director or president of the institution. At the time of his death he was president of the bank, having held the office for more than a quarter of a century. Mr. Robbins was one of the only two survivors of the original stall-holders in the Quincy market, and was at one time the sole owner of Gray's wharf. Among the many boys whom Mr. Robbins brought up and graduated to business, and who have become wealthy and honored men in the communities in which they have located, are his two brothers, Amos and Eli Robbins of New York, who are both millionaires, being worth from $2,000,000 to $5,000,000 each, and who are the largest poultry and game dealers in the United States, and are, as was their elder brother, honored and respected by all who know them. At the present day under the management of Mr. Olny Robbins the stalls are very carefully fitted up and kept, and the arrangements are the best that can be devised for facilitating the transaction of business. Mr. Olny Robbins is in possession of excellent facilities for procuring supplies from the best sections of the country, and is always enabled to offer the choicest game and poultry in America at extremely low prices. Personally Mr. Olny Robbins is highly esteemed by the community for his enterprise and integrity, and enjoys the entire confidence of his numerous patrons.

ROBERT MORSE, Wholesale Commission, Dealer in Wines, Liquors, Etc., No. 11 Central Street (Room 47).—Robert M. Morse senior, is to-day the oldest of the class of men, who were largely engaged in the grocery and produce business in Boston more than sixty years ago. He just passed the eighty-second year of his life and he still occupies an office in Central Street, where he still keeps up the sign of commission business if only for some occasional transactions and the pride of the thing as well as the associations of the past. He is still active and bears the unmistakable signs of health and contentment in his cheerful countenance. He was born on the 8th of January, 1807, in Windham County, State of Vermont in Newfane, the third town of the county—the one part set off as Fayetteville and another as Williamsville, where his enterprising father to meet the wants of the early settlers had built, saw and grist mills, and a good sized mansion which has for more than seventy years been occupied as a county tavern. When a little past thirteen years of age, Mr. Morse, against the expressed judgment and will of his guardian but with the consent and approbation of his mother, determined to try his fortune in Boston. It was the time of the old stage coaches and delayed by floods on the Connecticut, he failed to reach Boston in season to secure a place which had been thought desirable. He had but little money and the only alternative was to persevere and get a place or go back to be laughed at in the village of his birth. He determined to persevere, not only to find a place but to get one better than the one for which he seemed destined, one that should seem to give signs of permanency. In this spirit he went forward day by day, visiting only the stores which seemed to be engaged in a large and respectable business, and before the end of a week he succeeded in obtaining a clerkship in the employ of one of the oldest importers of hosiery and gloves from England, France and Germany—Smith & Gore, who had a branch store in New York. This firm stood high in credit and kept their business in an accurate and systematic way. In short they were ready and prompt in all their ways when they sent orders abroad for goods, generally a bill of exchange went with the order. Their account books were a model in the way of book keeping and bold and beautiful penmanship. In this way the subject of this sketch was trained in business ways, and when on his twenty-first birthday, 1828, his time was up, he received from his masters a small balance due him for service, and parted in mutual good feelings and went directly to a spacious store at No. 9 South Market Street, where aided by a man of experience, he commenced business in the grocery and produce line, and remained in that store over twenty-eight years, constantly increasing his business till it compared well in extent and amount with some twenty of the largest dealers in that line; for seven years a partnership existed with Asa F. Cochran of Pembroke, N. H. and during this period the business was done under the name of Cochran & Morse, and Cochran, Morse & Co.; and at this time it owned and had many small coasting vessels employed in various ways, in the states and in foreign countries, principally in trade with Cuba the south and the south side and in the Gulf Trade with Mexico, which at one time was profitable, and during this period there arose a new industry, importing and manufacturing of palm leaf hats which were sent to every port and place of consequence in the United States, France, Africa and South America. This business continued after the partnership with Cochran closed in March, 1836, and when the style of the firm became Robert M. Morse & Co. In the long course of these years of uncertain enterprise the lessons of his early life and apprenticeship always exerted a powerful influence on the business character of Mr. Morse. He held it as the first principle of his life to deal fairly and honestly with all men and never to misrepresent any important fact in a case but to keep his word of truth as his bond, to sell good goods at fair prices. In the best period of his business his sales even in low priced times amounted to about $700,000 annually, and in his times the firms of which he has been a member, have done a business of many millions and nobody ever complained of any intentional injustice.

A. G. ALLEN, Hardware, Brass Handles, Antique and Modern, Desk Rails, Castors, Etc., No. 157 Washington Street.—This gentleman deals at both wholesale and retail in hardware of every description, brass handles, both antique and modern desk rails, castors, etc., making a leading specialty of cabinet hardware, and has been established in the business here for a period of full forty years. The specialties in many articles here displayed are of a nature, and bear such a character for utility and usefulness, as to command universal attention and general patronage. All goods are purchased direct from manufacturers and first hands in vast quantities and at advantageous rates, and their superiority and low prices have secured the appreciation of an array of patrons in this and other countries, the trade of the house extending not only to all parts of the United States, but to Mexico, the Azores and other foreign ports. The supplies here recognized as standard in value wherever introduced, and have served to give this house a prestige and a popularity both at home and abroad. Mr. Allen was born in Boston and is known and honored as one of its representative merchants.

LIBERO PERETTI, Manufacturer and Importer of Fine Cigars, No. 30 Exchange Street.—Among the cigar houses of this city none is more worthy of honorable mention than that of Mr. Libero Peretti, who first began business in Harris Street in 1884, and afterwards removed to Nashua Street, then to North Street and finally, to Exchange Street, on August 15, 1888. Here he has a commodious workshop on the second floor, and this is equipped with all necessary appliances for the production of the finest brands of cigars, for which the house has become noted, and for which there is a very active demand. Six hands, skilled and experienced in the business, are employed in the manufacturing department, and the finest brands of cigars obtainable are produced here. Mr. Peretti, in addition to carrying a heavy stock of cigars of his own manufacture, has always on hand a fine and extensive assortment of foreign manufactured cigars, imported direct and carefully selected to meet the demands of a first-class trade. All goods sent out will be found to be exactly as represented, and in the matter of price this house defies competition for the same quality of goods. The trade is of both a wholesale and retail character, and extends over a large part of the New England States.

G. P. RAYMOND, Costume Parlors, No. 3 Pemberton Square.—This thriving and prosperous business was established about five years ago by the gentleman whose name heads the sketch, and from its inception the venture has proved a positive and permanent success. Keeping on hand at all times an extensive, varied and A1 assortment of everything in the line of costumes, courteous and attentive to patrons, and withal thoroughly conversant with the business, Mr. Raymond has been enabled to secure the hold on popular favor and patronage he deservedly enjoys. The premises occupied, including office, property, parlors and workrooms, are commodious and well-ordered, three efficient assistants being employed, while a complete line of costumes for masquerades, old folks' concerts, private theatricals, tableaux, etc., is constantly carried on hand all orders receiving immediate attention, and the patronage, which is large and influential, extends all over the New England States. Mr. Raymond's mother was one of the quartette who sang at the laying of the foundation of Bunker Hill Monument, and her mother one of the first who ascended to the top when finished.

ARTHUR S. DOANE & CO., Engravers and Commercial Printers, No. 27 Kilby Street.—Mr. Doane has been identified with this trade for a number of years, and was formerly connected with the firm of John A. Lowell & Co., of this city. In 1886 he started in business for himself, and has since met with the most gratifying success. Mr. Doane occupies a well equipped printing office on Broad Street, where he has every facility, including steam power for turning out the finest class of work. He is particularly noted for doing fine steel engraving work for business purposes, as well as wedding and visiting cards, of which he makes a specialty, while commercial printing in all its branches, bill and letter heads, notes heads, invoices, circulars, etc., is done in the best style of the art and in the promptest and most satisfactory way. The trade is of the finest description and is of large dimensions, constantly increasing. Mr. Doane, who is a Bostonian of middle age, pays the greatest attention to business and has a first-class reputation in the trade.

THE METROPOLIS OF NEW ENGLAND

CHARLES A. BRACKETT, Paper, Store and Shoe Boxes, No. 98 Hanover Street.—For the best made paper boxes in New England, the trade has gone to Mr. Charles A. Brackett, of No. 98 Hanover Street. He started in business here about twenty years ago, and early created a widespread demand for his product. He has had to repeatedly enlarge his facilities and now occupies the four upper floors of No. 98 Hanover Street, 40x80 feet in dimensions, and admirably adapted for the purposes of manufacturing. He here employs an average force of eighty-five hands in the manufacture of all descriptions of paper, store and shoe boxes of a quality nowhere else excelled and rarely duplicated. He exercises close personal supervision, while he brings to bear the widest range of practical experience coupled with an intimate knowledge of the wants of Boston's fine trade. Plush boxes are a specialty, and he controls the patronage of a large

age, was for twenty years, book-keeper of the Equitable Safety Insurance Company, and Mr. Clark, who is sixty-seven years old, was for a like period secretary of the same company. They formed their partnership in 1862 and are among the best known and popular fire and marine insurance brokers and agents in the city. They are members of the Brokers' Association, and represent the wealthiest and most responsible companies in the world. Their patronage is extensive and influential, and they are prompt and reliable. Both gentlemen are natives of Boston.

E. A. SHAW, Cotton Buyer, No. 18 Congress Street, Room 12 —Next to the trade in cereals, the cotton interests of the United States constitute the most important commercial factor. The transactions in this great staple commodity here in Boston alone in the course of a year for domestic consump-

section of the fancy goods trade. Here is headquarters for jewel and odor caskets of the most elegant and richly decorative character; also gilt, card-board, fancy leather and all other kinds for every possible use; mailing tubes are made to order in any size or length, this being the only place in the city where they are made by machinery. Mr. Brackett principally does a wholesale trade, and has extended his connections all over New England. He is a business man of sterling integrity, and has ever maintained the confidence and respect of leading financial and commercial circles. His establishment is a credit to his enterprise, ability and energy, and a valued factor in promoting the welfare and prosperity of the city of Boston.

LORING & CLARK, Insurance Agents, No. 19 Exchange Place.— No plan or system has ever yet been devised which has proved such an efficient handmaid in the development of the business interests of this country as insurance against losses by fire, and its advantages and usefulness was never more powerfully demonstrated than on the occasion of the vast and memorable conflagrations in Boston and Chicago, when street after street of buildings was reduced to ashes and insurance companies were called upon to pay out hundreds of millions of dollars to the sufferers. The insurance agent fills an important position between the companies and the policy holders he represents. Usually he represents a number of companies of good standing, and takes the contract for placing a line of insurance with such companies as he knows to be substantial and responsible, and saves his client much trouble and expense, and often much anxiety. The merchant or property owner needs but to be assured of the honesty and experience of the agent he employs and may then rest satisfied that his interests will be faithfully attended to, for the agent knows that if he is to be successful his reputation must be preserved unsullied. There are few agents who have had more practical experience in insurance matters than Messrs. John J. Loring and John Theodore Clark, the members of the firm of Loring & Clark, insurance agents and brokers of No. 19 Exchange Place. The former who is seventy-two years of

tion aggregate vast proportions. Indeed one of the extensive branches of business in this city is that devoted to the buying of this indispensable product for the New England cotton fabric manufacturers. Among the best known cotton buyers in the city may be mentioned the name of E. A. Shaw, whose office is located at No. 18 Congress Street, Room 12. Mr. Shaw, who is a man in the prime of life, and a native of Massachusetts, is a gentleman of entire probity in his dealings, as well as energy, sagacity and thorough knowledge of the wants of the trade. He has been engaged in this line since 1862—in the south twelve years, and in Boston six years —and is widely and favorably known in the trade. Mr. Shaw buys direct from the cotton growers of the Southern states for New England manufacturers on commission, having correspondents in the principal cotton centres of the south, and does a large and active business.

WM. CUSHING & CO., Real Estate and Mortgages, No. 15 Congress Street.—Few among the many responsible Boston real estate brokers, have been more fortunate in establishing a reputation for reliability and probity in their transactions, than that of Wm. Cushing & Co. They conduct a general real estate business, buying, selling and exchanging city and country property of every description on commission exclusively and also negotiate mortgages and loans. Rents are collected likewise, and estates taken in entire charge and judiciously managed; special attention being given to the handling of suburban realty, both improved and unimproved, while investments are desirably placed also, and insurance effected in staunch fire companies at lowest rates compatible with absolute security. This well and favorably known real estate and insurance agency, was originally established in 1873, by Duncan & Co., who conducted the business up to 1887, when they were succeeded by the present senior member, who continued it alone for about two years, when he associated with him in partnership, F. L. Whitney. Messrs. Cushing and Whitney are both men of unquestionable integrity in their dealings and business relations, as well as of sagacity and experience in this line.

DAMRELL & UPHAM, Old Corner Bookstore, Standard and Miscellaneous Books, etc., No. 283 Washington Street.—This is one of Boston's oldest landmarks and is surrounded with many pleasant historic associations. With one exception, it is the oldest building in the city. It was erected in 1712 by Thomas Crease, and previously its site was occupied by a dwelling in which Ann Hutchinson held her famous seances. Thomas Crease used the building as a store and dwelling, and eventually it was occupied as offices and again as a drug store. The last apothecary who was the tenant was Dr. Samuel Clarke, father of the Rev. James Freeman Clarke, who was born here. Dr. Clarke in 1828 was succeeded in the tenancy by Carter & Hendee, who first utilized the front part of the building as a book store, for which purpose it has ever since been devoted. The book business has been successively carried on by Carter & Hendee, Allen & Ticknor, William D. Ticknor & Co., Ticknor & Fields, E. P. Dutton & Co., A. Williams & Co. and Cupples, Upham & Co. Eventually in 1886 Messrs. Charles L. Damrell and Henry M. Upham assumed the management. This famous Old Corner Bookstore is one of the most popular resorts in Boston, the literary men of the city making it their chief rendezvous. Here men celebrated in literature in their day—Lowell, Longfellow, Hawthorne, Holmes, Whittier, Emerson and others noted in American letters—were accustomed to gather for the interchange of good fellowship and art. Its church department for works of devotion, bibles, prayer books, hymnals, etc., is now a very popular shopping place for ladies. Here is a department for medical, scientific and agricultural works; others for maps, globes and guide books, theological literature, illustrated works, sporting and yachting, juvenile literature, English books, American miscellaneous books, etc. There are also special counters for newspapers, journals, periodicals and novels. The establishment is never without the latest new thing in English, French, German or American literature. Messrs. Damrell & Upham conduct an extensive importing business, and pay special attention to supplying town and city libraries, clubs, etc. The firm have an establishment in London, England, at No. 7 Stationers' Hall Court, Ludgate Hill, through which they receive all the latest English publications with great regularity. Mr. Charles L. Damrell is a native of Portsmouth, N. H., while Mr. Henry M. Upham was born in Nantucket, Mass.

HILTON & WOODWARD, Dealers in Mutton, Lamb, Veal, and Lambs' Tongues, Nos. 5 and 7 Faneuil Hall Market.—The meat trade of Boston is one of the largest and most important industries carried on, and has many able and efficient exponents, among whom are Messrs Hilton & Woodward, the occupants of stalls Nos. 5 and 7 Faneuil Hall Market, who have gained deserved prominence and great success. The business of this enterprising firm was inaugurated some twenty-seven years ago by Mr. J. F. Hilton, and diligence, enterprise liberal and honorable methods quickly brought him substantial and influential custom. Year by year he experienced an increase of trade until it assumed dimensions of a large and prosperous character, requiring in its conduct the closest attention and unremitting energies. Then it was, some eleven years ago, that he admitted into partnership Mr. S. M. Woodward, a pushing, energetic man of business, who had a practical experience of fifteen years as clerk and afterwards partner with Hiscock & Co. The stall is a commodious one, is neatly and tastefully fitted up, and is kept constantly in a clean, inviting condition, while the stock is at all times large, fresh and choice. The stock embraces mutton, lamb, veal and lambs' tongues, newly slaughtered, and is carried in sufficient quantities to permit of the prompt filling of all orders, large and small. The transactions are of both a wholesale and retail character, and the distributing trade of the firm reaches to all sections of the New England States. The stall is connected by telephone, the call being 2102, and four assistants and a delivery wagon are kept busy in filling orders. Mr. Hilton is a native of Maine, and Mr Woodward was born in Massachusetts. Both gentlemen are well known both in the city and out of it, and are respected and esteemed by all with whom they have had dealings.

EPPLER & ADAMS SEWING MACHINE COMPANY, Andrew Eppler, Jr., President, G. W. Statham, Treasurer, No. 112 South Street.—The construction of machines for sewing shoes has for years occupied the attention of inventors and others and a number of ingeniously designed machines has been the result, but it could not be said that perfection had been reached until the introduction of the Eppler & Adams turn shoe sewing machine which is the simplest and most rapid curved needle sewing machine ever invented, and will sew all kinds of turn boots and shoes equal to the best hand work. These machines are manufactured by the Eppler & Adams Sewing Machine Company, and are leased to boot and shoe manufacturers upon satisfactory terms. They are in use in many of the leading factories throughout New England and other parts of the country and the work turned out is not surpassed, the goods made on these machines wearing well and giving the best satisfaction to the trade and the public. The operations of the company are widespread and extensive and for manufacturing purposes a three-story building having dimensions of 30x72 feet, is occupied at No. 112 South Street. It is well equipped throughout and a force of skilled practical machinists are kept constantly engaged. These machines have only been on the market three years, and in that time have been introduced in all parts of the country, and are fast superseding all others, and combine advantages of a superior character for doing the neatest, best and most substantial work. Mr. Andrew Eppler, Jr., the president of the company, is from the state of New Jersey. He has long been a resident of Boston, and conspicuous in the manufacture of boot and shoe-sewing machines. Mr. G. W. Statham, the treasurer, is a native of England. He has been in Boston many years, and was formerly with the Goodyear & McKay Sewing Machine Company.

FRED. C. NEWHALL, Manufacturer, Wholesale and Retail Dealer in Wood Easels, Folding and Fire Screens, Bamboo Chairs and Divans, also, Wire Door and Window Screens, Bamboo Work of all Kinds a Specialty, Factory and Office, Nos. 257, 259 and 261 Causeway Street.—Among the thriving industrial enterprises that have sprung up of late in this part of the city, there are few more worthy of notice in this review than that of Fred C. Newhall, manufacturer of easels, folding and fire screens, both wood and bamboo, also bamboo chairs and divans, and ordered work of all kinds, a specialty both wholesale and retail, whose office and well equipped factory are located at Nos. 257, 259 and 261 Causeway Street. The work turned out here is of a very superior character, the productions being articles of exceptional merit; and as a consequence they are in steady and growing demand in the trade throughout the New England States and also the British Provinces, with some in New York State likewise. They are not, in fact, surpassed, if equalled, by any similar articles produced in Boston, and of their superiority no more unfailing criterion need be offered than the enduring hold they have taken on popular favor everywhere. This prosperous business was established something over two years ago, on Beverly Street, but on account of increase of business, was compelled to move to the commodious quarters now occupied at the period mentioned. The factory occupies a 65x80 foot ground floor, and is supplied with ample steam power and all necessary machinery and facilities, while eight or more expert workmen on an average, are employed. Besides wood easels, folding and fire screens, in handsome designs and exquisite workmanship, Mr. Newhall manufactures also wire door and window screens, while he makes a leading specialty of bamboo work.

SAMUEL B. DEAN, Cut Soles and Leather, Nos. 70 and 72 South Street.—A reputable house in the leather trade of Boston is that of Samuel B. Dean, Nos. 70 and 72 South street. Mr. Dean has been identified with the business for the past fifteen years and was for five years, from 1883 to 1888, the senior member of the firm of Dean, Paten & Co. On its dissolution, January 1, 1888, he succeeded to the sole control and extended its operations in an energetic way. Mr. Dean occupies commodious premises 30x80 feet in dimensions, and carries a large stock of cut soles, having trade connections all over the city as well as throughout New England. His establishment is conducted on the strictest business principles and has the benefit of his constant supervision in every detail. Mr. Dean is noted for dealing only in the finest quality of leather of which he is an excellent judge. He is a resident of Boston and has a first-class reputation in commercial circles here.

THE METROPOLIS OF NEW ENGLAND.

JAMES E. WALL, Importer and Manufacturer of Bamboo Furniture, Bamboo Easels, Fire Screens, Folding Screens, Odd Chairs, Curtain Poles, Etc., No. 73 Cornhill.—The most widely known and successful importer and manufacturer of bamboo furniture, bamboo easels, fire screens, curtain poles, etc., is Mr. James E. Wall, whose trade is of a wholesale character principally, and is large and flourishing, extends all over the United States and Mexico. Mr. Wall, who is a gentleman of about thirty-six years old, and a native of this city, is a man of unmistakable energy and thorough practical skill in his line, with a complete

knowledge of the business in its every feature and detail. He established himself in business in 1878. Mr. Wall occupies ample and well equipped quarters as factory and salesroom at No. 73 Cornhill, having in service steam power and the latest improved machinery, while half a dozen or so expert hands are employed. A full and fine assortment is constantly kept in stock, including fine bamboo furniture of unique designs and exquisite workmanship, elegant bamboo easels, handsome fire screens, folding screens, odd chairs, curtain poles, etc. Mr. Wall imports India, Chinese and Japanese bamboo, while estimates for finishing rooms and stores in bamboo are promptly furnished upon application.

H. C. HASTINGS, Bookseller and Publisher, Scriptural Tract Repository, No. 49 Cornhill.—The old established and representative establishment of Mr. H. C. Hastings, bookseller and publisher, was founded in 1862, since which period he has built up an extensive patronage in all sections of the United States and Canada and also abroad. He occupies a spacious five-story building, which is fully equipped with every appliance and facility for the business. The retail department is on the second floor, the wholesale on the third and the composing and printing rooms on the fifth floor. Mr. Hastings keeps constantly in stock a superior assortment of bibles (90 varieties) prayer and hymn books, etc., and was one of the first importers of English Reference Bibles in the United States. He is likewise an able writer and well known public speaker, and delivered from 200 to 300 addresses a year. In a six months' tour through Great Britain in 1887, Mr. Hastings addressed crowded meetings, etc., 290 times. He is the popular publisher and editor of "The Christian" And "The Little Christian," the "Anti Infidel Library," and numbers of able and admirably written tracts and pamphlets. Mr. Hastings is also editor of a very useful and valuable pamphlet entitled "A few cold facts concerning preaching on Boston Common, presented at a public hearing in the City Hall, before a committee of the city council, on the petition to repeal the city ordinance prohibiting the unlicensed preaching of the Gospel on the public grounds of the city of Boston. In this pamphlet Mr. Hastings ably chastises the members of the city government, which taxes people to pay for Sunday jig playing on Boston Common contrary to the laws of the commonwealth, and fines and imprisons ministers and others for reading the Bible in the same place, and worshiping God in accordance with the state constitution and bill of rights. All Mr. Hastings' publications are forwarded post paid to any address in the United States and Canada, on receipt of price.

G. L. POND & CO., Real Estate Brokers, No. 320 Washington Street.—The secure market offered to the public by the real estate of Boston and its vicinity, both for speculative and investment purposes, has been duly appreciated, and both buyers and sellers realize that their investments when judiciously placed are absolutely secure. To certainly attain the greatest measure of security and the best results, the services of experienced brokers are always necessary, and prominent among their number in Boston is the firm of Messrs. G. L. Pond & Co., No. 320 Washington Street. Mr. G. L. Pond has been established in the real estate business for the last five years. He brings to bear on his business great practical experience, coupled with an intimate personal knowledge of the advantages of the residential and business sections of Boston and its suburbs. Mr. Pond conducts a general realty business, buying and selling houses, stores, lots and land in the city and elsewhere, placing loans, negotiating mortgages, arranging transfers, collecting rents, etc. His keen appreciation of values, present and prospective, together with a large acquaintance with business men, renders his services peculiarly valuable to parties dealing in realties. He is agent in Boston for a general line of patent novelties and supplies of all kinds for canvassing agents. He is also connected with the Pond Rubber Company, who are manufacturers of and dealers in ladies' and gents' rubber clothing and miscellaneous rubber goods of all descriptions. Mr. E. L. Pond, the manager, is the son of Mr. G. L. Pond, and has charge of the business. The company's goods are sold entirely through canvassing agents, who take orders to be made to measure, and all their goods are warranted. Mr. Pond is a native of Franklin, Mass., and was for thirty-five years in the wholesale shoe trade.

CODMAN & HALL, Importers, No. 164 Water Street.—Prominent among those who have contributed to the material progress of the city's commerce, is that of the well-known and reliable house of Messrs. Codman & Hall, formerly of No. 125 Milk Street, who are largely engaged in importing drugs, essential oils, chemicals and Mediterranean products of all kinds. This house was founded in 1881, by Mr. William C. Codman, Jr., and Mr. Henry G. Hall, and since that period the concern has always enjoyed a constantly increasing trade. In 1884, Mr. Arthur E. Butt became a member of the firm, who occupy roomy, handsomely appointed premises and possess every requisite facility for the successful prosecution of their business. The firm make a specialty of handling only the purest and most reliable goods, and their trade now extends throughout all parts of the east and west. They sell directly to jobbers, to whom they are in a position to offer exceptionally advantageous terms. All the members of the firm are pushing, enterprising young business men, and, in addition to being direct importers, they sell largely on commission.

PARKINSON & BURR, Bankers and Brokers, No. 35 Congress Street.—The financial firms of Boston are justly recognized as being as staple and reliable as those of any city in the United States, among them being that of Messrs. Parkinson & Burr, whose offices are situated at No. 35 Congress Street. This business was established in 1862 by Frank Hodghinson & Co., who were succeeded in 1880 by Peters & Parkinson. Eventually, in 1885, the present firm was organized, the copartners being Messrs. John Parkinson and F. T. Burr, Jr. In January, 1888, Mr. J. M Goodale, who had been engaged with this house for the last twenty-three years, became a member of the firm. Messrs. Parkinson & Burr deal in all kinds of stocks, bonds and government securities, and also buy and sell stocks and bonds on commission. The firm's correspondents in New York are Messrs. H. L. Horton & Co. and Ed. Sweet & Co., and the offices are connected by private wire with New York. The partners are members of the Boston and New York Stock Exchanges.

B. LEWIS, Periodicals, Stationery and Fancy Goods, No. 250 Hanover Street.—The stationery, periodical and fancy goods trade has a wide-awake representative in this portion of the city of Boston in the person of Mr. B. Lewis, of No. 250 Hanover Street, who has been long identified with this line of trade. The business was started twenty-two years ago on the opposite side of the street, and in 1885 was removed to its present quarters. The founder of the enterprise was Mr. E. S. Bliss, in whose service as assistant Mr. Lewis was for nine years. On December 1st, 1887, the latter purchased the business, which has continued to grow and prosper under his management. The premises occupied comprise a salesroom and basement, each having an area of 2x50 feet. The salesroom is elegant and attractive in its fittings and appointments, and the stock carried is a carefully selected, varied and comprehensive one. It embraces every description of plain and fancy stationery, stationer's sundries in great variety, books of all kinds, all the leading periodicals and the principal daily and weekly newspapers, plush goods, albums, toys, the finest brands of cigars in the market, etc. In connection with the business is a largely patronized circulating library of over twelve hundred volumes, which are issued at two cents per volume per day, or ten cents per week. Newspapers and periodicals are promptly and regularly delivered at residences or places of business of patrons. The leading specialties of the house are stationery, periodicals and cigars, and the patronage is a substantial and influential one. Mr. Lewis is a young, energetic and courteous business man, very popular with his customers.

McGREENERY BROS., Fine Cigars, and Jobbers in all the Leading Brands of Tobacco, No. 214 Hanover Street.—There are almost as many opinions as there are smokers as to what constitutes the proper flavor of a cigar, but we have observed that those who insist upon having a superior article find that the goods handled by Messrs. McGreenery Bros., fill the bill every time. This firm founded their enterprise in 1880, and have from very meagre beginnings built up a business which in its magnitude is unexcelled by that of any rival house in this section of the city. The store occupied has a frontage of twenty feet and a depth of forty feet, and is very tastefully fitted up and admirably arranged. Messrs. McGreenery Bros., carry in stock a full line of the most noted and popular brands of cigars, among which will be found the genuine favorites, Spanish Girl, J. and J., and La Norma, cigars, and other leading brands. The stock also includes the best grades of smoking and chewing tobaccos, and smokers' supplies of every description. The prices are always reasonable, and the service to all patrons is courteous and prompt. The transactions of the house are of both a wholesale and retail character, and a brisk trade is done throughout the city and its vicinity. The members of the firm are Messrs. J. J. and J. F. McGreenery, both of whom are natives of Boston.

LAWRENCE & ROBINSON, Real Estate, No. 15 Congress Street.—The real estate interests of Boston have in recent years attained proportions of such magnitude that they unquestionably represent the most important factor in Boston's financial strength, and have enlisted in their service the highest order of talent, energy and enterprise in the business world. Prominent among the best connected and most active and enterprising of the houses thus referred to is that of Messrs. Lawrence & Robinson, whose office is centrally and conveniently located at No. 15 Congress Street. The business of this firm was founded originally in 1877 by Mr. B. B. Lawrence, who is a resident of Linden, Mass., and was born in St. Andrews, N. B., whence he came to Boston more than a score of years ago. He conducted the enterprise alone until September, 1888, when he formed a partnership with Mr. B. F. Robinson, who is a native and resident of Saugus. Both gentlemen are middle-aged and have had an extended experience in real estate matters. They can be relied upon to give sound and reliable advice to persons seeking profitable investments in real estate, and have always in hand many desirable bargains in city and country property. The firm conduct a general real estate business, buying, selling, leasing, exchanging and letting, and also collect rents, take the entire management of estates, and negotiate loans on bonds and mortgages. The firm give particular attention to the handling of property in Malden, Somerville, Linden and Saugus, and make a specialty of selling medium-priced houses on easy terms. They also build houses to order at short notice, and are justices of the peace.

AMOS HAYNES, Manufacturer of Superior White Wine and Cider Vinegar and Refined Cider, Offices: No. 42 South Market and No. 4 Chatham Streets.—Boston is the centre of very important industrial enterprises; there is hardly an article of general consumption which cannot be had of home production, and notably is this the case with vinegar, as manufactured of absolute purity and the highest quality by Mr. Amos Haynes with headquarters at No. 42 South Market and No. 4 Chatham Streets. Mr. Haynes was born in Charlestown, Mass., and early in life became identified with the branch of trade in which he has achieved such marked success. He established this business upwards of forty years ago, and early achieved for his product the reputation of being the best in market. His facilities were repeatedly taxed to the utmost, and to-day his factory at Somerville is the best equipped, and one of the most extensive in New England. Mr. Haynes there employs twenty hands, in the manufacture of white wine and cider vinegars and refined cider. The enormous consumption of his vinegars affords ample proof of their purity, and superiority in general to all other brands. He numbers among his permanent customers leading jobbers and grocers all over the city and New England, and is ever solicitous of their best interests delivering his superior quality of product at prices as low as can be had elsewhere. He is a respected member of commercial circles, and has ever extended a hearty support to all measures best calculated to advance the permanent welfare and prosperity of this, the second greatest centre of commerce in the United States.

BEIERMEISTER & SPICER, Manufacturers of the Celebrated Anchor Brand Linen Collars, Cuffs and Shirts, Boston Salesroom, No. 38 Bedford Street.—One of the largest houses in Troy engaged in the manufacture of linen collars, cuffs and fine shirts, is that of Beiermeister & Spicer, whose goods, bearing their trade-mark, the Anchor brand, have a wide reputation throughout the United States and are always in demand by the trade, and have become staple on the market. For the purpose of supplying the trade branch houses have been established in New York, Chicago and Boston. The house in this city is in charge of Mr. Henry Beiermeister, a young man of excellent business qualifications, who has had quite a lengthened experience in the business, and who has by his enterprise and perseverance established a large, substantial trade throughout New England. He occupies very desirable premises at No. 38 Bedford Street, and keeps in stock a large general assortment of all the goods manufactured by the firm, and can offer inducements it would be difficult to obtain elsewhere. The goods are all of the highest standard quality, and are among the best in the market.

WELLS MANUFACTURING COMPANY, Manufacturers of Brass and Wire Goods, No. 65 Sudbury Street.—The widely and favorably known Wells Manufacturing Company was founded about eighteen years ago by a man by the name of Wells, and who was succeeded by Mr. L. Durnham. About three and a half years ago, Mr. E. H. Harding became sole proprietor. He is a native of this state, and a mechanical expert of great practical experience, and of equal importance of great inventive genius. He has here, a large factory fully equipped with the latest improved machinery for the manufacture of a wide range of brass and wire goods, including many specialties in light machinist work. Mr. Harding is the inventor and patentee of the Magic needle-threader for sewing machines. The seamstresses and all who toil long at, or only briefly use sewing machines, labor under a heavy obligation to Mr. Harding in view of the direct practical utility of this most ingenious, and really wonderful invention. It is handy, simple, easily worked, and is having a large sale all over the United States. Every owner of a sewing machine should have one. It will repay the slight cost a thousand times over. Dealers in sewing machines and supplies should keep a full stock on hand. Mr. Harding devotes close personal supervision to his factory, and all goods produced by him are of best quality, and prove highly satisfactory to the trade.

JOHN MATTSON & CO., Real Estate and Insurance Brokers; Room No. 69, No 28 School Street.—One of the most active and enterprising young brokers in real estate and insurance to be met with in this city is Mr. John Mattson, whose well appointed office is located very desirably at No. 28 School Street. Mr. Mattson is a native of Sweden, but came to Boston in 1884, after being several years a resident of Great Britain, having resided previously for about six years in Norway. Though a young man he has had a large business experience and has traveled very extensively in Europe. His first experience in business life was as a clerk in a large shipping house in Arandal, Norway. During the greater part of his residence in Great Britain he was connected with one of the largest firms engaged in importing American produce. Attracted by the opportunities offered ambitious, enterprising young men in the states, he embarked for Boston in 1884 as

already stated. May, 1888, he opened his present office and added real estate brokerage to his enterprise. Mr. Mattson does a general brokerage business, buying, selling and exchanging on commission all forms of city and suburban property, negotiating and purchasing mortgages, etc., and being well posted as to property values, and possessing sound financial judgment, his services are valuable to and in great demand among capitalists and investors generally. He has also superior facilities for placing insurable risks in the soundest insurance companies at the most favorable rates and with every assurance of prompt and equitable adjustment of losses. Mr. Mattson, although a young man, has built up a large and influential clientèle and is fast attaining a position among the representative city business men in his line.

WATTS & WILLIS, Commission Merchants, Butter, Cheese, Eggs, Etc., Basement No. 2 Faneuil Hall Market.—Prominent in the staple branches of the wholesale produce trade, the house of Messrs. Watts & Willis has developed influential connections of the most desirable character, and is the oldest firm, as one without change in partnership, in the Faneuil Hall Market. The business was founded by the late Dexter Follett, in 1826, who was succeeded by the firm of Follett & Alexander. In 1886, Mr. J. C. Willis, who had been with the house as clerk and manager from 1868, formed with Mr. Alexander the firm of Alexander & Willis; in 1888 the copartnership was dissolved, and Mr. Isaac Watts and Mr. Willis then formed the copartnership which has since permanently continued to exist. The firm has developed an important trade of great magnitude, with influential connections both among producers, shippers and buyers. They occupy basement No. 2 in the market, and are daily receivers of butter from the finest creameries, choice dairy butter, prime cheese, fresh eggs, poultry, game in season, and other produce. The firm have the capacity and connections to handle the largest consignments, making advances on same, and rendering prompt account sales. They are also sole agents for New England for the Improved Dry Air Refrigerator. The large and rapidly growing sales to produce merchants, grocers, butchers, hotels, restaurants and families show conclusively that this make gives much the best satisfaction of any. The principles embodied are practical and simple. The law of the atmosphere, that cold air seeks the lowest levels, while warm air rises, has been followed in the Improved Dry Air Refrigerators, and a continuous circulation is formed, the cold air from the ice passing through and into the food compartment, rapidly refrigerating the food, as it becomes warmer it passes into a flue and rises again in the ice holder, depositing its moisture and impurities, and again circulates over the food. It is the only refrigerator provided with two distinct dead air spaces, and secures the utmost economy of ice. All those in need of a refrigerator should visit basement No. 2, and see the improved in full operation.

SAMUEL DUDLEY KELLEY, Architect, Offices: No. 209 Washington Street.—The architectural advancement during the past decade of American development is as remarkable for its notable beauty and elegance, as it is for extreme utility and stability. Here in New England the work of leading local architects is of a character to elicit the warmest commendation of the public, and the favorable opinions of experts. A leading member of the profession is Mr. Samuel Dudley Kelley, with headquarters in the Rogers Building, No. 209 Washington Street. Mr. Kelley is devoted to his profession, and has designed the plans for, and superintended the erection of a number of the finest and handsomest buildings in Boston. Establishing himself about fourteen years ago, he brought to bear the experience of many years' close study and practical application of the science and art of the skilled architect, and early evinced marked originality and great executive ability in dealing with the difficult and ever varying problems and requirements of the building enterprises contracted for. It is thus a matter for congratulation that Mr. Kelley should have been commissioned to design and erect such prominent and ornate additions to Boston's architecture as the Hoffman House, corner of Columbus Avenue and Berkley Street; The Hotel Royal, corner Beacon and Exeter Streets; South Boston Stables and Car House; Middlesex Railroad Stables, Bunker Hill; the Hotel Beacon Winter Harbor, Maine; the residence for J. R. Whipple, Esq., on Commonwealth Avenue, another mansion on Commonwealth Avenue for Warren Sherburne, Esq., and many of the finest and most attractive modern residences in the Back Bay district. Mr. Kelley makes the same careful study of the interior requirements as of the exteriors, his computations are accurate, his plans thoroughly homogeneous and practical and style of architecture pure and symmetrical. His aim is to secure to the owner the best results within the limits of estimates and his close adherence to specifications and careful supervisions of builders and contractors point him out as a sound, conservative business man, as well as an architect of the highest professional attainments.

ROBERT J. MELLEDGE, Mortgages, No. 72 Equitable Building.—Among those paying especial attention to this line of business is Mr. Robert J. Melledge. Mr. Melledge is a native of Cambridge, and although quite a young man, is thoroughly versed in all legal questionings governing real estate, and has had some years of experience in the care of real estate and kindred subjects, and has developed a desirable business connection throughout the city and suburbs, and he transacts a general business in negotiating loans on bonds and mortgages, and numbers among his regular clients some of our leading capitalists, investors and property owners, confining himself to investments of a conservative class. Having a thorough knowledge of the Equitable Mortgage Company, of Kansas City, Mo., and New York, he offers for sale the guarantee mortgages and debenture bonds of that company. The Equitable is the largest company doing business in western mortgages, having a capital of $250,000, and conducting its business in a highly conservative manner, is constantly growing in the confidence of capitalists and investors. Mr. Melledge devotes especial attention to this department, and is prepared to give reliable information at all times to those seeking an outlet for their capital, and conducts his business on the most conservative methods, striving to give satisfaction by close personal attention to all matters committed to his care. Mr. Melledge has especial familiarity with matters of real estate in Cambridge, where he resides.

T. C. POWER, American and Nova Scotia Employment Company, No. 9 School Street, Near Washington Street.—An unbroken record of prosperity, extending over a period of nearly thirty-nine years, marks the history of the admirably conducted and responsible American and Nova Scotia Employment Bureau, T. C. Power, manager and proprietor. This flourishing enterprise was established in 1859 by the gentleman whose name heads the sketch. The premises occupied are spacious, convenient and neatly arranged, while an efficient corps of clerks are in attendance, and all persons having business here are assured of courteous attention and satisfactory treatment, everything about the place bespeaking order and excellent management. The company has always on its books an extensive and varied line male and female help of all kinds, and clerks, salesmen, book keepers, porters, waiters, gardeners, teamsters, hostlers, coach men, farm hands, mill and factory operatives, domestic servants cooks, nurses, etc., and is prepared to furnish the very best class of help at short notice for stores, offices, hotels, restaurants, private families, boarding houses, builders, contractors, brick yards, mills, factories, farms, gentlemen's places, stables, railroads, warehouses, etc., the office hours being from 9 A. M. to 6 P. M. Mr. Power, who is a gentleman in the prime of life and a native of the state of Maine, is a man of entire probity in his dealings, as well as energy, enterprise and ample experience, and is also engaged in the real estate, auctioneering and loan brokerage business.

BOSTON DASH STITCHING WORKS, J. L. Taylor, Proprietor, No. 28 Sudbury Street.—The Boston Dash Stitching Works, J. L. Taylor, proprietor, is about the leading and most responsible establishment devoted to this particular branch of industrial activity in Boston. This thriving enterprise was originally started in 1882 by the Eliott Dash Stitch Company, who were succeeded about four years ago by the present proprietor, who has since conducted the business with uniform success. The shop, which is located on the third floor of No. 28 Sudbury Street, is ample and completely equipped, steam power and all necessary facilities being at hand, while several expert workmen are employed. Dashers, wings and fenders are here covered, stitched and finished in the highest style of the art, and in the most expeditious manner, for the carriage and sleigh trade, the best grades of dash leather being constantly kept on hand, while all work executed in this concern is warranted to render satisfaction, Mr. Taylor referring by permission to the following well known carriage manufacturers—Sargent & Ham, James Hall & Son, R. Tyner & Co., F. A. Scott & Son.

BRIGHAM & COMPANY, Engravers on Metal, No. 912 Summer Street.—Perhaps no business is more indispensable than that which pertains to designing, engraving and cutting letters on metals and die sinking and stencil cutting, and among those engaged in it there are none more capable of doing this kind of work than Brigham & Co., whose establishment is one of the oldest and most prominent in Boston. It was founded in 1850 by Mr. Joseph H. Merriam who carried it on until 1870, when the present firm became his successor. For many years the business was carried on at No. 31 Cornhill, and some time ago was removed to the premises now occupied, which have an area of 40x100 feet and are perfectly equipped with special machinery and tools. From ten to twelve practical workmen are employed and steam power is used to facilitate the work which embraces designing and engraving on all kinds of metals and letter cutting and die sinking and manufacturing seal and embossing presses and brass dies for embossing and printing, steel stamps, alphabets and figures, hand stamps and ribbon and dating stamps, rubber stamps and stencils for all purposes, burning brands brass gilding dies, machinery, carriage and name plates and badges and medals and checks and tags of every description. Mr. W. C. Brigham who has the general management of the business is an experienced engraver on metals. He is a native of Boston.

THE FLORENCE SHIRT COMPANY, No. 791 Washington Street.—The Florence Shirt Company which was recently established has achieved a wide reputation and under the efficient management of Mr. J. August and Mr. R. Lewis, a substantial trade is being built up. They are both experienced practical shirt cutters and manufacture a fine class of goods and have become celebrated for the admirable fit and excellence of the work turned out. Shirts are made to order at from $6 per half dozen and upwards and as they are cut upon scientific principles, satisfaction is always guaranteed. The store occupied is 20x50 feet in area and very handsomely fitted up, and contains a general variety of gentlemen's garniture including besides fine white and colored shirts, neckwear, collars, cuffs, hosiery, underwear, gloves, etc., of all kinds, in short, all goods which pertain to the perfect costume of a gentleman. In the store three clerks are employed and every attention is given to those who favor Messrs. August & Lewis with their patronage. They established business with a determination to succeed and by their energy and perseverance have just cause to be proud of the success which has attended their efforts. They are liberal and fair in their dealings and as shirt makers can please all who leave orders with them and guarantee a perfect article of this kind, conducting in no small degree to repose in life and exemption from profanity.

BENJ. L. HAWKES, Stationery, Periodicals, Etc., No. 234 Hanover Street.—Mr. Hawkes is deserving of prominent mention in these pages and has been in business here for the past seven years, and has built up a trade of considerable importance and of a substantial and influential character. His store has an area of 22x50 feet, and in its arrangement and tasteful furnishings presents quite an attractive appearance. Here is a splendid display of mercantile and fancy stationery, stationers' sundries of every description, a fine assortment of current literature, daily and weekly newspapers, all the leading periodicals and a splendid selection of fancy goods of a varied character. Special attention is given to the handling of Swedish and Norwegian newspapers and books, a full assortment of which can always be found on the counters and shelves. Books, papers and periodicals of all kinds are procured to order expeditiously and at the lowest rates and the service is at all times courteous and prompt to all classes of customers.

W. F. BOWLER, Driving and Working Horses, Nos. 106 and 108 Canal Street.—This gentleman has been established in business here since 1874, and deals extensively at private sale, in New York and Pennsylvania horses, making a specialty of handling those suitable for use in the fire department and other city business, as well as for general trucking and carting. His stable is spacious in size, accommodating forty horses. Special care is taken by Mr. Bowler to select such horses as will meet the demands of his patrons and all in want of a first-class, reliable animal. Truck, cart, engine and hose horses are kept constantly on hand, and his facilities for filling orders in these lines and for supplying first-class stock at low prices are rarely equalled and never excelled in this city. He is in frequent receipt of carloads of horses, of a quality and character for both driving and working, that commend them to the confidence and patronage of close and critical buyers. Square dealing and the widely known worth of the proprietor have always inspired the fullest confidence and established this home in the general esteem as a reliable representative.

THOMAS W. HOBDAY, Mechanical Draughtsman, Room No. 11, No. 82 Water Street.—For thoroughly first-class work in the line of drawings for working models, experimental machinery, trade marks, tracings, etc., none have made a better reputation than Thomas W. Hobday, mechanical draughtsman. He is one of the foremost exponents of the art in Boston, and has a fine patronage throughout the city, state and the whole of New England. Mr. Hobday, who is an expert and has had several years' practical and successful experience in this exercise of his art, of which he is a complete master. He is prepared to make drawings for working models, special machinery and mechanical devices of every description in the most reliable and excellent manner, at short notice, giving particular attention to patent drawings, trade marks, lithographs, tracings and blue prints, while cams are laid out, etc., in first-class style; working models and the construction of experimental machines being his leading specialty.

JOSEPH F. JONES & CO., Dealers in Oils of all kinds, and Cotton Waste, No. 38 Haverhill Street.—The well-known name of Messrs. Frank Jones & Co., has been continuously before the public for the past thirty-seven years, and which has a character in the oil trade second to that of no other establishment. The business was organized in 1851, by the late Mr. Joseph Jones, who died in May, 1888. His son, Mr. J. Frank Jones, was in partnership with him for twenty years, and since his death his son has been the sole proprietor of the business, which consists of the handling, at wholesale and retail, of all kinds of oils, including engine,

38 years at present location.
MACHINERY AND CYLINDER OILS.
Axle and Gear Grease, Cotton Waste.
WHOLESALE AND RETAIL.
38 HAVERHILL STREET.

Petroleum for horses feet, Bicycle Lamp Oil, Lantern Oil, fine **Sewing Machine Oil.**
Special attention to Farmers' wants.

machinery and cylinder oils, also lard, sperm, paraffine, and neatsfoot, and a full line of animal-vig petroleum and fish oils, cotton waste, etc. The premises occupied for the business, comprise a well stocked store. Every facility is possessed for the prompt fulfillment of orders, and a brisk and extensive trade is done through out the whole of the New England States. We would call special notice to the Artic Cylinder Oil, as a pure, economical and perfect valve lubricator. It contains no animal oil to gum the rings, no stearic acid to go through packing, no gums to give it an appearance of great body, no salted stock to occasion rust, and it is liquid at zero. Mr. Jones is a native of Massachusetts, and a pushing and energetic business man.

THE SEWING MACHINE SUPPLIES COMPANY, No. 105 Summer Street.—The trade of The Sewing Machine Supplies Company is large and active and extends not only throughout the whole of the United States, Canada and Mexico, but they also export to Central America, Europe and Australia. This flourishing company, of which Geo. H. Bleloch (manager of the National Needle Company, Springfield) is president, and C. S. Leitwieler treasurer and manager, was organized on October 1, 1880, at Springfield, Mass., where the business was conducted up to 1882, when it was moved to this city. They occupy here commodious and well-ordered quarters, and keep on hand always a large and first-class stock, which comprises everything comprehended in sewing machine supplies, and manufacturers' findings, the following being their leading specialities. Standard machine needles, wax thread needles, McKay needles, parts of all sewing machines, belting and oils, channel knives, channel grooves, Amazena skiving knives, sewing-machine oilers and screw drivers, while a fine lined shoe findings also is constantly carried; all orders being attended to in the most expeditious and reliable manner. Mr. Leitwieler, the efficient manager of the concern, is a young man of energy and ample experience, and, prior to the inception of this prosperous enterprise, had been for some years with the National Needle Company at Springfield.

E. S. HARRISON & CO., Proprietors of Dr. Harrison's Peristaltic Lozenges, Chalybeate Tonic, Etc., No. 18 Marshall Street.—This firm has a wide reputation as the sole proprietors of Dr. Harrison's Peristaltic Lozenges, Chalybeate Tonic, Iceland Balsam, Pile Ointment and Diarrhea Cure. The business was founded thirty years ago by Dr. John S. Harrison, under Tremont Temple. Dr. Harrison died in 1876, and his widow succeeded to the control of the business, continuing the same under the present firm name, with marked ability and steadily increasing success. Dr. Harrison's Peristaltic Lozenges are approved by the most eminent of the medical faculty, and recommended by the medical journals throughout the country, as a positive remedy for costiveness and dyspepsia. They are a tonic and laxative, and give great satisfaction in all troubles arising from costiveness—the most common cause of headache, dizziness, piles, etc. They are alterative, and very effective in jaundice, pain in the side, loins and limbs, and a multitude of symptoms the result of congestion of the liver. They are so agreeable to the taste, and convenient in form, that children eat them readily after rejecting the usual nauseous remedies. In these symptoms supposed to indicate the presence of worms, these lozenges are a proper remedy, and will soon produce a healthy action of the stomach and intestines. To mothers these lozenges are a great blessing, for besides being superior as a laxative to castor oil, rhubarb, senna and all nauseous drugs, children never refuse them as they are agreeable as confections. For worms, fever turns, foul stomach, etc., they are just what is needed, and no family should ever be without them. The Iceland Balsam is another valuable specialty of this house, and is highly esteemed as a cure for bronchitis or sore throat, whooping cough, asthma, and all inflammation of the mucous membrane. Harrison's Remedy for the Piles is an ointment, prepared by this firm, and has been so thoroughly tested in so many different cases as to warrant it to be a relief to all who will give it a fair trial. One application at night never fails to relieve the greatest pain and anguish, and it invariably proves itself to be the safest, surest, speediest and cheapest cure for the piles extant. Harrison's Diarrhea Cure is the result of many years of experience and study, and is wonderfully efficacious in the worst cases of diarrhea and dysentery, as well as cholera morbus and cholera infantum. Certificates of the most surprising character can be furnished. These remedies are in steadily increasing demand by first class druggists throughout New England, New York and the west. Orders are filled with promptness and care in all cases.

WM. M. McADAMS, Stationer and Blank Book Manufacturer, No. 42 Kilby Street—This enterprise was founded between thirty and forty years ago, by the present proprietor's father, the late Mr. James McAdams, who died in 1884. The latter was then succeeded by his son, who was born and reared in the business, and who is thoroughly familiar with its every detail. The premises, which are eligibly located at No. 42 Kilby Street, are commodious and thoroughly equipped in every department for the successful prosecution of the business. Mr. McAdams promptly attends to all classes of paper ruling and book binding, and he possesses facilities equal to those of any other house in the city for filling orders promptly, artistically and in a perfect manner. His material generally, as well as the different machines used in the business, is of the best quality. Blank books are manufactured and paged at short notice, and printing of every description is executed with neatness and dispatch. A full and complete assortment of plain and fancy stationery, and stationer's sundries is always kept on hand, and a speciality is made of copying books and presses. Mr. McAdams is an energetic young business man and a native of Newtonville, Mass. He is well qualified by experience to sustain the old reputation which this house has always maintained as a thoroughly representative concern. They also make a specialty of perforating, numbering, eyeletting, punching, and paging for the trade.

M. D. CRESSY & CO., Teamsters and Forwarders; Office, No. 167 South Market Street.—For promptness, reliability and general service, none in their line in this city maintain a higher reputation than M. D. Cressy & Co., teamsters and forwarders, one of the leading and most responsible firms engaged in this branch of the business in Boston. The firm was established in 1874, and from the inception of the enterprise has steadily grown in public favor and confidence. The firm have in regular service twenty-four reliable horses and twenty-two trucks and wagons, while twenty-five in help are employed, including experienced drivers, loaders, etc. Teaming and forwarding of every description are attended to in the most expeditious and excellent manner, the transferring of fruits, produce and market stuffs being the specialty, all orders receiving immediate attention, while the proprietors exercise close personal supervision over every feature and detail of the business, promptness being their motto. The firm consists of Messrs. M. D. Cressy and A. W. Preston, both comparatively young men and natives of Manchester, N. H., and Beverly, Mass., respectively.

SAMUEL WALKER & CO., Oils, Naphtha Fluid, Etc., No. 33 India Street.—This firm are extensive wholesale dealers in kerosene, paraffine, spindle, sperm, lard, native and lubricating oils; also naphtha fluid and Brilliant White Safety oil. The foundation of the business was laid in 1859 by Mr. Samuel Walker, who commenced that year the manufacture of oil from coal imported from Scotland. In 1867 he gave up manufacturing and devoted his time and attention to supplying the trade throughout New England with oils of every description. In 1870 Mr. I. P. Waitt was admitted to partnership, remaining in the firm until his death in February, 1888, since which date Mr. Walker has continued the business as sole proprietor. He naturally brings to bear the widest range of practical experience, and gives his close personal attention to the selection and purchase of all stock. His spacious warehouses, in the adjoining town of Somerville, are stocked to repletion at all times. The illuminating oils handled by this responsible house are among the very best ever offered to the trade they burn freely, are of fine color, thoroughly safe and reliable, and produce a clear, soft and brilliant light. The cylinder oils work splendidly on all steam cylinders, contain no need to corrode or grit to wear out the metal. Only the finest grades of refined oil are sold, and the prices quoted are invariably fair and equitable. Sales are made principally to retail grocers throughout New England. Mr. Walker is a native of Langdon, N. H., a prominent citizen of Watertown, Mass., and known and honored in this city and throughout New England as a reliable leader of his branch of enterprise.

CHARLES T. A. BENT, (Manufacturers' Agent,) Boots and Shoes, No. 23 South Street.—Mr. Bent is a native Bostonian and although young in years has had a very large experience in the handling of boots and shoes, which, with his natural abilities have given him a very enviable reputation in the trade. He established himself in business on his own account in 1883, and since that time has built up a patronage which is extent is seldom accorded to houses much longer in the same business. The premises utilized are eligibly located and comprise a very neatly and appropriately fitted up office and sample room. In the latter will be found a full and complete assortment of samples from nearly all of the principal boot and shoe manufacturing houses in this portion of the United States, and which are offered to customers at manufacturers' prices at the factory, at which places all orders are filled and shipped direct to dealers. The products handled by Mr. Bent require no laudatory comment at our hands, as they are made by the most prominent and reliable houses in the country, while all goods sold are guaranteed to be as represented. The trade is very large and steadily increasing throughout the New England States.

A. W. PAINE, Tailor, No. 493 Washington Street (Room 2).—For the past fifteen years, Mr. A. W. Paine has been engaged in business for himself as a merchant tailor, and his thorough practical knowledge and long experience have been prime factors in securing for him his present success. Mr. Paine has occupied his present premises since 1872, and has fitted up his show room and custom work department, with everything needed to facilitate his labors in this branch of business. He caters to the best trade in the city, and makes a specialty of repairing, altering, cleaning and pressing gentlemen's clothing, in the most satisfactory and efficient manner, while the garments manufactured by him for men's wear, on all occasions are warranted to be perfect in fit, comfortable, stylish and reliable in quality, and thoroughness of workmanship. A fine line of the latest novelties imported and domestic cloths, cassimeres and vestings is advantageously displayed. Mr. Paine is a native of Barnstable, and a man of most excellent rating in the community.

JAMES H. CLEAVES (Successor to Joshua Cleaves), Weigher and Gauger, No. 31 India Street.—In a great centre of trade and commerce like this city, the official weigher and gauger fills an exceedingly useful and important function. Among those engaged in this line in Boston there is perhaps not one who is better known, than Mr. Cleaves. He is a comparatively young man, and a native of Salem, is a thoroughly competent weigher and gauger, of ample experience and has a complete knowledge of every feature and detail appertaining thereto. He has been established on his own account since January, 1888, when he succeeded his brother Joshua Cleaves, who in 1880 had succeeded his father Nathaniel Cleaves, who had been in business in the same line since 1843. Mr. Cleaves occupies ample quarters, and employs an efficient force of assistants, while all necessary appliances and facilities are in service. Hides, cotton, wool, iron, metals, cereals, etc., are accurately and reliably weighed, while oils, spirits, liquors and liquid products of all kinds are correctly and promptly gauged, and all business entrusted to this gentleman is certain to be attended to in the most expeditious and satisfactory manner.

SIMON SCHMIDT, Tortoise Shell Comb, Eye Glass and Jewelry Manufacturer, No. 274 Washington street.—For nearly forty years the establishment conducted by Simon Schmidt, tortoise shell, eye-glass and jewelry manufacturer, has been in prosperous existence. It is one of the oldest concerns devoted to this branch of industrial activity in the city. The business was started in 1846 by A. K. Joslyn, who conducted the same up to 1874, when owing to his death, which occurred at this period, the present proprietor, who had formerly worked in the concern for twenty years, assumed control. Mr. Schmidt occupies ample and well-equipped quarters, which are supplied with steam power and all necessary facilities, while a competent assistant is employed, also. The productions include everything in the line of tortoise shell ornaments, eye-glasses and jewelry specialties, while combs, jewelry and kindred articles are repaired, likewise, in the very best style of the art, at reasonable rates. Mr. Schmidt was born in Germany, and has been in this country for thirty-five years, and is a practical and expert workman of long and varied experience.

BURRILL & DUTTON, (Successors to Berney & Burrill,) Dealers in and Repairers of all Kinds of Saws, Corner Beverly and Travers Streets.—The enterprise in which Messrs. Burrill & Dutton is engaged is one of the most important of its kind in the city, and is also one of the oldest, and was originated in 1848 by William Berney, and subsequently carried on by Henry Kruger, and afterwards by Berney & Burrill, whom the present firm succeeded four years ago. The scope of operations embraces dealing in all kinds of saws, of which a full and varied assortment is kept in stock, and also repairing saws and gumming and trueing circular saws, and grinding edge tools. Five practical workmen are employed and premises of ample dimensions are occupied. Steam power is used and the workshop is replete with all the necessary requisites. An extensive business is carried on, orders being received from all parts of New England. Mr. John Burrill and Mr. George E. Dutton, the copartners, are both practical and experienced business men. Mr. Burrill is a Bostonian by birth, and Mr. Dutton was born in Newburyport.

O. NICHOLS & CO., Manufacturers of Patent Resilene Meeling, Factory, Nos. 154 and 156 Federal street.—The firm of O. Nichols & Co., is known all over the United States as manufacturers of Patent Resilene Meeling. They have been established in the business since 1869 and have occupied their present large factory since 1884. This building, which is five stories, 30x50 feet in dimensions, is furnished throughout with the best machinery and facilities, the former being driven by an engine with a capacity of twenty-five horse power. The patent Resilene paste manufactured by the firm is an admirable paste for shoe manufacturers, while Nichol's Resilene paste is peculiarly adapted for paper hangers, paper box manufacturers, etc., and is warranted stronger, more adhesive and to dry in less time than any other paste.

GEO. V. DeLUE & CO., Carpenters and Builders, No. 32 Tyler Street. Near Kneeland.—Among the prosperous industrial enterprises which line this busy trade avenue will be found that of Messrs. Geo. V. DeLue & Co., carpenters and builders. The premises are commodious and well arranged and the general appointment embraces all requisite facilities for the advantageous prosecution of the business. Everything pertaining to this branch of skilled industry is executed in the best manner and some of the finest work to be met with in this vicinity bears evidence of the superior handicraft of the firm. Mr. DeLue, the proprietor of the enterprise is a practical and skillful exponent of the carpenters' trade, and has had a wide experience in the business.

THE METROPOLIS OF NEW ENGLAND. 247

CHAS. W. ORNE, Butchers' Scales, Saws, Etc., No. 32 Faneuil Hall Square.—Some thirty-three years ago this thriving business was established by Mr. F. S. Orne, who conducted the same up to 1874, when it passed into control of his son and successor, the gentleman whose name heads this sketch. Mr. Orne, who is a native of this city, and a young man of push and industry, as well as practical skill and experience, occupies commodious and well equipped quarters as store and shops, and has in service complete and excellent facilities, including electric motor, while two expert assistants are employed, special attention being given to repairing and sharpening butchers' fixtures and tools. A large and first-class stock is always kept on hand, including butchers' scales, saws, knives, steels, boning chisels, axes, cleavers, scrapers, hooks, steelyards, money drawers, hammers, whetstones, shears, shovels, grass hooks, hack, hand and wood saws, while lawn mowers are sharpened, razors honed and concaved, and scales, saws, tools, etc., repaired in the most expeditious and excellent manner, at very reasonable rates.

H. C. TOWER, Commission Merchant and Dealer in Flour, Produce and Tea, No. 66 Commercial Street.—This establishment was organized in 1886 under the firm style of Tower & Joy, and this was the title of the concern until 1889, when the firm was dissolved and after about two years Mr. Tower became the sole representative of the business of the old firm. The premises occupied are desirably located at No. 66 Commercial Street, and comprise one floor, having an area of 25x75 feet, and provided with every convenience and facility for the transaction of business. A very large and comprehensive stock is carried. The house deals in all grades and qualities of flour, from the cheapest kinds to the best patented new processes, the finest grades of Vermont dairy butter, country produce of every description, ground and prepared cereals of all kinds, etc., and these are disposed of to jobbers and retailers in the city and surrounding country. The trade is extensive and among the best class of buyers. All orders are filled and shipped with promptness and regularity, a fact well appreciated by Mr. Tower's numerous customers.

GEO. H. DUNNING, Beef, Pork, Lard, Hams, Pigs' Feet, Tripe, Sausages, Smoked Beef, Etc., Nos. 23 and 25 Faneuil Hall Market.—One of the most prominent among the merchants in the provision trade in Faneuil Hall market is Mr. George H. Dunning, who has been identified with it for some years. The business he is now so successfully carrying on was established about thirty-five years ago by S. N. Learned and afterwards continued by Learned & Dunning, the latter gentleman being the father of the present proprietor, who succeeded to it in 1886. Two assistants are employed and a business of considerable magnitude transacted in beef, pork, lard, hams, pigs' feet, tripe, sausage, smoked beef and provisions, a specialty being made of the Yorkshire pork product. Mr. Dunning is a native Bostonian. His trade is principally in this city and vicinity, and his operations are extensive and widespread.

W. J. SCHOFIELD, Book and Job Printer, No. 105 Summer Street.—Mr. W. J. Schofield has been identified with the book and job printing trade from his youth up. In 1859 he ventured into business on his own account and opened an establishment on Summer Street that in the great fire of 1872 was reduced to ashes. In the January following the big fire he resumed business at his old place and finally located at No. 105 Summer Street, and from the start has maintained an excellent reputation for not only being a thorough master in the craft, but for turning out work of a higher order of perfection. His office has a capacity of 75x45 feet, and is equipped with a complete assortment of type—modern, antique, plain and fancy—new and improved machinery, and everything necessary for successfully carrying on the printing business. Anything in the shape of printing, from a card to a book, can be procured here in a short space of time, executed in the most artistic manner, and at reasonable charges. A specialty is made of commercial work—the printing of cards, note and letter headings, memoranda forms, bill heads, catalogues, circulars, handbills, checks, delivery notes, etc. An efficient staff of operatives is in service, and the patronage is drawn from the leading mercantile houses in the city. Under its proprietor's able management this house has taken a most creditable position in the trade. Mr. Schofield is a Bostonian by birth.

MISS A. M. GENDRON, Photographer, No. 15 Tremont Row.—Among the foremost exponents of the photographic art in this city may be mentioned the name of Miss A. M. Gendron, the talented artist, who has won an enduring reputation for skill and ability in her profession—few better in Boston; the cabinet photos, at $2.00 and $2.50 per dozen made in this studio, being pictures of exceptional merit. Miss Gendron, who is a young lady of energy and excellent business qualifications, as well as a thoroughly practical and expert photographer, has been established something over two years, and from the first she has received a very flattering share of recognition. The premises occupied, including reception parlor, studio, operating room, etc., are neatly appointed and completely equipped in every respect, all the latest improved appliances, apparatus and general appurtenances being in service, while five competent assistants are in regular attendance also. Photography in all its branches is executed in the highest style of the art, at extremely moderate prices; fine portraits being a leading specialty, while crayon, pastel, India ink and kindred artistic work is attended to likewise in the most prompt and excellent manner; the pictures leaving this establishment being first-class in every feature of merit—in beauty of design, execution, fidelity and finish.

J. MURRAY HOWE, Real Estate Agent and Broker, No. 5 Court Street.—In the line of real estate, one of the most successful men in the city is Mr. J. Murray Howe, whose handsome offices are at No. 5 Court Street, corner of Washington Street. This business was established by Mr. Howe in 1879, and has been conducted with the greatest ability and energy from the start. Mr. Howe handles all kinds of real estate in town and country, buying, selling and exchanging, procures loans on bond and mortgage, manages estates, and is a general real estate agent and broker. He makes a specialty of Cambridge property, with which he is intimately acquainted, and has been one of the largest dealers in realty in that flourishing suburb. He also deals very largely in seashore lands, especially those on the Maine coast, which offer beautiful building sites for summer homes. Mr. Howe's judgment in regard to the value of Boston property is appreciated by a large number of owners and speculators in the city, who consult him on every important transaction they undertake. He is a native of Brookline, lives at Milton, and is highly esteemed by all with whom he has come in contact.

S. T. SHARP, Custom House, Foreign Exchange and Insurance Broker, No. 41 Kilby Street.—For many years S. T. Sharp, the well-known custom-house, foreign exchange and insurance broker, has been actively engaged in this line of business. Mr. Sharp, prior to starting in business on his own account had been employed in a responsible position in the banking house of Kidder, Peabody & Co., for about twelve years. Mr. Sharp attends to everything comprehended in custom house broking, and has a complete knowledge of every feature and detail connected therewith, merchandise being pushed through and forwarded to destination with despatch. He also negotiates foreign exchange, while insurance is placed with first-class companies at the lowest rates, and all business entrusted to this gentleman is certain to be attended to in the most prompt and satisfactory manner.

W. F. PAUL, Foreign and Domestic Paper Stock, No. 18 Post Office Square, Room A.—Mr. W. F. Paul, wholesale commission dealer in foreign and domestic paper stock, has, for a period of twenty years, conducted business in this line with uniform success. Mr. Paul, who is an old and respected Boston merchant, is a man in the prime of life, active and energetic, with some twenty odd years experience in this line. He handles everything in the line of foreign and domestic paper stock, but chiefly rags, while he makes a specialty of new cuttings, which he sells to the mills throughout New England; and is prepared to fill all orders for anything in the paper stock line in the most prompt and reliable manner.

GEO. F. STRATTON, Western Mouldings, No. 78 Portland street.—Western manufacturers of mouldings have an active and vigilant representative in Boston and New England in the person of Mr. George F. Stratton of this city. He is the New England agent for the following firms: Leonard Laurence & Co., Detroit, Mich., prepared mouldings and backing; the Adley Manufacturing Company, Chicago, Ill., plain and ornamented hardwoods and California walnut; the Adam J. Press Manufacturing Company, Chicago, Ill. comp. gold and bronze mouldings; C. O. Baxter & Co., St. Louis, Mo., plain and ornamented room mouldings. Mr. Stratton was formerly for eight years in the service of Messrs. Leonard Laurence & Co., and in February, 1888, established his present agency, which has been attended by the most satisfactory and encouraging results. He keeps in stock a full line of samples from the above well-known manufacturers. Combined they form the most extensive and complete line ever shown in the city of Boston, and include ornamented hardwood mouldings, plain and antique oak mouldings, cherry and mahogany mouldings, composition gold mouldings, electro bronze mouldings, imitation ebony and gilt mouldings, California walnut mouldings, imitation oak and cherry mouldings, imitation rosewood and walnut mouldings, imitation hardwood mouldings, velvet and plush linings, composition gold and bronze linings bronze and gilt back mouldings, plain and stencilled linings, plain silver and patent gilt mouldings, mouldings for home decoration, plain and bamboo beads, panel, angle and bean mouldings; birch bark, bamboo and palm mouldings; chair-rails and cornice mouldings, hardwood room mouldings, ornamented and plain gilt mouldings, antique bronze mouldings, bamboo and palm pattern mouldings, burnished copper mouldings, plain mouldings and linings in the white, ornamented linings in the white, car beads and mouldings in the white, hardwood mouldings in the white, finished car and casket mouldings, Leonard Laurence & Co.'s soft and seasoned Michigan pine backing, L. L. & Co.'s patent looking-glass backs, L. L. & Co.'s cut-out backing for shippers' use. He travels throughout all sections of the New England States, and orders are shipped direct from the mills promptly. The trade is exclusively of a wholesale character. Mr. Stratton was born in England, and has resided in the United States for the past fourteen years.

BASTEY & SUTHERLAND, Manufacturers of and Dealers in Harnesses, Saddles, Russet Reins, and Horse Clothing, Etc., No. 103 Portland Street.—This popular and prosperous firm was established something over one year ago, and were formerly located at No. 254 State Street, whence they moved to the present commodious quarters a few months since. They occupy here a compact store and shop, employing two experienced hands, and keep constantly in stock a full and fine assortment of light and heavy harnesses, saddles, bridles, collars, russet reins, horse boots, leather specialties, blankets, robes, whips, carriage washers, sponges, combs and kindred articles. Harnesses and saddles are made to order likewise in the most expeditious and excellent manner, fine custom work being a specialty, while repairing is neatly and promptly executed also, and all work done by the reliable firm is fully warranted to render satisfaction. Messrs. J. A. Bastey and W. A. Sutherland, who are both Nova Scotians by birth, but several years in Boston, are practical and expert harness makers, of ample experience, and are thorough masters of their art in all its branches.

J. P. HAWES, Broker in Fertilizers, No. 54 Kilby Street.—Among those contributing most largely to the sum of commercial activity in this line in Boston, may be mentioned the name of J. P. Hawes, the well-known broker in fertilizers, whose business connection extends all over the Atlantic Coast and throughout the British Provinces, with some export also to Europe. Mr. Hawes, who is a native of this city, is a gentleman of thorough experience in this line, and prior to starting in business on his own account, twelve years ago, had been a member of the firm of A. F. Turner, Jr., & Co. Mr. Hawes does a general brokerage in fertilizer stock, buying for and selling to manufacturers on commission, and is prepared to fill all orders for anything in this line in the most prompt and reliable manner; while his trade, which is large and active, affords evidence of steady increase.

J. M. RUSSELL, Publisher of Sheet Music and Russell's Musical Library, No. 40 Hamilton Place.—One of the most popular among the many attractive business houses in this city, is that of Mr. J. M. Russell, publisher of sheet music and Russell's Musical Library, which is at No. 40 Hamilton Place. Mr. Russell has been engaged in this line of business over thirty-five years, and previous to locating in this city in 1853, carried on quite an extensive establishment in New York. The business he is now conducting, was founded by Gilmore & Russell on Court street, and afterwards continued by J. M. Russell & Co., for many years at No. 126 Tremont Street. About six years ago it came under the sole control of Mr. Russell, who has since carried it on with marked success and ability, and in 1887 removed to the very commodious, desirable premises now occupied, which have an area of 25x60 feet. Mr. Russell makes a fine display of music, and publishes and has on sale all the new sheet music and instruction books, and musical merchandise generally, and also plain and ornamented picture frames of every description. He is one of the leading representatives in this line in the city, and controls besides a first-class city custom, a large influential business throughout the New England, United States and Canada, where Russell's Musical Library has an immense sale. Born and brought up in Vermont, Mr. Russell is held in high regard, and is very popular as a music dealer and publisher, and as a useful, influential citizen. Three clerks assist him in his business operations.

E. ALLEN & CO., Woolens, No. 34 Harrison Avenue Extension.—The business of this house is now being managed by the third generation of the Allen family. It was originally founded in 1828 by Mr. E. Allen, and after his death it was conducted by his sons, and since 1884 his grandsons, Messrs. F. P. and W. E. Allen, who were born and reared in the business, have been the proprietors. Throughout its long career this house has been distinguished as a leader in its line of trade. The firm occupy one of the finest business establishments on the avenue, their salesroom having an area of 40x150 feet. It is handsomely fitted up and admirably lighted, while for variety, freshness and completeness of assortment, the stock of woolens here displayed has few equals, and no superiors, in America. The firm make a prominent specialty of importing the finest lines of foreign goods and handle the out-put of many of our leading domestic manufacturers, and do a trade which literally extends throughout the entire United States. A staff of experienced travelers is kept on the road, while a large force of clerks, salesmen, packers, etc., is employed on the premises. The proprietors have vast practical experience at their command, and a perfect knowledge of the wants of the trade in its every detail. The firm are noted for their honorable business methods and enterprise, and enjoy a wide-spread popularity.

F. P. JEWETT, Coffee Broker, No. 21½ Central Street.—Viewed from a commercial standpoint, there are but few among the great staple food products entering into general consumption of greater importance than coffee. The transactions in the raw bean in the course of a year in this city represents many millions of dollars, while the volume of business grows apace annually. The traffic in this article of commerce on the Boston Market through the medium of the broker is of very extensive proportions; and among those contributing most largely to the sum of activity in this line here can be named F. P. Jewett, the popular and responsible coffee broker of No. 21½ Central Street. None engaged in the business in Boston sustains a higher reputation in the trade, and few enjoy a larger measure of recognition; having an active and substantial business connection with wholesale dealers and jobbers to whom he sells for importers. This well and favorably known house was established in 1865 by D. E. Jewett, (deceased,) who conducted the same up to 1885, when owing to his death which occurred at this period, the business passed into the control of his son and successor, the gentleman whose name heads the sketch, and under whose judicious management it has since been continued with uninterrupted success. Mr. F. P. Jewett, is a gentleman of strict probity in his business relations, as well as a young man of energy, sagacity and thorough experience in the coffee trade, and maintains an A1 standing in commercial life.

THE METROPOLIS OF NEW ENGLAND.

J. NARDI & CO., Manufacturers of Moorish and Nubian Figures, No. 145 Charlestown Street.—It is a matter of interest to trace the careers of many of the leading Italian citizens of Boston. Mr. Nardi is a native of sunny Italy, and in 1873, came to the United States to try his fortune and better his condition, which he has succeeded in doing. He first established himself in business in New York city, and in 1856 removed to Boston and began the manufacture of Moorish and Nubian figures at No. 68 Leverett Street. In May, 1888, he removed therefrom to his present location, where he occupies a four story building, 20x40 feet in dimensions. This is equipped with all necessary mechanical appliances for the successful carrying on of the business, and em-

ployment is afforded to from six to ten hands in making all kinds of small clay statues, and particularly Moorish and Nubian figures, decorated in the most artistic colors. Having every facility for economical production, and in service the most talented and experienced artists, the firm are not only able to compete successfully in point of quality with imported goods of this class, but to offer their manufactures at less than half the prices paid for foreign made figures. A large assortment of subjects is kept constantly in stock, and the trade, which is of a wholesale character, extends to all parts of the United States and Canada. The firm are to be complimented upon the success achieved.

TARBOX & CLARKE, Wholesale and Retail Dealers in Flour, Grain and Hay, Nos. 66 and 68 Commercial Street.—In 1885 Mr. George W. Tarbox, who is a native of Newburyport Mass., formed a partnership with Mr. Greenleaf Clarke a native and resident of Atkinson, N. H., and the enterprise has resulted in a greater expansion of trade, for which the firm have excellent facilities and business relations of a most advantageous character. They are members of the Chamber of Commerce, and occupy for the purposes of their business three floors, each possessing a capacity of 25x75 feet. A very heavy stock of grain and hay is carried, and in these commodities the sales are of a jobbing character, a specialty being made of car-load lots. Their distributing trade extends to all parts of New England, and they are in a position to offer to dealers goods and prices that cannot be surpassed, if equaled, in this market.

JOHN HOLMAN & CO., Bedding and Bed Lounges, Etc., No. 188 Hanover Street, corner Cross Street.—One of the most reliable and extensive manufacturing establishments of the kind in Boston, is that of Messrs. John Holman & Co., manufacturers of spring mattresses, bedding, etc., whose office, factory and salesroom are located on Hanover Street. This business was established in 1859 by John Holman, who eventually admitted his sons Mr. John C. Holman in 1878, and Mr. W. A. Holman in 1881. In 1885 Mr. John C. Holman retired and in 1886 Mr. John Holman the founder died after a long, honorable and successful career. He was succeeded by the present firm, the copartners being Messrs. W. A. Holman and E. D. Lacount. The premises occupied are spacious and well equipped and comprise the basement of three adjoining buildings, and the four upper floors. The firm in the various departments of their business employ fifty skilled operatives. They manufacture all kinds of bedding, bed lounges, fine hair mattresses, upholstered spring beds, etc. They also keep on stock feathers, curled hair, tickings, burlaps, extra purified feathers and patent down pillows. At their mill in Reading, Mass., they make all their bed lounge frames, etc. All the goods turned out by this responsible house are unrivalled for quality, utility, reliability and excellence, and have no superiors in this city or elsewhere, while the prices quoted in all cases for all kinds of bedding are extremely moderate. The salesrooms are always filled with a heavy stock of choice goods, and all orders are promptly filled, while all bedding, mattresses, etc., are fully warranted to be exactly as represented. Mr. Holman is a native of Cambridge, Mass., while Mr. Lacount was born in Spencer, Mass. The partners are highly respected in commercial circles, attend personally to the direction of their affairs, and are widely known for their honorable and liberal business policy.

L. W. PICKENS, Proprietor of the West Boston Planing and Moulding Mill, Etc., No. 99 Beverly Street.—The enterprise so successfully conducted by Mr. L. W. Pickens, as proprietor of the West Boston Planing and Moulding Mill, was originally established in 1864, at the corner of Causeway and Merrimac Streets, and was removed to the present site in 1887. The premises here occupied comprise four floors, 22x60 feet each, thoroughly equipped with the latest improved wood working machinery, operated by steam power, and steady employment is provided for a large force of skilled and experienced workmen. The principal business to which attention is devoted is the manufacture of every description of mouldings used by builders, together with window frames, and a valuable line of inside and outside ornamental finish, suited to the requirements of the trade and the public, and which, by reason of its superior excellence in both material and workmanship, is in heavy and influential demand in this city and throughout all the surrounding country. The facilities here possessed for the prompt execution of orders and commissions are of the most complete and perfect character; the lumber is received direct from the forests and first hands, and prices are placed at the lowest point of moderation. Success which is well deserved has crowned the efforts of the proprietor in catering to the demands of his patrons in this direction of trade. Mr. Pickens is a native of Middleboro, Mass., a resident of Somerville, and eminently popular in this city as an accomplished, reliable and substantial business man.

A. G. HADLEY, Stair Builder, No. 21 Beverly Street.—Stair building has now become a separate and distinct branch of industry, and one of the oldest and most prominent leaders in this line is Mr. A. G. Hadley whose establishment is located at No. 21 Beverly Street. This gentleman has been in business in this line for upwards of thirty years, and is widely known among builders and architects as an expert. He occupies a commodious, well-equipped workshop, and has in service constantly an adequate force of experienced workmen. Specimens of his work are to be found in the houses on Fifth Avenue, New York; the Fifth Avenue Hotel, in that city; Parker House, Boston, Tremont Temple, Boston, etc. The patronage is large and influential, and Mr. Hadley is prompt and reliable in the carrying out of all contracts. He is a native of Boston and a resident of Arlington, and a popular business man well liked by all who come in contact with him.

RUGGLES & BUSS, Commission Merchants in Grain and Mill stuffs, No. 16 Broad Street.—Although established in business as a co-partnership but a comparatively short time, Messrs. Ruggles & Buss, the well-known commission merchants and shippers' agents for the sale of grain and mill-stuffs, No. 16 Broad Street, have long been engaged separately in this branch of commercial activity, and are well and favorably known to the trade. F. H. Ruggles and H. L. Buss, who compose the firm, are both gentlemen of ample experience and thorough responsibility, as well as men of energy and sagacity, and are prominent members of the Chamber of Commerce. After conducting business, each on his own account, for over ten years, they consolidated in 1888, and the unequalled success that has attended their joint efforts from the first abundantly attests the wisdom that inspired the venture. The firm carry on a general commission business in corn, wheat, oats, barley, rye meal, mill-feed, etc., selling on the Boston market in car-load lots exclusively; and are agents for W. P. Harvey & Co., Chicago; Harper & Co., Peoria, Ill.; F. H. Pavey, Minneapolis, Minn.; H. F. Shaffer, Dayton, Ohio, and Durant, Elmore & Bliss, of Albany, N. Y. The transactions of this popular and responsible firm are conducted on strict business principles, and all orders placed with these gentlemen are certain to be attended to in the most expeditious and satisfactory manner; while the trade of the concern, which is very active, gives evidence of steady and substantial increase.

ALEXANDER McDONALD, Manufacturer of Trunks, Bags, Etc., No. 11 School Street.—For more than thirty-six years the productions of Alexander McDonald, the well known trunk and traveling bag manufacturer, of No. 11 School Street, have been noted for their excellence. The goods turned out by this gentleman are of a very superior character, being neat in design, strong in construction, reliable, and of first-class workmanship and material; and for general excellence are not surpassed by any articles of the kind produced to-day in Boston. Mr. McDonald was born in Montreal, but has been in this city upward of forty years; being one of the oldest (in point of priority) in his line in Boston. He is a practical and expert workman himself, of long and varied experience, in the exercise of his art having been established in business since 1852, and from this period to the present day he has enjoyed a highly flattering patronage, his trade coming principally from the wealthy residents of the Back Bay district. He occupies a neat good foot store, with factory on third floor, and employs several skilled workmen; only fine goods being manufactured. The productions include sole-leather trunks, overland trunks, light French trunks, continental trunks, ladies' trunks, gentlemen's trunks, theatrical trunks, and trunks of every size, shape, style and variety; also the Gladstone, Harvard and Oxford bags, portmanteaus, valises, satchels and leather specialties, while repairing is neatly and promptly executed also, at reasonable rates; all work done here being warranted to render satisfaction.

JOHN J. RINK, Blacksmith and Wheelwright, Nos. 65 and 65 Beverly Street.—Among those prominently identified with the trade of the blacksmith and wheelwright, we desire to call attention to Mr. John J. Rink, who has been established in this business since 1878, and for four years was a member of the firm of Rink & Sawyer, whom he succeeded and has continued to conduct it and has achieved a high reputation for the standard character of the work he turns out. He manufactures all kinds of light and heavy wagons which are thoroughly constructed and finely finished and are fully equal in every respect to the best made in the city. Blacksmithing in all its branches and making to order carriage and wagon iron and wood work and repairing receives Mr. Rink's attention, and all his work is fully guaranteed. He is well-known in this community as an expert blacksmith and wheelwright and builder of wagons, and is doing a first-class substantial business. He employs five skilled, practical workmen and occupies commodious premises consisting of a blacksmith shop 20x70 feet in area, and a wheelwright shop adjoining, 20x35 feet in size, which are well equipped in every respect and replete with all appliances for rendering the work executed of an enduring character. Mr. Rink is a native of Germany, but for many years has resided in this country and is well known in his line in Boston.

WM. A. SMITH, Importer of Diamonds, No. 283 Washington Street.—This gentleman is a connoisseur and expert of wide celebrity, and is recognized by the trade as one of the finest judges of diamonds in America. He is a native of Cambridge, Mass., identified with this special branch of trade since 1853, and established his present enterprise here in 1861. In gems and stones of worth, in which this house may be said to be second to none in the Western Hemisphere, the display made is one of the largest and choicest on this side of the Atlantic. Diamond and emerald, ruby and beryl, opal and pearl, sard and peridot, jacinth and spinel, topaz and turquoise—all these and more "captain jewels in the carcanet" are fittingly represented. Here are diamonds in all conceivable shapes, of unequalled whiteness and clearness, and of absolute faultlessness, gems of purest ray serene—rivière solitaire, cluster and pendant, panache and aigrette, necklace and bracelet, chains, earrings and chatelaines; in fact, every article for personal adornment meets the eye and delights the sight. With the assistance of a number of highly skilled artisans, diamond jewelry is here produced to order of a character unsurpassed by the best houses in Paris or London; while loose stones are purchased and set in the best manner, after the most approved fashion, and in original designs. Many matched stones of rare beauty are here exhibited, which cannot be readily duplicated. Of one thing Mr. Smith justly boasts, and that is of the fact that none but genuine articles are kept at his establishment. The goods of this representative house go to all parts of the country, and its trade is especially heavy and valuable throughout New England. Mr. Smith enjoys a national reputation as a leader in the trade.

CURTIS CLARK, Fire, Marine and Accident Insurance, No. 85 Water Street.—The very best channel through which to effect fire insurance in this city is that afforded by Mr. Curtis Clark, as he represents some of the strongest and wealthiest companies in the world, quotes reasonable rates of premium, and guarantees the prompt and liberal adjustment of all losses. Without reflecting in any way upon other offices, it is but just to say that Mr. Clark has secured a leading position in his line, and now, after being in business for twenty-eight years, enjoys the respect and esteem of all classes of property-holders, and a connection and patronage of the most influential character. He is an agent and broker for fire, marine and accident insurance. Mr. Clark places his risks with the best class of companies at the minimum rates. His forms for policies are clearly worded, explicit, and devoid of technicalities. He gives personal attention to all losses sustained by his customers, which are honorably adjusted and promptly paid. He controls the insuring of important lines of business, residential and manufacturing property, stocks of merchandise, leases, rents, and household effects, and is steadily extending his circle of customers in the city and country. He is a recognized authority in his line, and has a thorough knowledge of every department of the business, rendering him eminently safe as an agent or broker while he is a prominent member of the Boston Underwriters' Association. Mr. Clark was born in Jefferson County, N. Y., and settled in Boston in 1880, and is recognized as one of its solid, substantial citizens and representative business men.

CARTER'S BAND, T. M. Carter, Leader, Office, No. 179 Washington Street, Over Thompson and Odell's Music Store.—Probably not one among Boston's many excellent bands is maintained at a higher degree of excellence than Carter's Military Band and Orchestra. It is one of the best equipped and most popular organizations of the kind in this city, and receives a highly flattering patronage. This band was organized in 1871, and during the nearly eighteen years since intervening it has steadily grown in favor, furnishing music throughout the whole of the New England states, except Connecticut. The organization comprises twenty-five members, among them many expert performers, while the leader is a cornet player and violinist of A1 repute. Military and orchestral music is furnished for all occasions—parades, balls, parties, etc.—in first-class style at reasonable rates, and satisfaction guaranteed in every instance. Instructions on the cornet, violin and other instruments being given also at moderate terms. Mr. Carter, the efficient leader and manager, is a native of New Hampshire, but has lived in Boston upward of twenty-five years.

THOMAS J. GRAHAM & CO., Manufacturers and Wholesale Dealers in Trunks, Bags and Umbrellas, Nos. 44 and 46 Lincoln Street.—The manufacture of trunks, bags, valises and kindred goods is an industry of no mean importance, and it is one of an indispensable character. In this line of enterprise Boston has long held a leading position, and the industry is one which is constantly undergoing expansion. Among the most energetic and successful firms on this line that of Messrs. Thomas J. Graham & Co., of Nos. 44 and 46 Lincoln Street, is deserving of special mention. The business was organized in 1883 under the style of Byrne, Graham & Co. In August, 1885, Mr. Byrne died, and since then the enterprise has been continued by Mr. Graham under the style which forms the caption of this sketch. The premises occupied are very commodious, consisting of a five-story building, 30x72 feet in dimensions. The upper floors are devoted to manufacturing and storage, and here some twenty-five hands are employed constantly. The manufacturing department is equipped with all the newest and best modern mechanical appliances and here are made to order and for stock trunks, bags and sample cases of every description, while special attention is given to all kinds of repair work. The stock carried is a very extensive and comprehensive one and embraces an almost endless variety of trunks, bags and umbrellas. The trade is wholesale and retail. The business of the house is mainly confined to the New England States, but the firm send many of their trunks and leather bags in alligator and other fancy leathers to distant parts of the Union and to Canada. They make a specialty of light theatre trunks for traveling. The prosperous career of this house is an evidence of the just policy upon which the business is conducted and Mr. Graham, who is a native of this city, is one of our most esteemed merchants.

SAMUEL HATCH & CO., Auctioneers, No. 9 Congress Street.— An old established, popular and responsible firm of auctioneers in this city is that of Samuel Hatch & Co., whose office is located at No. 9 Congress Street, and which for upward of half a century has maintained an enduring hold on public favor and confidence. This is, in fact, the oldest firm of the kind now in existence in Boston, and has a large, active and permanent patronage, fully sustaining its old time reputation for integrity and reliability. This flourishing business was established in 1838 by the present senior member, who conducted it alone up to 1866, when he associated with him in partnership Francis S. Tent, who was connected with the concern for fifteen years previously, while Edward Hatch (nephew of the founder) was admitted into the firm in 1876. No house in this line in the city maintains a higher standing in commercial and financial circles, as few if any receive a more liberal share of merited recognition, its business already of a very substantial character, growing apace annually. They conduct a general auctioneering business, selling houses, building lots, farms, and city and suburban property of all kinds, also household effects, furniture, stocks and merchandise of every description, special attention being given to sale of real estate and bankrupt chances. All sales entrusted to this firm are certain to be handled in the most judicious and satisfactory manner. The operations of the house are carried on a large scale. Mr. Hatch having made one sale of real estate of over one million dollars. The Messrs. Hatch and Mr. Tent, are all natives of Boston, are gentlemen of the highest personal integrity as well as men of thorough experience, sagacity and energy, and are well and favorably known in the community.

JOHN B. BURKE, Undertaker and Embalmer, Office and Warerooms, No. 60 Leverett Street.—This gentleman has been in business at his present location for the past eighteen years, and his career has been one of uninterrupted success. He is the accomplished master of his vocation, and is eminently qualified in every way to render the most satisfactory and finished service. He occupies a handsomely furnished store and office, 22x40 feet in dimensions, and here he has at all times a large and carefully selected stock of coffins, caskets, metallic burial cases and funeral merchandise in general, suited to all means and tastes; the assortment, in fact, being one of the most desirable and comprehensive to be found anywhere. Mr. Burke has every facility and convenience for the successful prosecution of the business, furnishes everything required for the plainest or most imposing ceremonies, takes charge of the dead, and superintends every detail of the last sad rites of burial, and the afflicted have always a melancholy pleasure in securing the professional services of this considerate gentleman. Mr. Burke is an experienced and competent embalmer, is skilful and precise, and preserves bodies entrusted to his care for any required period. His charges are always reasonable and just. He has not only a large city, but an extensive suburban patronage, and can always be relied upon for prompt and effective service. He is aided by competent assistants, and his office is kept open at all hours. Mr. Burke is a native of this city.

M. L. H. LEAVITT, Ph.G., Pharmacist, No. 65 Cambridge Street, And Nos. 27 and 29 Charles Street.—The well known popular pharmacy, located on the corner of Cambridge and Chambers Street, is one of the oldest drug stores in the city. The business was founded as far back as 1852 by Mr. Daniel Henchman, who, in 1878, was succeeded by his son, Mr. Russell B. Henchman. From the latter Mr. M. L. H. Leavitt purchased the business in the spring of 1888, and has since fully maintained the high reputation the establishment has so long enjoyed. In 1886 Mr. Leavitt also purchased from Mr. Ellis the noted drug store at Nos. 27 and 29 Charles street, and he is now conducting both establishments with marked success. Both stores are of ample dimensions, are handsomely and attractively fitted up and appointed, and are provided with every appliance and convenience for the successful prosecution of the business carried on. Each store contains a full and complete and carefully selected stock of fresh, pure drugs and chemicals, proprietary preparations and medicines of acknowledged merit, and a fine assortment of toilet accessories, fancy articles and druggists' sundries of every description. Special attention is given to compounding physicians' prescriptions and family recipes, every care being taken to secure accuracy, while only the purest drugs are used. Duly qualified assistants are employed and Mr. Leavitt exercises a close surveillance over every department of his business. He is a native of Portland, Me., and is a graduate of the Massachusetts College of Pharmacy.

A. TROEDER, Eliot Loan Company, No. 45 Eliot Street.—The business of making advances on collateral is conducted in a liberal, honorable manner by the Eliot Loan Co. Mr. Troeder, who has the entire charge of the business, is well known in this community, and numbers among his patrons many of the leading citizens. He is an experienced, practical business man and has been established in the loan business since 1872. The premises occupied are very commodious and neatly fitted up. As a merchandise and money broker, Mr. Troeder makes liberal advances on diamonds, watches, and all kinds of goods and personal property, and watches and diamonds are sold for half their value, and in his transactions Mr. Troeder will be found upright and square. He is from Amsterdam, Holland, and came to this country in 1862, and during his long residence in Boston has acquired a wide reputation as an honorable business man and useful citizen. He always has a number of unredeemed pledges to dispose of and can offer the very best inducements to those who will call upon him.

MRS. B. SPRAGUE, Dry and Fancy Goods, Etc., No. 95 Green Street.—One of the most enterprising and best conducted houses in this line in the west end of Boston, is that of Mrs. B. Sprague, dealer in dry and fancy goods, millinery, etc. Mrs. Sprague who had a long experience in the trade and was well qualified by her natural aptitude to conduct a first-class business, opened the establishment in February, 1888, and from the first was successful in drawing a large custom. She occupies a handsome corner store of ample dimensions 40x20 feet in extent and fitted up throughout in a manner to display to the best advantage, the varied and first class stock she carries on the premises. Besides a splendid line of the finest millinery which she has always made a specialty of, Mrs. Sprague keeps everything in dry and fancy goods, under wear, gents' furnishing articles, smallwares, plated jewelry, etc., and makes a specialty as well of stamping and stamping materials, while she is also agent for the Troy Laundry. Mrs. Sprague does an extensive business and employs from five to eight assistants.

R. G. CHASE & CO., Prop'rs of The Chase Nurseries, New England Office, No. 23 Pemberton Square.—Among the reliable nurseries of the United States, very prominent are those of which Messrs. R. G. Chase & Co., are the popular proprietors. The firm's nurseries and packing grounds, which have an area of 170 acres are located at Geneva, N. Y., and the house has likewise branches in Philadelphia and Boston, its New England office being at No. 23 Pemberton Square. Th's extensive business was established thirty-five years ago at Geneva, N. Y., and the Boston branch was opened in 1868. The members of this copartnership are Messrs. Roscoe G., Howard A. and George H. Chase, all of whom are thoroughly practical nurserymen. Mr. Roscoe G. Chase has charge of the nurseries at Geneva, N. Y., Mr. Howard A. Chase of the Philadelphia and Mr. George H. Chase of the Boston branch. The firm keep constantly on hand large supplies of all kinds of fruit and ornamental trees, vines, evergreens and hardy flowering shrubs, roses, hardy plants, bulbs, etc. Messrs. R. G. Chase & Co. do not claim to sell cheaper than other firms, but they do assert, that quality of stock considered (with the care exercised in packing and delivering) they are not undersold by any responsible concern. They likewise claim that wherever Geneva trees have been fairly compared with trees from eastern or southern nurseries, they have plainly shown their superiority. The reason of this is to be found, not only in the increased care and attention which competition always brings and the improvements which experience suggests, but in the fact that—first, the Geneva soil is sufficiently strong to grow trees without the application of strong fertilizers; second, the climate is so natural for producing healthy timber that a tree attains the age of three or four years perfectly healthy, and with vitality enough to be transplanted into the most fickle climate with perfect safety. Western New York is pre-eminently suited for growing healthy trees, and the fact that a large percentage of the trees planted in the country are grown within fifty miles of Geneva, demonstrates that this section is well adapted to the business. Every section in the country is suited for something, some for sweet potatoes, others for tobacco. Geneva is the place for raising young trees. Messrs. R. G. Chase & Co. are very particular to have their agents offer only those varieties of tree that do best in the section where they are selling. With the care they exercise in classifying for the different sections, a customer in New England or Maryland can make his selection of varieties with the same assurance of getting those best adapted to his particular latitude, as one living in Geneva. This responsible firm employs only first-class men as agents, who will do justice to patrons and the house.

ISBURGH & CO., Carriage Dealers, Nos. 8, 10 and 12 East Street, and No. 205 Essex Street.—The most popular source of supply for fine carriages of every description, and the best-known market for both horses, carriages and harnesses at auction, in this city, is the establishment of Messrs. Isburgh & Co. This enterprise was founded in 1858, by Messrs. Isburgh & Rowland, who were succeeded by the present firm in 1879. Their motto is "justice to owners, protection to buyers." The premises occupied for the business cover an area of 80,000 feet, and comprise a fine brick structure, extending through the block, and having three stories on East and one story on Essex Street; affording ample conveniences for the prosecution of the business. Here is exhibited one of the largest and finest assortments of vehicles to be seen in all New England, embracing all the latest novelties from the principal manufacturers of the country, including new designs in six seat rockaways, coupe rockaways, carryalls, beach wagons, Goddard buggies, phaetons in great variety, side-bar top buggies, piano box open wagons, Concord wagons, pony phaetons, landaus, coaches, surries, brouches, road wagons and track sulkies. The proprietors take a proper pride in maintaining their house at the head of the trade, laboring assiduously to that end, and only ask an opportunity to compete with other dealers and to demonstrate in that way their ability to confer benefits in all respects equal to any, either as regards style, quality, finish or price. Regular auction sales are held every Saturday, at a. m. for the disposal of horses, carriages and harnesses to the highest bidder, and are attended by a large concourse of critical, experienced and discriminating buyers, who rely with confidence and safety upon the good faith of all transactions. The co-partners, Messrs. C. B. Isburgh and J. F. Lothrop, are Massachusetts men by birth and training, of large and valuable experience in this branch of trade.

E. J. BROWN & CO., Dealers in Cotton, No. 27 Kilby street.—As the greatest manufacturing district on the continent in textile fabrics, New England is the principal and most active market for the best grades of cotton grown in the Southern States. Vast capital is invested in this branch of trade, and the leading factors are distinguished for their enterprise and energy. Prominent among the number is the old-established house of Messrs. E. J. Brown & Co., of No. 27 Kilby street. The firm was formed in 1833, and has always been respected for its honest and upright dealings. The members of the firm are Mr. E. J. Brown and his brother, Mr. F. L. Brown, both gentlemen being natives of Massachusetts and closely identified with the direct purchase and shipments of all the grades of cotton from the Southern States. In this branch of commerce everything depends on sound judgment, thorough knowledge of all the varying growths and grades, and perfected facilities for receiving, handling and supplying the cotton to the consumers, and in these essentials but few houses have achieved such an enviable reputation as that of Messrs. E. J. Brown & Co. They are buyers of cotton, specially adapted to the wants of the leading cotton mills of New England. They are regular receivers direct from southern ports of lots of even classed cotton, and carry in the public stores a large stock subject to the varied wants of the spinners. Their office are of a central and convenient location, at No. 27 Kilby street, where full lines of samples are shown and lowest prices quoted in every grade of this great staple.

C. D. STEVENS, Fashionable Millinery, No. 18 Hanover Street.—Of the many and varied establishments that contribute to the general sum of mercantile activity, there is not one that attracts more attention than the well ordered millinery emporium of C. D. Stevens. there being here always displayed a full and fine assortment of French millinery goods, including the latest Parisian novelties; also a complete and first-class line of hair and mourning goods, while bonnets and hats are altered, trimmed and made to order, likewise, in the very best style of the milliner's art, at popular prices. This well and favourably known store was established in 1877, being conducted at the present location about six years. The premises here occupied are compact, ample and nicely appointed, while eight or more competent assistants are employed, including expert designers, trimmers, etc., particular attention being paid to orders, and no pains are spared to render the fullest satisfaction in every instance to patrons. A large and A1 stock is constantly carried, embracing bonnets and hats, both trimmed and untrimmed, in exquisite shapes and patterns, superb feathers, flowers, ribbons, plushes, velvets and everything in the line of fashionable millinery trimmings in great variety; also, hair and mourning goods, laces, etc., while straw hats and bonnets are bleached and pressed in the latest style, and altogether Mr. Stevens has a flourishing trade. Mr. Stevens is a native of the state of Maine, but has resided in Boston since 1852.

H. J. COON & CO., Grain Shippers and Commission Merchants, No. 5 Broad Street, J. A. Yantis, Boston Agent.—A representative and influential Chicago firm, extensively engaged as grain shippers and commission merchants is that of Messrs. H. J. Coon & Co., whose Boston agency, under the able careful management of Mr. J. A. Yantis, is located at No. 5 Broad Street. Messrs. H. J. Coon & Co. have also agencies in New York City, Buffalo, N. Y. and Portland, Maine. Their Chicago office is at No. 20 Pacific Avenue. Their facilities are in every respect strictly first-class. They fill orders for car-load or cargo lots of grain at the lowest ruling market prices, shipments being made direct from the west to consumers. They also possess opportunities, and quote prices on round lots, that can seldom, and with the greatest difficulty be secured in the east for similar grades of grain. Mr. Yantis is a member of the Boston Chamber of Commerce, and has been agent for Messrs. H. J. Coon & Co for the last five years, and has reared the business second to none in their line in the New England states.

THE METROPOLIS OF NEW ENGLAND.

H. MARSHALL & CO., Steam Job Printers, No. 35 Sudbury Street.—One of the most successful exponents of the printer's art in this city is the house of H. Marshall & Co. This firm are deservedly prominent and popular as steam job printers, making a leading specialty of fancy color work. The business was established in 1874, by Messrs. Marshall and Sparrell, the present firm succeeding to the control in 1880. The premises occupied are spacious in size, well adapted for the purposes of the business, and fully equipped with the latest improved self-feeding and delivering presses, and other modern appliances, tending to facilitate rapid and perfect work. This firm is in a position to guarantee good work, promptness and bottom prices; and to execute all kinds of printing, such as show cards, labels, business cards, call cards, tags, bill heads, note heads, letter heads, circulars, programmes, price lists, dodgers, stickers, postal cards, wood cut printing, etc. It possesses excellent facilities for the production of every size, description, regular or irregular shape of labels. The office contains, among others, two automatic presses, which, taking paper from rolls, feed, print, (in one or several colors of ink) and cut to the required size at one operation; capacity 250,000 impressions per day. Show cards are printed in black or colored inks or gibbed, and cut by machinery either square, round, oval, diamond or almost any shape desired. Original designs for any kind of label, show cards or any other commercial printing furnished to customers, and wood engraving done to order. Mr. Marshall, the active member of the firm, was born in Concord, N. H., and has been in Boston for the past twenty-five years. His skill in printing is equal to any of his contemporaries either at home or abroad, and he has achieved a reputation that meets with wide recognition, orders being constantly received from all parts of the country.

LOUIS VALENTIN, Ladies' Tailor, No. 34 Boylston Street.— One among the well-known young business men in this city is Mr. Louis Valentin, the popular ladies' tailor. His offices are elegantly fitted up and in charge of courteous, polite lady assistants. Mr. Valentin is a practical, expert fashioner and designer of ladies' costumes, garments, cloaks, riding habits, etc., and is very successful in pleasing his patrons. He is certainly one of the most accomplished ladies' tailors in the city, and learned the art in the French capital, where he resided many years. He is a Hungarian by birth, but most of his life has been spent in Paris. He came to Boston in 1884, and for the past two years has been established in his present business, and is enjoying a success as well merited as it is unbounded.

RICHARD SCHWARZ, Importer of German, French and English Toys, Fancy Goods, Games and Lawn Tennis, Nos. 484 and 486 Washington Street.—There is no store in the city like that of Mr. Richard Schwarz, the leading importer of toys, fancy goods and games. It was a small affair when the enterprising proprietor first opened it in 1870, but to-day it comprises a splendid five-story and basement building, 19x75 feet in dimensions, the largest in its line in the city, and one of the most attractive and best patronized establishments on this great bustling thoroughfare. It is a bazaar and fancy goods emporium combined. For toys, fancy goods, games and novelties of every conceivable description, we commend the curious searcher for the rare, the novel, the unique and the useful, to visit Schwarz's. Of German toys, French toys, English toys and Yankee toys, toys for girls and toys for boys, there is an immense assortment. Mr. Schwarz imports direct from the most famous European houses, securing the latest productions from England, Germany and France, and always gets the best. There are games of all sorts, including lawn tennis, croquet, base balls and bats, racquet, parlor billiards, etc.; also, bric-a-brac of every description, gold and silver ornaments, articles of vertu, ivory and leather goods, fans, pocket books, albums, cards, brass goods, ornamental fire sets, umbrella stands, and knick-knacks of every kind. Then there is the display of the practical and the serviceable, including fine merino cloaks, infants'

lace caps, embroidered slippers, zephyrs, worsteds and other ladies' goods, while in the line of novelties we must not forget to mention the admirable collection of athletic goods, sporting goods and willow ware. A corps of experienced clerks and salesman, numbering from twenty-five to thirty, contribute to the satisfactory operations of the house. The trade is brisk and lively at all seasons, and the house is universally recognized as the leader in novelties, and low prices. Mr. Schwarz is a native of Germany, and a resident of this country for many years.

HENRY D. CASEY, Manufacturer and Gilder of Bronze and Gold, Landscape, Portrait and Looking-Glass Frames, No. 98 Hanover Street.—Mr. Casey has been identified with this line of trade for a quarter of a century, and in 1868 he started business on his own account. He met with substantial recognition from the first and has developed a very extensive business connection throughout the city and suburbs. His premises comprise two spacious rooms, one of which is utilized as an office and show and ware-room, and the other is used as the workshop, which is equipped with all the latest improved mechanical appliances known to the trade. Seven skilled and experienced assistants are employed in manufacturing bronze and gold landscape, portrait and looking-glass frames, mouldings in white, or ornamented, ovals, panels, etc. Old frames are regilded, and a special feature is made of ship and steamboat ornamenting and gilding. Mr. Casey justly prides himself upon the superiority of all work executed upon his premises or by him, and he is an acknowledged expert and most careful man at his trade. Many beautiful specimens of his handiwork in original designs are shown, and at the thirteenth exhibition of the Massachusetts Charitable Mechanic Association, Mr. Casey was awarded a gold medal for superiority of frames put on exhibition by him. He is a native of England and for forty-two years has resided in America to which he was brought when five years of age.

WOOD, KILBOURNE & CO., Agents for the Celebrated Wm. Bourne & Son Piano fortes. Warerooms, No. 66 Washington Street.—This business was founded under the present auspices in 1884, and from its inception has had a substantial and rapid growth. The spacious warerooms are fitted up in a tasteful and elegant style, and the stock of piano fortes shown represents the best makes, a specialty being made of the celebrated Wm. Bourne & Son instruments, for which the firm are agents. Pianos are sold for cash or upon the installment plan, also rented upon the most equitable terms. Instruments are also tuned and kept in general repair upon yearly contract, the charges being as low as is compatable with good and reliable service. The firm have already secured a large and continually increasing patronage and the general business is of most prosperous annual aggregate. Mr. J. B. Wood, the head of the firm is a practical man in the piano business, having been for twenty-five years prior to embarking in the present enterprise, in the employ of Messrs. Wm. Bourne & Son, piano manufacturers. Mr. F. H. Kilbourne, until engaging in the present pursuit, was a teacher in the Institution for the Blind at South Boston. Both gentlemen are natives of Boston.

FRANK W. MORRILL & CO., Butter, Cheese and Eggs, No. 5 North Market Street.—The house of Frank W. Morrill & Co. has been established since 1878 and occupies a foremost position among those in the trade in dairy and farm products. Mr. Frank W. Morrill, who is at its head, and has charge of the business affairs, conducts it upon upright and liberal basis, and is always in a position to afford extraordinary advantages to its patrons. The connections of the house are of the most satisfactory character and a large local and out of town trade has been built up. The premises utilized for the purposes of the business have an area of 20x60 feet, and every convenience is provided to facilitate operations. Choice creamery and dairy butter and cheese and fresh eggs and farm produce is received daily, and a wide-spread wholesale demand is supplied. Mr. Morrill, who is a native of Amesbury, in this state, has lived in Boston many years and is a prominent member of the Produce Exchange.

H. H. FOSTER & CO., Coal and Wood, No. 149 Beach Street.— The business conducted under the above heading was originally established upwards of half a century ago and is one of the oldest city enterprises in the coal and wood trade. In 1885, Mr. H. H. Foster, who had for some years previous been identified with the business succeeded to the proprietorship and by his well directed efforts has fully maintained the old time prosperity and popularity of the house. The premises on Beach Street are spacious, well arranged and convenient; all requisite facilities being at hand for the advantageous conduct of the business. The stock of coal is large, comprehensive and complete, embracing all sizes and the best grades of stove and furnace coal, and the stock of wood is equally desirable and fully up to the requirements of the trade. Mr. Foster has also a branch establishment in South Boston, No. 135 O Street, which is a favorite source of supply for the trade of that vicinity. The general business is both large and lucrative and the patronage received is drawn from the best family, hotel and other custom. Mr. Foster is a native of Boston, experienced and able in his business and has long been esteemed as one of the most active and enterprising merchants in his line in this city.

W. S. HODGDON, Manufacturer of Tongues, Stays, Button Flies, Tips, etc., No. 116 Bedford Street.—This responsible and strictly first-class business house is engaged in the manufacture of tongues, stays, button flies, tips, etc., and also in dealing in all kinds of leather and sheepskin remnants. The founder and proprietor of the enterprise, Mr. W. S. Hodgdon, started business in Haverhill, Mass., in 1872, and in the great fire which destroyed the principal business section of that city, in 1882, his establishment was included in the general destruction. He then removed to Boston and resumed business on the corner of Congress and High Streets, where he remained until 1887 when he removed to his present location. Here he occupies one floor, with a capacity of 40x72 feet, and here is in use all the latest improved machinery and other appliances appertaining to the trade, and a large force is employed. The tongues, stays, flies, tips, etc., manufactured here have an excellent reputation among the shoe manufacturers throughout the whole of New England, with whom he has established a permanent and extensive business connection. A heavy stock of these goods and also of leather and sheepskin remnants is constantly kept on hand, and the facilities of the establishment for promptly complying with all orders at the lowest possible rates are of a most adequate character. Mr. Hodgdon is a native of New Hampshire and an energetic, pushing business man.

A. YERETSKY, Fine Tailoring, No. 63 Cambridge Street.— This is the oldest tailoring establishment extant in the West End, and commands a patronage of a large and influential character. It was founded in 1870 by the present proprietor, who, by turning out stylish fits and first-class work, treating every customer courteously and fairly, has attained an enviable position as one of the leading merchant tailors of the city. His store has a frontage of twenty five feet, and a depth of forty feet, and is elegant and inviting in its appointments, arrangements, and in the order which prevails. The stock is a large and carefully selected one, and embraces fabrics of the very latest patterns from the best French, English, German and American looms. The most popular novelties in woolen and worsted suitings, cassimeres, cloths, checks, plaids, tweeds, serges, meltons, etc., are to be found here and at prices that cannot be surpassed. Customers can always rely upon getting excellent value, first-class work and satisfactory treatment in this reliable establishment. Mr. Yeretsky is a practical cutter of ability and long experience and he sees to it that no garment shall be permitted to leave his establishment that will not bear the closest scrutiny. He has been a resident of this city since 1867.

D. F. HALL, Meats, Provisions, Butter, Game, Vegetables, Fruit, Etc., No. 31 Charles Street.—Mr. Hall is a general dealer in all kinds of meats, provisions, game, vegetables, foreign and domestic fruits, butter, eggs, etc., and in these lines has won a very large and influential city and suburban trade. It is now thirty-five years since he first established himself in this line of trade, and for twenty-eight years has been located on Charles Street. Since 1865 he has occupied his present store, which has an area of 20x60 feet. It is very appropriately and elegantly fitted up, and admirably arranged for the accommodation of the stock and the convenience of customers. The stock is selected with great care and excellent judgment to meet the demands of a critical class of customers, and being frequently replenished can always be depended upon as being fresh and wholesome. Supplies are secured direct from the producers, and the prices ruling here are the lowest in the market. The result is a brisk and growing trade, necessitating the constant employment of six assistants, and the unremitting service of two teams. The business is entirely retail in its character, and purchases made here are promptly delivered in any part of the city free from extra charge. The telephone call is 177, Fremont, and prompt attention is given to all orders. Mr Hall is a native of Massachusetts, and is a most energetic and reliable merchant.

MISS M. B. STEWART, Type Writer Copying from Copy or Dictation, Room 51, No. 50 State Street.—One of the most talented and successful exponents of type-writing in the city of Boston is Miss M. B. Stewart, who has been established in the practice of her profession here since November, 1886, and is prepared to do type-writer copying, from copy or dictation, of every description, including patent specifications, and legal work of all kinds, supplying a stenographer by the hour, when desired. She has already gained a reputation and a patronage in this city that places her in the front rank of enterprise and success, and her services are in constant and influential demand among patent solicitors and city attorneys. She is prompt, accurate and methodical in all her methods, carefully guarding and intelligently promoting all interests committed to her care. She places her terms and prices at an eminently fair and reasonable figure. Miss Stewart is a resident of the city, and highly esteemed in social and professional life.

THE METROPOLIS OF NEW ENGLAND.

ANDREW C. BERRY, Engraver and Stationer, No. 12 West Street.—A deservedly popular exponent of the engraver's Art in Boston is Mr. Andrew C. Berry. There are few men in the business possessing a larger share of experience in this noble art than Mr. Berry, who received a very careful training in his calling in his youth, and is an admitted expert in every branch of his business. In 1867 he entered into business as a member of the firm of Berry & Reeve, and on the dissolution of the partnership in 1875, he assumed sole control of the enterprise, which he has developed into one of the leading and most successful concerns in its line in the city. The premises occupied are commodious and convenient, and are fully equipped with all the latest improved mechanical appliances and tools essential to the successful prosecution of the business. From five to six engravers and designers of skill and experience are employed, and all orders are promptly filled. While making a specialty of the very finest work in all departments of engraving, Mr. Berry gives close attention to general engraving, wedding and visiting cards, invitations, coats of arms, crests, monograms, street dies, etc., and in this department has a valuable business connection. He also carries in stock constantly a fine assortment of wedding and other fancy stationery, and is in a position to meet all the demands of his patrons with the most artistic work and at prices to insure a repetition of orders. He is a gentleman of middle age, a native of the city, and a highly esteemed business man.

THE COSMOPOLITAN DINING ROOM, E. K. Brooks & Son, Proprietors, No. 13 Eliot Street.—The business of catering to the appetites of the Bostonians seems to be well understood by Messrs. E. K. Brooks & Son, proprietors of the popular Cosmopolitan Dining Room, as they are doing a flourishing business and are highly complimented on the excellence of the fare provided by all who patronize their establishment. The firm first opened in 1876, on Washington Street, and in the spring of the present year occupied the very desirable premises, No. 13 Eliot Street, which are very commodious and afford a space of 35x70 feet in area for seating guests and general purposes. The dining room is furnished and fitted up in good taste in modern style, and contains all the conveniences for the accommodation of from 100 to 150 patrons at one time. It is admirably conducted, scrupulously neat and tidy, and always presents an attractive and inviting appearance; and is liberally patronized by a first-class custom of both ladies and gentlemen. The menu each day includes all the substantials and delicacies when in season, which are well cooked and carefully served by those who are thoroughly competent. Mr. E. K. Brooks, and his son and copartner, Mr. Brooks, are both Bostonians and experienced caterers, knowing what is required by their fellow citizens. Since removal to the present location the business has increased, but with extra facilities and help, prompt attention is accorded all.

A. E. KENNEY, Furniture, Carpets, Stoves, and Furnishing Goods, at the lowest prices; Second hand Furniture Bought, Sold and Exchanged, No. 52 Leverett Street.—Mr. Kenney has been established four years at the above address and shown his eminent fitness to conduct the affairs of a large establishment with profit to himself and the most complete satisfaction to the trading public. He occupies a commodious and well arranged store at No. 52 Leverett Street, in an admirable location, and carries a splendid stock of new and second-hand furniture in the finest upholstering as well as plainer goods, carpets of every description, Brussels, Turkish and Axminster, stoves and ranges to suit the requirements of large and small families and general household furnishing goods, making his establishment a complete depot for anything in the household goods line. He deals also largely in second hand furniture, buying, selling and exchanging, trading in the most liberal manner. Mr. Kenney has for some time been exclusively engaged in the storage of furniture and other goods, having three spacious floors for the purpose at No. 19 Blossom Street. He is noted for the particular care he has taken of the articles consigned to his keeping and the extremely moderate charge he has for the safekeeping of all furniture and other goods. Mr. Kenney, who is a native of Massachusetts, is one of the foremost business men of Boston in his line of trade.

M. T. J. KEENAN, Glass Cutter, No. 71 Sudbury Street.—Great advances have been made of late centuries in the production of glass, and innumerable are the uses to which it is now put. The business of the glass cutter is one of the most important branches of the industry, and requires considerable skill and thorough training in order to follow it successfully. A gentleman who has achieved signal success in this line in Boston is Mr. M. T. J. Keenan, who has been established for the past three years, and has during the intervening period developed a most desirable trade which continues to steadily assume greater proportions. The workshop is equipped in the most complete style with all apparatus and appliances peculiar to the trade and the motive power is furnished by steam. Mr. Keenan is a skilled exponent of his vocation, personally attends to all the work of his establishment and executes glass cutting in all its branches, cutting and beveling door and coach lights, plate glass shelves, making and cutting gas and kerosene globes, and performing general jobbing of all kinds, making, however, a leading specialty of beveled clock glasses. The prices charged are uniformly reasonable, while satisfaction is guaranteed in every instance. Mr. Keenan is a native of Brooklyn, N. Y., but has resided in Boston since 1883, and has become so well known to the trade that anything we might add of a personal nature would be superfluous.

HITCHCOCK & BROWNE, Druggists, No. 203½ Leverett Street.—An important acquisition to the drug trade of Boston is the establishment opened in July last, by Messrs. Hitchcock & Browne. The store is one of the handsomest and best equipped in this section of the city, and is fast becoming popular headquarters for all who esteem purity and excellence in stock, and enterprise and reliability in management. A large and valuable stock is carried, consisting of pure drugs, chemicals, standard proprietary and family medicines, dyes and colors, essences and extracts, surgical instruments and appliances, toilet goods and perfumery, fancy articles and holiday presents, beside that multitude of supplies coming under the head of druggists' sundries. None but the purest and most reliable goods are handled. The prescription department is under the most experienced supervision, and the utmost precision and safety is assured in all cases. Those who favor this house with their patronage can be sure of receiving reliable goods and equitable prices. The copartners are W. S. D. Hitchcock, M. D., and Mr. William A. Browne. Dr. Hitchcock is a native of Boston, a graduate of the College of Physicians and Surgeons. Mr. Browne is an accomplished pharmacist and is also a native of Boston.

BROADWAY HAT STORE, William McCarthy, Proprietor; No. 913 Washington Street.—The leading representative hat store on Washington Street is that familiarly known as the Broadway. It is 25x50 feet in dimensions and contains an immense stock of seasonable hats and caps of all kinds in perfect accord with the fashionable ideas of the day, so that no one, not even the most fastidious, can fail to make a selection of something new, beautiful in shape and becoming, at a fair, reasonable price. The Broadway is the recognized fashion resort in this section of the city. A large business is carried on and Mr. William McCarthy, the courteous proprietor, is justly entitled to the reputation he enjoys as a leader in his line of business. He is a native Bostonian and a wide awake, live, enterprising business man, and has been established in the hat and cap business since 1881, and has occupied his present handsomely fitted up store for the past three years.

PETER F. DOWLING, Fish and Oysters, No. 27 Leverett Street.—The excellent fish and oyster market conducted by Peter F. Dowling was established by the present proprietor about ten years ago, the business being carried on at the commodious quarters now occupied since 1885. The store is compact, ample and well kept, several competent assistants being in attendance, while a large and first-class stock is constantly carried on hand, including everything in the line of fresh fish in its season, also salt, dried and smoked fish, of every variety, and the choicest brands of oysters, clams, etc.; all orders being promptly and reliably filled at the lowest consistent prices.

D. C. SHEEHAN, Wholesale Dealer in Fruit and Produce, No. 7 Richmond Street.—Prominent among the wholesale commission merchants in fruit and produce is Mr. D. C. Sheehan, who controls a trade of great magnitude in these commodities. Mr. Sheehan, who has had a very extended experience in his line of enterprise, started his present flourishing business at No. 123 Atlantic Avenue, in 1886, and a year ago he removed to his present location. Here he occupies a commodious store, having a frontage of thirty feet and a depth of sixty feet. It is provided with every convenience and appliance for the speedy handling and storage of stock. While dealing in every description of fruit and produce, the house makes a specialty of potatoes, onions and apples, and the trade done in these is one of vast volume. Mr. Sheehan confines his operations to the handling of superior goods at the lowest market rates, and the trade is of such extent as to permanently require the services of five assistants. The stock is at all times kept fresh and choice, and daily renewed by the arrival of consignments from the best producing sections of the country. Controlling the large distributing trade which he does, Mr. Sheehan is in a position to offer the best of facilities to producers and dealers. He is a native of Lowell, Mass.

JOHN W. HARMON, Manufacturer of Spirit Levels and Leveling Instruments, No. 65 Haverhill Street.—One of the most noted and ingenious manufacturers in this department, as well as one of the most experienced, is Mr. John W. Harmon. Mr. Harmon was born in New Hampshire and thirty-five years ago came to Boston to learn the trade in which he is now an acknowledged expert. Since 1864 he has been in business at the address already indicated, and here he occupies the second floor of the building, which is 22x95 feet in dimensions. The manufacturing department is equipped with steam power, specially devised machinery, and all mechanical equipments essential to the successful carrying on of the business. Mr. Harmon is the inventor of valuable surveyor's instruments and spirit levels, which are shipped to all parts of the United States, and wherever used have met with deserved commendation. His improved levelling instrument, patented August 1st, 1882, is remarkable for the simplicity of its construction, and for its adaptability for ordinary work, where commonly a more expensive instrument is used. It is claimed that it will cover more points than any other low-priced instrument in the market. Constant employment is given to a competent staff of workmen, and special attention is given to the repairing of spirit levels. Mr. Harmon is a resident of Winchester.

E. F. SMITH, General Photographer, No. 22 Milk Street.—A Boston artist who has gained a well merited reputation, is E. F. Smith, who is in all respects one of the leading exponents of the art in this city. Mr. Smith was born at Bridgeton, Me., but has resided in Boston many years. He is a practical and expert photographer, of long and varied experience in his profession, and is a thorough master of the photographic art in all its branches. Mr. Smith established himself in business in 1862, and has occupied the present spacious quarters about thirteen years. The business premises, including studio, gallery and ware-rooms, occupy four 50x75 foot floors, with ample and complete facilities, while half a dozen or so competent assistants are employed. A general line of photographic work is executed; special attention being given to merchandise, machinery, buildings and views; and the pictures, leaving this establishment can be relied upon to be A1 in every feature of merit, alike in fidelity, execution, design and finish; while the patronage, which is very large, extends to all parts of the New England States. Mr. Smith is a well and favorably known member of the Massachusetts and the National Photographer's Associations.

D. B. HATCH, Manufacturer of and Dealer in Paper and Wood Boxes, No. 29 Bedford Street.—The manufacture of paper and wood boxes is carried on quite extensively by Mr. D. B. Hatch, who has been identified with it for many years, and is one of the oldest and most prominent in the city. The business he is now conducting, was established in 1871 by Hatch & Wade, and a year later came under the control of Hatch Bros., who continued it for a time. Mr. D. B. Hatch succeeding to it in 1873. From that time the business increased rapidly, necessitating greater facilities and help, and to meet the demands made upon him, in 1882 he removed to the premises now occupied at No. 29 Bedford street, where from twenty to thirty hands are kept constantly employed. Every facility and convenience have been provided, including the latest improved machinery and appliances, and he is prepared to give estimates and manufacture boxes of paper or wood in any size or style that may be desired at the very lowest prices. Plain boxes of every description are always kept on hand, and large wholesale and retail business is carried on, a specialty being made of order work. He is from New Hampshire, originally. He can always offer superior inducements to the trade and can turn out as well made paper and wood boxes as any other establishment in the country.

HAWKES & CRAWFORD, Plumbers and Sanitary Engineers, No. 50 Howard Street.—This is an old established concern having first been founded in 1865, in Cambridgeport, by the present proprietors, where they still carry on business under the firm style of Levi Hawkes & Co. The store in this city was opened in March, 1878, and has proved a very successful venture, greatly augmenting the firm's resources and largely increasing their volume of trade. The premises occupied are commodious, excellently arranged, and contain a superior stock of plumbing supplies of every description. The firm's extensive patronage demands the employment of a force of twenty hands, and the facilities are of such advantageous order that contracts of any magnitude are undertaken and all work brought to a satisfactory completion in the most expeditious manner. Particular attention is devoted to ventilation and sanitary plumbing, in which the utmost care and skill is exercised, in order to achieve the best results. As to the matter of terms it is sufficient to state that this house can safely meet all competition in this direction. The copartners, Messrs. Levi Hawkes and John Crawford, are natives of Cambridge, and are very favorably regarded wherever known.

T. E. SMITH, Manufacturer and Dealer in Havana and Domestic Cigars, Tobacco, and Smokers' Articles, No. 572 Washington Street.—Mr. Smith has been a manufacturer of cigars and a trader in smokers' articles of every description since the year 1869, and since 1876 has been doing business on the corner of Washington Street and Chickering Place, where he has a cozy, elegant store fitted up with every convenience for himself and his patrons. The stock is a superior and miscellaneous one, and embraces Havana and domestic cigars by other popular makers as well as the favorite brands of his own manufacture. Red Cross and T. E. S. smoking and chewing tobaccos of the finest brands, meerschaum and other pipes, and smokers' requisites of every description are found in ample display, and the prices which prevail are not excelled by any other establishment. Mr. Smith is a Bostonian by birth, and is very popular both as a merchant and private citizen.

F. H. BACON, Manufacturer, Wholesaler and Retailer in Fine Shirts, Etc., No. 50 Hanover Street.—An old and leading Boston shirt emporium and men's haberdashery store is the well known and popular establishment of F. H. Bacon, which is one of the oldest and foremost establishments of the kind in this quarter of the city, having been conducted at the present location by the gentleman whose name stands at the head of the sketch for thirty odd years. Only A1 goods are handled, and bed-rock prices also prevail, while the shirts to order made by Mr. Bacon have long been noted for their general excellence, alike as to neatness, comfort, finish and fabric; perfect fit being guaranteed in every instance. The store, which is 26x80 feet in size, is handsomely furnished and tastefully arranged, four efficient assistants being in attendance, while an extensive and first-class assortment is constantly carried on hand. The stock embraces fine dress and fancy colored shirts, novelties in underwear, rich neck dressing, elegant hosiery, gloves, suspenders, umbrellas, collars and cuffs in newest styles, handsome scarf-pins, sleeve buttons and everything comprehended in gents' furnishing goods—fine custom shirts being a specialty. Mr. Bacon, is a Vermonter by birth, but has resided in this city some forty years and has succeeded in rearing a very fine trade.

THE METROPOLIS OF NEW ENGLAND.

W. W. WINSHIP, Manufacturer of Trunks, Bags, Etc., No. 7 Elm Street.—In the production and sale of trunks, valises and bags in Boston, the position of supremacy is by common consent awarded to Mr. W. W. Winship. This gentleman has an international reputation as a manufacturer and wholesale and retail dealer in trunks, valises, bags, etc., making a leading specialty of sample trunks and bags, and has been established in the business here for fully fifty years. The present store has been occupied by Mr. Winship since 1878 and comprises a five story building, 25x100 feet in dimensions divided into manufactur-

ing and sales departments, and giving ample accommodations for supplying the most extensive demand. The sample trunks and cases of this widely-known and responsible house are rarely equalled in this or any other country for quality of materials, fine finish, thorough durability, elegance, and are the embodiment of skilled workmanship of the highest order of perfection. The best test of a reliable, well made trunk is the length of time it will stand the hard usage of luggage masters and expressmen, and the fact that the Winship trunks have withstood years of continual wear is a guarantee of the claim of the house for superiority and reliability of make. The specialties here produced are not only in heavy and permanent demand in this country, but are ship-

ped in large quantities to Africa, South America and other foreign countries. They are offered to customers at extremely low prices, and are preferred by dealers over all other makes wherever introduced on account of their great salability and solid merits. The history of this responsible house is a pleasant proof of the certainty with which energy and probity will win their way, and that honesty in representation and action is always the best policy. Mr. Winship is a native of Boston, a well-known citizen of Malden, and honored and respected in business, financial and trade circles for his honorable and successful career.

WILLIAM KERR & SON, Wholesale and Retail Dealers in Watches and Jewelry, Silverware, Clocks, Etc., No. 29 Hanover Street.—It is fully thirty years ago since Mr. William Kerr started in business on Hanover Street. By pursuing a policy of small profits and handling only the best goods in the market, whether solid or plated, his reputation became widespread and his house is to-day one of the leading representatives in this line in New England. In connection with his establishing in Boston, it an extremely interesting reminiscence. Mr. Kerr, who was born in Scotland, came to the United States thirty eight years ago and was in New York city for a couple of years. In 1862 he was sent from New York to the old dry goods house of Beebe, Morgan & Co., to enter the employ of that firm, at which time, Hon. Levi P. Morton, the present vice-president of the United States was a member of the firm. Mr. Kerr's business as jeweller and dealer in watches, clocks, silverware steadily enlarged, and in 1878 he removed to his present premises, at No. 29, where he has a very finely fitted up jewelry store. Two years ago, Mr. Albert B. Kerr, his son, was admitted into copartnership, under the existing name and style. He is a young business man of marked ability, and has been actively connected with the business for twelve years prior to entering the firm. Messrs. Kerr & Son carry a heavy stock of the best American watches, including the finest movements, such as Elgin, Waltham, etc. In cases they can meet the most exacting taste, while all pockets can here find a watch they can afford. In jewelry, their stock is always freshly assorted and covers the entire range from diamonds and gold jewelry to the elegant and beautiful designs in rolled plate, etc. This is headquarters for fine sterling silver, and silver plated goods, clocks, bronzes, etc. All goods are warranted as represented. Mr. W. Kerr was one of the founders of the Boston Caledonian Club, and was the chief of same in 1892-3-6-7-8. He is an esteemed member of the Masonic order; of the Order of Oddfellows, and Royal Arcanum.

H. W. MUNCH, Successor to C. R. Munch, Jr., Manufacturer of Ribbon Badges for Societies, Etc., No. 579 Washington Street. The oldest and most prominent house in Boston engaged in a very important branch of this business is that which is conducted by Mr. H. W. Munch, successor to C. R. Munch, Jr., manufacturer of ribbon badges, etc. Mr. H. W. Munch was born in Somerville in 1864, and has been connected with this line of trade from early years, and, desiring to engage in business on his own account, purchased this special branch in 1886. He occupies premises of ample dimensions, which are fully equipped with all the necessary appliances and devices for turning out first-class work, and employment is found of it to a number of skilled and competent operatives, and a full and complete assortment of original and adopted designs and samples of his work can be found at his establishment at all times. He is prepared to furnish in any quantities all kinds of ribbon badges, with suitable and tastefully delineated emblems, for all kinds of societies, such as Knights Templar, Masonic, I. O. O. F.; K of P.; A. O. of F.; S. O. T.; G A. R.; F. M.; T. A. B.; A O.H., and any of the prevailing organizations for funeral, festival, picnic, convention, parade, ball display and exhibition occasions. Especial attention is given to officers, committee, master of ceremonies and other orders for fine work. None but the best qualities of materials are used, and the work is of the highest artistic merit, while the designs are the very latest, most unique and attractive. College, Academic, athletic and all organizations out of the city are furnished with designs, on applications from which to make selections, and all orders are faithfully executed.

JOHN W. McKEY, Crockery, China and Glassware, No. 761 Washington Street.—Mr McKey is an extensive dealer in crockery, china and glassware, fine kitchen furnishing goods, silver-plated ware and lamp goods, and carries the finest stock of goods in this line ever brought to this city. The store is 20x100 feet in size, elegant in all its arrangements and appointments, and perfect in convenience for inspection and sale. The attractiveness of the stock and its artistic arrangement bespeak the taste and systematic methods of the management, and in the showrooms can be seen the most delicate china, decorated mantel and table ware, baccarat glass ware, porcelain, cut glass and the charming Bohemian glassware in vast variety; bisque statuettes of exquisite beauty, brica brac in bewildering array, articles of vertu, and hundreds of pieces for ornament or use, all displayed in a manner befitting the proprietor's distinguished enterprise and ample resources. He has source of supply in London, Paris, Berlin, Vienna and other European capitals, and is in a position to afford the American public unsampled opportunities for securing the most beautiful wares known to civilization. The stock speaks for itself and is full and complete to the extreme, while the prices challenge competition with any contemporary establishment in the country.

C. A. FAXON, ESQ., General Agent Cheshire, Central Vermont and Del. & Hudson Canal Company's Railroads; Office, No. 228 Washington Street.—As one of the greatest railroad centres on the Continent, Boston is headquarters for several of the best conducted and most important lines of passenger travel in the United States and Canada. Notably is this the case with the popular Cheshire and Central Vermont Line, whose extensive Boston traffic has been so long, and so ably conducted by Mr. C. A. Faxon, the widely and favorably known General Agent. The Fitchburg and Cheshire Line has had its general agency in Boston for over forty years past, and since 1867 has been prominently in charge of Mr. Faxon, whose practical experience, widespread influential connections, renders him specially qualified for the discharge of the onerous duties devolving upon him. The routes over which he sells tickets are the most direct to all points in the north-eastern part of the state, and Keene in New Hampshire; Rutland, Burlington and St. Albans in Vermont, with direct connections to all the points of scenic interest, or of industrial and commercial importance, in the northern and central sections of New York. Tickets can be best secured here for any points in the Lake George and Lake Champlain region, and the Adirondacks. Another important class of business, very largely controlled by the Cheshire Line is the direct passenger travel to all points in Canada—to Montreal, Quebec, Ottawa, &c. From Rouse's Point passengers now travel direct by the new Canada Atlantic to Ottawa. New and luxurious parlor and sleeping cars accompany through trains leaving Boston, and tickets and chairs or berths can best be secured at 228 Washington Street. Mr. Faxon was born in Quincy, Mass., and has all his life been actively identified with the business of passenger and freight transportation. He is one of the best-known general agents in New England, a prominent member of the Association of Railroad and Steamboat Agents of Boston.

C. S. SANBORN & CO., Produce Commission Merchants, Poultry, Game, Eggs, Etc.; Nos. 29 North Market and 29 Clinton Streets.—This popular and responsible firm was established in 1866, and during the twenty-three or so years of its existence has maintained an unbroken record of prosperity. Conducting the house on strict business principles, prompt and reliable in meeting all obligations, and withal thoroughly conversant with the trade, it is only in the nature of things that this firm should have attained the full measure of success that invariably attends energy and ability when well directed. The premises occupied are commodious, ample and well kept, some half a dozen in help being employed, while a heavy and fine stock is always carried on hand, including poultry, game, eggs, fruits, vegetables and country produce generally. The firm make a leading specialty of the sale of fowls in summer and of poultry and game in winter, handling large consignments of each daily in their respective seasons, and altogether a flourishing business is carried on, the trade extending all over the New England States. Mr. Sanborn, who is the sole member, is a gentleman of middle age, and a native of New Hampshire, but has long been a respected merchant in this city, and is a well-known member of the Chamber of Commerce. The reference of the house is Faneuil Hall National Bank.

GILLESPIE & HUTCHINSON, Dry and Fancy Goods, Etc., Nos. 58, 60 and 62 Green Street, Corner Staniford.—Conducting their business on a liberal, enterprising and equitable business policy, this firm have not been slow to adopt every position of vantage, so that it is ever found in the foreground, both as regards the newest goods and the latest styles that enables their patrons to speedily satisfy their tastes as to shades and patterns. The establishment has a frontage of sixty feet on Green Street, is ornamented with four handsomely-dressed show windows, while the interior is fitted up in keeping with the correct taste and sound judgment of the proprietors. The store is one of the busiest in its line in the west end, its counters being daily thronged with patrons from all classes of the community. Each department is complete within itself, while the employees are all noted for their courtesy and obliging manners, combining, with a thorough knowledge of their duties, a faculty for anticipating the wants of patrons, laying before them a full variety of textures, patterns and shades from which to choose, so that, when the excellence of the stock is taken into consideration, it is not surprising that rapid sales are made, and general satisfaction given to buyers. Customers can here obtain an outfit not alone of dry and fancy goods, but many articles both for use and adornment, including shirts, undershirts and drawers, hosiery, gloves and neckwear, collars, cuffs and general outfittings for gentlemen; corsets, Jersey waists, skirts and bustles; laces, ribbons and embroideries, and a splendid assortment of fancy goods, notions and small wares of every description. Mr. Gillespie is a native of Scotland, and a resident of this country for forty years, while Mr. Hutchinson was born in Maine. They are both experienced merchants.

H. STEWART, Manufacturer and Dealer in Fine Carriages of every Description; Factory, Nos. 5 to 9 Pitts Street; Salesroom, No. 15 Green Street.—This gentleman has been engaged as a manufacturer and dealer in fine carriages of every description since 1882, making a leading specialty of Berlin coaches, and also giving prompt and skilled attention to repairing in all its branches. His factory comprises two floors, 50x50 feet each, fully equipped with all modern conveniences tending to facilitate rapid and perfect production, and steady employment is given to a force of thirty-five expert workmen. All the operations of the works are conducted under the immediate personal supervision of the proprietor, thus insuring to customers only such products as will withstand the most critical tests, both in regard to the materials used in their construction, and the workmanship employed. The salesrooms on Green Street give ample accommodations for one hundred carriages, and the stock here carried is of a character to command the confidence and patronage of critical and discriminating buyers. The carriages and coaches of this responsible house are highly esteemed wherever introduced for their strength, lightness, ease of draft and elegance of finish, and have no superiors in the market. Business relations with the house may rely upon the promptness and liberality of all transactions. Mr. Stewart is a native of the North of Ireland, and a resident of this country for the past thirty years.

P. W. LYDON, Music-Plate Printer, No. 296 Washington Street.—Mr. P. W. Lydon, the well known music-plate printer, enjoys an A1 reputation for fine work in this line: being, in fact, one of the foremost exponents of the art in Boston. Mr. Lydon, who is a New Yorker by birth, is a practical and expert music plate and general job printer of long and varied experience at the case, and is a thorough master of his art in all its branches. He was formerly of the firm of Blair & Lydon established in 1880, whom he succeeded in July, 1887, and has since conducted the business alone with uninterrupted success. Mr. Lydon occupies commodious and well-equipped quarters here and has in service two presses and ample facilities, while a competent assistant or two is regularly employed. Music-plate printing of every description is executed in the most prompt and excellent manner, all orders receiving immediate attention while the lowest prices consistent with first-class work and reliability at all times prevail in this reliable establishment.

G. H. WHEELER, Real Estate, Mortgages and Insurance, No. 666 Washington Street.—In the line of real estate, mortgages and insurance one of our most successful and reliable houses is that of G. H. Wheeler. This well conducted business was established by Mr. Wheeler in 1867 in the old Boylston building, where it was carried on up to 1887 when the demolition of that well-known structure necessitated the removal of the offices, until the rebuilding of the hall, to the present address. Mr. Wheeler occupies here a fine suite of offices, and continues to push his business with the greatest success. He is an extensive handler of realty throughout the city, knowing intimately the value of every parcel throughout the city where he was born and where he has resided all his life. He also attends to the leasing and management of properties, procures mortgages at the best rates and generally acts as an agent of every kind in connection with real estate and has built up a first-class patronage, representing some of the leading institutions of the country as well as the leading foreign companies. Mr. Wheeler expects to remove to the new Boylston building, with which site he has been so long identified in a short time.

THE METROPOLIS OF NEW ENGLAND. 259

EZRA E. ROCKWOOD, Apothecary, No. 127 Leverett Street.— This gentleman established his business here in 1883, and has achieved a reputation and acquired a trade that places him in the front rank of enterprise and success. His store is spacious in size, eligibly located for trade purposes, and attractive in all its arrangements and appointments. It contains at all times a large and varied stock of the finest drugs and chemicals, proprietary medicines of acknowledged merit, fancy toilet articles, perfumery, and druggists' sundries of every description. There is no department of the drug business so important as the careful, conscientious and intelligent compounding of physicians' prescriptions and family receipts, and this branch holds a permanent position in this establishment. For this purpose the proprietor is supplied with the purest possible drugs, and the utmost accuracy and precision is assured in all transactions. The leading specialty of the business is the manufacture of Phora, a veterinary ointment, made by the Phora Ointment Co., Rockwood & Lamb, proprietors, which is fast superseding all other preparations in the market. It is put up in half-pound tin-boxes, and sold in bulk in any quantity desired. Mr. Rockwood is a native of Massachusetts and an accomplished pharmacist.

W. S. CONDELL, New England Freight and Passenger Agent for the Union Pacific Railway; No. 290 Washington Street.—We confer a favor upon the public when we point out the office of Mr. W. S. Condell, New England Freight and Passenger Agent of the Union Pacific Railway at No. 290 Washington Street, as the most desirable medium in this city for securing transportation to the far west. This is the only direct route to all points in Kansas, Nebraska, Wyoming, Idaho, Dakota, Oregon, Montana, Colorado, Utah and Nevada, and for Los Angeles, San Diego, San Francisco, Sacramento and all points in California, and this office is the only place where passage tickets are purchased and freight is furnished to this section of the country with the least possible annoyance to the public and at the lowest minimum of expense. Freight must be marked "via Union Pacific Railway," and safe conveyance and prompt delivery is invariably assured. The speed, comfort and safety of passengers on this great popular route is becoming to be a proverb to those who have traveled much in the west, and its accommodations are not surpassed by any line in the country, west or east. Mr. Condell has been in the railroad business since April, 1867, and was appointed to his present position in October, 1887. He is a member of the Association of Railroad and Steamship Agents of Boston, and stands deservedly high in social and business circles in this city.

GEO. S. WINSLOW & CO., Provisions, Poultry, Butter, Eggs Produce, Etc., No. 112 Blackstone Street.—This thriving business was established in 1879 by the present senior member, who conducted it alone up to October last, when he admitted into partnership Charles West. They occupy here a compact and neatly kept store and basement, with ample and complete storage facilities, and keep constantly on hand a large, first-class stock, which includes besides choice fresh beef, mutton, lamb, veal and pork; also prime corned, salt, pickled and smoked meats of all kinds, fine dairy butter, cheese, eggs, lard, vegetables, fruits and country produce generally. They handle nothing but reliable and excellent goods, and the trade of the firm, is large and active. Mr. Winslow, who is a man of middle age, was born in Maine, and has resided in Boston since 1868, and Mr. West, who is a comparatively young man, is a native of England, but was brought to this country at the age of six months.

HATCH & CO., Steel and Stencil Letter Cutting, No. 69 Cornhill Street.— Among the different industries of Boston is that of steel and stencil letter cutting. It is carried on quite extensively by the firm of H. Hatch & Co., successors to Smith & Hatch, who established it in 1856. The present firm has continued the business since 1872, and as may be inferred, the transactions are extensive enforcing the conclusion that the facilities for executing the best class of work and filling orders are of the most complete character. For some years the operations were carried on at No. 223 Washington Street, but recently the very eligible premises now occupied at No. 69 Cornhill, were secured which are perfectly equipped for doing all kinds of work pertaining to the business, which includes the manufacture of burning brands for cigar manufacturers and fish packers, and steel stamps for marking wood, leather, steel, silver, etc., and seals for societies, notaries and wax seals for druggists, banks and express companies, and stencils for business purposes and marking clothing and also rubber stamps of all kinds, cancelling stamps, check protectors, door plates, badges and numbers, baggage and key check, etc., and stamps for patentees, cutters and jewelers. Indelible ink, stencil paste, brushes, etc., are also furnished and every attention is given to work for the trade and customers. He also pays particular attention to making music engravers, tools to order of every description in the best manner at reasonable prices, and fully guarantees all his work. He was born and brought up in Charlestown.

JOHN P. CULLEN, Provisions, No. 113 Cambridge Street.—An establishment which is a leader in its special department of industry in this section of the city, is the provision mart of Mr. John P. Cullen. Mr. Cullen, who is a native of Canada, came to Boston in 1872, and in the same year established himself in business at No. 97 Cambridge Street, remaining there until 1879, when his growing trade demanded more commodious quarters, and he removed to the store which he still continues to occupy. The premises are amply commodious, are fitted up in the most tasteful, convenient manner, and are provided with all requisites for the care and handling of stock, and the expeditious handling of trade. The large stock at all times carried embraces the choicest fresh and salt meat of all kinds, and vegetables of every description in their season, and are the best of the kind obtainable in the market. Employment is furnished seven clerks and assistants, and customers have their wants promptly and courteously attended to, while goods are delivered to any part of the city or its vicinity free of charge. Mr. Cullen keeps his stock at all times up to the highest standard of efficiency.

WILLARD M. BACON, Architect, No. 85 Water Street.— Among the most popular and accomplished members of the architectural profession in Boston must be mentioned Mr. Willard M. Bacon. Mr. Bacon was born in Pennsylvania and at an early age began the study of architecture, for which he has a great natural aptitude, and his training for his chosen profession was the best that could be secured for him. He has had ten years hard practical experience and for the past three years has been in business on his own account in Boston, where he has resided for seven years. Numerous fine buildings in all parts of the city and New England attest his knowledge and good taste as an architect and building superintendent. Mr. Bacon is prepared with all the necessary facilities to execute or carry out any architectural undertaking, not only promptly, but with that intelligent apprehension of design which make his efforts so highly appreciated. He will be found prompt, liberal and enterprising, never unsolicitous for the benefit of his patrons, and always prepared to offer advantages in keeping with such a reputation.

J. P. PERRY & CO., Plumbers, Gas and Steam Fitters, No. 123 Devonshire Street.—In the important business of plumbing, together with gas and steam fitting the firm of Messrs. J. P. Perry & Co., No. 123 Devonshire Street, has secured a well earned reputation, and their establishment has now become recognized as one of the most reliable in the city of Boston. This business was established in 1852 by E. W. Norton & Co., who conducted it till 1868, when the present proprietors, Messrs. James P. and George W. Perry, succeeded to the management. The premises occupied comprise a spacious basement 35x60 feet in area, which is fully stocked with a well selected and complete assortment of plumbers' and gas fitters' supplies of every description. Everything in the way of plumbing, ventilating gas and steam fitting is executed in a first-class manner. Contracts for the complete fitting of buildings are satisfactorily performed at the lowest possible prices consistent with the best materials and superior workmanship. Only competent plumbers and mechanics are employed, while all work is executed under the immediate and personal supervision of the partners. The firm make a specialty of sanitary plumbing, and employ twenty workmen, and their trade now extends throughout all sections of Boston and its vicinity.

VIRGINIA, TENNESSEE AND GEORGIA AIR LINE, C. P. Gaither, New England Agent, No. 20 Washington Street.— In the purchase of railway and steamship tickets the question "where to buy" is very frequently more important to decide than "how to buy," and one that appeals forcibly to every prospective traveller on the principal routes of travel. As an aid to those going south from Boston we would direct attention to the advantages offered by the routes represented by Mr. C. P. Gaither, the New England agent for the Virginia, Tennessee and Georgia Air Line, the Shenandoah Valley Route, the Kennesaw Route and the Norfolk Route; also soliciting agent for the celebrated Merchants' and Miners' Transportation Company; with offices eligibly located at No. 20 Washington Street. Mr. Gaither has been closely connected with the railway and transportation business since 1872, and was appointed to his present position in 1878. He is widely experienced, thoroughly informed and brings to bear every facility tending to insure the safety, convenience and comfort of passengers securing transportation through him on any of the above routes. He has resided in Boston for the past thirteen years and is known here as a responsible business man of sterling integrity, who has ever retained the confidence of leading commercial and financial circles, building up for the lines he represents a popularity and a patronage of wide influence by a faithful discharge of his duties to the companies whose interests he represents and to the public which he serves conscientiously and creditably in all respects. Mr. Gaither was born in the State of Maryland in 1850, was in the employ of the Bay Line and Atlantic Coast Lines at Baltimore for several years, is a member of the Railway and Steamboat Agents Association of Boston, and stands high in the esteem and confidence of corporations and commercial circles as a reliable agent and an energetic and successful business man.

J. TINKHAM, Furnishing Undertaker, and Coffin Warerooms, No. 20 Howard Street.—Mr. Tinkham is the oldest exponent of his profession in Boston, having been engaged in it for the lengthy period of forty-five years. The business which he controls was founded some forty years ago by Mr. L. L. Tarbell, and fifteen years later Mr. Tinkham succeeded him to the management. Under his proprietorship the house has attained its present foremost position, and become recognized as a leader among its contemporaries. The premises occupied as office and warerooms consist of a store 25x100 feet in dimensions finely appointed and equipped in the most approved style with every convenience. A full stock is constantly kept on hand of coffins, caskets, burial cases and funeral furnishings of all kinds, and the establishment is amply prepared to meet all demands that may be made upon its resources. The proprietor has three fine hearses and they are kept in his own stable. Funerals are taken entire charge of, every detail being given the most careful supervision, and all services are conducted in the most considerate manner. Mr. Tinkham is a native of Massachusetts, and his reputation for honorable dealing is established far beyond the requirements of praise.

D. AVENPORT, PETERS & CO., Lumber Merchants, Offices: Mason Building, No. 70 Kilby Street.—The oldest concern engaged in this branch of trade is that of Messrs. Davenport, Peters & Co. This business was established in 1811 by Mr. Edward D. Peters, and who was succeeded by his son Mr. George H. Peters, under the style of George H. Peters & Co. In 1886 after a lengthy and prosperous mercantile career, Mr. G. H. Peters retired and the new firm of Davenport, Peters & Co. was formed, composed of Mr. George H. Davenport, Mr. G. Gorham Peters and Mr. William Bacon. They deal direct with headquarters of the various lumber regions as sources of supply for their customers, and are in a position to offer substantial inducements in regard to prices and quality of every description of hardwood lumber, white and yellow pine, cargo and car lots of oak, ash, maple, whitewood, sycamore, black walnut, cherry, etc. Michigan and Canada pine, yellow pine and cypress lumber and shingles, are delivered direct by them to their customers in all parts of New England. They handle several million feet annually and do one of the most active and enlarging trades in this line in the Eastern States. Mr. G. H. Davenport was born in Boston, and is an able and respected member of commercial circles. He became connected with the house in 1865 and went into copartnership in 1876. He has built up a large trade on the substantial basis of equity and due care of customers' interests. Mr. G. Gorham Peters was born in Boston, and is the son of Mr. George H. Peters, founder of the concern. He has had an intimate identification with the trade from youth up. Mr. William Bacon, is also a native Bostonian, who became a member of the firm in 1886. The house is an active member of the Lumber Dealers Association.

FRANK X. OBERLE, Manufacturer of the Bostonia, Qui Vive, Vega 41, and other brands of Fine Cigars, No. 1 Central Wharf.—This gentleman is deservedly prominent and popular as an extensive manufacturer of fine cigars, and has been established in the business here since 1872. He occupies spacious and well equipped premises, and gives steady employment to twenty skilled and experienced hands. The specialties manufactured by this responsible house include the Boquet le Bostonial Bostonia, Qui Vive, Vega 41, and other brands, all of which are of prime quality and have a wide sale owing to their reliability and uniform excellence. It has always been the aim of Mr. Oberle to make a thoroughly good cigar, that will be readily enjoyed by connoisseurs, and to keep his brands up to a high and uniform standard of excellence. His cigars are handled by the best retailers, hotels and restaurants in this city, and are eagerly sought for by lovers of good smoking everywhere. Only fine goods are manufactured. Mr. Oberle is a native of Germany, a resident of this city since his boyhood, and a young man of large practical experience as a manufacturer.

M. E. GOODRIDGE, Eliot Street Stables, Nos. 129 and 131 Eliot Street.—This is undeniably the largest and best ventilated stable in the city, and was opened for the accommodation of the public in August, 1888, by the present proprietor, who had for some years previously been engaged in the business at Haverhill, Mass. The building is of brick, containing four stories and a basement, and possesses first-class accommodations for two hundred and fifty horses. Particular attention is paid to boarding and baiting, while a splendid line of equipages is kept for hire at moderate rates. The stock of horses comprises those suitable for ladies and invalids' use, as well as others noted for speed and staying qualities. Some of the finest turn-outs to be seen in the city come from this establishment, including coupés, coaches, victorias, landaus, T carts and road wagons in great variety. The facilities of this house for boarding horses are not equalled in the city. Competent and careful grooms and stablemen look after the comforts of the stock. The institution is a credit to the enterprise and ability displayed in its management. Mr. Goodridge is a native of Haverhill, Mass.

D. W. FITZPATRICK, Artist Tailor, No. 114 Court Street.—This gentleman started in business originally in East Cambridge, in 1869, subsequently settling in California, where he resided for thirteen years, and returning to Boston in 1884. His business premises are spacious in size, eligibly located for trade purposes, and perfect in convenience for display, inspection and sale. Here is exhibited one of the finest stocks of cloths and trimmings ever brought to this city. The very best sources of American and European production contributing to its wealth. It is complete in material, design and novelty, and gives the limit of manufacture in high-class goods. Mr. Fitzpatrick devotes his time and talents to fine custom work only, and the garments produced here are simply perfection in style, fit and artistic workmanship. To be found among his permanent customers are many of Boston's best-dressed citizens, gentlemen old and young, who understand the merits of a thoroughly first-class tailor, and who find in Mr. Fitzpatrick's establishment not only a line of goods that is at all times superior, but a place where the general make-up, fit and trimming of a garment is a matter of careful consideration and study. When it is learned that a force of fifty-five skilled hands is employed, the extensive business that is here transacted can be fully appreciated. Mr. Fitzpatrick is one of Boston's most successful business men, eminently fair and conscientious in all his dealings, and widely popular as a thoroughly accomplished master of his art.

THE METROPOLIS OF NEW ENGLAND.

THOS. J. HOLMES, Specialist in Atomizing Tubes, Etc., No. 50 Sudbury Street.—Atomizers should be in every house, as their use is extremely beneficial in the sick room, diffusing disinfectants and thereby purifying the atmosphere, and at the same time making the room more comfortable and conducive to health. In this connection special reference is made in this commercial review of Boston to Mr. Thomas J. Holmes, specialist in atomizing tubes for all purposes, and proprietor and manufacturer of the Mammoth Atomizer, Boston perfumer, Centennial Atomizer, Favorite perfumer, etc. Mr. Holmes established this business in 1870, since which period he has built up a liberal, influential and permanent patronage, not only in all sections of the United States and Canada, but also in Central and South America, Europe and Japan. There is nothing better for moistening plants. By the use of an atomizer the leaves and vines may be kept moist, as are the garden flowers, by the falling dew. For throwing medicaments they are useful beyond compare. The throat may be sprayed by the "Reversible Atomizer," and more thoroughly than is possible by gargling, or by any other process. The same atomizer may be reversed to throw the spray upward behind the soft palate, and Catarrh alleviated and cured. For perfuming the room with grateful odors, there is nothing so well adapted. They are for sale by all druggists and apothecaries and by dealers in fancy goods throughout the United States and Canada, and are

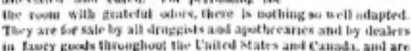

general favorites wherever introduced, always commanding a ready sale. Mr. Holmes was born in New York, but has resided in Boston for the last sixteen years.

VINTON & JENKINS, Manufacturers of Boots and Shoes, Stoneham, Mass. Boston Office, No. 16 Lincoln Street.— Among those who devote themselves exclusively to the manufacture of women's, misses' and children's boots and shoes are Messrs. Vinton & Jenkins, of No. 16 Lincoln Street. This concern was founded in 1876, and ranks among the foremost in the trade. Their headquarters and factories (two) are at Stoneham, Mass. From the outset the firm have kept themselves abreast of the times in adopting the most improved machinery, and it would be difficult to find shoe factories anywhere better equipped than those of Messrs. Vinton and Jenkins, who have every known facility for turning out the very best machine sewed and standard screw goods in large and ever multiplying quantities. A large force of hands is employed, and about 1500 pairs are produced daily and shipped to all parts of the New England and western states. The Boston office, where is kept on view a fine sample stock, representing the products of the factories, is under the management of Mr. F. M. Carter. Orders are shipped direct from the factories, and all transactions are guaranteed to afford satisfaction in every case.

GEO. C. ROCKWELL & SON, Produce Commission Merchants, No. 75 Richmond Street.—Among the many firms considered prominent and influential in the produce commission business in this city we may note the house of Geo. G. Rockwell & Son, which has been established many years. It dates its existence from 1851, when it was established by Rockwell, Bigley & Co., and afterwards continued by Rockwell & Adams, who were succeeded by Rockwell Bros., who carried it on until 1871 when the firm was dissolved, Mr. Geo. C. Rockwell continuing the business, and four years ago admitted his son to an interest. As commission merchants the firm is daily in receipt of consignments of farm and dairy products of all kinds, and handle in large quantities fresh, dried and pickled fish, poultry, and game when in season. Potatoes and eggs are a specialty and a large local wholesale trade is supplied. Both members of the firm are familiar with this line of business, and consignors may depend upon their making the proceeds fully commensurate with the market rates. They are honorable, reliable business men, and stand foremost among the solid commission merchants of this city, and are in a position to afford extraordinary advantages to those who patronize their house. Mr. Geo. C. Rockwell, who was born in Nova Scotia, has resided in Boston many years. His son, Mr. J. W. Rockwell, is a native of Boston.

JOHN H. WEBB, Practical Engraver, No. 75 Hanover Street.— The art of engraving on metals is well represented in this city by Mr. John H. Webb, who has been established in the business for the past thirteen years. Mr. Webb has had quite an extended experience in the art, and executes work which is not surpassed. He is doing a first-class business, and engraves door plates in script or solid letters; also, numbers and metal signs, and badges and name plates for machinery, and makes to order dies, stencils, &c., and is particularly expert in engraving jewelry and silverware, originating many beautiful designs in monograms and ornamental letters. He is well equipped and is provided with every facility for executing the very best class of work, and receives a liberal patronage. Mr. Webb, who was born in England, has lived in this country since childhood. He was born in 1870, and during his long residence in Boston has become very popular in all circles.

J. CALEY & CO., Engravers and Manufacturers of Metal and Brass Signs, No. 88 Kingston Street.—A representative concern, is that of J. Caley & Co., engravers and manufacturers of metal signs. This business was founded in 1879 by Mr. Caley who by superior work and prompt and satisfactory business methods has built up what may well be termed a representative city enterprise in his line. The commodious shop is supplied with all requisite facilities for the advantageous prosecution of the work, and a full and complete stock of materials is carried. Metal signs of all sizes and in many styles, are manufactured, a specialty being made of brass signs. Experienced and skilful artisans are employed and the work turned out has a standard reputation for the highest degree of excellence. Mr. Caley is practical and skillful at his trade and has long occupied a prominent and representative position.

J. M. HALL & CO., House Painters, Etc., No. 113 Standard Street.—The business of the painter and interior decorator is an important one and is ably represented by Messrs. J. M. Hall & Co. The firm have every facility requisite for the purposes of the business, and as they are both practical men of long experience can always guarantee the best class of work and full satisfaction. They are well known as artistic fresco painters and are pronounced fully equal to the best in the city. Particular attention is also given to house painting and graining and glazing, and estimates are furnished and contracts made for painting of every description. The store occupied is 27x65 feet in area, in which is kept everything in the line of painters' supplies, white lead, colors, ready mixed paints, brushes, etc. Messrs. J. M. Hall and Geo. Hall, the copartners, are both natives of Boston and as business men and citizens, are held in high esteem. They occupy a leading position among those who give their attention to house painting and the decoration of the interior of buildings, and dealers in paints, oils, and painters' supplies.

J. S. ZIEGLER & CO., Real Estate and Mortgages, Room 6, No. 15 Congress Street.—The buying and selling of real estate and negotiating loans is a business well represented by a number of enterprising men of high standing standing and sterling worth. Prominent among them is the firm of J. J. Ziegler & Co., whose office is in Room 6, No. 15 Congress Street. The operations are conducted by Mr. J. J. Ziegler, the head of the firm, who is a gentleman well-known in this city, and one in whom the utmost confidence can be placed. He has had quite an extended experience in the purchase and sale of realty, and his judgment can always be relied on. He is familiar with all the desirable sites in and around Boston, and always has very desirable properties to dispose of to those seeking first-class investments, and by his faithful and conscientious zeal he has secured a substantial clientage whose confidence and esteem he enjoys in the highest degree, and owing to the wide range and high character of his connections he is enabled to effect transactions satisfactory to all concerned. Loans on bond and mortgage are also negotiated by Mr. Ziegler, who gives his prompt attention to all orders entrusted to him. Mr. Ziegler is a native of Switzerland, but has been a citizen of Boston since 1871. His patronage is large and steadily increasing, and he stands high in business and financial circles and in the estimation of all who have dealings with him.

HENRY KELLOGG, JR., Note Broker, Nos. 25 Congress Square and 65 Devonshire Street.—Prominent among the reliable note and insurance brokers in this city is Mr. Henry Kellogg, Jr. This gentleman is actively engaged in buying and selling notes, discounting commercial paper, and is a licensed insurance broker, bringing to bear upon every branch of his business the widest range of experience and knowledge of financial matters, values and properties. He established his business here in 1872, and numbers among his permanent patrons many of the wealthiest and most reputable citizens of Boston and its surrounding towns, while his reputation for affording accurate information and valuable aid to investors and property owners is second to none of his contemporaries. He is prepared to place insurance policies in any company desired, quoting the lowest rates of premium and guaranteeing the prompt and liberal adjustment of all losses. No more reliable, well-informed and conscientious broker can be found in the city, and his success and popularity has been honestly won. Mr. Kellogg is a native Bostonian.

NEWHALL & ENGLISH, Costumers, No. 47 Hanover Street, Fred. P. Baxter, Manager.—Among Boston's leading and most popular costumers may be named Newhall & English, whose well-equipped establishment is under the efficient management of Fred. P. Baxter. Here can be found at all times an extensive, complete and varied assortment of elegant costumes in every size, style, variety and description, for balls, parties, weddings, masquerades, private theatricals, &c., at exceedingly moderate rates, while out of town parties are served also in the most expeditious manner at lowest terms. This thriving business was established in 1878, and was formerly conducted at No. 7 Tremont Row, whence it moved to the present commodious quarters four years ago, and has since been continued here under Mr. Baxter's management with highly gratifying success. Everything in the costuming line may here be found always, while all orders receive immediate attention, and the patronage of the firm, which extends all over Massachusetts, Maine and New Hampshire, is large and influential. Mr. Baxter, its manager, is a native of Bath, Me., but has resided in this city since three years ago. He is a gentleman thoroughly conversant with the business in its every feature and detail.

B. F. BARTLETT, Periodicals, Cigars, Pictures and Framing, No. 67 Stamford Street.—A large business is carried on by Mr. B. F. Bartlett the well-known dealer in periodicals, cigars, pictures, frames, etc. He has been established for the past ten years and recently moved to the neatly fitted up store now occupied. The premises have dimensions of 20x55 feet and are specially arranged for the purposes of the business and contain a large, valuable assortment of of the finest brands of all the popular brands, and all the leading desirable smoking and chewing tobacco, cigarettes, pipes of all kinds, and all those articles required by those who use tobacco in its many forms. Mr. Bartlett also makes a fine display of all the various periodicals, magazines and the popular literature of the day, and also plain and fancy stationery, blank books, albums, chromos, photos, and all kinds of pictures and frames, and a general line of fancy goods. Framing pictures and photos is a special feature of the business, Mr. Bartlett filling orders promptly in the most acceptable manner. He occupies a very desirable location and is conducting a first-class, substantial business.

J. A. BARRY, Millinery, No. 717 Washington Street.—A popular millinery establishment in this city, and which is a recognized leader of fashions, is that conducted by J. A. Barry who has been established in business here since 1886, and during this period has built up a large, first-class trade through her artistic ability, and the popular prices which have been followed in her dealings. The fine large store occupied has a frontage of eighteen feet and a depth of eighty feet, is tastefully furnished throughout, and is one of the finest and most attractive establishments in its line on the street. The store is filled with a large stock of bonnets, hats, caps, flowers, feathers, ornaments, etc., in all the latest fashions of the day. A staff of six expert milliners is employed, and careful attention is given the execution of orders for stylish hats or bonnets, the most artistic effects being attained in this line, while the prices are as reasonable as could be expected for such excellent goods. Miss Barry devotes her entire attention to the direction of her affairs, and is an expert in her business. She is a native of Boston.

GOULD'S Hat, Trunk, and Glove Depot, No. 747 Washington Street.—The business of this representative establishment was originally started in another store on Washington Street by the present proprietor, Mr. Gould, in 1880, and in June, 1888, it was removed to its present quarters at No. 747 Washington Street. Mr. Gould, who is a Bostonian by birth, and a gentleman of middle age, was formerly a manufacturer of hats on Chauncy Street, and has had vast experience in business affairs and is fully conversant with the best methods of management. The premises occupied for the business are neat and compact, and are fitted up in the most attractive manner, while every convenience and accommodation are at hand for the handling of trade. The fine display of goods to be seen here, embraces a full assortment of stylish hats and caps of all kinds, also a choice line of gloves, trunks, and traveling bags in great variety. None but the most reliable grades of goods in the lines named, are kept on hand, and the brisk trade supplied, enables the proprietor to sell to his customers at prices that cannot be surpassed for cheapness. Mr. Gould devotes his entire attention to his large business, and aims to give the fullest satisfaction to all who have dealings with him. Mr. Gould makes a specialty of children's hats, caps, etc., and sells at wholesale and retail.

W. H. LITTLEFIELD & CO., Apothecaries, No. 55 Green Street.—One of the leading and best equipped pharmacies in this quarter of the city is the neat and well ordered drug store of W. H. Littlefield & Co. Physicians' prescriptions and family receipts are here compounded in the most careful and accurate manner, in every instance from absolutely pure ingredients, while bottom prices also prevail. The store, which is 20x60 feet in size and situated on a busy corner, is tastefully appointed and admirably kept, while two experienced assistants are in attendance; the proprietors exercising close personal supervision over the laboratory. A large and carefully selected stock is constantly carried, embracing besides fresh and pure drugs, chemicals and standard medicines of all kinds, acids, extracts, herbs, roots, barks, medicinal liquors, mineral waters, proprietary remedies of merit and pharmaceutical specialities in great variety, also a full and fine assortment of toilet articles, perfumes, fancy soaps, sponges, chamois and choice cigars; special attention being given to prescriptions. This excellent and well known pharmacy was originally established about twenty years ago, and in 1886 came into control of the firm whose name heads the sketch. Mr. W. H. Littlefield, who is sole proprietor, is an experienced apothecary, and fully merits the large measure of popular favor he enjoys.

JOHN HATCHMAN, Manufacturer of Mouldings and Picture Frames, No. 1019 Washington Street.—In the gilding trade in Boston, no one is better known or has a longer or more honorable record than John Hatchman, who is also a manufacturer of mouldings and picture frames. Mr. Hatchman has been identified with the trade for over half a century and has carried on business with great success during that long period. He occupies a fine factory, 30x75 feet in dimensions and has every modern facility and improvement for turning out the finest kind of work. He is the oldest gilder in Boston, and as a matter of course has long enjoyed a trade of large dimensions both in ornamenting and gilding work, samples of which may be found in most of the principal houses and establishments of the city. For a number of years he has also been extensively engaged in the manufacture of mouldings and picture frames and he has besides a department devoted to funeral designs in immortelles, which is under the able management of Mrs. Harris. Mr. Hatchman is a native of Boston, and since his earliest days has been working at the gilding trade.

C. F. TUTTLE, Real Estate, No. 113 Devonshire Street.—This gentleman is a well-known citizen of West Newton, prominent in the business circles of this city, and has been established as a dealer in real estate and as a commercial broker since 1873. He possesses an intimate knowledge of the best residential and business properties in the city and its adjoining towns, and has upon his books some of the choicest bargains in real estate to be found in Boston. As the agent for the purchase and sale of realty and in the management of all interests connected therewith, in the collection of house and ground rents, in the adjustment of taxes and assessments, in expert appraisements of property, in the negotiation of loans on bond and mortgage, in the careful and skillful management of estates, and in the arbitration of complicated property interests, Mr. Tuttle brings to bear large experience and thorough knowledge of every detail. Mr. Tuttle was born in New Hampshire, settling in West Newton twenty-two years ago, and is a gentleman of wide acquaintance and high repute in social and business circles.

WILLIAM L. SEXAUER, Manufacturer and Dealer in Havana and Domestic Cigars, Etc., No.460 Washington Street.—A well known prominent business man of this city engaged in the manufacture and dealing in cigars is Mr. William L. Sexauer. He has been established in business since 1876, and by energy and enterprise he has achieved a wide popularity for superiority and excellence. The dimensions of the premises are 15x50 feet, and contain a large stock of choice cigars of his own manufacture, and also a general line of all the favorite brands of Havana and domestic goods together with smokers' articles of every kind, and fine cut and plug chewing and also smoking tobacco made by the best manufacturers in the country. These goods are all of high standard quality and are sold at prices as low as any others on the market. Mr Sexauer, who is a New Yorker by birth, is about forty years of age. He came to Boston in 1866, and has since become closely identified with the affairs of the city. He is a practical cigar maker, and turns out a line of fine and medium grade Havana and domestic goods that are unexcelled for quality or flavor.

MISS V. A. MILLS, Corsets and Panniers, No. 12 West Street.—Prominent among the enterprising business women of Boston is Miss V. A. Mills, of No. 12 West street (Rooms Nos. 9 and 10), who is a reliable manufacturer of corsets and panniers to order, and has, since the inception of the enterprise in 1875, built up a widely extended and permanent patronage among many of the best known residents of the city. Miss Mills is practically experienced in every detail of the business engaged in, and gives her personal supervision to the work of the eight skilful and painstaking hands whom she employs. She makes a speciality of corsets and panniers to order, and guarantees the quality, fit and general excellence of these goods to be strictly reliable in every particular, as well as reasonable in cost price. Miss Mills keeps in stock a fine assortment of sample goods, and has fitted up her establishment with all needed conveniences and facilities. She is a native of Boston, and a highly respected member of the community.

A. J. CHILD, Mercantile Boarding and Baiting Stable, No. 37 Richmond Street.—A stable that has gained not only a high reputation, but an extensive and solid permanent patronage, is that conducted by Mr. A. J. Child. Mr. Child founded the business here in 1877 and in 1886 he formed a partnership with Mr. H. S. Coolidge, under the firm style of Child & Coolidge. In December, 1887, Mr. Coolidge retired, and Mr. Child again became the sole proprietor. He is a horseman of long experience and has had a systematic and thorough training in the care and treatment of the noble animal. The stable is a two-story brick building, measuring 80x90 feet, and this is equipped and provided with all modern improved stable equipments of the most acceptable kind. The building is well lighted, and thoroughly drained and ventilated, and first class accommodations are afforded for one hundred horses and an equal number of vehicles. About two hundred horses are fed here daily, and fourteen experienced stablemen are permanently employed. Special terms are offered for permanent boarders, and the establishment is a very popular one with horse owners in this section of the city. Mr. Child was born in Connecticut in 1841, and during the Civil War he served with the Union forces for three years. For thirty years he has been a resident of Boston.

C. E. LINDALL, Manager Lindall's Band, No. 180 Washington Street.—There is perhaps not one among the many excellent bands that have come into existence of recent years in this city that has secured firmer hold on popular favor than Lindall's Military Band and Orchestra, C. E. Lindall, Manager. This band was organized on April 17, 1887, and from its inception has steadily grown in popularity and patronage on absolute merit; excellent music, promptness and reliability being the special features contributing to its well merited success. The band comprises twenty-five members, and the leader is prepared to furnish first-class music for all occasions, including balls, picnics, weddings, street parades, etc., at popular prices. Mr. Lindall, who is the efficient leader and manager, is a thoroughly competent and experienced musician, and prior to establishing himself in business here had been for some years with Chandler's Band, of Portland, Me., his native city. Mr. Lindall also gives lessons on the cornet and piano, and is an expert performer on both instruments.

THOS. McMAHON, Wholesale and Retail Dealer in Cigars, Tobacco, Etc., No. 20 Hanover Street.—Mr. Thomas McMahon has had quite an extended experience in the business, and during the two years he has been established in his present location his trade has been steadily growing. The store is well arranged and is stocked with a choice assortment of goods, including all the favorite brands of imported and domestic, fine and medium grade cigars, and also the best brands of chewing and smoking tobaccos and cigarettes; also, snuffs and pipes of all kinds, and smokers articles generally. Besides the retail trade, Mr. McMahon has built up quite an extensive wholesale business and supplies a demand derived from the city and adjacent sections. Mr. McMahon, who has lived in Boston for about eleven years, was born in Kings County, Nova Scotia.

N. M. LADD, Boots, Shoes and Rubbers, No. 19 Leverett street.—The popular shoe store conducted by N. M. Ladd, is a neat, well kept and reliable establishment, and one of the leading stores of the kind in this vicinity, as well as one of the oldest. The business was originally started about thirty years ago by a Mr. Colby, and in 1884 came into control of the gentleman whose name heads this sketch. Nothing but first-class goods are handled, while the very lowest prices consistent therewith always prevail, purchasers being assured of receiving excellent value and satisfactory treatment here. The store is compact, ample and nicely fitted up, two efficient assistants being in attendance, while a large and well selected stock is kept constantly on hand, including ladies', misses', gents', youths', boys' and children's boots and shoes in all sizes, widths, styles and grades, and also rubbers and slippers. Mr. Ladd is a native of Andover, Mass., but a resident of Boston some years, and fully merits the liberal measure of popular favor he enjoys.

C. H. SiMONDS & CO., Printers, No. 45 Temple Place.—The steam job printing establishment of Messrs. C. H. Simonds & Co. was founded in 1852 by Mr. C. H. Simonds, who in connection with his son still continues the business. When Mr. Simonds first commenced business, the hand press was the only mechanical contrivance for taking an impression of movable type, and the impressions were limited to from one to three hundred per hour, according to the nature of the work. Now with the aid of steam and modern printing presses, thousands of impressions are made each hour. Messrs. Simonds' establishment has kept well in the front rank with modern improvements, and to-day is one of the best equipped printing houses in the city of Boston. The premises occupied comprise a spacious floor 30x125 feet in dimensions, which is equipped with every requisite for the systematic and successful prosecution of the business. Here forty skilled printers are constantly employed, and the trade of the house is by no means confined to Boston, but extends to all sections of New England. Mr. Simonds is prepared to execute all kinds of newspaper and book composition and job work, also plain and ornamental printing in the highest style of art at the lowest possible prices consistent with first-class work. All kinds of printing are executed promptly and satisfaction is guaranteed. Mr. Simonds, Sr., was born in Boston, and is an accomplished master of his art.

ADAMS, BLODGET & CO., Bankers, No. 20 Congress Street.— This house was established in January, 1886, the copartners being Messrs. Walter B. Adams, Wm. Blodget and E. P. Merritt, all of whom possess great practical experience, and being an intimate knowledge of the stock and bond markets to bear on their business, in connection with the prompt and faithful execution of the orders of their numerous customers. The firm transact a general banking business, receiving deposits subject to draft at sight. As brokers, Messrs. Adams, Blodget & Co. fill all orders promptly for the purchase or sale of all stocks, bonds, government and miscellaneous securities as listed on the Boston or New York Stock Exchanges, strictly on commission, and there is no firm in the city better qualified to handle the accounts of capitalists or active operators. Mr. E. P. Merritt represents the firm on the Stock Exchange, and the New York correspondents of this reliable house are Messrs. Winslow, Lanier & Co., and Messrs. Spencer Trask & Co. The firm have a private wire to New York.

T. W. TOWNSEND, Justice of the Peace, Real Estate, Etc.; No. 113 Devonshire Street.—Prompt and faithful attention to the interests of clients will always bring the sure reward of success to the agent or attorney who practices these virtues. Such has been the result in the case of Mr. T. W. Townsend, the well-known Real Estate Agent and Justice of the Peace, whose office is located at No. 113 Devonshire Street. This gentleman has been established in the real estate business here for a period of twenty-five years, and has a reputation and standing in the real estate market second to none of his contemporaries. He is at all times prepared to buy, sell, rent and exchange city and country property of all kinds, on the most reasonable rates of commission, while he makes a leading specialty of Somerville realty. His patrons come from all parts of the state, and his services are in special and constant demand by leading capitalists, investors and property-owners in this city. He has always on his books desirable properties to sell or rent, and he is also prepared to take the entire management of estates, to collect rents, make investments, and to negotiate loans on bond and mortgage. Mr. Townsend is a native of the State of Maine, and is also Justice of the Peace for the Commonwealth of Massachusetts.

CLARK POWERS, Musical Goods, Violins, Strings, Etc., No. 45 Court Street.—Mr. Powers is a practical violin maker and has achieved a wide celebrity for his success as a skilful maker and repairer. He gives particular attention to repairing and making violins to order and executes orders for all parts of the United States. Besides manufacturing violins, Mr. Powers carries a large valuable assortment of all kinds of musical instruments and musical merchandise, and is doing a large first-class substantial business. A native of Vermont but for some years a resident of Boston, Mr. Powers has always been popular in this community and was for a time connected with the firm of Elias Howe.

WARREN'S MILITARY BAND AND ORCHESTRA. John P. Warren, Leader and Agent, No. 116 Court Street.— Warren's Military Band and Orchestra, is, in all respects, one of the leading best-equipped and most popular bands of Boston. Mr. Warren, the leader and manager of the organization, is a gentleman of thirty-six, and a native of Reading, Mass. He is an expert cornet player and an experienced musician of many years' practical and successful experience, as well as a young man of energy and enterprise. Warren's Military Band and Orchestra was established in 1873, and during the fifteen years of its existence has steadily strengthened its hold on popular favor. It numbers thirty performers, this number being increased to fifty at short notice when necessary, and music is furnished for all occasions, including balls, parties, weddings, picnics, theatricals, &c., in first-class style at reasonable rates. Mr. Warren has furnished the music during the past two seasons for J. F. Folsom, at Oak Island by the sea, the popular summer resort at Revere Beach.

SLAYTON & BOYNTON, Commission Merchants for the sale of General Produce, No. 19 Blackstone Street.—This well-ordered and stanch concern was established in March, 1887, and from its inception Messrs. Slayton & Boynton have steadily pushed their way to favor and prosperity. Consignments placed with these gentlemen for disposal are judiciously handled, while returns for the same are promptly furnished in every instance; this being a special feature of the house. The firm occupy a commodious store, with ample cool storage quarters elsewhere also, and carry on hand at all times a large and fine stock, which includes butter, eggs, cheese, poultry, beans, butter, cheese, eggs and beans being specialties. Consignments are received from all parts of the United States, and all orders by telephone (No. 1783) or otherwise, are filled in the most expeditious and satisfactory manner, some half a dozen experienced assistants being in attendance. Messrs. J. C. F. Slayton and W. W. Boynton are both natives of Vermont and have resided in Boston for a number of years. They are popular and respected members of the Chamber of Commerce.

JOHN S. RICE & CO., Tin Can Manufacturers, Etc., Nos. 19 to 23 John Street.—This thriving enterprise was started in 1866, and during the twenty odd years of its existence the firm has maintained an unbroken career of prosperity, its trade which is wholesale altogether, being at once large and active, and extends throughout the whole of the New England States. The work and warerooms are spacious and commodious, ample and complete manufacturing and storage facilities being at hand, while from twelve to twenty expert workmen are employed. The productions include oil cans, bakers' cans, tin kettles and tin and sheet-iron vessels of every description; also Evenden's Patent Wood-Jacket can, cracker boxes and varnish cans, while jobbing of all kind likewise is done to order in the most expeditious and excellent manner; all work executed in this establishment being fully warranted. Mr. Rice, who is the sole proprietor, is a gentleman in the prime of life, and a native of Wayland, Mass., but has lived in this city some thirty years. He is a practical and skilful tin and sheet iron worker himself of many years' experience in the exercise of his art, and is thoroughly conversant with the business in all its branches.

CHAS. KIMBALL, Photographer, No. 140 Court Street.—Mr. Kimball, who is a native of Connecticut, came to Boston when a young man and in 1868 opened a photographic gallery, achieving a first-class reputation from the start. His present establishment, which he has occupied for the past five years, includes commodious reception and operating rooms fitted up with excellent taste and provided with all the latest scientific photographic apparatus and appliances and having every modern convenience at hand. Mr. Kimball does a large business in all branches of the art, his customers being found not only in the city, but largely out of town. He has been singularly successful in every case in reproducing the expression and characteristics of sitters, giving a warmth to the picture and making a real souvenir of the subject's appearance at the time. He is especially successful in grouping, having the true instinct of pose and softening all those peculiarities which more or less distinguish every individual, so difficult to obtain in groups.

THE METROPOLIS OF NEW ENGLAND.

M. E. NASH, Furnaces, Stoves, Ranges, Grates, Etc., No. 38 Essex Street.—This first-class concern was established in 1866, by Fawcett, & Hawkes, who conducted it under that style up to 1876, when the firm became Hawkes, Nash & Co. Two years later Mr. M. E. Nash succeeded to the sole control of the business which he still retains. The premises occupied are 18x50 feet in dimensions with a shop in rear 40x30 feet. A large stock of furnaces, stoves, ranges, grates, etc., is carried in the store, the principal line being Nash's improved Furnaces, which are made entirely of cast iron and are so constructed as to combine

perfect combustion of fuel with great radiating power, durability, and ease of management, qualities which render them the most economical and desirable in use. Several thousands of these furnaces have been placed in churches, school houses, stores, public buildings, private residences, etc., and have given universal satisfaction. Mr. Nash employs from six to eight men in his establishment both in manufacturing and in repairs for Fawcett & Hawkes' furnaces and ranges. The trade is extensive all over New England.

CLARENCE A. DORR, Note Broker, No. 55 State Street.—Mr. Dorr has had vast experience in his branch of financial enterprise, and on November 1, 1869, embarked in business on his own account. For sixteen years he has been located in the same building in which his office now is, and he has occupied his present office for more than a dozen years. His long experience and his natural adaptability and sound judgment well fit him for the successful and satisfactory carrying on of the important and responsible business entrusted to him. Mr. Dorr deals in all kinds of commercial paper corporation, city, town and railroad loans, and also collateral loans for savings banks and trusts, etc. He controls a very large business, and is possessed of every facility by telephone, private telegraphic and correspondence service for securing the latest quotations on the principal exchanges in the country for all classes of securities. For prompt and faithful execution of all commissions entrusted to him, Mr. Dorr is thoroughly reliable. He was born in Burlington.

JOHN DAVIS & SON, Ship Stores, etc., No. 304 Commercial and No. 179 Fulton Streets.—Among the most popular, old established and reliable concerns engaged in this line of trade in the city is that of Messrs. John Davis & Son. When this business was established in 1849, it was founded by the firm of Davis & Howe. The firm afterwards underwent three or four changes. First it became John Davis & Son, then Davis & Coley, and 1876, John Davis & Son again. The senior member of this firm died in 1880, and under this firm name the business has since been conducted by his son, Mr. J.

E. Davis, who was reared in the business and is familiar with it in every detail. He is a native of Boston and resides at Cambridge, is an owner of vessels and a business man of considerable prominence and deserved popularity. His store has an area of 25x125 feet, and is fitted up and appointed with every appliance and convenience for conducting business on a large scale. The stock is a large and comprehensive one, and it embraces everything in the line of staple and fancy groceries, flour, molasses, ropes, cordage, oils, paints, and everything required in the provisioning of ships. A large trade is done with vessels coming to this port, and the business partakes of both a wholesale and retail character. Several assistants are employed and orders are filled promptly and at the lowest possible rates.

C. F. ROBINSON, Produce Commission Merchant, and Dealer in Butter, Cheese and Eggs, No. 71 Blackstone Street.—The reliable and well known house of C. F. Robinson, general produce commission merchant and dealer in butter, cheese and eggs, was established about eighteen years ago by the firm of Brooks and Robinson, who conducted the same up to 1874, when Mr. Robinson assumed sole control, and has since continued it alone with uninterrupted success. Everything in the line of fruits and country produce is handled on commission, while a general jobbing business is carried on also in dairy products, cheese, etc., and consignments placed with this concern are judiciously disposed of, and returns promptly made for the same in every instance. Mr. Robinson occupies a spacious basement store with ample and excellent facilities, and employs several experienced salesmen. A large and carefully assorted stock is constantly carried on hand, comprising butter, cheese and eggs, poultry and game in season, beans, apples, onions, potatoes, domestic fruits vegetables, etc., eggs being a leading specialty of the house, and the trade, which is principally of a jobbing nature is quite extensive. Mr. Robinson was born in the state of Maine, but has resided in this city over twenty-one years. He is a man of thorough experience in the trade, is a well known member of the Boston Fruit and Produce Exchange.

G. H. LAW, Musical Instruments, No. 158 Washington Street.—In the sale of brass and string instruments and musical merchandise generally, the house of Mr. G. H. Law, may be said to have attained its well known reputation by a combination of both the essentials mentioned. In supplying the trade throughout the country, and in furnishing bands and orchestras with the above named goods to order, this house has unquestionably been given a prominence to which but few of its compeers in the country can lay claim to. The proprietor established his business here in September, 1883, and quickly secured a national reputation and built up a trade that is now co-extensive with the country. The demands of brass bands and orchestras are promptly met with every description of instruments and supplies needed, and the house also deals extensively in sheet music and miscellaneous merchandise, besides furnishing music for all occasions. Mr. Law is a native of Littleton, Mass., and is known in this city and in musical circles throughout the land as a reliable, progressive business man.

A. D. CARLETON, Silver and Gold Plater, No. 73 Hanover Street.—No industry perhaps is more indispensable than that which pertains to the art of gold, silver and nickel plating. Mr. Carleton has been engaged in this business since 1851. He was formerly located on Washington street, and afterwards for fifteen years on Brattle Street, and two years ago moved to the very desirable premises now occupied. He does plating for the trade and to order, and his knowledge of all branches of the business is second to none. He gives particular attention to plating harness mountings, carriage trimmings and hardware, and makes a special business of replating table ware, and keeps in stock a great variety of plated letters, and escutcheons, pew numbers and door plates, etc., and also repolishes and laquers old brass work of every description. He also makes to order and repairs old fashioned hall clocks. All work executed by Mr. Carleton is warranted. He is a native of Vermont, and came to Boston more than forty years ago, and has acquired a well deserved reputation as an electro-plater.

ROBERT CARRINGTON, Book-binder, No. 299 Washington Street.—The book binders' trade is one of the branches of skilled industry to which much and able attention is accorded in this great commercial mart, and in this connection as one of the most popular exponents is mentioned Mr. Robert Carrington whose premises occupy an eligible business site at No. 299 Washington Street, opposite the Old South Church. The commodious and well arranged establishment is equipped with the newest and best improved book-binding methods and appliances and all work pertaining to the trade is executed in the highest degree of artistic and mechanical excellence. Mr. Carrington employs a full complement of experienced hands and is prepared to execute promptly and satisfactorily morocco, tree calf, and English colored calf work, with gilt, red and marbled edges at the lowest rates, compatible with first class work. He enjoys a large and liberal patronage composed of the best city custom and the general business is of most prosperous aggregate. Mr. Carrington was born in England, where he early learned and became an expert at the book-binders' trade. He came to Boston in 1881 and in the following year embarked in the enterprise with which he has since been both prominently and prosperously identified.

ALLEN & GINTER, Manufacturers of Cigarettes and Smoking Tobacco, E. K. Danbrow, Manager, No. 61 Hanover Street.—One of the leading concerns in this country engaged in the manufacture of superior grades of cigarettes and smoking tobaccos are Messrs. Allen and Ginter, whose extensive factories are located at Richmond, Virginia, and London, England, and whose trade extends not only to all parts of the American Continent, but abroad. The firm have for some years had a wholesale branch establishment at No. 61 Hanover street, Boston, which is under the management of Mr. E. K. Danbrow, who, two years ago, succeeded Mr. Charles G. Clark in the control of the business in this city and throughout the New England States. Mr. Danbrow was, prior to his removal to Boston, engaged in the firm's New York house. Mr. Danbrow occupies a commodious office, where he carries a fine sample stock, and goods are shipped from the factory direct to dealers in all parts of the New England States. A very extensive and growing business is done through this house, and dealers find it a profitable one at which to trade. Messrs. Allen & Ginter's cigarettes and smoking tobaccos are regarded by consumers as of superior excellence, and their goods have such a universal sale and appreciation as to be beyond the limit of praise.

C. BERRY, Bottler of Lager Beer, also Wholesale Dealer in Ales, Wines and Liquors, No. 84 Leverett Street.—A popular house in Boston is that of Mr. C. Berry, who carries on an active business as a bottler of the Ph. Best Brewing Co.'s Milwaukee, and Roessle's Centennial Premium lager beer, and also as a wholesale dealer in ales, wines and liquors. He established his enterprise ten years ago, in Cambridgeport, continuing there until the passage of the local prohibitory law in 1887, when he removed to this city, where his trade has since become largely increased. The spacious store occupied has dimensions of 20x90 feet, and is equipped with every facility for the convenient and satisfactory transaction of business. Employment is afforded six experienced hands. A large stock is carried and a leading specialty is made of catering to a first-class family trade. The patronage is desired from all parts of the city and its suburbs. Orders by mail or express are given the promptest attention, and goods are delivered at the shortest notice and without delay. Mr. Berry, who was born in Switzerland, has resided in the United States for the past twenty years. He is thoroughly acquainted with all the demands of the trade in which he is engaged.

DUBIN & CARROLL, Manufacturers of Fine Cigars, No. 8 Central Wharf.—The firm name of Dubin & Carroll is celebrated throughout all this section of the country as that of manufacturers of the finest and most popular cigars extant. Their fame is based strictly on the merits of their goods, which are pronounced unrivalled by the most critical experts. Amongst their brands are included the Boston Dandy, D. C. & S., New England Star, Gladiator, No. 8, and A No. 1. This firm occupy spacious and well-equipped quarters at No. 8 Central Wharf, and have been established in the business, as manufacturers of fine cigars only, since 1884. To-day the house ranks first every way, and the partners, Messrs. Samuel Dubin and James W. Carroll, are worthy exponents of one of the leading American industries. The premises occupied for trade purposes comprise two floors, 25x75 feet each and employment is given to from twenty to twenty-five expert cigar-makers. Such brands of cigars as Number Eight and the New England Star are practically supplanting all rival productions wherever they are introduced, the trade of the house is rapidly increasing. The copartners are both natives of Russia, practical cigar-makers of large experience and young men of marked business ability.

ARTHUR L. HAYDEN, Manufacturer and Dealer in Gent's Fine Boots and Shoes, No. 116 Washington Street.—A largely patronized and excellent Washington Street shoe store, is the popular emporium of Arthur L. Hayden, manufacturer and dealer in fine boots and shoes. The goods to be found in this establishment are of a very superior character, alike as to neatness, quality of material and workmanship; Mr. Hayden receiving orders from all parts of the country. The store is compact and neat, with shops attached, and several expert hands are employed—fine custom work being a specialty. A first class assortment of hand-made boots and shoes, of every size, style and variety, is always kept in stock, and patrons can rely upon getting an A1 article and satisfactory treatment in every instance here, while the prices prevailing also are maintained at the very lowest figures consistent therewith. Mr. Hayden, who is a gentleman of middle age, and a native of Quincy, Mass., is a practical and experienced workman himself of many years' experience. He established himself in business here in Boston in 1873, occupying the present quarters since 1880, and from the start he has enjoyed an excellent patronage.

R. F. MURRAY, Dealer in Provisions, No. 16 Leverett Street.—One of the oldest, most popular and representative retail dealers in provisions in Boston, is Mr. R. F. Murray who has been established in the business here since 1848. He conducts an extensive retail trade in meats, fruits and vegetables, handling daily, immense quantities of these supplies, fresh from the hands of the producer, and delivering them to all parts of the city. He gives the business the benefit of his large and valuable experience and close personal attention in all its departments, and is in a position to place all transactions upon a thoroughly substantial and satisfactory footing. His store is a model of neatness, cleanliness and orderly management. Here is to be found at all times the finest stock in the market, including beef, pork, lamb, veal and mutton, smoked, salt and corned meats, lard, hams and sausage, green and dried fruits, and vegetables in their season. The meats handled by Mr. Murray are the choicest that can be secured from any section of the country, and are supplied to patrons at prices which are invariably fair and equitable. Mr. Murray is a native of New Hampshire, and known throughout this community as a popular tradesman.

DR. A. J. HOLLAND, Dentist, No. 1050 1-2 Washington Street.—Among the most successful and foremost dental practitioners in this section of the city, may be mentioned the name of Dr. A. J. Holland. Dr. Holland, who is a young man and a native of Limerick, Maine, is a thoroughly practical and expert dentist, with many years' experience in the exercise of his profession, and is a thorough master of the art both in its mechanical and scientific features, having acquired his skill in one of the leading dental offices in the city. He commenced practice on his own account in 1884, and soon established himself in popular favor and confidence owing to the general satisfaction rendered to those employing his professional services. Dr. Holland occupies finely appointed and well equipped offices, all the latest improved apparatus and dental appliances being at hand, and attends to everything comprehended in modern dentistry in the most reliable and excellent manner. Teeth are extracted, filled and adjusted with judgment and skill, at popular rates, gas or ether being administered, when desired, with absolute safety, while plates are inserted and gums skillfully treated also, and artificial work likewise in all its branches is executed in the very best form of the art.

ADOLPH WOLFF, Watch Maker, Jeweler and Optician, No. 1 Kneeland Street and No. 1525 Tremont Street.—Among the well-known and prominent local exponents of the jewelry trade will be found Mr. Adolph Wolff, watchmaker, jeweler, and optician. Mr. Wolff is a native of Germany, where he early acquired an expert knowledge of his dual trade. In 1872 he came to Boston and in the following year began business at No. 1525 Tremont Street, in the Highlands, where he still has a fine store and prosperous trade. In the early part of 1886 he increased the compass of his enterprise by opening the Kneeland Street store. The spacious salesrooms, 15x30 feet in size, is fitted up in a convenient and attractive style, and an the large show window and wall and counter cases, is shown a remarkably fine stock of diamonds, jewelry, silverware, watches, clocks and optical goods, carefully selected in each department, from the best makes and newest styles and novelties. Everything in the line of repairing of all kinds of complicated work is skillfully done. Several assistants are employed, and among his many and highly desirable patrons Mr. Wolff is regarded as one of ablest and deservedly successful city exponents of his trade.

OSCAR C. PULLEN, Central Market, Nos. 285 to 289 Tremont Street.—A leading and representative establishment in its important branch of trade in this part of the city is that of Mr. Oscar C. Pullen, proprietor of the "Central Market." The spacious premises are most attractively fitted up with natural wood finish and fixtures, marble slabs, etc., and the large double front is composed entirely of plate glass show windows. In the general complete equipment are represented all the modern conveniences and facilities for the advantageous handling and display of goods, it is the largest and finest retail family market in the city, and the stock of beef, pork, mutton, veal, etc., etc., is large, comprehensive and carefully selected from the best sources of supply. Twelve assistants are required in attending to the wants of the numerous patronage which represents and largely includes the high class family restaurant and hotel trade on this side of town. Mr. Pullen is a native of Maine, and a practical and experienced merchant in his line. He has been established since 1882, and, in the interval, by well directed and enterprising management, has reared what may well be termed an eminently successful and representative business in the local provision trade.

HENRY SIEBERT, Leather and Shoe Findings, No. 52 Eliot Street.—One of the most successful of the business houses in Boston in the special line of trade is that of Mr. Henry Siebert, dealer in leather and findings, and manufacturer of boot and shoe uppers. Mr. F. F. Siebert established the business in 1862 and conducted it with marked ability until 1893, when he was succeeded by his son, a business man of ability, having a thorough knowledge of the details connected therewith. The dimensions of the premises are 20x72 feet, and as regards equipment and facilities are perfect and complete. From three to five hands are employed and a large business is carried on, the stock of leather and findings, embracing everything in that line, including French and American calf skin and sole leather of the best quality. All kinds of boot and shoe uppers are manufactured, a specialty being made of ordered work. Mr. Siebert, who was born in Boston, is a very popular business man.

HENRY H. GOLDBERG, Manufacturer of Fine Cigars, No. 77 Cambridge Street.—This gentleman began his present business in April, 1897, and has since had the good fortune to enjoy a steadily increasing trade, winning permanent customers both in the city and the surrounding towns. The business premises are compact and amply commodious, comprising a store and work shops, excellently fitted up with all necessary conveniences. Four hands are employed and an active business is carried on in the manufacture of first class cigars. Only the best quality tobacco leaf is used, and the goods turned out are much praised for general superiority and for the enjoyable smoke which they yield. A leading specialty is made of the "Middlesex," a ten cent cigar, and "147" and "77," a five cent straight cigar, which are held in high favor by judges of first quality goods. Both a wholesale and retail trade is catered to. Mr. Goldberg, has resided in the United States for the past sixteen years.

GAY & JEFFREY, Provisions, Foreign and Domestic Fruits, and Country Produce, No. 152 Cambridge Street.—For more than forty years this has been a popular house for meat supplies of every description, and has always commanded a liberal, substantial and influential patronage. For a considerable period the business was run by Mr. James G. Jeffery, in whose service Mr. Fred. H. Jeffery, one of the present proprietors, was for a period of eight years. In the early part of 1898, Mr. Fred. H. Jeffery and Mr. Gay formed a partnership and purchased the business which they have conducted with great success. The market is spacious in size, fitted up with all conveniences for facilitating the trade, and for the preservation of meats and perishable articles during the hot terms. The firm carry a fine stock of slaughtered meats, including beef, pork, lamb, mutton, veal, sausages, hams, shoulders, tongues, tripe, salt, corned and smoked meats, all of which are kept fresh and pure. The firm have also always on hand a full line of foreign and domestic fruits and country produce of all kinds. Competent assistants are employed, and customers are treated with liberality and promptness. The proprietors are both natives of this state.

FRANK M. PARKER, Provisions, Fruits, Vegetables, Etc., No. 61 Cambridge Street. Mr. Parker founded his business two years ago, meeting with the best of success from the start, and has continued to carry on a steadily increasing trade. The commodious store occupied, 22x80 feet in dimensions, is fitted up in the most approved style with all the requisite appliances and conveniences, and it is at all times kept in neat, cleanly order. A large stock is kept for sale, supplies being received fresh daily from the most reliable sources of supply and the finest grades of fresh and salt meats, beef, mutton, lamb, pork, poultry, lard, butter, eggs, fruits and vegetables are at all times to be found here—all offered at the lowest market prices. A staff of intelligent assistants are employed, and customers are waited upon in the most prompt and considerate manner. Orders are taken and goods sent free to any part of the city. Honest weight and fair prices are fixed rules in this establishment. A native of Massachusetts, Mr. Parker enjoys a large business and social acquaintance.

J. P. JOHNSON, Produce and Provisions, No. 80 Shawmut Avenue.—A leading local establishment in its important field of commercial activity is that of Mr. J. P. Johnson, dealer in produce and provisions. The spacious and attractively fitted up market is supplied with all the modern conveniences and facilities for the advantageous handling and display of goods and the stock of meats, vegetables, fruits and country produce generally, is carefully selected in each department from the best sources of supply and with due regard for the requirements of the high-class family and other trade from which his large and liberal patronage is chiefly derived. Mr. Johnson is a gentleman of wide experience in his line of business. After acquiring a thorough knowledge of the trade, he established for himself in 1878 in South Boston. In 1885 he removed to the present site. Mr. Johnson employs three experienced assistants and two delivery teams which are kept busy delivering goods to all parts of the city.

A. V. HEALD, Meats, Fruits, Vegetables, Etc., No. 166 Eliot Street.—The history of this house since the inception of the business in 1871, marks a record of unbroken prosperity. Before Mr. Heald began business on his own account he was identified as an employee with the provision trade, and upon his enterprise he brings long practical experience and great business ability to bear. His store, which has an area of 25x40 feet, is excellently equipped and arranged for the business, is adequately provided with cold storage, and is at all times a model of cleanliness and order presenting a neat inviting appearance. The stock is abundant to meet all demands and is maintained at the highest standard of excellence. It embraces the choicest cuts of beef, mutton, lamb, veal, pork, etc., hams, sausages, poultry, foreign and domestic fruits and vegetables in season, etc. A brisk trade is done, not only in the city, but in the suburbs, and courteous and prompt attention is given to all customers. Three assistants are employed and a delivery wagon is in constant service.

PHENIX HOTEL, I. M. Southwick, Proprietor, Nos. 21-31 Green Street.—One of the most popular and best patronized among the low-priced hostelries in this quarter of the city is the well-known Phenix Hotel, I. M. Southwick, proprietor. It is centrally located, horse cars and coaches passing the door every two minutes up to midnight, and is kept open all hours. The hotel premises occupy the four upper floors of a substantial five story structure, and contain about fifty commodious, airy, neatly appointed bed-rooms, and is neatly furnished throughout, the terms being 50c, 75c and $1.00 per day for rooms, for each person, singly or en suite. Special rates also are made for regular patrons and persons sojourning for an extended period. The hotel is thoroughly ventilated, well lighted and excellently heated, and withal admirably conducted; and for those desiring quarters, security and solid comfort at cheap rates is unsurpassed by any establishment of the kind in the city. This deservedly popular house was established many years ago, and after several changes in 1874 came into control of the present proprietor, under whose judicious and excellent management it has since been conducted with uniform and gratifying success. Mr. Southwick is a Vermonter by birth and a man of thorough business ability, and fully merits the very liberal patronage the Phenix has enjoyed ever since he assumed control of the house.

EDWARD A. LANE, Painter, Glazier, Decorator, Paper Hanger, Etc., No. 96 New Stamford Street.—For the past seventeen years Mr. Lane has been engaged in the same line of business at Manchester by-the-Sea, where he now has a finely equipped store and workshop, and where his headquarters are located. In October, 1886, he opened a branch establishment in Boston, at No. 1 Province Court, and in January, 1888, he removed therefrom to his present address, No. 96 New Stamford Street. Here he occupies a handsomely appointed store, connected with which is a well equipped workshop. Mr. Lane carries on hand here a large and first class assortment of paints, oils, varnishes, glass, brushes, painters' and artists' materials of every description, together with a complete line—representing all the latest novelties—of wall papers, borders, dados, frieze, and picture mouldings. Papers are furnished and put on by experienced workmen at the lowest prices, and estimates are furnished for the supply of large quantities. Painting and decorating in all the branches, including sign writing, interior and exterior work, lettering, and frescoing are executed in the highest style of the art. Glazing also forms a prominent feature of the business. All contracts are executed in the most superior and expeditious manner. From ten to thirty hands are employed in the business and satisfaction is guaranteed to all patrons. Mr. Lane is a native of Gloucester, Mass., a practical painter, and an enterprising business man.

THOS. J. CONDON, Provisions, Teas, Coffees, Spices, Flour, Butter, Etc., No. 96 Washington Street.—One of the most enterprising houses in the grocery and provision trade in the city, is that of Mr. Thomas J. Condon, who succeeded in 1887 the firm of O'Brien & Condon which established the business in 1886. Mr. Condon occupies a commodious store at No. 96 Washington Street, 15x45 feet in dimensions and carries a large and select stock of the finest provisions, teas, coffees, spices, flour, butter, etc., which he sells at the lowest cash prices, being able to compete with the leading houses in the trade both in this respect as well as in the quality of the goods he carries in stock. He has already built up a large trade in the neighborhood and employs three clerks to attend to its various details. Mr. Condon, who is a young man, was formerly clerk with one of the foremost houses in the grocery trade here, and has a thorough knowledge of the requirements of a first-class business. Recognized in trade circles as a reliable and pushing merchant, he has been enabled to take a leading position in his line in a comparatively brief period and has justified in every way the high opinion his friends entertained of his mercantile capacity.

ORMAND F. NIMS, Apothecary, No. 85 Cambridge Street.—Mr. Ormand F. Nims, the well-known apothecary has been established in the business here since March, 1854, and has developed an influential and extensive patronage not only with the general public, but also with the medical profession, with whom no house in the city stands in better favor. The premises occupied are very commodious and well appointed. The various departments are under the personal supervision of the experienced proprietor, and the stock displayed embraces the purest drugs and chemicals, standard proprietary and family medicines, essences and extracts, surgical instruments and appliances, perfumery, toilet articles, and druggists' sundries generally. The goods are selected with special reference to their strength and freshness. A specialty is made of Nims' Syrup of Tar and Wild Cherry a valuable remedy for colds, and Nims' Expectorant and Croup Compound for tightness of the chest and lungs. Popular prices prevail in all branches of the business. Mr. Nims is a native of New Hampshire, a resident of Boston for the past forty-five years, and highly regarded in the city.

FRANK E. GILLIS, Photographer, No. 164 Leverett Street.— Mr. Frank E. Gillis the artistic photographer, has, after years of earnest and patient endeavors, gained the reputation of doing artistic work in all branches of the photographic art. It is not necessary to particularize or call attention to his work in general, as he lays claim to no one particular specialty, but does claim to do the best of work in the making of all kinds of negatives. His life-size portraits, made from the negative are much admired, as they should be, by those who are conversant with works of art. Another feature that he gave more than ordinary attention to is his cabinet pictures, in which he has achieved such success as to be entitled to the distinction of artistic photographer. Mr. Gillis started business in his present premises in 1881 and has since developed a patronage of a most substantial and influential character. He occupies the second floor of a two story building and this is divided into reception room, operating room, etc. The establishment throughout is tastefully and appropriately fitted up and is equipped with all the latest improved photographic appliances, including the instantaneous process. Mr. Gillis is aided by two experienced and competent assistants, and his portraits are distinguished by their life-like character and beauty of finish. To these facts are to be attributed the large patronage accorded, both in the city, Cambridge and Somerville. Mr. Gillis is a native of Buffalo, N. Y., and has resided in Boston for the past seven years.

J. SMITH & SON, Fresh, Pickled and Smoked Fish, Etc., No. 470 Tremont Street.—Among the most prominent and popular of the dealers in all kinds of fish in this section of the city are Messrs. J. Smith & Son. The business is an old established one, having been founded in 1863, on Washington Street, by the senior member of the firm, who, in 1878 took his son, into partnership. In 1884 the business was removed to its present quarters, which comprise a neatly appointed store, 20x45 feet in area, and which is always kept in a clean, inviting condition while a first-class, extensive stock is ever presented for the choice of customers and at prices unsurpassed by those of any other house in the trade. The firm handle all kinds of fresh pickled and smoked fish, oysters, lobsters, scallops, quahaugs and South Shore clams, and a specialty is made of New York and Monmouth oysters. Fresh supplies are received daily, and prompt and satisfactory attention is given to the filling of all orders in the city or suburbs. The firm have the finest of connections, and transact a large and permanent trade. The proprietors are native of Boston.

T. S. SWIFT, Horse Shoer, No. 53 Pitts Street.—Mr. Swift began business here eight years ago, and has built up a trade connection of a substantial and influential character. He occupies a commodious work-shop, which is thoroughly equipped with the latest improved mechanical appliances for securing the most satisfactory results, and three competent and experienced workmen are permanently employed. Mr. Swift shoes horses upon correct principles, and is particularly successful with interfering horses and those troubled with quarter crack. The work is always neatly executed, and as an evidence of the skill exercised by Mr. Swift it need only be added that he is highly endorsed and recommended, and is in the full enjoyment of a large and prosperous business. Mr. Swift has had a vast experience in his line, and is prompt and reliable in the fulfilment of all orders entrusted to him. He is a native of Massachusetts, and a resident of Cambridge.

J. E. POWER, Designer and Engraver, No. 15 Cornhill.— A recent addition to the manufacturing establishments of the city is that of J. E. Power, manufacturing engraver. Mr. Power, who is a young man and a native Bostonian, has had an experience of seven years in the designing and engraving business and is thoroughly trained in every department of the trade. Six months ago he opened his present establishment at No. 15 Cornhill Street, and has already earned a place in the front rank of engraving specialists for the fine character of the work he has executed. His line of work is not confined to any particular class, and extends from furnishing

small class medals to large church memorials in old brass; he also is a furnisher of door plates, badges for police, firemen, societies and others. The furnishing of original dies for regimental badges is an important branch of the business and in which a marked success has been achieved. His trade has steadily advanced and his patronage extends not only in New England, but through the west and south. Mr. Power is a young man of advanced ideas, intelligent and industrious, and will continue to uphold the standard of fine work for which he is celebrated. Knowing that an increase of business is the only result that can accrue from such efforts, he is in the way of building up a splendid permanent business.

A. C. HOWES, Dealer in Hotel and Restaurant Supplies, and Manufacturer of the celebrated Brunet Baking Powder, No. 4 Liberty Square.—Mr. Howes was one of the founders of, and was for some time connected with, the Boston Baking Powder Company. In the summer of 1888 he founded his present enterprise, and the venture has been attended by the most marked and encouraging success. He devotes his energies exclusively to the manufacture of the celebrated Brunet Baking Powder and to furnishing hotels and restaurants with baking powder, tea, coffee, salads, chow-chow and other supplies. He carries an extensive stock and has the best of facilities for promptly filling all orders on terms that cannot be easily duplicated by any other concern. He has within a short period developed a very extensive trade in all parts of Massachusetts, and his business connection in Boston is a most active and prosperous one, demonstrating at once that the proprietors of hotels and restaurants find it to their advantage to place their orders in his hands. Mr. Howes is a gentleman of middle age, an energetic, reliable business man, and a resident of Somerville.

COL. WM. BEALS, Public Decorator, Etc., No. 96 Court Street. —The oldest and most successful public decorator in New England is Col. Wm. Beals. Colonel Beals, who is now seventy-two years old established this business forty years ago, since which period he has built up a liberal, influential and permanent patronage in all sections of the United States. He occupies three commodious rooms, and keeps in stock a superior assortment of flags and all kinds of decorations for banquets, public celebrations, balls, etc. He is ably assisted by Mr. Geo. W. Greenlief, and the flag department is carefully supervised by his wife Mrs. Wm. Beals. Col. Beals manufactures promptly to order all kinds of tinsel ornaments for decorations on public occasions, also stars, tinsel knights, gold eagles, spears, banners, shields, etc., while his prices in all cases for the finest artistic work is exceedingly moderate. He did a large amount of first-class decorative work for the Centennial and latterly made the splendid banner carried by the Massachusetts Republicans to the Chicago Convention. This banner was six by nine feet, velvet, bound with gold, and had 100 letters inscribed on it with three eagles. The motto of this banner was, "Home Market Club, Boston, American Wages for American Workmen; American Markets for People; Home Markets for Home Manufacturers; Protection for American Homes." This banner was greatly admired by experts and created great enthusiasm among all classes of Republicans, owing to its beauty, artistic design, and superior finish. This banner under which General Harrison was nominated at Chicago is to go to Washington and will be used at the inauguration next March. Col. Beals knows more people in New England, than any other man. He was present in 1825 at the laying of the corner stone of the Bunker Hill Monument, where Lafayette was there, also at the foundation of the Pilgrim Monument, Plymouth. In 1834 he organized a Volunteer Corps of boys under fifteen years of age, which was reviewed by General Jackson on Boston Common. Many of these boys have since become very prominent men. The Colonel was born in Boston.

EDMUND W. NOYES, Printer, No. 63 Kilby Street.—An experienced and accomplished representative of the printers craft is Mr. Edmund W. Noyes, of No. 63 Kilby Street, who first began business in 1871 as a member of the firm of Noyes & Poole. This firm was dissolved in 1876, and Mr. Noyes has since conducted his business alone and with a success that demonstrates he is a thorough master of it and affords abundant satisfaction to all who favor him with their patronage. For his printing department he occupies two floors. The equipments are full and complete and embrace every variety of modern, antique, fancy and plain types, four steam-power presses and all the paraphernalia incident to a first-class printing office. Six operatives are in service, and all kinds of fine mercantile printing are executed here and in the highest style of the art. The specialty of the house is commercial work, and the relations subsisting between this establishment and many leading mercantile houses of the city are such that prove Mr. Noyes to be a favorite in his line of trade. His success has been great, and the secret of it lies in the turning out of first-class work promptly at reasonable prices.

THOMAS SINGLETON & SON, Manufacturers of Rich Cut and Plain Glass Ware, Nos. 39 and 41 Beverly Street.—The firm of Thomas Singleton & Son manufacturers of rich cut and plain glass-ware, enjoy an excellent reputation for fine work; the articles produced being maintained at a very high standard of excellence. This enterprising and prosperous firm (which enjoys the additional distinction of being the only one in its line in Boston) was established a few months since, but from its inception the venture has proved a positive success. They occupy ample and well-equipped quarters with full steam power and all necessary facilities being in service, while some half a dozen skilled workmen are employed. The productions include everything in the line of fine cut and plain glassware, in exquisite designs and artistic workmanship; a superb assortment being constantly carried on hand, and all orders are promptly and reliably filled, while estimates are cheerfully furnished upon application. Messrs. Thomas Singleton, senior and junior, are both practical and expert workmen themselves, of many years' experience, and are complete masters of their art.

W. A. SYLVESTER, Mechanical Draughtsman, Pattern and Model Maker, No. 35 Haverhill Street.—In the construction of machinery and mechanical apparatus, castings of brass, composition, iron and steel are necessary. In order to produce these, patterns—usually of nice seasoned pine, cherry or mahogany—are required. These patterns are moulded in damp loamy sand, then withdrawn, the cores—necessary to cast holes that cannot be drawn from the patterns—are set, the moulds firmly clamped together and are then filled with the molten metal. After the castings have got cooled off, the moulds are broken up, the castings taken out, cleaned and snagged, and sometimes pickled—and then ready to use. The patterns are very nearly duplicates of the castings, but have to be made larger to allow for the contraction of the metal in cooling, brass and composition shrinking about 3-16 inch per foot, iron from 1-16 to 1-8 inch per foot, varying with the kinds of iron used, the size and form of the casting, and also whether the mould is of green sand, dry sand or loam, and steel varying from 1-16 to 3-8 inch per foot according to the mixture used by the various foundries. While very much depends on the foundrymen, it is of the greatest importance that the patterns shall be thoroughly constructed so as to be able to withstand the severe usage they receive, also that the dimensions be correct and the necessary draft allowed so that they can be easily withdrawn from the moulds. Then it is often necessary to provide lugs and bars in the castings in order to facilitate matters for the machinist who has to bore and plane up these castings. There is probably no branch of the mechanic arts that an intelligent judgment and skill are required more than in pattern making, for the workmen must be able to make drawings, to read very complicated drawings, and must be familiar with foundry practice and machine shop practice, and take into consideration the shrinkage to allow, must decide which of several methods is the best method to mould the pattern, and finally must be a good joiner and wood turner in order to build a good durable pattern. Then again when many castings of small or fragile patterns are wanted, metal patterns have to be made and gated. The pattern maker is usually a good model maker also. In all that is requisite to make first-class patterns we know of no one who is better able to fill the bill than W. A. Sylvester of No. 35 Haverhill Street, who started in business in 1883. His workshops are light and roomy and are fitted up with the best of modern machinery. From five to twelve men are employed. Being a practical draughtsman also, he is frequently able to assist customers in developing their ideas and in laying out the work for the pattern maker.

BARNARD'S BAKERY, No. 132 Cambridge Street.—This popular and prosperous house was originally founded in 1865, and about eight years ago it passed into the possession of the present proprietor. The premises occupied consist of a store with a capacity of 18x40 feet, and this is very tastefully fitted up, and presents at all times a neat, clean, orderly and an inviting appearance. In the rear of the store is the bakery, and this is equipped with all the latest improved appliances known to the bakery trade. Three hands are employed, and here are manufactured all kinds of bread, rolls, tea biscuits, cakes, etc. These goods are fresh, light and nutritious, and there is an active demand for them throughout the city and vicinity. A heavy stock is constantly carried, and Mr. Barnard is always in a position to fill all orders promptly and satisfactorily. He is a native of England, and has been a resident of America for the past seventeen years.

E. W. FAVOR, Flour and Fine Groceries, Butter, Cheese, Etc., No. 150 Cambridge Street.—This is one of the oldest grocery houses in this locality, having been established in 1830, and in 1865, when the proprietors were Messrs. Flagg & Forbes, Mr. E. W. Favor became an employé of the firm. In 1875 he succeeded to the business, and he has from that date enjoyed a permanent trade of influential proportions, owing to the very superior quality of the merchandise sold by him, and the popular prices at which the same have been dispensed. The commodious premises occupied for the purposes of the enterprise consist of a store and basement, each 25x60 feet in dimensions. The salesroom is neatly arranged and fitted up, and is equipped throughout with every convenience and facility for the storage and handling of stock and the accommodation of customers. A large and very carefully selected stock is at all times carried, the assortment embracing a splendid variety of staple and fancy groceries, fruits and vegetables, flour, butter, cheese, eggs, canned goods, etc., including the finest grades of teas, and fresh roasted coffees and spices, which form a specialty with the house. The trade supplied is principally retail, and extends throughout the city and its vicinity. A staff of competent clerks and a delivery team form the working force, and all orders are filled and sent to their destination without delay. Mr. Favor is a native of Maine.

DANIEL W. FOSTER, Manufacturer and Wholesale Dealer in Horse Blankets, Carriage Robes, Etc., No. 59 Sudbury Street.—We desire to call the attention of our readers to the advantages offered in the well ordered and conducted horse furnishing goods establishment of Mr. Daniel W. Foster, where he pilotly occupies a spacious and handsomely appointed store with Mr. H. B. Snodgrass, manufacturer and dealer in fine harness, etc. The business had its origin in 1855, when it was founded by Mr. Nye Foster. In 1860 he was succeeded by Foster & Colburn, and in 1867 the firm became Foster, Colburn & Co., which partnership was dissolved in 1881, at which time it was at the head of its line of trade. In 1884 Mr. Foster opened his present place of business at the address already indicated, and here he carries on a wholesale trade in horse blankets, carriage robes, saddlery, hardware, green waulen dusters, linen horse sheets, etc.; and is agent for extra quality Swede's Iron Jacks and Amos Bollinger's superior oak harness leather. Special goods in these lines are made to order promptly and at the lowest possible rates. Mr. Foster is a very prominent dealer in his line and controls an active and large trade in the city and vicinity. In his line he is enabled to offer special inducements to the trade. He is also the agent for several life insurance companies of substantial growth and high standing. He is a native of Maine, and for the past thirty years has resided in Melrose, Mass.

C. A. TWITCHELL & CO., Engravers, No. 183 Washington Street.—This popular and well known firm was established in 1868, and during the twenty years of its existence has maintained a position in the front rank in its line; no concern of the kind in this city bearing a higher reputation for skill or reliability. The shop is ample and well equipped, all necessary facilities being at hand, while a competent assistant or two is regularly employed likewise. Metal engraving in all its branches is executed in the very best style of the art, at short notice, while badges, stencils, presses, stamps, seals, etc., are made to order in the most superior and prompt manner. And a complete and fine assortment is constantly carried in stock, including door plates, badges of every design, stencils, seals, and seal presses, steel and rubber stamps; all orders for the trade receiving immediate attention. Mr. Twitchell, who is the sole member, is a native of this city, and a man of long and varied practical experience in the increase of his art of which he is a thorough master in all its branches.

J. H. WILLARD, Pictures Framed to Order, No. 50 Green Street.—One of the most reliable and best known houses in the picture trade is that of J. H. Willard, which has been conducted in a successful manner for many years. Mr. Willard has been in Boston for the long period of forty-five years, having come here from Vermont, his native place, when a young man. Shortly after his arrival he started in business as a baker and was engaged in that line up to 1874 when he gave it up for the picture frame trade. He occupies a neat store, 15x40 feet in dimensions and carries a splendid assortment of the most attractive pictures for a family trade, which together with frames in ebony, bronze, walnut and other materials, he sells at the most reasonable prices, doing an extensive business on the instalment plan. His principal line, however, is in framing pictures for customers who find in his establishment, the largest variety of patterns to choose from, and can always place the greatest reliance in the character of the work performed. Mr. Willard has been ten years at his present location. Conscientious to a degree, he strives to render his work equal to any test, and judging from his first-class reputation has succeeded in a remarkable degree.

T. KELLY & CO., Importers and Dealers in all kinds of Foreign and Domestic Birds and Animals; Wholesale and Retail, No. 92 New Stanford Street.—Though founded so recently as August, 1888, this house has rapidly gained a prominence to which older establishments in the same line of trade would be glad to lay claim to. The store devoted to the business has an area of 25x65 feet, is well lighted by two fine show windows, and is admirably fitted up for the accommodation and display of the large and varied stock carried. Here are shown fancy birds of every plumage and from every clime; pigeons, canaries, parrots, cockatoos, prize poultry, etc., also dogs, rabbits, rats, squirrels, and curiosities of all kinds in the animal kingdom. The firm manufactures a bird sand that is highly commended, and keep in stock all kinds of fresh seeds and special foods for birds and animals. They are the agents for Nabhre's Tablet Soap for dogs (imported); Clarke's Buffalo Meat Biscuits; Barbone's celebrated Mocking Bird Food, suitable for all soft-billed birds, and warranted to keep any length of time in any climate; Barbone's Improved Sands, acknowledged to be the best in the market; and Barbone's Mange Cure and medicines of all kinds for dogs. The transactions of the house are of both a wholesale and retail character, and all orders are promptly and satisfactorily attended to. Mr. T. Kelly, who is the sole proprietor, is a native of England.

C. J. F. SHERMAN & SON, Watches, Clocks, and Fine Jewelry, No. 220 Hanover Street.—The watch and jewelry establishment of Messrs. C. J. F. Sherman & Son, has had an honorable career covering a period of over half a century. The business was founded in 1839 by Mr. C. J. F. Sherman who many years ago took into partnership his son, Mr. H. H. Sherman, who was born and reared in the business and has a life's acquaintance with its every detail. The founder died eight years ago, and his son, who then succeeded to the entire control of the business, has since conducted it under the old style of C. J. F. Sherman & Son. The store has an area of 20x30 feet, and is finely furnished and fitted up with plate glass show cases, etc. The stock displayed is a large and carefully selected one embraces an excellent assortment of gold and silver watches of domestic and foreign manufacture, clocks in great variety, watch chains, rings, diamonds and other precious stones, bracelets, ear-rings, shawl and scarf pins, broaches, studs, sleeve and collar buttons, and jewelry of every description of the finest and most reliable quality. Every article sold and every representation made is guaranteed in every particular. A special feature of the business is the repairing of all kinds of jewelry, and the cleaning, repairing and regulating of fine watches, and all work is guaranteed to afford the fullest satisfaction. Five assistants, practical and experienced in the business, are employed.

JAMES TREGURTHA, Machinist, No. 69 Haverhill Street.—The expert machinist is now a most valued artisan in every community, and prominent among those of this class in Boston is Mr. James Tregurtha. This gentleman was born in England, where he learned his trade, and twenty four years ago came to America. Eighteen years since he began business on his own account at his present location, where his workshop has an area of 25x70 feet, and is equipped with steam power, lathes, drilling and other mechanical contrivances essential to the successful carrying on of the business. Mr. Tregurtha is a general machinist of exceptionally fine ability, and is as adept in the designing and construction of special machinery, and especially of experimental and model work. He builds and repairs all kinds of electrical, numerical, perforating, indicating and other machinery, and makes a speciality of developing and elaborating the crude work of inventors. Employment is given to a staff of skilled artisans and prompt and satisfactory service is rendered all patrons.

J. W. MARSTON & CO., Wholesale Lobster Dealers, No. 26 T Wharf.—This business was originally established in 1831 by John Marston, who conducted it till 1868 when he retired, and was succeeded by his son J. W. Marston. In 1881 Mr. J. W. Marston died, and the present firm assumed the management. The business is still conducted under the old name of J. W. Marston & Co. The members of the copartnership, Messrs. J. E. Newcomb and J. C. Smith have had great experience in the wholesale lobster trade, and have an interest in several vessels engaged in this industry. They make a specialty of dealing in lobsters, and offer advantages and inducements very difficult to be secured elsewhere. All orders are promptly filled at the lowest ruling market prices, and the trade of the house now extends throughout all sections of the United States. Mr. Newcomb is a native of Boston, while his partner Mr. J. C. Smith was born in Sandusky, Ohio. Mr. Smith is a member of the Massachusetts Fish Exchange. Both partners are highly esteemed in trade circles for their enterprise and just methods, and are well worthy of the large measure of success, which has rewarded their persevering efforts.

PARKE SNOW, Ladies' and Gents' Furnishings; Agent for Laundry Work, No. 299 Shawmut Avenue.—This business was started under the firm name of Eldridge & Snow in 1883, and this continued until 1888, when Mr. Snow succeeded to the sole proprietorship. The store is a fine corner apartment with large plate glass show windows on two sides and the interior apartment embodies all the modern ideas of combined elegance and convenience. The stock shown comprises everything in the line of fancy goods, notions and ladies' and gentlemen's furnishing goods, the best grades, newest novelties and latest popular styles being represented in each department. Mr. Snow has also the agency for the National Steam Laundry of Malden, and orders for all laundry work receive prompt attention, while the work executed is unexcelled in point of general excellence. Three assistants are employed, and the numerous patronage received is drawn from the best custom of the vicinity. Mr. Snow is a vigorous and active young business man, and is one of the deservedly successful young merchants of this, his native city.

M. J. MURPHY, Undertaker and Embalmer, No. 42 Hanover Street.—This enterprise was started by Mr. Murphy in 1878 at his present address, and has steadily won his way to prosperity, his patronage growing steadily from the first. The premises occupied comprise a store, 20x40 feet in dimensions, and this is neatly and appropriately fitted up. A full and fine stock of funeral requisites is constantly carried, embracing elegant coffins and caskets of every size, style and variety, also grave clothes, shrouds, trimmings, embalming apparatus and everything comprehended in funeral requisites. Mr. Murphy, who has had ample experience in his line of business, assumes the entire charge of funerals, provides all the necessary requisites, and performs all his duties intelligently and in the most satisfactory manner. He is aided by competent assistants, and gives prompt attention to all calls, day or night. He has a large and influential patronage, not only in the city, but in East Boston and Brighton. Mr. Murphy is a native of New Bedford, Mass., and has resided in Boston for the past eighteen years. He is a capable and efficient undertaker and embalmer, and is thoroughly conversant with every feature and detail incident to disposition of remains, the management of funerals and the procuring of interments.

GEORGE C. APPLETON, Real Estate Broker, No. 27 State Street, Room 17.—A representative real estate broker of this city is Mr. George C. Appleton, who has been actively engaged in this line of business for the past twenty two years, developing a widespread connection and an extensive patronage, and including among his customers many of our leading capitalists and property owners. Mr. Appleton is a recognized authority in regard to values of residential and business properties throughout the city and its neighboring towns, and intending investors can rely upon his sound judgment and judicious advice with perfect confidence in purchasing property. He gives his prompt personal attention to the purchase, sale and leasing of real estate, the negotiation of mortgages, and the collection of rents, dividends and interest. In obtaining loans on bond and mortgage, he is eminently popular with those property owners in need of financial assistance. Both in the line of city and country property, Mr. Appleton possesses facilities for the purchase, sale and lease of all descriptions of houses, flats and stores, and those in search of something in either of these lines are sure to be suited as regards both location, size and price by calling on him. Mr. Appleton is a native of Roxbury, and of high standing in the real estate business.

ATWOOD & CO., Wholesale Commission Merchants in Fish of all kinds, No. 52 Long Wharf, next to T Wharf.—Among the leading firms engaged in this line in the city may be mentioned that of Atwood & Co., wholesale commission merchants in fish of all kinds, whose transactions annually aggregate very substantial proportions, handling as high as 50,000 lbs. of blue fish and about the same amount of mackerel per day during the season. This well and favorably known house was established in 1873 by John Atwood, who four years subsequently admitted into partnership his son, W. I. Atwood, who since the retirement of the senior member in 1884, has conducted the business alone with uninterrupted success. The business premises occupy three 25x50 foot floors and are well ordered and equipped throughout every convenience and facility being at hand, while half a dozen or more in help are employed. Consignments are received daily from Cape Cod and Nova Scotia, including fresh fish of every description; mackerel and blue fish being the specialties of the house during the summer months, and smelts, salmon and ground fish of all kinds during the winter months. Sales are made as soon as the market opens thereby realizing the highest prices for the consignor. Mr. W. I. Atwood, who is the sole member, is a native of Provincetown, Mass., and has resided in this city since 1873, and enjoys an A1 reputation in the trade.

JAMES H. EARLE, Publisher, Importer and Bookseller, No. 178 Washington Street.—This house was founded in 1868, for the publication of books of all descriptions, both religious and non-sectarian, and in 1872 Mr. Earle began the publication of The Contributor, a monthly paper, devoted to religious subjects, with no denominational bias, but with a view of doing the greatest good to the greatest number. This paper has given the publisher a prestige throughout the Union which could not be acquired in any other way. He also does an extensive trade in books chiefly at wholesale, with booksellers in all parts of the United States, and carries at all times a very large and valuable collection of standard works both of his own and also of contemporaneous publication. At his office are wont to gather men conspicuous in the pulpit, in literature, and in authorship, in this city and from other portions of the country, for the interchange of information upon congenial topics. The house has become to be recognized not only as a complete book publishing establishment, but, from its history and literary attractiveness, a place of special interest to literary men and strangers visiting the city. Some considerable retail business is transacted. Mr. Earle is a New Yorker by birth, but received his college education in Massachusetts, well equipped as an editor, expert and accomplished as a publisher, and reliable and responsible as a business man.

M. H. KEENAN, Job and Commercial Printer, No. 15 Water Street.—For a period extending over thirty-five years M. H. Keenan, the well-known job printer, has been successfully engaged in the exercise of his art. He is one of the oldest established and best known exponents of the art preservative in this part of the city, being located at the present quarter since 1881. Mr. Keenan, who is a gentleman of about sixty-four but active, energetic and devoted to his business, was born in Ireland, and has been in this country since early childhood. He is a practical and expert workman, with long and varied experience at the case, and is a thorough master of his art in all its branches. Mr. Keenan occupies a commodious room on the third floor and has in service ample steam power, three presses and complete facilities, while several first-class hands are regularly employed. General job printing of every description is executed in the most expeditious and excellent manner, at the lowest rates, special attention being given to fine commercial work.

JOHN KEENAN, Wool and Wool Stock, Nos. 285 and 287 Commercial Street.—The large business done by Mr. John Keenan in woolen rags and wool stock during the past twenty years has given him a wide celebrity in commercial circles. He is a heavy buyer and dealer, and through his connections in the west and south conducts extensive transactions and has a large trade with the woolen mills throughout New England. He handles from twelve to fifteen tons of wood and wool stock each week and employs from twelve to fifteen hands in the business.

When Mr. Keenan began operations in 1860 he was located on Ferry Street, and afterwards removed to Fulton Street. Two years ago he secured the premises now occupied, which consist of a four-story substantial building, having dimensions of 25x55 feet, and well adapted in every way for storage purposes and to facilitate transactions. Mr. Keenan is a native of Ireland. He has lived in Boston a long while and is very popular, and an honorable and upright gentleman.

SAMUEL JACOBS & BROS., Manufacturer of Fine Cigars, No. 76 Cambridge Street.—An ably conducted establishment in the West End engaged in the cigar manufacturing industry is that of the Messrs. Samuel Jacobs & Bros. The business was inaugurated six years ago by the present firm, the individual members being Messrs. Samuel, Abram and Benj. Jacobs. These gentlemen are all practical cigar makers, expert at the trade, and being bright, energetic young business men, they have been deservedly successful in building up an active, flourishing trade, and their store is very popular with admirers of a choice weed. The brands which find particular favor with buyers are the Franklin Park, a ten cent cigar, and the United Three, which sells for five cents. The neat store occupied contains a good stock of imported and domestic cigars, also, cigarettes, smoking and chewing tobaccos. The firm also pay particular attention to the manufacture of special brands of cigars for the trade, and are prepared to fill all orders in this line on the most advantageous terms. The Messrs. Jacobs are natives of Philadelphia and have resided in Boston for the past ten years.

J. REARDON & CO., Engraved and Painted Signs, No. 78 Kingston Street.—Mr. Reardon has been engaged in the manufacture of engraved and painted signs in this city for the past fourteen years—since Oct. 1878, at the present site—and in the interval has built up a reputation for superior work unexcelled by that of any other exponent of his trade. The shop, 30x70 feet in dimensions, is equipped with all requisite facilities for the advantageous conduct of the business, including a full stock of paints, oils, and other materials incident to the trade. A goodly corps of experienced hands is employed, and the many and various styles and designs of signs turned out embody in every instance the highest degree of artistic and mechanical excellence. Mr. Reardon makes a specialty of the popular brass signs for dry goods commission, brokerage, banking and other mercantile houses, which are executed in many new and attractive designs. He enjoys a large and liberal patronage from the best city custom.

H. C. HILTON, Commission Merchant and Dealer in Fruits, No. 91 S. Market Street.—Mr. H. C. Hilton, the well-known commission merchant and wholesale dealer in foreign and domestic fruits, has a trade which is very large in Boston and extends throughout the New England States. He began about four years ago, and having had lengthened experience in the trade, fully understands how to meet the demands of the public in a satisfactory manner. He is constantly receiving consignments of farm produce, and as a wholesale dealer in fruits, both foreign and domestic, supplies a large demand, and controls a first-class order trade. He is one of the representative dealers in fruits in the city, and always has the choicest bananas, lemons, oranges, nuts, figs, &c., that are brought to this market. Mr. Hilton, who was born in Maine, is a young man of energy, and has a fine business connection and many friends.

HALEY'S Fashionable Millinery, No. 109 Hanover Street.—The millinery establishment of Mrs. Catherine Haley is the most fashionable on that thoroughfare. Mrs. Haley is a lady of exquisite taste and knows what is becoming and suitable for her patrons, and always has something new and beautiful in seasonable fashionable millinery, to please those who may favor her neat, handsome, attractive establishment with a visit. Trimmed hats in great profusion are displayed which are lovely to look upon and exceedingly rich in the blending of colors and trimmings. Mourning millinery is made to order at the shortest notice and every care and attention is given to customers. Mrs. Haley is very popular with the ladies and is highly commended by all her patrons.

THE METROPOLIS OF NEW ENGLAND.

GEO. T. HOYT & CO., Sail Makers, and Manufacturers of House and Store Awnings, Tents, Flags, Piazza Curtains, Etc., No. 45 South Market Street.—The leading representative of its branched industry in this city is the house of Messrs. Geo. T. Hoyt & Co., the well-known sail makers, and manufacturers of house and store awnings, tents, flags, piazza curtains, etc., at No. 45 South Market Street. This house has been in successful operation since 1851, and controls a vast trade in the various articles of its manufacture. The premises occupied for the business are spacious in size,

and every facility is at hand for insuring rapid and perfect production and for the prosecution of the business under the most favorable auspices and upon a large scale. The specialty of the business is the manufacture of awnings, tents, and flags, which are in active and permanent demand in this city and throughout the state. Tents are made for all purposes and in any shape, fitted up with sundry conveniences. Lawn and seaside tents are made picturesque, graceful and methodical, at the same time can be easily and expeditiously set and removed, and are not burdensome in transit. Particular attention is given to the manufacture

of silk flags and banners, embroidered or gold letters, yacht suits and signals, poles, gold balls, spears, halliards etc. Tents are kept on hand to let, awnings are taken down and stored; canvas signs, horse and wagon covers are for sale, also old canvas. The awnings made by this firm are unsurpassed for beauty, elegance, durability and artistic workmanship by any other first-class house in the trade, and are sold at prices which are safe from successful competition.

D. A. CARR, Stoves, Ranges and Furnaces, Nos. 33 and 35 Leverett Street.—Mr. D. A. Carr is an extensive dealer in stoves, ranges, and furnaces, tin and sheet iron ware and general house furnishing goods, and gives special attention to hotel and restaurant work, plumbing, gas-

fitting and general jobbing, and to the lining and repairing of stoves, ranges and furnaces. He succeeded to the control of the business here in 1882, and has steadily maintained a position in the front rank of the trade in this city. His business premises comprise a fine double store, 40 by 60 feet in dimensions, a spacious basement, workshop and storage room, and unsurpassed facilities are at hand for conducting all branches of the enterprise under the most favorable conditions and upon the largest scale. In his splendid warerooms can be found everything needed in the line of stoves, tinware and kitchen furnishings, including the latest improved cooking stoves and ranges, the praises of which are repeated by cooks and housewives all over the land ; the handsomely ornamented parlor-heaters, the praises of which are sung to the music of the piano ; a great variety of portable furnaces, a thing of beauty and a joy forever ; and the new summer cooking ranges and gas stoves. In plumbing materials, tin, sheet-iron and copper ware and domestic utensils the stock is complete. A large force of skilled and expert workmen are employed in the different departments of plumbing, gas fitting, tinsmithing, jobbing and general repairs, and satisfaction is confidently assured to all who patronize this house in any of these branches of industry.

C. H. LALLEY, Wholesale Dealer in Bottles, No. 83 Fulton Street.—This gentleman started business in 1882 on Harrison Avenue, whence he removed in 1885 to his present location. Here he occupies a suitable, well appointed store and basement, each 25x50 feet in dimensions, and appropriately fitted up and arranged for the business. The stock carried is at all times a very extensive one and consists of champagne, wine, brandy, claret, hock, porter, ale, mineral and other bottles and jugs of every description, secured direct from the manufacturers and offered at prices which are not surpassed in the trade. The business of the house is exclusively of a wholesale character, and heavy shipments are made to order to all parts of the New England and New York States. Owing to the extensive stock always carried and the possession of all necessary facilities for the successful prosecution of the business the proprietor and his assistants are always in a position to fill all orders promptly and satisfactorily. The standing of the house in mercantile circles is of the highest, and Mr. Lalley is a most pleasant gentleman to establish business relations with.

A. & J. E. TUTTLE, Mechanical Draughtsmen and Pattern Makers, No. 73 Haverhill Street.—In this department of enterprise the establishment of Messrs. A. & J. E. Tuttle, of No. 73 Haverhill Street, has been a noted and successful one for the past thirty years. It was founded in 1858 by Mr. George Blake, who conducted the business until 1872, when he was succeeded by the present proprietors, who have developed a wide spread trade connection of a substantial and influential character. The firm are general mechanical draughtsmen and pattern makers, and make models and designs for steam engines, steam and gas fittings, stoves, furnaces, ranges and all kinds of machinery. Their business premises comprise one floor with an area of 60x90 feet, and this is fully equipped with all necessary machinery, which is operated by steam power. From five to ten hands are employed, and all business commands meet with prompt and satisfactory attention. The co-partners have had vast practical experience in their business. Mr. A. Tuttle, who was born in Boston, resides in Lockport, and Mr. J. E. Tuttle, who is a native of Rockport, is a resident of Chelsea.

FRANCIS STANWOOD, Cotton Buyer, No. 4 Post Office Square.—Prominent among the cotton buyers of this city is Mr. Francis Stanwood, who does a strictly commission business, buying for cotton goods manufacturers all over the eastern states, filling orders direct from the south and is prepared to buy in any quantity ranges, car-load lots and in smaller amounts, while his business which is large and active gives evidence of steady improvement. Mr. Stanwood, who is a comparatively young man and a Bostonian by birth, is a gentleman of thorough reliability as well as energy, and is fully conversant with the wants of the trade. He succeeded his brother, L. Stanwood, who had been established since 1848, on the event of that gentleman's death, February, 1886.

LEWIS WHARF TOW BOATS, Nath'l P. Doane, Agent, Office No. 105 Commercial Street, and Pier 2, Lewis Wharf.—The Lewis Wharf Tow Boat Company is one of the leading and best known enterprises in the city of its kind, and is eminently deserving of honorable mention in these pages. It was founded some twenty years ago, under its present management and title, with Messrs. Rodgers and Sayers as agents, and in 1884 the present agent of the company, Mr. Nath'l P. Doane, succeeded to the control. The main offices of the company are at No. 105 Commercial Street, and Pier 2, Lewis Wharf, each of which is furnished with telephone connection. The tugs owned and operated by the company, are the Nath'l P. Doane, Leader, Nellie and Blanche, and with these staunch boats, vessels are towed in and about this harbor and to all neighboring ports. The Nath'l P. Doane, is a fine new boat recently built, and is the largest of the fleet. It has all the modern improvements, including wrecking pumps, etc., and is superior in every detail. Passing years have only served to add to the strength, influence and popularity of this company. Its engagements are invariably met at the time agreed upon, contracts and commissions are fulfilled with scrupulous care and promptness, and all interests committed to its care are zealously watched and safely guarded. Its tariff of rates is fair and satisfactory to patrons, and the utmost confidence in its reliability and responsibility is always fully justified. Mr. Doane, the popular agent, is a native of Mass., in the active prime of life, a member of the Chamber of Commerce and a part owner in the Lewis Wharf Tow Boat Company.

DAVIS, STEBBINS & CO., Hardware, Mechanics' Tools, Cutlery, &c., Nos. 31 and 33 Sudbury street.—This well known and popular firm was established in 1872, and from the start has enjoyed a very liberal and growing patronage. The premises occupied, which are desirably located at the corner of Portland Street, include a neat 25x35 store and basement, three experienced clerks attending to the wants of customers, while a large and well selected stock is constantly kept on hand, comprising shelf and builders' hardware of all kinds, mechanics tools in great variety, pocket and table cutlery, steel and iron goods, nails, screws and small wares, household specialties, cordage, rope, wire, garden tools and in short, everything that is to be found in a leading hardware store, and the trade which extends throughout the city is quite substantial. The firm is composed of Messrs. S. H. Davis and M. B. Stebbins, both gentlemen of middle age, active and energetic, and natives of New Hampshire, but old and respected Boston merchants.

L. B. ROLLINS & CO., Commission Merchants for the sale of Butter, Cheese, Eggs, Beans, Poultry, Etc., No. 17 Blackstone Street, and No. 20 John Street.—Although a comparatively young firm L. B. Rollins & Co., have a standing in the trade and established a business connection second to few engaged in this branch of commercial activity hereabouts. Established about two years since, this enterprising and responsible firm at its very inception may be said to have bounded into prominence and prosperity, building up in a short time a large, active and flourishing trade. All consignments placed with this concern are judiciously handled, and returns promptly made for the same in every instance, this latter being a special feature here. The premises occupied are commodious, ample and well equipped, every convenience and facility being at hand, while three experienced salesmen are in attendance also. A heavy and first-class stock is always carried (consignments being received regularly from all sections of the country), comprising prime butter, cheese, eggs, poultry, beans, apples, onions, potatoes, and everything in the line of country produce; butter, cheese and eggs being specialties, and the trade is wholesale exclusively. Mr. Rollins, who is the sole member, was born in New Hampshire, but has been a resident of Boston since 1863, and was formerly with the firm of Foster, Weeks & Co., same line, for fourteen years. He is a well known member of the Chamber of Commerce.

B. F. HUMPHREY, Blank Book Manufacturer, No. 114 State Street.—This gentleman brings to bear vast practical experience and a thorough knowledge of all the wants and requirements of manufacturing blank books of all kinds, having been established in the business here since 1865. Previous to that time he had been in the employ of Messrs. S. G. Simpkins & Co., and purchased their bindery and blank book manufacturing department at that date, continuing in the business with steadily increasing success. He is essentially a first-class blank book manufacturer and binder, and is in a position to guarantee prompt, systematic and successful work in all branches of his business. His manufactory is equipped with a full outfit of the most improved machinery and appliances for binding and blank book making, and every facility is at hand for insuring rapid and perfect production and the execution of all orders at the time promised. His blank books are in steady and permanent demand among the leading stationers in the city, being recognized as standard staples in their line, and selling readily throughout the mercantile and financial community. Mr. Humphrey is a native of Pelham, Mass., a resident of Somerville, and known in this city as a reliable and responsible business man and an accomplished master of his trade.

S. THOS. WOODWARD, Wholesale Lumber Commission Merchant, No. 11 Central Street (Room 15).—A wholesale commission house doing an immense and thriving business, in lumber, is that of Mr. S. Thomas Woodward, whose office is located in Room 15, No. 11 Central Street. This gentleman founded his enterprise in February, 1886, and from its inception to the present has been attended by the most marked success. He is the representative here of some of the most extensive manufacturers of lumber in the east, west, south and north, with whom he has telegraphic communication, and his customers are supplied with hard and soft lumber, in such dimensions as desired, in car and cargo lots, direct from the forests immediately upon order. His facilities for prompt service and at the lowest rates in the trade, are not surpassed by those of any other wholesale concern in the city, and the more this fact has become known the more has his trade increased, until now it extends all over the New England States. Mr. Woodward is a Bostonian by birth, a young and enterprising business man, of much promise, and, being in the morning of commercial usefulness, the future prospect of his house is exceedingly bright.

THOMAS HENRY HEARN, Apothecary, Harrison Avenue Cor. Kneeland Street.—A well stocked and well-conducted pharmacy is an important acquisition to any community, and in this connection, as a representative local establishment, is mentioned that of Mr. Thomas Henry Hearn. The spacious and attractive premises are fitted up in a style appropriate to the business and a full and complete stock of pure drugs, chemicals, proprietary medicines, toilet and fancy articles, etc., is carried. Prescriptions of all kinds are compounded with the utmost skill and care, and the large and liberal patronage received is drawn from the best medical and family custom of the vicinity. Mr. Hearn is a native of Boston, and a practical and skillful pharmacist of twenty-two years experience in the business. He embarked for himself in the present enterprise in 1880, and has built up what may be termed a representative local business in his line.

GEORGE H. WARE, Steam Printer, No. 43 Lincoln Street.— Among the best known and most popular city establishments in its line, should be mentioned the book and job printing enterprise of Mr. George H. Ware. Mr. Ware succeeded to an old established business at the present site in the early part of the present year, and by his well directed and able management has materially augmented the old time popularity and prosperity of the enterprise. The premises are spacious, well-arranged and convenient, and the plant embraces the newest and best improved printing methods and appliances, the motive force being supplied by steam. A competent corps of experienced assistants are employed, and anything in the line of commercial printing is executed in the highest degree of artistic and mechanical excellence. The business received is both large and lucrative, and the patronage is derived from the best commercial custom. Mr. Ware is a practical and skillful exponent of his trade, and fully merits a classification among the ablest young business men of his day.

CHANDLER & FARQUHAR, Wholesale and Retail Dealers in Hardware Tools, Machinists' and Manufacturers' Supplies, Nos. 177 and 179 Washington Street.—The leading and best patronized headquarters for hardware, iron and kindred supplies, in this city, is the establishment of Messrs. Chandler & Farquhar. This firm are extensive dealers in this class of goods, at both wholesale and retail, and have been established in the business since 1882. The premises occupied for trade purposes comprise a fine store and basement, 25x80 feet each, and part of second floor, while a branch store is also operated at Nos. 23 and 25 Purchase street, devoted principally to the sale of machinery. The several departments are filled with an elaborate and diversified stock, embracing builders' and general hardware, shelf goods and cabinet hardware, carpenters', machinists' and mechanics' tools, locksmiths', butchers' and manufacturers' supplies; Stubbs' Swiss and American files, bolts, set, cap and machine screws, wires and sheet metals, drills, taps and dies, chucks and reamers, foot and hand lathes, bar iron and steel, table and pocket cutlery, and implements and tools for all trades. This house is also prominent as New England Agent for the W. F. and John Barnes Foot-Power Machinery. All the above supplies are purchased in vast quantities direct from the manufacturers. Significant advantages are extended to the trade and consumers in the matter of terms and prices. Both a wholesale and retail business is transacted, and in addition to a large local trade, a heavy demand is ministered to coming from all parts of the New England and western states, and all orders are guaranteed prompt and perfect fulfillment. The individual members of the firm are Messrs. F. Chandler and C. S. Farquhar, the former being a native of Augusta, Me., and the latter of this state; and the reliable, liberal and trustworthy policy they have ever pursued in their dealings, have made these gentlemen exceedingly and deservedly popular with the public and the trade.

JOSEPH D. ELLIS, Wholesale Dealers in Paper and Linen Collars, No. 78 Bedford Street.—The wholesale handling of men's furnishing goods in Boston, is represented in the trade by some solid and noteworthy houses, and among these may be mentioned that of Joseph D. Ellis, wholesale dealer in paper and linen collars, cuffs, neckwear, etc. Mr. Ellis is a native of Fair Haven, Mass., and a man of enterprise and energy, and is thoroughly conversant with the trade. He bears a very creditable war record also, serving throughout the late rebellion in the navy under Admiral Farragut, and was appointed Ensign on the Flag Ship in 1861 when but a very young man. Returning to Fair Haven at the close of the war, Mr. Ellis embarked in the business of manufacturing collars at his native place, and in 1868 moved to Boston, establishing himself in the present line in which he has been uniformly successful from the start. The salesrooms, which are spacious and attractive, occupy a 25x72 foot floor and basement, and several efficient salesmen are in attendance, while a large and fine stock is constantly carried embracing everything in the line of paper and linen collars and cuffs, neckwear in great variety, white and fancy colored shirts, underclothing, hosiery and gents' furnishings generally, and the trade which is principally of a jobbing nature, is quite substantial, extending all over the New England States.

CHAS. E. ELLIOT & CO., Tailors, No. 419 Washington Street—Among the oldest and best known merchant tailors of this city is Mr. Chas. E. Elliot. Mr. Elliot was born in Maine, but came to this city forty-five years ago, and here served his apprenticeship and acquired an expert knowledge of the tailors' trade. As far back as 1848 he began business with a copartner under the firm name as above, and although alone since 1885, he still maintains the old time-honored title. The present premises which have been occupied since 1879, consist of a spacious and elegantly fitted up salesroom containing a full and complete stock of imported and domestic suitings, trouserings, overcoatings, etc., carefully selected from the best grades and most popular patterns and styles. Mr. Elliot has an old established and highly desirable city trade, made up of the best society and business custom. His work has a standard reputation for the highest degree of artistic and mechanical excellence, and he has long been respected and esteemed as one of the leading and representative Boston tailors.

H. P. HALMA, Sailmaker and Manufacturer of Italian Awnings, Tents, Flags, Etc., No. 76 North Market Street.—The occupation of Mr. H. P. Halma as sail maker and especially manufacturing awnings, tents, flags, water proof covers, etc., is an important one and is carried on by him quite extensively. His experience in the business extends over thirty-two years, and he has been established in it since 1876 on his own account. For six years he occupied the premises at No. 29 North Market Street, and afterwards in order to meet the demands of his growing business he moved to the commodious premises at No. 26, on the same street. A number of workmen are employed during the season and a large business transacted in the manufacture of Italian and other kinds of awnings, lawn and field tents of all sizes and ship and yacht sails and flags, also water proof covers, canopies, etc. Repairing receives attention and large or small tents are kept on hand for sale or to let, on reasonable terms and new and second hand sail cloth for covers. Wheel ropes are spliced and put up, and canopy awnings are rented for special occasions. Yacht sails and flags are made to order and in this branch of the business Mr. Halma is pronounced one of the best in the city, and can always guarantee perfect work and full satisfaction. He is originally from Denmark, has been in the United States twenty years, building up a business which extends to various sections of the state of Massachusetts. He is a prominent member of the Masonic Order and also of the Dorchester and South Boston Yacht Clubs.

LAROY E. NICHOLS, American Watches and Clocks, Jewelry and Optical Goods, No. 215 Hanover Street.—There is probably not one among the many well kept jewelry stores that have sprung up in this vicinity of late years, that has been attended with more gratifying prosperity than that of Laroy E. Nichols. It is a neat, compact and well-ordered establishment, where is always displayed a complete and first class assortment of American watches and clocks of every description; also a full and fine line of jewelry, including novelties in rings, pins, chains, charms, lockets and emblematic designs; while purchasers can rely upon receiving an excellent article, courteous attention and satisfactory dealing in every instance in this reliable establishment. Here can also be found everything in the line of optical goods, opera glasses, spectacles, eye-glasses, etc., also society emblems in quite a variety, in unique designs and artistic workmanship; bottom prices likewise prevailing. Watches, clocks, jewelry, etc., are neatly and promptly repaired at reasonable rates; fine watch repairing being a specialty, while a competent assistant is regularly employed, and all work executed in this establishment is fully warranted to render satisfaction. Mr. Nichols, is a native of New Hampshire, and a practical and expert jeweler, of many years' experience. He established himself in business in Boston, in 1884, moving to the present location, May 9th, 1888, and from the start he has enjoyed a very nice patronage. Mr. Nichols is a popular member of the order of Red Men and also of the Good Fellows.

HEWES & MAYO, Successors to A. P. Boyer, Sign and Office Painters, No. 31 Cornhill Street.—Boston has many experts in the painting and decorative line, and among these are numbered Messrs. Hewes & Mayo. The business of this concern had its origin in 1887, when it was founded by Mr. A. P. Boyer, who, in 1885, was succeeded by Messrs. Hunting & Hewes. In the early part of 1888 this firm was reorganized, and became, as now, Hewes & Mayo, the copartners being Mr. James B. Hewes and Mr. William B. Mayo. The former is a native of England and resides at Arlington, and the latter was born on Cape Cod and lives at Everett. Both these gentlemen are practical sign and general painters of long experience, and in their line have produced the most artistic work. They give special attention to glass lettering, cloth signs, marble lettering, metal signs, wire screen lettering, carved signs, show cards, etc., and permanent employment is afforded to a force of skilled workmen. The firm occupy roomy premises, and their appliances and facilities are such as to admit of the speedy and effective execution of orders. Having seen some specimens of the work of this house we can in full confidence commend the firm to the patronage of our readers as one competent to do first class work in every respect.

L. DICKEY, Manufacturer of Fancy Whips, Thongs, Lashes, Knotted Bone, and Named Whips, Old Whips repaired, No. 60 Sudbury Street.—In 1862 the well-known gentleman whose name heads this sketch, and who is now a man in the prime of life, came to this city from the Empire State, and began business in a modest way on Sudbury Street. From the inception of the venture he has steadily pushed his way to a forefront rank in his branch of trade, in which he has had a practical experience extending over a period of forty-six years. Mr. L. Dickey is a manufacturer of fancy whips, thongs, lashes, knotted bone and named whips. His premises are adequately equipped with all necessary mechanical appliances, and here a staff of competent and skilled artisans are permanently employed in making whips towards and for the trade. A large and varied assortment of whips is constantly carried in stock, and all orders are promptly and satisfactorily filled. The business is of both a wholesale and retail character, and it extends throughout the New England States. Mr. Dickey is a native of Rochester, N. Y., and is one of the best known and most popular whip makers in this section of the country.

N. C. WHITAKER & CO., Manufacturers of Fine Tortoise Shell and Horn Goods, Combs, Pins, Bracelets, Jewelry and Novelties of Every Description in Shell and Horn, and Manufacturers' Agents for Ivory and Cloth Buttons, No. 353 Washington Street.—As manufacturers of fine tortoise shell and horn goods, combs, pins, bracelets, jewelry and novelties of every description in shell, horn etc., this firm have obtained deserved success and have won a large and influential patronage both at home and abroad. The enterprise was originally founded in 1874 by Messrs. Zates, Whitaker & Kane, and two years later the firm was changed to Zales & Co., who, in 1878, were succeeded by Whitaker & Proctor. This firm was dissolved in August, 1888, and Mr. N. C. Whitaker, on becoming the sole proprietor removed the business to its present location, where he occupies finely appointed offices and sample room and a spacious factory in the rear. The latter is equipped in the most thorough manner with the latest improved machinery appertaining to the trade, and the machinery is operated by steam power. The tortoise shell and horn goods made here are of the finest quality and are noted for their beauty of design and elegance of finish. A prominent feature is made of the repairing of combs, jewelry and fans, and the firm are manufacturers' agents for ivory and cloth buttons, and the facilities of the house are such as ensure the prompt and satisfactory fulfillment of all orders. The trade of the house is very extensive and influential, its products being shipped not only to all parts of the Union, but to South America, and the transactions of the house, which are exclusively of a wholesale character, are yearly increasing in volume.

ELMER E. GRAY, Commission Merchant, Butter, Cheese, Eggs and Poultry, No. 131 Blackstone Street.—This representative and progressive house was established in 1885 by Mr. Gray, who has built up a large trade and through his extensive connections controls a large business. Consignments of choice creamery and dairy butter, cheese and fresh eggs are received daily, and also live and dressed poultry. Promptitude and quick sales form the policy upon which the business is conducted and the stock is always choice and fresh. Mr. Gray is in the possession of the best facilities for procuring supplies direct from the producers and can supply the trade at the lowest market prices. The premises are of ample dimensions for the requirements of the business and a force of clerks are kept constantly employed. Liberal advances are made on consignments and in all matters pertaining to this special line of trade Mr. Gray is prepared to transact business in a manner satisfactory to all concerned. He supplies dealers, hotels, restaurants and families, and is enjoying a well merited success. He was born in East Boston twenty-seven years ago and is well known in Boston business circles.

FOSS & GAULT, Importers and Dealers in Ladies', Gentlemen's and Children's Fine Hosiery and Underwear, No. 22 Temple Place. A newly established mercantile enterprise, but one which is fast assuming a position in the front rank of the great houses which form the basis of the trade, wealth and importance of this great shopping district is that of Messrs. Foss & Gault, importers and dealers in ladies', gentlemen's and children's fine hosiery and general furnishing goods, also umbrellas and parasols, recovered and repaired. Messrs. Chas. E. Foss and J. E. Gault, composing the firm, are young men thoroughly conversant with the business on hand, having served a long clerkship in the well known house of C. F. Hovey & Co. In September, 1888, they embarked for themselves at the present site, and their business from its inception has had a substantial and rapid growth. The salesroom, 25x60 feet in dimensions, is a model of systematic and convenient arrangement and its appointment is in accord with the best modern ideas of artistic elegance. The large, comprehensive and complete stock represents the newest novelties, latest fashionable styles and finest fabrics in the goods above enumerated, a large force of experienced clerks is employed and the liberal patronage received is drawn from the best town and suburban custom. Messrs. Foss & Gault are thoroughly active, go-ahead business men, generally respected as among the representative and rapidly rising young merchants in their line, of this, their native city.

JESSE SCOTT, Fine French and American Confectionery, Ice Cream, Soda and Mineral Waters, No. 122 Court Street.—One of the best known among the many attractive establishments on Court Street is that of Mr. Jesse Scott, successor to Joseph Fowler, located at No. 122 of that thoroughfare. Mr. Scott, who is a practical business man, assumed control and became sole proprietor of this popular and reliable house in October, 1888, and by courtesy and liberal dealing has made many friends whose confidence and esteem he enjoys in the highest degree. The handsome store is neatly and tastefully fitted up with plate glass show cases and ornamental fixtures and a fountain of new novel design. In the rear of the store is a finely furnished saloon parlor, which is provided with every convenience for the accommodation of the public. Mr. Scott manufactures all kinds of fine French and American confectionery and candies from pure cane sugar and other materials, and ice cream and ices, and supplies a large demand. The store and saloon is liberally patronized by an appreciative public, and Mr. Scott, who is a ready, courteous, polite, attentive gentleman, has just came to be proud of the success which has attended his well directed efforts. He fills all orders promptly and guarantees the best service in the line of his business of any merchant in the city. A Bostonian by birth, he is very popular as a business man and citizen.

C. R. MÜNCH, Jr., Hat Tip Printer, No. 339 Washington Street.—A deservedly successful house engaged in hat tip printing is that which is conducted by Mr. C. R. Münch, Jr. Mr. Münch is a Swede by birth and learned his trade in this city, after which he was employed in some of the best houses engaged in his special line, and after acquiring a thorough experience in all its details, he founded this establishment originally in 1877, on Bedford Street. The large and influential trade he received by his close attention to business executing first-class work and honorable dealings, compelled him to seek more comfortable and spacious quarters, and in 1884 he removed to his present address. Here he utilizes a finely fitted up establishment of spacious dimensions, which contains all the conveniences and latest improved machinery and appliances required in the trade. He employs a sufficient force of skilled and experienced workmen in order to meet all the demands of his large and constantly increasing business, and is prepared to execute all orders of any magnitude at the shortest notice. A specialty is made of fine printing in gold or silver leaf, on silk, satin or leather, in which all the latest and newest designs are produced, while he is in constant receipt of new patterns, suitable for trade marks and other branches of the business. His trade is very large and includes a large portion of the most prominent and leading hat manufacturers in this city and throughout New England. Mr. Münch has had many years experience in his business.

THE METROPOLIS OF NEW ENGLAND. 277

S. W. CHAMBERLIN, Steam Cookers, No. 25 Union street.— The improvements made in the art of cooking have occupied the attention of inventors and scientific men for an indefinite period, and the most important result of their labors is shown in the Chamberlin Steam Cooker, manufactured by Mr. S. W. Chamberlin, the patentee, at No. 25 Union Street, in this city. This cooker is an article constructed on scientific principles, giving concentrated heat, together with steam pressure, which makes it an important factor in household economy. The invention was originally patented February 29, 1876, and the business of their manufacture was established by Mr. Chamberlin, at Montague, Mass., removing to Boston in 1877. The business premises comprise three floors, 25x100 feet each, thoroughly equipped with new and improved machinery, operated by steam power, and every modern facility is afforded for insuring rapid and perfect production. The Chamberlin is recognized wherever introduced as the only perfect self-regulating steam cooker in the market. It has always been upheld by learned scientists that the cooking of food by steam is the most desirable, and now that a perfect cooker has been invented there will be less dyspepsia and indigestion among our epicures. This invention is not only a health-saving affair, but gives great relief to the over-burdened housewife or cook at all seasons of the year. Its construction is simple, requiring no attention except to keep the water supplied, which may be replenished without removing the cover or disturbing the food. It is the only steamer that controls the steam; there are no odors or steam arising from the cooking of food; no intermixture of flavors, no loss from forgetfulness as nothing burns, no heavy pots of water to lift; is easier to clean than the pots, gives economy of store room, and can be used on gas, kerosene or common stoves; makes the food more nourishing, palatable and digestible; sweet vegetables become sweeter, and twenty per cent is saved in shrinkage. The seamless rim was never used before, and the whistle which gives the alarm when the water is low is an improvement peculiar to this cooker alone. Over eighty thousand of these cookers have already been sold, and diplomas and medals have been awarded it at the fair of the Massachusetts Charitable Mechanic Association, at Boston; the New England Fair, at Worcester, Mass.; the State Fair, at Lewiston, Me., and many others. They are in heavy and increasing demand throughout all the United States, and shipments are also freely made to Australia and many other foreign ports. Mr. Chamberlin, the enterprising proprietor, was born in New Salem Franklin County, Mass., and is recognized in this city as an accomplished inventor and manufacturer, and a reliable and progressive business man.

R. & J. BESSES, Caterers, No. 167 Tremont Street.—These gentlemen are natives of Switzerland, and came to New York where they first established themselves in 1872. In 1878 they removed to Hartford, Conn., where they still operate the leading house in their line, and in April, 1884, opened their elegant establishment in this city at the address above indicated. Although a recent candidate for popular favor, this firm have already won a leading position and an extensive, influential and steadily increasing patronage. They are prepared to execute all orders that are entrusted to their care with the utmost promptness, and to guarantee perfect satisfaction. Their salesrooms are spacious and elegantly appointed, and a large and varied stock is displayed of fancy cakes, ice creams, pastry, imported fruits, salted almonds, and other specialties. The assortment of fancy cakes here supplied comprise pastile, chocolate bisque, iced cakes, hazel nut cakes, meringues, kisses, chocolate eclaires, cream cakes, pound cake, angel cake, lady cake, sponge cake, baba, savaren, brisse, macha, pistach cakes, genuise cakes, santanore, corne al crem, macaroons, almond praline, pignoli, wafers, almond wafers, etc., etc. The line of fancy ice creams includes neapolitan, harlequin, bisque glace, parfait aux cafe, mousse aux cafe, bisque torioni, creme praline, nougaten, sistori and tutti frutti; while puddings, pudding glace, punch glace and pastry of every description are but features of an array of good things which is rarely duplicated elsewhere. Then there are varieties of oysters, salads, pates, sandwiches, croquettes, etc., which are here served in the very finest style, as well as every other article which could by any reasonable stretch of the imagination be included in a caterer's bill of fare. Special attention is given to serving wedding and reception parties, also balls and picnics, for which a complete supply of silver, glass and china ware is kept on hand, while waiters and cooks in any number desired are furnished on short notice.

FISK'S Lunch and Dining Rooms, No. 132 Essex Street.—That Mr. Fisk knows how to minister to the wants of the inner man, is fully attested by the large and successful patronage he has built up within the past few years. He was born in this city some fifty-five years ago, and for about thirty years was in business as a truckman. In 1883, he opened the lunch room on the first floor of the building, No. 126 Bedford Street, and this has an area of 50x100 feet. It was fitted up in the most elegant and attractive manner, yet convenience and comfort were not sacrificed to mere display, attraction and comfort. Wholesome, relishable lunches were provided at popular prices, and merchants, clerks and others have soon discovered that this was a place in which to take "mine ease in mine Inn," that the appetite could here be appeased with everything it could crave for, and a' reasonable prices. In 1884 he fitted up the second floor of the building as a general dining room. He has recently removed to No. 132 Essex Street. This is a finely fitted up lunch room, and visitors find here a cordial welcome, every comfort and convenience, civil attendance, food of the finest quality and of great variety, and charges the most reasonable. It is just the place for a hungry man to get into, and when he gets out of it he will do so feeling good, and that he has had his money's worth. Mr. Fisk believes in giving satisfaction, and that is the secret of his success and popularity.

HOLWAY BROS. & WOODBURY, Sail Makers, No. 150 Commercial street.—The old established concern of Messrs. Holway Bros. & Woodbury, was organized in 1864 under the style of Holway & Woodbury. In 1868 the firm was reorganized and became as now, Holway Bros. & Woodbury, the co-partners being Messrs. Lemuel and James O. Holway and Mr. Nelson Woodbury. Throughout its career the concern has had a successful and enviable record and its trade relations extend to all parts of the New England and the United States. The premises devoted to the business comprise two floors, each floor having an area of 25x125 feet, and provided with every modern mechanical appliance necessary to the successful carrying on of the business, and employment is afforded to from five to fifteen hands. In the way of tents a large variety of styles are made, and for all purposes, including A tents, round or ball tents, croquet and lawn tennis tents, wall tents, and lawn canopies, as well as large tents for picnics, agricultural fairs, etc. The house manufactures sails of every description, and of all sizes. In the manufacture of sails for yachts and awnings the firm have gained, as in the other departments of their business, a very high reputation, all the material entering into their work being of a thoroughly reliable character, while the work itself is first class and prompt in execution. The firm buy and sell second-hand sails and second hand duck for covers, and have always in stock sails to let and hire. The members of the firm are all practical workmen in the business, and their long experience has given them a knowledge which is a great benefit to consumers. The brothers, Holway, are natives of Cape Cod, and Mr. Woodbury was born at Gloucester, Mass., and are well-known in their line.

L. SISKIND & CO., Five and Ten Cent Goods, Etc., No. 106 Leverett Street.—The business conducted by L. Siskind & Co., is a bazaar and fancy goods emporium combined, and has been in successful operation for the past four years, and is headquarters for all kinds of five and ten cent goods. The store is spacious in size, attractive in all its arrangements and appointments, and stocked to overflowing with a brilliant bewildering display of crockery, china, glass and tinware, dry and fancy goods, cutlery and stationery, toys and games. For general holiday goods and novelties of every description we commend our readers to visit Siskind's. Of French toys, German toys, Yankee toys, toys for girls, and toys for boys, there is an immense assortment. Then there are books and games, bric-a-brac of every description, ivory and leather goods, ornamented buttons, fans, pocket books, brass goods and small articles in endless variety. There is also a display of the practical and serviceable, handsomely ornamented toilet sets, breakfast, dinner and tea sets, ranging in value from the plainest to the most elaborate; dress goods, laces and embroidery, fine stationery, etc. Bargains are here offered that have no equal in the city, while at holiday time the store is thronged. Customers are waited upon promptly and courteously. Mr. Siskind, the active member of the firm, is a native of Russia. From three to four assistants are employed and as they are courteous and polite, none go away dissatisfied.

FAMILY GROCERY AND WINE STORE, P. H. Desmond, Manager; No. 24 Leverett Street.—For thirty odd years or more the popular and excellent family grocery and wine store now conducted by P. H. Desmond, has maintained an enduring hold on public favor. The reliable and well known store was originally established in 1856 by Charles Jarvis, who was succeeded on February, 1868, by the firm of Ennis & Dewey, and on the following May came under the management of Mr. Desmond, under whose judicious management the business has since been continued with gratifying success. The premises occupied are compact, ample and well kept, two efficient clerks being in attendance, while a large and excellent stock is constantly carried, including choice teas and coffees, fresh and pure spices, condiments, sauces, pickles and table delicacies, canned goods in great variety, dried fruit, fine creamery butter, cheese and eggs, best brands of flour, meal, beans, peas, rice, lard, sugars, syrups, molasses, vinegar, salt, soda, fish, soaps, starch, etc.; also pure wines, liquors, ales, and bottled goods, for medicinal and family use, and the patronage, which is large and prosperous, gives evidence of steady increase. The manager, Mr. Desmond, who is a native of Ireland, but a resident of this country thirty-two years, is a man of energy, sagacity and good business qualities and well merits the liberal measure of popular favor he enjoys.

C. E. WHITE, Cigars, Tobacco, Etc., No. 273 Hanover Street.—This gentleman has been established in the business here for a period of twenty years, and has built up a reputation and a trade of which he may well be proud. He deals extensively at both wholesale and retail in cigars and tobacco, and all other smokers' articles, supplying a large and first-class trade throughout New England, and also exporting tobacco to England and other foreign countries. As fine an assortment of cigars, tobacco and smokers' articles are kept in stock as can be found in the city. A large storehouse is operated on Central Wharf to accommodate surplus stock, and the resources of the house enable it to guarantee the prompt and perfect fulfillment of all orders, of whatever magnitude. The best possible facilities are possessed for reaching the best manufacturers both at home and abroad, and the best supplies are secured at such advantageous rates as enable the proprietor to offer the rarest inducements to his patrons. Mr. White is a native of Maine, of large and valuable experience in business.

HENRY S. LOMBARD, Clothing and Gentlemen's Outfitter, Nos. 46-52 Clinton Street.—In the clothing and gentlemen's outfitting trade, a house which is well known in Boston is the old established one of Henry S. Lombard, Nos. 46-52 Clinton Street. This flourishing business dates its establishment back to the year 1855. Mr. Lombard has occupied the same premises during all that time, comprising a store having a frontage of sixty feet, and two upper floors, where he carries a large stock of clothing. He makes a specialty of all styles of butchers' frocks, which he manufactures, and carries one of the largest stocks to be found in Boston and at prices which defy competition, as well as yachtsmen's outfits of which he keeps a splendid variety. Four assistants are employed in the business which has long been of an extensive description, owing to the fine quality of goods which Mr. Lombard has invariably kept and the reasonable prices he has always charged for the same. Mr. Lombard is a native of Truro, Mass. He is an active business man and stands high in the commercial community of Boston.

NEW ENGLAND SUPPLY COMPANY, Clothing, Dry Goods, Jewelry Etc. Office: No. 86 Court Street.—This enterprise had its origin five years ago, and in 1888 it came under the direction and control of Mr. J. Waxman, who has built up a trade of considerable magnitude in clothing, dry goods, jewelry, furniture, carpets, etc., on the weekly payment plan at strictly cash prices. The company have a well appointed office at the address indicated, but do not carry any stock. Arrangements have been made with the leading houses in the various branches of business in the city, and customers of the company are given orders upon these houses, where they can secure anything they need, the company being responsible to such houses. Thus customers are afforded the most ample choice of goods at cash prices, while they have the advantage of meeting the cost by weekly payments of an easy character. Through its good offices many persons with small wage earnings have been enabled to secure in times of necessity most useful goods and to enjoy the use of them while they were paying for them in sums regulated to come within their means. Mr. Waxman, the manager, is a most energetic and wide-awake business man. He was born in Poland, but lived in England and Australia most of his life before coming to the United States, ten years ago.

J. WARREN GILL, Fish, Oysters, Lobsters, Clams, Etc., No. 88 Staniford Street.—Notable among those who have for years been supplying the citizens of Boston and vicinity with fish, oysters, etc., is Mr. J. Warren Gill, who has unusual facilities for securing the finest oysters, clams, lobsters, and all the various kinds of fish, and supplies a large, first-class custom. The market is kept neat and clean and every morning is supplied with the choicest sea food and also river and lake fish when in season. He is one of the largest dealers in the section of the city in which he is located, and can always offer the best inducements to his patrons. He has been in the business since 1873 and was formerly located at Nos. 54-56 Green Street, removing in May last to the very desirable premises now occupied at No. 88 New Staniford Street. Mr. Gill, who is a native of Cape Cod, is thoroughly posted and familiar with every detail of the fish and oyster business, and is very popular in this community.

A. H. LIVERMORE, Surgeon and Mechanical Dentist, No. 140 Court Street.—For fully a quarter of a century, Dr. A. H. Livermore, surgeon and mechanical dentist, has occupied a distinguished position in his line and enjoyed a successful practice among the best people of Boston, as well as the surrounding country. Dr. Livermore, who is a native of New Hampshire, has been a resident of this city for thirty-four years and nine years after his arrival, entered upon the practice of his profession, achieving in a short time a distinguished name for the successful manner he performed all operations, whether in the extracting, filling or re-arrangement of teeth. He occupies a handsome suite of rooms, embracing an elegant reception room, operating room and private office and has every modern convenience and requisite in the dental art, including the latest scientific and artistic apparatus, making the establishment one of the best appointed offices in the city. Dr. Livermore's long experience and first-class record put him among the leading surgeon and mechanical dentists of Boston. He is still one of the deftest men in his profession and is looked upon with respect both by his confreres and the general public because of his honorable methods and excellent workmanship.

THE METROPOLIS OF NEW ENGLAND. 279

BOSTON MERCANTILE BUSINESS COMPANY, F. D. Frisbie, Manager, No. 22 School Street.—The Boston Mercantile Business Company was organized in 1888, and in the same year opened an office, and began business on Bromfield Street. In July, 1888, Mr. F. D. Frisbie became the proprietor, and removed the business to its present desirable site at No. 22 School Street. The Boston Mercantile Business Company furnishes duly qualified and properly attested employees for all positions in the higher walks of commercial and professional life, the method pursued being as follows: A merchant, banker, lawyer, et al, wishes to engage a competent clerk, cashier, stenographer, type-writer, etc. He hasn't the time, nor inclination, perhaps, to secure his man through the common method of advertising and subsequent tedious examination of applicants, hence he writes the company, describing the position to be filled, with a commission to secure a proper party. This the company promptly does, and the applicant secures an employee thoroughly competent and fully vouched for as to integrity, moral character, etc., these matters being a distinctive feature of the business, for which the company assumes the responsibility. Mr. Frisbie, the enterprising young proprietor, is a son of the celebrated physician of that name, in Newton, Mass., and a gentleman in every way eminently well fitted for the business in hand. Although but little more than fairly started, he has already secured a large and influential patronage. Mr. Frisbie has recently added to his enterprise a first-class short hand and type writing school.

J. T. GILMAN, Apothecary, No. 173 North Street.—No name is more closely identified with the drug trade in Boston than that of Mr. J. T. Gilman. The business was founded in 1850, by George Wilson, who died in 1862, and who was succeeded by Geo. K. Lane. The business afterwards was conducted by Mr. Richmond and finally in 1869 came into the hands of Mr. Gilman, who has carried it on with the greatest success ever since. Mr. Gilman is the oldest business man on North Street. He was born in New Hampshire, studied medicine when young with his uncle at Winterport, Maine, and has been a resident of Boston since 1847, when he went to work in a drug store on North Street, remaining here up to the present time. The store is a neat and commodious one, 25x70 feet in dimensions, and contains a full line of the purest and freshest drugs and chemicals, as well as proprietary medicines of various kinds, surgical and fancy goods, etc. The preparations of the house are well-known, and include first-class cough and diarrhoea medicines, which are highly popular throughout the city. Mr. Gilman has a large family and prescription trade and bears the highest reputation in his line for reliability and skill. He sells no alcoholic articles of any kind, having kept no liquors in his establishment since it came under his control.

JAMES LAPWORTH, Carving, Designing and Mould Sinking, No. 25 Sudbury Street.—Barbarian and civilized races of all ages have cultivated this art, perfecting it and carrying it forward from generation to generation, until to-day artistic carving is as much appreciated as it ever could have been in the days of old. In his line Mr. Lapworth is an expert, and his ability is backed by an experience of a practical character extending over a period of thirty years. He was born in England, and twenty-two years ago came to America. In 1866 he began business in Boston at No. 100 Sudbury Street, and on Nov. 1, 1888, removed to No. 35, where he has commodious quarters, well equipped for executing all kinds of carving, designing and mould-sinking. He has a fine business connection throughout Massachusetts, is a resident of Melrose, and a gentleman who is prompt and reliable in all his dealings.

ELLA C. McLEAN, Artist, 560 Washington Street.—Miss McLean, who is a native of Boston and a young artist of pronounced natural ability, after the careful study and practical experience of several years, established herself as an exponent of the profession in 1885, and has since won a liberal share of public favor and the patronage of many of the best-known residents of the metropolis. Miss McLean occupies an elegantly appointed apartment as her studio, and is prepared to give the most satisfactory and conscientious attention to painting of all kinds for decoration, as well as to pupils of all ages, and stages of advancement in the art "beautiful." Her charges for painting lessons by the quarter are exceedingly moderate, and a specialty is made of giving lessons to classes or private pupils on Tuesday or Friday evenings, when the studio is lighted by electric lights and every facility is at hand for achieving the most satisfactory results in every branch of art decoration, portrait painting, etc. Miss McLean deservedly enjoys the most exemplary of reputations as a faithful, able and conscientious teacher. The number of her patrons increase each year, and she occupies a leading position among the best-known and most clever lady artists in the city.

CLYDE C. CLARK, Printer and Publisher of the Spirit of the Hub, Nos. 10 State, and 194 Washington Streets.—The house of Mr. Clyde C. Clark, the printer of the popular sporting paper the Spirit of the Hub, has long enjoyed an enviable reputation for the excellence of its productions. As a book and job printer, Mr. Clark is highly regarded as a master of his art in all its details, and is prepared to promptly meet every demand of the public in this line of enterprise. His premises are spacious and commodious, handsomely fitted up, conveniently located and thoroughly equipped with every requisite necessary for the successful prosecution of the business. He is prepared to execute every description of plain and ornamental printing at the shortest notice and most reasonable prices. His specimens of programmes, bill-heads, cards and invitations to balls, weddings and parties show the utmost skill and a just conception of the artistic in designing new and novel styles. The Spirit of the Hub has a wide and steadily increasing circulation, is a model of excellence in typography, and edited with ability. All the news in sporting matters are given in an entertaining vein, and the information it contains may be relied upon as accurate and trustworthy. Mr. Clark is a native of Stoughton, Mass., a practical printer of large experience and high reputation.

WETMORE & STORY, Merchant Tailors, No. 17 Essex Street.—Messrs. Wetmore & Story are practical skilled cutters of judgment and taste, which with their experience in the business combine to make their services desirable by those who wish to be well and fashionably dressed. The handsomely fitted up store is admirably arranged, and upon the counters is displayed a large and valuable assortment of fine woolens, suitings, cloths, etc., of both foreign and domestic productions, in all the new and beautiful styles and fashionable designs. The goods have been carefully selected, expressly for a fastidious custom, and every attention is given to cutting, making and trimming of all garments ordered. Mr. O. F. Wetmore and Mr. L. J. Story, the copartners, are both young men, natives of Boston, and are among the most popular exponents of the merchant tailoring art in the city. They have been associated in business for seven years, and since 1885 have occupied the very eligible premises at No. 17 Essex street, and number among their patrons many of the leading citizens.

H. M. SCRIBNER & CO., Portrait Artists and Photographers, No. 63 Court Street.—In reviewing the establishments devoted to this interesting and useful branch of art, more than passing notice should be given that of Messrs. H. M. Scribner & Co., the talented and well known artists, who have long won favor and recognition for skill and reliability. This popular and prosperous studio was established in 1877 by the Alden Photo Co., who conducted the same up to April, 1888, when they were succeed by Ward & Scribner, the style changing to H. M. Scribner & Co., (A. J. Alden) in November last. The premises occupied are commodious and well equipped, all the latest improved apparatus and photo appliances being in service, while several competent assistants are employed. Everything comprehended in modern photography, including pictures of every size, style and variety, from a life size portrait to the most diminutive finger ring, is done in the most satisfactory manner, at prices immeasurably lower than those prevailing for the same class of work in Boston; old photographs being copied and enlarged in A1 style, fine portraits being a specialty. Pictures are finished in crayon, oil, pastel, India ink, etc., while outside work is promptly and reliably executed likewise, this firm being agents for the Alden Photo Co., which make this a special feature.

BARKER & STARBIRD, Headquarters for Amateur Photographers, Photographic Apparatus, Dry Plates and Chemicals, Picture Frames, Etc., No. 56 Bromfield Street.—A leading house in Boston engaged in this line of trade is that of Messrs. Barker & Starbird, whose headquarters for amateur photographers, and photographic apparatus, is located at No. 56 Bromfield Street. The individual members of the firm are Mr. F. E. Barker a native of this city, who was formerly in the starch business with his father on Commercial Street, and Mr. N. W. Starbird, until lately a buyer for the Danvers Hospital at Danvers, Mass., and is also a Bostonian by birth. The business was founded originally by Mr. C. B. Selee in 1880, and continued by him very successfully until 1888 when Mr. Barker was admitted as a partner, and the business was conducted by them for a short time under the firm name of Selee & Barker, and upon the retirement of the former in October the same year, Mr. Starbird entered into the business, since which date the business has been carried on with increased patronage and influence under the present firm title. The premises occupied are spacious and commodious, and are fitted up with every convenience for the display of goods and all facilities for the transaction of business. They keep constantly on hand a full and complete stock of amateur photographers' supplies, embracing entire outfits, such as cameras, tripods, lenses, slides, caps, drop shutters, dry-plates, baths, sensitized paper, chemicals, chloride of gold, etc., in fact everything pertaining to a perfect outfit. They also carry a fine supply of frames, materials for mounting, albums, etc. These goods are all received direct from producers and are sold at the very lowest prices. They deal in first-class articles only and have a very large patronage throughout the New England States. Polite and attentive assistants are employed. A specialty of this house is promptness and care in filling all orders, a matter well worthy of consideration to purchasers. Both Messrs. Barker and Starbird are well worthy of the large and increasing patronage they now enjoy. In connection with their establishment they have a desk room and reading room for the free use of their customers.

ROBERT MILLER & CO., Manufacturers of Sails, Awnings, Etc., No. 230 State Street.—One of the oldest industries in Boston is that of sail making, and it is one that dates back to the days of the first settlers of New England. For more than thirty years the establishment of Mr. Robert Miller, the sail and awning manufacturer, of No. 230 State Street, has been a noted one in the trade, and has earned a high reputation among ship builders for the strength and durability of its sails. The late Mr. Robert Miller, senior, started this business in 1854 and continued it until December, 1884, when he was succeeded by his son, Mr. Robert Miller, who was born and reared in the business, and is familiar with its every detail. The premises occupied for the business comprise the three upper floors of a five-story building, and these are equipped with every modern mechanical appliance necessary for the successful operation of the business, which consists of the manufacture of sails of all kinds (especially of yacht sails), awnings, horse, wagon and piano covers, canopies, flags, tents, etc. Tents from the smallest round or bell patterns, to the largest for houses, agricultural fairs, etc., are made to order, and tents can either be purchased or hired. In the manufacture of yacht sails the house has gained a high reputation for excellence of material, neatness of finish and promptness of execution, also in the making of canopies, awnings and flags; a full stock of awning goods and flag materials being constantly kept on hand. A specialty is made of gymnasium goods and his aim is to use only the best materials obtainable, to employ only the most experienced hands, and to put his manufactures on the market at the lowest possible price. The strict adherence to these points, coupled with the integrity and straightforwardness on the part of Mr. Miller, in all his business relations, has led to the house having meted out to it a large and substantial patronage.

STEPHEN P. BROOKS, Manufacturer of Pianos, No. 55½ Sudbury Street.—Mr. Brooks has been engaged in this special line of manufacture since 1854, and has made many valuable improvements in the action and arrangement of the sounding board which greatly adds to the effectiveness of the instrument in quality of tone and ease of touch. He manufactures both grand and upright pianos in elaborate, new style, highly polished cases, and can furnish an instrument equal to the best made in the country at the low price of $150. Mr. Brooks is a Massachusetts man and has lived in Boston forty years, and was for sometime engaged in business as a builder and contractor, and also in the clothing trade. He patented in 1854 an iron frame with a sound-board attached thereto without a wood back. In 1865, an upright piano-forte action, in 1865, a piano-forte action. In 1877, he found that an upright piano with a light frame would not stand in tune because the blow of the hammer being struck towards the pin, was liable to start the pin, so he arranged to string the piano with nuts and screws, and put bars on the plate so the string was drawn in the centre of the bars. Later he patented a piano in which the outer case and cover, act as a sound-board, and a string plate hung within a sound board; also an improvement in stringing with nuts and screws when one nut runs beneath the other, also, a piano with two sets of strings drawn in different angles, and crossing, one on the plane of the other set at the striking point. Also, an elastic hammer, where the portion that gives the blow is open or hollow.

ALLEN BROTHERS, Manufacturers and Dealers in Rubber and Steel Stamps, No. 156 Washington Street.—A widely known Boston firm engaged in the manufacturing of stamps, stencils, presses and kindred devices, is that of Allen Brothers. It is one of the leading and best equipped concerns of the kind in this city, and has a large and flourishing trade throughout the New England States, besides a fine local patronage, with some export also to South America and Europe. This business was established in 1854, and under the firm name that heads this sketch has since been conducted with uniform success, a branch store having been opened in 1888. They occupy ample and well equipped quarters, and employ some eight or more expert hands, the articles produced being of a very superior character. The firm manufacture and keep in stock everything in the line of steel and rubber stamps, burning brands, check protectors, stencils, seal presses, dog collars, etc., and all orders for the trade are executed in the most expeditious and excellent manner. Mr. N. H. Allen, who is the sole member of the firm since the retirement of his brother, J. E. Allen in 1883, is a man of long, practical experience in this line of business.

S. C. HAYES & CO., Commission Merchants, and Receivers of Hay, Straw and Grain, No. 106 Canal Street.—Twenty odd years of uninterrupted prosperity sums up in brief the history of the well-known and responsible firm of S. C. Hayes & Co., commission merchants, and receivers of hay, straw and grain. The firm carries on a general commission business in baled hay, straw, oats, corn, rye, barley, meal and millfeed. Keeping on hand at the various railroad freight depots in the city a big stock—carloads being sold on the track, and the trade of the firm, which is of a wholesale nature exclusively, extends throughout Boston and surrounding cities and towns. Mr. S. C. Hayes, who is and has always been the sole member, is a gentleman of middle age, and a native of New Hampshire, but a resident of this city many years. He is a man of entire probity in his business relations, as well as of energy and judicious enterprise, thoroughly conversant with the trade, and enjoys an excellent reputation.

CHAS. F. LIBBIE, Jr., Proprietor Libbie's Show Print, No. 11 Hayward Place.—One of the largest establishments in the printing trade in Boston, is that of Chas. F. Libbie, Jr., No. 11 Hayward Place, which is well known in connection with show printing of all kinds. Mr. Libbie, who is a Boston man in his twenty-eighth year, has had a long experience in his line, and is well fitted by first-class business aptitude to conduct the large concern under his control in a successful way. He established the business in 1886, the premises he acquired being of the most commodious description, comprising three floors, 25x90 feet in dimensions, provided throughout with every convenience for the trade, elaborate fonts of the largest job type in a multitude of styles, and every requisite of a thoroughly equipped office for show printing of the finest kind. Two cylinder presses of the fastest make and four job presses are kept running in the establishment, while twenty men find constant employment in the various departments of the business.

WRIGHT BROTHERS & CO., Manufacturers of Umbrellas and Parasols; Warerooms, Nos. 63 and 65 Essex Street, Boston; Factories: Nos. 6, 8, 10, 12, 14, 25 and 27 Hudson Street, Philadelphia.—An extensive business conducted under the above title constitutes the Boston branch of the old, time-honored and representative house of that source whose large manufactories are among the foremost industries of Philadelphia

and New York—the manufactory being located in the former, and the main distributing depot in the latter cities. The Boston branch was established in 1870 on Chauncey Street but was removed to the present eligible site in January last. The spacious salesroom, 37x72 feet in dimensions, is fitted up in a manner appropriate to the business and every facility is at hand for the advantageous display of the fine stock of goods. The umbrellas and parasols manufactured by the Messrs. Wright Bros. & Co., are too well known and have too wide a celebrity to require an extended discretion at our hands. Suffice it to say, therefore, they represent the highest degree of artistic and mechanical excellence while in point of variety and general beauty of design, excellence of workmanship, durability, etc., they stand unrivalled in the trade. In the attractive salesroom in this city will be found a large comprehensive and complete stock of these famous goods which are supplied to the trade throughout New England at factory prices. Mr. G. P. Howlett, the Boston manager, is a gentleman thoroughly conversant with the business in which he has had a large and varied experience.

LOUIS JESELSOHN, Tobacconist, No. 213 Hanover Street.— Mr. Louis Jeselsohn began business in 1882, and here he has built up a trade of such magnitude that reflects the highest credit upon his business ability. He occupies a handsomely appointed and well arranged store, which has an area of 25x55 feet, and it is at all times stocked with a well selected and extensive assortment of the most popular brands of cigars of both foreign and domestic manufacture, together with all the leading varieties of smoking and chewing tobaccos, meerschaum pipes and cigar holders, and smokers' articles of every description. Mr. Jeselsohn does an important trade in the importing of cigars, both hand and mould made, and of fine and medium grades. The business is a brisk one, and extends throughout the city and suburbs. Dealers can secure here the best goods at the most liberal prices and prompt service, while consumers can always rely upon securing cigars and tobaccos of the finest quality at the most reasonable rates with courteous attention. Mr. Jeselsohn was born in Germany, and for the past eighteen years has resided in the United States.

ROBERT H. CARLETON & CO., Manufacturer and Wholesale and Retail Dealers in Boots and Shoes, No. 196 Hanover Street.—This enterprising house was founded in 1873 by Mr. Carleton, and he conducted the business alone until 1886, when he took into partnership, Mr. Henry F. Hagen, who is a native of New Brunswick, and a gentleman who has had a long practical experience in the shoe trade. Mr. Carleton, is a native of Massachusetts, has a thorough knowledge of the business, and the stock carried by the firm is at all times a thoroughly representative one of all that is stylish and popular in every description of foot-wear. The store has an area of 18x40 feet, and is tastefully and attractively fitted up. A brisk local patronage is enjoyed and every satisfaction is given to patrons in the quality of goods and prices.

T. W. GLEESON & CO., Electricians, No. 62 Sudbury Street.— Nowhere in America or Europe has there been made more progress both in scientific and mechanical branches appertaining to electricity than here in Boston—its very birthplace, so to speak—which justly boasts of a number of electricians of exceptional ability. Among those referred to may be mentioned the name of T. W. Gleeson, doing business under the style of T. W. Gleeson & Co., at No. 62 Sudbury Street, and who sustains an A1 reputation for skill and reliability. Mr. Gleeson, who is a comparatively young man and a native of this city, is a thoroughly practical and expert electrician, of several years experience in his profession, and is a complete master of the art in all its branches, while he was, prior to starting in business on his own account a few months since, assistant to Prof. Bell, some four years and subsequently foreman for Williams & Co., for six years. Mr. Gleeson occupies ample and well equipped quarters, having steam power and all necessary appliances in service, and employs half a dozen competent assistants. He is prepared to enter into contracts for everything in the line of electrical work, experimenting being a leading specialty, and also manufactures, to order, electric and magnetic batteries and kindred apparatus of every description, in the most reliable manner, at short notice. A complete and first-class assortment is always carried on hand, likewise, including telegraph and electrical instruments, galvanic batteries, medical batteries, electric bells, burglar alarms, gas lighters, annunciators, etc., while jobbing also is promptly attended to, and all work executed by this firm is fully warranted to render satisfaction.

SHURTLEFF BROTHERS, Commission Merchants and Wholesale Dealers in Fruits and Produce, No. 47 Commercial Street.—This pushing and responsible firm was started in April, 1888, and by judicious enterprise and untiring energy, coupled with sterling integrity, soon won favor and recognition, acquiring in a short time a flourishing business. All the transactions of the house are conducted on sound and conservative business principles; a special feature being made of prompt returns for consignments in every instance. Messrs. Shurtleff handle foreign and domestic fruits of every variety in their season; also vegetables, nuts, berries and country produce generally; fruits being a specialty, however, and employ four experienced salesmen. A heavy and carefully assorted stock is constantly carried on hand, including oranges, lemons, apples, tropical fruits, etc. all orders receiving prompt and satisfactory attention, and the trade of the firm, which is principally located in and around the city, is large and substantial. Messrs. Charles L. and Jesse P. Shurtleff are Canadians by birth, but have resided in Boston a long time, and are respected members of the Fruit and Produce Exchange.

H. B. HOBBS, Carriage, Sign and Fancy Painter, No. 304 Commercial Street.—For strictly A1 work in the line of plain and artistic painting, or for promptness and reliability, not one in the business in this quarter of the city anywhere excels H. B. Hobbs, the well known carriage, sign and fancy painter. Mr. Hobbs has resided in this city for nearly a quarter of a century. He is a practical and expert painter of long and varied experience, and is a thorough master of his art in all its branches. He established himself in business in his native place in 1861, and four years subsequently moved to Boston, opening a shop on Commercial Street, whence he moved to the present commodious quarters some three years since. He occupies here one 50x75 foot floor, and keeps constantly on hand a large and complete assortment of paints, oils, colors, varnishes, whitelead, gold and bronze powders, glass signs, show cards, and kindred articles, while a competent force of workmen are employed. Painting in all its branches is executed in the highest style of the art at reasonable rates, special attention being given to fancy sign and carriage painting; also marbling, graining and artistic work; while ship's carving, etc., are gilded, and cabins filled and polished in the most superior style, at short notice. Show cards and glass signs are made to order, likewise in novel and attractive designs, while cloth lettering is done also in the most prompt and excellent manner, the proprietor exercising close personal supervision over all work executed.

JOHN H. WOODMAN, Manufacturer and Dealer in Gent's Hand and Machine-made Boots and Shoes, No. 13 Devonshire Street.—In the department of industry devoted to the manufacture of gentlemen's fine footwear, we find a leading establishment in Boston to be that of Mr. John H. Woodman. This gentleman is a skilled expert in every department of his vocation, gives his personal attention to all the details of his business, employs none but the most experienced workmen, and his goods are the acme of perfection in every respect. The business of this house was inaugurated over twelve years ago by C. L. Stearns & Co., by whom it was conducted until 1871, when the present proprietor succeeded to the control. Under his able management the volume of trade has steadily increased, and the house has permanent patrons in various parts of Boston and the surrounding towns. The store and workshops are amply spacious and are provided with the most improved facilities for the successful carrying on of the business. A force of skilled workmen are given constant employment, only the best of materials are utilized in the production, and the range of manufacture embraces the finest of French and American calf and horse-hide hand and machine sewed boots and shoes for gentlemen's wear. These are made to order and for stock, a good assortment constantly being carried on hand, and all goods purchased from this establishment may be depended upon to be the best that human hands can produce. Mr. Woodman, who is a native of this state, enjoys a superior reputation in mercantile circles, and invariably wins the fullest esteem of his customers.

F. THOMAS, Manufacturer of Pure Candies, No. 65 Temple Place.—One of the most prominent and reliable houses in Boston engaged in the manufacture of specialties in fine confections and pure candies is that of F. Thomas. This is an old and popular stand and has been under the control of the present proprietor since 1884. The premises occupied for the business are spacious in size, elegant in all their arrangements and appointments, and possessing every modern improvement for insuring rapid and perfect production. This house is the recognized headquarters among critical consumers in this city for delicate flavors, finest quality and popular prices. The output is one of great magnitude and variety, including creams, chocolates and caramels, gum drops, lozenges and candy sticks, bonbons, choice confections and pure candies, also a full line of the basket, boxes and chocolate novelties of the most desirable description. Purity is the main essential with these goods, and mail and express orders to all parts of the country are promptly filled. Mr. Thomas, the enterprising proprietor, is a well known Boston man, born and bred, and justly merits the success and popularity he has achieved.

W. J. FITZEMEYER, Plain and Ornamental Japanner, No. 138 Blackstone Street.—An old established, representative japanner in Boston is Mr. W. J. Fitzemeyer, who has been in the business nearly a quarter of a century. He commenced in a small way on Union Street, where he remained only about six months, when he moved to the premises now occupied. His establishment is well equipped with all the requisite appliances, and he is kept constantly engaged filling orders. Several competent workmen are employed, and plain and ornamental japanning in all branches is executed, in the best manner, Mr. Fitzemeyer also makes a special business of lettering tin signs to order and bronzing, gilding and graining. He is an expert, practical skilled workman and is prompt in his attention to all work entrusted to him. He was born in Germany, and came to this country nearly thirty-five years ago.

NICHOLS & FISH, Manufacturers of Cigar Boxes, and Dealers in Ribbons, Labels, and Cigar Manufacturers' Supplies, No. 40 Lincoln Street.—Boston has within it many establishments devoted to the manufacture and handling of cigar manufacturers' supplies, and in this line Messrs. Nichols & Fish occupy a distinctive and prominent position. The leading specialty of this firm is the manufacture of cigar boxes, while they also control a very large trade as dealers in ribbons, labels and cigar manufacturers' supplies of all kinds. The business was founded originally in 1883 by Mr. F. M. Holmes, with whom Mr. C. N. Fish entered into partnership in 1887. In September, 1888, Mr. C. N. Nichols purchased Mr. Holmes' interest in the enterprise, and thereupon the style of the concern became, as now, Nichols & Fish. The firm's factory comprises one floor, having an area of 30x100 feet, and this is equipped with all the latest improved modern machinery and is complete with every convenience. Fifteen hands are employed in this department and about three thousand boxes are produced weekly. The firm also occupy a commodious floor in the adjoining building for storage purposes, and have always on hand not only cigar boxes in vast numbers, but an almost endless assortment of labels, ribbons and cigar manufacturers' supplies of every description. In addition to their large city trade, the firm have an extensive business connection throughout the New England States. Both partners are Bostonians, young energetic business men, who are worthily making the best of their opportunities.

RICHARD HILLS, Watch Maker, and Dealer in Watches and Jewelry, No. 544 Washington Street.—This first-class business was founded in 1860 by Mr. Hills, who had many years' experience as a practical watchmaker and was well qualified to carry on a business which would depend for success on the fine character of the work done. In 1871 he removed to his present fine location, which is 22x35 feet in dimensions, and is fitted up throughout in first-class style. Mr. Hills carries a fine line of gold and silver watches of the leading movements in plain and ornamental casings, diamonds, jewelry of every description, silverware, etc., which offers a splendid selection to the purchasing public at prices as low as those of any other first-class house. He employs two assistants, and does repairing of all kinds on watches and jewelry at the lowest rates and in the promptest manner. His trade is very extensive throughout the city, and his customers are to be found among the best class of people. Mr. Hills is a native of the State, sixty-two years of age, and is justly held to be one of the most skilled and reliable watchmakers in Boston.

FRANK H. HOWLAND, Men's Furnishings, No. 129 Court Street.—An old established and excellent men's furnishing store is the well ordered emporium conducted by Frank H. Howland. This thriving business was established many years ago, and after several changes, about three years since came into control of the present proprietor who completely remodelled the establishment, and from the first has conducted it with uniform success. Nothing but fine goods are handled, and purchasers can rely upon finding a very superior article, courteous attention and satisfactory treatment in every instance here. The store is compact, ample and very tastefully fitted up. A large and A1 stock is constantly carried including fine dress shirts, novelties in neckwear, collars and cuffs in all the recent styles, elegant underwear in great variety, hosiery, gloves, suspenders, umbrellas, handkerchiefs, scarfpins, sleeve buttons, shirt studs and everything comprehended in gents' furnishings, fine custom shirts being a specialty, while laundrying is attended to also in first-class style, at very reasonable rates. Mr. Howland, who is a native of this city, is a gentleman of thorough reliability in his dealings.

DOANE & CO., Ship Brokers, No. 105 Commercial Street.—The business of this concern was originally started in 1868, in the name of Doane & Cowell, and this was the style of the house until 1885, when the firm dissolved partnership. Since then the enterprise has been conducted by Mr. Z. S. Doane alone under the firm name of Doane & Co. This gentleman, who is widely known among shippers and merchants of this port, is a native of Cape Cod and sixty-seven years of age. He is an old resident in Boston, and is personally largely interested in the shipping business. He has an interest in thirteen vessels and is the agent for two others, and is also a member of the Vessel-Owners' Association, where he is highly esteemed for his business promptitude, reliability and integrity. He is fully conversant with every detail and feature of ship broking and the requirements of patrons. He has every facility for transacting his extensive and steadily increasing business, and he promptly places vessels at most favorable rates on all the leading trans-atlantic and other foreign routes as well as for coast service. Freight is also punctually shipped to any desired port at satisfactory terms and persons having shipments cannot in any place make better rates than with this house.

B. O. & G. C. WILSON, Wholesale Botanic Druggists, No. 28 Merchants Row.—The name of Wilson will ever be honorably and prominently identified with the wholesale drug trade of Boston, and the country at large. The business was established in 1812 by Mr. B. O. Wilson and Mr. G. C. Wilson, two brothers, natives of Boston, who early became identified with the trade in which they achieved such success. Their father was also a member of the firm for thirty years and then retired. He is still living, a hale, hearty old man of ninety-one years of age, and whose reminiscences go back to a very early period of the trade. Mr. G. C. Wilson died in 1861, and since that date, Mr. B. O. Wilson has continued the business as sole proprietor under the honored old firm name. The business has had a continuous growth, and has frequently required enlarged premises and facilities. Eight years ago, Mr. Wilson moved to his present centrally located premises in Merchants Row, between State Street and Faneuil Hall, five stories in height, and 25 feet by 60 feet in dimensions. The stock stands far ahead of anything of the kind either in Boston or elsewhere in the United States. Here are all manner of herbs and their extracts, barks, roots, leaves, gums, essential oils, tinctures, infusions, etc. There is a splendidly equipped laboratory in the establishment and all additional facilities. This is the only wholesale drug house in Boston that grinds its own drugs, and is the leading one in the preparation of staple pharmaceutical products. Mr. Wilson has an intimate knowledge of botany and pharmaceutic science, and is likewise a keen and able business man, who secures his herbs, roots and drugs from the best direct sources.

F. J. McFARLAND, Grocer, No. 425 Hanover Street.—This gentleman first began business on Clark Street in 1872, and in 1880 removed to his present location, where he occupies a neatly arranged salesroom, 25x35 feet in dimensions, and a basement of similar proportions. From the outset the business of this establishment has been conducted on fixed business principles, and its management characterized by energy, ability and judicious enterprise, and it has been characterized by a record of steady and substantial progress. A heavy and fine stock is constantly carried, embracing pure teas, coffees, spices and canned goods in great variety; condiments, sauces, preserves and table luxuries; choice dairy butter and best brands of family flour, household articles, sugar, molasses, rice, lard and a complete assortment of shelf goods and staple groceries. Competent and attentive assistants are employed and customers can always rely upon courteous and prompt service, and upon obtaining the purest and most wholesome goods in the market at prices which cannot be surpassed by those of any other house in the trade. The business is of a retail character and altogether a large and flourishing business is done. Mr. McFarland, who is a native of Boston, is a gentleman of push and excellent business ability and is respected by all who come in contact with him.

D. W. KEYS & CO., Produce Commission Merchants, and Dealers in Country Produce, No. 116 South Market Street.—Messrs. D. W. Keyes & Co., have been catering to a first-class trade for more than forty years, and by keeping excellent goods, making satisfactory prices, treating every customer with uniform courtesy and politeness and delivering purchases promptly, they have succeeded in building up and retaining a custom extending widely throughout the city and suburban towns, and even beyond. The firm are general produce commission merchants and dealers in butter, dried apples, etc., and all kinds of country produce, and the business has been conducted at its present location, No. 116 South Market Street, for the past thirteen years. The premises occupied are very commodious and are equipped with all appliances and conveniences for the successful operation of the business, which is exclusively of a wholesale character. Consignments are daily received from the best farming sections of the country, and the stock is at all times fresh and choice and kept up to the highest standard of excellence. Courteous and experienced assistants are employed and all orders are filled with dispatch and at the lowest market rates. The proprietor, Mr. D. W. Keyes, was the founder of the business, and no merchant in his line of trade is held in higher repute. He is a native of New Hampshire.

W. M. STEARNS & CO., Wholesale Grocers, Etc., No. 60 Chatham Street.—This time-honored and deservedly popular house was founded more than seventy years ago by the late Mr. William Stearns, who, at the time of his death, in 1876, was one of Boston's oldest, most able and respected merchants, and a gentleman who did much to advance the commercial importance and general welfare of the city. For half a century Mr. J. B. Hutchinson, who is a native of Vermont, has been a member of the firm; and his son, Mr. H. D. Hutchinson, who was born in Boston, has been a partner since 1888. The premises occupied for the business comprise a building containing four floors and basement. The establishment is fitted up tastefully and provided with every convenience for the successful carrying on of the heavy and important trade of the house. A splendid stock is carried, and it embraces everything the retail grocer needs to keep in stock, from clothes pins and soap to the finest grades of teas and coffees, of which a specialty is made. The trade is exclusively wholesale and extends to all parts of New England. The proprietors are members of the Wholesale Grocers' Association, and their rank and reputation in the trade are A1. They have increased their importing department the last few years, and have connections with a large number of foreign houses.

FRED H. HAINES, Jeweler and Optician, No. 3 Leveret Street.—One of the most expert and reliable jewelers and opticians in this part of the city is Fred H. Haines. Mr. Haines, who is a native of Boston, is a thoroughly practical and skillful workman, of fifteen years' experience in his profession, and is a complete master of his art in all its branches. He started in business on his own account about five years ago, and from the first he has enjoyed a very flattering patronage. He keeps constantly on hand a full and fine assortment of watches of all kinds, clocks, jewelry in quite a variety, solid silver and plateware, art novelties, opera, field and marine glasses, spectacles, eye glasses and optical goods of every description, particular attention being given to adjusting watches; French clocks, jewelry, etc., are repaired in the very best style of the art, all work executed in this establishment being fully warranted to render satisfaction. Only first-class goods are handled, and patrons can rely upon getting a very superior article, prompt and polite attention and satisfactory treatment in every instance, while the very lowest prices consistent with honest value and straight-forward dealing at all times prevail.

CALL & CARLTON, Wholesale and Retail Dealers in Butter, Cheese and Eggs, No. 99 Washington Street.—An enterprising house in the butter, cheese and egg business, is that of Call & Carlton, the individual partners of which are H. A. Call and A. G. Carlton respectively. This young firm began business in June, 1889, both partners having had an extensive experience in the line as clerks with one of the leading establishments in the city. They occupy an attractive store, 12x40 feet in dimensions, and fitted up in a superior manner with marble slabs, etc., and hardwood finish of the best kind. Messrs. Call & Carlton are wholesale and retail dealers in butter, cheese and eggs, which they receive daily fresh from consignors throughout New England. During the brief period since their establishment they have built up a first-class trade, which requires the services of two clerks, while the members of the firm gave themselves the closest attention to its details. They are both young men, and natives of the city.

EDWARD L. BRAY, Patentee and Manufacturer of Bray's Patent Balance Spring Curtain Fixtures, No. 122 Eliot Street.—This business was originally founded by the late Mr. Benjamin Bray, in Salem, Mass., in 1854. In 1863 it was removed to Boston, and for the past seventeen years it has been conducted in the premises now occupied. The factory is efficiently equipped with the best mechanical facilities pertaining to the business, while from six to eight hands are afforded permanent employment. Mr. Stevenson, who has managed the business for the past twenty years, exercises a close surveillance over all the affairs of the establishment and sees to it that the fulfillment of orders is in no way unnecessarily delayed.

CHARLES BILLMAN, Rigger, Loft: No. 81 Commercial Street. —Rigging and fitting out vessels forms one of the important industries that is carried on in Boston, and among those actively identified with it, there are none more thoroughly competent to do this kind of work than Mr. Charles Billman who has been engaged in the business for many years, and from 1870 to 1882 was a member of the firm of Billman & Wilson, and for three years of Billman & Co. In 1886 he succeeded to the business and has since conducted it on his own account and has become well known in shipping and commercial circles. A loft 25x125 feet is occupied at No. 81 Commercial Street, and everything in the way of ropes, block and tackle, is at hand and in the busy season a large force of practical workmen are employed. Mr. Billman furnishes everything required in rigging ocean, bay and river craft, and also fishing vessels, and is particularly expert in rigging yachts which with him is a special business and in his time has rigged some of the fastest boats belonging to the clubs and individuals along the Atlantic coast. He also furnishes rigging and blocks and tackle, and derricks for builders' uses and for lifting and moving heavy and bulky machinery, buildings, stone, etc. Mr. Billman, who was born in Stockholm, Sweden, came to this country in 1847 and since 1854 has lived in Boston.

B. B. RUSSELL, Publisher of Subscription Books, Maps, Charts and Engravings, No. 57 Cornhill Street. —This gentleman has been engaged in this business for a period of twenty-three years, and enjoys a national reputation as a prominent educator of the public. He brings to bear the widest range of practical knowledge, while by far the most worthy and valuable books, maps, charts and engravings are published by him of any subscription house extant. He makes a leading specialty of religious and historical works, by the best authors. He always is enabled to furnish plenty of work to good agents, supplies them with an outfit at very small expense, and pays them liberally and promptly for their services. His stock of books gives the widest range for selection, and the agent who handles these publications will never want for aid and encouragement from the hands of lovers of good literature or from Christian people anywhere. The name of B. B. Russell is a talisman of good luck to the canvasser, insuring him good returns and the gratitude of those who buy from his stock. Agents and traveling men will do well to communicate with this old-established and ever-reliable house. Mr. Russell is a native of Maine, a business man of Boston for thirty-eight years, and a reputable member of social and literary circles.

EDWARD W. LUNDAHL, Photographic Printer, No. 363 Washington Street. —Among those who devote their attention to photography, there are perhaps none better known than Mr. Edward W. Lundahl. He is a thorough master of all the details of the profession and is recognized as one of the most careful and correct printers in the business, and is perfectly equipped for executing the very highest class of work. His services are constantly in demand by photographers by whom he is considered one of the best in his special department of the art, and he is also eagerly sought after by amateurs who are well aware he can bring out their work and make it as perfect as it is possible to be done, and he is always actively engaged in printing portraits, groups, views, scenes, and commercial photography, and amateur work which he executes unexcelled in quality or permanence. Mr. Lundahl is a native of Sweden. He keeps five competent assistants in his employ and as he is provided with every convenience for printing and finishing photographic work, he can always guarantee to give perfect satisfaction.

N. R. VARNEY, Watchmaker, No. 75 Hanover Street. —Mr. N. R. Varney the well-known watchmaker has had an experience extending over thirty-five years, twenty of which were with the Waltham Watch Co. For ten years he was employed in the springing and setting up department, and for four years at matching and adjusting the escapement and also assisted in perfecting the pendant set watch and case. He has not only had a varied experience in factory work, but has also devoted many years to general repairing and is pronounced by all who have availed themselves of his services one of the most accurate and best in the city. He can make any new parts of a watch and is practically proficient in making repairs, and regulating watches and chronometers, and as an evidence of his skill and ability it is only necessary to state that he is highly endorsed and recommended by the following well-known gentlemen, who are prominent and well-known in this vicinity: Morrill Bros. & Co., No. 405 Washington Street, Boston; Hon. Henry N. Fisher, foreman escapement department, James N. Hammond, foreman repairing department, and C. V. Woerd, late superintendent, American Watch Co., Waltham, Mass.; and A. L. Logan, hair spring manufacturer, Waltham, Mass. He is also endorsed by the trade and during the past two years, the time he has been established on his own account, his business has steadily grown. Mr. Varney is from New Hampshire originally, and is very popular in this community and enjoys the esteem and confidence of the trade.

C. SOWDEN, Signs and Show Cards, No. 118 Washington Street. —For variety and originality of design in signs and show cards, or fine workmanship and finish, probably none in this business in Boston excels Mr. Sowden, who is a practical and expert workman himself of many years' experience, and is a thorough master of his art in all its branches. He has been in business on his own account at the present location since 1873, and has acquired a good patronage. Mr. Sowden occupies ample and well equipped quarters here, and employs a competent assistant. He is prepared to furnish signs and makes a specialty of plain and fancy show cards to order in the most prompt and superior manner, keeping constantly on hand also a first-class assortment of everything in this line, while lettering is done on tin, wood, doors, posts, etc., in the best style of the art at short notice, all work executed by this gentleman being fully warranted in every particular.

FRED F. HALLETT, Commission Merchant in Fruits and Vegetables, No. 106 Clinton Street. —One of the best known houses engaged in handling fruits and vegetables in the city is that of Mr. Fred. F. Hallett. Mr. Hallett has been in the business for a number of years, having opened his present establishment in 1878. He has occupied the stall at No. 106 Clinton Street, during this period and carries a fine stock of foreign and domestic fruits of all kinds in season, as well as a first supply of vegetables which he receives fresh daily. He established the best connections with shippers and is enabled to supply the largest orders on the shortest notice and at rates which place his house on a footing in this respect with the largest houses in the city. Mr. Hallett has built a flourishing trade all over Boston and the vicinity and has an assistant employed in his store. He was born in Chenryville and has lived in Boston for the past nine years.

F. F. STOCKWELL, Engraver, No. 99 Court Street. —Mr. F. F. Stockwell in his special department of metal engraving, has achieved a high reputation and produces work bearing the impress of a master-hand. He has been established in the business twenty-three years, and in his specialty of choice work in monograms, letters, names and ornamental work has no successful compeer. His work is executed with neatness and will bear the closest examination and inspection. Jewelry and silver plate is engraved to order, also name plates, numbers, metal signs, etc., and he is well equipped for doing all kinds of work in his special department of the art. He is a native of Worcester County, Mass., and learned his trade in Boston, where he has resided many years, and is one of the leading artists in his line in the city.

CAMPBELL BROTHERS, Loan Brokers, No. 699 Washington Street. —The business in which the Campbell Brothers is engaged is a great convenience to the citizens and business men. They are gentlemen of large means and have a wide acquaintance among capitalists and negotiate loans on personal property of every description and merchandise, and all articles of value. The proprietors, Mr. C. N. and J. W. Campbell are from Minnesota originally, where for some years Mr. C. N. Campbell was engaged in the banking business, and his brother was engaged in the grocery trade. Both are well qualified to conduct operations as loan brokers. A handsome office is occupied where they may be consulted daily, between the hours of nine a. m. and five p. m.

R. M. YALE & CO., Sail Makers, Etc., No. 29 South Market Street.—One of the most reliable and old established houses in Boston engaged in sail making, etc., is that of Messrs. R. M. Yale & Co., which was established in 1842, by Mr. R. M. Yale, who is sole proprietor. Mr. Yale has had great experience as a sail maker, and his patronage is by no means confined to the United States, but extends to the British Provinces and Upper Canada. He occupies two commodious and well-equipped floors, and manufactures largely Italian awnings, tents, flags, wagon coverings, sackings, and store awnings of every description. Mr. Yale makes a specialty of yacht flags, and also supplies promptly canopies for weddings, reception parties, etc. An excellent assortment of awning stripes of various patterns are kept constantly on hand, and all orders are carefully attended to at extremely moderate prices. Mr. Yale keeps in stock  a large number of tents of all sizes and flags of all nations, which are let upon reasonable terms. All awnings and other goods manufactured by Mr. Yale are made of the best materials and are unrivalled for finish and workmanship. Mr Yale was born in Maine, but has resided in Boston the greater part of his life. He is one of the original members of the Boston Yacht Club, which was founded in 1866, and has been a member of the Ancient and Honorable Artillery Company of Boston, and of the Mechanics' Association for the last thirty years.

NEW ENGLAND FURNITURE EXCHANGE, Special Credit Investigations; Albert T. Knapp, Manager: Boston Office: No. 174 Hanover Street.—Special reference is made to the reliable and trustworthy New England Furniture Exchange, whose Boston office, under the able and careful management of Mr. Albert T. Knapp, is located at No. 174 Hanover Street. The headquarters of this company are situated in New York City at No. 62 Bowery. The New England branch was organized in 1874 and incorporated under the laws of Massachusetts in 1879. This company makes special credit investigations in the furniture, carpet, upholstery, wall paper, window shade, glass, picture frame, undertaking and cabinet wood trades—and guarantee promptness and reliability in credits and collections. Members and their agents can use all of the Lyon Associations for credit reports and legal advice. The Lyon Reference Book is the acknowledged standard register of these special trades. It gives all the dealers' names, addresses and credit ratings. Issued every January and July (Adopted and revised by the official Furniture Trade Associations.) This book also gives the railroad, bank, express company and population of each town. Lyon's Furniture Report—issued to members every week, gives all the business and credit changes, corrections, warnings and notifications; also all the mortgages, judgments, attachments, conveyances, assignments, etc. in these trades throughout the United States. Lyon's Detailed Credit Reports—furnished to members on application, regarding the standing of any parties engaged in these trades,—or in any other trades when required. The Lyon reports are noted for their thoroughness, detail and reliability. Special cautionary or daily reports are likewise furnished confidentially with a list of such persons, whose members desire to have closely watched,—any necessary information affecting their credit is at once forwarded to members of their agents. Yearly membership dues with reference books and all privileges are only $50 per annum.

BOSTON PLATING COMPANY, No. 90 Sudbury Street, Room 2. —One among the best known concerns in this city doing an extensive business in gold silver and nickel plating is the Boston Plating Company. The foundation of the business dates from 1879 when it was established by W. S. Burton who was succeeded by W. H. Fisher. In May last the present company was formed with Mr. A. N. Smith president and Mr. G. F. Knight manager, and from that time it has been vigorously prosecuted and the trade extended. The premises occupied for the purposes of the business are on the second floor and have dimensions of 25 × 40 feet. Steam power is used and the equipment in every respect is perfect and complete for executing the very best class of work with promptness and dispatch. Plating is done to order for the trade and also oxydizing, particular attention being given to watch cases and jewelry and also railroad and to carriage trimmings, saddlery hardware, etc., and also to repairing and replating old ware, knives, forks, etc. This is the best fitted up shop for railroad work such as headlights, car trimmings, etc., the company doing a large business for the different railroads. The work executed by the company is warranted and every confidence can be placed on its giving satisfaction. Mr. Smith the president of the company lives at North Adams. Mr. Knight the manager who has charge of the business is a practical man to the trade. He was born in Cambridgeport where he resides. The company is doing a large business and is prepared to execute work in any quantity and orders by mail or express receive strict attention.

B. F. BRADBURY, Pharmacist, No. 463 Washington Street.— In elegance, reliability and extent of trade the pharmacy of Mr. B. F. Bradbury, occupies a leading position in Boston. The proprietor first established himself as a pharmacist in 1846, in Bangor, Me., and came to Boston in 1872, and purchased the present business which had been in operation since 1820. The career of the house had been prosperous and successful from the start, and under the present enterprising and efficient management the volume of transactions has been greatly augmented. The store is directly central to the best business portion of the city, is spacious in size, and all its appointments are handsome, attractive and appropriate, no pains or expense being spared to make it as complete as possible in its every feature. A very large stock is carried of pure drugs, chemicals, pharmaceutical preparations, essences and extracts, wines and liquors for medicinal purposes, toilet and fancy goods, druggists' sundries of all kinds, and, in fact, everything kept in a first class establishment devoted to this trade. The proprietor makes his purchases from the most reputable sources. The prescription department is carefully and intelligently directed. It is in charge of experienced compounders, and the limit of precision and safety is reached in every case. Patrons are waited upon promptly and courteously, and the prices which prevail are eminently low and attractive. Mr. Bradbury is a native of Maine, and is highly regarded in the community as an accomplished pharmacist.

H. H. WOOLSON, Tailor, No. 433 Washington Street.—The merchant tailoring trade has many able representatives in Boston, but probably none are coming faster into prominence for fine work than the gentleman whose name appears in the caption of this article. Mr. H. H. Woolson is a native of New Hampshire and very early acquired an expert knowledge of his trade. He subsequently came to Boston and for a number of years filled the responsible position of cutter in the well known house of Robbins & Rowell, and while there employed built up an enviable reputation for superior work. In March, 1883, he embarked for himself in the enterprise with which he is rapidly becoming both popularly and prosperously identified. His tasty and convenient salesroom contains a choice selection of the finest of imported goods only, which are made up by the most skillful workmen obtainable. Mr. Woolson counts among his constantly growing patronage many of the leading society and business men of Boston and he is generally regarded as one of the ablest city tailors.

D. S. BANKS, Tea Broker, No. 215, Central Street.—A tea house that has been established for close upon a quarter of a century is that of Mr. D. S. Banks, tea broker, who is one of Boston's oldest and best known business men. This gentleman was born in Maine. He embarked in his present line of business in 1864, and for the past ten years has occupied his present office and he controls a large trade. During all these years Mr. Bank's career has been a progressive and successful one, and he has earned a reputation for fair and honorable dealing and for handling first-class, reliable goods that he may justly be proud of. Mr. Banks represents some of the largest tea importing houses in New York, and sells directly to wholesale houses all over New England. His facilities for filling orders promptly and to the entire satisfaction of all concerned are of the most ample character.

E. L. ATWOOD, Teas, Coffees, Groceries and Ship Stores, Nos. 153 Hanover and 118 Blackstone Streets.—A representative house, and one of the oldest in this section of the city, in its line is that conducted by Mr. E. L. Atwood. This time-honored and popular establishment was founded as far back as 1852 under the style of Messrs. L. R. Crosby & Co., of which firm E. L. Atwood was a member and one of the founders. The partnership between Mr. L. R. Crosby and Mr. Atwood subsisted for the long period of forty-four years. In 1876 Mr. Atwood became the sole proprietor of the business with which he has now been identified for fifty-six years. He is to-day probably the oldest merchant still actively engaged in business on the street. His enterprise has about it all the evidences of youthful vigor and push, and is kept abreast with the age in the introduction of all the novelties and attractions which characterize the most modern and first-class grocery houses of New England's metropolis. The store has an area of 25x50 feet, and a basement of equal dimensions is occupied in connection with the business. A heavy stock of teas, coffees, staple and fancy groceries, ship stores of all kinds and grocers' sundries of every description is constantly carried, and the large business done requires the permanent services of from four to five assistants. Mr. Atwood is a native of Wellfleet, Cape Cod.

HARRIS STAHL, Manufacturer of fine Havana Cigars, Wholesale and Retail, No. 47 Green Street.—One of the most popular and excellent cigar stores in this quarter of the city, is the well and favorably known establishment of Harris Stahl, manufacturer of fine havana cigars. The goods produced here are of a very superior character, alike as to quality, flavor and make, and as a consequence they have gained a firm hold on popular favor throughout Boston and environs, and also outside the state. This thriving business was established in 1877 as a retail smokers' emporium, the manufacturing and wholesale department being added about three years ago, and from the first Mr. Stahl has enjoyed quite a liberal patronage. The store is compact, neat and well kept, while several expert cigar makers are employed in the shop, the favorite brand Bay State turned out here being an article of exceptional merit. A large and first-class assortment is constantly carried on hand including besides Mr. Stahl's own products, also choice imported and domestic cigars, all the favorite brands of cigarettes, smoking and chewing tobaccos, snuff, pipes and everything in the line of smokers' articles, and also makes a specialty of handling private brands and offers special inducements to patrons purchasing for cash, the trade of the concern, both wholesale and retail, afford evidence of steady increase.

JOSEPH MEASURES, Brass Founder, No. 29 Pitts Street.—A well known and prominent establishment engaged in this line of industry is that conducted by Mr. Joseph Measures. Mr. Measures was born in this city, and has long been identified with the brass trade, in which he is an acknowledged expert. The business was founded originally in 1877, and from the outset the proprietor has always had a large and influential trade. Until June 1st, 1888, the enterprise was conducted at No. 141 Portland Street, whence it was transferred to its present location. The foundry comprises the whole of the lower floor of the building, which has a capacity of 100x55 feet. The entire establishment is thoroughly equipped with all the newest and most improved machinery, which is operated by steam power, while constant employment is afforded to a large force of skilled and efficient workmen. Mr. Measures manufactures a large and comprehensive line of brass work, and all kinds of composition, brass, German silver and zinc castings; also copper castings for electric light work, lining metal, etc. He is prepared to execute all kinds of work in these lines with promptitude, and he justly prides himself upon the accuracy and superior excellence of all the work emanating from his establishment. Estimates are duly furnished, contracts entered into and executed in the most satisfactory manner.

KOSCHWITZ & CO., Lithographic Engravers and Printers, No. 76 State Street.—The art of lithography has been developed to a high plane of perfection. A leading member of the calling is Mr. T. Koschwitz, the active member of the firm of Koschwitz & Co. This gentleman established his business here four years ago, and through the thorough knowledge which he possesses of his vocation, has since built up a large and influential patronage, derived from the leading business men in the central part of the city, and has won a reputation of the most enviable character for the superiority of his work. The commodious premises occupied are equipped in the most complete manner, being provided with four fine lithographic presses, and all necessary appliances used in this branch of industry. Mr. Koschwitz attends personally to the management of his establishment, employs none but competent workmen, and is prepared to execute lithography and Illuscraphic printing in all their branches. He makes a leading specialty of commercial work of all kinds, performing the finest and most delicate operations in this line in a manner that never fails to gain the fullest appreciation. All orders are promptly executed and at the most reasonable prices. Mr. Koschwitz, who is a native of Germany, has resided in the United States since 1865.

C. R. MUGRIDGE, Carpenter, No. 1285½ Cambridge Street.— Mr. C. R. Mugridge is a practical carpenter of large experience and established reputation, and as such carries on an extensive jobbing trade both in the city and its vicinity. Mr. Mugridge was born and reared in Maine, where he learned his trade, with which he has been identified for nearly a quarter of a century. Nine years ago he removed to Boston, and in 1884 started business on his own account at No. 33 Endicott Street, whence he removed to his present central location. Here he has a well equipped workshop, equipped with all necessary tools and appliances for the successful prosecution of the business. Every description of carpenter work is carefully executed and in a thoroughly workmanlike manner. Special attention is given to the altering and fitting up of stores, offices, etc., and to jobbing of every description. From one to eleven hands are employed, according to the nature of the work in operation, and Mr. Mugridge exercises a close surveillance over the execution of all work entrusted to him. He has earned the reputation of being a first-class workman, of honestly fulfilling all his obligations.

H. W. PINKHAM, Choice Provisions, Etc., Pinkham's Market, No 280 Tremont Street.—Among the well-conducted and deservedly popular local establishments in the provision trade should be mentioned that of Mr. H. W. Pinkham—familiarly known as "Pinkham's Market." The spacious and well arranged market is attractively fitted up in hardwoods, and every facility is at hand for the advantageous handling and display of goods. Here is at all times to be found a full and complete stock of choice beef, lamb, mutton, pork, lard, poultry, game, vegetables, etc.; also, fresh-laid eggs and fine creamery and dairy butter. These goods are carefully selected from the most reputable sources of supply, with due regard for the requirements of the high-class family and hotel trade from which the large patronage is chiefly drawn. Employment is given to four experienced assistants besides the proprietor. Mr. Pinkham has been engaged in his present enterprise since 1881, and in the interval has reared a business which entitles him to classification among the representative young merchants in his line, of this, his native town.

A. J. LOVELL, Grocer and Tea Dealer, Nos. 62 and 64 Cambridge Street.—One of the principal establishments in the West End engaged in the grocery trade, and which has for many years occupied a foremost position in the favor of the public, is that of Mr. A. J. Lovell. The house was first opened in 1860 by the present proprietor. The spacious store occupied has a frontage of 30 feet, and a depth of 100 feet. Its interior is arranged in the most convenient and systematic manner, every appliance or accommodation peculiar to the business being provided. The heavy stock carried embraces a complete line of staple and fancy groceries of every description, including the choicest teas, coffees and spices, canned and bottled, its immense variety, baking and laundry supplies, and fruits and vegetables. The custom supplied extends to the surrounding neighborhoods and the suburban towns. A full staff of clerks and assistants is employed, and all orders invariably meet with the same prompt and satisfactory fulfillment. Mr. Lovell is a native of this state, having been born in West Boylston.

THE METROPOLIS OF NEW ENGLAND. 287

JOHN R. FARRELL, Tailor, No. 755 Washington Street.—Mr. John R. Farrell is one of the oldest and best known tailors in the city, and has long been recognized as a tower of strength in the trade. Establishing his business forty years ago, in Boylston Hall, he has by his enterprise, liberality and special acquirements in his profession, built up a large, first class and permanent patronage in this city and throughout the country. His business premises have been occupied by him since July, 1887, and includes an elegant and spacious salesroom, 30 by 112 feet in size, handsomely fitted up and perfect in convenience of arrangement for inspection and sale. Here is exhibited the largest and finest stock of cloths and trimmings ever brought to this city. It is complete in material, design and novelty, giving the best of manufacture in high-class goods, and the very best sources of American and European production have contributed to its wealth. Mr. Farrell devotes his time and talents to fine custom clothing, making a leading specialty of military work, and the garments here made are recognized as simply perfection in style, fit and artistic workmanship. He makes all the uniforms for the high schools of Boston, while to be found among his permanent customers are very many of the best dressed citizens of this city and its suburban towns. Unusually fine facilities are afforded for guaranteeing the prompt and satisfactory fulfillment of all orders, including a large force of skilled workmen and an experienced and artistic cutter, while prices are placed at the lowest figure consistent with first-class service. Mr. Farrell is one of Boston's most prominent and successful business men. He has served his fellow citizens as a member of the State Legislature for several terms, was Captain of Co. G, 9th Massachusetts Infantry during the war, and organized the Ninth Regiment, M. V. M., of which he was commissioned Lieutenant Colonel, after having recruited Company A, which was the nucleus of the regiment.

W. H. WHITE, Jr., & CO., Dealers in Boots and Shoes, No. 100 Court Street.—The business was established some twenty years ago, and come into the control of the present owners in 1883. Under their vigorous, energetic management the enterprise has flourished and the trade developed to extensive proportions, the patronage being derived from all parts of the city and the surrounding towns. The store occupied is amply spacious, and is well furnished and attractively fitted up for the convenience of a large trade, and the accommodation and display of an extensive stock of goods. The assortment of boots, shoes, slippers and rubbers is one of the finest as well as most complete to be found in the city, embracing, as it does, the latest and most desirable styles of foot wear. A staff of polite clerks are employed and customers are waited upon promptly and shown every courteous attention. The goods are all guaranteed to be as represented, while the prices are unquestionably of the most reasonable character. The members of the firm, Messrs. W. H. White, Jr., and G. P. Soule, the former a native of Boston, the latter of Maine, are business men of thorough experience and of excellent standing in commercial circles, and are thoroughly deserving of their popularity.

D. McELWIN, Turning and Band Sawing, Manufacturer of Show Cases, Parlor Furniture, odd pieces, and General Jobbing, No. 37 Haverhill Street.—Among the enterprises meriting mention is that prosecuted by Mr. D. McElwin, who has had some twenty years' experience in wood turning and band sawing, and in the manufacture of show cases, parlor furniture and odd pieces of artistic furniture. For five years he has been in business at his present location, and controls a trade that is not only extensive, but influential. His premises comprise the second and third floors of the building, and each are 28x40 feet in dimensions, equipped with steam power and the most efficient modern wood working machinery. Six skilled and experienced artisans are employed and all orders are filled with promptness. Mr. McElwin has always on hand a very fine assortment of show cases of all sizes and forms and choice specimens of artistic parlor furniture. A specialty is made of the manufacture of odd pieces and of general jobbing. While Mr. Elwin does not conduct his business on as large a scale as some concerns that we could name, we know of none that can surpass his work in point of quality. He is a native of Boston and resides at Charlestown.

ALBEE, BROWN & CO., Wholesale and Retail Dealers in Stoves, Ranges and Furnaces, Ship Stoves, Etc., No. 63 Blackstone Street.—One among the oldest of the well known houses in the stove trade in Boston is that of the firm of Albee, Brown & Co. It was established as long ago as 1843 by J. M. Reed. About a year ago Messrs. Albee, Brown & Co., succeeded Mr. Reed and continued the business until a few months ago, when Mr. Brown retired and Mr. Albee has since continued it under the old firm name. The premises which have an area of 25x 60 feet, are admirably arranged and contain a large and varied assortment of all kinds of stoves, ranges and furnaces in all the new styles, containing the latest improvements, also ship stoves, which form a special feature of the stock. All kinds of sheet iron work is done to order, and general jobbing and repairing receives that attention its importance demands. Cooking and heating stoves and ship stoves are put up, and Cabooses lined with tin or sheet iron and ranges are set, cleaned and repaired by competent workmen, under the immediate supervision of Mr. Harry L. Albee, the proprietor, who is a practical workman himself. A large city and suburban, and a trade with the shipping is carried on, and the business is conducted in an able, efficient manner. Born in Hopkinton, in this state, Mr. Albee who for many years had lived in Boston, is well known and popular.

M. PELONSKY, Dry and Fancy Goods, Etc., No. 23 Cambridge Street.—Among the most popular and prosperous mercantile establishment that have come into existence of recent years in this vicinity may be mentioned the thriving and well stocked emporium of M. Pelonsky, dealer in dry and fancy goods, ladies' wear and men's and boys' clothing. This business was established about three years ago, and from the start Mr. Pelonsky has steadily pushed his way to public favor and patronage. The premises occupied include a commodious store and basement, and an extensive and varied assortment is constantly carried, comprising fine dress fabrics and trimmings, silks, shawls, cloaks and millinery in quite a variety, novelties in underwear, corsets, gloves, hosiery, notions, umbrellas and everything in the line of fancy goods; also staple dry goods, calicoes, cottons, ginghams, flannels, shortings, towellings and domestics. The stock also includes a full line of mens' and boy's clothing, shirts, suspenders, neckwear, etc., while five efficient assistants are in attendance, no pains being spared to render the fullest satisfaction in every instance to patrons.

JAMES M. KNAPP, Machine and Tool Forging, No. 12 Bowker Street.—The enterprise of Mr. James M. Knapp, the well known machine and tool forger, has been in successful operation since January, 1887, and has become celebrated not only in this city but in the vicinity, while the substantial and influential patronage it enjoys is the strongest possible evidence that the work turned out is of no ordinary grade of excellence. The workshop has a capacity of 25x40 feet, is finely equipped with forges, machinery, steam power and all other necessary accessories for conducting the business economically and satisfactorily. All kinds of machine blacksmithing and general job work are given prompt attention, tools of every description and for every conceivable use are made to order, and a specialty is made of steel forging. Mr. Knapp is a practical man at his trade, and a patron can always rely upon having his instructions carried out in the most minute detail. Mr. Knapp is a native of Maine, and his business success is fully deserved.

BARBER BROS., Wholesale and Retail Dealers in Cigars, Tobacco, Cigarettes, and Smokers' Articles, No. 15 Green Street.—This pushing and popular firm was established in June last, and at its very inception may be said to have fairly bounded into prominence and prosperity. The firm occupy commodious and neatly appointed quarters, and carry constantly on hand an extensive and first class assortment, which includes finest and medium grades of imported and domestic cigars, all the favorite brands of cigarettes, smoking and chewing tobaccos of every description, snuff, pipes in great variety, and everything comprehended in smokers' articles; while the trade, both in the wholesale and retail departments, gives evidence of steady and substantial increase.

A. A. ROWE & SON, Forwarding Agents and Truckmen, No. 35 India Wharf.—In every great commercial community forwarding agents and truckmen necessarily fill a very useful and important position, and their duties invariably are of a very onerous and responsible character. It is essential to success that they be men of the highest repute and intelligence, and prompt in the carrying out of all orders. These are the characteristics of the members of the firm of A. A. Rowe & Son, the well-known and popular forwarding agents and truckmen, of No. 35 India Wharf. The business of this concern was organized in 1868 by the senior member of the firm, who quickly secured a very flattering patronage, which has been increasing year by year. Mr. A. A. Rowe, who is a native of New York State, has resided in Boston, for upwards of twenty-three years, and in 1887 admitted into partnership his son, Mr. A. H. Rowe, who was reared in the business. The firm have a neat, well appointed office, and this is connected by telephone. They have fifteen hands and sixteen horses in constant service, and undertake the removal of all kinds of merchandise from and to any places desired, and they receive and forward goods of all kinds to any and all points at reasonable rates. Promptitude and efficiency of service to all patrons is the ruling principle upon which this firm conducts its business, and immediate attention is accordingly given to all orders. The firm have a large, vigorous, growing trade, and the standing of Messrs. A. A. Rowe & Son in the mercantile community is one of the highest.

THOMAS G. SNOW, Dealer in Specialties, and Manufacturer of Commonwealth Salad Cream, Etc., No. 130 Commercial Street.—The steady and increasing demand that has developed of late years in this country for choice grades of table delicacies and condiments, such as dressing for cold meats, fish and salads of all kinds, has resulted in very notable improvement. For purity, flavor and general excellence, none produced in this section of the country compares with the delicious and wholesome Commonwealth Salad Cream, manufactured by Thomas G. Snow. This is an article of exceptional merit, and has secured an enduring hold on popular favor, as also has the Hub Mustard Dressing, which is noted for its superior quality, and which for the purposes intended—fish, game, roast meat, steaks, chops and made dishes—is unsurpassed. Besides the manufacture of the Commonwealth Salad Cream and the Hub mustard dressing, Mr. Snow deals extensively also in sauces, catsups, preserves, flavoring extracts, essences, condiments and grocers, specialties, and is well and favorably known in the trade. Mr. Snow, who is a young man of push and enterprise, started in business in 1877, as a dealer in grocers' sundries, and commenced the manufacture of the Commonwealth Salad Cream and the Hub Mustard Dressing about three years ago. He occupies for business purposes two commodious floors, and carries constantly on hand a large, first-class stock, while half a dozen in help are employed, besides several traveling salesmen, and the trade of the concern, which is very active, extends throughout the whole of the United States.

M. CANTWELL, Practical Plumber and Gas Fitter, No. 60 Pitts Street.—A prominent and most reliable house engaged in this business in this section of the city, is that of Mr. M. Cantwell. It was founded in 1875 by the present proprietor, who has gained an excellent reputation for first-class work. The premises occupied are of spacious dimensions, and comprise a store with work-shop attached, in which six skilled and competent workmen are constantly employed. The store is neatly and tastefully fitted up, and contains a fine assortment of all kinds of plumbers' supplies, such as bath tubs, faucets, urinals, closets, wash-bowls, lead, iron and earthenware drain pipes, gas fixtures, chandeliers, brackets, and, in fact everything pertaining to all branches of the business. Mr. Cantwell is prepared to furnish estimates and enter into contracts of any magnitude for the plumbing, ventilating, lighting and heating of public buildings in this city and vicinity, and, being a practical man, one of the greatest advantages about his work is that, when once completed, it will remain perfect for years. Mr. Cantwell makes a specialty of sanitary plumbing and of the ventilation of dwelling houses in which line he is an expert. He is a native of Ireland and has resided in Boston for the past twenty years.

GEO. F. HAYDEN, Costumer, No. 725 Washington Street.—This business was established in 1873 by Mr. Hayden, who was originally an actor. He occupies the second floor 30x112 feet in area, which is elegantly fitted up and fully stocked with a splendid assortment of theatrical goods, society regalia, wigs, beards, dress suits, reception dresses, play books, standard plays, also with uniforms and lodge supplies. He likewise keeps in stock Chas. Meyer's paints, powders and cosmetics and all articles and specialties for making up the face. Mr. Hayden is recognized authority for all matters pertaining to theatrical costumes, society regalia, etc., and his goods without exception are quite equal to the best productions of famous costumers in London, Paris or New York, while his prices in all cases are exceedingly moderate. All orders are promptly and carefully filled, and the trade of the house now extends throughout the principal cities and towns of New England and New York. Mr. Hayden is a native of Stoughton, Mass., but lived the middle years of his life in the south. He is highly regarded in theatrical circles for his integrity, skill and enterprise, and justly merits the liberal and influential patronage secured in this artistic industry. Mr. Hayden is presiding officer of the Wapiti Tribe, I. O. R. M., and a prominent member of the Elks, I. O. O. F., and Knights of Pythias.

JAMES A. YOUNG, Wholesale Dealer in Lobsters, No. 76 Commercial Wharf.—An extensive and well-conducted concern in the lobster trade, is the well-known house of James A. Young, which has been identified with the business for a number of years. Mr. Young is a native of Boston, and enjoys a first-class name in the business community here. In 1878 he founded the house which he has since brought to so flourishing a condition, and has occupied his present commodious premises, comprising two floors, 25x50 feet in dimensions, for the past twelve years. Mr. Young is a wholesale dealer in lobsters of all grades, and puts up packages of the various sizes demanded by the trade, which he sells largely to local houses, as well as ships in extensive quantities all over Massachusetts and New York. He employs three clerks in his establishment and is fast increasing the dimensions of his trade each year. Mr. Young is a first-class business man who is eminently worthy of the success he has achieved in his enterprise.

JOHN DRISCOLL, Manufacturer of Fine Cigars, No. 292 Atlantic Avenue.—Among Boston's most active and successful cigar manufacturers, is Mr. John Driscoll. The premises occupied are roomy, and admirably adapted for the purposes to which they are devoted. They are equipped with every appliance and convenience for facilitating the operations of the business, which consists of the manufacture of the finest grades of cigars known to the trade. The business of this house was founded in 1886, under the firm style of Driscoll & Goldberg, and in the following year, on the retirement of Mr. Goldberg, Mr. Driscoll became the sole proprietor. He is a native of Ireland and has resided in the United States for the past twenty-two years. He is a practical cigar-maker of extended experience and is an excellent judge of tobaccos, the best leaf of which he selects for the purposes of his business. Constant employment is afforded to nine hands, and the products of the house have an extensive and brisk sale throughout Massachusetts and New Hampshire, as they are very popular among and highly appreciated by lovers of the weed. The leading favorites are the D & G, five cent cigar and the Elcho, ten cent cigar. The business is entirely of a wholesale character.

J. W. SHERMAN, Stationary, Toys, Etc., No. 115 Cambridge Street.—The business career of this gentleman embraces a period upward of thirty busy, prosperous years. He was born in Newport, Rhode Island, in 1824, and is a brother of the late General T. W. Sherman, and during his long residence in Boston has won the confidence of the public and enjoyed a large profitable trade. He has always been located in the premises now occupied. The store is neatly and tastefully arranged, and well stocked with a large and varied assortment of stationary and school supplies, blank books and periodicals, toys of all kinds, and a general line of fancy goods for use or ornament. Mr. Sherman is well deserving the success which has attended his efforts.

THE METROPOLIS OF NEW ENGLAND.

C. H. EUTEBROUK, Importer and Gun Maker, No. 17 Portland Street.—There is probably not in this entire city to-day a more skillful or reliable workman in his particular line than C. H. Eutebrook. Mr. Eutebrook, who is a man of middle age, was born in Belgium and has lived in Boston since 1870. He is a thoroughly practical and expert gunsmith, of nearly forty years' experience, in his calling, and is a complete master of the art in all its branches. He started in business on his own account here some ten years ago, moving to the present location in 1888, and from the first he has enjoyed a very liberal share of pop-

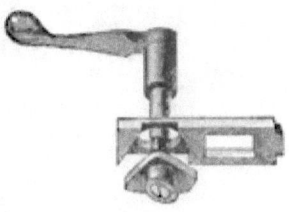

ular favor. Mr. Eutebrook occupies a well-kept store and shop, keeping constantly on hand a complete and fine assortment of fire arms, ammunition and kindred sporting goods,—shot guns, rifles and fishing tackle, while guns are let by the day at fifty cents each, or by the week at $2.50. Fowling pieces, rifles and guns of every description are made to order in the most prompt and excellent manner, at lowest figures, while repairing in all its branches is

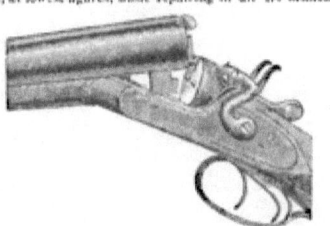

reliably executed, at short notice; and, altogether Mr. Eutebrook has a very nice patronage. Barrels are re-bored to shoot close and hard and guns are made to order from $10 and up. Mr. Eutebrook has five patents in firearms which are valuable to sportsmen and gun clubs in the United States.

LUCIUS SLADE, Dealer in Butter, Cheese and Eggs, No. 24 Faneuil Hall Market.—One of the oldest established and most enterprising firms in this line, is that of Mr. Lucius Slade. This business was established thirty-seven years ago by Slade & Rust, who continued it till 1856, when, on the retirement of Mr. Rust, Mr. Slade became sole proprietor. Mr. Slade occupies a commodious store and cellar, and handles largely butter, cheese and eggs, large quantities of which are daily received from the best producing sections of the country. He numbers among his permanent customers many of the best-known shippers, jobbers, wholesale and retail grocers of Boston and the neighboring cities. Mr. Slade handles only the choicest and most reliable produce. He makes liberal advances on consignments when required, and is noted for his promptness and accuracy when making returns. Mr. Slade was born in New Hampshire, but has been a resident of Boston for the last forty-four years. He is a popular member of the Produce Exchange, and was the third president of this Institution. Mr. Slade has also been an Alderman for eight years, member of the City Council, member of Massachusetts Senate and Boston School Board, and during the civil war was captain of the National Lancers.

BOSTON PASTE COMPANY, Manufacturers of Noah's Patent Improved Machine Paste, No. 46 Beverly Street.—The steady and increasing demand that has grown up in the shoe, book binding and paper hanging trades for a superior grade of paste has, in the nature of things, resulted in marked improvement having been affected in this useful and indispensable article of late. For general excellence, none yet offered for sale in Boston or the New England States compares with Noah's Patent Improved Machine Paste, manufactured by the Boston Paste Company, which for more than twenty-one years has maintained an enduring hold on popular favor. Noah's Patent Improved Machine Paste is an article of exceptional merit—effective, reliable durable and in all respects the most superior paste for the purposes intended yet introduced—and of this assertion no better criterion need be offered than the steady and extensive sale it finds in the trade, not only throughout the Eastern States, but west as far as St. Louis. This thriving enterprise was started in 1867 by George G. Noah, after whom the paste is named, who conducted it up to 1882, when he was succeeded by the present proprietors, Messrs. I. W. Hamlin and A. C. Noah, (son of the founder,) and by these gentlemen the business has since been continued. They occupy as factory and store a commodious first floor and basement, having in service ample steam power and complete manufacturing and storage facilities, while several in help are employed. They produce a very superior grade of paste for the use of shoe manufactory, book-binders, paper hangers, paper box makers, etc., special attention being given to the manufacture of paste of any consistency or quality, adapted to any work, and satisfaction is guaranteed in every instance. It is put up in barrels, half barrels and kegs.

GEO. W. SMYTH, Insurance Agency, Fire, Marine and Life Insurance, No. 74 Kilby Street.—A leading agency for fire, marine and life insurance in this city is that conducted by Mr. Geo. W. Smith, who has been established in the business here since 1871. He numbers among his clientele many of the solid citizens and largest property holders in this city and its suburban towns. His standing in insurance circles is best shown by the list of companies which he represents, including some of the foremost insurance corporations in the world. Representing, as he does, many millions of dollars of assets and resources, Mr. Smith is prepared to promptly place the largest risks, distributing the same in the most judicious manner, quoting the lowest rates of premium, and guaranteeing a speedy and liberal adjustment of all losses. He controls the insuring of many of the choicest lines of business and residential property in this city, and is deservedly popular with all classes of patrons carefully guarding and intelligently promoting every interest committed to his care. Mr. Smith is a native of Boston, a member of the Underwriters' Association, thoroughly experienced and reliable in all matters relating to insurance.

JAMES S. NEWELL & CO., Mechanical Engineers and Machinists, Manufacturers of Presses, Dies, Etc., Nos. 200, 202 and 204 Federal Street.—Among the best known practical and popular mechanical engineers and machinists in Boston are Messrs. James S. Newell & Co., of Nos. 200, 202 and 204 Federal Street (between Beach and Kneeland Streets). This business was founded in 1840 by Chas. Graves, who was succeeded by Messrs. Bray and Newell in 1867, and on the dissolution of their partnership in 1868 Mr. James S. Newell became the sole proprietor, and since then he has conducted the business under the style which forms the caption of this sketch. The business has been carried on at its present location since 1884, and the premises occupied comprise two floors, each having an area of 90x72 feet. The equipments include the most efficient tools and the latest improved machinery, which is operated by a fifty horse power steam engine, while permanent employment is afforded to between thirty and forty hands skilled and experienced in the business. The firm manufacture all descriptions of presses and dies, design and build all sorts of new machinery, and give special attention to the development and elaboration of inventors' plans. Models, patterns and mechanical drawings are made and gear cutting executed to order promptly and satisfactorily. Mr. Newell is a native of Worcester County, Mass.

M. F. HOWARD & CO., General Mercantile, Book and Job Printers, No. 164 Hanover Street.—For strictly first-class, all around work in the typographic line, or for promptness and reliability in executing orders, none in the business in this vicinity, enjoy a better reputation than M. F. Howard & Co. This popular and well known firm was established in 1887, and from the start has enjoyed a very liberal share of recognition, having a large and growing patronage from secret orders. The quarters occupied as office and shop are commodious and well equipped, every facility and convenience being at hand, while several expert printers are employed. Everything in the line of mercantile, book and job printing is done in the most prompt and excellent manner, at the lowest consistent prices, special attention being given to secret society work, including printing to order for the Golden Cross, Temple of Honor, Nazarite Legion, G. A. R. and the Women's Relief Corps. A full and fine assortment of society badges, gold watch charms, lodge seals, solid gold pins, etc., can always be found on hand and all orders for anything in this line as well as in the typographic way receive immediate attention, while sample copies of assessment and due notices, etc., are promptly furnished on application. Mr. Howard, who is the sole member, the company being nominal, was born at Plymouth, Mass., and is a thorough master of the art in all its branches.

J. F. WASSERBOEHR & SON, Manufacturers of Fine Cigars, No. 149 Court Street.—This business was established thirty years ago by Mr. J. F. Wasserboehr, who eventually admitted his son, Mr. H. P. Wasserboehr into partnership. In 1875 Mr. J. F. Wasserboehr died, after a successful and honorable career and was succeeded by his son, who is now sole proprietor. Mr. Wasserboehr's factory, which gives constant employment to a competent force of skilled cigar makers, is in the Third District of Massachusetts. In the manufacture of his cigars, he uses only the finest domestic and Havana tobaccos, and makes a specialty of the popular H. P. W., ten cent; 149 and Peacock, five cent cigars, and numerous other brands. These cigars are unrivalled for quality, flavor, and uniform excellence, while the prices quoted necessarily attract the attention of careful buyers. Mr. Wasserboehr likewise deals largely in imported and domestic wines and liquors. Only the best liquors, etc., are handled and the trade of the house which is wholesale entirely, now extends throughout all sections of New England. Mr. Wasserboehr was born in Germany, but has resided in Boston for the last thirty-one years.

G. O. HALL, Dentist, No. 96 Court Street.—Dr. Hall, who is a native of Maine, has resided in Boston for the past twenty years. He is a regularly registered dentist, and established the business six years ago, and has since that period, through his perseverance, thorough knowledge of his vocation, and his close application to the interests of his customers, built up a large, active patronage. He occupies admirably equipped premises, fitted up with the most modern dental appliances, and every facility necessary is at command. Dr. Hall performs dentistry in all its branches, including the extraction of teeth, cleaning, filling, etc., and the making of partial or entire sets of artificial teeth. All work is executed in a careful, conscientious and skillful manner. While all work done is in every case reliable and finished in character, the prices charged are remarkably reasonable. Dr. Hall treats all his patrons with the same uniform courteous attention, and persons requiring dental work done will find him at his office daily from 8 a. m to 6 p. m.

W. H. MARTIN, Window Tickets, Show Cards, Signs, Etc., No. 216 Washington Street.—Among the many and varied features of advertising that obtain at the present day, there are few that have secured such an enduring hold on public favor as fancy show cards, attractive board signs and kindred devices. And in this connection it may be observed that very notable improvements have been effected in the cards, signs and window tickets displayed of recent years. Among those who have acquired a reputation for artistic work in this line in Boston may be mentioned the name of W. H. Martin, who ranks among the foremost in this business in this city. Mr. Martin, who is a comparatively young man was born in Boston and is a practical and skillful workman—an expert in fact—of many years' experience and is a thorough master of his art in all its branches. Mr. Martin occupies ample and well equipped quarters, on the fourth floor, and employs two competent assistants. Show cards, board signs and window tickets in every size, design and variety are made to order in the very best style of the art at short notice, while a complete and fine assortment is always kept on hand, and lettering of all kinds likewise is executed in the most prompt and excellent manner, the lowest prices consistent with first-class work at all times prevailing.

WM. N. CONNER, Propr. London Hair Store, No. 485 Washington Street.—This progressive and flourishing business house was founded in 1874 by the present proprietor, who has since developed a trade of a very extensive and influential character, having a thorough knowledge of every detail of the hair business, and giving every department the benefit of his experience. The store is a corner one, and is commodious and handsomely and attractively fitted up. Mr. Conner has in service an able staff of assistants, and manufactures hair work of all kinds, especially for the use of ladies for the house and street, supplying dealers and filling individual orders from all quarters. He pays special attention to keeping up with and leading the styles in ornamental work, and makes a specialty of ventilated goods in the shape of waves, crimps, switches, etc., which have proved a great success. His wigs, fronts, etc., are pronounced most natural in appearance and durable in quality ; and his general goods please the ladies of all classes while he numbers among his patrons many from the wealthiest and highest circles. All kinds of crimps, switches and hair goods in every shade and color are promptly and satisfactorily made to order. Possessing every facility for the work, neatness, beauty of style and artistic taste, form, the rule in every department, and his customers, both wholesale and retail, reside in all parts of the New England States. Mr. Conner is a native of New Hampshire, but has long resided in Boston, and is held in the highest esteem by all to whom he is known.

HAMLIN & MARTIN, New and Second Hand Furniture, Carpets, Stoves, Etc., No. 70 Kneeland Street.—This business was founded in 1880, by Mr. Henry J. Martin, who was joined under the firm name and style as above by Mr. Frank W. Hamlin in 1885. From its inception the house has become a favorite purchasing depot for the surrounding residents. The spacious and attractive salesroom is literally packed with household goods of every description, furniture, carpets, stoves, kitchen utensils, etc., etc., new and secondhanded. The goods handled are all of excellent quality and carefully selected with due regard for the current want and fancy. The highest cash prices are paid for second hand goods and many desirable opportunities are offered for profitable bargains in this connection. The gentlemen composing the firm have had a wide experience in the business and are thoroughly conversant with the wants of the trade.

ANDREWS & CO., Truckmen, General Office, No. 404 Atlantic Avenue.—Perhaps the best known truckmen in Boston, are Messrs. Andrews & Co., whose general office is situated at No. 404 Atlantic Avenue, with stands at Nos. 61 Broad, 29 and 30 India, 45 Pearl, and the corner of Commercial and Clinton Streets. Established in the business here for a period of twenty years, and from the outset doing all business with a promptitude and faithfulness that is ever appreciated, this firm enjoy a very substantial and enviable reputation. They are prepared to do all kinds of trucking, handling free goods only, and make a specialty of the wholesale house trade. For the execution of all orders and commissions with the least possible annoyance or delay to customers this firm employ thirty-one experienced hands and forty-two horses, and are consequently in a position to grant their patronage every advantage and benefit known to the trade. Charges are placed at the lowest point of moderation, and all the great resources, accumulated through long years of identification with a particular industry, are used to promote the interests of patrons. The members of this firm are Messrs. E. and H. D. Andrews. The senior partner has resided in this city for the past thirty years. Both are natives of Maine.

THE METROPOLIS OF NEW ENGLAND. 291

MAX WEISS, Globe Clothing House, Nos. 46 and 46½ Howard Street.—An establishment whose popularity demands special mention at our hands, is that of The Globe Clothing House. The enterprise was founded ten years ago by the present proprietor, Mr. Max Weiss, and has since been conducted with unfailing success. The neatly furnished store is filled with a first-class assortment of new and second-hand clothing of every variety and at prices to suit all means. The highest cash prices are paid for gents' misfits and cast-off garments, while careful attention is given to the cleansing, repairing and pressing of clothing, orders being expeditiously executed at the lowest charges. Directly opposite this store, Mr. Weiss also carries on a merchant tailoring establishment. He occupies commodious, tastefully appointed quarters, and keeps constantly on hand a splendid assortment of foreign and domestic fabrics for coating, vestings and suitings, also a full and complete stock of gents' furnishings, the display embracing all the latest and most fashionable patterns. Measures are accurately taken, only the most skilled labor is employed, and the garments when ready for delivering are unsurpassed for perfection of fit, finish of workmanship, and genuine excellence, while the prices are placed on the most reputable basis. Mr. Weiss is by birth a German, but has resided in the United States for the past twenty-five years. He has won success in business life by a close study of his patrons' interests, and his fair dealing.

THORNDIKE BROS., Wholesale Dealers in Beef, Mutton and Lamb, corner Blackstone and Clinton Streets.—Among the enterprising and prosperous firms engaged in the wholesale handling of fresh meats in this vicinity, can be named that of Thorndike Bros. This popular and well-known firm was established in 1883. They handle nothing but prime stock, and all orders receive immediate attention. Messrs. Thorndike devoting close personal attention to every detail of the business. The firm occupies a spacious basement, with capacious refrigerator and complete storage and other facilities, while several efficient salesmen are in attendance. A heavy and first-class stock is kept on hand at all times including choice beef, mutton and lamb, and their trade, which is of a wholesale character entirely, is large and active, extending all over the city and suburban towns. Messrs. A. B. and C. W. Thorndike who are natives of Maine, but residents of Boston a number of years, are men of energy and thorough reliability in their dealings.

B. F. SILSBY, Confectioner, No. 101 Cambridge Street and No. 6 Chamber Street.—The business of this concern was founded originally at No. 1 Bowdoin Square by the present proprietor, Mr. B. F. Silsby, in 1878, and a year later it was removed to No. 101 Cambridge Street. In September 1885 he started a branch store at No. 6 Chamber Street, which has ever since been conducted with the most gratifying success. The premises occupied at No. 101 Cambridge Street, comprise a handsomely appointed store, 18x30 feet in dimensions, and a basement of like proportions, the latter being used for manufacturing purposes and provided with the latest improved mechanical appliances and other facilities for the manufacture of confectionery and ice cream of every description. Purity is the main essential in this line of goods, and Mr. Silsby, whose reputation is so high for making none but the purest and best goods, is at once manifest. All kinds of confectionery are made fresh daily, fine cream caramels forming a specialty. Ice cream of a superior quality is supplied at short notice. An extensive, brisk retail trade is done, using on an average of 290,000 boxes a year. Mr. Silsby is a practical confectioner of long experience, and he exercises a close surveillance over every department of his business. He was born in Aurora, Me., and has long been a resident in Boston.

HOYT & TRIPP, Mechanical Draughtsmen, Pattern and Model Makers, Etc., No. 17 Chardon Street.—Among those whose reputation stands high in this special department of mechanical art, we find Mr. F. A. Hoyt and Mr. B. F. Tripp, who are thorough, ingenious, practical draughtsmen, and pattern and model makers, whose experience extends over many years. They have been associated as copartners about a year. Messrs. Hoyt & Tripp are skilled mechanics, and are particularly expert in designing and making draughts of intricate and complicated mechanism, and make patterns and models from designs, with that intelligent apprehension and promptness that has given them a reputation not excelled by any others in the city. All kinds of working and experimental models, and patterns are made to order at short notice, and special attention is given to turning, jig, band and circular sawing. The workshop on the fourth floor of the building above mentioned, is 28x75 feet in area, and is perfectly fitted up and equipped with special machinery and appliances operated by steam power, and on an average from three to five skilled workmen are employed, and orders are filled not only from the city and adjoining towns and villages, but from all parts of New England. Both members of the firm are well known to inventors and manufacturers, and their ideas, suggestions and opinions are sought for and appreciated. Mr. Hoyt is a Massachusetts man, and Mr. Tripp is from New Hampshire.

E. W. THOMPSON, New England Passenger Agent of the Chicago, Rock Island and Pacific Railway, No. 296 Washington Street.—This gentleman has been filling his present position here since 1883, and has been connected with the railroad business of the country for the past twelve years. Mr. J. H. Mills is the New England freight agent for this railroad, and occupies office quarters with Mr. Thompson at the above address. Both freight and passengers are accommodated through this agency, passage tickets and bills of lading being given to all parts of the western country by the most direct route possible. The C., R. I. and P. Railway is celebrated as one of the best routes on the continent, and the safety, comfort and speed of passengers are favorably assured by its management. Western bound travelers should consult this office before purchasing tickets elsewhere, as they will be accorded advantages and accommodations unequalled by any other company. Mr. Thompson is a Vermonter by birth, while Mr. Mills is a native of Massachusetts; both are members of the Association of railroad and steamship agents of Boston.

BOYNTON & CO., Commission Merchants, Wholesale Dealers in Foreign and Domestic Fruits and Produce, No. 413½ Commercial Street.—This prosperous business was established in 1883 by Chas. E. Robinson & Co., who conducted the same up to about one year ago, when they were succeeded by the pushing and popular firm whose name heads the sketch. They handle everything in the line of foreign and domestic fruits, nuts, country produce and berries in season, including oranges, lemons, bananas and tropical products, and solicit consignments, a feature being made of prompt returns. The firm occupies commodious quarters, and carry on hand at all times a heavy and first-class stock, while several experienced salesmen are in attendance, and the trade of the house, which is of a wholesale character entirely, extends all over the New England States, besides a fine local connection. Mr. George C. Boynton, was a partner in the old firm. He is a young man of excellent business qualities, as well as thoroughly reliable in his dealings, and is a popular member of the Fruit and Produce Exchange.

FRED'K KOELLER, Cutler, No. 48 Hanover Street.—Mr. Fred'k Koeller, the well known cutler, has had a long experience in this special trade, and in 1883 was a member of the firm of Chas. & Fred'k Koeller, which was dissolved about two and a half years ago, when he established the business he is now conducting with such success. The premises are ample for the purposes of the business, and a large, well assorted stock of fine table and pocket cutlery, surgical instruments, etc., is always kept on sale. Special attention is given to grinding and polishing cutlery and tools, and to engraving razors in the best German, English and American styles, and to grinding and polishing all kinds of metal. Mr. Koeller warrants every razor coming from his hands, and can sell a new full concaved razor at $1.00 and $1.25. A native of Germany, Mr. Koeller came to this country in 1879. In his workshop steam power is used, and several expert workmen are employed in repairing and redressing cutlery and also in concaving razors, a process which greatly prolongs their usefulness. Mr. Koeller also makes a special business of silver and nickel plating.

JERE A. DENNETT, Dealer in Paper Hangings and Interior Decorations, No. 23 Bromfield Street.—This business was founded originally in 1850, by Messrs. Dennett, Bliss & Jones, and was continued under that firm name for some years, when changes in proprietorship occurred, and resulted in Mr. Dennett retiring from active business life; but the mantle of idleness became irksome to him and he began the same line of industry again in 1883, and has built up a very flourishing trade from among his old patrons, and new ones, who are constantly increasing in numbers. He occupies a very neatly and appropriately fitted up store, which is fully equipped with every convenience and appliance necessary for the attractive display of the large and handsome stock of goods on hand. The assortment embraces a line of wall papers that rank as high in the estimation of art critics, and interior decorators as any goods in the same line of industry in any portion of the world; and comprises gold and highly colored parlor and drawing-room papers, with beautiful dados and friezes to match, while rich library paperings in imitation of leather, carved oak and walnut are shown, with plain and embossed flocks, and other superior paper-hangings in bewildering variety and lavish profusion, while extremely rich and pleasing effects are obtained in comparatively inexpensive goods. The trade of this house is derived principally from among our leading and most distinguished citizens, and the facilities enjoyed by Mr. Dennett for procuring the very latest designs and styles from the leading manufacturers enable him to offer his customers the best and newest of everything in his line of business, at the very lowest prices. Mr. Dennett is a native of Boston, and has had many years' practical experience in his business.

JOHN H. McCARTHY, Commission Dealer in Mutton, Lamb and Veal, No. 12 Clinton Street.—Among the active enterprising business men on Clinton Street, there are probably none having a wider reputation than Mr. John McCarthy, commission dealer in mutton, lamb and veal. He has been established in the business the past ten years and has built up a large wholesale trade with the dealers throughout the city and vicinity. The premises is a spacious cellar, which contains every facility for the purpose of the business, including ample refrigerator for use in summer, and three employees are kept constantly busy about the establishment. Mr. McCarthy handles only the very choicest mutton, lamb and veal, and his connections are such as to enable him to supply the trade with the freshest and choicest that comes to the city. Consignments are received daily and the stock is always in prime condition, and extensive in its character. Promptitude, quick sales and low prices form the policy upon which the business is conducted. Mr. McCarthy is a native of Charlestown.

H. E. GUSTIN & CO., Country Produce, No. 104 Clinton Street.—The firm of H. E. Gustin & Co., is prominently identified with the produce business in Boston as one of the most energetic houses engaged in the line. The business was established by Mr. Asa Andrews in 1878 and was carried on by him till 1889, when the present proprietor assumed control, and brought a first-class business training to bear on the conduct of the concern. Mr. Gustin employs three assistants and does a large commission business in country produce of all kinds, having first-class connections all through New England who consign to him potatoes, etc., fresh every day. Mr. Gustin secures a ready market for these consignments at the most favorable figures, and gives the greatest satisfaction to customers in all his transactions. He has also an extensive stall trade and is known in the city and suburbs in connection with the reliable character of the goods he handles. Mr. Gustin is a young man and is a native of Winchester, Mass. He lives in Somerville.

E. J. HARTNETT, Fashionable Millinery, No. 697 Washington Street.—Nearly twenty years ago Miss E. J. Hartnett started in business for herself as a fashionable milliner and fancy goods' dealer, and during her lengthy career she has built up a widely extended and influential trade among the leading families in the community. In 1877 Miss Hartnett moved into her present eligibly located quarters, and has fitted up her spacious and commodious store in the most elegant and tasteful manner, besides supplying the millinery parlors and salesroom with every improved facility and convenience. Miss Hartnett handles the choicest assortment of imported and domestic novelties in trimmed and untrimmed hats and bonnets, ribbons, laces, feathers, flowers, velvets, plumes, mourning bonnets, etc., all of which are of superior quality. A force of ten thoroughly experienced milliners and clerks is constantly employed. Miss Hartnett is a native of Boston and a lady of pronounced business ability.

NATIONAL PLATING CO., Nickel, Gold, Silver and Copper Plating, Albert G. Webb, Manager, No. 82 Sudbury Street.—The National Plating Co., is one of the best known in its special line of business in Boston, and was established and has been under the management of Mr. Albert G. Webb, for six years. He is an experienced practical man to the trade, and his knowledge of all kinds of plating is second to none in the business. The premises occupied on the 3rd floor of the building, No. 82 Sudbury Street, contain every facility including steam power and special appliances for executing the very best class of work in nickel and copper plating, and metal polishing for the trade and satisfaction is guaranteed. Skilled workmen are employed who are under the immediate direction of Mr. James D. Campbell, and all work emanating from the establishment is warranted. Mr. Webb is a native of Norwood, where he resides. Mr. Webb has acquired a well deserved reputation for attention to the high standard and character of the work turned out.

WM. H. VAN DALINDA, Manufacturer and Wholesale Dealer in Barbers' Supplies, No. 298 Washington Street.—Mr Van Dalinda, who is a native of New Jersey, is a practical and experienced barber, and up to 1885 when he started in this line, had been engaged in the exercise of his art. He occupies ample and compact quarters, and keeps always on hand a full and fine assortment of barbers' supplies, including the following specialties: Van Dalinda's Egg Shampoo Cream, perfumed Petrolatum Pomade, and French rose cosmetique; Cantana jelly, Foley's cream, Damascus razors, shaving soaps, hair oils, Florida and Lavender waters, essential oils, fine hones, straps, bay rum, etc.; and is prepared also to decorate shaving mugs in the very best style of the art at short notice, and at reasonable rates. Mr. Van Dalinda likewise attends to grinding and concaving, which are executed in the most prompt and excellent manner at lowest prices, and altogether, he receives a very nice patronage.

WHITE & JOHNSON, Provisions, Butter, Eggs, Fruit, Vegetables, Etc., No. 219 Eliot Street.—The well conducted establishment of Messrs. White & Johnson, is one of the leading sources of local supply in this section of the city. The premises in size are 35x30 feet, and neatly and tastefully fitted up with handsome fixtures and are kept in a faultlessly clean condition. Mr. George G. White and Mr. Harry F. Johnson, the proprietors, are young practical business men and have been associated as copartners for the past two years. They are well equipped and provided with every convenience for conducting business upon a large scale and deal in only the choicest and best provisions of all kinds, and the finest creamery and dairy butter, eggs and farm produce generally, and vegetables and foreign and domestic fruits. Messrs. White & Johnson, are thoroughly worthy of all patronage that may be tendered them.

BRADLEY'S Troy Laundry, No. 9 Harrison Avenue.—One of the best equipped and best conducted establishments of its kind in this section of the city is Bradley's Troy Laundry. The proprietor, Mr. G. E. Bradley, had had vast experience in his line before he ventured into business on his own account, and this he did in 1882. In May, 1888, he removed to his present eligible premises, in which all the most improved Troy washing and ironing machinery is in use, while constant employment is afforded to a number of experienced hands. Those who send their linen to this laundry will have it returned white as when in its virgin purity, and polished in a manner that can be truthfully called artistic. A speciality is made of doing up lace curtains. Goods are called for and delivered in any part of the city, and all telephone orders are promptly attended to. Mr. Bradley is a native of the city, is vigilant and attentive to all the affairs of his establishment,

THE METROPOLIS OF NEW ENGLAND.

JOHN POWER, Cork Manufacturer, No. 98 Union Street.—The oldest cork manufacturer in the city is Mr. John Power. Mr. Power has been in this line for the past forty-eight years, twelve years before he came to the United States from Ireland, where he was born. He has been established here for the past twelve years, and occupies the second and third floors at No. 98 Union Street. Mr. Power, besides manufacturing largely him-

self, deals in all kinds of capsules, imported corks, brewers' supplies, corkscrews, tin foil, etc., and carries a large stock of all these various lines on hand. He is the patentee of the celebrated Power's Patent Corking Machines, which are in such general use throughout the country, and are justly considered the most perfect machines of the kind in the market.

SAMUEL E. CROWELL, Ship Broker, No. 150 Commercial Street.—Samuel E. Crowell, ship broker, No. 150 Commercial Street, was formerly a member of the firm of Doane & Co., from which he withdrew in 1886, and engaged in business alone at the place indicated, and where he has secured a patronage of a permanent and gratifying character. Mr. Crowell charters and insures vessels for coast and international service, secures freights for all ports, buys and sells merchandise of every description on commission at home and abroad. He is himself interested in several vessels, and is prompt and reliable in all his dealings. Mr. Crowell has a splendid connection among merchants, shippers and producers, and he covers every branch of his field of activity with intelligent attention to the requirements of his numerous patrons. He is a prominent and esteemed member of the Vessel Owners' Association. Mr. Crowell has a neat, well appointed office, is aided by several assistants, and is untiring in his zeal to afford satisfaction in the carrying out of all orders. He is a native of Cape Cod and is a resident of Somerville.

A. H. BROWN & BROS., Millers' Agents, No. 129 State Street.—Among the solid and substantial firms engaged in this branch of commercial activity in Boston can be named that of A. H. Brown & Bros., Millers' agents. This well known and responsible house was established in 1884, and its history from the start marks an unbroken record of prosperity. The firm represent several western millers, and handle consignments of flour, grain of every description and mill feed, on commission, shipping direct from the mills in car loads, and their trade which extends throughout New England, is large and active. Messrs. A. H. and F. H. Brown who compose the firm, are young men, and natives of this city, well and favorably known to the trade, and are members of the Chamber of Commerce, and are now enjoying the fruits of their business ability.

E. J. BOYCE, Manufacturing Jeweler, No. 383 Washington Street.—Among the most successful and progressive manufacturing establishments on this line is the well known and popular concern of Mr. E. J. Boyce. Mr. John Jennings founded this business in 1859; in 1882 Messrs. Boyce & Wainwright became the proprietors, and on the dissolution of this firm, in 1886, Mr. Boyce assumed sole control of the enterprise. He was a partner with Mr. Jennings when the latter founded the business. He was born in England, learned his trade and worked there as a journeyman, and after coming to this country in 1875, and until he formed a partnership with Mr. Jennings, he was employed as a workman. His experience and ability qualify him as an expert in the trade, and he closely supervises all work executed in his establishment, which is 80x10 feet in dimensions, and fully equipped with improved tools and machinery operated by steam power. Eight skilled and experienced hands are employed, and the products of the establishment comprise gold and plated bracelets, pins, rings and jewelry of every description, a specialty being made of rings, plain and chased, and in many different styles and patterns. The trade is brisk and growing, the goods produced here being in high favor with both wholesale and retail dealers, and meeting with a ready sale, throughout the whole of the New England States. Mr. Boyce is well spoken of in mercantile circles, and merits the great degree of popularity to which he has attained.

LEWIS WOOD, JR., Manufacturer of Custom Cabinet Work, Fine Store and Office Fittings, Moulding, Sawing, Turning, Etc., No. 16 Beverly Street.—Actively engaged as a manufacturer of custom cabinet work, fine store and office fittings, we find Mr. Lewis Wood, Jr., who has been established in the business here for upward of thirty years. He occupies large and commodious quarters, equipped with new and improved machinery and ample steam power, also gives steady employment to ten or a dozen skilled hands. He is prepared to execute all kinds of moulding, sawing and turning, also pattern and model making; while he makes a leading specialty of old pieces, in which branch of his business he is known to excel all his competitors. His large and permanent trade, broadly distributed throughout the state, and especially heavy and influential in this city, is the direct result of the superior character and fine finish of his various productions. In all departments of the business it has always been the aim of Mr. Wood to secure the highest standard of excellence in design, workmanship and finish. His work is always promptly and faithfully performed, and his terms are placed at an eminently reasonable figure. Mr. Wood was born in South Acton, Mass., and is now a well known and honored citizen of Everett, Mass., in which place he is as well known as in Boston.

E. C. DOW, Outer and Inner Soles, Taps, Etc., No. 10 South Street.—This house was established originally by Mr. E. C. Dow in 1869, which subsequently became Messrs. Dow & Son in 1884, the latter having been admitted in 1878, and the present proprietor assumed sole control of the business. The business office on this city is under the charge of his son, W. E. Dow, where a full and complete assortment of all the higher grades of goods in their line of production are kept constantly on hand. The office is very neatly and economically fitted up with every facility for the proper transaction of the business, orders are received both at the office and factory, and also shipped from either place. The factory at Haverhill, Mass., is of ample dimensions and fitted up with all the latest improved machinery required, and a full force of the best and most skilful workmen are constantly employed, whose operations are conducted under the immediate and personal supervision of the proprietor. Mr. Dow is particularly careful in the selection of stock for his goods, and none but the very best grades of sole leather are used in the outer and inner soles, also taps prepared by him. The goods from this establishment have always occupied a very high position among the best boot and shoemakers, and are used by them throughout this state and other portions of New England. Mr. Dow is a native of Mass., and has been in this line of business over a quarter of a century. The reputation of Mr. Dow's establishment is constantly increasing, while his methods of upright and honorable dealings are proverbial among those having business transactions with him.

W. A. HUSTON, Druggist, No. 160 Hanover, Corner Salem Street.—The drug store of Mr. W. A. Huston, has for more than three-score years been one of the prominent business institutions in this section of the city. It was founded as far back as 1820, and since 1879 it has been under the direction of the present proprietor. The situation of this fine, largely patronized store is a most eligible one, and with its marble floor and counters, handsome soda-water fountain, splendid plate glass show cases, its finely arranged stock and electric lights the place has at all times an attractive and pleasing appearance. Mr. Huston has at all times on hand a stock of drugs, chemicals, proprietary preparations, medicines, etc., all pure and fresh, and a stock of toilet accessories and fancy articles, druggists' sundries, etc., that will compare favorably with that of any similar establishment in the city. Special attention is given to compounding physicians' prescriptions and family recipes, this department being in charge of thoroughly competent pharmacists. No druggist in Boston is better or more favorably known than Mr. Huston, who is a native of Maine, a pharmaceutical graduate and a pharmacist of long experience. The policy upon which his business is conducted is characterized by a careful regard for the interests of his patrons.

A. M. LELAND, Music Goods, No. 161 Tremont Street.—Mr. Leland is an extensive dealer in the celebrated Postawka taborets, fine violins and mandolins at various prices, the very best strings for the violin, banjo, guitar and mandolin; piano chairs, stools and ottomans; piano chairs with adjustable backs and seats, piano tuners' outfit, piano polish, etc. He has been closely identified with the piano and music trade for the past fifty years, being intimately conversant with all the details and requirements of the business, and established his present enterprise here in 1887. His intimate and influential connections with the best manufacturing sources in this line, both in this country and Europe, enable him to offer the public a line of specialties that cannot readily be obtained elsewhere. The stock bears such a character for utility, novelty, value and usefulness as to command universal attention. The demands of teachers, tuners, pupils and musicians of all grades are here met with intelligence and promptness, and orders are filled with conscientious regard for the best interests of patrons. Mr. Leland is a Massachusetts man by birth and education, well and favorably known in this city and throughout the state as a thorough musician and an enterprising and reliable dealer.

A. McCLEAN & CO., Lumber and General Commission Merchants, No. 102 State Street.—The well-known firm of A. McLean & Co., lumber and general commission merchants, has from its inception to the present day maintained a record of steady progress. The concern carries on a general business, making a specialty of lumber, however, and enjoys especially favorable facilities for executing all orders in their line. The business of the firm extending to New York, besides Boston and New England. Special attention is given to soft and hard-wood lumber for export orders, viz.: white pine, whitewood, white oak, first and second-growth ash, hickory, black walnut lumber and logs. Mr. McLean, who is the sole member of the Co., being nominal, is a Nova Scotian by birth, but came to this city in 1858, being now a gentleman in the prime of life. He is a man of wide practical experience, active and energetic, and of entire probity in his dealings, and enjoys an enviable reputation in commercial life.

E. R. BURBANK, Real Estate Broker and Auctioneer, Room 4, No. 235 Washington Street.—The Boston real estate market has come to be recognized as the leading financial interest of the metropolis. Investments in Boston realty are more than ever sought for, and those who effect their purchases through the reliable house of E. R. Burbank, real estate agent and broker, will find the investment profitable. He is a native of Lowell, Mass., but is an old resident in Boston, where he has long been identified with real estate matters, and he brings to bear on his business not only vast practical experience, but likewise an intimate knowledge of the respective merits of the various residential and business sections of the city, as a talented and popular real estate agent. Mr. Burbank started in business in 1883, and has been accorded a very substantial and influential patronage. As a broker, he possesses the most superior connections and ample facilities to promptly buy or sell property of every description, and has carried through to a successful issue many heavy transactions. He conducts sales of real estate with ability and credit.

C. M. WARD & CO., Manufacturing Jewelers, No. 69 Washington Street.—Among the prosperous concerns engaged in the manufacture of jewelry will be found that of C. M. Ward & Co. The commodious premises on the third floor are systematically and conveniently arranged and all requisite facilities are at hand for the advantageous prosecution of the business. Mr. Ward manufactures all kinds of jewelry—as scarf and lace pins, ear rings, finger rings, brooches, etc., in gold, silver and other materials, and special attention is given to repairing and diamond setting. Five skillful and experienced assistants are employed, and the work turned out in all departments embodies the highest degree of artistic excellence. Mr. Ward was born in England but came to this city twenty years ago, and here learned and became an expert at his trade. In 1872 he established for himself under the name and style as above, and in the period elapsed by superior work and fair and equitable dealing has secured a large and highly desirable patronage.

G. A. CLARKE, Designer, No. 9 Milk Street.—For variety, originality and beauty of designs in the lines of business cards, letter-heads, book-covers, etc., or for promptness and reliability in executing work, but few, if any, in Boston, surpass G. A. Clarke, designer. He is unquestionably among the foremost exponents of this branch of art in the city, and receives an excellent city and out of town patronage. Mr. Clarke was born in Littleton, N. H., and has been in Boston some years. He is a thoroughly practical and expert designer, of ample experience in his profession, and is a complete master of the art in its every detail. He has been established in business for himself something over three years, and from the first he has constantly won his way to favor and recognition owing to the excellence of his work. Mr. Clarke is prepared to execute designs for business cards, letter-heads, book-covers, railroad-bills, etc. in the most superior and artistic manner at short notice, special attention being given to commercial and railroad work, and all orders receive immediate attention.

MARINER & WILLIAMS, Shipping Agents, No. 192 Commercial street.—Boston is the home of many sea captains and sailors whose services are always in demand to man the various vessels sailing from the port. To secure crews, owners and consignees call in the services of the shipping agents, such for instance as Messrs. Mariner and Williams, who are experienced, practical men, well known to masters and sailors, and who can furnish crews at short notice and secure berths for long or short voyages for all who apply at their office. Mr. G. G. Mariner and Mr. S. J. Williams have been in partnership since 1882 and occupied their present location about a year and a half. Mr. Mariner is a native of Mt. Holly, N. J. He has been a sailor, and for twenty-five years was captain of the staunchest vessels hailing from ports in his native state and from Boston. Mr. Williams who was born in Bath, Maine, is an old-time resident of Boston. He is a practical seaman well known in the coasting trade.

R. M. LOWELL, Plumber and Dealer in Plumbing Materials, No. 36 Brattle Street.—One of the oldest and best known plumbers of the city is Mr. R. M. Lowell, of No. 36 Brattle Street, nearly opposite the Quincy House. Mr. Lowell, who is a native of Maine, and is now in his sixty-third year, came here at an early age, and learned the trade in which he has since become a leading representative. At the age of twenty-three he established his present business and succeeded from the start in obtaining a first-class trade in the neighborhood and throughout the city, which has steadily grown to its modern large dimensions. Besides his extensive business in doing practical plumbing of all kinds, especially of a sanitary description, he is in a position to undertake contracts for the plumbing work of new buildings at the lowest rates, having three men employed in his establishment and is likewise ready to do repairs on the shortest notice.

SAGE'S TRUNK DEPOT, Nos. 658 and 660 Washington Street.—The leading headquarters for trunks and travelling bags in this city is the establishment of Mr. G. F. Sage, familiarly known as Sage's Trunk Depot. The proprietor learned the trunk-making trade in early life, and established business for himself in 1861, at No. 596 Washington Street, removing to his present quarters in 1876. Here he occupies a fine corner store, in the business heart of the city, specially suited for trade purposes, and three floors above for manufacturing. His reputation has become firmly established throughout New England as a manufacturer and wholesale and retail dealer in the finest grade of ladies' and gent's, trunks, travelling and shopping bags, fancy leather goods and tourist articles of every description known to the trade; and, as making a leading specialty of basket trunks, in which branch of the trade he is known as excelling all competitors. The stock here displayed presents an exhibition of the possibilities of production in this line, and is an interesting and instructive exhibit of the useful and the beautiful, the unique and the ornamental, in the trunk and travelling-bag industry. This is the centre from which radiates a trade extending to all parts of the New England States. The wants of dealers, tourists, travellers and all classes of consumers are here ministered to with eminent success and satisfaction in all cases. Mr. Sage was born in Macon, Ga., but came to this city in his boyhood. His life-long connection with this trade has given him a detailed knowledge of the business that is always employed to the advantage of those who deal with the house.

WHITON & KNIGHT, Mercantile and Theatrical Ticket Printers, No. 57 Washington Street.—This popular and responsible firm was established in 1883, and was formerly located on Bromfield Street, where the business was conducted up to some four years since, when it was moved to the present commodious quarters. They occupy here ample premises on the third floor, with steam power and the latest improved printing appliances, first-class outfit of type and complete facilities for executing all orders, small or large, with despatch; while half a dozen expert hands are employed, and the office is connected by telephone (2168). General mercantile, novelty and ticket printing of every description is done in the very best style of the art and in the most expeditious manner, at the lowest prices consistent with first-class work and honorable business principles, special attention being given to theatrical ticket printing and numbering, while theatrical blanks of all kinds are printed to order; lithographing and engraving also being promptly and reliably attended to, and all work leaving this concern is executed under the close personal supervision of the proprietors. Messrs. E. E. Whiton and S. D. Knight, who compose the firm, are both men of many years' practical experience and are thoroughly conversant with the business in all its features and details.

GEO. E. CROSBY & CO., Printers, No. 293 Washington Street, Opp. head of Franklin Street.—The book and job printing business is one of vast importance and extent in Boston. Among those who have gained eminence and distinction in this line are Messrs. Geo. E. Crosby & Co. Mr. Crosby, who was born in Milford, N. H., forty-three years ago, has been identified with the typographical art in all its phases from his youth up, started business on his own account in Cambridge in 1880, and in May, 1886, he purchased the business at its present quarters from Messrs. Johnson & White, who had founded it and conducted it since 1873. In Mr. Crosby's hands the patronage of the establishment has grown and multiplied and the trade is now one of considerable magnitude, requiring the constant employment of about twenty hands. The printing office has a capacity of 35x100 feet, and the mechanical facilities include three cylinder and seven job presses, which are operated by a twelve horse power steam engine. Types of every description—modern, antique, plain and fancy—are abundant and varied, and all the paraphernalia of a first-class, thoroughly equipped printing establishment are there at hand. Printing of all kinds, from a small business card to an elaborate and finely-finished book, is executed with promptness and despatch and at prices which no other concern in the trade can excel. This house justly prides itself upon the neatness and uniform excellence of the work turned out, and the success it has achieved since founded is fully merited.

WALTER LOCKETT & CO., Merchandise Brokers, Canned Goods, Etc., No. 7 Broad Street.—A firm which ably serves the best interests of the most prominent manufacturers in certain staple lines is that of Messrs. Walter Lockett & Co., general merchandise brokers and jobbers in canned goods, etc. The founder and proprietor of this business, Mr. Walter Lockett a native of Massachusetts, is an old resident in Boston, and is a widely known and respected member of the mercantile community. He embarked in his present line of business in 1880, and the wide-spread trade he has built up and the success he has achieved sufficiently demonstrate his ability to satisfy the most exacting demands of his patrons. The firm are the sole agents for E. D. Mallory & Co., "Arrow" Brand Canned Goods; Gibbs Preserving Company, Bull Head Brand Canned Goods; Kraft & Wonderimer, Justice Brand Canned Goods; C. A. Rutledge & Bro., Rutledge Brand Canned Goods; Erie Preserving Company, Erie Brand Canned Goods; L. Ladd, Ladd's Brand Canned Squash; J. S. Johnson, Johnson's Brand Bahama Pineapple; W. Underwood & Co., Sardines, Blueberries, Etc.; S. M. Donger & Son, Pickles, Etc. The firm are also connected, directly and indirectly, with all the leading packers throughout the country. They occupy a neatly appointed sample room, where a large and well assorted stock is at all times displayed. All orders are shipped direct from the canneries, and the trade is direct with jobbers, who are supplied at manufacturers' lowest quotations. The business relations of the house extend to every section of the United States, and are particularly active in the New England and western states.

BARON & CO., Manufacturers of Cigars, H. H. Sacker, Manager, New England Depot, No. 38 Central Street.—Although but a comparatively short time established here in Boston, Baron & Co., the widely known cigar manufacturers, with capacious factory at Nos. 1007-1009 East Pratt Street, Baltimore, this city, have already achieved a degree of success and built up an eastern connection that more than attests the wisdom that inspired the venture. The Boston branch was established in June, 1886, with W. H. Sacker as manager, and from its inception has proved a highly gratifying enterprise. The secret of the firm's prosperity in the New England states is not far to seek, however; fine goods, reliable dealing and excellent management being the special features contributing to its well-deserved success. The office and salesroom at No. 38 Central Street are compact and ample, while a complete and first-class sample stock is constantly carried, including the following favorite brands manufactured by Baron & Co.: La Baronesa, Signet, El Tasso, Inside View, etc., and the trade done in this city, which is principally with jobbers and retailers is at once large and active. Mr. Sacker, the efficient manager here, is a man of energy and many years' business experience, and prior to assuming charge of the New England depot for Baron & Co., had been long a member of the coffee and spice firm of Davis, Sacker & Perkins of this city.

COUSENS & PRATT, Sail Makers, No. 3 Commercial Street.—No concern engaged in the sail making business in this city enjoys a better reputation for skill or reliability, as few, if any, receive a larger measure of merited recognition, than the firm of Cousens & Pratt. This well and favorably known firm was established in 1851 and from this period down to the present day has received an excellent patronage from the vessels plying between this port and all the seaports of the world. In 1880 William Pratt, Jr., one of the members, was removed by death, and the business has since been conducted by the surviving partner, C. A. Cousens, alone with uninterrupted success under the original style of firm. Mr. Cousens, who is a man in the full prime of life, and a native of Cohasset, is a practical and expert sail maker, of long and varied experience, and is a thorough master of his art in all its details. He occupies a 25x125 foot floor, which is completely equipped in every respect with all necessary facilities, and employs from three to a dozen experienced hands, according to season. Sails of every description are made to order in the most expeditious and excellent manner, while a large and first-class assortment of new and second hand sails are constantly kept on hand, and all orders for anything in this line receive prompt and satisfactory attention.

LENT & BRAHAM, Importers of Tailors' Trimmings, No. 116 Tremont Street, Studio Building, W. J. Hyde, Agent.—The trade in this line of goods in Boston has grown to vast proportions within the last few years, and the enterprising firm of Lent & Braham, to better accommodate their large and rapidly increasing patronage in this city, established this house in 1874 with Mr. Hyde as their agent, and since its inception has been the recipient of a very substantial and constantly growing trade. Mr. Hyde is a native of New York, and prior to his advent here was employed for many years as traveling salesman for the popular and influential house he so ably represents. His office and salesrooms are of ample dimensions, and are very conveniently arranged for the display of the large line of samples constantly on hand, which embraces everything known in the line of tailors' trimmings, such as buttons of all sizes and quality, sleeve and body linings for dress, business and overcoats, vest linings, trouser trimmings, facings, canvasses, hair and stiff cloths, silk, linen and cotton threads, silk twists, etc. These goods are received direct from the main house in New York, whose proprietors are in constant communication with foreign manufacturers, which connection enables them to place on the market all the very latest novelties and designs in tailors' trimmings simultaneously with their appearance in the Paris and London markets. The system which prevails in this establishment, under the direction of Mr. Hyde, indicates thorough skill and intimate acquaintance with every minute detail of a critical and exacting trade. The prices are the same as those of the parent house, and customers can save time and money both by selecting from sample and ordering through this house, as all orders receive special and prompt attention. The trade of this house is not confined to the city of Boston, but extends throughout the United States. Mr. Hyde is also the accredited agent for the old, reliable and popular New York Life Insurance Company, and does a very extensive business for it in this city.

NICKERSON & GLIDDEN, Commission Merchants and Dealers in Shoe Findings, Twines, Sash Cords, Tapes, Etc., No. 48 South Street.—Among the most noted and successful of the younger houses in this line, and which are in keen competition with the old established concerns for first place, is that of Messrs. Nickerson & Glidden, who are doing business at No. 48 South Street. The members of this firm are Messrs. Augustus Nickerson and George B. Glidden, both young, enterprising Bostonians. Mr. Nickerson had previously been in the steamship business; Mr. Glidden was reared and trained in the shoe-finding trade, and knows all about it, from first to last, and how to meet the wants of shoe manufacturers and dealers with first class goods at bottom prices. For about one year Mr. Glidden was in business on his own account on Bedford Street, and in March, 1888, he formed a partnership with Mr. Nickerson. They have a fine office and sample room, 35x50 feet in dimensions, and here they conduct a most flourishing and wide-spread jobbing trade in all kinds of shoe-findings, twines, sash cords, tapes, etc. They represent several extensive manufacturers in these lines, and are in a position to fill the most extensive orders at the shortest notice.

CHARLES F. PEASE, Pease's Durable and Household Bindings for Carpets and Oil Cloths, Etc., No. 45 Kingston Street.—This gentleman is the proprietor of Pease's Durable and Household Bindings for carpets and oil cloths; also, excelsior (worsted warp) carpet binding, and handles extensively zinc and brass oil-cloth bindings. He also deals in curtain fixtures, worsted and wire picture cord, picture knobs, moulding hooks and screw eyes, shade pulls, drapery loops, window screen cloth, carpet thread, etc. Mr. Pease commenced business in Boston in 1865, as a member of the firm of Fowle & Pease, succeeding to the sole control of the business in 1884. Mr. Pease has made a special study of the trade in bindings and is a recognized authority in the market, and displays a full and complete stock of the above-named specialties and supplies at all times. Pease's Durable and Household Bindings are held in high repute wherever introduced, and are in heavy and permanent demand in many states of the Union, being preferred in many markets above all other makes for their great salability and solid worth. Mr. Pease is a well known citizen and business man of Boston, and has ever retained the confidence and esteem of commercial and trade circles.

WM. READ & SONS, Importers and Dealers in Guns and Sporting Goods, and Military Contractors, No. 107 Washington Street.—This business was founded in 1826 by Mr. Wm. Read, who died in 1884, after a successful and honorable career. He was succeeded by his sons, who are now carrying on the business under the old firm name of Wm. Read & Sons. The premises occupied are spacious and comprise a superior five-story and basement building, 6x100 feet in area. The salesrooms are fully stocked with a splendid and varied assortment of guns, rifles, revolvers, ammunition and shooting and fishing tackle of every description. They offer guns of every description, comprising all the prominent English and American makes in laminated steel, Damascus, and steel twist barrels, breech-loading double guns of Scott, Wesley Richards, Purdey, Moore & Harris, Hollis, and other English makers; also Colt, Parker, Harrington & Richardson, Remington, and all other American makes. W. & C. Scott and Sons' fine hammerless guns a specialty. Breech-loading rifles of all kinds, single and double barrel; Maynard, Winchester, Sharp's, Wesson's, Ballard, Remington, and others. Colt's, Smith & Wesson's and all other American pistols at retail or in quantity for shipping. All the American shells, wads, etc. James Dixon & Son's fine shooting tackle. All articles adapted to the manufacture of guns, locks, stocks, cones, barrels, etc. A full assortment of fishing tackle, etc. The firm are the agents for the Yates breech-loading cannon, invented by Colonel Theodore Yates of the United States Army, an exact model of eight inch gun now being made for the United States Government by the South Boston Iron Company under appropriations made by Congress. It is believed to be the strongest and best breech-loading gun in existence. In their factory at Chicopee, they manufacture the New Mail Bicycles, which are so largely used. The business is both wholesale and retail, and extends not only throughout the entire United States and Canada, but also to Mexico, Central and South America, the East Indies, China, Japan, South Africa and Australia, their export business being very large.

ELLIOTT J. HYDE, Insurance and Notary Public, No. 31 Milk Street, Room 6.—One of the best known and most popular among the younger insurance brokers doing business in this city is Elliott J. Hyde, whose office is located at No. 31 Milk Street, Room 6, and than whom few in this line that have come to the front within recent years in Boston have been more fortunate in securing a hold on public favor. Mr. Hyde, who is a gentleman of about thirty-two and a native of Newton, is a young man of entire responsibility in his dealings as well as energy and ample experience in insurance matters, and prior to starting in business on his own account in 1884 had been for many years associated with his father in the same line. He carries on a general insurance brokerage, placing all classes of desirable risks with staunch and reliable companies at the lowest rates consistent with absolute security, while he is also a competent notary public; and altogether, he is an active and constantly improving business. Mr. Hyde is a popular member of the Boston Tariff Reform Association, and is noted for his honorable and straightforward business methods.

BOWEN & CO., Real Estate and Business Brokers, No. 178 Washington Street.—This firm began operations in 1863, and since then have developed a large, active and influential patronage. This success has been achieved through a close application to the interests of patrons and by the satisfactory services which have in every instance been given. The active member of the firm is Mr. O. O. Bowen, who is a recognized authority in all matters affecting the present or prospective values of realty, improved or unimproved. He negotiates properties of all kinds, buying, selling, leasing and renting, taking entire charge of estates, negotiating loans on bond and mortgage, loaning money on personal security, and buying and selling business chances. In all cases he strives to promote the best interests of his patrons by a close study of their needs, and of the opportunities the market presents. Mr. Bowen is a resident of Charlestown, and is familiarly known throughout the community. He is Deputy Supreme Justice of the order of the Iron Hall, and Grand Sentinel of Athenæum Council, No. 161, and a member of the Royal Conclave of Knights and Ladies.

GOULD & COMPANY, Wholesale Paint Dealers, Nos. 69 and 71 Union Street.—The business of this concern was founded as far back as thirty-six years ago under the firm style of J. Porter & Co., manufacturers of Porter's Patent Burning Fluid, of which firm Mr. J. A. Gould was a member. The son of the latter, Mr. George L. Gould, also became a member of the firm in 1872. On the retirement of Mr. Porter Messrs. J. A. and G. L. Gould continued the business under the present style of Gould & Company, and they have developed the trade to large proportions, the house being in all respects a representative one in its line. The firm occupy commodious premises, consisting of a salesroom 25x80 feet in dimensions, and a basement of equal size, and these are admirably fitted up and provided with every facility for the successful prosecution of the business. Messrs. Gould & Company are manufacturers of equal and shellac varnishes and japans, Gould's "imperial" carriage gloss paints and natural wood stains; and Gould's "silver light" high test oil. They are also the New England agents for Benj. Moore & Co.'s calson finish, for walls and ceilings; Lucas' greens and prepared paints; "granite" floor paints, Crockett's specialties, Pratt's liquid dryer, Whiting's brushes, Moses's absolutely pure oil colors,—warranted full strength; and for the Ulster White Lead Company, of New York city, the factory being located in Saugerties, N. Y. The "Ulster" lead is noted for its extreme fineness, whiteness and covering qualities. This firm carries on hand an immense stock of painters supplies of every description and offer these at prices which effect a brisk sale and a trade extending to all parts of the New England States. The business is exclusively of a wholesale character and dealers and painters everywhere will find it advantageous to establish business relations with this concern. Both members of the firm are Massachusetts men by birth; and are widely known and esteemed in both commercial and social circles, the senior partner being a resident of Chelsea and the junior partner resides at Malden.

F. HOLDEN & CO., Beef, Pork, Lard, Hams, Etc., Nos. 49 and 51 Faneuil Hall Market.—The supply of the choicest meats and provisions has long been a prominent feature in the trade of Boston, and among the leading firms engaged in catering to the wants of the community in this direction is that of Messrs. F. Holden & Co., at Nos. 49 and 51 Faneuil Hall Market. This firm are widely known as wholesale and retail dealers in beef, pork, lard, hams, etc. The business was originally established in 1826 by Mr. F. Holden, who died in 1878, and was succeeded by the firm of Holden & Glidden, the senior member of which, Mr. F. Holden, succeeded to the sole control in 1883, under the present firm name. He staff in fitted up with special reference to the trade, and thoroughly supplied with cold storage for the preservation of perishable articles in hot weather, while order and system prevails in all branches, and the entire place is a model of neatness and cleanliness. Mr. Holden is determined that everything leaving his establishment to be served to customers shall be of the very best that is reared and handled, and spares no pains nor expense in securing the choicest supplies, while his facilities for so doing are not surpassed by any of his contemporaries. He handles none but the very best meats and provisions, noted far and near for their freshness, prime quality, flavor and excellence, and every detail of the management receives his most careful supervision. His trade is large, first-class and influential in this city and throughout the surrounding country, and is annually increasing in volume and importance. Mr. Holden is a native of Boston, liberal and courteous in all his dealings, and eminently popular with his host of patrons.

THE PENINSULAR NOVELTY COMPANY, Manufacturers of Button Attaching Machines and Fasteners, No. 88 Lincoln Street.—As manufacturers of button attaching machines and fasteners, this company has become within a comparatively short space of time one of the most important and best-known of Boston institutions, whose works and products are known throughout the length and breadth of the land. It was but four short years ago that this company became incorporated and opened an office in this city, establishing its works at about the same time, in Boylston. The factory of the company at Boylston, contains three stories and a base ment, 30x90 feet in dimensions thoroughly equipped with new and improved machinery, operated by a fifty horse-power steam engine, and steady employment is furnished to fifty skilled hands. The salesrooms in this city are spacious in size, eligibly located, well stocked and ably managed, and every facility is at hand for the prompt and perfect fulfillment of orders of any magnitude. A branch factory and office is also operated at Toronto, Canada, in charge of the well known shoe finding dealer, Phillip Jacobs, and another in London, England, while the connections of the company are practically worldwide. In the construction of their specialties this company have placed all the skill and experience attainable, and the result is a product unique, utilitarian, useful, novel, and the perfection of mechanical genius and the highest order of practical ingenuity and skill. It is placed upon the market at prices which bring them within the reach of all classes of buyers, and which are satisfactory to the trade. The officers of the company at present comprise Edward O. Ely, vice-president; Geo. E. Parker, treasurer. Mr. Ely is a native of New York, while Mr. Parker is a Boston man.

THE ALLIANCE INSURANCE ASSOCIATION, of New York, Robert A. Boit, Manager, No. 40 Kilby Street.—Mr. Robert A. Boit is the authorized agent of the Commercial Union Insurance Company, of London, and the Alliance Insurance Association, of New York, in this city, and is also prominent and popular as a general fire insurance broker. The agency was originally established here in 1878, by Messrs. Crosby & Boit, the present proprietor succeeding to the sole control in 1883. His long experience in the insurance business is the best possible guarantee that he fully understands all its details, and that he can offer the very best indemnity furnished by responsible insurance corporations. He possesses unusual facilities for placing large blocks of insurance on mills, manufactories, churches, business blocks, public institutions and private residences at reasonable rates, while the officers and managers of the companies that he represents have entire confidence in his ability and integrity. This enables him to secure equal and exact justice to all parties in interest when a loss occurs, while all classes of desirable risks are placed with stable and reliable companies, perfect indemnity is offered, the prompt adjustment and speedy payment of all honest claims are guaranteed. Mr. Boit was formerly connected with the New York office of the Commercial Union, where he acquired a foundation understanding of the details and requirements of the fire insurance business. He is a prominent member of the Boston Underwriters Association and the New England Insurance Exchange.

WM. A. PERRY, Real Estate and Insurance, Room 26 Globe Building, No. 211 Washington Street.—Not many among the younger real estate and insurance brokers of Boston have been more fortunate in establishing a reputation for integrity and reliability than Mr. William A. Perry, who is a native of Rhode Island, born in Providence, but for several years a resident of this city. He has been engaged in this line since 1885, and has occupied the present quarters in the Globe Building, No. 211 Washington Street (room 26), for about two years. Mr. Perry conducts a general real estate business, and also negotiates mortgages, effecting loans at honest rates, while special attention is given to the management of estates, which are taken entire charge of and judiciously managed. Insurances placed with first-class companies, likewise, including the following staunch institutions, for which Mr. Perry is agent: The Imperial Insurance Company, of London, Eng.; the Sun Fire Insurance Company, of London, and the Continental, of New York; and altogether, quite a large and growing business is transacted.

DREW BROS., Wholesale and Retail Dealers in Flour, Tea, Coffee and Spices, and Choice Family Groceries, Etc., No. 98 Cambridge, Corner of South Russell Street, and No. 55 Anderson Street.—The reputation of this firm is of the highest, both as regards the quality of goods carried, and for enterprise and liberality in business management. The firm deal, chiefly at retail, in flour, teas, coffees and spices, and choice family groceries of all kinds, making a leading specialty of fine creamery butter. All the specialties handled by the house are bought direct from producers, trusted agents securing and transporting them daily in such quantities as the trade of the house demands. No inferior goods are kept, the custom of the house and the high character of the proprietors prohibiting the sale of any but the choicest in the market. Messrs. Drew Bros. are also the originators of the "Boston Cash Indicator and Cash Recorder," and are largely interested in the Boston Cash Indicator and Recorder Company, who are now offering to the public their new and perfected cash registering machine, the simplicity, accuracy and perfect working of which, surpasses anything of the kind yet invented. It records plainly every purchase, and foots up accurately the total amount of each day's sales. It does not make mistakes, but corrects carelessness and errors on the part of either proprietor or clerks. The Massachusetts Mechanic Association, at their last exhibition, awarded this company a silver medal and diploma. The particular points mentioned in the diploma were for ingenuity, accuracy, and simplicity in cash registering apparatus. It is patented in the United States and in England. The company is officered by Mr. James H. Wright as president, and Mr. W. W. Drew, treasurer, with the Boston office at No. 98 Cambridge Street. The firm of Drew Bros. is composed of Messrs. W. W. and Oscar Drew, born in Canada of New Hampshire parents.

DANIEL RUSSELL, Wrought Iron, Steam and Gas Pipe, and all kinds of Brass and Iron Fittings, Etc., No. 18 Howard Street.—An old established and highly successful house which has earned a reputation as a leader in its special line of trade, and which is, therefore, entitled to special commendatory notice in this volume is that of Mr. Daniel Russell, of No. 18 Howard Street. The business of this representative concern was inaugurated some twenty-one years ago by the above gentleman, in company with Mr. Thomas F. Burke, and was carried on under their joint control until 1887, when Mr. Burke's lamented death occurred. Mr. Russell conducts a general line of operations as a dealer in wrought iron, steam, and gas pipe and all kinds of brass and iron fittings, coils, heaters, pumps, steam and gas fitters' tools, hot water and steam, warming and gas lighting apparatus. He enters into contracts for steam and hot water heating, plumbing and gas piping, also sinks tubular and artesian wells, and applies hot water attachments to hot air furnaces. Estimates are furnished at the shortest notice, the prices being fixed at the most moderate scale, and contracts are carried through to completion in a manner reflecting the highest degree of finished workmanship. The premises occupied for the business have dimensions of 25x100 feet, and are equipped with the most approved mechanical devices for the prosecution of the industry. A heavy stock is constantly kept on hand of goods in the lines above named, the resources of the house being complete for meeting all demands made upon its resources. A large force of skilled workmen are employed and expedition as well as care marks the manner in which all work is executed.

WINSLOW FURNITURE CO., Furniture, Carpets, Bedding, Etc., S. Winslow, Manager, Nos. 28 and 30 Portland Street.—This enterprise was founded in 1882, upon a scale far from so extensive as that upon which it is now carried on. Year after year, however, the business has increased, capital and facilities augmenting in proportion, and new and more ample quarters occupied. In 1888 the business had so much increased, that more commodious premises became a necessity, and a removal was effected to the premises now occupied, at Nos. 28 and 30 Portland Street, near Hanover Street. These premises comprise an entire building of three floors, each 20x80 feet in dimensions, and these are stored with a complete and varied stock of goods from first hands, embracing all the newest patterns in upholstery, and the latest designs in furniture, from the most reliable manufacturers of the country. Everything which may properly belong to furnishing a house may be found here, including wilton, axminster, velvet, brussels, tapestry and ingrain carpets, oil cloths, rugs, parlor, chamber and kitchen furniture, spring beds, mattresses, bedding, curtains, draperies, folding and mantle beds, roll top desks, etc., all of which are offered at the lowest possible prices, and lower than those of most houses in the trade. A specialty is made of furnishing hotels, and here those of moderate means as well as the affluent have opportunities to gratify their tastes and desires. The manager, Mr. S. Winslow, is a native of Massachusetts, and a business man of tact, push and enterprise. The standing and reputation of the house is of the highest character, and the establishment is one meriting the liberal support it receives.

FRANK J. TRIGGS; Representing Arthur & Bonnell, Lithographers, New York; No. 12 Post Office Square.—Foremost among those who have gained a national reputation as lithographers are Messrs. Arthur & Bonnell, the noted lithographers, of No. 55 Cedar Street, New York City. This firm have been in the business since 1869, and from a small beginning have developed a trade which is only confined by the limits of the country. Their business premises have grown with their trade, and to-day their printing works are among the largest in the Union. They execute every description of lithographic work, whether for illustration of fine books or catalogues, or for securing ornamentation and neatness in design of bill heads, cards, letter headings or any kind of papers and books used in business transactions. They also manufacture blank books, account books, etc., for merchants, factories, banks, insurance companies, etc., in all forms and sizes desired, and at the lowest rates. Since 1882 the firm have had a branch office and an extensive business connection in Boston at No. 12 Post Office Square, and the establishment here is under the management of Mr. Frank J. Triggs, who has control of the whole New England trade, and who is always prepared to furnish samples and estimates for all descriptions of work desired. In his hands the business has grown and is growing.

WILLIAM WEST & CO., Manufacturing Confectioners, Cakes, Etc., No. 37 Hanover Street, 3 doors from Court Street.—One of the oldest leading confectionery and fancy bakery establishments in Boston is that of Messrs. William West & Co. This business was founded in 1851 by Mr. John Fernhoffer, to whom Mr. William West succeeded in 1868. Upon his lamented decease in 1885, his son, Mr. William West, Jr., succeeded to the proprietorship, and has actively and successfully conducted the concern. He brings to bear a wide range of experience and caters to the most refined circles of Boston society. He has here a large store, elegantly fitted up, and two spacious basements devoted to the manufacture of the choicest, pure and delicious confections of all kinds. Mr. West also produces superior wedding cakes, of the richest ingredients, and iced and ornamented in the most elaborate style. This is recognized headquarters for all kinds of cakes of the finest quality, both at wholesale and retail, and Mr. West supplies customers all over New England. He offers great inducements to the trade in handling only the purest and choicest goods.

E. E. BUTLER & CO., Produce Commission Merchants, Etc., No. 104 Commercial Street.—Among the prominent and responsible produce houses doing business on Commercial Street may be mentioned that of E. E. Butler & Co., commission merchants, and dealers in butter, cheese and eggs. This reliable and well known house was established in 1868, by the present senior member, who conducted it alone up to August last, when he admitted into partnership H. F. Upham, and thus formed the popular and prosperous firm whose name heads this sketch. They occupy for business purposes a 25x75 foot floor and cellar of equal area, and carry constantly on hand a large and fine stock, which includes butter, cheese, eggs, poultry and game in season, beans, peas, etc., while several competent assistants are in attendance. The firm handles a general line of country produce on commission, consignments being judiciously disposed of and returns for the same promptly made in every instance, and the trade of the house which is wholesale entirely is quite extensive, all orders receiving immediate attention.

THE METROPOLIS OF NEW ENGLAND.

L. STRECKER & CO., Manufacturers and Jobbers of Pants and Vests, specialty in Thin Coatings, No. 167 Summer Street.—This house was founded originally by Messrs. Strecker and Brother in 1860 at which date they embarked in the manufacture of hats and caps, and in 1870 they went into the present line of trade which was conducted under the original firm title until January, 1886, since which period it has been carried on by Mr. L. Strecker under the present firm name. The proprietor was born in Germany in 1828, but has been a resident of the United States for over half a century. He occupies spacious and commodious premises, having a frontage of forty feet with a depth of nearly three times that distance. The store, office and salesrooms are very neatly and appropriately fitted up with all the latest conveniences for the display of the large stock of goods kept constantly on hand and with every facility for the proper transaction of the large and constantly increasing business. The stock embraces a full and complete assortment of pants and vests, made up from the very finest and best imported and domestic materials in the latest styles. A careful inspection of the stock reveals the fact that the goods are made with the greatest care by experienced workmen a large force of which are kept in constant employment. The putting of these garments is performed by a full force of the most competent and artistic cutters to be found in the city, while the prices are so low as to defy competition. In addition to the manufacturing of pants and vests Mr. Strecker makes a specialty of thin coatings, and in his extensive assortment of goods in that line will be found the very best fabrics both imported and domestic, all of the very latest styles and patterns, which are offered to the trade at the lowest prices. The connections of this establishment are very large and not only embrace the city and suburbs, but extend throughout the entire New England States.

J. V. FLETCHER, Wholesale and Retail Dealer in Beef, Pork, Lard, Hams, Tallow, Pigs' Feet, Tripe, Etc., Nos. 66 and 68 Faneuil Hall Market.—A business concern conducted for the long period of fifty-six years with uninterrupted success by one person is of such a rare occurrence in these days of commercial vicissitudes as to warrant prominent mention in this work. Such is the achievement of Mr. J. V. Fletcher, the widely known and popular wholesale and retail dealer in beef, pork, lard, hams, tallow, pigs' feet, tripe, etc., occupying stalls Nos. 66 and 68 Faneuil Hall Market. Mr. Fletcher is a native of Westfield, Mass., and there he established himself in business in his present line of trade in 1828. Nine years later he removed to Faneuil Hall Market, and here for a period of fifty-one years he has been one of the most prominent and successful business men in that mart of trade, while he is now one of the, if not the oldest stall-holders in the market. He now controls a large business, in the management of which he is ably assisted by his two sons, George V. and J. H. Fletcher, both of whom were born in Charlestown. His stalls are commodious, and finely fitted up and well equipped with all necessary appliances for facilitating the transactions of the extensive business done. A very large stock is carried at all times, and as this is daily renewed it is always kept fresh, choice and wholesome. The business demands the permanent employment of seven efficient and experienced assistants, and delivery wagons are in constant service. In a wholesale way Mr. Fletcher's trade reaches to all parts of New England, and his city and near-by trade is one of considerable proportions.

CRAFTS & CO., Druggists and Apothecaries, No. 148 Commercial Street.—A time-honored and well-equipped Boston drug store is the commodious and admirably conducted establishment of Crafts & Co., druggists and apothecaries, which for upward of half a century has maintained an enduring hold on public confidence. It is, in fact, one of the oldest, largest and leading establishments of the kind in this section of the city. Physicians' prescriptions and family recipes are here prepared in the most careful and reliable manner in every instance from absolutely pure and fresh ingredients. This well and favorably known drug store was established over fifty years ago by E. Crafts, who conducted it alone up to 1872, when he associated with him in partnership H. G. Nelson, thus constituting the popular firm whose name heads the sketch, and under this style the business has since been continued with uninterrupted success, although the founder retired in 1881 and Mr. Nelson was removed by death two years later. The present proprietors are Messrs. J. W. Hunnewell & Co., the senior member of which has had a practical experience of thirty years, while the establishment is under the capable management of Dr. C. A. Place, a thoroughly competent pharmacist and skilful physician of several years' practical as well as thorough experience in the laboratory. The business premises occupy four 25x75 foot floors, including a spacious and well kept pharmacy, while three experienced assistants are in attendance. An extensive and carefully selected stock is always carried on hand, comprising everything comprehended in drugs, medicines and chemicals, extracts, acids, herbs, barks and pharmaceutical specialties, minerals, standard proprietary remedies, sanitary preparations, toilet articles, perfumery, soaps, sponges, chamois and druggists' sundries in great variety, while ships' medicine chests are furnished and also replenished in the most superior and satisfactory manner, and the trade, which is both wholesale and retail, is very large, the firm having an extensive marine patronage with coasting vessels.

PRAY & TILLSON, Diamond Cutters, Recutting a Specialty, No. 383 Washington Street, Room No. 2.—A thoroughly representative and successful house engaged in this line of business, and very popular with the trade is that of Messrs. Pray & Tillson, the individual members of which are Mr. A. B. Pray and Mr. John Tillson, both natives of the old Bay State and for many years residents of Boston, where they served a long and faithful apprenticeship in learning all the intricacies and delicate work of diamond cutting. After acquiring a thoroughly practical experience under the personal tuition of the late Henry D. Morse, they formed a copartnership and embarked in the business on their own account in May, 1887, succeeding to the wholesale trade of The Morse Diamond Cutting Co. They occupy premises of ample dimensions, of easy access at No. 383 Washington Street, (Room 2,) which are thoroughly fitted up and equipped with all the latest and best improved machinery and appliances required in the successful prosecution of their trade, being possessed of all those facilities and with their experience and knowledge of the business they are prepared to execute all orders for cutting, polishing and matching of diamonds promptly in the best manner known to the trade at very lowest prices. Their machinery is driven by steam power and none but the most experienced and skilful workmen are employed, whose operations are conducted under the immediate personal supervision of the firm. A particular specialty is made of polishing and recutting and all work of this character receives the most careful attention. Messrs. Pray and Tillson are perfect masters of their business and enjoy the fullest confidence of the trade.

ROBERT LAYCOCK, Merchant Tailor, No. 19 Bosworth Street. —Among the enterprising merchant tailors in Boston, we desire to call attention to Mr. Robert Laycock, a gentleman who has had an experience in the business extending over thirty years and who has become well known and enjoys an excellent reputation for liberal dealing and the high character of his goods and workmanship. He occupies a very desirable location under Horticultural Hall at No. 19 Bosworth Street. Mr. Laycock displays fine taste and excellent judgment in selecting his stock and exhibits a handsome assortment of new, elegant goods in the piece, embracing everything that is new and of the latest style in both foreign and domestic fabrics in suitings, trouserings, etc. Every attention is given to the cutting and fitting of wearing apparel, which is done under the immediate supervision of Mr. Laycock, who numbers among his patrons many of the leading citizens. As an expert practical cutter, he is not surpassed, and as he employs the best skilled workmen and is careful in the making and trimming, he can always guarantee the best satisfaction. No goods leave the establishment without undergoing his careful inspection and he will be found careful and accurate and indefatigable in his endeavors to please all who favor him with their patronage. Mr. Laycock who was born in Ireland, came to Montreal, Canada when quite young, where he learned his trade, and soon after located in Boston. He has been established in business on his own account only since Sept. 1888.

LANE & SMALL, Machinists, No. 280 Atlantic Avenue.—In the construction of light mechanical devices, models and electrical apparatus no firm in their line in this city excels Lane & Small, the well-known machinists, model makers and die-sinkers, whose well-equipped shop is located at No. 280 Atlantic Avenue. They are, in fact, among the leaders in their special line in Boston, and have a large, active and growing business. Messrs. F. Lane and F. E. Small, who compose the firm, are comparatively young men and natives of this city. They are both practical and expert machinists of several years' experience, and are thorough masters of the art in all its features and phases, while Mr. Lane is a skillful electrician likewise. They commenced business on their own account in November, 1885, moving to the present commodious quarters in 1887, and the unequivocal success that has attended their efforts from the start abundantly attests the excellence of the work turned out as well as the wisdom that inspired the venture. They occupy a 25x75 floor, with ample steam power and all necessary machinery and general appurtenances, and employ a competent force of skilled mechanics. Light mechanical work of every description is executed in the most expeditious and excellent manner; fire alarms and electrical appliances being specialties, while punches, dies and kindred devices are made to order in first-class style at short notice. Models are constructed, also, with the utmost fidelity to drawing, particular attention being given to patents and experimental work, and all work done in this establishment is executed under the close personal supervision of the proprietors.

KILBORN, WHITMAN & CO., Manufacturers of Fine Parlor Furniture, Etc., No. 46 Canal Street.—Prominent among the various houses of enterprise and refinement in the city of Boston, successfully engaged in the manufacture and sale of fine parlor furniture, etc., is that of Messrs. Kilborn, Whitman & Co. The factory of the house, which is fully supplied with modern tools, machinery and appliances, and furnishes constant employment to 100 skilled cabinet-makers and operatives, is situated at Chelsea. The business was established eighteen years ago by Palmer & Whitman, who conducted it until 1878, when, on the retirement of Mr. Palmer, Mr. Whitman became sole proprietor, and is now carrying on the business under the firm name of Kilborn, Whitman & Co. He manufactures extensively all kinds of fine parlor furniture, easy chairs, reclining chairs, lounges, rockers, stands, etc., and makes a specialty of odd pieces. Much of his parlor furniture is made from the rarest woods, including mahogany, cherry, cocobla, French walnut, rosewood, ebony, etc., which, from their fine grain and richness of color, always sustain such a high finish. His upholsteries are of the finest quality, the richest stuffs, of all desirable shades and textures, being used in his parlor suits. Mr. Whitman promptly fills all orders at the lowest possible prices, and his trade, which is chiefly wholesale, extends throughout the United States and New Brunswick. The premises occupied in Boston comprise a spacious six-story building, 25x120 feet in area, with one floor of the adjoining store. These are fully stocked with a superior assortment of furniture and specialties of his own manufacture. Mr. Whitman was born in Pembroke, Mass., but has resided in Boston for the last thirty years.

UNION STEAM SPONGING WORKS, M. Crohn, Proprietor; No. 17 South Street.—The Union Steam Sponging Works, under the proprietorship of Mr. M. Crohn, was established originally upon a small scale by Mr. Louis Crohn, father of the present proprietor, in 1858, and since that date has always enjoyed a very liberal and substantial patronage. Mr. M. Crohn succeeded to the business in 1873, and owing to the rapidly increasing trade was obliged to seek more commodious quarters, and accordingly removed to his present stand in 1883. The premises utilized are spacious and commodious, eligibly located and fitted up with all the latest improved machinery and conveniences, in order to be able to meet the constantly increasing demands of the trade. Steam power is used for driving the machinery and constant employment is furnished to a sufficient force of competent and reliable workmen whose operations are conducted under the immediate supervision of the proprietor. The trade is derived principally from among the very best class of merchant tailors and ready made clothing manufacturers of this city and vicinity. By the aid of the steam power and machinery employed Mr. Crohn is prepared to do all kinds of sponging fine cloths, cassimeres, suitings, etc., at the very shortest notice and in the most satisfactory manner, and at rates that cannot fail to suit customers. He is also prepared to execute all orders for rolling, folding and unfolding all kinds of fabrics which may be shelf worn, in the neatest and most workmanlike manner, making such goods have a new and bright appearance.

HOWARD COON & CO., Masons, Contractors and Builders, Office, No. 17 Milk Street.—One of the best equipped and most responsible among the leading firms engaged in the general building trade in Boston is that of Howard Coon & Co., masons, contractors and builders, whose office is located at No. 17 Milk Street, with capacious wharf and storehouse at No. 57 Main Street, Cambridgeport. This popular and reliable firm was established some ten years since, and its career from the start has been a record of steady progress, constructing some notable pieces of work, among which may be mentioned the pavilion of the Boston base ball grounds, W. L. Lockhart's block, and several other substantial pieces of architecture. The firm is prepared to enter into contracts for stone or brick work, constructing either part or the whole of buildings, but makes a leading specialty of large and massive structures; while estimates on all classes of masonry and building are promptly furnished, and all work entrusted to this firm is certain to be executed in the most expeditious and excellent manner. An efficient force of skilled hands are regularly employed, while a complete equipment and all necessary facilities are in service; and the trade of the firm, which extends throughout the New England States, is of a highly flattering character. Mr. Coon, who is the sole member, the "Co." being nominal, is a native of this city. He is a practical and expert mason, of ample experience, and is an active and well-known member of the Master Builders' Association and Mechanics' Exchange.

PATTEN & STRATTON, Photographer, No. 47 Hanover Street.—Patten & Stratton photographers, by turning out first-class work at reasonable prices, have gained control of a large and constantly increasing patronage. The business was founded some twenty years ago by a Mr. Turner, and in 1876 the style of the house became J. D. Patten & Co., which, in 1888, was changed to the present one of Patten & Stratton. The office and reception room are located on the third floor, and are elegantly furnished and provided with every accommodation. The operating room, on the fourth floor, is equipped with all the latest improved appliances known to the profession. Every description of photographic work is executed in the highest style of the art, a specialty being made of instantaneous photographs. Particular attention is also given to enlargements in oil, chromo, water colors, india ink, etc., for which class of work the house has special facilities. The productions of this house will bear the most rigid criticism, as no picture is permitted to leave the establishment that is not perfect in every detail.

H. & A. MORSE & CO., Coal, No. 104 State Street.—Messrs. H. & A. Morse & Co. established their business here in 1874. They handle Philadelphia & Reading Coal & Iron Company's coals, hard white ash, free burning white ash, North Franklin, Shamokin, Lorberry and Lykens Valley coals; Old Company's Lehigh and Jermyn white ash coal; also George's Creek and Cumberland coal, and possess unsurpassed facilities for the prompt filling of all orders by car and cargo lots, shipments being made direct from the mines to customers in all parts of New England. The coals above named have no rivals as powerful heat producers, and sustain combustion in a manner that insures the greatest economy for manufacturing, steam and domestic purposes; while all coal purchased of this responsible house is guaranteed to maintain in every respect the highest standard of excellence, and holds the front rank as regards the care exercised in its preparation for the market, coming as it does from the best-equipped collieries in America. The resources of the house are such that the largest orders can be filled at short notice, while all connections sustained with mines and miners enable the firm to offer the rarest inducements in terms and prices.

THE METROPOLIS OF NEW ENGLAND. 301

HENRY L. ALBEE & CO., Manufacturers of Folding Beds, Etc., Nos. 30-36 Washington Street.—Few articles of furniture are so useful at the present day as a good folding bed, largely met by the folding bed, which pays for itself in a few months by saving the rent of an extra room. In this connection we desire to make special reference in this commercial review of Boston, to the representative and successful firm of Messrs. Henry L. Albee & Co., manufacturers of folding beds, etc., whose office and salesrooms are located at Nos. 30-36 Washington Street. The factories of this reliable house are at Melrose and No. 163 Friend Street, Boston. Mr. Henry L. Albee who is sole proprietor, established this business in 1872, since which period he has secured a liberal and influential patronage in all sections of New England.

His salesrooms are spacious, and are fully stocked with an excellent assortment of folding beds, curled hair, feathers, mattresses, pillows, cushions and fine bedding, which are unrivalled for quality and reliability, and have no superior in this country. His folding beds include the varieties known as the upright wardrobe, folding cabinet, desk and book case, lounge and couch beds, also chiffonnier beds and Albee's famous parlor sofa bed. Mr. Albee's parlor and sofa bed was awarded a medal in 1882 at the Massachusetts Charitable Mechanics' Association for its superiority over all competitors. For many years the parlor and sofa beds have been greatly admired by householders for their beauty and convenience, but their high price has hitherto prevented many from using them; this obstacle has now been removed by Mr. Albee, who has brought them within the reach of all. Mr. Albee is a native of Boston.

D. T. CHARD & CO., Manufacturers and Dealers in Fine Cigars No. 150 Water Street.—A leading representative house in the manufacture and sale of fine cigars in this city is that of D. T. Chard & Co., located at No. 150 Water Street. The business was originally established in 1882 by Messrs. Little & Chard, the present firm succeeding to the control in January, 1888. The premises occupied for manufacturing and trade purposes comprise four spacious floors, and every modern facility is at hand for conducting the business under the most favorable auspices and upon the largest scale. Employment is given to some fifty skilled hands, and the output is one of great magnitude and variety. The leading brands of cigars here manufactured comprise the Pullman, La Fortuna, D. T. C., Pantello, 150, and others, while special and private brands are made to order. The specialties above named have attained an enormous consumption all over the country, and have been conscientiously maintained at the highest standard of excellence. They are handled by the best retailers in this city and elsewhere, and are recognized as staples wherever introduced. They are deservedly popular for the splendid quality of tobacco used, as well as for purity and care in their manufacture, and are considered by connoisseurs and critical judges as the most fragrant, agreeable and reliable cigars in the market. To those tobacconists who desire to cater to the best class of trade and to attract new custom, we would recommend this house as every way worthy of their confidence and patronage. All orders and commissions are promptly filled at terms which preclude successful competition.

EDWARD D. HOLMES, Lumber and Lime, No. 71 Kilby Street.—As prime factors in the building trade, lumber and lime in the very nature of things, are articles of surpassing importance the handling of which constitutes one of the great branches of commercial activity in every large city. The transactions in these useful and indispensable products through the medium of merchants here in Boston, reach vast magnitude annually, while the volume of business grows apace. Among the rising and responsible dealers in lumber and lime in this city, can be named E. D. Holmes, whose office is at No 71 Kilby Street (Room 12), and who, although established in business on his own account but a comparatively short time, has built up a very substantial connection. Mr. Holmes, who is a young man and a native of Boston, is a gentleman of entire probity in his dealings, as well as a man of energy and experience, and prior to establishing himself in business, in 1886, had been for a number of years actively connected with several prominent lumber firms. Mr. Holmes handles northern, western and southern lumber, both hard and soft, also lime, and does a good business, selling principally to dealers and large consumers, by the car load, and is prepared to fill all orders for anything in his line, in the most prompt and reliable manners.

WOOD BROTHERS, Paints, Oils, Etc., No. 12 Sudbury Street.—This popular and prosperous firm was established fourteen years or more ago, and from the start Messrs. Wood have enjoyed an excellent patronage. They occupy ample and compact quarters at No 12 Sudbury Street, with commodious storehouse, also at Central Wharf, while four or more clerks and store hands are employed. A heavy and very fine stock is constantly carried on hand, comprising everything in the line of paints, oils, varnishes, colors, putty, glass, brushes and painters' supplies in great variety, the firm being proprietors of the following meritorious articles: Falcon Ivory Black in Japan, Harvard Ready Mixed Paint, Harvard Green, German Vermilion, Hamburg Red; and are sole agent for House and Villa Ready Mixed Paint, Steamboat Paste Paint, Mander's English Varnishes, Bigelows' Fine Varnishes, Parrotts' Fine Varnishes, Littlefields' Enamel Top Dressing, Masury's Japan and Oil Colors; and the trade of the concern extends all over the New England states.

HARRISON, BEARD & CO., Manufacturers of Furniture and Fine Cabinet Work, No. 129 Friend Street, Factory; No. 425 Medford Street, Charlestown.—This concern, the leading representative in its line dates its inception back to 1870, when the firm of Daniels, Harrison & Co., was formed. In 1873 they dissolved and the present firm was then organized, composed of Samuel J. Harrison, James M. Beard and Albert T. Johnson. Their business has been a marked success, and has grown at a rapid ratio, both the retail trade and public at large, recognizing the superiority, originality, elegance and durability of their product. Their factory is in the Charlestown District, and is extensive and fully equipped with the latest improved machinery and appliances. Upwards of fifty of the most skillful cabinet makers and carvers obtainable are there employed in the manufacture of full lines of the finest furniture, wainscotings, mantels, and interior fittings, carvings, etc., for the finest mansions. The firm exercise the greatest care in the selection of their materials, using only the choicest of mahogany, rosewood, French walnut, oak, ash, cherry, maple, and numerous other rare woods both foreign and domestic. The firm originate designs which are of the highest order of merit and are sought for in fashionable circles, and turn out elaborate parlor and chamber sets. They also manufacture all descriptions of library and dining-room, furniture, hall stands, chairs and racks, tables, desks, etc., and all kinds of high-class cabinet work generally. In their Friend Street salesrooms they make the most attractive display known to the trade, and one that offers the most substantial inducements to purchasers, both as to price and quality.

DUNSHEE & CO., Photographers, No. 3 Tremont Row.—This firm enjoy a high reputation and a widespread patronage as artist photographers, possessing a prestige and a popularity that place them in the front rank, not only in this city but throughout the entire country. The business was originally established in 1866 by Mr. E. S. Dunshee, who was succeeded in 1878 by his nephew, Mr. F. F. Dunshee, and in 1886 the present firm was organized by the admission of Mr. F. H. Maxfield to partnership. The premises occupied include a handsomely furnished reception room and a well equipped operating room, and every modern facility is afforded for conducting all branches of the business under the most favorable conditions. Photography in all its branches is executed in the highest style of the art, and crayon, pastel, India ink, oil and kindred artistic work being accomplished in the most superior and expeditious manner, and all at popular prices. A specialty is made of coupon tickets, which are issued in an unlimited number, and good until used, for one dozen cabinet photographs at $3.00. Mr. Dunshee is a native of Toledo, Ohio, and resides in the town of Malden. Mr. Maxfield was born in the state of Maine, and is a resident of Chelsea.

GEO. A. WARE, Wholesale Dealer in Barbers' Supplies, Manufacturer of Cosmetique, Soap, Camphor Ice, Oils, Bay Rum, Mustache Wax, Etc., No. 21 School Street.—An important business, well-represented by Mr. George A. Ware, is that of manufacturing and dealing in barbers' supplies. It was established about two years ago by J. C. Hursell & Co.; Mr. Ware being a member of the firm, and succeeded to the business some six months ago. The third floor of the building, No. 21 School Street, is occupied. It is of ample dimensions and affords every facility for manufacturing purposes and the display of a large stock of goods, which includes a great variety of articles belonging to the business. Mr. Ware is the sole manufacturer of cosmetique, camphor ice, hair oils, bay rum, mustache wax, and, also, Hursell's Purity, and is the New England agent for J. S. Kirk's shaving soap. The business is conducted on a wholesale and retail basis, and is not confined to the city and vicinity, but extends to all parts of New England. Mr. Ware also decorates shaving mugs to order in all styles, and furnishes ornamental bay rum and tonic bottles, and is doing a large business buying and selling new and second-hand barbers' chairs, furniture, etc.

M. F. HANSON, Boarding, Hack and Livery Stable, No. 32 Charles Street and No. 3 Willow Street.—This enterprise has been in operation for some forty years, and under the proprietorship of Mr. Hanson since 1883. The stable is a substantial brick structure, two stories high, 60x80 feet in dimensions, thoroughly equipped with every requisite, well ventilated, lighted and drained, and possessing first-class accommodations for thirty-two horses. The best of conveniences are at hand for baiting, and every possible care and attention is given to horses entrusted to the charge of this house by experienced grooms and stablemen. The proprietor owns a large number of the most stylish equipages to be seen in the city, and his stock of horses kept for hire include those suitable for ladies' or invalid's use, as well as others noted for their speed and staying qualities. Among the vehicles are to be found elegant coaches, carriages, coupes, landaus, hacks, buggies and road wagons, and stylish, safe and reliable turn-outs are let for business or pleasure, day and night, on very moderate terms. The house is also prepared to supply parties, funerals, weddings and excursions with any number of carriages at short notice, and first-class coupes and coaches are kept for shopping or visiting. A corps of fourteen hands contribute to the satisfactory operations of the house, and the patronage is large, first-class and permanent among the best classes of society. Mr. Hanson is a New Hampshire man by birth, a resident of Boston since 1853.

W. H. EMERSON, Importer and Dealer in Molasses and Sugar, No. 9 Central Street.—Mr. W. H. Emerson, the well-known importer and dealer in domestic sugar and molasses, has been established in the business here since 1874, while his experience in this line of trade covers a period of twenty-five years. He makes a specialty of supplying sugar refiners with raw goods, and his trade is not exclusively confined to the Boston market, but being a large receiver of New Orleans Molasses, (only one other northern house receiving as much) he does a large business in this line with the wholesale grocers of New York, Philadelphia and all the large cities of the north and east. His resources are large and ample and his connections abroad are thoroughly perfected. His relations with the foreign growers and shippers are of that intimate and influential character which enables him to command every favorable opportunity for procuring supplies in vast quantities and at advantageous rates, and to guarantee the prompt and satisfactory fulfillment of all orders. Mr. Emerson is a native Bostonian, in the prime of life, and a well-known citizen of Cambridge. He is largely interested in the Oxnard Sugar Refinery on Atlantic Avenue, in this city.

H. E. CLEMENT & CO., Watches, Jewelry and Diamonds, No. 19 Milk Street, Room 56.—This thriving and responsible firm was established in 1883, moving to the present location in October 1887, and from the start has steadily pushed its way to popularity and patronage, building up a large trade throughout the city and state. At their place of business, No. 19 Milk Street, (Room 56), will be found a full and first-class assortment, which embraces fine gold and silver watches, diamonds, solid silver and plated ware, opera glasses and optical goods. Watches, jewelry, etc., are repaired likewise in the most prompt and excellent manner at very reasonable rates; fine watch repairing being a specialty, and all work executed here is fully warranted to render satisfaction. Goods are sold either for cash or on easy payments by the week or month, and purchasers are assured of getting honest value and satisfactory treatment at the very lowest figures consistent with a first-class article and upright dealing.

E. M. WILSON, D. D. S., Dentist, No. 116 Court Street.—Among those well known and prominent as dentists in this city there are none more popular or more successful than E. M. Wilson, D. D. S., who has been practicing his profession for the past twenty years and has occupied the handsome commodious office, No. 116 Court Street, since 1886. Dr. Wilson is a regular graduate of the Boston Dental College, and is a practical expert in all branches of the science. He is particularly skillful in filling and preserving the natural teeth and in making artificial teeth singly or in sets and extracts teeth by the latest improved methods. The doctor numbers among his patients many of the leading families of this city and vicinity and is highly recommended for his care and skill in all operations.

W. F. DOWLER, Draying and Working Horses, Nos. 196 and 198 Canal street.—This gentleman has been established in business here since 1874, and deals extensively at private sale, in New York and Pennsylvania horses, making a specialty of handling those suitable for use in the fire department and other city business, as well as for general trucking and carting. His stable is spacious in size, accommodating forty horses. Special care is taken by Mr. Dowler to select such horses as will meet the demands of his patrons and all in want of a first-class, reliable animal. Truck, cart engine and hose horses are kept constantly on hand, and his facilities for filling orders in these lines and for supplying first-class stock at low prices are rarely equalled and never excelled in this city. He is in frequent receipt of carloads of horses, of a quality and character for both driving and working, that commend them to the confidence and patronage of close and critical buyers. Square dealing and the widely known worth of the propels he have always inspired the fullest confidence and established this house in the general esteem as a reliable representative. Mr. Dowler is a native of New York State, and a resident of Charlestown.

I. COHN, Clothing, Gent's Furnishing Goods, Etc., Nos. 39 and 41 Kneeland Street.—One of the leading and popular local establishments in its important branch of mercantile industry, is that of Mr. I. Cohn, dealer in clothing, gent's furnishing goods, hats, caps, boots and shoes. The spacious premises consist of two floors of a building 75x35 feet in surface dimensions and the salesrooms are fitted up in a remarkably neat and attractive style. The stock displayed is carefully selected from the best markets and represents the finest goods, newest novelties, and latest and most fashionable styles in the staple goods above enumerated. Four experienced clerks are in courteous attendance upon the many patrons, and the house has an enviable reputation for first-class goods and fair and equitable dealing. Mr. Cohn, although still a young man has had a wide business experience, and possesses a comprehensive and valuable knowledge of the trade, he having served for some years as a clerk.

GUSTAVO PRESTON, Commission Merchant, No. 37 Central street.—The wholesale handling of sugar, syrups and kindred grocers' specialties, and the products of the West Indies and Spain through the medium of commission houses in Boston, annually reaches enormous proportions. Prominent among those engaged in this particular line in this city is Gustavo Preston, the well known commission merchant and importer of Chanze's triple flavor bay rum, sugar, molasses, salt olives, Almeira grapes, etc. Mr. Preston was born at Porto Rico, West Indies, but has lived in Boston since boyhood. He has been established in business since 1882, and from the first has been uniformly successful; his trade, which is large and active, extending throughout the New England States, and also to New York. Mr. Preston handles besides the goods enumerated, also a general line of Spanish and West India products, and is a direct importer and commission merchant, receiving consignments regularly; and is prepared to fill all orders for the trade in the most expeditious and reliable manner.

S. B. LOGAN, Auctioneer, Real Estate and Insurance Agent, No. 47 State street.—Mr. S. B. Logan, the popular and reliable auctioneer, real estate and insurance agent and a Justice of the Peace, likewise has been engaged in this line for over twenty years, and has established an extensive and substantial business connection throughout Boston and environs, numbering among his clientele some of the staunchest citizens in the community. He carries on a general real estate business, buying, selling, exchanging and renting city and country property of all kinds, and also negotiates mortgages; while rents are collected likewise; special attention being given to the care and management of estates. Insurance is effected in first-class fire companies at lowest rates, Mr. Logan being local agent also for the insurance company of North America. In short, everything connected with the purchase, sale and management of realty and the insurance brokerage is attended to in the most judicious and satisfactory manner. Mr. Logan was born at Halifax, N. S., but has resided in Boston some forty odd years, and is a prominent member of the Fire Insurance Brokers' Association.

I. L. PRATT & CO., Metals, New and Old; No. 34 India street.—A firm who have established a first-class name as dealers in metals, new and old, is that of I. L. Pratt & Co., of No. 34 India Street. This well-conducted concern was established in 1886 by I. L. Pratt who had a long experience in handling metals and business capacity of the highest order. In the spring of 1888 he admitted into partnership his son, L. T. Pratt and under their joint management the house has extended its operations in a marked degree. The premises occupied by the firm from the start comprise the store and cellar of a fine four story building, in dimensions 25x106 feet with a factory at Border Street, East Boston. Messrs. I. L. Pratt & Co. are large dealers in metals, new and old, ingot copper, spelter, lead, tin, ingot brass, etc., and make a specialty of old metals which are melted in their furnace and sold to founders throughout the country. They employ several men in their establishment and have a trade extending all over New England as well as Missouri, Ohio, New Jersey, New York, Baltimore and various points west.

R. S. HOOD, Broker in Old R. R. Iron and Scrap, No. 249½ Central Street.—Mr. R. S. Hood, broker in old railroad iron and scrap, buys for and sells to foundries, rolling mills etc., old iron of every description, but makes a specialty of old rails; transactions being by car lots exclusively, and his trade which extends throughout the New England States, is of a very substantial character. He has been engaged in business on his own account over five years, and has established a large permanent connection; and is prepared to fill all orders for anything in this line in the most reliable manner. Mr. Hood, who is a native of Nova Scotia, is a young man of ample experience, and enterprise, and prior to starting in business for himself in 1889, had been employed for some time as bookkeeper in the same line.

J. N. BROOKS, Cotton Buyer, Room 68, Nos. 53 and 55 Kilby Street.—For more than twenty-three years Mr. Brooks has been actively and successfully engaged in this important branch of commercial activity, and during the entire period he has conducted business in the same building which he at present occupies with unbroken prosperity. He handles cotton, on commission exclusively, and buys for manufacturers of cotton fabrics throughout the New England States, shipping direct from the south to the mills, and has a fine business connection. Mr. Brooks, who is a gentleman in the prime of life, active and energetic, was born in New Hampshire, but has been a resident of this city many years.

E. A. COSTIGAN, Shipwright & Caulker, No. 94 Commercial Street.—A well-known representative in this business is Mr. E. A. Costigan who has been established in it for thirty years, and located in the premises now occupied, since 1878. He has always conducted a large business and employed at times upwards of half a hundred competent workmen. A native of Charlestown and a resident of Dorchester, he has for many years been prominently conspicuous in the business affairs of Boston, and is well-known in shipping and commercial circles. He does the best class of work and is highly endorsed and recommended as a thoroughly reliable master workman. He furnishes estimates for all work in his line, and makes contracts and gives his prompt attention to all orders entrusted to him. He is one of the oldest shipwrights and caulkers in the city.

MAURICE REARDON, Manufacturer of Horse Collars, Nos. 44 and 46 Sudbury Street.—Mr. Maurice Reardon is a celebrated manufacturer of horse collars. His are the best in the United States without exception. They are as perfect a fit as fine custom shoes for men. Mr. Reardon started in business here thirty five years ago, and early achieved an enviable reputation for the superiority of his product. He is recognized by leading horse owners, as being the most expert manufacturer of horse collars in the country, and also promptly attends to the repairing of collars and harness. His collars are all hand work, possessing features of excellence not found in any other make, and every man interested in securing to his horse the greatest comfort and capacity for work or speeding, should have one of Reardon's collars. It will prove an invaluable investment.

304   ILLUSTRATED BOSTON.

T. McCOSKER, Portrait and Commercial Photographer, No. 51 Washington Street.—Mr. T. McCosker is a thorough artist and fully understands all the details necessary to complete a satisfactory photograph and in his fine portrait work there is always a pleasing variety, the pose being characterized by an ease and grace and a superiority of finish seldom obtained. Mr. McCosker takes pride in all his work, and copies and enlarges pictures which are finished in ink, crayon, oil, water colors or pastile as may be desired, with a neatness, elegance and perfection unequalled. He also gives particular attention to commercial photography and in this direction executes orders for many of the leading representative manufacturing and business houses in this city and vicinity. A native of New York, Mr. McCosker, who has been established in business since 1861, has been located in the premises now occupied during the past five years and has established a reputation placing him in the front rank among the most distinguished artists in the city. The premises which consist of a neatly, handsomely arranged parlor and thoroughly equipped operating room, 25x60 feet in area, contains many beautiful specimens of his artistic handiwork. Among his customers are to be found many of the leading citizens of Boston and suburbs, and to assist him in his operation, four skilled photographers are employed.

D. TOY, Tailor and Draper, No. 31 Charles Street.—One of the most genial, popular and marked by skillful and painstaking custom tailors and drapers of Boston is Mr. D. Toy, who brings to bear an experience of over thirty-three years, derived from permanent connection with the best circles of the trade in Europe and here, and since starting in business in 1874, he has developed a widespread, desirable connection. Fashionable tailoring is done here on correct principles, and gentlemen can here be measured with a guarantee of securing the latest styles, choicest imported fabrics and superior workmanship. Mr. Toy's skill as a cutter has long been recognized; he is remarkably successful in accurately meeting the requirements of every figure, and spares no pains to suit the most fastidious. He carries a large and most desirable stock of imported fabrics, including all the newest shades, patterns and textures in coatings, pantaloon stuffs, for overcoats, etc. He makes to order from measure with a guarantee of perfect fitting garments and has the permanent patronage of many of the leading citizens and merchants of Boston and New England, also a trade all over the United States. His old customers find themselves better suited here, and both as to style, durability comfort and fine finish every essential is a certainty with garments emanating from this well-known establishment.

OLD COLONY GROCERY, Wm. C. Coolidge, Proprietor, No. 235 South Street.—A well ordered and first-class general grocery establishment is the popular and well known Old Colony Grocery. Wm. C. Coolidge, proprietor, where can always be found a full and fine assortment of everything comprehended under the head of fancy and staple groceries, and patrons are assured of getting honest weight and measure, as well as a very superior article and prompt and polite attention in every instance here, while the prices prevailing maintained at the lowest figures, consistent with excellent goods and honorable dealing. This prosperous business was established many years ago by the father of the gentleman whose name heads the sketch, and was formerly conducted on Beach Street, where the present proprietor assumed control some twenty years since, subsequently moving to Kneeland Street, whence it was removed to the commodious quarters now occupied about four years ago. The store, which is 30x72 feet in dimensions, is finely fitted up and well arranged, while two competent assistants are in attendance. A large and first-class stock is kept constantly on hand, comprising choice teas and coffees, pure, fresh spices, condiments, baking powder, pickles, preserves, canned goods in great variety and table delicacies, sugars, syrups, prepared cereals, dried fruit, fine wines, liquors and bottled goods, prime dairy and creamery butter, cheese and fresh eggs, lard, smoked meats and fish, best brands of family flour, oatmeal, cornmeal, rice, beans, peas, soda, salt, saleratus, soap, starch, shelf goods, etc., etc.; all orders receiving immediate attention.

WILLIAM EGIN, Manufacturer of Pipes, No. 41 Beverly Street.—For the past twenty-six years William Egin, manufacturer of all kinds of iron pipes and general sheet-iron worker, now located at No. 41 Beverly Street, has been engaged in business on his own account, and during this entire period he has maintained a well deserved reputation for skill and reliability, while his trade, which is large and prosperous, extends throughout the greater portion of the New England States, with a fine local patronage also. Mr. Egin, who is a man in the prime of life, and a native of Boston, is a thoroughly practical sheet-iron worker himself, of long and varied experience, and is a master of his art in all its branches. He occupies as shop a 50x75 foot (third) floor, with ample and excellent facilities, and employs a large force of skilled workmen. Mr. Egin manufactures everything in the line of iron pipes for piping blowers for shavings, saw dust, emery wheels, rag and cotton pickers, grain elevators, foul air, gas, smoke, etc., also hot air pipes of every description; in short, pipes of all kinds and sizes, piping blowers being a specialty, while estimates are cheerfully furnished upon application. Sheet-iron work of all kinds is executed also in the most expeditious and superior manner, and jobbing likewise promptly and reliably attended to; all orders receiving immediate attention.

H. P. EMERSON & CO., Manufacturers' Agents, Fancy Goods and Small Wares, No. 15 Kingston Street.—This firm established business here in 1874, and have built up a reputation and a trade that places them in the front rank of enterprise, popularity and success. They occupy spacious and well-appointed salesrooms, and are in a position to conduct their business under the most favorable conditions. They handle the choicest productions known to the trade in fancy goods and small wares, as agents for the manufacturers, and make large and valuable shipments to all parts of the United States and Canada. They carry a full and complete assortment in stock, including the latest styles and freshest novelties in every line, while the favorable conditions under which purchases are made enable them to offer inducements to customers in terms and prices that are of the most advantageous character. The lines represented will be found as rich and attractive as it is possible to make them, while the selections are made with that taste and judgment which involve a thorough and intimate knowledge of the wants of the trade.

WM. A. CARRIE, Bank Stationer, Lithographer and Printer, No. 84 Devonshire Street.—Among the active, energetic young business men in this city, there are probably none more enterprising than Mr. Wm. A. Carrie, the popular bank stationer, who occupies the commodious basement under the National Bank of the Commonwealth. He has had many years' experience in this line of business and during the three years he has been established he has built up a large flourishing business, derived from the banks, insurance companies and merchants, and is fully equal in every respect to that of any other dealers in the city. Lithographing and commercial and general printing, is a feature of the business which is carried on extensively, the work being executed in every variety of style. Mr. Carrie is a native of Ontario, Canada, but has been a resident of the United States many years, and was brought up in Chicago. He has had eleven years' experience in the stationery and printing business, and was for a long time with the firm of J. C. Hall & Co., of Providence, R. I.

J. M. RODONACHI, Importer of Smyrna and Mediterranean Products, No. 79 Milk Street, Room 21.—An old-established and responsible Boston merchant, engaged in the handling of Smyrna and Mediterranean products, is Mr. J. M. Rodonachi, whose office is located at No. 79 Milk Street (Room 21). He is one of the very oldest and foremost merchants in this particular branch of commercial activity in Boston. Mr. Rodonachi was born in Smyrna, Asia Minor, but has resided in this city since 1858, having been the Greek Consul here for some twenty four years. Mr. Rodonachi is a direct importer of general products from Smyrna and the Mediterranean ports, making a leading specialty, however, of the importing of figs and emery, and is prepared to fill all orders for anything in this line in the most prompt and reliable manner. His business connection extends throughout the whole of the United States.

ISAAC H. DINNER, Ladies' Travelling Caps and Tennis Caps, No. 117 Summer Street.—In no industry has enterprise been so plainly demonstrated as in the manufacture of hats and caps. Thus, we find one house making a cheap line of silk hats, another a superior grade of the same article, another devoting all its energies to straw goods, another to the production of

caps, and so on through the whole category. A prominent manufacturer in this city, who was one of the first to recognize the advantages to be derived from making a special line of caps, is Mr. Isaac H. Dinner, of No. 117 Summer Street. This gentleman started business on Chauncy Street, in 1878 as a member of the firm of Alexander, Foster & Dinner. Subsequently the firm was changed to Alexander & Dinner, and in 1881 Mr. Dinner became the sole proprietor. Five years ago he removed to his present premises, No. 117 Summer Street, where he occupies two floors, each 30x100 feet in dimensions. One of these is used as a stock room, and the other for manufacturing purposes. Mr. Dinner confines himself to the production of superior grades of ladies' travelling and ten-

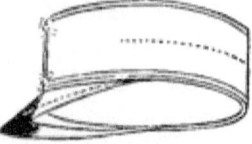

nis caps, making a specialty of children's fancy caps, and to selling direct to the trade. His newly patented driving cap protects the forehead from the sharp, penetrating wind in severe winter weather, and is the most comfortable and most salable cap yet placed on the market. They are made of the finest beaver and elysian goods in blue, brown and black, for the best trade only. The business has been a remarkably successful one from the start, and a large distributing trade has been established throughout New England, the West and Canada. Mr. Dinner, who is a native of Germany, has resided in Boston since boyhood, and has gained success by deserving it.

G. LAMKIN & CO., Manufacturers of Boots and Shoes, No. 28 Tremont Row.—Prominent among the representative and reliable boot and shoe manufacturers of the city of Boston, is the popular firm of Messrs. G. Lamkin & Co., whose office and salesroom are located at No. 28 Tremont Row. This business was established thirty-five years ago by Mr. G. Lamkin, who conducted it till 1881, when Mr. G. L. Boyce became a partner. The firm's factory, which is one of the best equipped in the country and furnishes constant employment to 500 operatives, is situated at Milford, Conn. They manufacture largely all kinds of ladies', misses' and children's fine shoes, also men's, boys' and youths' boots and shoes, and they likewise deal extensively in rubbers. Their boots and shoes are made from the best materials, and none but first-class hands are employed in their manufacture, while every detail as to quality and reliability of stock, character of workmanship, style and finish, is carefully supervised by experts, before the goods are allowed to leave the factory. In the Boston store of the firm, a large stock of all descriptions of boots and shoes is constantly on hand, and the prices quoted necessarily attract the attention of close and careful buyers. At the Massachusetts Charitable Mechanic Association, 1881, G. Lamkin & Co., were awarded a medal for their fine shoes. The trade is both wholesale and retail, and now extends throughout New England, New York, the Middle and Western States. Mr. G. Lamkin was born in Vermont, but has resided in Boston for the last forty years, while his partner, Mr. Boyce, is likewise a native of Vermont. They are highly regarded in trade circles for their enterprise and integrity, and those interested requiring first-class boots and shoes cannot do better than give their orders to this responsible house, where they will obtain advantages in goods and prices, very difficult to be secured elsewhere.

STEPHEN L. BARTLETT, Teas, Cocoas and Chocolates, Sole Importer of Bensdorp's Royal Dutch Cocoas and Chocolates, No. 27 Broad street.—Among the most successful and best known houses engaged in the wholesale handling of teas, cocoas and chocolates that have come into existence of recent years in Boston may be named that of Stephen L. Bartlett, whose office and salesroom are located at No. 27 Broad Street. This prosperous business was established in 1880 by the firm of W. L. Hill & Co., of which the present proprietor was the junior member, and under the style mentioned was conducted up to June, 1888, when Mr. Bartlett assumed sole control, and has since continued it alone with uninterrupted success. He handles a general line of teas, cocoas and chocolates, importing direct, and makes a speciality of fine grades of cocoas, while he is sole importer of Bensdorp's Royal Dutch cocoas and chocolates. Mr. Bartlett occupies for office purposes the whole of a 25x75 foot floor, and carries constantly on hand a complete and first class stock, while several competent salesmen are in attendance. The transactions of the house are with wholesale dealers and jobbers; all orders for the trade being promptly and reliably attended to, and the business which embraces the sale in the United States and Canada, is large and active and very extensive; giving evidence of steady and substantial increase.

MILLER & SON, Manufacturing Confectioners, Factory, No. 170 Canal Street.—Among the leading and best known candy manufacturers that have come into prominence of recent years in Boston may be named Miller & Son, manufacturing confectioners, whose productions are in steady and growing demand in the trade throughout New England, owing to their general excellence. The goods produced by this firm are of a very superior quality, being made from absolutely pure and fresh ingredients, and are of choice flavor, their old fashioned molasses candy being an article of exceptional merit; while their penny goods have secured an enduring hold on popular favor. This prosperous business was established about four years ago by Messrs. Charles H., Charles N., and W. A. Miller, father and sons respectively, and under their joint management was conducted up to July last, when the senior member was removed by death, the sons continuing the business alone since under the original firm name with uninterrupted success. The factory occupies three commodious floors, and has ample and complete manufacturing facilities, while a dozen or more hands are employed. The productions include plain, fancy and mixed candies delicious and toothsome confections in quite a variety, the specialties being old-fashioned molasses candy and penny goods, while an A1 assortment is constantly carried in stock.

MERWIN B. WINEGAR & CO., Stationery, Fancy Goods Etc., No. 403 Cambridge street.—Mr. Winegar started this business in May, 1888, and bringing an unbiased store of enterprise, energy and ability to bear upon his operations has acquired a success as gratifying as it is pronounced. He has developed a trade of permanent and influential character as a fair dealing and honorable merchant. The store is 15x36 feet in dimensions, and is well adapted in every respect for the purposes of the business. It is fitted up in a tasteful, attractive style, and contains a very superior assortment of stationery, articles of every description, fancy goods in great variety, foreign and domestic toys in profusion and suitable for holiday seasons, blank books, novels, periodicals and magazines, novelties in cards, pictorials, juvenile books, cigars of the choicest brands, and all the principal daily and weekly newspapers. The establishment is also a laundry agency, in connection with which the service is prompt and reliable. Papers and periodicals are promptly and regularly delivered at the addresses of customers at the lowest rates. An active, steadily increasing trade is enjoyed. Mr. Winegar is a native of New York city, and has resided in Boston for the past fifteen years,

www.ingramcontent.com/pod-product-compliance
Lightning Source LLC
Chambersburg PA
CBHW030403250426
43670CB00050B/435